P9-AQV-031

This Book
presented to the

CHURCH
LIBRARY
IN MEMORY OF

Emmet Edwards

BY

Haltom Convalescent Center

Code 4386-23, No. 3, Broadman Supplies, Nashville, Tenn. Printed in USA

BIRDVILLE
BAPTIST CHURCH
LIBRARY

THE MACARTHUR NEW TESTAMENT COMMENTARY

MATTHEW 8-15

John MacArthur, Jr.

MOODY PRESS / CHICAGO

© 1987 by
THE MOODY BIBLE INSTITUTE
OF CHICAGO

All rights reserved. No part of this book may be reproduced in any form without permission in writing from the publisher, except in the case of brief quotations embodied in critical articles or reviews.

Unless noted otherwise, all Scripture quotations in this book are from *The New American Standard Bible,* © 1960, 1962, 1963, 1968, 1971, 1972, 1973, 1975, and 1977 by The Lockman Foundation, and are used by permission.

Library of Congress Cataloging in Publication Data

MacArthur, John F.
  Matthew 8-15.

  (The MacArthur New Testament commentary)
  Bibliography: p.
  Includes index.
1. Bible. N.T. Matthew VIII-XV—Commentaries.
I. Title. II. Series: MacArthur, John F. MacArthur
New Testament commentary.
BS2575.3.M243 1986   226'.2077   86-23748
ISBN 0-8024-0763-3

1 2 3 4 5 6 7 Printing/RR/Year 91 90 89 88 87

Printed in the United States of America

To Dr. John Stead,
my partner in ministry
at The Master's College
and my lifelong friend

BIRDVILLE
BAPTIST CHURCH
LIBRARY

Contents

Preface

It continues to be a rewarding divine communion for me to preach expositionally through the New Testament. My goal is always to have deep fellowship with the Lord in the understanding of His Word, and out of that experience to explain to His people what a passage means. In the words of Nehemiah 8:8, I strive "to give the sense" of it so they may truly hear God speak and, in so doing, may respond to Him.

Obviously, God's people need to understand Him, which demands knowing His Word of truth (2 Tim. 2:15) and allowing that Word to dwell in us richly (Col. 3:16). The dominant thrust of my ministry, therefore, is to help make God's living Word alive to His people. It is a refreshing adventure.

This New Testament commentary series reflects this objective of explaining and applying Scripture. Some commentaries are primarily linguistic, others are mostly theological, and some are mainly homiletical. This one is basically explanatory, or expository. It is not linguistically technical, but deals with linguistics when that seems helpful to proper interpretation. It is not theologically expansive, but focuses on the major doctrines in each text and on how they relate to the whole of Scripture. It is not primarily homiletical, although each unit of thought is generally treated as one chapter, with a clear outline and logical flow of thought. Most truths are illustrated and applied with other Scripture. After establishing the context of a passage, I have tried to follow closely the writer's development and reasoning.

My prayer is that each reader will fully understand what the Holy Spirit is saying through this part of His Word, so that His revelation may lodge in the minds of believers and bring greater obedience and faithfulness—to the glory of our great God.

Jesus' Power over Disease (8:1-15)

And when He had come down from the mountain, great multitudes followed Him. And behold, a leper came to Him, and bowed down to Him, saying, "Lord, if You are willing, You can make me clean." And He stretched out His hand and touched him, saying, "I am willing; be cleansed." And immediately his leprosy was cleansed. And Jesus said to him, "See that you tell no one; but go, show yourself to the priest, and present the offering that Moses commanded, for a testimony to them."

And when He had entered Capernaum, a centurion came to Him, entreating Him, and saying, "Lord, my servant is lying paralyzed at home, suffering great pain." And He said to him, "I will come and heal him." But the centurion answered and said, "Lord, I am not worthy for You to come under my roof, but just say the word, and my servant will be healed. For I, too, am a man under authority, with soldiers under me; and I say to this one, 'Go!' and he goes, and to another, 'Come!' and he comes, and to my slave, 'Do this!' and he does it." Now when Jesus heard this, He marveled, and said to those who were following, "Truly I say to you, I have not found such great faith with anyone in Israel. And I say to you, that many shall come from east and west, and recline at the table with Abraham, and Isaac, and Jacob, in the kingdom of heaven; but the sons of the kingdom shall be cast out into the outer darkness; in that place there shall be weeping and gnashing of teeth." And

Jesus said to the centurion, "Go your way; let it be done to you as you have believed." And the servant was healed that very hour.

And when Jesus had come to Peter's home, He saw his mother-in-law lying sick in bed with a fever. And He touched her hand, and the fever left her; and she arose, and waited on Him. (8:1-15)

Matthew 8 begins where chapter 4 leaves off, with the Sermon on the Mount as a sort of parenthesis in between. At the end of chapter 4, Jesus was "going about in all Galilee, teaching in their synagogues, and proclaiming the gospel of the kingdom, and healing every kind of disease and every kind of sickness among the people. And the news about Him went out into all Syria; and they brought to Him all who were ill, taken with various diseases and pains, demoniacs, epileptics, paralytics; and He healed them. And great multitudes followed Him from Galilee and Decapolis and Jerusalem and Judea and from beyond the Jordan" (vv. 23-25). Jesus then "went up on the mountain" (5:1), where He preached His great sermon, and then came down from the mountain, still followed by "great multitudes" (8:1).

In the Sermon on the Mount Jesus turned the religious beliefs and practices of popular Judaism, especially those of the scribes and Pharisees, topsy-turvy. He had told them, in effect, that their teaching was wrong, their living was wrong, and their attitude was wrong. Virtually everything they believed in, stood for, and hoped in was unbiblical and ungodly. The Lord overturned their entire religious system and exposed them as religious hypocrites and spiritual phonies.

Unlike other Jewish teachers of that day, Jesus did not quote the Talmud, the Midrash, the Mishnah, or other rabbis. He recognized no written authority but the Old Testament Scripture and even put His own words on a par with Scripture. "The result was," Matthew explains, "that when Jesus had finished these words [the Sermon on the Mount], the multitudes were amazed at His teaching; for He was teaching them as one with authority, and not as their scribes" (Matt. 7:28-29).

In establishing Jesus' messiahship Matthew demonstrated His legal qualification through His genealogy, His prophetic qualification through the fulfillment of prophecy by His birth and infancy, His divine qualification by the Father's own attestation at His baptism, His spiritual qualification by His perfect resistance to Satan's temptations, and His theological qualification through the teaching of the Sermon on the Mount.

In chapters 8 and 9 Matthew dramatically sets forth still another qualification: Jesus' divine power. Through the miracles of these two chapters, Matthew shows beyond doubt that Jesus is, in fact, the very Son of God, because only God could perform such supernatural feats. In an astounding display of power, Jesus cleansed a leper, healed two paralytics, cooled a fever, calmed a storm at sea, cast out demons, raised a girl from the dead, gave sight to two blind men, restored speech to a man made dumb by demons, and healed every other kind of disease and sickness.

These two chapters are particularly critical to understanding the life and ministry of Christ. In this section Matthew records a series of nine miracles performed by the Lord, each one selected out of the thousands He performed during His three-year ministry. The nine miracles of Matthew 8-9 are presented in three groups of three miracles each. In each group Matthew recounts the miracles and then reports the Jews' response.

Jesus' miracles were the supreme proof of His divinity and the irrefutable credentials of His messiahship. Matthew's purpose in recording the miracles, like Jesus' purpose in performing them, was to confirm His deity and His claim to be the Messiah of Israel and the Savior of the world. In many ways this section is the heart of Matthew's message.

When Jesus first called His twelve disciples, He charged them not to go to Gentiles or Samaritans but "to the lost sheep of the house of Israel. 'And as you go, preach, saying "The kingdom of heaven is at hand." Heal the sick, raise the dead, cleanse the lepers, cast out demons; freely you received, freely give'" (10:5-8).

. Tragically, however—and inexplicably from a human point of view—many of the Jews who saw Jesus' miracles concluded that He performed them by demonic rather than by divine power (Matt. 12:24). As more and more Jews rejected Him, Jesus turned His attention to the establishment of the Gentile church. He also began to speak more in parables, which the unbelieving Jews could not understand because of their spiritually hardened hearts (13:11-13).

It should be noted that the apostle John also recorded the miracles in his gospel as proof signs of Jesus' divinity and messiahship. When the Jewish leaders criticized Jesus for healing on the Sabbath, accused Him of blasphemy, and then sought to kill Him for claiming to be equal to God, "Jesus therefore answered and was saying to them, 'Truly, truly, I say to you, the Son can do nothing of Himself, unless it is something He sees the Father doing; for whatever the Father does, these things the Son also does in like manner. For the Father loves the Son, and shows Him all things that He Himself is doing; and greater works than these will He show Him, that you may marvel. For just as the Father raises the dead and gives them life, even so the Son also gives life to whom He wishes'" (John 5:16-21). A short while later He further explained, "The works which the Father has given Me to accomplish, the very works that I do, bear witness of Me, that the Father has sent Me" (v. 36).

Still later Jesus said to His Jewish listeners, "I told you, and you do not believe; the works that I do in My Father's name, these bear witness of Me. . . . I and the Father are one" (John 10:25, 30). When "the Jews took up stones again to stone Him," Jesus said, "I showed you many good works from the Father; for which of them are you stoning Me? . . . If I do not do the works of My Father, do not believe Me; but if I do them, though you do not believe Me, believe the works, that you may know and understand that the Father is in Me, and I in the Father" (vv. 31-32, 37-38).

To His troubled disciples, who even late in His ministry could not comprehend His relationship to the Father, Jesus had to explain again, "Do you not believe that I am in the Father, and the Father is in Me? The words that I say to you I do not speak on My own initiative, but the Father abiding in Me does His works. Believe Me that I am in the Father, and the Father in Me; otherwise believe on account of the works themselves" (John 14:10-11; 15:24).

3

In his stated purpose for writing this gospel, John says, "Many other signs therefore Jesus also performed in the presence of the disciples, which are not written in this book; but these have been written that you may believe that Jesus is the Christ, the Son of God; and that believing you may have life in His name" (20:30-31).

The first three miracles reported in detail by Matthew (cf. 4:23-24) all involve the healing of physical affliction. In New Testament times disease was rampant and medical science as we know it did not exist. If a person survived a serious disease it was usually because the malady had run its course. Whether or not it was fatal, most disease caused great pain and suffering, for which there was little remedy. Sufferers were often left scarred, deformed, crippled, or otherwise debilitated for the rest of their lives. Plagues would sometimes wipe out entire villages, cities, or even regions. The list of diseases was long, and life expectancy was short.

Many diseases are mentioned in Scripture. We read of various forms of paralysis and atrophy, which would encompass such things as muscular dystrophy and poliomyelitis. The Bible frequently speaks of blindness, which was rampant because it could be caused by countless forms of disease, infection, and injury. Deafness was almost as common and had almost as many causes. We are told of boils, infected glands, various forms of edema, dysentery, mutism and other speech disorders, epilepsy, intestinal disorders, and many unidentified diseases.

When Jesus healed, He did so with a word or a touch, without gimmicks, formulas, or fanfare. He healed instantaneously, with no drawn out period of waiting or of gradual restoration. He healed totally, not partially, no matter how serious the disease or deformity. He healed everyone who came to Him and even some who never saw Him. He healed organic as well as functional afflictions. Most dramatically and powerfully of all, He even raised the dead.

It is small wonder, therefore, that Jesus' healing miracles brought such immediate and widespread attention. For people who seldom had means to alleviate even the symptoms of disease, the prospect of complete cure was almost too astounding to be believed. Even the rumor of such a thing would bring a multitude of the curious and hopeful. For those of us who live in a society where basic good health is accepted largely as a matter of course, it is difficult to appreciate the impact Jesus' healing ministry had in Palestine. Jesus instructed the disciples not to take any money, because people would have paid them all they had for health, and that could easily have corrupted the disciples' motives and objectives (see 10:8-9). For a brief period of time disease and other physical afflictions were virtually eliminated as Jesus went through the land healing thousands upon thousands (see Matt. 4:23-24; 8:16-17; 9:35; 14:14; 15:30; 19:2; 21:14; etc.). As Jesus Himself said on several occasions, His miraculous works alone should have been more than enough reason to believe in Him (John 10:38; 14:11). Such things had never happened before in the history of the world and could only have a divine cause. That is what made the rejection of the scribes, Pharisees, Sadducees, and others so self-condemnatory. No one could deny that Jesus performed the miracles, and only the most hard-hearted resistance to the truth could make a person reject His divinity in the face of such overpowering evidence. Those who would not believe in Jesus were indicted by every miracle He performed.

In the first three miracles of Matthew 8 the Lord healed a leper, a paralytic, and a woman with a fever. Beside the fact that each of them involved healing, these three miracles have four other common characteristics. First of all, in each of them Jesus dealt with the lowest level of human need, the physical. Although even earthly life involves much more than the physical, the physical part has its importance, and Jesus was lovingly sympathetic to those with physical needs. He thereby revealed the compassion of God toward those who suffer in this life.

Second, in each of the first three miracles Jesus responded to direct appeals, either by the afflicted person himself or by a friend or relative. In the first case the leper himself asked Jesus to make him clean (8:2); in the second the centurion asked in behalf of his servant (v. 6); and in the third (v. 14), several unnamed friends or relatives asked on behalf of Peter's mother-in-law, as we learn from the parallel account in Luke 4:38.

Third, in each of the first three miracles Jesus acted by His own will. Though He was sympathetic to the needs of those who were afflicted and was moved by the appeals for help, He nevertheless acted sovereignly by His own volition (vv. 3, 13, 15).

Fourth, in all three miracles Jesus ministered to the needs of someone who, especially in the eyes of the proud Jewish leaders, was on the lowest plane of human existence. The first person He helped was a leper, the second was a Gentile soldier and his slave, and the third was a woman. We learn from John that Jesus first revealed His messiahship to a despised Samaritan adulteress in Sychar (John 4:25-26), and we learn from Matthew that these three miracles of His early ministry served the humblest members of society. Our Lord showed special compassion toward those for whom society had special disdain.

THE WRETCHED MAN: A LEPER

And when He had come down from the mountain, great multitudes followed Him. And behold, a leper came to Him, and bowed down to Him, saying, "Lord, if You are willing, You can make me clean." And He stretched out His hand and touched him, saying, "I am willing; be cleansed." And immediately his leprosy was cleansed. And Jesus said to him, "See that you tell no one; but go, show yourself to the priest, and present the offering that Moses commanded, for a testimony to them." (8:1-4)

The **great multitudes** that **followed** Jesus **when He had come down from the mountain** did not do so because they adored Him as their Messiah. Most of the crowd, no doubt, was simply curious, never before having seen anyone perform miracles or heard anyone speak with such authority (4:23-25; 7:28-29). They were uncommitted observers, amazed by what Jesus said and did but not convicted of their need of Him as Lord and Savior.

The root word behind *lepros* (**leper**) means "scaly," which describes one of the earliest and most obvious characteristics of leprosy. There continues to be much debate among scholars as to whether or not the disease commonly called Hansen's disease today is the same as biblical leprosy. Many biblical terms for diseases simply describe observable symptoms that could apply to several different physical afflictions. In addition to that, some diseases change over the course of years, as immunities develop and new strains of infectious microorganisms are formed.

Most medical historians believe that leprosy originated in Egypt, and the leprosy bacillus called myobacterium leprae has been found in at least one mummy that also showed the typical scaly evidence of the disease on its skin. The Old Testament scholar R. K. Harrison maintains that the symptoms described in Leviticus 13 "could presage clinical leprosy" (Colin Brown, ed. *The New International Dictionary of New Testament Theology* [Grand Rapids: Zondervan, 1975], 2:465). It seems safe to assume, therefore, that ancient leprosy was virtually the same as contemporary Hansen's disease.

This severe form of leprosy was the most feared disease of the ancient world, and even today it cannot be totally cured, though it can be kept in check by proper medication. Although some 90 percent of people in modern times are immune to such contagion of leprosy, it was much more communicable in ancient times. Spongy, tumorlike swellings would eventually grow on the face and body, and the bacillus would become systemic and affect internal organs, while the bones would begin to deteriorate. Untreated in ancient times, it produced a weakness which made the victim vulnerable to tuberculosis or other diseases.

In order to protect His chosen people, God gave strict and specific regulations to Moses regarding leprosy, the details of which are found in Leviticus 13. A person suspected of having the disease was taken to a priest for examination. If he showed signs of having more than a superficial skin problem, he was isolated for seven days. If the symptoms became worse, the person was isolated for seven more days. If, at that time, the rash had not spread further, the person was pronounced clean. If, however, the rash had become worse, he was pronounced unclean. When leprosy was immediately evident from a person's hair turning white and his having raw, swollen flesh, he was pronounced unclean on the spot and no isolation period was involved. A less serious type of disease caused the entire skin to turn white, in which case the affected person could be considered clean. That disease was probably a form of psoriasis, eczema, vitiligo, tuberculoid leprosy, or perhaps a condition which Herodotus and the great Greek physician Hippocrates called leukodermia. When a person was found to have the serious form of leprosy, his clothes were to be torn, his head uncovered, his mouth covered (to prevent spread of the disease), and he was to cry, "Unclean! Unclean!" wherever he went to warn others to stay clear of him. Lepers were legally ostracized and forbidden to live in any community with their fellow Israelites (Num. 5:2). Among the sixty-one defilements of ancient Judaism, leprosy was second only to a dead body in seriousness. The Talmud forbade a Jew from coming closer than six feet to a leper, and if the wind was blowing, the limit was one hundred fifty feet.

Recent medical studies confirm that Hansen's disease can be passed on to others when it is inhaled through the air—a good reason for a leper to cover his mouth, as the Leviticus regulations required. People have also contacted the disease from touching an object handled by a leper—again showing the value of the Leviticus standard, which required the burning of contaminated clothes.

In his book *Unclean! Unclean!* L. S. Huizenga describes some of the horrors of leprosy.

> The disease which we today call leprosy generally begins with pain in certain areas of the body. Numbness follows. Soon the skin in such spots loses its original color. It gets to be thick, glossy, and scaly. . . . As the sickness progresses, the thickened spots become dirty sores and ulcers due to poor blood supply. The skin, especially around the eyes and ears, begins to bunch, with deep furrows between the swellings, so that the face of the afflicted individual begins to resemble that of a lion. Fingers drop off or are absorbed; toes are affected similarly. Eyebrows and eyelashes drop out. By this time one can see the person in this pitiable condition is a leper. By a touch of the finger one can also feel it. One can even smell it, for the leper emits a very unpleasant odor. Moreover, in view of the fact that the disease-producing agent frequently also attacks the larynx, the leper's voice acquires a grating quality. His throat becomes hoarse, and you can now not only see, feel, and smell the leper, but you can hear his rasping voice. And if you stay with him for some time, you can even imagine a peculiar taste in your mouth, probably due to the odor. (Grand Rapids: Eerdmans, 1927, p. 149; cited in William Hendriksen, *The Gospel of Matthew* [Grand Rapids: Baker, 1973], p. 388)

Although advanced leprosy is generally not painful, because of the nerve damage it is disfiguring, debilitating, and can be repulsive in the extreme, and has therefore for millennia been one of the most dreaded of diseases. One ancient rabbi said, "When I see lepers I throw stones at them lest they come near me." Another said, "I would not so much as eat an egg that was purchased on a street where a leper had walked."

An up-to-date look at modern leprosy reveals more of its character. Dr. Paul Brand, world-renowned expert on the treatment of Hansen's disease has provided much help in understanding the unique nature of this affliction.

> Hansen's disease (HD) is cruel, but not at all the way other diseases are. It primarily acts as an anesthetic, numbing the pain cells of hands, feet, nose, ears, and eyes. Not so bad, really, one might think. Most diseases are feared *because* of their pain—what makes a painless disease so horrible?
>
> Hansen's disease's numbing quality is precisely the reason such fabled destruction and decay of tissue occurs. For thousands of years people thought HD caused the ulcers on hands and feet and face which eventually led to rotting flesh and loss of limbs. Mainly through Dr. Brand's research, it has been established that in 99 percent of the cases, HD only numbs the extremities. The destruction follows solely because the warning system of pain is gone.
>
> How does the decay happen? In villages of Africa and Asia, a person

with HD has been known to reach directly into a charcoal fire to retrieve a dropped potato. Nothing in his body told him not to. Patients at Brand's hospital in India would work all day gripping a shovel with a protruding nail, or extinguish a burning wick with their bare hands, or walk on splintered glass. Watching them, Brand began formulating his radical theory that HD was chiefly anesthetic, and only indirectly a destroyer.

On one occasion, he tried to open the door of a little storeroom, but a rusty padlock would not yield. A patient—an undersized, malnourished ten-year-old—approached him smiling.

"Let me try, sahib, doctor," he offered and reached for the key. With a quick jerk of his hand he turned the key in the lock.

Brand was dumbfounded. How could this weak youngster out-exert him? His eyes caught a telltale clue. Was that a drop of blood on the floor?

Upon examining the boy's fingers, Brand discovered the act of turning the key had gashed a finger open to the bone; skin, fat, and joint were all exposed. Yet the boy was completely unaware of it! To him, the sensation of cutting his finger to the bone was no different from picking up a stone or turning a coin in his pocket.

The daily routines of life ground away at the HD patient's hands and feet, but no warning system alerted him. If an ankle turned, tearing tendon and muscle, he would adjust and walk crooked. If a rat chewed off a finger in the night, he would not discover it missing until the next morning. . . .

. . . Stanley Stein (author of *Alone No Longer*) went blind because of another cruel quirk of HD. Each morning he would wash his face with a hot washcloth. But neither his hand nor his face was sensitive enough to temperature to warn him that he was using scalding water. Gradually he destroyed his eyes with his daily washing. (Philip Yancey, *Where Are You God When It Hurts?* [Grand Rapids: Zondervan, 1977, pp. 32-34)

Leprosy is a graphic illustration of sin. Like leprosy, sin infects the whole person, and it is ugly, loathsome, corrupting, contaminating, alienating, and incurable by man. Lepers in ancient Israel were vivid object lessons of sin.

Yet a leper was the first to be healed by Jesus in this series of miracles in Matthew, and the fact that the **leper came to Him** was astounding in itself, because lepers were forbidden to come close to nonlepers.

Four things about this particular leper stand out. First of all he came to Jesus with confidence. He obviously sensed a love and tenderness in Jesus that allowed him to approach **Him** without fear of reprisal (such as being stoned) or even of reprimand. He somehow knew that Jesus was neither afraid of him nor ashamed to associate with him. He did not shout to Jesus from a distance, as he was supposed to do, but approached Him directly and without hesitation. Because he realized Jesus was not ashamed of him, he was less ashamed of himself. He thought of nothing but his great need and of Jesus' ability and willingness to meet that need.

Second, the man came to Jesus with reverence. His boldness did not come from presumption but from humble adoration. When he reached Jesus he **bowed down to Him.** *Proskuneō* (from which comes **bowed down**) literally means to prostrate oneself and is most often translated "to worship" (see Matt. 2:2; 4:9, 10; John 4:20-24; Acts 7:43; Rev. 4:10; 19:10). From the reverential nature of his request it seems that the leper addressed Jesus as **Lord** not simply in the sense of "Sir," but as an acknowledgment of deity. He felt he was in the presence of God and that therefore Jesus could heal him of his terrible disease. It is both interesting and instructive to note that the scribes and Pharisees who were doubtlessly in the multitude that day were beautifully and richly attired, yet were inwardly corrupt, proud, and unbelieving. By contrast, the **leper** appeared loathsome and repulsive on the outside, but inwardly he was reverent and believing.

Third, the leper came to Jesus with humility. He came expectantly but not demandingly, saying, **Lord, if you are willing.** He asked to be healed only if it were the Lord's will. He did not claim to be worthy or deserving, but left himself in the Lord's hands to do as He would. The implication seems to be that the leper was quite willing to remain leprous if that were the Lord's will. Obviously he wanted to be healed, but he did not explicitly ask Jesus for healing, almost as if that were too much to presume. He simply acknowledged Jesus' ability to heal him. How far that humble spirit is from the demands of many Christians today who make claims on God's healing, blessing, and favor as if those were their inherent rights. This man claimed no rights, and his first concern was not his own welfare at all, but the Lord's will and glory.

Fourth, the leper came with faith, declaring, **You can make me clean.** He literally said, "You have the power to make me clean." That is faith at its highest—the absolute conviction that God is able, coupled with humble submission to His sovereignty in the exercise of His power. The man knew that Jesus was not obligated to heal him, but he also knew that He was perfectly capable of doing it. He had the faith of Shadrach, Meshach, and Abed-nego, who declared to Nebuchadnezzar, "If it be so, our God whom we serve is able to deliver us from the furnace of blazing fire; and He will deliver us out of your hand, O king. But even if He does not, let it be known to you, O king, that we are not going to serve your gods or worship the golden image that you have set up" (Dan. 3:17-18).

The leper came with confidence because he believed Jesus was compassionate, with reverence because he believed Jesus was God, with humility because he believed Jesus was sovereign, and with faith because he believed Jesus had the power to heal him.

In response to that faith, Jesus **stretched out His hand and touched him, saying, "I am willing; be cleansed."** Jews were forbidden by the Mosaic law to touch a leper, because he was unclean (Lev. 5:3). To do so was to expose themselves to both ceremonial and physical contamination. They could not help a leper by touching him, but only harm themselves. Yet it is certain that lepers yearned for the touch of another human being. In their isolation and social stigma they no doubt would have given anything for even brief intimate contact with someone besides other lepers.

Jesus could have healed with only a word, as He did on numerous other occasions. But He made an obvious point of touching this man. That simple act in itself was amazing, not in the sense of being sensational and spectacular—as are the supposed miracles of many modern healers—but simply in the fact that the Son of

God lovingly condescended to touch the outcast of outcasts whom no other man would even come near.

The healing was instantaneous: **immediately his leprosy was cleansed.** Jesus did not need to heal in stages, although at times He chose to do so (Mark 8:22-26; John 9:6-7). When He touched defilement it went away. The scene on this occasion must have been startling—to see a deformed, shriveled, scaly, sore-covered, derelict suddenly stand upright, with perfect arms and legs, with his face smooth and unscarred, his hair restored, his voice normal, and his eyes bright. The marvels of modern medical science pale beside such miraculous restoration.

The first requirement of faith is obedience, and as soon as the leper was cleansed, **Jesus said to him, "See that you tell no one; but go, show yourself to the priest, and present the offering that Moses commanded, for a testimony to them."** Before he celebrated his new lease on life, and even before he testified to others about his miraculous cleansing, the man was to fulfill the requirements of the Mosaic law by having the temple priests attest to his cure.

This process, described in Leviticus 14, involved taking two birds and killing one of them over running water. The live bird, along with cedar wood, a scarlet string, and some hyssop, was then dipped in the blood of the slain bird. The former leper was then sprinkled seven times and pronounced clean by the priest, and the live bird was set free. The cleansed person was then to wash his clothes, shave off all his hair, and bathe himself. He could then rejoin Israelite society, although he had to remain outside his tent for seven days. The final act on the eighth day was to bring the required guilt, sin, and grain offerings—according to what could be afforded—and to be anointed by the priest on various parts of the body.

Jesus may have told the man not to say anything about his healing in order not to increase the crowd's adulation of Him simply as a miracle worker, or perhaps He wanted to discourage their looking to Him as a political deliverer. It may have been that the Lord was still in His period of humiliation and that His exaltation by the crowd at this time would have been premature in the divine plan.

All of those reasons could have been involved, but Jesus' instruction to **go, show yourself to the priest, and present the offering that Moses commanded,** was specifically given **for a testimony to them,** that is, to the multitude and especially to the Jewish leaders. Although Jesus devastated the hypocritical, superficial, and unbiblical standards and practices of the scribes and Pharisees, He did not want the people to think He was violating the requirements of God's law—which He had just declared He came to fulfill, not destroy (5:17). In addition to that, when the priest declared the man clean—as he would have to do because of the obvious healing—Jesus' miracle would be officially confirmed by the Jewish establishment. It is likely also for this reason that Jesus told the man not to tell anyone else before he presented himself to the priest for examination. If word that his healing was done by Jesus reached Jerusalem ahead of the man, the priests would no doubt have been reluctant to verify the cleansing.

Sadly, the man who had shown such confident and humble faith in his joyous exuberance did not also show immediate obedience. We learn from Mark that he became so excited that "he went out and began to proclaim it freely and to spread the news about, to such an extent that Jesus could no longer publicly enter a city, but stayed out in unpopulated areas; and they were coming to Him from everywhere" (Mark 1:45).

As Jesus remarked several times in various words, "Which is easier, to say, 'Your sins are forgiven,' or to say, 'Rise and walk'?" (Matt. 9:5; cf. Mark 2:9; Luke 5:23). The Lord's greatest purpose was to cleanse sin, not sickness, and even His physical cleansings became illustrations of the spiritual cleansing He offered. The healing of leprosy was especially powerful in that regard, because its great physical destructiveness, pervasiveness, ugliness, and incurableness represent the even greater destructiveness, pervasiveness, ugliness, and incurableness of sin. Just as leprosy destroys physical health and makes a person an outcast with other men, so sin destroys spiritual health and makes a person an outcast with God. But just as Christ can cure leprosy, He can also cure sin; and just as His cleansing from leprosy restored men to human fellowship, His cleansing from sin restores them to God's.

Much modern evangelism and personal witness is weakened by failure to confront men with the terribleness and danger of their sin. Coming to Christ is not getting on a popular bandwagon of religious sentimentality. It is facing and confessing one's sin and bringing it to the Lord for cleansing. True conversion takes place when, like the leper, desperate people come to Christ humbly confessing their need and reverently seeking His restoration. The truly repentant person, like this leper, comes with no pride, no self-will, no rights, and no claim to worthiness. He sees himself as a repulsive sinner who has absolutely no claim to salvation apart from the abundant grace of God. He comes believing that God can and will save him only as he places his trust in Jesus Christ.

After a person is saved from sin, Jesus' first requirement is that he henceforth obey the Word of God. Only a life-style of holy living can give proper testimony to what Jesus Christ has done in saving us. It is best to say nothing of our relationship to Jesus Christ unless our living reflects something of His holiness and will. When a Christian lives obediently, then both his actions and his words testify to Christ's goodness and power.

THE RESPECTED MAN: A GENTILE

And when He had entered Capernaum, a centurion came to Him, entreating Him, and saying, "Lord, my servant is lying paralyzed at home, suffering great pain." And He said to him, "I will come and heal him." But the centurion answered and said, "Lord, I am not worthy for You to come under my roof, but just say the word, and my servant will be healed. For I, too, am a man under authority, with soldiers under me; and I say to this one, 'Go!' and he goes, and to another, 'Come!' and he comes, and to my slave, 'Do this!' and he does it." Now when Jesus heard this, He marveled, and said to those who were following, "Truly I say to you, I have not found such great faith with anyone in Israel. And I say to you, that many shall come from east and west,

and recline at the table with Abraham, and Isaac, and Jacob, in the kingdom of heaven; but the sons of the kingdom shall be cast out into the outer darkness; in that place there shall be weeping and gnashing of teeth." And Jesus said to the centurion, "Go your way; let it be done to you as you have believed." And the servant was healed that very hour. (8:5-13)

Many commentators believe that the first three miracles of Matthew 8 occurred on the same day. If so, Jesus entered **Capernaum** only a short while after healing the leper. Because Jesus pronounced a curse on it (Matt. 11:23), the ancient city no longer exists, except in the form of the ruins of a synagogue and of a few houses, including, according to tradition, that of Peter. It was a lovely town in Jesus' day and He spent considerable time there, much of it perhaps in Peter's home (see 8:14).

The **centurion** who **came to Him** not only was a Gentile but an officer in the Roman occupation army, a man who ordinarily would have been greatly hated by the Jews. Such soldiers were often hated still more because the Romans usually chose alien residents of a region to make up its occupation force—making those soldiers not only oppressors but traitors in the eyes of the populace.

We learn from Luke that this **centurion** actually **came to** Jesus through some Jewish intermediaries, because he felt spiritually unworthy of approaching Jesus personally and perhaps also because he thought he would be rebuffed because of his military position. He was probably in the troops of the wicked Antipas and was possibly even a Samaritan, a half-breed Jew who was traditionally hated even more than Gentiles by "pure" Jews. Yet this man was held in great esteem by the Jews of Capernaum, because, as they told Jesus, "He is worthy for You to grant this to him; for he loves our nation, and it was he who built us our synagogue" (Luke 7:2-5). Like Cornelius (Acts 10:2), this **centurion** was undoubtedly a God-fearing Gentile. It is noteworthy that each of the Roman centurions mentioned in the New Testament are spoken of favorably. And from the biblical record it seems likely that each of them became a believer in Christ.

Pais, here translated **servant,** literally means a young child. Luke calls him a slave (*doulos*), indicating he was probably born into the slave household of the centurion. In any case, the boy "was highly regarded" by the centurion, who was now afraid that his servant would die (Luke 7:2). **Lord,** he said to Jesus through his emissaries, **my servant is lying paralyzed at home, suffering great pain.** Whatever the disease was, it was paralyzing, painful, and fatal. Like the leper, it seems the centurion was reluctant to ask Jesus specifically for a healing, since he simply states the young man's terrible condition—although the request is clearly implied.

The fact that the **centurion** cared so much for his **servant** set him apart from the typical Roman soldier, who could be brutally heartless. The average slave owner of that day, whether military or civilian, had no more regard for his slave than for an animal. The great Greek philosopher Aristotle said there could be no friendship and no justice toward inanimate things, not even toward a horse, an ox, or a slave, because master and slave were considered to have nothing in common. "A slave," he said, "is a living tool, just as a tool is an inanimate slave" (*Ethics*, 1161b). The Roman law expert Gaius wrote that it was universally accepted that the master possessed the power of life and death over his slave (*Institutes*, 1:52). Still another Roman writer, Varro, maintained that the only difference between a slave, a beast, and a cart was that the slave talked (*On Landed Estates*, 1:17.1). Cato the Elder advised those in economic difficulty to look over their livestock and hold a sale. They should sell their worn-out oxen, their blemished cattle, sheep, wool, and hides, their old wagons and tools, their old and sickly slaves, and whatever else was superfluous (*On Agriculture*, 2.7).

But the **centurion** from **Capernaum** had no such inhumane ideas. He was a seasoned and capable fighting man or he would not have been a centurion—who, as the title indicates, was responsible for a hundred men. He was a man's man, and a soldier's soldier. Yet he had deep compassion for his dying slave boy and felt unworthy to approach Jesus personally. Jesus knew the man's heart and did not need to hear a direct request, either from the centurion or from the Jews who came in his behalf. He simply responded in love, saying, **I will come and heal him.**

When Jesus came near to his house, **the centurion** saw Him and sent some friends out to meet Him (Luke 7:3). In his behalf they **answered and said, "Lord, I am not worthy for You to come under my roof."** He felt genuinely unworthy for Jesus to go to that much trouble for him, and no doubt also did not want Him to break the Jewish tradition of not entering the house of a Gentile in order to avoid ceremonial contamination.

The centurion's twice addressing Jesus as **Lord** indicates much more than courtesy. Jesus testified of the man that He had not seen such great faith in all of Israel (v. 10). The man here affirmed the divine lordship of Christ, believing that Jesus was indeed God and consequently had the power to heal his paralyzed servant. Because the servant was too ill to be carried out to Jesus and because he felt unworthy to have Jesus come into his house, the centurion said to Him, **Just say the word, and my servant will be healed.** From the many reports he had doubtlessly heard of Jesus' healing power, and perhaps from having witnessed some of the healings himself, he knew that distance presented no barrier.

The centurion also understood delegation of power. **For I, too, am a man under authority, with soldiers under me,** he said. **And I say to this one, "Go!" and he goes, and to another, "Come!" and he comes, and to my slave, "Do this!" and he does it.** He recognized **authority** when he saw it, even in a realm in which he had no experience or understanding. He knew that if he had the power to make his soldiers and slaves do his bidding by simply giving them orders, Jesus' supernatural powers could even more easily allow Him simply to **say the word** and cause the **servant** [to] **be healed.**

Now when Jesus heard this, He marveled, and said to those who were following, "Truly I say to you, I have not found such great faith with anyone in Israel." Although, as God, Jesus knew all men's hearts, in His humanness He was amazed that this Gentile soldier showed more genuine **faith** in Him than He had found **with anyone in Israel.** Many Jews had believed in Jesus, but none had shown the sincerity, sensitivity, humility, love, and depth of faith of this Gentile soldier. Even to His disciples Jesus would say a short time later, "You men of little faith" (8:26). Still later in His ministry He would say to Philip, "Have I been so long with you, and yet you have not come to know Me?" (John 14:9).

This Gentile would not be alone in his belief. Jesus went on to say, **many shall come from east and west, and recline at the table with Abraham, and Isaac, and Jacob, in the kingdom of heaven; but the sons of the kingdom shall be cast out into the outer darkness; in that place there shall be weeping and gnashing of teeth.** Those who had less spiritual advantage and less opportunity to know God's truth—the Gentiles **from east and west**—would show greater response to the gospel than God's own chosen people, who considered themselves to be **the sons of the kingdom** simply by virtue of racial descent.

The gospel came through Abraham's seed, as Matthew has already attested through Jesus' genealogy. But the benefit of the gospel, which is salvation, is appropriated by faith, not by genealogical descent. The Jews played an integral part in God's bringing the Messiah and His gospel, and they are yet destined to play an important role in the end times. It was integral to God's plan of salvation that His own Son be born, live, and die as a Jew. But the fact that **Abraham, Isaac, and Jacob**—or any other Jew—will be **in the kingdom of heaven** will not be because of their Jewishness but because of their saving faith.

Jesus' words to those Capernaum Jews was startling in the extreme. What He said utterly contradicted everything taught by their rabbis. The twenty-ninth chapter of the apocryphal book of Second Baruch pictures what Jews believed would be the great heavenly feast at which all Jews were going to sit down and eat behemoth, the elephant, and leviathan, the giant sea monster, or whale—symbolic of an unlimited amount of food. In the eyes of many Jews, one of the most significant and appealing things about the feast was that it would be totally free of Gentiles.

But at that meal, Jesus said, many Gentiles would be present and many Jews absent. The presumed **sons of the kingdom shall be cast out into the outer darkness; in that place there shall be weeping and gnashing of teeth.** To the Jews God had given the unique promises and privileges of His kingdom, but because they rejected the King when He came to them, they disqualified themselves from God's blessing of light and destined themselves for **outer darkness,** where, instead of feasting throughout eternity, they would suffer forever in the horror of **weeping and gnashing of teeth.** Jewish tradition taught that sinners—a term synonymous with Gentiles in their thinking—would spend eternity in the outer darkness of gehenna. Jesus concurred with them about the destiny of condemned sinners (see also Matt. 22:13; 24:51), but He declared them totally wrong about the identity of those condemned sinners.

Hell is a place both of darkness and of fire, a combination not found in our present world. Part of the supernatural quality of hell is that it will be a place of fire, pain, and torment that will continue for all eternity in total darkness.

Being a physical descendant of Abraham was a great privilege and advantage (Rom. 3:1-2), but in spite of what most Jews believed, it did not guarantee salvation. It is the children of Abraham's spiritual faith, not the children of his physical body, whom God adopts as His own children (Rom. 8:14-17; Gal. 3:7-9, 26-29; cf. Rom. 4:11, 16). Those who reject Christ, even though they are physical descendants of Abraham, will have no place **at the table with Abraham, and Isaac, and Jacob, in the kingdom of heaven.** By their rejection of the Son of God—especially in light of the irrefutable evidence of His miracles—they prove they are really sons of Satan (John 8:42-44). Because they are false **sons of the kingdom,** they annul the divine promise, forfeit the divine blessing, and are forever barred from the divine **kingdom.** That was the substance of Jesus' brief but sobering message to the unbelieving Jews just before He pronounced the healing of the centurion's slave.

Jesus again reaffirmed the greatness of the centurion's faith as He said to him, **"Go your way; let it be done to you as you have believed." And the servant was healed that very hour.** That the **servant was healed** was Jesus' affirmation that **the centurion** truly **believed,** because otherwise his servant would have remained sick and probably soon died. The servant's healing was *according to* the centurion's faith (**as you have believed**), and because the healing was complete so had to have been the faith. And if the centurion had such great faith before the miracle, how much greater must it have been when he saw his beloved young friend get up from his deathbed and go about his work in perfect health and without pain?

Jesus did not give the principle **as you have believed** as a universal promise to all believers. The principle of healing in proportion to faith was sovereignly applied as the Lord saw fit (see also, e. g., Matt. 9:29). Paul had absolute faith in God's ability to heal him, and he personally experienced, and was often used as the instrument of, God's miraculous healing. But when he prayed three times in great earnestness for his "thorn in the flesh" to be removed, the Lord's answer to him was, "My grace is sufficient for you, for power is perfected in weakness" (2 Cor. 12:7-9).

THE RELATIVE: A WOMAN

And when Jesus had come to Peter's home, He saw his mother-in-law lying sick in bed with a fever. And He touched her hand, and the fever left her; and she arose, and waited on Him. (8:14-15)

The first thing many male Jews did every morning was to pray, "Lord, I thank Thee that I was not born a slave, a Gentile, or a woman." In the first two miracles of Matthew 8, Jesus showed mercy and compassion not only to an outcast leper but to an outcast Gentile and his slave. Now He shows mercy and compassion to a woman. The proud, self-righteous Jewish men could not have missed Jesus' point: physical health, race, social status, or gender made no difference to Him. None of those things in itself was an advantage or disadvantage as far as His ministry and message were concerned. That the disadvantaged more often received His blessing was due to their more often being humble and aware of their need. Likewise, that the advantaged more often failed to receive His blessing was due to their more often being proud and self-satisfied.

Mark tells us that when Jesus, Peter, Andrew, James, and John arrived at

Peter's home, some of the group discovered that Peter's **mother-in-law** was ill, "and immediately they spoke to Him about her" (Mark 1:30). Luke adds the information that her fever was high and that the unidentified friends or relatives "made request of Him on her behalf" (Luke 4:38). In response to their request, Jesus then went to her room and **saw** her **lying sick in bed with a fever.**

We do not know the cause of the fever, but the facts that it was high and that the woman was too sick to get up suggest an extremely serious and probably life-threatening illness. The demands of everyday living did not allow most people in that day the luxury of going to bed whenever they felt bad. Physical pain and discomfort were a regular part of life, and, unless they were severe, did not normally interfere with a person's responsibilities.

Again Jesus' response and healing were immediate. **And He touched her hand, and the fever left her; and she arose, and waited on Him.** We know from both Mark and Luke that she also served the other people there (Mark 1:31; Luke 4:39), but Matthew emphasizes her special ministry to Jesus: **she waited on Him.** His healing touch had instantly removed her fever and pain, and most likely saved her life. We can be sure she served her gracious Lord with special attention and care.

Although Peter's mother-in-law obviously was a woman, she was also a Jew. It may therefore be that, after His strong words of verses 11-12, Jesus did not want to leave the impression that God had forsaken His chosen people, even though most of them had forsaken Him. That the kingdom was open to faithful Gentiles certainly did not mean it was closed to faithful Jews. As Paul makes clear in his letter to the Romans, "God has not rejected His people whom He foreknew. . . . There has also come to be at the present time a remnant according to God's gracious choice. . . . For if you [Gentiles] were cut off from what is by nature a wild olive tree, and were grafted contrary to nature into a cultivated olive tree, how much more shall these who are the natural branches be grafted into their own olive tree?" (Rom. 11:2, 5, 24).

What Keeps Men from Christ? (8:16-22)

2

And when evening had come, they brought to Him many who were demon-possessed; and He cast out the spirits with a word, and healed all who were ill in order that what was spoken through Isaiah the prophet might be fulfilled, saying, "He Himself took our infirmities, and carried away our diseases."

Now when Jesus saw a crowd around Him, He gave orders to depart to the other side. And a certain scribe came and said to Him, "Teacher, I will follow You wherever You go." And Jesus said to him, "The foxes have holes, and the birds of the air have nests; but the Son of Man has nowhere to lay His head." And another of the disciples said to Him, "Lord, permit me first to go and bury my father." But Jesus said to him, "Follow Me; and allow the dead to bury their own dead." (8:16-22)

After Jesus had healed the leper, the centurion's slave boy, and Peter's mother-in-law, Matthew reports that the crowd brought Him countless other people to be healed. Because these were brought to Him **when evening had come,** it is possible that the first three healings had been done on the Sabbath. Because of their religious leaders, many Jews were afraid to ask Jesus to heal on the Sabbath, and since it ended at sundown, they now felt free to bring **many who were demon-possessed; and He cast out the spirits with a word, and healed all who were ill.**

As He had done before (see 4:23-24) and many times afterward (see 14:14; Luke 5:17; 9:6; etc.), Jesus here performed mass healings, without regard to individual faith or circumstances. Whether the problem was spiritual, as with the **demon-possessed,** or physical, as with those **who were ill, He healed all.** He was giving evidence of His deity and messiahship, and everyone who came for healing was healed. As mentioned in the previous chapter, for all practical purposes Jesus banished sickness and disease from Palestine during the course of His earthly ministry.

Through His healing miracles Jesus participated in human pain and sorrow in that **He Himself took our infirmities, and carried away our diseases.** He participated first of all by sympathizing with man's pain and sickness. Jesus knew men's hearts and all of their inner feelings. He knew the agony, the bewilderment, the confusion, the despair, and the frustration that disease and sickness bring in addition to physical pain. Repeatedly the gospel writers tell of Jesus' having compassion on those who came to hear Him teach and to experience His healing touch (Matt. 9:36; 15:32; Mark 1:41; Luke 10:33). Just as surely as then, He now knows the agonies of His children, "for we do not have a high priest who cannot sympathize with our weaknesses" (Heb. 4:15). It was not that Jesus **carried away our diseases** by contracting them, but by experiencing vicariously the pain they bring.

Second, Jesus **took our infirmities, and carried away our diseases** in the sense that He saw and felt the destructive power of their root cause, which is sin. Jesus did not weep over Lazarus' tomb in remorse over the death of a dear friend, because He knew His friend would soon be raised from the dead. He wept because of the evil, sinful power that brought suffering and death to every man. He could not see the pain of sickness and death without feeling the pain of sin. Sin, sickness, and death are all inextricably tied to the curse. That is why Jesus asked rhetorically, "Which is easier, to say, 'Your sins are forgiven,' or to say, 'Rise, and walk'?" (Matt. 9:5). Neither is easier or harder. The same cause is behind both sin and sickness, and only divine power can remove either.

Third, and most supremely, Jesus **took our infirmities, and carried away our diseases** in that His victorious redeeming work dealt with sin in such a devastating way that ultimately all sickness and disease will be **carried away.** The King was offering His kingdom and was previewing its marvelous and glorious elements, one of the most wonderful of which will be the removal of all illness and sorrow for all eternity.

Jesus healed because of His divine and loving compassion for those who were suffering and for their loved ones who suffered with them. He healed because He hated sickness and disease, which were never part of God's plan for mankind and which came about because of sin. But He also healed in order to give a preview of His coming kingdom, in which there will be no more sin, no more death, no more sorrow, no more pain. Just as on the mount of transfiguration He pulled back the veil of His flesh and gave His three disciples a glimpse of His divine glory, through His vast healing miracles Jesus gave a vision of His glorious kingdom—when all disease and sickness would be banished, not in a small corner of the world or for a few brief years, but throughout the whole world and forever (see Rev. 21:1-4).

But before He established His earthly kingdom that would be free of suffering and death, the Messiah Himself would have to suffer and die to redeem men from sin. He would be "pierced through for our transgressions, . . . crushed for our iniquities; the chastening for our well-being [would fall] upon Him, and by His scourging we [would be] healed" (Isa. 53:5). And before He suffered and died He would give evidence of His divine power by bearing our griefs and carrying our sorrows (v. 4). It is that verse to which Matthew refers when he says that Jesus **healed all who were ill in order that what was spoken through Isaiah the prophet might be fulfilled, saying, "He Himself took our infirmities, and carried away our diseases."**

Disease and death cannot be permanently removed until sin is permanently removed, and Jesus' supreme work, therefore, was to conquer sin. In the atonement He dealt with sin, death, and sickness; and yet all three of those are still with us. When He died on the cross, Jesus bruised the head of Satan and broke the power of sin, and the person who trusts in the atoning work of Christ is immediately delivered from the penalty of sin and one day will be delivered from the very presence of sin and its consequences. The ultimate fulfillment of Christ's redeeming work is yet future for believers (cf. Rom. 8:22-25; 13:11). Christ died for men's sins, but Christians still fall into sin; He conquered death, but His followers still die; and He overcame pain and sickness, but His people still suffer and become ill. There is physical healing in the atonement, just as there is total deliverance from sin and death in the atonement; but we still await the fulfillment of that deliverance in the day when the Lord brings the end of suffering, sin, and death.

Those who claim that Christians should never be sick because there is healing in the atonement should also claim that Christians should never die, because Jesus also conquered death in the atonement. The central message of the gospel is deliverance from sin. It is the good news about forgiveness, not health. Christ was made sin, not disease, and He died on the cross for our sin, not our sickness. As Peter makes clear, Christ's wounds heal us from sin, not from disease. "He Himself bore our sins in His body on the cross, that we might die to sin and live to righteousness" (1 Pet. 2:24).

In some ways it is hard to understand why any person would fail to accept Jesus Christ as Lord and Savior after even once hearing Him speak or after seeing even one miracle of healing. It is still harder to understand why people continued to reject the incomparable, gracious, loving Son of God after hearing Him preach many times and seeing Him heal dozens, or perhaps hundreds, of people of every sort of affliction. It seems totally incredible, however, that God's own chosen people—who were given His covenant, His law, His prophets, and His many special blessings – would reject the Son of their own God, the Messiah their own Scriptures prophesied, the very Deliverer whom they claimed to look and long for.

Yet as one studies the gospel accounts, that was exactly the response of most of the Jews. Their unbelief and rejection flew in the face of everything Christ said and did in their very midst. The proofs of His divinity, His power, and His goodness were obvious and beyond contradiction. Yet, as the evidence increased, so did resistance and rejection. At the beginning of his gospel, John prepares us for that response, telling us that "He came to His own, and those who were His own did not receive Him" (John 1:11). From the beginning Jesus knew that rejection would exceed acceptance, and He said to those who sought to kill Him, "You do not have His word abiding in you, for you do not believe Him whom He sent. You search the Scriptures, because you think that in them you have eternal life; and it is these that bear witness of Me; and you are unwilling to come to Me, that you may have life" (John 5:38-40). Like the rebellious citizens in one of Jesus' parables about the kingdom, those who rejected Christ said, in effect, "We do not want this man to reign over us" (Luke 19:14).

Those who rejected Jesus Christ even after witnessing His miracles were like a judge or jury who, after hearing an open and shut court case, makes a decision that is the exact opposite of what the evidence calls for. Jesus' authority was evident, as the people recognized from the beginning of His ministry (Matt. 7:29). His teaching was unique, as the officers reported to the chief priests and Pharisees who had sent them to arrest Jesus. "Never did a man speak the way this man speaks," they said (John 7:46). To the unbelieving Jewish leaders who questioned him about his healing by Jesus, the former blind man said, "Well, here is an amazing thing, that you do not know where He is from, and yet He opened my eyes. . . . Since the beginning of time it has never been heard that anyone opened the eyes of a person born blind. If this man were not from God, He could do nothing" (John 9:30, 32-33). When representatives from the Pharisees and the Herodians tried to entrap Jesus with a question about paying taxes to Caesar, He answered, "Render to Caesar the things that are Caesar's; and to God the things that are God's." His answer was so astute that His questioners "marveled, and leaving Him, they went away" (Matt. 22:21-22). The Jews were amazed at His teaching in the Temple, saying, "How has this man become learned, having never been educated?" (John 7:15). Although many accusations were leveled against Jesus, no one could convict Him of falsehood or any other sin (John 8:46). When Jesus healed the paralytic, the multitude was "filled with awe" (Matt. 9:8), and after He cast out a demon they said, "Nothing like this was ever seen in Israel" (v. 33). When Jesus wept over the grave of Lazarus, the Jews said, "Behold how He loved him!" (John 11:36). Jesus' composure was also beyond the human. When He stood before Pilate, who had the power to release Him or order Him crucified, Jesus would not give a single word in His own defense, "so that the governor was amazed" (Matt. 27:14).

Everything about Jesus was astounding, marvelous, and humanly unexplainable. It is no wonder that, when the people marveled at Him but would not accept Him, Jesus would Himself marvel at their unbelief (Mark 6:6). How can people witness God's power over and over again, admit that it is marvelous and even divine, and yet refuse to accept and follow the One who does such wonderful things?

Jesus Himself explained that some people run from the truth because it exposes their sin, which they do not want to give up. "The light is come into the world, and men loved the darkness rather than the light; for their deeds were evil. For everyone who does evil hates the light, and does not come to the light, lest his deeds should be exposed" (John 3:19-20). Others are attracted to Jesus' charisma and power. They marvel at the wonderful things He says and does, but they take nothing to heart. They follow Jesus from a distance, wanting to be thrilled but not changed, entertained but not saved. Often they are willing to be identified as a follower of Jesus Christ, but their commitment is superficial and they have no staying power.

In 9:18-22 Matthew shows us two of the things that often keep such people from genuine conversion: personal comfort and personal riches.

The Barrier of Personal Comfort

Now when Jesus saw a crowd around Him, He gave orders to depart to the other side. And a certain scribe came and said to Him, "Teacher, I will follow You wherever You go." And Jesus said to him, "The foxes have holes, and the birds of the air have nests; but the Son of Man has nowhere to lay His head." (8:18-22)

Jesus and His disciples were on the western shore of the Sea of Galilee, and the **crowd** became so massive that He **gave orders to depart to the other side.** Though He was completely God, Jesus was also completely human. He needed occasional rest and respite from the never-ending demands of those who came to Him for help.

When Jesus decided to cross the lake, the issue of commitment was pressed for several men who apparently were reevaluating their relationship to Him. From Mark we learn that some of the crowd got into other boats in order to go across the lake with Jesus (4:36), but three men (a third is mentioned in Luke 9) obviously did not want to leave and they approached Jesus just before He departed.

The first man was **a certain scribe,** who **said to Him, "Teacher, I will follow You wherever You go."** Since he did not ask Jesus a question or a favor, we can only guess at the man's motive for making that statement to Jesus. As **a scribe** he would have broken with the majority of his fellow scribes had he become a dedicated disciple of Jesus. He knew such a decision would be costly, and perhaps he wanted to see how Jesus reacted to his declaration of allegiance.

The scribes were authorities in Jewish law, and were closely associated with the Pharisees. They were highly educated and were the scholarly class of Jewish society. They were fiercely loyal to the system of religious traditions that many of their forerunners had been instrumental in devising. Typically the scribes were teachers, not followers of teachers, and they were especially reluctant to follow a teacher such as Christ, who not only was not educated in a rabbinic school but actually denounced the traditions they held sacrosanct.

For **a scribe** to address Jesus as *didaskalos* (**Teacher**) was therefore a considerable concession in itself, and no doubt the crowd, as well as the inner circle of the twelve disciples, were impressed that the Lord was spoken to so favorably by one of the Jewish leaders. In his own mind the man no doubt believed what he said to Jesus was true, just as Peter was later convinced in his own mind that he would never forsake Jesus (Matt. 26:33, 35). But neither man knew himself as well as he thought. The **scribe** may have sincerely thought that Jesus was the greatest **Teacher** he had ever heard and the greatest miracle worker the world had ever seen. He probably sincerely recognized that Jesus' teaching and power were from God and that He was in some uniquely special way God's man for the hour. He found Jesus appealing and wanted to be associated with Him. **I will follow You wherever You go,** he said to Jesus.

Unlike many Christian churches and organizations today, who are eager to embrace any famous personality who makes a profession of Christ, Jesus knew that a strong profession does not necessarily reflect strong commitment. Even without knowing men's hearts as He did, Christians today can benefit from taking that truth into account.

Jesus responded to the scribe's statement by making a statement of His own. He did not verbally question the man's sincerity but simply mentioned some demands of true discipleship the man had never considered. **Jesus said to him, "The foxes have holes, and the birds of the air have nests; but the Son of Man has nowhere to lay His head."** At first glance Jesus' words seem unrelated to the scribe's affirmation. He was saying. in proverbial form, that in spite of His divine authority and miracle-working power, self-indulgence was not in His plan, and He had fewer physical comforts than many animals. **Foxes have holes** they can call their own, and **birds of the air have nests** to which they can return and rest.

The Messiah is first referred to as **the Son of Man** in Daniel 7:13. Jesus is called by that title over eighty times in the gospels and it was the most common name that He used for Himself. It was a term of His humiliation, and was especially appropriate in the figure of His having **nowhere to lay His head.** In His humiliation He did not even have the basic comforts of life. Jesus had no place of His own—no house or property, not even a tent. After the dispute about Jesus' healing of the blind man, "everyone went to his home," John tells us: "But Jesus went to the Mount of Olives" (John 7:53–8:1). Whereas others went home to spend the night, Jesus spent it alone under the stars, in prayer with His Father. We are told of His often spending time in the home of Peter in Capernaum and of Mary, Martha, and Lazarus in Bethany, but we are never told of His spending even an hour in His own house, because He had none.

Jesus' purpose in making such a statement was obviously to make the **scribe** take stock of the genuineness of his commitment. Impressive words of affirmation are easy to make, especially when one does not know the cost of commitment involved. The Lord knew that the initial declared faith of many of His followers was shallow and superficial. When Jesus was in Jerusalem during the first Passover after He began His ministry, "many believed in His name, beholding His signs which He was doing." Yet, John goes on to say, "Jesus on His part, was not entrusting Himself to them, for He knew all men, and because He did not need anyone to bear witness concerning man for He Himself knew what was in man" (John 2:23-25). The Lord had no faith in their faith because He knew it was not genuine. Those people were only committed to the wonder and excitement that accompanied His work, not to Him as Lord or to the work of the gospel itself. Jesus repeatedly refused to take advantage of temporary popularity, which He knew would soon turn to permanent rejection.

In the parable of the sower, Jesus gives a vivid illustration of such people. They are the rocky places that do not have much soil. The seed immediately springs up and gives the appearance of a strong and healthy plant. But because it has no root it is soon scorched by the sun and withers. "This is the man," Jesus says, "who hears the word, and immediately receives it with joy; yet he has no firm root in himself, but is only temporary, and when affliction or persecution arises because of the word, immediately he falls away" (Matt. 13:5-6, 20-21).

Jesus knew human nature is fickle, unstable, and self-centered, and that many people are attracted to Him by excitement, glamor, or the hope of personal benefit, such as being healed or fed. They are quick to jump on the bandwagon when things are going well, but as soon as the cause becomes unpopular or demands sacrifice they want to jump off. At first they look as if they are alive for Christ and often give glowing testimonies, but when their association with Him begins to cost more than they bargained for they lose interest and are never seen again in the church or in Christian work. As the Bible commentator R. C. H. Lenski observes, such a person "sees the soldiers on parade, the fine uniforms, and the glittering arms and is eager to join, forgetting the exhausting marches, the bloody battles, the graves, perhaps unmarked" (*The Interpretation of St. Matthew's Gospel* [Minneapolis: Augsburg, 1961], pp. 338-39).

Jesus knew the **scribe** was too eager to declare his allegiance. He did not count the cost of discipleship, which involves self-denial, sacrifice, and quite possibly suffering. Jesus' proverb about the **foxes** and **birds** represented the relatively minimal sacrifice of being homeless—yet even that cost was obviously too high, because the **scribe** simply disappears without another word said by or about him. The Lord's words hit him where he was weak and unwilling, and his true loyalty only to his own comfort was quick to show itself.

Sugarcoating the message of the gospel, trying to make it appear to be less demanding than it is—or even not demanding at all—not only compromises God's Word and does disservice to the Lord but also does disservice to those to whom we witness. Jesus did no such thing. He warned His disciples with sobering candidness, "Behold, I send you out as sheep in the midst of wolves" (Matt. 10:16). He then continued to tell them, "And brother will deliver up brother to death, and a father his child; and children will rise up against parents, and cause them to be put to death. And you will be hated by all on account of My name, but it is the one who has endured to the end who will be saved. . . . A disciple is not above his teacher, nor a slave above his master. It is enough for the disciple that he become as his teacher, and the slave as his master. If they have called the head of the house Beelzebul, how much more the members of his household!" (vv. 21-22, 24-25).

Toward the end of His ministry the Lord said to His disciples, "They will make you outcasts from the synagogue, but an hour is coming for everyone who kills you to think that he is offering service to God" (John 16:2). Paul assures us that "all who desire to live godly in Christ Jesus will be persecuted" (2 Tim. 3:12). After presenting the long list of faithful Old Testament saints, the writer of Hebrews says of them that some "were tortured, not accepting their release, in order that they might obtain a better resurrection; and others experienced mockings and scourgings, yes, also chains and imprisonment. They were stoned, they were sawn in two, they were tempted, they were put to death with the sword; they went about in sheepskins, in goatskins, being destitute, afflicted, ill-treated (men of whom the world was not worthy), wandering in deserts and mountains and caves and holes in the ground" (11:35-38).

The **scribe** who came to Jesus on the shore of the Sea of Galilee was not willing to pay any such price for his faith. He merely wanted to add excitement to his life, have the prestige of being identified with a popular leader, or some other equally self-centered objective.

An explorer may have many volunteers to go with him on an expedition—until he explains that the team will be working in scorching heat, sub-zero cold, or sweltering swamps, with only subsistence rations, few chances to take a bath, and little contact with the outside world for months at a time. A young athlete may dream of winning a gold medal in the Olympics—until he learns about the rigorous training, strict diet, limited social life, and fierce competition he would have to face for many years.

There is no thrill like the joy of knowing and following Christ, but it is not a thrill that the world can understand or appreciate. Jesus Christ gives great peace to those who belong to Him, but His peace is not the kind the world gives or seeks (John 14:27). His joy and peace come by the way of ridicule, suffering, and the cross, which His disciples must take up when they follow Him. "If anyone wishes to come after Me," He said, "let him deny himself, and take up his cross, and follow Me" (Matt. 16:24). The Christian life is not adding Jesus to one's own way of life but renouncing that personal way of life for His and being willing to pay whatever cost that may require.

THE BARRIER OF PERSONAL RICHES

And another of the disciples said to Him, "Lord, permit me first to go and bury my father." (8:21)

This man, like the scribe of verse 19, was one of Jesus' **disciples** in the sense of being a follower who was unofficially identified with Him. He was not one of the twelve, but a hanger-on who had perhaps followed Jesus about the countryside for a few weeks or months.

Like the scribe, he assumed that his relationship to Jesus was all it should be, and he made what seems to have been a reasonable request: **Lord, permit me first to go and bury my father.** Since the Jews did not practice embalming, a dead body had to be quickly prepared and buried. Not only that, but Jewish tradition required that a person mourn for his deceased father or mother for a period of thirty days. The final act of devotion to parents was seeing that they were properly buried. Since Jesus was about to go to the other side of the Sea of Galilee, a burial obviously could not wait until His return.

The man's asking for permission to **bury** [his] **father**, however, did not mean that his father was already dead. The phrase was a common Near Eastern figure of speech that referred to a son's responsibility to help his father in the family business until the father died and the inheritance was distributed. Obviously such a commitment could involve a long period of time, thirty or forty years or more if the father was relatively young.

The expression is still used in parts of the Middle East today. A few years ago a missionary asked a rich young Turkish man to go with him on a trip to Europe, during which time the missionary hoped to disciple the man. When the young man replied that he must bury his father, the missionary offered his sympathy and expressed surprise that the father had died. The man explained, however, that his father was alive and healthy and that the expression "bury my father" simply meant staying at home and fulfilling his family responsibilities until his father died and he received his share of the inheritance.

Since a man's inheritance was customarily lost or reduced if he did not fulfill his expected responsibilities to the family, the phrase "I must bury my father" was frequently equivalent to "I want to wait until I receive my inheritance."

This second superficial disciple did not want to risk losing his inheritance by committing himself fully to Jesus. He wanted to be associated with Jesus in name, but the focus of his life was on his personal prosperity and well-being, not on serving the Lord. Jesus therefore **said to him, "Follow Me; and allow the dead to bury their own dead."** Like "foxes have holes, and the birds of the air have nests" (v. 20), the seemingly nonsensical expression **allow the dead to bury their own dead** was a proverbial figure of speech. It meant, "Let the world take care of the things of the world." The spiritually dead can take care of their own things.

In his parallel account of this story, Luke adds Jesus' further instruction, "As for you, go and proclaim everywhere the kingdom of God" (9:60). The man's primary responsibility as a disciple of Jesus Christ would be to proclaim the gospel, to bring the good news of eternal life to the spiritually **dead**. The Christian's responsibility is not to follow and mimic the world but to be a witness to the world in Christ's name and power. His citizenship is in the living, eternal kingdom of God, not in the dead and decaying realm of this world.

Again like the scribe, this second of the **disciples** who approached Jesus on this occasion also disappears without further mention. Apparently neither man wanted to discuss the matter further. Jesus' demands were too high, and the appeal of discipleship vanished. Like the rich young man who asked Jesus what good thing he must do to inherit eternal life (Matt. 19:16-22), when this professing disciple heard Christ's answer, he lost his enthusiasm for the things of the Lord.

For **Jesus** to say, **Follow Me,** is for Him to say, "Deny yourself and take up your cross" (Matt. 16:24). It is not that any amount of self-denial or sacrifice can earn salvation, but anything that is held more dearly than Christ is a barrier to Christ and will stand between the unsaved person and salvation.

Luke tells us of a third man who came to Jesus on this occasion and made a profession of discipleship. "I will follow You, Lord," he said; "but first permit me to say good-bye to those at home" (9:61). As with the other two men, this man's statement seems perfectly reasonable. It would take but a few days, or a few weeks at the most, for him to pay his parents the simple courtesy of saying good-bye.

But Jesus knew the man's heart and that his motivation was weak and his loyalty divided. He was not yet ready to give himself wholeheartedly to Jesus as Lord. He was still tied to his parent's apron strings and was under their dominance and control. The decision to follow Jesus Christ is the most uniquely personal decision that can be made. It is wonderful when friends and relatives encourage someone to decide for Christ, and it is tragic when they advise against Christ. But whatever the outside influences may be, the commitment is the individual's alone to make. Jesus therefore replied, "No one, after putting his hand to the plow and looking back, is fit for the kingdom of God" (v. 62). These words were perhaps adapted from a proverb attributed to the famous Greek poet Hesiod, who lived around 800 B.C.—"You can't plow a straight furrow when looking backward." A person cannot satisfactorily do the job at hand if he is continually looking back to his past work and loyalties. A person cannot follow Jesus Christ if he still longs for the ways of the old life.

Of these three men who came to Jesus and then disappeared, William MacDonald aptly says, "They left Christ to make a comfortable place for themselves in the world and to spend the rest of their lives hugging the subordinate."

Jesus made it clear that commitment to Him is total and unreserved or it is not commitment at all. "Do not think that I came to bring peace on the earth," He said. "I did not come to bring peace, but a sword. For I came to set a man against his father, and a daughter against her mother, and a daughter-in-law against her mother-in-law; and a man's enemies will be the members of his household. He who loves father or mother more than Me is not worthy of Me; and he who loves son or daughter more than Me is not worthy of Me. And he who does not take his cross and follow after Me is not worthy of Me" (Matt. 10:34-38). If a person allows anything to hold him back from full allegiance to Christ, he is not worthy of the kingdom of God. Jesus is not here talking about Christian service but about salvation. God will save no one who comes to Him with strings attached.

Throughout the centuries many people have marveled at Jesus, acclaiming His authority, His love, His wisdom, His purity, His power, His provision, His healing, and even His deity—but have failed to give themselves to Him. They praise and profess Jesus, and then walk away. Bishop J. C. Ryle wrote, "The saddest road to hell is the one that runs under the pulpit, past the Bible, and through the middle of warnings and invitations."

Jesus' response to the three men who came to Him on the shore of Galilee seems to contradict His promise that "all that the Father gives Me shall come to Me, and the one who comes to Me I will certainly not cast out" (John 6:37). Those men personally came to Christ, and they seemed to come positively, speaking well of Him and proclaiming their desire to follow Him. But Jesus' further words in John 6 explain why so many people who profess to come to Christ do not really come to Him at all. He said, "He who eats My flesh and drinks My blood has eternal life, and I will raise him up on the last day" (v. 54). In other words, belief in Jesus Christ is total identity with Him. There is no such thing as partial belief or partial salvation. A person who does not totally commit himself to Christ disbelieves in Him, no matter how many positive things he may have to say about Him. Jesus therefore went on to say, "There are some of you who do not believe," and shortly after that we are told that "as a result of this [that is, of all of the hard sayings Jesus had just given], many of His disciples withdrew, and were not walking with Him anymore" (vv. 64, 66).

Coming to Jesus Christ is coming on His terms, not our own. The person who comes to Christ comes in humility, meekness, a needy beggar in spirit who hungers and thirsts for God's righteousness, who cries for mercy, and is willing to be hated, reviled, and persecuted for the sake of his Lord (Matt. 5:3-12). The Lord may not take away comforts, money, or relationships with others, but all of those things—and everything else besides—must be given over to Him, to do with as He pleases. Otherwise He is not Lord, no matter how much allegiance to Him is professed.

BIRDVILLE
BAPTIST CHURCH
LIBRARY

Jesus' Power over the Natural (8:23-27)

And when He got into the boat, His disciples followed Him. And behold, there arose a great storm in the sea, so that the boat was covered with the waves; but He Himself was asleep. And they came to Him, and awoke Him, saying, "Save us, Lord; we are perishing!" And He said to them, "Why are you timid, you men of little faith?" Then He arose, and rebuked the winds and the sea; and it became perfectly calm. And the men marveled, saying, "What kind of a man is this, that even the winds and the sea obey Him?" (8:23-27)

At creation God ordained man to be king of the earth, to "rule over the fish of the sea and over the birds of the sky and over the cattle and over all the earth, and over every creeping thing that creeps on the earth" (Gen. 1:26). But when man fell into sin, he was dethroned and lost his sovereignty over the earth. He lost his God-given majesty along with his innocence. With the rest of the earth man was cursed and corrupted. He lost his dominion, and both man and earth lost their glory. The control of earth fell into the hands of the usurper, Satan, who now reigns as ruler of this world and age (John 12:31; 14:30). Man's sin, earth's corruption, and Satan's rule have brought sickness, pain, death, hardship, sorrow, war, injustice, falsehood, hunger, natural disaster, demonic activity, and every other evil that plagues the world.

But from the beginning, and even before the beginning, God planned the redemption of both man and the earth, reversing the curse. According to His divine plan, God's own Son would come to earth twice in the process of that redemption—the first time to redeem man and the second time to redeem the earth. In His first coming Jesus Christ came in humility, going to the cross and rising from the grave to redeem man from sin. In His second coming He will come in blazing glory and establish His thousand-year kingdom, the Millennium, and after that a completely new heaven and earth—redeeming the whole of creation for all eternity.

In the coming kingdom of God, His ultimate plan for earth will be restored—without sin, pain, disease, hatred, hardship, sorrow, disaster, or demons. There will be only holiness, righteousness, truth, peace, love, and beauty. Everything that now blights man's happiness, that breaks his heart, that frustrates his hopes, that disrupts and perverts his dominion will be removed forever. For all time and eternity the universe will be redeemed.

As we look at mankind and the present earth, however, it is glaringly obvious that man himself could never effect such changes. Man cannot solve the natural problems of environment, weather, droughts, famines, disease, and sickness. Someone has said that for every problem science solves, six others are created in its place. The greater our advancements, the more severe the complications.

Even less can man solve his moral and spiritual problems. As we become more advanced in psychology, sociology, criminology, and diplomacy, we also become more engulfed in psychological disorders, sociological problems, and in crime and war.

The power to reverse the curse and bring a new heaven and a new earth not only is infinitely beyond man but is inconceivable to man. We cannot imagine the power necessary to make such a radical recreation of the universe, any more than we can imagine the power it took to create it in the first place and to sustain it. Man has the capability to destroy his world, but not the power to perfect it.

The psalmist tells us that "power belongs to God" (Ps. 62:11). He speaks of "the greatness of Thy power" (79:11) and of the one "who dost establish the mountains by His strength, being girded with might" (65:6). David cried out, "O God, Thou art my God; I shall seek Thee earnestly; my soul thirsts for Thee, my flesh yearns for Thee, in a dry and weary land where there is no water. Thus I have beheld Thee in the sanctuary, to see Thy power and Thy glory" (Ps. 63:1-2). Paul reminds us that, "since the creation of the world His invisible attributes, His eternal power and divine nature, have been clearly seen, being understood through what has been made" (Rom. 1:20).

The more man delves into the universe, the more amazing and awesome the wonder of creation becomes. Telescopes can take us some four billion light years—about twenty-five sextillion miles—into space, and yet we have not come near the edge of the universe. We have discovered certain gravitational principles that keep the stars and planets in their orbits, yet we are far from fully explaining those principles, much less duplicating them. The earth spins on its axis at a thousand miles an hour at the equator, travels in a five-hundred-eighty-million-mile orbit around the sun at about a thousand miles a minute, and, with the rest of its solar system, careens through space at an even faster speed in an orbit that would take billions of years to complete. The energy of the sun has been estimated to be equivalent to five-hundred-million-million-billion horsepower. There are at least one-hundred-thousand-million other suns in our galaxy, most of them larger than ours.

God is also creator and sustainer of the microcosm. A teaspoon of water contains a million-billion-trillion atoms, which themselves are composed of still smaller particles of energy. Smaller subparticles of those particles are still being discovered.

We know Jesus Christ "upholds all things by the word of His power" (Heb. 1:3). He energizes every atom and every atomic particle and subparticle in the universe. That is the power of our God and Savior! If He has power to create and sustain the earth, surely He has power to recreate it. He has the power to bring back Eden and, indeed, create a new earth that far surpasses Eden.

Jesus Christ came into the world, in part, to demonstrate that power, to show for all who would see it that He was indeed the Son of God. The promised Messiah and King had power to redeem man from sin and to give him renewed sovereignty over a renewed earth. As noted in the previous chapter, Matthew has already shown that Jesus had the right genealogy, the right birth, the right baptism, the right success over temptation, and the right message. God had said that the One who would reverse the curse would come through the line of David, and Jesus did. God had said this Deliverer would be born of a virgin, and Jesus was. God had said He would be approved by the Father, and Jesus was. God had said He would be more powerful than Satan, and Jesus proved that He was. God had said His Son would speak the truth, and Jesus did. God had said He would have power over disease and death, and Jesus proved that He did.

Above all else the miracles were foretastes of kingdom power. When Jesus healed diseases and restored broken bodies, He previewed the kingdom, in which there would be no sickness or deformity. When He cast out demons, He previewed the kingdom, in which there would be no demonic activity. When He raised the dead, He previewed the kingdom, in which there would be no death.

After Jesus had both forgiven and healed the paralytic, He said that He had done so "in order that you may know that the Son of Man has authority on earth" (Matt. 9:6). When the multitudes saw Jesus' miracles, "they were filled with awe, and glorified God, who had given such authority" (9:8). To prepare them for His transfiguration, Jesus told His disciples, "'Truly I say to you, there are some of those who are standing here who shall not taste death until they see the kingdom of God after it has come with power.' And six days later, Jesus took with Him Peter and James and John, and brought them up to a high mountain by themselves. And He was transfigured before them; and His garments became radiant and exceedingly white" (Mark 9:1-3). As He taught in the Capernaum synagogue one Sabbath, the people "were amazed at His teaching, for His message was with authority" (Luke 4:32). When He cast a demon out of a man in that synagogue, they were still further amazed and exclaimed, "With authority and power He commands the unclean spirits, and they come out" (v. 36). In the opening words of his letter to the Romans, Paul speaks of Jesus' being "declared the Son of God with power" (1:4), and in First Corinthians speaks of Him as "Christ the power of God and the wisdom of God" (1:24). The supreme proof of Jesus' divinity and messiahship was His absolute authority and power over everything on earth.

In Matthew 8:23-27 Jesus demonstrates His unlimited power over the natural world. His stilling the storm is the first miracle of the second group of three miracles presented in chapters 8 and 9.

THE PARTICULARS

And when He got into the boat, His disciples followed Him. And behold, there arose a great storm in the sea, so that the boat was covered with the waves; but He Himself was asleep. (8:23-24)

After confronting the three superficial followers with the true cost of discipleship (8:18-22; Luke 9:61-62), Jesus **got into the boat** to go to the other side of the Sea of Galilee, which is about 13 miles long and as much as 8 miles wide.

The **disciples** who **followed Him** included the twelve, some of whom were in the same boat as Jesus, along with other followers who went in separate boats (Mark 4:36). Because Jesus healed many people and talked with the three professing disciples after "evening had come" (v. 16), it was probably well into the night when the small flotilla departed.

Mathētēs (**disciple**) simply means a follower, learner, or pupil. The word itself has no spiritual connotation, and it is used of superficial followers of Jesus as well as of genuine believers. Because the Sermon on the Mount is essentially a message on salvation, the disciples who gathered on the mountain to hear Jesus (Matt. 5:1) obviously included unbelievers. The two men who approached Jesus just before He entered the boat are called disciples (Matt. 8:21; cf. v. 19), but their leaving Him proved them to be false disciples. The men of Jesus' inner circle are often referred to as disciples (Matt. 10:1), yet unbelieving Judas ended up betraying the Lord.

At least four categories of disciples are seen in the gospels. The broadest group were the curious, those who followed Jesus for a while simply to find out what He was like. They were fascinated and intrigued by what He said and did, but they would not surrender to Him as Lord and Savior. We see some of these disciples in John 6. When Jesus proclaimed, "Truly, truly, I say to you, unless you eat the flesh of the Son of Man and drink His blood, you have no life in yourselves, . . . Many therefore of His disciples, when they heard this said, 'This is a difficult statement; who can listen to it?' . . . As a result of this many of His disciples withdrew, and were not walking with Him anymore" (John 6:53, 60, 66).

The second category of disciple included those who were intellectually convinced of Jesus' divine message and power. When Nicodemus came to Jesus at night, he said, "Rabbi, we know that You have come from God as a teacher; for no one can do these signs that You do unless God is with him" (John 3:2). But at that point he was not yet committed to Jesus. As the Lord went on to point out, Nicodemus was not born again and consequently had no spiritual relationship to God, no participation in His kingdom, and no eternal life (vv. 3-15).

The third category of disciple was composed of secret believers. Joseph of Arimathea was such a clandestine follower until he asked Pilate for permission to bury Jesus in his own tomb and thereby proclaimed allegiance to his Savior (Matt. 27:57-58).

In the fourth category of disciples were the true and open believers, those who were publicly and permanently committed to Jesus Christ. The small group of **disciples** who **followed Him** was more than just the twelve and no doubt included all four kinds.

The **boat** was probably a small, open fishing craft of the type commonly used by fishermen such as Peter, James, and John. The Sea of Galilee lies just over 600 feet below sea level, near the northern end of the Jordan River. Mt. Hermon rises 9,200 feet to the north, and strong northerly winds often plummet down the upper Jordan valley with great force. When they meet the warmer air over the Galilee basin, the intensity is increased. Hitting the cliffs on the eastern shore, the winds swirl and twist, causing the waters beneath them to churn violently. The fact that they come quickly and with little warning makes the storms all the more dangerous and frightening.

Seismos (**storm**) literally means a shaking and is the term from which we get seismic, seismograph, and related terms. The storm was so violent that it shook the water in the lake as if it were a glass of water in the hands of a great giant. The exclamation **behold** intensifies the rapid and surprising manner in which **there arose a great storm in the sea.** The storm became so fierce that **the boat was covered with the waves,** and Mark explains that "the waves were breaking over the boat so much that the boat was already filling up" (Mark 4:37).

Yet Jesus **Himself was asleep,** no doubt being exhausted from the long day's work of healing and teaching. Just before we see one of His most awesome demonstrations of deity, we see a touching picture of His humanness. The Lord was bone weary, and He slept so soundly that not even the tossing of the boat, the noise of the wind, or the blowing water in His face awakened Him. He was soaked to the skin while lying on hard planks with only a cushion for His head (Mark 4:38).

Yet this was all part of the divine plan. The storm was howling, the wind and waves were about to swamp the boat as it tossed about on the water like a cork—and the Creator of the world slept soundly in the midst of it all. Although in His divinity He was omniscient, in His humanness He was at this time oblivious to the turmoil that surrounded Him.

THE PANIC

And they came to Him, and awoke Him, saying, "Save us, Lord; we are perishing!" And He said to them, "Why are you timid, you men of little faith?" (8:25-26*a*)

Several of the twelve disciples were fishermen, and we can be certain they had done everything possible to save themselves. They were probably just as tired as Jesus was, but were far too afraid to sleep. They had nowhere else to turn but to Jesus and were exactly where God wanted them to be. Sometimes the Lord has to bring us to a point of absolute desperation before He can get our attention, and that is what He did with those disciples whose boat was about to be swamped or torn to pieces. They had run out of human solutions and had only Jesus to turn to. Perhaps the one who could cleanse lepers, restore sight to the blind, and heal every other sort of disease also had power over the wind and the sea. Their great fear was mixed with a glimmer of faith as **they came to Him, and awoke Him, saying, "Save us, Lord; we are perishing!"** Had they had the confidence in Jesus that He had in His Father, they would have been as calm and unconcerned as He.

The story is told of a hardened old sea captain who was quite vocal about his atheism. One night during a storm he was washed overboard and his men heard him crying out to God for help. When he was finally rescued one of the men asked him, "I thought you didn't believe in God." He replied, "Well, if there isn't a God, there ought to be one for times like this." Many people turn to the Lord only when every other resource has been exhausted. When sickness, death, loss of job, or some other tragedy comes, they cry out to God much as the disciples did to Jesus.

God is always pleased when men turn to Him, especially for salvation. People can be healed, comforted, saved from financial ruin, and helped in many other ways without God's direct intervention, but the person who is not saved has absolutely no resource but the Lord. God loves to hear a sinner's cry of desperation, because realizing one's own inadequacy is the first step in turning to Him. He also loves to hear His own people cry out to Him, even in desperation, because that is a sign they remember to whom they belong.

Even the greatest saints of God have at times forgotten their heavenly Father and become swamped by circumstances. The psalmist cried, "Why dost Thou stand afar off, O Lord? Why dost Thou hide Thyself in times of trouble?" (Ps. 10:1). The writer of Psalm 44 lamented: "But for Thy sake we are killed all day long; we are considered as sheep to be slaughtered. Arouse Thyself, why dost Thou sleep, O Lord?" (vv. 22-23). Even Isaiah was dismayed at God's seeming inability to help His people. "Awake, awake," he cried out, "put on strength, O arm of the Lord; awake as in the days of old, the generations of long ago" (Isa. 51:9). Like the disciples during the storm, he wondered why God slept while His people were perishing.

Jesus' first response to the disciples' plea was to rebuke them gently for their lack of faith. **He said to them, "Why are you timid, you men of little faith?"** *Deilos* (**timid**) has the basic meaning of being fearful or cowardly, and the disciples must have wondered why Jesus wondered at them. How could He ask why they were afraid and **timid,** when they obviously had everything to be afraid of? The great question in their minds was why *Jesus* was *not* afraid. It was the middle of the night, the storm was sure to wash them overboard or sink the boat, and any response but fear seemed foolish and unnatural. Jesus' calmness so perplexed the disciples that they accused Him of insensitivity: "Teacher, do You not care that we are perishing?" (Mark 4:38).

But Jesus turned the rebuke back upon them. **Why are you timid,** He asked, and then gave the answer as part of the question: **you men of little faith?** They were fearful because they were faithless, **timid** because they had **little faith.** "Don't you believe in Me and in My power?" He asked, in effect. "Haven't you seen enough of My power and experienced enough of My love to know you are perfectly safe with Me? You have seen Me perform miracle upon miracle, even on behalf of those who never trusted in Me or even bothered to thank Me. You have seen My power and My compassion, and you should know that because of My power I *can* help you and that because of My compassion I *will* help you. Even if you should drown, don't you know that would mean instant heaven? What, then, do you have to be worried about?"

The disciples knew the Psalms. Many times they had heard and repeated the words of Psalm 89: "O Lord God of Hosts, who is like Thee, O mighty Lord? Thy faithfulness also surrounds Thee. Thou dost rule the swelling of the sea; when its waves rise, Thou dost still them" (vv. 8-9). They had sung, "God is our refuge and strength, a very present help in trouble. Therefore we will not fear, though the earth should change, and though the mountains slip into the heart of the sea: though its waters roar and foam, though the mountains quake at its swelling pride" (Ps. 46:1-3). They knew well the majestic and comforting words of Psalm 107:

> Those who go down to the sea in ships, who do business on great waters; they have seen the works of the Lord, and His wonders in the deep. For He spoke and raised up a stormy wind, which lifted up the waves of the sea. They rose up to the heavens, they went down to the depths; their soul melted away in their misery. They reeled and staggered like a drunken man, and were at their wits' end. Then they cried to the Lord in their trouble, and He brought them out of their distresses. He caused the storm to be still, so that the waves of the sea were hushed. Then they were glad because they were quiet; so He guided them to their desired haven. (Ps. 107:23-30)

It was a literal fulfillment of those verses that Jesus was about to accomplish on the Sea of Galilee.

The believer who is aware of God's power and love has no reason to be afraid of anything. Because God both can and will take care of His children, there is no hardship or danger through which He cannot or will not take them. God's power and love will see us through any storm, and that is the essence of what we need to know and consider when we are in trouble.

Yet every believer realizes from his own experience that knowing about God's power and love and trusting in them do not always go together. Our weaknesses and frailties are so much a part of us that, even after we have witnessed God doing marvelous things, we still fall into doubt and fear. In fact, like Elijah after the great miracle on Mt. Carmel and the disciples after the great miracles in Capernaum, we sometimes are most afraid just after we have been overwhelmed with God's greatness. We marvel at His greatness, but as soon as trouble comes we forget His greatness and see only the trouble.

Faith needs constant strengthening, as the disciples eventually came to realize. "Increase our faith!" they pleaded of Jesus (Luke 17:5). Even believers are subject to disbelief, and the more we believe, the more we also want to cry out with the father of the boy with the unclean spirit, "I do believe; help my unbelief" (Mark 9:24). We know God can provide, but we also know how easily we can fail to trust in His provision. We know God loves us, but we also know how easily we can forget His love. We know He gives peace that passes understanding, but we also know how easily we can fall into worry and despair. When it is coupled with **little faith**, even much knowledge about God leaves us **timid** and afraid when trouble comes.

THE POWER

Then He arose, and rebuked the winds and the sea; and it became perfectly calm. (8:26b)

Jesus **arose, and rebuked the winds and the sea,** saying, "Hush, be still" (Mark 4:39). At the word of the Creator the storm could do nothing but become **perfectly calm.** The winds stopped, the waves ceased, the air cleared, and the water became as glass. Storms normally subside gradually, with winds and waves diminishing little by little until calm is restored. But this storm subsided faster even than it had come; it came suddenly and ceased instantly. Though small in comparison to hurricanes and typhoons, that storm on the Sea of Galilee had generated multiplied millions of units of horsepower. Yet Jesus stopped it with a word—an easy feat compared to His bringing the entire world into existence with a word.

The one who had control over diseases and demons also had control over nature. And as Matthew would proceed to show, He also had power to forgive sins and to raise the dead.

THE PORTENT

And the men marveled, saying, "What kind of a man is this, that even the winds and the sea obey Him?" (8:27)

Thaumazō (**marveled**) refers to extreme amazement and can carry the idea of portending. **The men** could not imagine **what kind of a man** Jesus was, **that even the winds and the sea obey Him.** Mark reports that, along with their great amazement, the men were also "very much afraid" (4:41). They were now more afraid of the one who had stilled the storm than they had been of the storm itself. Many of them had encountered dangerous storms, but none had encountered such supernatural power as Jesus here displayed.

After God had declared His great power and majesty, Job exclaimed, "I have heard of Thee by the hearing of the ear; but now my eye sees Thee; therefore I retract, and I repent in dust and ashes" (Job 42:5-6). When Isaiah "saw the Lord sitting on a throne, lofty and exalted, with the train of His robe filling the temple," he declared, "Woe is me, for I am ruined! Because I am a man of unclean lips, and I live among a people of unclean lips; for my eyes have seen the King, the Lord of hosts" (Isa. 6:1, 5). After Daniel beheld the Lord, he testified: "No strength was left in me, for my natural color turned to a deathly pallor, and I retained no strength. But I heard the sound of his words; and as soon as I heard the sound of his words, I fell into a deep sleep on my face, with my face to the ground" (Dan. 10:8-9). When Peter saw Jesus miraculously provide the great catch of fish, "he fell down at Jesus' feet, saying, 'Depart from me, for I am a sinful man, O Lord!'" (Luke 5:8). When Paul encountered the risen Christ on the Damascus road, "he fell to the ground. . . . And though his eyes were open, he could see nothing" (Acts 9:4, 8).

God's majesty is so overwhelming that when He displays Himself in even a small part of His glory men cannot stand in His presence. These disciples suddenly realized that God was standing in the very boat with them, and they were terrified by His power and His holiness. On a similar and later occasion Peter walked on the water. But when the wind came up, he became afraid, and Jesus not only held up His faithless disciple but also caused the wind to stop. "And those who were in the boat worshiped Him, saying, 'You are certainly God's Son!'" (Matt. 14:29-33).

Isaac Watts wrote:

> We sing the mighty power of God,
>   Who bade the mountains rise.
> Who spread the flowing seas abroad,
>   And built the lofty skies.
> We sing the wisdom that ordained
>   The sun to rule the day.
> The moon shines full at His command,
>   And all the stars obey.
> Lord, how Thy wonders are displayed
>   Where e'er we turn our eyes,
> When e'er we view the ground we tread,
>   Or gaze upon the skies.
> There's not a plant nor flower below,
>   But makes Thy glories known,
> And clouds arise and tempest blow,
>   By order of Thy throne.

He closes with the beautiful lines:

> On Thee each moment we depend,
>   If Thou withdraw we die.
> O may we ne'er that God offend,
>   Who is forever nigh.

The same Christ who stilled the Sea of Galilee is the Christ who keeps every atom and every star in its orbit. He keeps the universe in balance and provides for each plant and animal. One day He is coming to restore the world that sin defiled, to make completely new the heavens and the earth. Even now He is the God who gives eternal life to those who trust in Him, and who will calm their every storm and give strength for their every tragedy.

Jesus' Power over the Supernatural (8:28-34)

4

And when He had come to the other side into the country of the Gadarenes, two men who were demon-possessed met Him as they were coming out of the tombs; they were so exceedingly violent that no one could pass by that road. And behold, they cried out, saying, "What do we have to do with You, Son of God? Have You come here to torment us before the time?" Now there was at a distance from them a herd of many swine feeding. And the demons began to entreat Him, saying, "If You are going to cast us out, send us into the herd of swine." And He said to them, "Begone!" And they came out, and went into the swine, and behold, the whole herd rushed down the steep bank into the sea and perished in the waters. And the herdsmen ran away, and went to the city, and reported everything, including the incident of the demoniacs. And behold, the whole city came out to meet Jesus; and when they saw Him, they entreated Him to depart from their region. (8:28-34)

Matthew adds to the convincing evidence of Jesus' messiahship and divinity by showing His power over the supernatural as well as over disease, deformity, and the natural world. For Jesus to redeem the earth and reverse the curse, He would have to have total power over Satan and his demon hosts. In order to rescue fallen humanity He would have to be able to overpower the evil forces that hold men in physical, mental, and spiritual bondage. Throughout the gospel record, therefore, we repeatedly find accounts of Jesus' ability to cast out demons from those under their evil control. He exercised His power instantaneously, authoritatively, and with total success—often by the use of but a single word, as in the present instance.

In the wilderness temptations Jesus demonstrated His power to resist Satan; now He demonstrates His power to overcome and completely subdue Satan. In His dealing with the kingdom of darkness He not only would not bend to Satan but made Satan bend to Him. As the apostle John tells us, "The Son of God appeared for this purpose, that He might destroy the works of the devil" (1 John 3:8). The Lord became a Man and came into the world in order to destroy the works of Satan. When He comes again to establish His kingdom He will incarcerate Satan for a thousand years, at the end of which, after a brief freedom, he and his evil co-workers will be cast into the lake of fire, where "they will be tormented day and night forever and ever" (Rev. 20:2, 7-10). By casting out demons during His earthly ministry, Jesus gave dramatic, powerful, and repeated evidence of His power over Satan. As He explained to a multitude near Jerusalem, "If I cast out demons by the finger of God, then the kingdom of God has come upon you" (Luke 11:20).

When the disciples tried to cast out demons they found out how extremely difficult it is. Although Jesus had given them "power and authority over all the demons" (Luke 9:1), they discovered that casting out demons was not as easy for them as for Him (Matt. 17:16, 19). Many Jews of New Testament times were involved in exorcism by means of various formulas and rituals, with no real success. That is why Jesus' total success was so surprising. "What is this? A new teaching with authority!" exclaimed the incredulous Jews at Capernaum. "He commands even the unclean spirits, and they obey Him" (Mark 1:27). Because Jesus cast out demons with such ease, some of the people concluded that He must therefore be in collusion with the devil, and they declared, "He casts out demons by Beelzebul, the ruler of the demons" (Luke 11:15). When the seven sons of Sceva tried to cast an evil spirit out of a man by the power of "Jesus whom Paul preaches, . . . the evil spirit answered and said to them, 'I recognize Jesus, and I know about Paul, but who are you?' And the man, in whom was the evil spirit, leaped on them and subdued all of them and overpowered them, so that they fled out of that house naked and wounded" (Acts 19:13-16).

In the account of the two demon-possessed men, Matthew first describes the possession by the demons, then the power of Christ over the demons, and finally the perspective of the people in regard to Jesus.

THE POSSESSION BY THE DEMONS

And when He had come to the other side into the country of the Gadarenes, two men who were demon-possessed met Him as they were coming out of the tombs; they were so exceedingly violent that no one could pass by that road. And behold, they cried out, saying, "What do we have to do with You, Son of God? Have You come here to torment us before the time?" Now there was at a distance from them a herd of many swine feeding. And the demons began to

entreat Him, saying, "If You are going to cast us out, send us into the herd of swine." (8:28-31)

After the miraculous stilling of the storm, Jesus and His disciples continued across the Sea of Galilee **to the other side.** By now it was daylight and the group of boats (see Mark 4:36) landed in **the country of the Gadarenes.** Those whom Matthew calls **Gadarenes** were also called Gerasenes (Mark 5:1; Luke 8:26) or Gergesenes, as found in some Greek texts. The small town of Gerasa, or Gergesa (from which come *Gerasenes* and *Gergesenes,* respectively) was on the northeast shore of the Sea of Galilee, about six miles across the water from Capernaum, and the steep cliffs nearby fit the geographical setting described here. The town of Gadara (from which comes **Gadarenes**) is located farther south and is inland; but the general region, including Gerasa, was often referred to as **the country of the Gadarenes.**

THE RECEPTION BY THE DEMONS

two men who were demon-possessed met Him as they were coming out of the tombs; they were so exceedingly violent that no one could pass by that road. (8:28b)

In their accounts of this incident, Mark (5:2) and Luke (8:27) mention only one demon-possessed man but do not state that only one was present. For their particular purposes they chose to focus on the more dominant of the **two men.** *Daimonizomai* (**demon-possessed**) simply means to be demonized, to be under the control of a demonic spirit, without regard to the kind or degree of control. Although its accounts of demonized people reflect many different conditions and degrees of control, Scripture does not clearly distinguish between being possessed, obsessed, or oppressed by demons.

Demonization may be defined as a condition in which one or more demons inhabits and gains control over a human being. Demons can attack men spiritually, mentally, and physically. In the spiritual realm they promote false religions, demon worship, the occult, and innumerable kinds of immorality, including murder (Rev. 9:20-21; 18:23-24). In the intellectual and psychological realm they promote such things as false doctrines; insanity and masochism, as in this **demon-possessed** man, who gashed himself with stones (Mark 5:5); and inability to speak and suicidal mania (see Mark 9:17-22).

Demon domination was a common affliction in New Testament times, even among God's chosen people, the Jews. In the apostolic church, the gift of miracles, or powers, was the ability to cast out demons. It is interesting, however, that we read of no account of demon possession in the city of Jerusalem. Throughout history, including modern times, that particular aspect of Satan's activity seems to appear more commonly in rural and unsophisticated areas than in sophisticated urban society. It is also more common where animistic religion and its accompanying fear and worship of evil spirits are strong. In more advanced societies, a person who is seriously deranged by demons is likely to be considered insane and placed in a mental institution, and it seems certain that many people who are diagnosed as mentally ill are actually demonized.

It is significant that Jesus never blamed a person for being either diseased or demon controlled. He recognized them as victims of powers beyond their own control and as in need of deliverance, not exhortation or condemnation.

As we see with these **two men who were demon-possessed,** the personality and voice of a demon can at will, and sometimes continuously, eclipse the personality and voice of the occupied person. When Jesus asked one of the men, "What is your name?" the demon responded through the man's mouth, saying, "My name is Legion; for we are many" (Mark 5:9).

These men lived in burial chambers that were commonly hewn out of rock hillsides or cliffs on the outskirts of a town or city, and as they saw Jesus approaching they **met Him as they were coming out of the tombs.** It is possible they were Jews, for whom touching a dead body was the greatest ceremonial defilement. If so, their being forced by the demons to live in a cemetery was an additional humiliation and torment.

They were so exceedingly violent that no one could pass by that road. We learn from the other gospel accounts that at least one of the men wore no clothes and that he had such great strength that no chain could keep him bound. He was often driven into the desert by the demons and spent much of his time ranting and raving, "crying out and gashing himself with stones" (Mark 5:4-5; Luke 8:27-29).

THE RECOGNITION BY THE DEMONS

And behold, they cried out, saying, "What do we have to do with You, Son of God? Have You come here to torment us before the time?" (8:29)

What do we have to do with You meant, "What are You doing here and why are You bothering us?" By addressing Jesus as **Son of God** the demons showed that they immediately recognized who He was. Mark reports that one of the men "ran up and bowed down before Him" (5:6). The word from which "bowed down" comes (*proskuneō*) is usually translated "worship," because it represents the most common Near Eastern act of adoration and reverence. The term carries the idea of profound awe and respect. Demons hate and loathe everything about God, yet they are powerless to do anything but bow down before Him when in His presence—just as one day at His name every knee will "bow, of those who are in heaven, and on earth, and under the earth" (Phil. 2:10).

Demons are fallen angels, and before they joined Satan in his rebellion against God they knew intimately each member of the Trinity. Though they had never before seen Him in human form, they instantly recognized Jesus as the second Person of the Godhead. As spirits, they recognized His spirit. They knew intuitively that they were standing in the presence of the **Son of God,** the "Son of the Most High God," as Mark

(5:7) and Luke (8:28) report. As we learn from another encounter of Jesus with demons, they also "knew Him to be the Christ," that is, the Messiah (Luke 4:41).

They knew Jesus was their divine antagonist and that He had full power and authority to destroy them at will. By their question, **Have You come here to torment us before the time?** they acknowledged that they knew there was a divinely appointed **time,** not yet come, when He would indeed judge them and punish them with eternal damnation. Their eschatology, like the rest of their theology, was factually correct. As James tells us, "the demons also believe, and shudder" (James 2:19). They shudder because their belief is that of recognition but not acceptance, and they fully realize the consequence of rejecting God.

In light of their knowledge about His divine power and plan it seems strange that Satan and his fallen hosts bothered to tempt and attack Jesus. But the supreme deceivers are also supremely self-deceived, and in their evil delusions they somehow hoped to frustrate Christ in His humanity. By inducing Him to sin, perhaps they could drag Him down to the lake of fire with them when judgment came. Perhaps they thought He was somehow less powerful and righteous on earth than they knew Him to have been in heaven. In any case, it is the nature of Satan and of those who belong to him to oppose God, no matter what the consequences or prospect for success.

The demons understood much more about Jesus' identity and about the divine plan of redemption and judgment than did the twelve disciples at that time. It was much later that Peter confessed before Jesus, "Thou art the Christ, the Son of the living God," a truth he came to know only by divine revelation (Matt. 16:16-17).

The demons knew they were not destined for judgment until after the Millennium and they consequently wondered why Christ now had dealings with them. It was much too early for their scheduled **time** of **torment,** and yet they sensed that Jesus was about to interrupt and destroy their present evil work.

THE REQUEST OF THE DEMONS

Now there was at a distance from them a herd of many swine feeding. And the demons began to entreat Him, saying, "If You are going to cast us out, send us into the herd of swine." (8:30-31)

In desperation the demons looked around for a way of escape, and they spotted **a herd of many swine feeding** in a pasture. The great size of the **herd,** which numbered 2,000 animals (Mark 5:13), indicates that the number of demons was also large (see also Mark 5:9). **If You are going to cast us out** was not a statement of uncertainty or mere possibility. The idea is, "In light of the fact that You are about to cast us out, . . ." Knowing Jesus' compassion for men and His divine plan to destroy the works of the devil, the demons knew He would not let them continue to inhabit and torment the two men.

The request of the demons seems bizarre, and we are not told why they asked to be sent **into the heard of swine.** Perhaps they thought the Lord had changed His timetable for judgment and would otherwise immediately throw them into the great abyss. Even inhabiting pigs would be immeasurably better than that. Because **swine** were the most unclean of all unclean animals to the Jews, perhaps the demons thought Jesus would not care if the demons took control of them. Or, by inhabiting and then destroying the pigs, perhaps they could cause the pigs' owners and others in the area to turn against Jesus. Perhaps Jesus would be killed for killing the pigs. Whatever the reason for the demons' request, it was predicated on the clear understanding that Jesus would not allow them to remain where they were.

THE POWER OF CHRIST

And He said to them, "Begone!" And they came out, and went into the swine, and behold, the whole herd rushed down the steep bank into the sea and perished in the waters. (8:32)

When the disciples cast out demons even with God's commissioning and empowering, it often required considerable time and persistence as well as prayer and fasting (Matt. 17:21; Mark 9:29). But Jesus cast the entire legion of demons out of the two men with but a word: **Begone!** He gave permission to the demons (see Luke 8:32) in the form of a command which they were powerless to disobey, and immediately **they came out, and went into the swine.**

Again we can only wonder at the demons' reason for doing what they did. Whether they directed **the whole herd** to rush **down the steep bank into the sea** where they **perished in the waters,** or whether that was simply the animals' frenzied response to being inhabited by the evil spirits, it seems likely the demons knew the outcome in advance. But we do not know why they did what they did or what happened to them after the pigs drowned.

As fallen angels, demons are extremely powerful beings (see 2 Kings 19:35; Ps. 103:20; 2 Pet. 2:11). When an angel was sent with a message for the prophet Daniel, he was delayed by a demon (called "the prince of the kingdom of Persia") for three weeks, and the Lord had to send the archangel Michael to his aid (Dan. 10:13). It is therefore hardly surprising that Paul warns us that even as God's own children we cannot withstand the attacks of demons apart from the Lord's armor, especially the shield of faith (Eph. 6:16).

Demons have superior intelligence (Ezek. 28:3-4), superior strength (Mark 5:4; Acts 19:16), superior supernatural powers to perform "signs and false wonders" (2 Thess. 2:9), and the superior experience of having existed long before the creation of the world, first as holy angels and then as fallen. They not only have great knowledge of God's nature and power but also great knowledge of man's nature and weaknesses. As spirit beings they are not limited by time, space, or form. Only the Lord Jesus Christ has the power to bruise Satan's head and it will only be by the Lord's power that he will be bound and cast into the abyss and eventually into the lake of fire and brimstone (Rev. 20:3, 10). It required tremendous power to cast out so many demons as Jesus did in the country of the Gadarenes, yet He did it in an instant.

Many people wonder why Jesus would allow so many animals, even unclean pigs, to be destroyed just to cater to the bizarre request of a bunch of demons. But animals were created for man's use and consumption, and those pigs were destined for slaughter anyway. Their being drowned brought considerable financial loss, but if the owners were Jews—as they may well have been—they had no business raising pigs in the first place. But the souls of the two possessed men were of infinitely greater value than the two thousand animals, and Jesus did not hesitate to permit such a relatively small sacrifice to be made on the men's behalf.

The primary lesson of this passage, however, does not have to do with the right to raise or eat pigs or with the relative value of pigs and human beings. The Lord's supreme purpose in casting out the demons and Matthew's purpose in reporting it were to demonstrate Jesus' authority and power over Satan and his forces. The fact that the demons **went into the swine** and the swine reacted in the frenzy they did was dramatic and convincing evidence that they had left the two men. Their fierceness and violence was transferred to the pigs and there could be no doubt in the minds of observers as to what had happened.

THE PERSPECTIVE OF THE PEOPLE

And the herdsmen ran away, and went to the city, and reported everything, including the incident of the demoniacs. And behold, the whole city came out to meet Jesus; and when they saw Him, they entreated Him to depart from their region. (8:33-34)

When **the herdsmen** saw what happened to their pigs, they **ran away.** The fact that they **reported everything, including the incident of the demoniacs,** indicates they realized the connection between the two demon-possessed men and what had happened to the animals. The pigs' mass suicide proved that Jesus had indeed cast the demons out of the men. Further evidence, which the **herdsmen** and the others discovered when they returned to the scene, was that one of the men—and presumably the other as well—was clothed and sat in his right mind at Jesus' feet (Luke 8:35).

The townspeople, probably including the owners of the pigs, were so amazed by the report that **the whole city came out to meet Jesus.** That they came specifically **to meet Jesus** shows that He was the focus of attention. He was of greater concern to them than either the pigs or the two previously possessed men. Contrary to the suggestion of many interpreters through the centuries, there is no indication in the text that the response of the people was due to their materialistic concern over the loss of so many pigs. Though they were possibly present, the owners of the pigs are not mentioned in any of the three gospel accounts. The issue was not the demons, the pigs, or the two men, but **Jesus.**

The people of the **city** (probably Gerasa) did not even give Him the reluctant reverence shown by the demons. They did not seem the least interested in finding out who He was or why He had come to their area. They wanted nothing to do with Him, and **entreated Him to depart from their region.** They had at first simply come out "to see what it was that had happened," but when "they came to Jesus and observed the man who had been demon-possessed sitting down, clothed and in his right mind, the very man who had the 'legion'; . . . they became frightened" (Mark 5:14-15). They were not angry or resentful but scared.

When unholy men come face-to-face with the holy God, they are terrified. Again we are reminded that when Isaiah "saw the Lord sitting on a throne, lofty and exalted," he exclaimed, "Woe is me, for I am ruined! Because I am a man of unclean lips, and I live among a people of unclean lips; for my eyes have seen the King, the Lord of hosts" (Isa. 6:1, 5). After Peter witnessed Jesus' miraculous provision of fish that nearly swamped two fishing boats, "he fell down at Jesus' feet, saying, 'Depart from me, for I am a sinful man, O Lord'" (Luke 5:8). When the storm came on the Sea of Galilee, the disciples were afraid, but when they saw Jesus still the storm they were even more afraid (Mark 4:38-41). They were more afraid of Jesus than the storm, because they realized that God Himself was in the boat with them. The sinner who knows he faces God can only see his sin, and the result is fear.

We are not told exactly what the people from the **city** thought of Jesus. We only know that they had a glimpse of the supernatural and it caused them to panic. They saw One who could control demons, who could control animals, and who could restore shattered minds to sanity—and they wanted nothing to do with Him.

Here we find the first opposition to Jesus recorded in the gospels. The people did not ridicule or persecute Jesus; they simply asked Him to leave them alone. Perhaps they resented His righteousness exposing their sin, His power exposing their weakness, or His compassion exposing their hardness of heart. Perhaps they could not tolerate Jesus because of His perfection. But unlike the scribes and Pharisees, these people showed no interest at all in who Jesus was or in His teaching or work. They seemed totally indifferent to His person and ministry. They did not care if He was the Messiah. They did not seem to care whether His powers were good or whether He was from God. They did not care anything about Him, except that He would go away. Their rejection of Jesus was in the form of great indifference, the same indifference to God shown by most men throughout history—the indifference that wants to let God alone and to be left alone by God. The Lord was an intrusion with whom they did not want to be bothered.

In great contrast to the attitude of those people, one of the men who had been demon-possessed begged Jesus "that he might accompany Him" (Mark 5:18). He was so grateful to Jesus for deliverance and so drawn to Him in love and adoration that he could not bear to be separated from Him. But Jesus had other plans for the man, and "He did not let him, but He said to him, 'Go home to your people and report to them what great things the Lord has done for you, and how He had mercy on you'" (v. 19). Jesus sent the man back to his own people—quite probably the very people who had asked Jesus to leave—to testify to them of the Lord's love and mercy. The man was to be an evangelist and missionary to his own people, living testimony that the One whom they had rejected nevertheless loved and sought to redeem them. Even to those who entreat **Him to depart,** Jesus extends His grace.

Jesus' Power over Sin (9:1-8)

5

And getting into a boat, He crossed over, and came to His own city. And behold, they were bringing to Him a paralytic, lying on a bed; and Jesus seeing their faith said to the paralytic, "Take courage, My son, your sins are forgiven." And behold, some of the scribes said to themselves, "This fellow blasphemes." And Jesus knowing their thoughts said, "Why are you thinking evil in your hearts? For which is easier, to say, 'Your sins are forgiven,' or to say, 'Rise, and walk'? But in order that you may know that the Son of Man has authority on earth to forgive sins"—then He said to the paralytic—"Rise, take up your bed, and go home." And he rose, and went home. But when the multitudes saw this, they were filled with awe, and glorified God, who had given such authority to men. (9:1-8)

The most distinctive message of Christianity is the reality that sin can be forgiven. That is the heart and lifeblood of the gospel, that men can be freed from sin and its consequences. The Christian faith has many truths, values, and virtues, each of which has countless applications in the lives of believers. But its supreme, overarching good news is that sinful man can be fully cleansed and brought into eternal fellowship with holy God. That is the message of Matthew 9:1-8.

Matthew has been focusing on various miracles of the Lord, all of which are meant to demonstrate Jesus' divinity. Even more specifically, they precisely and completely fulfilled the Old Testament prophecies of the Messiah's kingdom work. The miracles recorded by Matthew under the inspiration of the Holy Spirit therefore have a uniquely Jewish and Old Testament character and significance.

Concerning the natural realm, the Old Testament prophesied that the Messiah would have power over the curse in the physical world. Isaiah predicted there would be in His reign an abundance of rain and crops not known since the Fall (Isa. 30:23-24) and that one day even the wilderness would blossom profusely, as waters break forth and the scorched land and thirsty ground become pools and springs of water (35:1-2, 7; cf. 41:17-18; 51:3; 55:13; Ezek. 36:29-38; Joel 3:18). Animals which had been natural enemies of man and of other animals would no longer destroy or devour, and human longevity would increase so that a person who died at a hundred years of age would be considered to have died young. By the stilling of the storm (Matt. 8:23-27) Jesus gave a foretaste of His eventual taming of the entire natural world.

Concerning the supernatural realm, the Old Testament speaks of Satan and his evil forces who have so long oppressed and persecuted God's people (Dan. 7:24-27; 8:23-25; 11:36-12:3; Zech. 3:1-2) and who the Messiah would have to conquer before His righteous kingdom could be established on earth. By resisting Satan's temptations and casting out his demon servants (Matt. 8:28-34) Jesus proved His power was superior to Satan's.

Concerning the spiritual realm, the Old Testament tells us that Messiah's kingdom will be marked by forgiveness and redemption (Isa. 33:24; 40:1-2; 44:21-22; Ezek. 36). By His forgiveness of the paralytic recorded in this passage and many others Jesus further demonstrated power that is reserved to God alone and that Scripture had prophesied would characterize the Messiah.

It was Jesus' specific, complete, and dramatic fulfillment of these and all other messianic prophecies that made His rejection by the Jews—especially that of the scribes and Pharisees, who were students of Scripture—so heinous and inexcusable.

Matthew's arrangement and presentation of the three sets of miracles in chapters 8 and 9 show progressive development in revealing Jesus' credentials as the divine Messiah. First we see Him heal a leper with the touch of His hand (8:3), heal a centurion's servant without having seen the afflicted person (8:13), and then heal Peter's mother-in-law of a serious fever (8:15). Next He went beyond physical afflictions and demonstrated His authority and power over the spiritual kingdom of Satan by casting out many demons with a word (8:16), by demonstrating His power over the great natural forces by stilling the storm on Galilee (8:26), and by again demonstrating His authority over Satan by casting out a legion of demons from two possessed men of Gadara (8:32).

In the first of the last three miracles in these two chapters Jesus ascends still higher in the drama of supernatural acts as He deals with sin, the root of all man's physical and spiritual troubles and misery as well as the cause of his separation from his Creator. Christ Jesus demonstrates His power to remove the pollution and guilt of sin in those who trust in Him. The Great Physician not only can heal the sick, still the storm, and cast out demons, but can bring to the human soul the thing that it needs most: forgiveness of sin.

Matthew majors on the authority of Christ. At the end of the Sermon on the Mount he reports that Jesus "was teaching them as one having authority, and not as their scribes" (7:29). Those great teachings demonstrate His moral and theological authority. Throughout the book His miracles demonstrate His authority over both the natural and spirit worlds, and at the end of the book He declares, "All authority has been given to Me in heaven and on earth," and then sends out His disciples to teach and minister in that authority (28:18-20).

In all of those ways Jesus declared and demonstrated His sovereign authority to rule. In the present passage He demonstrates His sovereign authority to redeem.

We do not know how much time elapsed between Jesus' healing of the two demoniacs and His **getting into a boat,** by which He **crossed over** to the west shore of the Sea of Galilee **and came to His own city.** Matthew's concern here is not so much with the chronology or full details of Jesus' ministry as with the significance and progression of His miraculous signs.

Although Nazareth was the city of Jesus' childhood, He had been rejected by the people there, who would have thrown Him over a cliff to His death had He not passed through their midst unnoticed. From there "He went His way" a few miles east "and He came down to Capernaum, a city of Galilee" (Luke 4:29-31), as a prophet rejected in His own country (see Matt. 13:57). At this time He probably took up temporary residence with Peter, in whose home He healed Peter's mother-in-law (8:14-15). Jesus' **own city** was therefore now Capernaum (cf. Mark 2:1).

The events and teachings of Matthew 9:2-8 can be represented by six key words: faith, forgiveness, fury, forensic, force, and fear.

FAITH

And behold, they were bringing to Him a paralytic, lying on a bed; and Jesus seeing their faith (9:2a)

Before He went across the Sea of Galilee to the country of the Gadarenes, Jesus had generated massive interest in His ministry, and it was partly to get away from the crowds for a while that He took the trip (8:18). It was natural, therefore, that when He returned, the news quickly spread and the crowds returned.

We learn numerous additional details about this story from Mark and Luke. As already noted, Jesus had now made Capernaum His home city and was staying in Peter's house, where Jesus "was at home" (Mark 2:1). Two-story houses were common in Palestine and it is likely that the room with the overflow crowd (see v. 2) was on the second floor, where most visiting and socializing were done. Such upper rooms were common, and it was in one of these that the Lord ate the Last Supper with His disciples. The roof of the house was often used as a place for relaxation in the cool of the day, and frequently for sleeping on hot nights. The outside stairs were therefore usually built all the way to the roof.

Because the afflicted man's friends could not get into the crowded room where Jesus was, they carried the litter up to the top of the house and proceeded to dismantle the roof until they made enough room to lower the man into Jesus' presence (Mark 2:3-4; Luke 5:19). It is to these four friends or relatives that **they** refers.

Because the **paralytic** (*paralutikos*) had to be brought to Jesus **lying on a bed,** his paralysis obviously was severe, and he may well have been a quadriplegic. No wheelchairs or other such equipment were available to those who could not walk, and they had to rely on others to carry them around. Cripples have always suffered social stigma and neglect, but in the Jewish culture of Jesus' day the stigma was made immeasurably worse by the belief of most Jews that all disease and affliction was the direct result of someone's sin. The idea was common even in the days of Job, who may have lived as early as the time of Abraham. Eliphaz asked Job, "Who ever perished being innocent?" (Job 4:7) and Bildad said to him, "If your sons sinned against Him, then He delivered them into the power of their transgression" (8:4). The same attitude was clearly reflected in the disciples' question to Jesus as they passed a man who had been blind from birth: "Rabbi, who sinned, this man or his parents, that he should be born blind?" (John 9:1-2).

Though it is true that affliction, pain, and hardship of every sort are the result of the presence of sin in the world, they are not necessarily brought on by some specific sin of the person who is suffering. Not all sickness is chastening, but all sickness is a graphic demonstration of the destructive power at work in the world because of sin.

Like his fellow Jews, the **paralytic** no doubt believed his paralysis was direct punishment for his own sin or that of his parents or grandparents, and that thought must have added immensely to his suffering. In his own mind and in the minds of most of the people who saw him his paralysis was a vivid representation of his own sinfulness and of God's judgment. That belief gave crippled and diseased people even more reason to shun crowds.

But this man was determined to see Jesus at any cost. Because he associated the paralysis with his sin, his first concern was for forgiveness, which to his thinking would have automatically brought healing. And although his theology may have been erroneous, he was right in believing that his first and greatest need was spiritual.

By their persistence, the man and his four friends evidenced their strong conviction that Jesus could help. They had carried the man to the house, and when they could not get into the room with Jesus, they carried the stretcher all the way up to the roof, tore the roof open, and lowered the man on his **bed** down to Jesus' feet. Jesus not only saw this outward evidence but also saw their hearts. And **seeing their faith** by their aggressive approach to Him, the omniscient Lord also read the believing hearts of these five men just as He read the unbelieving hearts of the scribes who thought He was blaspheming (vv. 3-4).

Because the **paralytic** said nothing to Jesus it is possible to conclude that the paralysis had affected his vocal chords or his tongue. Or the man, despite his **faith**, may have been overcome with awe as he came face-to-face with the One who had power to heal all kinds of disease. Perhaps he now wondered if He could also heal hearts. In any case, he willingly and silently exposed himself to Jesus and to the whole crowd in all his physical, moral, and spiritual ugliness. He was literally at Jesus' feet, and in his heart he threw himself on Jesus' mercy. He approached the Lord in true humility, in the poverty of spirit God requires of the seeking heart (Matt. 5:3).

Jesus sometimes healed people who had little faith and even some who had no faith, but He was especially disposed to heal those with great faith, such as this man and his friends demonstrated. It was the kind of great faith shown by the centurion (8:10) and that would soon be shown by the man whose daughter had died (9:18).

FORGIVENESS

said to the paralytic, "Take courage, My son, your sins are forgiven." (9:2b)

Jesus' first words **to the paralytic** were, **Take courage, My son.** Knowing the man's fearful heart from being overwrought with sin and now being thrust into the very presence of incarnate God, Jesus spoke tender words of comfort and encouragement. How thrilling it must have been to hear the holy One who knew his sin, grief, and humiliation to say **take courage.**

Tharseō (**take courage**) refers to subjective courage, that which is deep and genuine—in contrast to *tolmaō*, which refers to outward boldness. *Tolmaō* would be characterized by gritting the teeth to help endure pain or whistling in the dark to stave off fear. It is the kind of courage that tries to master fear by sheer will power and determination. But *tharseō* represents the **courage** that eliminates fear. Jesus was saying, "Don't be afraid, because you no longer have anything to be afraid of." It was not that the man's fears had not been real and well founded. An unrepentant sinner is separated from God and under divine judgment. But when he repents in faith he no longer has reason to fear, because he is no longer under judgment. Knowing the paralytic's faith, Jesus therefore said to him, **take courage.**

Addressing the man as **My son** gave further comfort. *Teknon* (**son**) refers to a child of any age or sex. It is here translated **son** because Jesus was speaking to a man. **Son** was used in that day as it often is in our own, as a term of friendship and identity—sometimes even with a person just met. Because the paralytic repentantly identified himself with Jesus, Jesus lovingly identified Himself with the paralytic.

But Jesus' supreme words to him were, **your sins are forgiven.** Those words represent a divine miracle that is perhaps the greatest of all miracles and certainly the most desirable for the recipient—holy God forgiving the sins of an unholy man. Just as with a word Jesus stilled the storm, with a word He dismissed the paralytic's sins and gave him His most gracious gift to meet his greatest need.

Aphiēmi, the verb behind **are forgiven,** has the basic idea of sending or driving away, of doing away with. "As far as the east is from the west, so far has He removed our transgressions from us," David declared (Ps. 103:12). When God forgives sins He casts them "into the depths of the sea" (Mic. 7:19). Paul rejoiced that, even though he "was formerly a blasphemer and a persecutor and a violent aggressor," he was yet "shown mercy" (1 Tim. 1:13). "It is a trustworthy statement, deserving full acceptance," he goes on to say, "that Christ Jesus came into the world to save sinners, among whom I am foremost of all" (v. 15).

When missionaries in northern Alaska were translating the Bible into the language of the Eskimos, they discovered there was no word in that language for forgiveness. After much patient listening, however, they discovered a word that means, "not being able to think about it anymore." That word was used throughout the translation to represent forgiveness, because God's promise to repentant sinners is, "I will forgive their iniquity, and their sin I will remember no more" (Jer. 31:34).

When I was in college I was asked to visit a girl in the hospital who had been accidentally shot in the neck. The bullet severed her spinal cord and she was paralyzed from the neck down. I had never met the girl but was told she was a cheerleader at her school and had been very active and vivacious. When I came into the hospital room she was lying on a sheepskin pad, unable to do anything but speak. After we talked a while she confessed that, if she were able, she would commit suicide, because she did not want to face a future of helplessness. I presented Christ to her and, after some questions and discussion, she received Christ as her Lord and Savior. I went back to visit her several times, and one day she said to me, "I can honestly say now that I'm glad the accident happened. Otherwise I may never have met Christ and had my sins forgiven."

Forgiveness of sin is God's greatest gift because it meets man's greatest need. Sin is a transgression of God's law (1 John 3:4) and defiles His image in man, staining his soul with Satan's image (John 6:70; 8:44). Sin is hostility and rebellion against God (Lev. 26:27; 1 Tim. 1:9). It is ingratitude toward God (Josh. 2:10-12), is incurable by man himself (Jer. 13:23), affects all men (Rom. 3:23), and affects the total man (Jer. 19:9), body, mind, and spirit. It brings men under the dominion of Satan and the wrath of God (Eph. 2:2-3), and it is so persistent in the heart of man that even the regenerate person needs to continually fight against it (Rom. 7:19). It subjects man to trouble (Job 5:7), emptiness (Rom. 8:20), lack of peace (Isa. 57:21), and to eternal hell if he does not repent (2 Thess. 1:9).

Because of that bleak picture, the best news anyone can receive is the word that his **sins are forgiven.** When Jesus spoke those words to the paralytic, He must have tasted the bitterness and agony of Calvary, knowing that the words could be effective only because He would take the man's sins upon Himself. Every time He forgave sin He knew and anticipated the cost.

FURY

And behold, some of the scribes said to themselves, "This fellow blasphemes." (9:3)

Luke tells us that some Pharisees were also present with **the scribes** and that they thought within **themselves** Jesus was blaspheming by claiming to forgive sins (5:21; cf. Mark 2:7). They were right that only God can forgive sins (Isa. 43:25; Mic. 7:18-19), but because they refused to recognize Jesus' divinity, they could only conclude that **this fellow blasphemes.**

Unlike the paralytic, those men saw no need for forgiveness, because they considered themselves already to be righteous. They resented Jesus' offering forgiveness, not only because they did not believe He was God but also because they considered it unjust for a person to be forgiven simply by asking for it—instead of by earning it, as they thought they had done. The two great barriers to salvation have always been refusal to recognize the need for it and the belief that it can be earned or deserved.

These **scribes** had probably seen many miracles of Jesus and heard the testimony of others who had been healed of disease and cleansed of demons. But they refused to recognize His power as coming from God, much less that He Himself was God. Their thinking **this fellow blasphemes** reflected the pattern of growing rejection and persecution by the Jewish leaders that led ultimately to Jesus' crucifixion. They accused Him of being immoral because they saw Him "eating with the tax-gatherers and sinners" (Matt. 9:11) and they even declared the greatest blasphemy themselves by accusing Jesus of being satanic, of casting "out the demons by the ruler of the demons" (v. 34).

Their hearts were so hardened against Christ that every miraculous evidence of His divinity and messiahship drove them to deeper unbelief rather than to repentance. Even His most gracious and loving words and acts drove them to greater fury against Him.

FORENSIC

And Jesus knowing their thoughts said, "Why are you thinking evil in your hearts? For which is easier, to say, 'Your sins are forgiven,' or to say, 'Rise, and walk'? But in order that you may know that the Son of Man has authority on earth to forgive sins" (9:4-6a)

The word that best describes the fourth aspect of this event is forensic, which refers to discussion, debate, or argument. Because only Jesus' words were spoken aloud, we know the scribes' side of the interchange only because the Lord omnisciently revealed to us what was in **their thoughts.**

Jesus "did not need anyone to bear witness concerning man for He Himself knew what was in man" (John 2:25). "The Lord looks at the heart" (1 Sam. 16:7) and knows the hearts of all men (1 Kings 8:39). He even "searches all hearts, and understands every intent of the thoughts" (1 Chron. 28:9; cf. Jer. 17:10; Ezek. 11:5). When Ananias and Sapphira tried to deceive God, Peter told them, "Why has Satan filled your heart to lie to the Holy Spirit?" (Acts 5:3).

An **evil . . . heart** is a heart that plots against God (see Acts 5:3-4, 9; 8:20-22), and in saying those words to the scribes and Pharisees Jesus not only laid bare *what* they were **thinking** but exposed the wickedness behind the thoughts. In claiming to defend God's holiness they showed themselves to be utterly against it, because they were **thinking evil** of the Son of God whom they refused to acknowledge.

Jesus' first argument was in the form of a rhetorical question: **"For which is easier, to say, 'Your sins are forgiven,' or to say, 'Rise, and walk'?"** The scribes and Pharisees had seen irrefutable evidence of Jesus' power to heal disease. "Why, therefore," He asked in effect, "do you think it impossible for Me to forgive sins? Is one **easier** than the other?" Sin and disease are inseparable, just as are sin and demons, sin and death, sin and disaster, and sin and the devil. The One who brought the kingdom would have to deal with sin or else He could not deal with the rest; and the One who could deal with the rest could also deal with sin. If Jesus could not deal with sin by putting it away, He could not deal with anything else related to sin. But He could deal with both sin and its symptoms.

His opponents said nothing, but the answer was obvious: both things are equally impossible for men and both are equally possible for God. The point was that no one but God could either heal disease with a word or could forgive sins, and He can do both with the same divine ease. Even their own distorted theology should have led the scribes and Pharisees to believe in Jesus' divinity. If, as they believed, sickness and disease were the consequences of sin, then removing disease would be connected to dealing with the sin that caused it. In their thinking, *all* healing of disease would have to involve at least some forgiveness of sin—which by their own declaration only God can grant. They were trapped in their own theology and logic.

Jesus may have emphasized the word **say.** If so, His point was that *saying* something is always easier than *doing* it. It is also much easier to make a claim that cannot be verified than to make one that can be. The scribes and Pharisees had no visible way to verify the paralytic's forgiveness, but they were about to receive abundant evidence of his healing, which would force the conclusion that Jesus could and did deal with sin.

"But in order that you may know that the Son of Man has authority on earth to forgive sins," Jesus continued, "I will demonstrate again My power to heal disease. You cannot see the results of My forgiveness," He implied, "but you can easily see the results of My healing." So in order that they might know He could forgive sin, which they could not see, He did what they *could* see—by dealing with sin's symptoms.

The scribes and Pharisees knew well the Old Testament predictions that miraculous healings would accompany the Messiah when He came to **earth,** and **the Son of Man** (the title of His humiliation) was now about to give them a special, front-row view of one of those miracles. If all He said were, "Your sins are forgiven," no one could verify what happened. But to make the paralyzed man able to walk would give proof for everyone to see—just as seeing the two thousand pigs run off the cliff to their deaths gave proof that the demons had indeed gone from the two possessed men into the animals, just as Jesus gave them permission to do (8:32).

Many individuals and groups through the centuries have claimed the power to absolve sins, but they have had no proof. Any pretender can utter the words, "Your sins are forgiven," but only God's divine power can both tell a paralytic to walk and then make it happen.

FORCE

then He said to the paralytic—"Rise, take up your bed, and go home." And he rose, and went home. (9:6b-7)

As far as we know, no one but Jesus spoke during the whole episode. Neither the believing paralytic and his four friends nor the unbelieving scribes and Pharisees said a word. The scribes and Pharisees may have mumbled among themselves about the matter, and the healed man and his friends may have thanked Jesus, but we have no record of it.

As soon as Jesus **said to the paralytic—Rise, take up your bed, and go home,** that is exactly what the man did. The command to **rise** suggests that when Jesus spoke the healing had already taken place. No description of this act of healing is recorded, only the command to the paralytic to take advantage of it.

At Jesus' word, the man **rose, and went home.** Mark adds that he "immediately took up the pallet and went out in the sight of all" (Mark 2:12), a living testimony to Jesus' power both to heal and to forgive sins.

FEAR

But when the multitudes saw this, they were filled with awe, and glorified God, who had given such authority to men. (9:8)

When the multitudes saw this, they realized that such a miracle could only be done by God's power, and **they were filled with awe.** *Phobeō* (**filled with awe**) is the term from which we get *phobia* and is often translated "fear." But the most common use of it in the New Testament represents reverential awe, not cringing fright. It expresses the feeling of a person who is in the presence of someone infinitely superior.

Phobeō is used to describe the reaction of the disciples when they saw Jesus walking on the water (Matt. 14:26) and to describe the reactions of the people after the raising of the widow's son at Nain (Luke 7:16) and after the healing of the demoniacs at Gerasa (Luke 8:37). It is used to describe Zacharias's response to the appearance of the angel (Luke 1:12) and the spectators' response when he regained his speech (v. 65). It is used of the shepherds when they heard the angels sing (Luke 2:9), of the guards at the garden tomb when the angels rolled the stone away (Matt. 28:2-4), and of the women after they visited the empty tomb (v. 8). It is used to describe the feelings of the people who witnessed the signs and wonders of Pentecost (Acts 2:43) and of men in the midst of the shattering events of the last days (Luke 21:26). It is used of the response of the people to the deaths of Ananias and Sapphira (Acts 5:5, 11) and to the demons overpowering the unbelieving sons of Sceva who tried to cast the demons out in Jesus' name (19:16-17).

In the synoptic gospels and Acts the term is never used to speak of anything other than the feeling in a person's heart when he is confronted with divine power, and it is declared to be a part of the Christian's attitude as he seeks to faithfully serve the Lord (Acts 9:31). Reverential **awe** of God is a part of the truly repentant life (2 Cor. 7:10-11), the chaste life (1 Pet. 3:2), the holy life (2 Cor. 7:1), and the godly life (Phil. 2:12). Mutual ministry, love, and respect, as well as powerful evangelism and proper church discipline, are all grounded in reverential **awe** of the Lord (see 2 Cor. 5:11; Eph. 5:21; 1 Tim. 5:20). It is the substance out of which all right Christian worship, behavior, and service must come.

The multitudes' response to the great miracle of healing and forgiveness was commendable: they **glorified God, who had given such authority to men**. We do not know how much the crowd knew about Jesus, but they knew that what He did had to have been empowered by God and that He **had given such authority to men,** since Jesus was obviously a man. If they did not realize that He was the God-Man, they at least realized He was an extraordinarily godly man.

BIRDVILLE
BAPTIST CHURCH
LIBRARY

Receiving the Sinner/Refusing the Righteous (9:9-17)

6

And as Jesus passed on from there, He saw a man, called Matthew, sitting in the tax office; and He said to him, "Follow Me!" And he rose, and followed Him.

And it happened that as He was reclining at the table in the house, behold many tax-gatherers and sinners came and were dining with Jesus and His disciples. And when the Pharisees saw this, they said to His disciples, "Why is your Teacher eating with the tax-gatherers and sinners?" But when He heard this, He said, "It is not those who are healthy who need a physician, but those who are sick. But go and learn what this means, 'I desire compassion, and not sacrifice,' for I did not come to call the righteous, but sinners."

Then the disciples of John came to Him, saying, "Why do we and the Pharisees fast, but Your disciples do not fast?" And Jesus said to them, "The attendants of the bridegroom cannot mourn as long as the bridegroom is with them, can they? But the days will come when the bridegroom is taken away from them, and then they will fast. But no one puts a patch of unshrunk cloth on an old garment; for the patch pulls away from the garment, and a worse tear results. Nor do men put new wine into old wineskins; otherwise the wineskins burst, and the wine pours out, and the wineskins are ruined; but they put new wine into fresh wineskins, and both are preserved." (9:9-17)

God's receiving the sinner and refusing the righteous is central to the Christian faith. The gospel is not for good people but for bad people who know they are bad and who come to God for forgiveness and cleansing.

From the earliest part of his gospel, Matthew gives the message of God's forgiveness of repentant sinners. In the genealogy of Jesus in chapter 1 he specifically mentions a number of people whose lives were marked by terrible sin. Both Rahab and Ruth were from pagan, idolatrous, Gentile nations, and Rahab was even a prostitute. Although David was a man after God's own heart, he was also a murderer and adulterer.

As the forerunner of the Lord, John the Baptist prepared the people for the Messiah by preaching repentance from sin, and as they confessed their sins, he baptized them as a symbol of God's cleansing (3:2, 6, 11). Jesus began His own ministry with the preaching of repentance (4:17), and in the Sermon on the Mount He proclaimed God's offer of forgiveness for those who sincerely and humbly hunger and thirst for righteousness (5:3-6). In His model prayer He taught His followers to continue to ask God for forgiveness (6:12). From the day of Pentecost on, the early church preached repentance from sin as an integral part of the gospel message (Acts 2:38; 3:19; 5:31).

The object of men's repentance is God's forgiveness, and that is the dual theme of the gospel—men must turn from sin in order for God to forgive, cleanse, and save them. The only people who ever receive salvation and enter God's kingdom are those who acknowledge their sinfulness and repent of it. It follows, then, that those who consider themselves already to be righteous see no need for repentance or forgiveness—and thereby shut themselves out from salvation in the kingdom of God.

That is the central truth of Matthew 9:9-17. Here one discovers one of the most definitive, dramatic, insightful, and comprehensive statements our Lord ever made. It gives the divine perspective on His ministry and the basic rationale of the incarnation. It is among the most important statements ever recorded in the Bible: "I did not come to call the righteous, but sinners" (v. 13b). That truth gives the essence of the gospel and the purpose for the incarnation. Jesus came into the world to call sinners to Himself. For those who know they have a terminal spiritual illness and who have no trust or hope in themselves to be cured, Jesus says, "I am the way, and the truth, and the life" (John 14:6).

Those who are pleasing to God testify with the penitent tax-collector in the Temple: "God, be merciful to me, the sinner!" (Luke 18:13). Augustine pleaded, "Lord, save me from that wicked man, myself." John Knox, perhaps the greatest preacher in the history of Scotland, confessed, "In youth, in middle age and now after many battles, I find nothing in me but corruption." John Wesley wrote, "I am fallen short of the glory of God, my whole heart is altogether corrupt and abominable, and consequently my whole life being an evil tree cannot bring forth good fruit." His brother Charles, who penned so many great hymns, confessed, "Vile and full of sin I am." Augustus Toplady, who wrote the beloved hymn "Rock of Ages," said of himself, "Oh, that such a wretch as I should ever be tempted to think highly of himself. I am myself nothing but sin and weakness, in whose flesh naturally dwells no good thing."

As he beheld Jesus' great power and glory, Peter declared, "Depart from me, for I am a sinful man, O Lord!" (Luke 5:8). In his first letter to Timothy, Paul summed up the confession of every honest believer: "It is a trustworthy statement, deserving full acceptance, that Christ Jesus came into the world to save sinners, among whom I am foremost of all" (1 Tim. 1:15).

Had Jesus come to save the righteous, His incarnation would have been pointless. Righteous people need no salvation. But even more relevant to man's situation is the fact that there *are* no righteous people apart from the saving work of Jesus Christ. "There is none righteous, not even one; there is none who understands, there is none who seeks for God; all have turned aside, together they have become useless; there is none who does good, there is not even one" (Rom. 3:10-12).

Many people, like the scribes and Pharisees of Jesus' day, *consider* themselves to be righteous, and for them Jesus offers no hope or help, because they admit no need. The first declaration of the gospel is negative—that every man is sinful, separated from God, and condemned to hell. A person will not seek to be saved until he realizes he is lost. Therefore the first step in proclaiming the gospel is to tell men of their lostness, and the first step in receiving the gospel is to confess that lostness. A person will not seek healing until he is convinced he is sick; he will not seek life until he acknowledges he is dead. Conversion, then, occurs in one who is willing to accept the death sentence and also the acquittal of God. The man who does not recognize his condemnation to death has no hope for new life.

In the midst of his carefully selected accounts of Jesus' miracles that show His credentials as the predicted Messiah, Matthew presents that central truth of the gospel. The first three miracles (see Matt. 8:1-17) dealt with disease and displayed Jesus' power over sickness and the infirmities of the body. After those miracles came the response of three would-be disciples, whose unwillingness to pay the price of discipleship betrayed their lack of genuine faith (8:18-22; cf. Luke 9:57-62). The second group of three miracles displayed Jesus' power over nature, over demons, and over sin (see 8:23-9:8).

The response to those three miracles is set forth in the present text. The first part of the response is positive, evidenced in the acceptance of the gospel by a penitent sinner. The second part of the response is negative, evidenced in the rejection of the gospel by those who thought themselves already to be righteous.

After Jesus forgave the paralytic's sin (9:2), the questions in the minds of many people no doubt were: "How much sin is God willing to forgive? Whose sin can be forgiven, and whose not? What are the parameters and limits of His forgiveness? What are its conditions and how far does it go?" Those are the questions answered in verses 9-17.

THE POSITIVE RESPONSE

And as Jesus passed on from there, He saw a man, called Matthew, sitting in the tax office; and He said to him, "Follow Me!" And he rose, and followed Him.

And it happened that as He was reclining at the table in the house, behold many tax-gatherers and sinners came and were dining with Jesus and His disciples. (9:9-10)

As He left Capernaum, "His own city" (v. 1; cf. 4:13), **Jesus passed on from there** and **saw a man, called Matthew.** Mark calls **Matthew** by the name of Levi and identifies him as "the son of Alphaeus" (Mark 2:14; cf. Luke 5:27). It was not uncommon for men to be known by more than one name. Thomas was also called Didymus (John 11:16), Mark was sometimes called John (Acts 12:12), and Peter was also known as Simon (Matt. 4:18). It may be that the Lord renamed Levi as **Matthew** (which means, "gift of Jehovah, or Yahweh") just as He renamed Simon as Peter (which means, "stone"; see Matt. 16:18; John 1:42).

When we realize that **Matthew** penned these two verses about himself, we get a glimpse of his modesty and humility. In his own mind, the most important truth about the writer's former character is given in the words, **sitting in the tax office.** To Jews of his day, that single phrase established **Matthew** as the most despised, vile, and corrupt man in Capernaum.

Matthew was a *publicani* (whence the title *publican* in some translations), a man who served occupying Rome against his own people as a collector of taxes. By the nature of his position, his first loyalty had to be to Rome. Nationals of a country or province occupied by Rome could buy franchises that entitled them to levy certain taxes on the populace and on travelers. A franchise required collecting a specified amount of taxes for Rome and allowed anything collected beyond that figure to be kept as personal profit. Because his power of taxation was virtually unlimited and was enforced by the Roman military, the owner of a tax franchise in effect had a license for extortion. For those reasons the *publicani* were understandably considered traitors by their own people and were usually even more despised than Roman officials or soldiers.

Many tax collectors would accept bribes from the wealthy to reduce and falsify their taxes and would then exact proportionately more from the middle and lower classes, making themselves hated still more. They amassed great fortunes under the authority of the oppressor and at the expense of their own countrymen.

Most Jews believed that the only proper government over them was a theocracy—the rule of God through His appointed leaders such as they experienced under Moses, the judges, and the Jewish monarchy. Because they considered any foreign rule over them to be illicit, they considered taxation by any such government as both unjust and unholy. Taxation by Rome was therefore not only extortive but also made them compromise both their patriotism and their religion. It was those convictions that prompted the Pharisees to ask Jesus if it was proper to pay taxes to Caesar (Matt. 22:17). For Jesus to have answered yes would in their minds have marked Him both as a traitor and a reprobate.

The noted Jewish scholar Alfred Edersheim reports that a Jewish *publicani* was barred from the synagogue and was forbidden to have any religious or social contact with his fellow Jews. He was ranked with the unclean animals, which a devout Jew would not so much as touch. He was in the class of swine, and because he was held to be a traitor and a congenital liar, he was ranked with robbers and murderers and was forbidden to give testimony in any Jewish court.

Edersheim states that there were two categories of *publicani*. The first, whom the Jews called *gabbai*, collected general taxes, which included those on land and other property, those on income, and those referred to as poll, or registration, taxes. The basic land tax (the amount paid to Rome) was a tenth of one's grain and a fifth of one's fruit and wine. Income tax amounted to one percent of one's earnings, and the amount of the poll tax varied.

The second type of tax collector was called a *mokhes*, who collected a wide variety of use taxes—taxes similar to our import duties, tollway fees, boat docking fees, business license fees, and the like. The *mokhes* had almost unlimited latitude in their taxing powers and could attach a tax to virtually any article or activity. They could, for instance, levy a tax on a person's boat, on the fish he caught with it, and on the dock where he unloaded it. They could tax a traveler's donkey, his slaves and servants, and his goods. They had authority to open private letters to see if a taxable business of some sort might be related to the correspondence.

There were two kinds of *mokhes*. One kind, called the great *mokhes*, hired other men to collect taxes for them and, by virtue of partial anonymity, protected at least some of their reputation among their fellow countrymen. The other kind, called small *mokhes*, did their own assessing and collecting and therefore were in constant contact with members of the community as well as with all travelers who passed their way. The *gabbai* were despised, the great *mokhes* were more despised, and the small *mokhes* were despised most.

Matthew was obviously a small *mokhes*, because he himself was **sitting in the tax office** as Jesus passed through the outskirts of Capernaum. It was to that man, the most despised of the despicable, to whom Jesus said, **Follow Me!** It was clear to early readers of Matthew's gospel, as it was clear to those who witnessed this amazing encounter, that Jesus extended His forgiveness even to the outcasts of society.

Although we are given no details of any words Matthew may have uttered in reply to Jesus' call, it seems evident from the context that he had been under deep conviction of sin and spiritual need. Because of Jesus' considerable teaching and miracle working in the region around Capernaum, Matthew would have been well acquainted with His ministry, whether or not he had personally listened to Jesus preach or seen Him perform a miracle. And although he did not seek Jesus out as did the centurion (Matt. 8:5) and the paralytic (9:2), Matthew seems to have been yearning for the forgiveness that the perverted system of Judaism told him he could never have. Therefore, when the Lord called him, he immediately **rose, and followed Him.**

Because of his modesty, Matthew does not mention the fact, but Luke tells us that the moment Jesus called him, Matthew "left everything behind, and rose and began to follow Him" (Luke 5:28). That simple call by Jesus was more than enough reason for Matthew to turn his back on everything he was and possessed. Because of his position as an agent of Rome, he knew that once he forsook his post he would never be able to return to it. He knew the cost and willingly paid it. Of all the disciples, Matthew doubtlessly made the greatest sacrifice of material possessions; yet he himself makes no mention of it. He felt with Paul that "whatever things were gain to me, those things I have counted as loss for the sake of Christ" (Phil. 3:7).

When a person is truly converted, he cannot leave his old life fast enough. His old habits, standards, and practices no longer appeal to him and he gladly longs to leave them behind. Edersheim says of Matthew, "He said not a word, for his soul was in the speechless surprise of unexpected grace." Far from being depressed about what he left behind, his heart overflowed with joy. He lost a career but gained a destiny, lost his material possessions but gained a spiritual fortune, lost his temporal security but gained eternal life.

In one of her loveliest poems Amy Carmichael wrote,

> I hear Him call, "Come, follow";
> That was all!
> My gold grew dim.
> My heart went after Him.
> I rose and followed,
> That was all.
> Would you not follow,
> If you heard Him call?

Like many new converts, Matthew's first thought was to tell his friends about the Savior. He was so overwhelmed that he threw a banquet to present Jesus to his friends—all of whom, as **tax-gatherers and sinners,** were social and religious outcasts. We learn from Mark (2:15) and Luke (5:29) that the banquet was in Matthew's own house, another fact that he modestly omits in his own account.

The **tax-gatherers** no doubt included the local *gabbai* of Capernaum and perhaps even some fellow *mokhes* from neighboring communities. The **sinners** doubtlessly included robbers, murderers, drunkards, prostitutes, and other irreligious and ungodly people. They were the riffraff of the area and must have been intrigued and touched by the prospect of **dining with Jesus,** whom they knew to be a teacher of righteousness, **and His disciples.**

It was probably because of this banquet that Jesus first gained the reputation among His opponents as "a gluttonous man and a drunkard, a friend of tax-gatherers and sinners" (Matt. 11:19; cf. Luke 15:2). Most religious Jews, and especially the proud and self-righteous scribes and Pharisees, could not conceive of any Jew socializing with such a group of **sinners** unless he were one of their own kind.

The Jews of Jesus' day used the term *hamartōloi* (**sinners**) almost as a technical term for people who had no concern or respect either for the Mosaic law or rabbinic traditions. They were looked on as the vilest and most wretched and worthless of all people. Yet it was some of these that **Jesus and His disciples** joined at the banquet in Matthew's house.

Matthew's response to Jesus' call was immediate and positive, and his sincerity was evidenced by his eagerness to share his new faith and his new Master. In a similar way, the genuine faith of Zaccheus, another despised and wealthy tax-gatherer, was evidenced by his voluntary determination to share half his possessions with the poor and to repay four times whatever he had defrauded anyone (Luke 19:8).

We are not told what the group of **tax-gatherers and sinners** thought of Jesus either before or after the meal, but their response to Him was at least positive enough to eat with Him and listen to Him. The main point of the incident, however—and what most offended the Pharisees—was not that the **tax-gatherers and sinners** were willing to associate with Jesus but that *Jesus* was willing to associate with *them*.

THE NEGATIVE RESPONSE

And when the Pharisees saw this, they said to His disciples, "Why is your Teacher eating with the tax-gatherers and sinners?" (9:11)

The response of the **Pharisees** was quite different from Matthew's. They were outraged that this **Teacher** who claimed to uphold standards of righteousness even higher than their own (see Matt. 5:20) would willingly sit down and eat with such a flagrantly sinful group. No doubt they were also resentful and humiliated that Jesus had never shown them such favor. If He were really a man of God, they reasoned, why had He not given a banquet for them, the exemplars and self-appointed custodians of religious purity?

The **Pharisees** did not confront Jesus head-on but instead cornered **His disciples**. Having learned of the banquet, these Jewish leaders waited outside to see what would happen and to exact an explanation of the unorthodox activity. The words **Why is your Teacher eating with the tax-gatherers and sinners?** were more a rebuke than a query. In the Pharisees' own minds the question was largely rhetorical, and because they did not believe a satisfactory answer could be given, they were not asking a sincere question but were venting their hostility. The purpose was to put the **disciples** and their **Teacher** on the spot. As with their many other questions to and about Jesus, their motive was not to learn the truth but to entrap and convict this presumptuous upstart who was turning their religious system upside down.

Even at this relatively early stage in Jesus' ministry, the **Pharisees** were becoming resentful and vindictive. Jesus had already said and done more than enough to establish Himself as an iconoclast who was at complete odds with almost everything they stood for and held sacred. They could see no defects in themselves and no good in those who were not like them. They were so pleased with themselves that they considered their enemies to be God's enemies. They were so convinced of their own doctrinal rightness that any belief or standard contrary to their own was by definition heretical and ungodly. They were so convinced of their own moral and spiritual righteousness that anyone who questioned their holiness questioned God's. The only thing Jesus could do that was worse than snubbing them, the religious and moral elite, was to befriend **tax-gatherers and sinners,** the religious and moral dregs. And He did both.

The **Pharisees** did not think they needed God's forgiveness and were certain that **tax-gatherers and sinners** did not deserve it. Their "ministry" was not to help but to judge, not to restore but to condemn. They wanted no part of a Man who, contrarily, condemned their self-righteousness and offered forgiveness to obvious **sinners.**

THE ARGUMENTS

But when He heard this, He said, "It is not those who are healthy who need a physician, but those who are sick. But go and learn what this means, 'I desire compassion, and not sacrifice,' for I did not come to call the righteous, but sinners." (9:12-13)

When Jesus **heard this** accusatory question, He answered it for the disciples. His doing so doubtlessly embarrassed the Pharisees and added to their indignation. The fact that they had approached His disciples suggests that the Pharisees were afraid to confront Jesus Himself, and His overhearing and responding to their obvious indictment of His actions was more than a little disconcerting.

Although Jesus was fully aware of the Pharisees' true intent (cf. 9:4), He took their question at face value and explained exactly why He had done what He did. In His brief reply, He gave three arguments in defense of His gospel of forgiveness and reconciliation, the gospel that was reflected in His willingness to eat with the ungodly and immoral tax-gatherers and sinners.

THE ARGUMENT FROM HUMAN LOGIC

First of all, Jesus **said, "It is not those who are healthy who need a physician, but those who are sick."** "If," He was saying to the Pharisees, "you are really as spiritually and morally perfect as you claim to be, you do not need any help from God or other men. If you are indeed spiritually **healthy,** you do not need a spiritual **physician.** On the other hand, these tax-gatherers and sinners—who you declare, and they themselves admit, are spiritually **sick**—are the self-confessing sinners who need God's way of salvation presented to them. They are the one's who seek the spiritual **physician,** and that is why I am ministering to them."

The analogy is simple. Just as a **physician** is expected to go among people who are **sick,** a forgiver should be expected to go among those who are sinful. Jesus was giving Himself to those who recognized their deepest need. What sort of doctor would spend all his time with **healthy** people and refuse to associate with those who are **sick?** "Are you doctors," He implied to the Pharisees, "who diagnose but have no desire to cure? Will you tell a person what his disease is and then refuse to give him medicine for it?" What an indictment of their self-righteous hardheartedness! Those whom they diagnosed as sinful they were quite willing to let remain sinful.

As the Lord charged them later, the scribes and Pharisees were hypocrites who were careful to "tithe mint and dill and cummin" but had no regard for the matters of true righteousness, the "weightier provisions of the law" such as "justice and mercy and faithfulness" (Matt. 23:23). They had outward form but no inward holiness, much ritual but no righteousness. They loved to condemn but not uplift, to judge but not help, They loved themselves but not others, and proved themselves to be without the compassion and mercy that God's law required—the law they vigorously claimed to teach, practice, and defend.

How could the Pharisees have missed or forgotten God's wonderful and merciful declarations such as, "I, the Lord, am your healer" (Ex. 15:26). How could they neglect, and even resent, the healing of those whom God Himself desired to heal? Those who claimed to be well proved themselves to be sickest of all!

THE ARGUMENT FROM SCRIPTURE

Jesus' second argument was directly from Scripture. **"Go and learn,"** He said, **"what this means, 'I desire compassion, and not sacrifice.'"** He pinned the Pharisees to the wall with their own Scripture. The phrase **go and learn** was commonly used in rabbinic writings to rebuke those who did not know what they should have known. Jesus used the Pharisees' own most honored authorities to rebuke them for their ignorance of God's true nature and of their failure to follow His clear commandments.

Jesus here quotes the prophet Hosea, through whom God said, "I delight in loyalty rather than sacrifice, and in the knowledge of God rather than burnt offerings" (Hos. 6:6). "It is the perfect Word of God and not the flawed words of men that you should be concerned about," Jesus was saying; "and His Word calls you to be merciful and forgiving, not judgmental and condemning."

The fact that the quotation was from Hosea made it all the more pointed. The story of Gomer's unfaithfulness to her husband Hosea was a living illustration of Israel's own unfaithfulness to God; and Hosea's continuing love and forgiveness of Gomer was a picture of the continuing love and forgiveness God offered Israel. And just as God then desired **compassion** rather than **sacrifice,** He still did. Without **compassion,** all the rituals, ceremonies, and sacrifices of the Pharisees were unacceptable to God. Without **compassion** they proved themselves to be more ungodly even than the despised tax-gatherers and sinners, who made no pretense of godliness.

God had divinely instituted the sacrificial system, and when the prescribed offerings were made to Him in a spirit of humility, penitence, and reverence, they were pleasing to Him. But when offered insincerely and in a spirit of self-righteousness and self-satisfaction, they became instead an abomination. The rituals and ceremonies were only as valid as the contriteness of the worshiper. And the person who sacrificed to God in genuine reverence would serve his fellow man in genuine **compassion.** Conversely, the person who is cold toward other people proves he is also cold toward

God, no matter how orthodox his theology and how impeccable his external moral standards. The person who sees obvious sinners as those only to be condemned proves himself to be a greater sinner than they. Those who are furthest from giving mercy are furthest from receiving it (see Matt. 6:15; 18:23-35).

God is never pleased with religious routine and activity that does not come from sincere love of Him and of other people. Ritual separated from righteousness is a sham and an affront to God. "I hate, I reject your festivals," God declared to Israel. "Nor do I delight in your solemn assemblies. Even though you offer up to Me burnt offerings and your grain offerings, I will not accept them; and I will not even look at the peace offerings of your fatlings. Take away from Me the noise of your songs; I will not even listen to the sound of your harps. But let justice roll down like waters and righteousness like an ever-flowing stream" (Amos 5:21-24).

THE ARGUMENT FROM HIS OWN AUTHORITY

Third, Jesus defended His work on the basis of His own authority: **I did not come to call the righteous, but sinners.** He gladly associated and identified with tax-gatherers and other **sinners,** because they are the ones who needed Him. The parallel passage in Luke 5:32, and some Greek texts and English translations of Matthew 9:13, include the ending phrase, "to repentance." It is the repentant person, the person who is sinful and who acknowledges and turns from his sin, who is the object of Jesus' divine **call.** The person who is sinful but thinks he is **righteous** shuts himself out from God's mercy, because he refuses to acknowledge his need of it. He rejects Jesus' **call** to salvation because he rejects the idea of his lostness.

In response to a later similar charge by the Pharisees and scribes that He "receives sinners and eats with them" (Luke 15:2), Jesus gave three illustrations of God's concern for and forgiveness of the penitent sinner. Through the stories of the lost sheep and lost coin He pointed up the truth that "there will be more joy in heaven over one sinner who repents, than over ninety-nine righteous persons who need no repentance" (v. 7; cf. v. 10). In the story of the prodigal son He dramatically illustrated the double-sided truth that God is overjoyed with a humble sinner who repents and is grieved by the self-righteous person (represented by the older brother) who is himself unforgiving of others and even resents God's forgiveness of them (see espec. vv. 21-32).

Kaleō (to **call**) was often used of inviting a guest to one's home for food and lodging. The inference here is clear. Jesus did **not come to call** the self-**righteous** to salvation for the same reason He did not call the Pharisees to recline with Him at the dinner in Matthew's house. They were too good in their own eyes to condescend to such humiliation. And because they would not identify themselves with fellow **sinners,** they could not be identified with Christ, who offers salvation only to sinners who willingly acknowledge they are **sinners.**

"Because you consider yourselves already **righteous,**" the Lord was saying, "I have not come to **call** you. Because you are satisfied with yourselves, I will leave you to yourselves." The Pharisee who stood proudly in the Temple and thanked God for his own goodness saw no need for forgiveness and thus was not forgiven. But the penitent, heart-broken tax-gatherer who beat his breast and cried out, "God, be merciful to me, the sinner! . . . went down to his house justified" (Luke 18:10-14). At that same Temple, Jesus said to a group of Pharisees, "I go away, and you shall seek Me, and shall die in your sin; where I am going, you cannot come" (John 8:21; cf. v. 24). The one who thinks he is **righteous** and spiritually safe without Christ has no part in Christ, who came **to call . . . sinners.** He cannot seek and save those who will not recognize they are lost (see Luke 19:10). Logic, Scripture, and Jesus Himself together affirm that forgiveness is for the sinful and salvation is for the lost.

In one of His last parables Jesus graphically portrayed that truth. He pictured His kingdom as a great royal wedding feast for the king's son, for which the king had sent out many invitations. When the previously invited guests, who represented Israel, were called at the appointed time but were unwilling to come, the king several times sent his servants out again to plead with them to reconsider. When they still refused, and mistreated and killed some of the servants, the enraged king ordered his armies to destroy the murderers and set their city on fire. He then sent servants throughout the rest of the kingdom, even to the most out-of-the-way places, to gather all they could find and bring them to the feast (see Matt. 22:1-10; cf. 21:33-46). That was the message He gave to the Pharisees at Capernaum. As Jews, they were the already invited guests to the Lord's banquet, but they refused to attend and acted with hostility toward the messengers. Therefore, just as they stood outside Matthew's house and watched the tax-gatherers and sinners eat with Jesus, they would also stand outside God's kingdom and watch every sort of repentant sinner and outcast be welcomed into it.

The kingdom of God is for the spiritually sick who want to be healed, the spiritually corrupt who want to be cleansed, the spiritually poor who want to be rich, the spiritually hungry who want to be fed, the spiritually dead who want to be made alive. It is for ungodly outcasts who long to become God's own beloved children.

THE ILLUSTRATIONS

Then the disciples of John came to Him, saying, "Why do we and the Pharisees fast, but Your disciples do not fast?" And Jesus said to them, "The attendants of the bridegroom cannot mourn as long as the bridegroom is with them, can they? But the days will come when the bridegroom is taken away from them, and then they will fast. But no one puts a patch of unshrunk cloth on an old garment; for the patch pulls away from the garment, and a worse tear results. Nor do men put new wine into old wineskins; otherwise the wineskins burst, and the wine pours out, and the wineskins are ruined; but they put new wine into fresh wineskins, and both are preserved." (9:14-17)

We do not know how long after Jesus' encounter with the Pharisees **the disciples of John came to Him,** but the logical relation of their question to that of the Pharisees is clear. Unlike that of the Pharisees, the question of John's disciples was sincere, but it reflected a similar concern about Jesus' teaching and activities that did not conform to the accepted religious standards.

Shortly after he baptized Jesus, **John** the Baptist in effect turned his disciples over to Jesus, saying, "You yourselves bear me witness, that I said, 'I am not the Christ,' but, 'I have been sent before Him.' . . . He must increase, but I must decrease" (John 3:28, 30). Not all of **the disciples of John** began to follow Jesus, however, and even long after Pentecost the apostle Paul encountered some of them in Ephesus who knew no more of the faith than "John's baptism" (Acts 19:1-3).

John the Baptist was then in prison (see Matt. 4:12), and those of his **disciples** who had not begun to follow Jesus were left only with their traditional Jewish ceremonies and practices. Unlike the Pharisees outside Matthew's house, they **came to Him** (Jesus) directly, **saying, "Why do we and the Pharisees fast, but Your disciples do not fast?"** The Old Testament prescribed only one fast, the one on Yom Kippur, the Day of Atonement (see Lev. 16:29, 31, where the phrase "humble your souls" [from the Heb. *'āna,* "to afflict or humble"] commonly included the idea of refraining from food). But Jewish tradition had come to require fasting twice a week (see Luke 18:12), and these **disciples** were careful to follow that practice.

Along with alms giving and certain prescribed prayers, twice-weekly fasting was one of the three major expressions of orthodox Judaism during Jesus' day. The scribes and Pharisees looked on these practices with great seriousness and were careful not only to follow them faithfully but to do so as publicly and ostentatiously as possible—ostensibly as a testimony to true godliness but in reality as a testimony to their own self-styled piety. When they gave alms, they blew trumpets "in the synagogues and in the streets" in order to "be honored by men" (Matt. 6:2). When they prayed "in the synagogues and on the street corners," they did so "to be seen by men" (v. 5). And when they fasted, they "put on a gloomy face" and neglected their "appearance in order to be seen fasting by men" (v. 16). They did not see religion as a matter of humility, repentance, or forgiveness, but as a matter of ceremony and proud display. And therefore the external rituals which they paraded as badges of godly righteousness actually marked them as ungodly hypocrites, as Jesus declared in each of the three verses just cited (cf. 5:20).

Religious ritual and routine have always been dangers to true godliness. Many ceremonies, such as praying to saints and lighting a candle for a deceased relative are actually heretical. But even if it is not wrong in itself, when a *form* of praying, worshiping, or serving becomes the focus of attention, it becomes a barrier to true righteousness. It can keep an unbeliever from trusting in God and a believer from faithfully obeying Him. Even going to church, reading the Bible, saying grace at meals, and singing hymns can become lifeless routines in which true worship of God has no part.

Jesus first replied to John's disciples by saying, **The attendants of the bridegroom cannot mourn as long as the bridegroom is with them, can they? But the days will come when the bridegroom is taken away from them, and then they will fast.**

In those days a wedding would usually last seven days, and the **bridegroom** would choose his best friends as **attendants** to be responsible for the festivities. The wedding celebration was not a time for them to **mourn** but to rejoice. Jesus' point was that it was inappropriate for His followers to **mourn** and **fast** while He was with them in person. The insincere, superficial, and hypocritical fasting practiced by the Pharisees was, of course, always out of place. But even sincere fasting was out of place as long as Jesus, the divine **bridegroom,** was still among His people. Their fasting was out of harmony with what God was then doing in their midst. There was no connection between their ritual and spiritual reality.

A fast is always meaningless if it is performed from habit and does not result from deep concern and mourning over some spiritual need. Going to church on Sunday is hypocritical if it is done apart from a genuine desire to worship and glorify God. Singing a hymn is only a pretense of worship if it does not come from a heart that seeks to praise the Lord.

The days will come, Jesus explained, **when the bridegroom is taken away. Taken away** is from *apairō,* which can carry the idea of sudden removal, of being snatched away violently. Jesus was obviously referring to His crucifixion, which would abruptly and violently take Him away from His followers, His faithful **attendants.** That will be the time for mourning, and **then they will fast.**

But for the present time, He was saying, fasting was inappropriate. When there is no reason to mourn there is no reason to fast. Fasting springs naturally from a broken and grieving heart, but fasting as a shallow spiritual ritual apart from such brokenness is an affront to God.

But an even more important issue was behind the question of John's disciples. Since they obviously had not become disciples of Jesus as John had instructed them to do, they had no basis for genuine faith. But it was clear to them, as it was to the Pharisees, that Jesus' teaching and activities were radically different from those of traditional Judaism. Consequently, behind their question about fasting may have been a deeper concern about forgiveness. "Why," they may really have been wondering, "do You emphasize internal things such as forgiveness, while our recognized religious leaders only emphasize external things such as fasting?"

Jesus' next two illustrations deal with that issue. He made clear that He was not teaching a reformed Pharisaism or a reformed rabbinicalism but an entirely different way of believing, thinking, and living. He did not come to improve the old system but to renounce and undermine it. His way had nothing to do with the old ways, and the old ways had no part in the new. The two ways cannot be connected to one another or be contained one in the other.

To illustrate the truth that His new way cannot be *connected* to the old way, Jesus went on to say, **No one puts a patch of unshrunk cloth on an old garment; for the patch pulls away from the garment, and a worse tear results. Cloth** of that day was primarily wool or linen, and both would shrink when washed. If **a patch of** new, **unshrunk, cloth** is sewn **on an old garment,** Jesus reminded them, then the first time the garment is washed, the new **patch** shrinks and **pulls away from the garment,** making **a worse tear** than before. In the same way, Jesus' new and internal gospel of forgiveness and cleansing cannot be attached to the old and external traditions of self-righteousness and ritual.

To illustrate the truth that His new way also cannot be *contained* in the old way, Jesus said, **Nor do men put new wine into old wineskins; otherwise the wineskins burst, and the wine pours out, and the wineskins are ruined.** Wine was often stored in animal skins that were specially prepared for that purpose. The hide would be uncut except at the legs and neck, and sometimes would be turned inside out. The leg openings would be stitched closed and sealed, and the neck was used as a spout, which was tied with a leather thong or string. **Old wineskins** would eventually dry out and become brittle, and if someone then **put new wine into** them, they would crack and **burst,** spilling **the wine . . . out.** The only suitable container for **new wine** is a **fresh wineskin.** In the same way, the only life that can contain true righteousness is the new life given by God when a person repents of his sin and trusts in Jesus Christ as Lord and Savior.

The pharisaical, legalistic, external, self-righteous system of traditional Judaism could neither connect with nor contain the ministry and message of Christ. Consequently, that system had only one option—to oppose and seek to eliminate Christ, which is what it did.

It should be made clear that Jesus' doing away with the old and bringing in the new did not refer to setting aside the divine law and ushering in grace—as many interpreters have claimed throughout church history, and as some still claim today. Nothing could be further from the truth. Jesus categorically declared that He did *not* come to destroy the law but to fulfill it and that any opponent of the law was an opponent of God (Matt. 5:17-19). God's law and His grace have always coexisted and have always been perfectly compatible. The **old wineskins** were not the teachings of the Old Testament but the rabbinical traditions that had come to overshadow, supersede, and often contradict the divinely revealed truths of the Old Testament.

In this passage we can discover three marks of the true believer. First, like Matthew, the true believer follows the Lord. He leads a life of unquestioning obedience. Matthew made no conditions or excuses; he simply "rose, and followed Him" (v. 9). During a postresurrection appearance, Jesus said to Peter, "Follow Me!" But "Peter, turning around, saw the disciple whom Jesus loved following them; . . . [and] therefore seeing him said to Jesus, 'Lord, and what about this man?' Jesus said to him, 'If I want him to remain until I come, what is that to you? You follow Me!'" (John 21:19-22). The true believer is not always questioning God's truth and resisting His standards for living.

Second, the true believer has compassion on the unsaved. Like Matthew, he has a deep desire to lead others to Christ. That desire may sometimes get cluttered over with selfish concerns, but it will be there. Because we know "the fear of the Lord, we persuade men" to come to Him for salvation (2 Cor. 5:11); and if "the love of Christ controls us" (v. 14), that love will prompt us to witness of Him to others. Both our love of the unsaved and our love of Christ motivate us to be His instruments as He seeks and saves the lost (Luke 19:10). The indwelling Spirit of Christ gives compassion for the lost, and the person who has no desire to win the lost has no basis for claiming Christ or His Holy Spirit.

Third, a true believer forsakes legalism and ritualism. He fasts only as an expression of genuine spiritual concern, and he does not try to attach his new life in Christ to his old ritual or religion or try to fit it somehow into his old patterns. He knows they are incompatible and utterly contrary. He knows that what is begun in the Spirit cannot be completed in the flesh (Gal. 3:3). The genuine righteousness of a forgiven and cleansed heart cannot be enhanced or supplemented by external religious works. Freedom in Christ has no part in the bondage of legalism.

In a hymn that chronicles his own conversion, John Newton movingly describes the transforming power of Christ:

> In evil long I took delight,
> Unawed by shame or fear,
> Till a new object struck my sight,
> And stopped my wild career.
> I saw One hanging on a tree,
> In agony and blood;
> He fixed His loving eyes on me,
> As near His cross I stood.
> How can it be, upon a tree
> The Savior died for Me?
> My soul is thrilled, my heart is filled,
> ﹍To think He died for me.

Jesus' Power over Death (9:18-26)

7

While He was saying these things to them, behold, there came a synagogue official, and bowed down before Him, saying, "My daughter has just died; but come and lay Your hand on her, and she will live." And Jesus rose and began to follow him, and so did His disciples. And behold, a woman who had been suffering from a hemorrhage for twelve years, came up behind Him and touched the fringe of His cloak; for she was saying to herself, "If I only touch His garment, I shall get well." But Jesus turning and seeing her said, "Daughter, take courage; your faith has made you well." And at once the woman was made well. And when Jesus came into the official's house, and saw the flute-players, and the crowd in noisy disorder, He began to say, "Depart; for the girl has not died, but is asleep." And they began laughing at Him. But when the crowd had been put out, He entered and took her by the hand; and the girl arose. And this news went out into all that land. (9:18-26)

Perhaps no man in modern times has seemed before the eyes of the world to have been more at peace with himself and others than Mahatma Gandhi. He was the image of a tranquil soul who possessed perfect inner harmony. Fifteen years before he died, he wrote, "I must tell you in all humility that Hinduism as I know it entirely satisfies my soul. It fills my whole being and I find a solace in the Bhagavad and

Upanishad that I miss even in the Sermon on the Mount." But just before his death he wrote, "My days are numbered. I am not likely to live very long, perhaps a year or a little more. For the first time in fifty years I find myself in the slew of despond." Even the tranquil Gandhi had to face the reality of death and the inability of his man-made religion to give him answers or comfort in face of it.

A Turkish watchmaker decided to build a special grave for himself that had an eight-inch window on top, an electric light, and a button beside the window connected to an outside alarm. In case he was accidentally buried alive and managed to revive, he could press the button to summon help. He instructed his friends to leave the light burning for seven days after his death and to turn it off only if they were sure he was actually dead.

Cemeteries have been a companion of man throughout history, a constant reminder that he is mortal. And as the earth's population grows, grave space is becoming extremely scarce in some places, and more and more people are turning to cremation. We live in a dying world, where before all of us looms the inevitability of death. We are deteriorating human beings in a deteriorating world that is marked by tragedy, sorrow, pain, and death. Since the Fall, there has been a curse on the earth, and that curse has sent the earth and all of its inhabitants careening and spiraling into disasters, tears, sickness, and the grave.

Most of us could recite a long list of those we know who have recently suffered painful illness, serious accident, loss of a loved one, breakup of a family, or some other tragedy. Children have lost a mother, parents have lost a child or are watching him daily grow weaker from a debilitating disease. Many people suffer continual pain for which even the strongest medicine has lost its effectiveness. Others face long months and years of rehabilitation as they seek to adjust their lives to the loss of limb, sight, hearing, or motor function.

When Mary came out to meet Jesus as He was approaching Bethany after the death of Lazarus, John reports that when He "saw her weeping, and the Jews who came with her, also weeping, He was deeply moved in spirit, and was troubled." Jesus Himself wept, and, "again being deeply moved within, came to the tomb" (John 11:33-38). Not only was the Lord touched by the grief of Mary, Martha, and her friends, but in the infinity of His mind He could also stretch His thinking back throughout all the eons of human history and perceive the immeasurable pain that sin brought to man. As a sympathizer beyond anything we could imagine, Jesus was deeply grieved, because He could see clearly and completely the pain and power of sin.

Sin was not God's purpose for man. All things in the world were created for the good and blessing of man, but sin corrupted that goodness and blessing and brought a curse in its stead. In God's time sin will one day have run its course and be forever destroyed. "Behold, the tabernacle of God is among men, and He shall dwell among them, and they shall be His people, and God Himself shall be among them, and He shall wipe away every tear from their eyes; and there shall no longer be any death; there shall no longer be any mourning, or crying, or pain; the first things have passed away" (Rev. 21:3-4).

The Old Testament prophets predicted that the Messiah would have power to bring back wholeness to life (Isa. 30:26; 35:5-6; 53:5; Mal. 4:2; etc.), and when Jesus came into the world He demonstrated that power. Though the final fulfillment of the prophecies regarding His power would be in the future, Jesus fully proved His ability to fulfill them during His ministry in Palestine—where He virtually banished disease, changed water into wine, multiplied food, calmed storms, cast out demons, forgave sins, and raised the dead. He gave a sampling of the great and glorious future kingdom in which there would no longer be need for healing or food or calming of storms or raising from the dead. When John the Baptist was facing imminent death in Herod's prison and sent his disciples to ask Jesus if He were truly the Messiah, Jesus told them, "Go and report to John what you hear and see: the blind receive sight and the lame walk, the lepers are cleansed and the deaf hear, and the dead are raised up" (Matt. 11:4-5).

Jesus' miracles were the verification of His divine might which He would reveal some day to reverse the curse and to restore righteousness, harmony, and peace in all of His creation. Already the people had "brought to Him many who were demon-possessed; and He cast out the spirits with a word, and healed all who were ill in order that what was spoken through Isaiah the prophet might be fulfilled, saying, 'He Himself took our infirmities, and carried away our diseases'" (Matt. 8:16-17; cf. Isa. 53:4). "Just as the Father raises the dead and gives them life," Jesus said, "even so the Son also gives life to whom He wishes" (John 5:21).

Although Jesus had great compassion on the suffering and afflicted people who came to Him (Mark 1:41; Matt. 9:36; 14:14), He did not heal and cleanse them and raise their dead simply for their own sakes. He performed those miracles to demonstrate His deity and to establish His credentials as the Messiah predicted by the Old Testament prophets (see Matt. 8:16-17; 9:35; 11:5).

In 9:18-26, Matthew gives the first miracle in his third set of three miracles (see 8:1-22 and 8:23-9:17)—a miracle that was actually a double miracle, a miracle within a miracle. He raised a young girl from the dead, and during the process restored health to a woman who was considered by society all but dead. He demonstrated His power to restore life to the whole body and to restore wholeness to any part of the body.

The Canadian scientist G. B. Hardy one time said, "When I looked at religion I said, I have two questions. One, has anybody ever conquered death, and two, if they have, did they make a way for me to conquer death? I checked the tomb of Buddha, and it was occupied, and I checked the tomb of Confucius and it was occupied, and I checked the tomb of Mohammed and it was occupied, and I came to the tomb of Jesus and it was empty. And I said, There is one who conquered death. And I asked the second question, Did He make a way for me to do it? And I opened the Bible and discovered that He said, 'Because I live ye shall live also.'"

That is the supreme, two-part question that all mankind faces. Has anyone conquered death? And if so, did he provide a way for others to conquer death? That is the question dealt with in the present passage.

Within this text we not only see a miracle within a miracle but also a beautiful picture of Jesus' response to people in need. We see the dual portrayal of His power and His sensitivity, His authority and His gentleness, His sovereignty and His openness, His majesty and His lovingkindness. We see in particular that Jesus was accessible, touchable, and impartial as well as powerful. Of the two principal characters in this account besides Jesus, one was an influential ruler and the other an outcast. The one was wealthy and the other poor. Yet in common they had great needs and a great Helper.

JESUS WAS ACCESSIBLE

While He was saying these things to them, behold, there came a synagogue official, and bowed down before Him, saying, "My daughter has just died; but come and lay Your hand on her, and she will live." (9:18)

While He was saying these things refers to the conversation Jesus had just been having with the critical Pharisees and confused disciples of John the Baptist (vv. 11-17), in which our Lord made clear that He had come to save only those who acknowledge and confess their sins and that the ways of the old life of the flesh and the new life of the spirit are totally incompatible.

Mark (5:22) and Luke (8:41) explain that the man who came up to Jesus was named Jairus and that he not only was an *archōn* (**synagogue official**) but was the chief official, or elder, of the synagogue, the *archisunagōgos* (Heb., *rosh hakeneseth*). He was therefore the highest ranking religious **official** in Capernaum, responsible for the total administration and operation of the synagogue. He supervised the worship services and oversaw the work of the other elders, which included teaching, adjudicating disputes, and other such leadership duties.

As the ranking member of the Jewish religious establishment in Capernaum, which would have included scribes and Pharisees, Jairus may well have been a Pharisee himself. As is clear from the earlier sections of Matthew and of the other gospels, the religious establishment in general was already developing strong opposition to Jesus even in this relatively early stage of His ministry. Jairus could not have escaped being aware of this opposition, and when he came to Jesus for help he knew he would face criticism and pressure from his peers.

Yet when he faced Jesus he did not seek to protect himself by going at night, as Nicodemus did, or by disguising his true motive and need with an involved and veiled religious question. We are not told what he then thought about Jesus' messiahship, but to have **bowed down before Him** was to offer an act of great homage and reverence—and the Greek term behind **bowed down** (*proskuneō*) is most often rendered "worshiped" (see Matt. 4:10; John 4:21-24; 1 Cor. 14:25; Rev. 4:10; etc.). The act involved prostrating oneself before the honored person and kissing his feet, the hem of his garment, or the ground in front of him.

Such acts of reverence were not, of course, always completely sincere.

Proskuneō is also used of the mother of James and John, who "came to [Jesus] with her sons, *bowing down*" (Matt. 20:20, emphasis added). Her seeming act of reverence was entirely external and self-serving. She did not desire Jesus' honor and glory but only that He would grant that "in Your kingdom these two sons of mine may sit, one on Your right and one on Your left" (v. 21).

By contrast, everything Jairus did proved his humility and sincerity. Like that of the mother of James and John, his request was in behalf of his child, but it was a selfless request that, by its very asking for the humanly impossible, honored Jesus' power, compassion, and grace. Whatever thoughts he may have had about the reaction of his fellow religious leaders, he knew that Jesus was the only source of help for his **daughter,** who had just **died.** Nothing else mattered as he came to the Lord in anguish and utter desperation.

From the more detailed accounts of Mark and Luke we learn that when Jairus first came to Jesus, his daughter was not yet dead but was "at the point of death" (Mark 5:23; cf. Luke 8:42). A short while later messengers from his house informed him that she had died and counseled him not to "trouble the Teacher anymore" (Mark 5:35). Matthew begins his story at that point.

The **daughter** was twelve years old, in the first year of her womanhood according to Jewish custom. The day after his thirteenth birthday a Jewish boy was recognized as a man, and a day after her twelfth birthday a Jewish girl was recognized as a woman. Jairus's **daughter** had just come into the flower of womanhood, but to her father she was still his little girl, whose life was dearer to him than his own. The sunshine of her childhood had turned into the shadow of death.

The Jewish establishment had no resources that would help a father facing such tragedy, and Jairus knew that the only hope for his daughter lay in the Man whom that religious establishment ridiculed and was coming to despise. God obviously had already been working in the father's heart, because his request evidences absolute conviction that Jesus was able to do what was asked: **Come and lay Your hand on her, and she will live.** His faith was without reservation or a hint of doubt. He swallowed his pride and his fear. He did not care what his neighbors, his family, or even his fellow religionists thought. Nothing would keep him from seeking Jesus' help.

So the first thing that brought Jairus to Jesus was deep need. Often some great tragedy drives a person to Christ. The person who feels no needs in his life has no hunger for God. That is why the first step in witnessing is to convince people of their need of salvation and therefore of Christ as the only means for obtaining it. As noted in the previous chapter, the person who does not see his sin and his lostness sees no reason to be saved from them. Similarly, the person who has a need but thinks it can be met by human resources sees no reason for coming to the supernatural Lord for help.

Jairus was already convinced that human resources could not save the life of his daughter, and he was also already convinced of Christ's power to do it. It may have been that, until it was obvious she was dying, he hesitated seeking Jesus' help. But now he knew he had only one hope for help. He did not come to Christ out of an entirely pure motive, because his first concern was his daughter's life and his own despair. He did not come primarily to adore or glorify Jesus but to seek life for his daughter and relief of pain and anguish for himself. But he trusted in Jesus for that help, and he found Him to be accessible.

That is the second thing that brought him to Jesus, his faith. He believed Jesus had the power to do what he asked of Him. Such great faith is especially amazing in light of the fact that Jesus had not yet performed a resurrection miracle. He had healed many life-threatening diseases, but He had not brought anyone back to life after dying. Yet without hesitation or qualification, Jairus asked Jesus to do just that—raise his daughter from death. **Come lay Your hand on her, and she will live.**

Jesus marveled at the faith of the centurion who believed that He could heal the man's servant by simply saying the word. "Truly I say to you," Jesus said, "I have not found such great faith with anyone in Israel" (Matt. 8:9-10). But Jairus even believed that a touch of Jesus' **hand** could raise his daughter from the dead. His faith also surpassed that of Martha, who believed Jesus could have kept her brother Lazarus from dying but gave up hope once he was dead (John 11:21). Even when Jesus said, "Your brother shall rise again," she thought the promise could only be fulfilled in "the resurrection on the last day" (vv. 23-24). With such great faith in Jesus' power to restore life, it is hard to believe that Jairus did not also trust that Jesus was as able to forgive his sins and raise him to spiritual life as He was able to raise his daughter to physical life.

Jesus was not a religious guru surrounded by servants to do His every bidding, nor was He a monastic who removed Himself from the life and activities of ordinary people. Nor did he establish a hierarchy of intermediaries through whom people would have to go before seeing Him, if they saw Him at all.

Even though He was the Son of God, Jesus "became flesh, and dwelt among us" (John 1:14), as a Man among men. He walked the streets of the cities, and visited the smallest villages. He talked with the great among men and with the humble, with the rich and poor, the healthy and the sick, the noble and the outcast. He talked with the educated and successful and the uneducated and deprived. He talked with young and old, male and female, Jew and Gentile.

Almost everywhere Jesus went He was in the midst of a crowd, because the people would not let Him alone. Among those crowds were three kinds of people— the critical and resentful religious leaders, especially the self-righteous scribes and Pharisees; the curious and uncommitted onlookers who saw Jesus only as a powerful, authoritative, and fascinating contrast to those religious leaders; and the guilty, hurting, desperate people who came to Jesus for help from sin, sickness, and tragedy. These people asked Jesus their deepest questions and brought to Him their profoundest needs, because He listened, cared, and acted in their behalf. The Creator of the universe, the Master of the world, the King of kings and Lord of lords was not too busy to stoop in mercy to serve His creatures.

JESUS WAS AVAILABLE

And Jesus rose and began to follow him, and so did His disciples. (9:19)

Jesus responded to Jairus by being available as well as accessible. Jesus could just as well have sent the power to raise the girl from where He was, but in a demonstration of self-giving love and compassion He **rose and began to follow** the grieving father to where his daughter now lay dead. Jesus was willing to be interrupted and to go out of His way to serve others in His Father's name. There were doubtlessly many other sick and hurting people where Jesus was, but the need of the moment demanded that He go with Jairus.

In somewhat similar fashion, in the midst of a highly fruitful ministry in Samaria, the Lord sent an angel to Philip saying, "Arise and go south to the road that descends from Jerusalem to Gaza" (Acts 8:26). As soon as Philip arrived there, he met "an Ethiopian eunuch, a court official of Candace, queen of the Ethiopians, who was in charge of all her treasure; and he had come to Jerusalem to worship" (v. 27). When the Holy Spirit told Philip to join the Ethiopian, Philip found an eager inquirer about God and proceeded to lead the man to faith in Jesus Christ (vv. 35-37). As soon as the new believer was baptized, "the Spirit of the Lord snatched Philip away; and . . . Philip found himself at Azotus" many miles away (vv. 39-40).

God not only is sensitive to the needs of the multitude but to the cry of an individual. He sometimes leads His servants, as He often led His own Son, to temporarily put a seemingly larger ministry aside in order to concentrate on one person. The Lord makes certain His promise that "the one who comes to Me I will certainly not cast out" (John 6:37).

Joining Jesus in the short trip to Jairus' house were **his disciples**, along with "a great multitude" (Mark 5:24).

JESUS WAS TOUCHABLE AND IMPARTIAL

And behold, a woman who had been suffering from a hemorrhage for twelve years, came up behind Him and touched the fringe of His cloak; for she was saying to herself, "If I only touch His garment, I shall get well." But Jesus turning and seeing her said, "Daughter, take courage; your faith has made you well." And at once the woman was made well. (9:20-22)

The multitude that followed Jesus and the disciples was "pressing in on Him" (Mark 5:24*b*), and in the crowd was **a woman who had been suffering from a hemorrhage for twelve years.** As Jesus was on His way to minister to a single desperate person among a large number of needy persons, His attention was called to still another single individual—one whom a less sensitive person might never have noticed. Again, an interruption became an opportunity.

Like Jairus, this **woman** knew that only Jesus could help her. And just as Jairus' daughter had known twelve years of life and laughter with her family, this woman had known **twelve years** of misery and ostracism from her family. The girl had known twelve years of sunshine and happiness, while the woman had known twelve years of shadow and tears.

The woman's **hemorrhage,** perhaps caused by a tumor or other disease of the uterus, caused her to be ceremonially unclean according to Old Testament law. Because she continually bled, she could not even be temporarily cleansed and was therefore continually unclean. Mark, not seeking to protect the medical profession, tells us that she "had endured much at the hands of many physicians, and had spent all that she had and was not helped at all, but rather had grown worse" (Mark 5:26). The physician Luke, perhaps concerned about the reputation of his profession, says that this particular case was humanly incurable, that she "could not be healed by anyone" (Luke 8:43).

The stigma and humiliation of such **a hemorrhage** were perhaps second only to those of leprosy. Such affliction was not uncommon, and the Jewish Talmud prescribed eleven different cures for it. Among the remedies, most of them superstitious, was that of carrying the ashes of an ostrich egg in a linen bag in the summer and in a cotton bag in the winter. Another involved carrying around a barleycorn kernel that had been found in the dung of a white female donkey.

The Mosaic law specified that a woman who suffered from such "a discharge of her blood many days, not at the period of her menstrual impurity, or if she has a discharge beyond that period, all the days of her impure discharge . . . shall continue as though in her menstrual impurity; she is unclean. Any bed on which she lies all the days of her discharge shall be to her like her bed at menstruation; and every thing on which she sits shall be unclean, like her uncleanness at that time. Likewise, whoever touches them shall be unclean and shall wash his clothes and bathe in water and be unclean until evening" (Lev. 15:25-27). After seven days without any bleeding a woman was considered ceremonially clean and could then offer the prescribed sacrifices (vv. 28-29).

But the **woman** who approached Jesus at Capernaum had had no remission of bleeding **for twelve years** and was therefore perpetually in a state of ceremonial uncleanness. Her condition caused her to be excluded from the synagogue and Temple, because she would contaminate anyone and everything she touched and render them unable to participate in worship. Even her associations with her own family, including her husband if she was married, had to be carried on from a distance. In addition to her social and religious isolation she was also penniless, having spent all her resources on ineffective treatments and probably a few charlatans.

According to biblical requirements, Jewish men were to "make for themselves tassels on the corners of their garments" and "put on the tassel of each corner a cord of blue" (Num. 15:38; cf. Deut. 22:12). The threads of the tassels and cords were woven in a pattern that represented faithfulness and loyalty to the Word of God and holiness to the Lord. Wherever a Jew went, those tassels reminded him and testified before the world that he belonged to the people of God. Consistent with their typical hypocrisy and pretension, the Pharisees lengthened "the tassels of their garments" in order to call attention to their religious devotion (Matt. 23:5). In much later times, persecuted Jews in Europe wore the tassels on their undergarments for the very opposite reason—to avoid identification and possible arrest. Modified forms of the tassel are still sewn on the prayer shawls of orthodox Jews today.

It was probably such a tassel that the woman with the hemorrhage took hold of. Having nowhere else to turn, she **came up behind** Jesus **and touched the fringe of His cloak.** The phrase **She was saying to herself** is more precisely rendered, "She kept saying to herself," which conveys the idea of repetition. She was saying over and over to herself, **If I only touch His garment, I shall get well.** The single thought on her mind was to get close enough to Jesus just to **touch His garment.**

When the godly Sir James Simpson lay dying, a friend said to him, "Well, James, soon you will be able to rest on the bosom of Jesus." In typical humility he replied, "I don't know that I can quite do that, but I do think I can take hold of His garment."

In her embarrassment and shame the woman who followed Jesus in the crowd wanted to be unnoticed. She would simply **touch His garment,** confident that even that indirect contact with Him was enough. Her confidence was not in vain, and in the touching she was immediately cleansed of her defilement.

Jesus turning and seeing her said, "Daughter, take courage; your faith has made you well." Luke tells us that she was healed before Jesus spoke. As soon as she touched His cloak, "immediately the flow of her blood was dried up; and she felt in her body that she was healed of her affliction" (Mark 5:29). Before Jesus Himself knew of her specifically (cf. Luke 8:46), she was healed. He became aware of the miraculous occurrence only when He realized that power had gone out of Him (Luke 8:46). His words of assurance, **your faith has made you well,** simply confirmed what had already happened. Jesus did not care that her touching even His clothing would make Him ceremonially unclean in the eyes of fellow Jews. He was touchable even by the untouchable.

Throughout His earthly ministry thousands of people came in contact with Jesus, and many hundreds of them talked with Him and touched Him; but many of them were not touched by Him. Throughout the history of the church, countless others—such as Mahatma Gandhi, mentioned above—have also come in close contact with Jesus; and many of them, too, have remained untouched by Him. He knows the difference between the person who approaches Him out of mere religious curiosity or a sense of adventure and the one who comes to Him in desperation and genuine faith.

The woman's expectations seem to have been almost superstitious, as she perhaps thought there was some power even in the clothing of this miracle worker. Yet Jesus spoke to her with words of tenderness, warmth, and intimacy: **Daughter, take courage.** Whatever else may have been in her mind, her **faith** was genuine and was acceptable to the Lord. It was enough to make her **well.**

The common Greek word for physical healing was *iaomai*, the term used by Mark when he explains that this woman "was healed of her affliction" (Mark 5:29, cf. 34). In saying that she "could not be healed by anyone," Luke used another word for physical healing, *therapeuō* (Luke 8:43), from which we get *therapeutic*. But the three references to being made **well** in Matthew 9:21-22, as well as those in the parallel passages of Mark 5:34 and Luke 8:48, use *sōzō*, the usual New Testament term for being saved from sin.

When the blind beggar Bartimaeus asked Jesus to restore his sight, Jesus replied, "Go your way; your faith has made you well" (Mark 10:52). Here *sōzō* ("has made you well") is also used in connection with the healed person's faith. Bartimaeus had repeatedly called Jesus the "Son of David" (vv. 47-48), a common messianic title. It therefore seems probable that his being made well, like that of the woman with the hemorrhage, included spiritual salvation as well as physical healing.

After Jesus forgave the sins of the prostitute who washed His feet with her tears and wiped them with her hair, He spoke to her exactly the same words (*hē pistis sou sesōken se*) that He spoke to the woman with the hemorrhage and to Bartimaeus, although the English translations of that phrase are not always the same. In Luke 7:50 it is rendered, "Your faith has saved you," clearly indicating that the restoration was entirely spiritual (because no physical healing was involved) and that it resulted from the forgiveness of sins based on trust in the Lord (v. 48).

In his account of the ten lepers who pleaded with Jesus to cure them, Luke reports that all ten "were cleansed" (from *katharizō*; Luke 17:14) but that it was only to the one man who glorified God and returned to give thanks that Jesus said, "Your faith has made you well" (*hē pistis sou sesōken se*; v. 19). Ten men were cleansed, but only one was saved.

It is unfortunate that most English translations do not make clear that all of the renderings of "made well" and "saved" just mentioned—which in each case the Lord Himself specifically said resulted from the person's faith—come from the same Greek verb (*sōzō*). That fact strongly implies that a redemptive aspect was involved in each of those incidents.

In the gospel accounts we read of multitudes of people being healed completely apart from any faith on their part or the part of another person. Jesus performed His miracles of healing by His sovereign will, often in response to faith, but not conditioned by it. The centurion's servant was healed without having any contact with Jesus and perhaps even without being aware that he might be healed. Jairus' dead daughter obviously could not have had faith. But no one is ever *saved* apart from faith, and there seems reason to believe that the woman who touched Jesus' garment that day trusted Him for spiritual as well as physical healing.

The two things that bring men and women to Jesus Christ are deep-felt personal need and genuine faith, and the woman with the hemorrhage had both.

The fact that Jesus ministered equally to the outcast woman and the leading elder of the synagogue certainly reveals His divine impartiality. He was not offended by the woman's taking hold of His tassel with her unclean hands. He did not resent her presuming to seek His help while He was engulfed by a demanding multitude and on His way to raise a young girl from her deathbed. No person in need ever interfered with Jesus' ministry, because "the Son of Man did not come to be served, but to serve, and to give His life a ransom for many" (Matt. 20:28). And as He had just declared to the self-righteous Pharisees, He "did not come to call the righteous, but sinners" (Matt. 9:13). He came to seek and save sinners who knew they were sinners—and such persons have always been more likely to be the poor and insignificant of the world.

"For consider your calling, brethren," Paul reminds the Corinthian believers, "that there were not many wise according to the flesh, not many mighty, not many noble; but God has chosen the foolish things of the world to shame the wise, and God has chosen the weak things of the world to shame the things which are strong, and the base things of the world and the despised, God has chosen, the things that are not, that He might nullify the things that are" (1 Cor. 1:26-28).

In their book *Fearfully and Wonderfully Made,* Paul Brand and Phil Yancey quote from the novelist Frederick Buechner, who wrote:

> Who could have predicted that God would choose not Esau, the honest and reliable, but Jacob the trickster and heel, that He would put the finger on Noah, who hit the bottle, or on Moses, who was trying to beat the rap in Midian for braining a man in Egypt and if it weren't for the honor of the thing, he'd just as soon let Aaron go back and face the music, or the prophets, who were a ragged lot, mad as hatters most of them . . . ?

Then Brand and Yancey add:

> The exception seems to be the rule. The first humans God created went out and did the only thing God asked them not to do. The man He chose to head a new nation known as "God's people" tried to pawn off his wife on an unsuspecting Pharaoh. And the wife herself, when told at the ripe old age of ninety-one that God was ready to deliver the son He had promised her, broke into rasping laughter in the face of God. Rahab, a harlot, became revered for her great faith. And Solomon, the wisest man who ever lived, went out of his way to break every proverb he so astutely composed.
>
> Even after Jesus came the pattern continued. The two disciples who did most to spread the word after His departure, John and Peter, were the two He had rebuked most often for petty squabbling and muddleheadedness. And the apostle Paul, who wrote more books than any other Bible writer, was selected for the task while kicking up dust whirls from town to town sniffing out Christians to torture. Jesus had nerve, in trusting the high-minded ideals of love and unity and fellowship to this group. No wonder cynics have looked at the church and sighed, "If that group of people is supposed to represent God, I'll quickly vote against Him." Or, as Nietzsche expressed it, "His disciples will have to look more saved if I am to believe in their Savior." (Grand Rapids: Zondervan, 1980, pp. 29-30)

How wonderful that God is more gracious than men. God never excuses disobedience, unfaithfulness, or any other sin. But He will forgive every sin that is placed under the atoning death of His Son, Jesus Christ. Position, prestige, or possessions give no advantage with Him, and lack of those things gives no disadvantage. As Peter learned only after much resistance to the idea, "God is not one to show partiality" (Acts 10:34; cf. 1 Pet. 1:17). In Christ "there is neither Jew nor Greek, there is neither slave nor free man, there is neither male nor female" (Gal. 3:28).

And when Jesus came into the official's house, and saw the flute-players, and the crowd in noisy disorder, He began to say, "Depart; for the girl has not died, but is asleep." And they began laughing at Him. But when the crowd had been put out, He entered and took her by the hand; and the girl arose. And this news went out into all that land. (9:23-26)

It is Jesus' power that most uniquely sets Him apart from other men. We can be accessible, available, touchable, and impartial, reflecting to some extent those qualities that He perfectly exemplified. But only He has power to heal leprosy, restore sight, overpower demons, forgive sins, and raise the dead.

After the interlude involving the woman with a hemorrhage, Jesus continued on His way and **came to the official's house,** where the young daughter of Jairus lay dead. We are not told how long she had been dead, but it was obviously long enough to have summoned the professional **flute-players** and for **the crowd** of mourners already to be **in noisy disorder.**

In great contrast to those in the western world of our day, funerals in most ancient cultures, including that of Israel in the time of Christ, were not occasions for quiet whispers and soothing music. They were instead characterized by the loud wailing of voices and the harsh dissonance of musical instruments such as those of the hired **flute-players** on this occasion. The result, not unintended, was great **noisy disorder.**

Jewish funerals involved three prescribed ways of expressing grief and lamentation. First was the tearing, or rending, of one's garment, for which tradition had developed some thirty-nine different regulations and forms. Among other things, the tearing was to be done while standing up, and the tear was to be directly over the heart if the mourner was the father or mother of the deceased. Otherwise it was to be near the heart. The tear had to be large enough to put a fist through, but could be sewn up with large, loose stitches for the first thirty days—to provide covering of the body while allowing the tear to be clearly noticeable. For sake of modesty, women would rip their undergarments and wear them backwards.

The second way of expressing grief was by the hiring of professional women mourners, who would loudly wail the name of the one who had just died. They would also intermingle the names of other family members who had died in the past. Sorrow was intentionally intensified as memories of old grief were added to the new. Every tender chord was touched, and agony was magnified with loud shrieks, wailing, and groanings.

The third way of expressing grief involved hiring professional musicians, most often **flute-players,** who, like the hired mourners, would play loud, disconcerting sounds meant to reflect the emotional discord and confusion of grief.

The Talmud declared that "the husband is bound to bury his dead wife and to make lamentations and mourning for her according to the custom of all countries. Also the very poorest among the Israelites will not allow her less than two flutes and one wailing woman." Reflecting such "customs of all countries," the Roman statesman Seneca reported that there was so much screaming and wailing at the death of the emperor Claudius that some onlookers felt Claudius himself probably heard the noise from his grave.

Because Jairus was the highest ranking religious leader in Capernaum and was no doubt a man of means, the number of paid mourners and musicians at his daughter's funeral was probably large. When Jesus came upon them He said, **Depart; for the girl has not died, but is asleep. Depart** was more a command than a request, the same command Peter used a number of years later when he sent the mourning widows out of the room where their dear friend Dorcas lay dead (Acts 9:40).

Jesus surprised and annoyed the mourners first of all by His asking them to leave. They were following the long-established and revered traditions set down by respected rabbis centuries earlier. What they were doing was not only proper but required. Jesus surprised and annoyed them even more, however, by daring to suggest that **the girl has not died, but is asleep.** In scorn and derision, **they began laughing at Him.** It was the hard, haughty laughter of those who gloat over a foolish act or statement by someone to whom they feel superior. That their weeping could so quickly turn to laughter, even mocking laughter, betrayed the fact that their mourning was a paid act and did not reflect genuine sorrow. It also betrayed their complete lack of faith in Jesus' power to raise the girl from the dead.

Jesus knew the girl was dead, just as He knew Lazarus was dead when He said to His disciples, "Our friend Lazarus has fallen asleep; but I go, that I may awaken him out of sleep" (John 11:11). As He explained to His incredulous disciples on that occasion, His reference to sleep signified actual death—though it was temporary—and not "literal sleep." Jesus then "said to them plainly, 'Lazarus is dead'" (vv. 13-14).

When the crowd of hired mourners **had been put out,** Jesus **entered** the room **and took her by the hand.** Mark informs us that Jesus allowed only Peter, James, John and the girl's parents to go into the room with Him, and that, as He **took her by the hand,** He also said to her, "'Talitha kum!' (which translated means, 'Little girl, I say to you, arise')" (Mark 5:40-41). At that time, "her spirit returned, and she rose immediately" (Luke 8:55). Jesus could just as easily have raised her by only speaking the words, or by saying nothing at all. But His touching and speaking to her manifest a compassion and tenderness that far exceeded what was only necessary.

It is hardly surprising that when Jesus performed His first miracle of resurrection **this news went out into all that land.** It was now evident that Jesus not only had power to heal disease, cast out demons, and forgive sins, but had power even to raise the dead! This account is the pinnacle of Matthew's presentation of Jesus' messianic credentials. The Son of Man has demonstrated His power over every enemy of man, including Satan and death. He truly holds "the keys of death and Hades" (Rev. 1:18).

In Christ there is no longer reason to fear sickness, disease, demons, deformity, tragedy, or even death. As believers, we can even rejoice in dying, because our Lord has conquered death. Though we will not be brought back to this life, we will be raised to new life. In Him is fullness of joy and life everlasting. "No longer must the mourners weep," a poet reminds us, "nor call departed children dead, for death is transformed into sleep and every grave becomes a bed."

When as a young man D. L. Moody was called upon to preach a funeral sermon, he began to search the gospels to find one of Jesus' funeral messages—only to discover that He never preached one. He found instead that Jesus broke up every funeral He attended by raising the dead person back to life. When the dead heard His voice, they immediately came to life.

Arthur Brisbane has pictured the funeral of a Christian as a crowd of grieving caterpillars, all wearing black suits. As they crawl along mourning their dead brother and carrying his cocoon to its final resting place, above them flutters an incredibly beautiful butterfly, looking down on them in utter disbelief.

Death can strike God's saints in unexpected, painful, and seemingly senseless ways. Yet He does not promise to give explanations for such tragedies. Instead He gives the wondrous assurance that "he who believes in Me shall live even if he dies" (John 11:25).

Miracles of Sight and Sound (9:27-33*a*)

And as Jesus passed on from there, two blind men followed Him, crying out, and saying, "Have mercy on us, Son of David!" And after He had come into the house, the blind men came up to Him, and Jesus said to them, "Do you believe that I am able to do this?" They said to Him, "Yes, Lord." Then He touched their eyes, saying, "Be it done to you according to your faith." And their eyes were opened. And Jesus sternly warned them, saying, "See here, let no one know about this!" But they went out, and spread the news about Him in all that land.

And as they were going out, behold, a dumb man, demon-possessed, was brought to Him. And after the demon was cast out, the dumb man spoke; (9:27-33*a*)

When God created man He gave him dominion over the earth. Adam was king of the earth, with full right to rule it under God. He was given authority to name the animals and to care for this incredibly amazing and wonderful creation of the infinite mind of God. As God presented it to Adam, it was a kingdom of great light, life, beauty, harmony, health, happiness, goodness, and glory. But when Adam sinned and lost his innocence, he also lost his crown and his dominion. Adam's sin allowed Satan to usurp man's dominion and to turn the kingdom of light into a realm of darkness. The beauty of God's creation became corrupted by ugliness, its harmony by confusion and disorder, its health by disease and decay, its happiness by sorrow and pain, its goodness by sin and evil, and its glory by guilt and shame. Sin turned man's life into the path to death.

Yet almost as soon as man fell, God promised He would some day use man to restore the kingdom of earth to its beauty and goodness and to restore man himself to his rightful dominion over it. The Lord declared that the seed of the woman would bruise Satan's head (Gen. 3:15), and from that point on the Old Testament is filled with increasingly more explicit promises about the Lord's great plan of redemption and restoration. God promised to send a King to restore the kingdom and to reestablish the rule of God and to destroy sin and its consequence, death. Disease, hardship, sorrow, pain, disappointment, and every other evil would be destroyed. Again and again the prophets tell of His coming as the Anointed One, the great King of kings, the destroyer of sin and death, the Healer, and the Righteous Ruler. The Jews knew Him as the Messiah (Greek, "Christ"), who would one day establish His eternal kingdom of righteousness; and earth, like heaven, would forever be under the perfect rule of God.

The gospels present a dazzling preview of Jesus' coming eternal kingdom. When He was transfigured on the mountain, the veil of His flesh was pulled back to reveal before the eyes of Peter, James, and John a glimpse of His divine majesty, a microcosmic display of His eternal reign in majestic glory (Matt. 17:2). The climax of Jesus' divine preview came at Pentecost, as the outpouring of His promised Holy Spirit fulfilled the prophecy of Joel that "'it shall be in the last days,' God says, 'That I will pour forth of My Spirit upon all mankind'" (Acts 2:16-17; cf. Joel 2:28). Throughout His entire ministry Jesus displayed a series of glimpses of the ultimate power He will demonstrate when He establishes His thousand-year rule on the present earth and then His eternal rule in the new heaven and the new earth.

As Matthew continues to present the third set of miracles that demonstrate Jesus' claim to messiahship (begun with the dual miracles of 9:18-26), he shows Jesus' power to restore sight to the blind and hearing to the deaf. In raising Jairus's daughter from the dead, the Lord demonstrated His ultimate power over death. And because death is the ultimate and inescapable penalty of sin, Jesus' power over death also demonstrated even more than did His power to heal disease that His claim to forgive sin (9:2-6) was not empty. In healing the woman with the hemorrhage (9:20-22), and now healing the blind and the deaf men, He continued to demonstrate His power over the physical evils and corruption that sin produces. Through the miracles of restoring sight to blind eyes and sound to deaf ears the Messiah again affirmed His ability not only to restore life to a body but also to restore life and function to any of its individual parts.

HEALING THE TWO BLIND MEN

And as Jesus passed on from there, two blind men followed Him, crying out, and saying, "Have mercy on us, Son of David!" And after He had come into the house, the blind men came up to Him, and Jesus said to them, "Do you believe that I am able to do this?" They said to Him, "Yes, Lord." Then He

touched their eyes, saying, "Be it done to you according to your faith." And their eyes were opened. And Jesus sternly warned them, saying, "See here, let no one know about this!" But they went out, and spread the news about Him in all that land. (9:27-32)

When He left Jairus's house in Capernaum after raising his daughter from death, **Jesus passed on from there** and **two blind men followed Him,** seeking deliverance from their great affliction. In this brief account we are shown a number of truths about these two men: their condition, their cry, their confrontation, their conversion, the command to them, their contrariness, and their commitment.

THE CONDITION OF THE MEN

Blindness was common in ancient times, as it still is in most underdeveloped parts of the world. The fact that Jesus healed more cases of blindness than any other kind of disease reflects its pervasiveness. Unsanitary conditions, infectious organisms, blowing sand, accident, war, malnutrition, and excessive heat all combined to make blindness a constant danger. Many infants were born blind because of various diseases suffered by the mother during pregnancy, and many others became blind a few days after birth by being exposed to venereal disease, especially gonorrhea, as they passed through the birth canal.

It was not uncommon for blind people to associate with others who were blind, and it is possible that these **two blind men** had been companions in darkness for many years.

THE CRY OF THE MEN

As they **followed** after Jesus, these men were continually **crying out** to the Lord, hoping somehow to gain His attention amidst the noise and confusion that usually accompanies a large group of people. Because they could not see Jesus, they could only guess as to how close to Him they might be. *Krazō* (from which comes **crying out**), basically carries the idea of shouting or screaming with great intensity, and the word had a broad range of application in New Testament times. It is used of the unintelligible babbling of a deranged person such as the demoniac of Gadara (Mark 5:5) as well of the shouts of the children in the Temple who were praising Jesus (Matt. 21:15). It is used of the Lord Himself on the cross, as He "uttered a loud cry, and breathed His last" (Mark 15:37). It is used in Revelation 12:2 of a woman screaming in the pains of childbirth.

The two blind men were **crying out** to Jesus in great anxiety and desperation and were determined to be heard over the hubbub of the crowd, knowing He was their only hope of deliverance from their afflictions. What they said as they cried out indicates they had both the right knowledge about Jesus and the right attitude toward Him.

The right knowledge about Jesus. The fact that the blind men addressed Jesus as **Son of David** indicates they acknowledged Him as the Messiah, because **Son of David** was one of the most common Jewish titles for the promised Deliverer. It was a royal title, denoting His lineage from the family of the great King David and His right to reestablish and rule over the coming kingdom of God.

As mentioned above, the first Old Testament promise of God's great Deliverer declared that He would be a man, the seed of woman. Later in the book of Genesis God reveals that the Messiah would be a descendant of Abraham (Gen. 12:3), specifically through his son Isaac (21:12) and his grandson Judah (49:10). Through the prophet Nathan, the Lord told David, "When your days are complete and you lie down with your fathers, I will raise up your descendant after you, who will come forth from you, and I will establish his kingdom. He shall build a house for My name, and I will establish the throne of his kingdom forever. I will be a father to him and he will be a son to Me; . . . And your house and your kingdom shall endure before Me forever; your throne shall be established forever" (2 Sam. 7:12-14*a*, 16). When the angel Gabriel announced Jesus' birth to Mary, he said of Him, "He will be great, and will be called the Son of the Most High; and the Lord God will give Him the throne of His father David; and He will reign over the house of Jacob forever; and His kingdom will have no end" (Luke 1:32-33). In his beautiful Spirit-directed song of praise and prophecy, Zacharias, the father of John the Baptist, exulted, "Blessed be the Lord God of Israel, for He has visited us and accomplished redemption for His people, and has raised up a horn of salvation for us in the house of David His servant" (Luke 1:68-69). When he registered in Caesar's census, Joseph took his expectant wife Mary with him "to the city of David, which is called Bethlehem, because he was of the house and family of David" (Luke 2:4).

Again and again the New Testament declares Jesus to be the promised descendant of David who would deliver God's people and establish His eternal kingdom (John 7:42; Acts 2:29-30; Rom. 1:3; 2 Tim. 2:8; Rev. 5:5; 22:16). The multitudes who threw down their garments and branches before Jesus as He made His triumphal entry into Jerusalem sang, "Hosanna to the Son of David; blessed is He who comes in the name of the Lord; hosanna in the highest!" (Matt. 21:9). To call Jesus the Son of David was to proclaim Him the Messiah, the Christ—as the unbelieving and envious Jewish leaders well knew (see Matt. 22:42).

Every Jew who heard the blind men call Jesus the **Son of David** recognized it as a clear confession of their belief in His messiahship. Publicly and boldly they affirmed Jesus as the promised Deliverer of Israel, and they came to Him seeking their own deliverance.

The right attitude toward Jesus. The cry of the blind men also reveals they had the right attitude toward Jesus. They pleaded, **have mercy on us,** by which they may have acknowledged their need not simply for physical help but for forgiving **mercy.** Although one cannot be dogmatic in assuming so, it seems reasonable to suggest that they felt a spiritual need that only Jesus could meet, and they came to him in hungering humility, openly throwing themselves on His grace. They knew they were undeserving of the Lord's help, but they also must have known that "the Lord is gracious and merciful; slow to anger and great in lovingkindness," that He "is good to all, and His mercies are over all His works" (Ps. 145:8-9). They heeded the call of Joel to "return to the Lord your God, for He is gracious and compassionate, slow to anger, abounding in lovingkindness" (Joel 2:13).

These two men came to Jesus not only with a right understanding of His great worthiness but also with a right understanding of their own great unworthiness. That is the attitude of heart that the Lord honors and accepts. Again it is made clear that the person who comes before God declaring his own goodness is rejected by Him, whereas the one who mourns over his sin and humbly cries out, "God, be merciful to me, the sinner!" is justified by the Lord (Luke 18:10-14).

The blind men came to the right person, because Jesus Christ was mercy incarnate. As I have written elsewhere,

> He was the most merciful human being who ever lived. He reached out to the sick and healed them. He reached out to the crippled and gave them legs to walk. He healed the eyes of the blind, the ears of the deaf, and the mouths of the dumb. He found prostitutes and tax collectors and those that were debauched and drunken, and He drew them into the circle of His love and redeemed them and set them on their feet.
>
> He took the lonely and made them feel loved. He took little children and gathered them into His arms and loved them. Never was there a person on the face of the earth with the mercy of this One. Once a funeral procession came by and He saw a mother weeping because her son was dead. She was already a widow, and now she had no child to care for her. Who would care? Jesus stopped the funeral procession, put His hand on the casket, and raised the child from the dead. He cared. (*Kingdom Living Here and Now* [Chicago: Moody Press, 1980], p. 107)

In behalf of himself and his fellow Israelites, Daniel prayed expectantly to God, "We are not presenting our supplications before Thee on account of any merits of our own, but on account of Thy great compassion" (Dan. 9:18). Jeremiah declared, "The Lord's lovingkindnesses indeed never cease, for His compassions never fail. They are new every morning; great is Thy faithfulness" (Lam. 3:22-23). The writer of Hebrews tells us that Jesus was "made like His brethren in all things, that He might become a merciful and faithful high priest" (Heb. 2:17). Paul reminds us of "the surpassing riches of [God's] grace in kindness toward us in Christ Jesus" (Eph. 2:7) and that "He saved us, not on the basis of deeds which we have done in righteousness, but according to His mercy" (Titus 3:5). Ours is a God of mercy, for healing and for saving.

It is interesting that Jesus at first showed no response to the pleas of the two blind men. They continued to cry out as the entire crowd moved along with Jesus and the disciples, and He let them keep pouring out their hearts as they persistently demonstrated their determination. He tested their faith, letting it run to the extremity that proved its sincerity.

Although we are not told specifically, the **house** to which Jesus went was possibly Peter's, where Jesus probably made His home while He was in Capernaum (see 8:14). After a demanding day of teaching and healing, Jesus finally went to one of the two places that could be considered His earthly home after He began His ministry. The other was the home of Mary, Martha, and Lazarus in Bethany. Our Lord endured three years of almost total lack of privacy. Not only were His disciples His constant companions, but throngs of people followed Him wherever He went.

THE CONFRONTATION OF THE MEN

It was not until **after He had come into the house** that **the blind men came up to Him.** They somehow managed to keep up with Him and then followed Him into the house where He was staying. Each of the healings recounted in chapter 9 involved such persistence. The paralytic and his friends were so intent on getting to Jesus that they actually tore a hole in the roof of the house and lowered the afflicted man to Jesus' feet. The synagogue official continued to seek Jesus' help even after his daughter was dead, and the woman with the hemorrhage was determined to take hold of the tassel of His robe in order to be healed. In each case Jesus led the persistent seekers to affirm faith in Him.

Now He asks the two blind men pointedly, **Do you believe that I am able to do this?** The question seems strange and almost cruel in light of the obvious determination of these men, who, in spite of their great handicap, had managed to follow Jesus for a considerable distance while contending with a great multitude of sighted people who also wanted to be with Him. The men had already acknowledged Jesus' messiahship by continually addressing Him as Son of David; and because Jesus knew their hearts, He was already aware that their faith in Him was genuine. His asking them about their faith must therefore have been for the purpose of drawing out a more complete public confession. "If you confess with your mouth Jesus as Lord," Paul wrote, "and believe in your heart that God raised Him from the dead, you shall be saved" (Rom. 10:9).

Such a confession Jesus drew out of the blind men, and it became a public testimony to others of what is required for salvation. **Yes** affirmed their belief that He was able to do what they asked of Him, and **Lord** affirmed their belief that He was the divine Messiah, the coming Savior long promised by the prophets.

The men's testimony also separated them from those who expected the Messiah to be a merely human political and military deliverer who would throw off the yoke of Rome and set up an earthly kingdom like that ruled by their ancient King David. Their testimony also affirmed the belief that Jesus was more than a highly competent and charismatic human leader. More than that, their testimony pointed to His being above all a spiritual leader, whose first concern was delivering individuals from their bondage to sin. Though Jesus' compassion for physical suffering was great, His compassion for lost souls was immeasurably greater. His healing of diseases was first of all to demonstrate both the compassion and power of God for the purpose of establishing His divine credentials as God's promised Messiah—in order that men might be convinced to trust in Him as their spiritual Savior. He healed bodies for the infinitely greater purpose of saving souls.

As discussed in the previous chapter, the gospels make clear that faith was not necessarily present in all cases of physical healing. The majority of Jesus' healings were performed apart from the mention of any sort of faith. Some healings, such as that of the centurion's slave, were performed without the afflicted person so much as seeing Jesus. Others, such as the raising of Jairus's daughter and Lazarus, were performed on those who were already dead when Jesus' power did its work in their bodies.

But faith is *always* involved in salvation, and Jesus prompted the two blind men to openly confess their trust in Him surely for the sake of the their spiritual, not their physical, restoration. They came to Jesus acknowledging Him as God's Messiah, the Son of David; and they came to Him asking for mercy, beyond simply healing. Although the term **Lord** was sometimes used merely as a title of respect, much as our "Sir," the context here convinces one that the two blind men looked to Jesus as their divine Lord, not simply as a man of great dignity. By leading them to confess Him as **Lord,** Jesus brought them to conversion.

THE CONVERSION OF THE MEN

Without the fanfare or superficial drama so common with self-proclaimed faith healers, **Jesus** simply **touched their eyes, saying, "Be it done to you according to your faith." According to your faith** signifies that the extent of Jesus' ministry to these men was based on the measure of their personal faith in Him. Faith is the means by which men receive the salvation God graciously gives. In light of their confession and of Jesus' specific mention of their **faith**, it seems certain that more than **their eyes were opened.** Their trust in Jesus Christ likely brought salvation as well as healing. He gave them spiritual life as well as physical sight.

Writing about this passage, Archbishop Richard Trench commented,

> The faith which in itself is nothing is yet the organ for receiving everything. It is the conducting link between man's emptiness and God's fullness, and herein lies all the value faith has. Faith is the bucket let down into the fountain of God's grace, without which the man could never draw water of life from the wells of salvation. For the wells are deep, and of himself man has nothing to draw with. Faith is the purse which cannot of itself make its owner rich, and yet effectually enriches by the wealth which it contains. (*The Miracles of Our Lord* [London: Kegan Paul, Trench, Trubner, & Co., 1902], p. 212)

THE COMMAND TO THE MEN

At this point **Jesus sternly warned them, saying, "See here, let no one know about this!"** Jesus was not simply making a suggestion. *Embrimaomai* (**sternly warned**) is an intensified form of an already strong verb and could even carry the idea of scolding (see Mark 14:5).

Jesus' reason for this command was not, as some suggest, to keep His miracle-working power from becoming known. He had already performed hundreds of public miracles and had become famous for them. His miracles were *meant* to be publicized, because they demonstrated His divine messiahship.

Nor was the command given to keep this particular miracle from becoming known for some reason. Relatives and friends of the men would have known of the miracle the instant they saw the men. And because of His fame as a miracle worker, they would immediately have concluded that Jesus was the Healer.

Obviously Jesus had another reason for commanding the men's silence. The best explanation seems to be that He did not want His messiahship proclaimed prematurely. As already noted, the men's calling Jesus the Son of David was a clear acknowledgment of His messiahship—and it was a title He did not reject and that His act of healing in fact confirmed.

Because Jesus did not develop His ministry through the Jewish establishment or come wielding the political-military power that many Jews associated with the Messiah, Jesus' messiahship would not be accepted by most Jews, especially the leaders. It was the very affirmation that He was indeed the prophesied King of the Jews that ultimately brought His crucifixion. But now was not the time for that truth to be spread abroad. He did not want to stir up premature opposition or encourage revolutionary Jews to begin rallying around Him as if He were a political deliverer.

It may also have been that Jesus commanded the men to be quiet in order not to overemphasize the miracle-working aspect of His ministry. Although His miracles were an essential part of His divine work, many people had come to see Him *only* as a great human healer and nothing more. Jesus chided the multitude who searched Him out after He miraculously fed the five thousand near Tiberias, telling them plainly, "Truly, truly, I say to you, you seek Me, not because you saw signs, but because you ate of the loaves, and were filled" (John 6:26). Most people did not perceive Jesus' miracles in their intended purpose as "signs" of His messiahship but simply as a supernatural, perhaps even magical, means of gaining a free meal or some other temporary physical benefit.

And perhaps Jesus told the two men not to broadcast their healing in order that others might draw their own conclusions about His messiahship. If they had boldly called Him by the messianic title Son of David *before* they were healed, how much bolder their declaration must have been *after* they received their sight by the touch of His hand! When John the Baptist was imprisoned and sent His disciples to ask Jesus, "Are You the Expected One, or shall we look for someone else?" Jesus did not answer directly, but rather said, "Go and report to John what you hear and see: the blind receive sight and the lame walk, the lepers are cleansed and the deaf hear, and the dead are raised up, and the poor have the gospel preached to them" (Matt. 11:3-5). Jesus was concerned that especially the Jews, as God's chosen people, accept His messiahship on the basis of His fulfillment of Old Testament prophecy, not simply on the basis of hearsay or mere verbal claims.

THE CONTRARINESS OF THE MEN

Despite Jesus' strict command to the contrary, the two men immediately **went out, and spread the news about Him in all that land.** Most believers need to say more about the Lord, not less. But for His own important reasons at this time, Jesus had ordered these two men to say nothing about what He had done for them; and yet they disobeyed. Because it *was* disobedience of the Lord, what they did was wrong; but it was a kind of sin that only a grateful, overflowing heart could commit. The men could not resist the overwhelming desire to tell everyone of their wonderful deliverance and of the Lord who delivered them.

THE COMMITMENT OF THE MEN

The translation **As they were going out, behold, a dumb man, demon-possessed, was brought to Him** suggests that other people brought the **dumb man** to Jesus while the two former blind men were leaving. But another possible rendering is: "As they went out, behold, they brought to him a dumb man" (KJV). The idea is that the two men themselves came across another needy person as they were leaving and immediately brought him to Jesus for healing. If this was the case, they evidenced genuine commitment to Christ by bringing others to Him.

The **dumb man** may have been a friend of the two blind men, who perhaps had acted as their eyes while they acted as his voice. In that case, the first thing they did after being healed and saved themselves was to bring their friend to Jesus for healing and salvation.

Kōphos (**dumb**) often included the idea of deafness (see Matt. 11:5), because inability to speak is frequently caused by inability to hear. As with blindness, deafness was common in the ancient world. Accidents and disease caused loss of hearing, and foreign matter could collect in the ear wax and become a breeding ground for infectious organisms that eventually destroyed hearing. In this man's case, however, dumbness was caused by being **demon-possessed,** and when he was delivered from the demon he was delivered from deafness.

HEALING THE DEAF MAN

And after the demon was cast out, the dumb man spoke; (9:33*a*)

We are not told how **the demon was cast out.** Whether Jesus touched the man, as He had the two blind men; verbally commanded the demon to leave, as He had done with the demons who possessed the Gadarene men (8:32); or used some other means, the **demon** immediately left, and **the dumb man spoke.**

Nothing is said of this man's faith, and no intimation is given of his salvation. As far as we know, he made no profession of faith in Jesus and received nothing from Him except physical healing. Perhaps through the continued witness of his two friends, he may later have placed his faith in Christ and received eternal life. But at this time his healing seems only to have been physical.

The primary focus of the passage is on the two blind men, and their story gives a beautiful analogy of the pattern of salvation. Their physical blindness is a picture of spiritual blindness. First of all, they acknowledged their need.

Second, the blind men acknowledged Jesus as the Son of David, the Messiah, just as the saved person must acknowledge Him as Lord and Savior. Third, they came seeking God's mercy, knowing that what they needed they did not deserve. How much less do sinful men deserve God's forgiveness of their sin, and how much more do they therefore need His mercy? Fourth, they trusted in Jesus for healing, just as the lost must trust in Him for salvation. On the basis of their faith they were converted. Fifth, by disobeying the Lord, they displayed the well-meaning weakness that often follows conversion. As babes in Christ they were undiscerning and careless, placing their own judgment above the Lord's. But, sixth, they were also useful to the Lord, because they brought others to Him.

Long ago, George Lansing Taylor wrote,

> O Saviour, we are blind and dumb,
> To Thee for sight and speech we come;
> Touch Thou our eyes with truth's bright rays,
> Teach Thou our lips to sing Thy praise.
> Help us to feel our mournful night,
> And seek, through all things, for Thy light,
> Till the glad sentence we receive,
> "Be it to you as you believe."
> Then swift the dumb to Thee we'll bring,
> Till all Thy grace shall see, and sing.

BIRDVILLE
BAPTIST CHURCH
LIBRARY

Responding to Jesus' Power (9:33*b*-35)

and the multitudes marveled, saying, "Nothing like this was ever seen in Israel." But the Pharisees were saying, "He casts out the demons by the ruler of the demons."

And Jesus was going about all the cities and the villages, teaching in their synagogues, and proclaiming the gospel of the kingdom, and healing every kind of disease and every kind of sickness. (9:33*b*-35)

A contemporary British writer has commented, "The problem with humanity is this: humanity stands at the crossroads, and all of the signposts have fallen down."

For Matthew, however—as for every other writer, preacher, and teacher of the New Testament and for every believer today—humanity's needed spiritual signposts are very much in place and are entirely reliable. The problem with humanity is not with the signposts but with those who ignore or reject the signposts God has made abundantly evident (see Rom. 1:18-23).

Among those signposts are the miracles that demonstrated Jesus' divine nature and messiahship, His power to save and His right to rule. In addition to demonstrating who Jesus was, His miracles also served to separate those who accept Him from those who reject Him. For some people, Jesus' miracles were a sign of divine power and glory that drew them nearer to Him; for some they were supernatural marvels by a good man, but a man who had no claim on their lives; and for others they were an affront to religious propriety that drove them even further from the Lord.

Jesus is the dividing line of history and the demarcation point that determines the ultimate destiny of every individual on earth. When Jesus was only about forty days old, His parents took Him to the Temple in Jerusalem to present Him to the Lord as their first-born male child and to perform Mary's rite of purification after giving birth. While they were there, a godly man named Simeon, whom the Holy Spirit had promised "would not see death before he had seen the Lord's Christ," took the infant Jesus in his arms. He praised God for the Child, saying of Him, "My eyes have seen Thy salvation, which Thou hast prepared in the presence of all peoples, a light of revelation to the Gentiles, and the glory of Thy people Israel" (Luke 2:26, 30-32). Then he blessed Mary and Joseph "and said to Mary His mother, 'Behold, this Child is appointed for the fall and rise of many in Israel'" (v. 34).

Those who reject Jesus "fall" into God's judgment and consequently into hell, whereas those who accept Him are saved from sin and death and "rise" into eternal life with God in heaven. Those are the only two possible destinies for a human being. Those who trust God are saved and are "like a tree firmly planted by streams of water, which yields its fruit in its season," while those who reject God are lost and "are like chaff which the wind drives away" (Ps. 1:3-4).

Even while Jesus was still in her womb, Mary praised God as "the Mighty One . . . [whose] mercy is upon generation after generation toward those who fear Him. . . . He has brought down rulers from their thrones, and has exalted those who were humble. He has filled the hungry with good things; and sent away the rich empty-handed" (Luke 1:49-50, 52-53). From her knowledge of the Old Testament Mary knew that God receives those who come to Him humbly and penitently and rejects those who proudly and arrogantly trust in themselves and see no need for His mercy or deliverance. At the beginning of His ministry Jesus declared,

> Blessed are you who are poor, for yours is the kingdom of God. Blessed are you who hunger now, for you shall be satisfied. Blessed are you who weep now, for you shall laugh. Blessed are you when men hate you, and ostracize you, and cast insults at you, and spurn your name as evil, for the sake of the Son of Man. Be glad in that day, and leap for joy, for behold, your reward is great in heaven; for in the same way their fathers used to treat the prophets. But woe to you who are rich, for you are receiving your comfort in full. Woe to you who are well-fed now, for you shall be hungry. Woe to you who laugh now, for you shall mourn and weep. Woe to you when all men speak well of you, for in the same way their fathers used to treat the false prophets. (Luke 6:20-26)

Those who are blessed are the saved, and those who fall under God's woes are the lost.

Using other figures to teach the same truth, Jesus said the saved are like those who build their lives on the rock of the Lord's righteousness and the lost are like those who build their lives on the sand of man's religion. Those who build on the rock withstand God's judgment, whereas those who build on sand do not (Matt. 7:24-27). Using still another figure, the Lord said, "For whoever wishes to save his life shall lose it; but whoever loses his life for My sake shall find it" (Matt. 16:25). On another occasion He said, "Everyone therefore who shall confess Me before men, I will also confess him before My Father who is in heaven. But whoever shall deny Me before men, I will also deny him before My Father who is in heaven" (Matt. 10:32-33). Those who identify themselves with God's Son, Jesus Christ, God will identify as His own children. Jesus made clear that His peace is only for those who belong to Him. For those who reject Him, He does not "bring peace, but a sword. For I came to set a man against his father, and a daughter against her mother, and a daughter-in-law against her mother-in-law; and a man's enemies will be the members of his household" (vv. 34-36).

In a parable addressed specifically to the unbelieving chief priests and elders in Jerusalem, Jesus said, "'A man had two sons, and he came to the first and said, "Son, go work today in the vineyard." And he answered and said, "I will, sir"; and he did not go. And he came to the second and said the same thing. But he answered and said, "I will not"; yet he afterward regretted it and went. Which of the two did the will of his father?' They said, 'The latter.' Jesus said to them, 'Truly I say to you that the tax-gatherers and harlots will get into the kingdom of God before you'" (Matt. 21:28-31). The second son represents irreligious and ungodly people who come to recognize their sin and repent of it, turning to God for salvation. The first son represents religious hypocrites who make an outward profession of God but are inwardly rebellious against Him. Whether religious or irreligious, only those who turn to God through Jesus Christ can be saved.

The apostle Paul wrote often on the theme that the human race is divided into believers and unbelievers—into the heaven-bound and the hell-bound, the blessed and the cursed, the glorified and the damned—and that the determining issue between them is their response to the Lord Jesus Christ. "Thanks be to God, who always leads us in His triumph in Christ, and manifests through us the sweet aroma of the knowledge of Him in every place," he wrote the Corinthian believers. "For we are a fragrance of Christ to God among those who are being saved and among those who are perishing; to the one an aroma from death to death, to the other an aroma from life to life" (2 Cor. 2:14-16). Christians touch all the world with the fragrance of God, but that fragrance is a pleasant blessing only to fellow believers. The more the saved hear and understand and fellowship with those who also believe the gospel that redeemed them, the more they rejoice and grow in their new life in Christ. But to those who are doomed to hell, who reject the good news about Christ, all that believers are and teach carries only the smell of death. The more they hear the gospel and see it manifested, the more repulsive it becomes to them and the deeper they entrench themselves in their lostness. Their continual rejection of the gospel serves to confirm their spiritual deadness.

The writer of Hebrews says, "How much severer punishment do you think he will deserve who has trampled under foot the Son of God, and has regarded as unclean the blood of the covenant by which he was sanctified, and has insulted the Spirit of grace?" (Heb. 10:29). The more the saving gospel of Jesus' sacrificial atonement for sin is denied and purposely rejected, the deeper becomes the spiritual darkness and the severer the punishment of eternity.

In Matthew 9:33b-35 we are first shown two superficially different but basically similar responses to Jesus' miracles, and then we are given a brief summary of His Galilean ministry, which is also a summary of His entire ministry until the time of His crucifixion.

THE RESPONSES OF THE PEOPLE

and the multitudes marveled, saying, "Nothing like this was ever seen in Israel." (9:33b)

After the first group of three miracles, the general response of the people is characterized by three men, each of whom was attracted to Jesus but found an excuse for not following Him (see 8:19-22; cf. Luke 9:57-62). The first response after the next group of miracles was the call and conversion of Matthew (9:9), which was followed by the insincere questioning of Jesus by the unbelieving Pharisees (v. 11-13) and the sincere questioning of Him by the confused disciples of John the Baptist (vv. 14-17).

Throughout Jesus' ministry—as throughout the New Testament and the history of the church—the responses to Jesus Christ show variations. Some people immediately recognize Him for who He is but fall short of seeking His salvation. Others acknowledge and trust Him and gain eternal life. Some at first reject Him but later accept Him, and some outwardly claim to accept Him but inwardly remain unchanged and unsaved. In every case, however, the response reflects one of only two basic decisions—that of true acceptance, which leads to salvation, or that of rejection, which leads to damnation.

In this text the Holy Spirit shows the responses given to Jesus after the third and last set of miracles recorded in Matthew 8-9.

THE RESPONSE OF THE MULTITUDE

The first response was that of **the multitudes,** who **marveled** at what Jesus was doing. They publicly testified that **nothing like this was ever seen in Israel.** They knew of the many miracles God wrought while Moses appealed to Pharaoh to release the Israelites from bondage, and of the deliverance through the Red Sea and the provision of water and manna in the wilderness. They knew of God's giving the law on Mt. Sinai on tablets of stone inscribed with His own finger and of His dramatic crumbling of the walls of Jericho. They knew of the great miracles of Elijah and Elisha. But in less than a year's time, they themselves had witnessed miracles of a greater and absolutely unique magnitude. Here was a display of divine power unequalled not only in the history of **Israel** but in the history of the world.

Thaumazō (**marveled**) means to be greatly amazed and astounded, to be overcome with awe. The intensified forms of the verb found in Matthew 27:14 and Mark 12:17 carry an even stronger meaning. As Jesus' miracles increased so did the astonishment of the crowds. They became amazed beyond amazement. When Jesus stilled the storm on the Sea of Galilee, the disciples were more afraid of the divine power that stilled it than they were of the storm itself. The vast number and variety of healings and other miracles made them both incontestable and incomprehensible. The people were therefore continually "amazed at the greatness of God" (Luke 9:43).

Yet, as astounded as the people were, most of them were fickle in their praise of Jesus. As He entered Jerusalem on the Monday preceding His death, "most of the multitude spread their garments in the road, and others were cutting branches from the trees, and spreading them in the road. And the multitudes going before Him, and those who followed after were crying out, saying, 'Hosanna to the Son of David; blessed is He who comes in the name of the Lord; hosanna in the highest'" (Matt. 21:8-9). But by Friday of that same week—persuaded by the religious leaders that Jesus was going against established Judaism and that He might even become a threat to their safety because of Rome—that same basic multitude chose to release Barabbas the criminal and to crucify Jesus the Savior (27:21). Because their fascination with Jesus' miracles was superficial and involved no submission to Him as Lord and Savior, the marveling multitude eventually screamed for His blood in death.

Great throngs of people praised Jesus and walked many miles along hot, dusty roads to see Him perform His amazing works; but they admired Him only from a distance. They did not lastingly identify with Him or submit to Him. They were always astonished and sometimes afraid, but never committed. They were mere onlookers, willing to cheer but not willing to participate. They came to Jesus out of curiosity and to be entertained.

In John 6:26-27, for example, Jesus said to the crowd, "Truly, truly I say to you, you seek Me, not because you saw signs, but because you ate of the loaves, and were filled. Do not work for the food which perishes, but for the food which endures to eternal life." They came to Jesus only for free food! And because that is all they sought, that is all they received. Eventually they turned away from Him and then turned against Him, because there is no other course for those who will not have Him as Lord and Savior.

History is replete with people who heap high praise on Jesus but who give no evidence of submitting to Him and in many cases flagrantly oppose the truth He taught. In front of Jesus' sworn enemies, Pontius Pilate declared Him to be innocent of any wrong and then a short while later approved His death sentence. The French philosopher Diderot said Jesus was the unsurpassed, and the great French emperor Napoleon said He was the emperor of love. D. F. Strauss, the liberal German theologian, said Jesus was the highest model of religion. The English philosopher and economist John Stuart Mill called Him the guide of humanity. William Leckey, the Irish historian, said He was the highest pattern of virtue, and James Martineau, the English theologian and philosopher, called Him the divine flower of humanity. The French historian Joseph Renan acknowledged Jesus to be the greatest among the sons of men. Theodore Parker, an American Unitarian clergyman, referred to Jesus as the youth with God in His heart, and the Welsh social reformer Robert Owen said He was the irreproachable. A popular musical refers to Him as a Superstar. Those are lovely sentiments, but they all fall short of saving truth.

The Pharisees and other leaders of Jesus' day loudly praised the Old Testament prophets, but their counterparts who lived when the prophets were alive were the ones who put the prophets to death—just as the Pharisees led the people to reject and crucify Jesus. Many people today praise and identify with the great Christian leaders of church history yet reject the central doctrines and standards those leaders taught and often died for.

A few years ago a group of Christian students at a state university held a series of meetings to present and defend the biblical standards of morality. As long as the presentation remained in general terms it was received fairly well. But when statements were made condemning homosexuality as unequivocally sinful in God's sight, an avowed homosexual faculty member stormed down the aisle of the meeting hall shouting obscenities at the speaker. Afterward, many of the gay students spit on the Christians who had attended.

As long as Jesus can be kept at arms' length, and as long as His demanding and confrontational teachings are ignored or denied, He is often acceptable to the world. But when He accuses of sin and demands repentance and submission, the world turns away. When man's need for salvation is preached and Jesus' claims of lordship are pressed, that is another matter. Those who once praised Him become His critics, and those who once marveled at Him become His enemies. People will often give the highest praise to Jesus, even acknowledge His divinity and perfection—as long as no mention is made of His condemning to hell the liar, murderer, adulterer, homosexual, thief, and every other sinner who refuses to repent and receive Him as Savior and Lord.

THE REJECTING RELIGIONISTS

But the Pharisees were saying, "He casts out the demons by the ruler of the demons." (9:34)

From that statement it is clear that many of the Pharisees not only were suspicious and envious of Jesus but already had determined Him to be an absolute enemy of traditional Judaism, of which they were the chief custodians. And in their minds, the enemy of their religion was the enemy of God.

Because they could not deny the fact of Jesus' miracles, they chose to deny the source. And because they refused to recognize Jesus as the Messiah of God, they declared Him to be an agent of Satan who **casts out the demons by the ruler of the demons.** They could not assail the miracles themselves, because they were too numerous, public, and provable; instead, they foolishly assailed the One who performed them.

A short while later Jesus exposed the elemental illogic of the accusation (slightly revised from the one in 9:34) that He "casts out demons only by Beelzebul the ruler of the demons" (Matt. 12:24). Beelzebul was probably a form of Baalzebub (which means, "lord of the flies"), the pagan Philistine deity considered to be the prince of demons, Satan himself. But as Jesus pointed out, "Any kingdom divided against itself is laid waste; and any city or house divided against itself shall not stand. And if Satan casts out Satan, he is divided against himself; how then shall his kingdom stand?" (vv. 25-27). The darkness, hardness, and anger of the Pharisees' hearts led them to attack Jesus with a foolish charge they hoped the people would believe—a charge that, in their blind and determined unbelief, they probably believed themselves. Truth cannot be contradicted with truth; it can only be denounced with falsehood.

When an unbeliever is determined not to believe, no fact or reason, no matter how obvious and convincing, can enlighten him. The person who is sold out to darkness refuses to recognize the light, even when it is blindingly clear. And the person who *praises* Jesus but rejects Him or *ignores* and rejects Him is just as damned as the person who *denounces* and rejects Him. Any response to Jesus but the response of faith amounts to rejection and results in damnation.

THE WORKS OF THE LORD

And Jesus was going about all the cities and the villages, teaching in their synagogues, and proclaiming the gospel of the kingdom, and healing every kind of disease and every kind of sickness. (9:35)

Following his presentation of the responses to the third set of miracles, Matthew gives another brief summary of Jesus' Galilean ministry (cf. 4:23).

We learn from the Jewish historian Josephus that at this time there were some two hundred cities and villages in the region of Galilee, an area about 40 miles wide and 70 miles long. "The cities are numerous and the multitude of villages everywhere," he wrote, "crowded with men owing to the fertility of the soil, so that the smallest of them contains above fifteen thousand inhabitants." Based on that assessment, Galilee then contained at least three million people, most of whom could have had direct exposure to Jesus.

Cities of that day were distinguished by having high surrounding walls for fortification, whereas **villages** were unwalled. During His brief stay in Galilee, Jesus visited **all** of them as He fulfilled His threefold ministry of **teaching, . . . proclaiming the gospel . . . , and healing.**

TEACHING

teaching in their synagogues, (9:35b)

Synagogues developed during the Babylonian exile (which began in 586 B.C.), and from that time on they were the centers of Jewish community life. The synagogue was a place of worship, a town hall, and a courthouse. Before the Exile all worship centered in the Temple at Jerusalem, from which every Jew in Palestine lived less than a hundred miles. But when they were separated from the Temple for those 70 years of captivity, they began to gather together in a synagogue, which simply means "place of assembly." Wherever at least ten Jewish men lived, a synagogue could be formed, and many large cities of the ancient world had numerous synagogues.

The synagogue was usually located on a hill or by a river, and was frequently built roofless—as was most of the Temple—in order for the people to look up to heaven as part of their worship. The synagogue was often identified by a long pole that went high into the air, much as a church steeple. A stranger in town could always find his way to the synagogue simply by traveling toward the pole.

Members of the synagogue would meet for worship on the Sabbath and on the second and fifth days of each week. They also met there to celebrate their many feasts, festivals, and holy days. Regular worship services were simply structured. They began with a time of thanksgivings or blessings, which included songs of praise and spoken testimony of the Lord's goodness. Prayer followed and was concluded by a congregational "Amen," a statement of affirmation that means "So be it." Jesus often used the term *amēn* (translated, "truly," or "verily"; see Matt. 16:28; Mark 9:1) to emphasize the truth of important teachings; and the early church, following the synagogue practice, used it as a response to prayer (see 1 Cor. 14:16).

After prayer was given in the synagogue service, a designated reader would stand up and read from the law of Moses, the first five books of the Bible (the Pentateuch). The passage was read in Hebrew and then translated into Aramaic, the common speech of Palestinian Jews (cf. Neh. 8:8). That would be followed by the reading, translation, and exposition of a passage from one of the prophets. The Jewish scholar Philo, who lived in Alexandria during the time of Christ, wrote, "Synagogues are mainly for the detailed reading and exposition of Scripture."

The practice of reading and expounding Scripture therefore began as early as the time of Nehemiah and remains the soundest way to preach and teach God's Word. The Master of such exposition was Jesus, and to the people of His hometown synagogue at Nazareth on one occasion He explained that He Himself was the fulfillment and true interpretation of Isaiah 61:1-2, which He had just read to them (Luke 4:16-21).

Because of the policy called "freedom of the synagogue," the exposition of the Scripture passage could be given by any qualified man of the congregation, and the privilege was frequently extended to visiting rabbis or dignitaries. Both Jesus and Paul took advantage of that privilege, which became instrumental in the spread of the gospel during the first century (see Matt. 4:23; 13:54; Luke 4:15-21; Acts 9:20; 13:5; 18:4; 19:8).

The typical worship service was closed by a benediction and a final congregational "Amen."

As already mentioned, the synagogue was also a place of instruction, as reflected in the Yiddish word for synagogue (*schul,* akin to our English *school*). It was the public school, or seminary, where Jewish boys were trained in the Talmud (the official commentaries on the law of Moses) and where many Jewish men (besides the elders and rabbis) often spent time studying the Scriptures (see Acts 17:11).

Religious and community affairs were administered by the ten elders, or rulers, of the synagogue, such as Jairus (Mark 5:22). All of the elders acted as judges, and from their number they selected a chief ruler, an interpreter of Hebrew for the worship services, a director of the school, and other such officers. All religious disputes were settled in the synagogues, and in most countries and provinces during New Testament times the Roman government permitted the Jews to handle many of their own civil disputes and even to administer punishment. Cases would be tried, judged, and the punishment carried out in the synagogue (see Matt. 10:17).

PREACHING

and proclaiming the gospel of the kingdom, (9:35c)

Proclaiming is from *kērussō*, which is often translated "to preach" (Matt. 4:17; 10:7; Mark 16:15). The basic meaning is to herald a message, to make a public announcement for everyone to hear.

Jesus not only taught in the synagogues but He went about **proclaiming the gospel of the kingdom** wherever He went—in a synagogue, on a street corner, on a hillside, or on the seashore. It was through **proclaiming the gospel** that He made His major evangelistic thrust, calling on His hearers not simply to believe what He taught but to believe in Him. In preaching **the gospel of the kingdom**, Jesus was not expounding the Old Testament, as He did when teaching in the synagogues, but He was **proclaiming** the New Testament, the New Covenant which He would seal with His own blood (Matt. 26:28). He was unfolding the mysteries that were mentioned but not explained in the Old Testament, hidden even from the most faithful believers of previous times. He was thus giving new revelation about God's plan of redemption.

Gospel (*euangelion*) means "good news," and in the New Testament it is used in particular of the good news **of the kingdom** of God, which Jesus not only proclaimed but of which He was both the entrance and the Ruler (Matt. 16:28; 18:3; Luke 22:29-30; John 14:6; 18:36).

Jesus' teaching about **the kingdom** was not just about the future kingdom, in its millennial and eternal states, but about His present spiritual kingdom, into which a person is born by forgiving, transforming grace the moment he trusts in the Son of God. Every Christian is a citizen of God's kingdom in this present life. Christ is the King, the Lord, of every believer. He rules our lives, supplies our needs, guarantees our salvation, and in every way is sovereign over us. **The kingdom** is the rule and reign of Christ—now in and over His saints on earth, eventually over all the earth during the Millennium, and ultimately and eternally over the new heavens and the new earth.

The dual tasks of teaching the Word and proclaiming the gospel are still the primary ministry of the church today. Our first calling is to teach men the truth of God's Word and to lead them to saving knowledge of Jesus Christ (Matt. 28:19-20).

HEALING

healing every kind of disease and every kind of sickness. (9:35*d*)

In his book *Counterfeit Miracles,* B. B. Warfield wrote, "When our Lord came down to earth, He drew heaven with Him. The signs which accompanied His ministry were but the trailing clouds of glory which He brought from heaven, which is His home" (Carlisle, Pa.: Banner of Truth, [1918] 1983, p. 3).

Jesus' ministries of teaching and preaching were verified as divine and true by the display of supernatural power in His ministry of miracles, manifested especially through **healing**. Those three activities summarize the public ministry of our Lord.

The Harvest and the Laborers (9:36-38)

10

And seeing the multitudes, He felt compassion for them, because they were distressed and downcast like sheep without a shepherd. Then He said to His disciples, "The harvest is plentiful, but the workers are few. Therefore beseech the Lord of the harvest to send out workers into His harvest." (9:36-38)

At this point Matthew has concluded the section on Jesus' attestation of His divine authority and His messianic credentials (chaps. 8-9). In chapter 10 Matthew focuses on Jesus' commissioning of the disciples and His initial instruction and training for their apostolic ministry (see 11:1). Verses 36-38 of chapter 9 form a bridge between these two sections, as Jesus temporarily turns away from His public ministry to the multitudes and begins to concentrate exclusively on discipling the inner circle of twelve.

This text marks a significant transition in Jesus' ministry. Until this point His disciples have simply been listeners and onlookers, observing and learning. All of the actual ministry—teaching, preaching, and healing—has been performed by Jesus Himself. Now Jesus shows the reason and need to begin involving the disciples (compare 9:35 and 10:1, 7-8, 27). In the three verses of our text we are given a glimpse of Jesus' motives and methods in preparing the disciples for their joint ministry with Him.

His Motives

And seeing the multitudes, He felt compassion for them, because they were distressed and downcast like sheep without a shepherd. Then He said to His disciples, "The harvest is plentiful," (9:36-37a)

Here is a marvelous disclosure of our Lord's heart, a revelation of His divine motive for ministry. We discover what prompted the Son of God to come to earth to teach, preach to, and heal a sinful people who deserved only the condemnation of hell. Three elements of that motivation are His own divine compassion, man's lost condition, and the coming consummation of judgment.

CHRIST'S DIVINE COMPASSION

And seeing the multitudes, He felt compassion for them, (9:36a)

Perhaps from the vantage point of a hillside, Jesus looked out over the great mass of people who had been His almost constant followers for many months. They were always there, wherever He went. If He entered a boat to cross the Sea of Galilee, they would either follow in other boats or run around the shore to the other side and meet Him there. They dogged Him from town to town, from house to house, from synagogue to synagogue, and gave Him no rest.

Many people came simply to watch and listen, eager to see and hear what the great miracle worker and teacher would do or say. They had never heard anyone speak the authoritative but gracious words He spoke, and they had never seen anyone perform the marvelous feats that He performed. Many other people, however, came to Him for specific needs in their own lives or in the lives of their loved ones or friends. Most of these came for physical healing or deliverance from demons.

But the divine eyes of Jesus saw infinitely greater need in their lives, a need that far surpassed a withered arm, a bleeding body, a possessed mind, or blind eyes and deaf ears. He sympathized with their physical pains, too, and would have been deeply moved had those been their only afflictions.

But in **seeing the multitudes** Jesus saw the deepness and pervasiveness of their sin and the desperate plight of their spiritual blindness and lostness. Consequently, **He felt compassion for them** as only God could feel. He cared for them because He was God incarnate and it is God's nature to love and to care, for "God is love" (1 John 4:8). Over and over in the gospel record we are told of Jesus' **compassion** and love for men. When He withdrew in a boat to be alone after hearing of the death of John the Baptist, the crowd discovered where He went and "followed

Him on foot from the cities. And when He went ashore, He saw a great multitude, and felt compassion for them, and healed their sick" (Matt. 14:13-14). After He had healed a great number of people on a mountainside in Galilee, He privately told His disciples, "I feel compassion for the multitude, because they have remained with Me now three days and have nothing to eat; and I do not wish to send them away hungry, lest they faint on the way" (15:32). It was not enough that He had healed the lame, the crippled, the blind, the dumb, and many others among them (vv. 30-31). When they were without food, He cared deeply about their hunger.

Splanchna, the noun form of the verb behind **felt compassion,** literally refers to the intestines, or bowels. In Scripture it is sometimes used literally, as when describing Judas's death (Acts 1:18). More often, however, it is used figuratively to represent the emotions, much in the way we use the term *heart* today. The Hebrews, like many other ancient peoples, expressed attitudes and emotions in terms of physiological symptoms, not in abstractions. As most of us know from personal experience, many intense emotions—anxiety, fear, pity, remorse, and so on—can directly, and often immediately, affect the stomach and the digestive tract. Upset stomach, colitis, and ulcers are a few of the common ailments frequently related to emotional trauma. It is not strange, then, that ancient people associated strong emotions with that region of the body. The heart, on the other hand, was associated more with the mind and thinking (see Prov. 16:23; Matt. 15:19; Rom. 10:10; Heb. 4:12). The heart was the source of thought and action, whereas the bowels were the responder, the reactor.

Jesus therefore used the common term of His day to express His deep **compassion** for the great crowds of people who were suffering. But His care was not merely figurative, because He felt in His own body the symptoms of His deep caring. If our bodies literally ache in pain and nausea when we experience great agony, remorse, or sympathy, we can be sure that the Son of Man felt them even more. Matthew tells us that, in order to fulfill the prophecies of Isaiah, Jesus "Himself took our infirmities, and carried away our diseases" (Matt. 8:17). It was not, of course, that Jesus Himself contracted the diseases or infirmities, but that in sympathy and compassion He physically as well as emotionally suffered with those who came to Him for healing—just as a parent can become physically ill from worry and concern over a child who is desperately sick or in trouble or danger.

When Jesus saw Mary and her friends weeping over the death of her brother Lazarus, "He was deeply moved in spirit, and was troubled," and He wept with them (John 11:33, 35). The phrase "deeply moved in spirit" carries the idea of physical as well as emotional and spiritual anguish. Jesus Himself was seized with grief as He saw His dear friend grieving; and He burst into tears. He knew that Lazarus would soon be alive again, and His grief was therefore not for the same reason as theirs. But it was the same feeling as theirs and even more intense. After some of the people there wondered aloud why Jesus had not prevented Lazarus' death, He was again "deeply moved within" (v. 38), a phrase that carries the idea of shuddering, of being physically racked with emotion.

When Jesus was arrested in the Garden, His concern was not for Himself but for His disciples. He said to the soldiers, "If therefore you seek Me, let these go their way" (John 18:8). When He was hanging on the cross, facing death and suffering great physical agony from the crown of thorns and the nails in His hands and feet, His concern was for His mother. "When Jesus therefore saw His mother, and the disciple whom He loved standing nearby, He said to His mother, 'Woman, behold, your son!' Then He said to the disciple, 'Behold, your mother!'" (John 19:26-27). In His incalculable compassion He would not give up His spirit until He had provided for His mother.

As He agonized over the rejection by His own people, He did not feel anger or vengeance but the deepest possible remorse for them. In one of the most poignant statements ever uttered, He lamented, "O Jerusalem, Jerusalem, who kills the prophets and stones those who are sent to her! How often I wanted to gather your children together, the way a hen gathers her chicks under her wings, and you were unwilling" (Matt. 23:37). Luke reports that when Jesus approached Jerusalem for the last time, "He saw the city and wept over it, saying, 'If you had known in this day, even you, the things which make for peace! But now they have been hidden from your eyes'" (Luke 19:41-42). As Isaiah had prophesied, Jesus was indeed "a man of sorrows, and acquainted with grief" (Isa. 53:3).

Jesus not only performed miracles of healings to establish His messianic credentials but also to show God's infinite love. He demonstrated *compassionate* power, a kind of power completely foreign to pagans and even to most Jews—who had long ago lost sight of the lovingkindness of the God who had called, guided, protected, and blessed them as His chosen people. The people who witnessed Jesus' healing touch and heard His healing words must surely have been as astonished by His **compassion** as they were by His power.

Dr. Paul Brand has spent many years in medical work among lepers. In his book *Fearfully and Wonderfully Made,* he writes,

> [Jesus] reached out His hand and touched the eyes of the blind, the skin of the person with leprosy, and the legs of the cripple. . . .
>
> I have sometimes wondered why Jesus so frequently touched the people He healed, many of whom must have been unattractive, obviously diseased, unsanitary, smelly. With His power, He easily could have waved a magic wand. . . . But He chose not to. Jesus' mission was not chiefly a crusade against disease . . . but rather a ministry to individual people, some of whom happened to have a disease. He wanted those people, one by one, to feel His love and warmth and His full identification with them. Jesus knew He could not readily demonstrate love to a crowd, for love usually involves touching.

Commenting on two statements about Jesus in the book of Hebrews ("For we do not have a high priest who cannot sympathize with our weaknesses," 4:15; and "Although He was a Son, He learned obedience from the things which He suffered," 5:8), Dr. Brand says,

A stupefying concept: God's Son learning through His experiences on earth. Before taking on a body, God had no personal experience of physical pain or of the effect of rubbing against needy persons. But God dwelt among us and touched us, and His time spent here allows Him to more fully identify with our pain. (Paul Brand and Philip Yancey, *Fearfully and Wonderfully Made* [Grand Rapids: Zondervan, 1980], pp. 140, 146-48)

That sympathetic compassion is unique to Christianity, because it is unique to Christianity's God. Hinduism is perhaps one of the most cruelly neglectful of all religious systems. Its caste system prohibits anyone from even touching those of an alien caste. Its treatment of the sick and dying is sometimes shocking and barbarous, because providing them help is thought to delay the process of karma and reincarnation. Brahmins, the Hindu priestly class, recognize no responsibility for the care of the afflicted and downtrodden. Islam, whose history runs red with secular and religious bloodshed, cannot be expected to show much pity for those in need. The primary motive behind Buddhist benevolence is that the act may lay up merit.

How different were Jesus' teaching and example. In the parable of the slave who owed an unpayable debt to his king, Jesus illustrated God's love through the grace of the king, who "felt compassion" on his slave "and released him and forgave him the debt" (Matt. 18:27). When the two blind men sitting by the road just outside of Jericho cried out to Jesus, "Lord, have mercy on us, Son of David!" He was "moved with compassion, . . . touched their eyes," and restored their sight (20:30, 34). When the leper came to Him, declaring, "If You are willing, You can make me clean," Jesus again was "moved with compassion," and He cleansed the man of his tormenting disease (Mark 1:40-41).

G. Campbell Morgan wrote on this passage,

There is no reason in man that God should save; the need is born of His own compassion. No man has any claim upon God. Why, then, should men be cared for? Why should they not become the prey of the ravening wolf, having wandered from the fold? It has been said that the great work of redemption was the outcome of a passion for the righteousness and holiness of God; that Jesus must come and teach and live and suffer and die because God is righteous and holy. I do not so read the story. God could have met every demand of His righteousness and holiness by handing men over to the doom they had brought upon themselves. But deepest in the being of God, holding in its great energising might, both holiness and righteousness, is love and compassion. God said, according to Hosea, "How shall I give thee up, Ephraim?" It is out of the love which inspired that wail of the Divine heart, that salvation has been provided. (*The Gospel According to Matthew* [Old Tappan, N.J.: Revell, 1979], pp. 99-100)

The great Puritan writer Thomas Watson said, "We may force our Lord to punish us, but we will never have to force Him to love us." The God of Scripture is the

God of love and compassion. How different are the gods of paganism. The supreme attribute of the ancient Greek gods was *apatheia*, apathy and indifference. Those supposed deities were supremely unconcerned about the welfare of mankind. Even the nature of the true God had been so distorted by the scribes, Pharisees, and rabbis that most Jews thought of Him primarily as a God of anger, vengeance, and indifference. Jesus brought an entirely new message.

Because the Lord is compassionate, believers who bear His name are also to be compassionate. "To sum up," Peter says, "let all be harmonious, sympathetic, brotherly, kindhearted, and humble in spirit; not returning evil for evil, or insult for insult, but giving a blessing instead" (1 Pet. 3:8-9).

MAN'S LOST CONDITION

because they were distressed and downcast like sheep without a shepherd. (9:36*b*)

Jesus' second motive for ministry was the knowledge of man's lost condition. He saw the people around Him in the reality of their need. He was moved by their diseases and sickness, and He healed every kind of them (v. 35). But He was moved even more deeply by the needs that most of the multitude did not know they had—to be freed from their bondage to sin. He was not fooled by their religious fronts and their spiritual facades. He saw their hearts, and He knew that inwardly **they were distressed and downcast.**

Skullō (to be **distressed**) has the root meaning of flaying or skinning, and the derived meanings of being harassed or severely troubled. It often connoted the ideas of being battered, bruised, mangled, ripped apart, worn out, and exhausted. Jesus saw the multitudes as being inwardly devastated by their sinful and hopeless condition.

Rhiptō (to be **downcast**) has the basic meaning of being thrown down prostrate and utterly helpless, as from drunkenness or a mortal wound. The Septuagint (Greek Old Testament) uses the word of Sisera as he "was lying dead with a tent peg in his temple" (Judg. 4:22). Jesus saw the **downcast** multitudes as **sheep without a shepherd** to protect and care for them. They were helpless and defenseless, spiritually battered, thrown down, and without leadership or supply.

Those who claimed to be their shepherds were the scribes and Pharisees, but it was those very "shepherds" who were largely responsible for the people's confusion and hopelessness. Their religious leaders gave them no spiritual pastures, nor did they feed them, give them drink, or bind up their wounds. Instead, they were spiritually brutalized by uncaring, unloving leaders who should have been meeting their spiritual needs. Consequently, the people had been left weary, desolate, and forlorn. In 10:6 Jesus calls them "the lost sheep of the house of Israel," God's chosen people who had been left to perish.

The scribes and Pharisees offered a religion that added burdens instead of lifting them. They had great concern about their self-made traditions but only superficial and hypocritical concern about the true law of God. And for them, the common people were the object of disdain not compassion, to be exploited not served. The scribes and Pharisees were true descendants of the false shepherds against whom the Lord had railed centuries earlier through Ezekiel: "Woe, shepherds of Israel who have been feeding themselves! Should not the shepherds feed the flock? You eat the fat and clothe yourselves with the wool, you slaughter the fat sheep without feeding the flock. Those who are sickly you have not strengthened, the diseased you have not healed, the broken you have not bound up, the scattered you have not brought back, nor have you sought for the lost; but with force and with severity you have dominated them" (Ezek. 34:2-4; cf. Zech. 11:5).

The scribes and Pharisees "tie up heavy loads, and lay them on men's shoulders," Jesus said; "but they themselves are unwilling to move them with so much as a finger" (Matt. 23:4). Worse than that, they "shut off the kingdom of heaven from men," not entering themselves and not allowing others to enter (v. 13). What an indictment.

Many religious leaders today are still endeavoring to keep people out of the kingdom by distorting and contradicting God's Word and perverting the way of salvation. They still keep them from the true Shepherd. By telling people they are already saved because "a good God would never condemn anyone to hell," they lead people to be content with themselves and to see no need for repentance and salvation—thereby shutting tight the gracious door God has provided. Or when people are told they can work their way into God's favor by avoiding certain sins or by performing certain good deeds or participating in some prescribed ritual, they are likewise deceived and left in their lostness. Those for whom Christ feels compassionate love are spiritually battered, bruised, and thrown down to lie helpless outside the sheepfold God has provided for them in His Son.

Jesus called such false teachers thieves and robbers, strangers from whom people should flee (John 10:1, 5). In his parting words to the Ephesian elders at Miletus, Paul warned, "Be on guard for yourselves and for all the flock, among which the Holy Spirit has made you overseers, to shepherd the church of God which He purchased with His own blood. I know that after my departure savage wolves will come in among you, not sparing the flock" (Acts 20:28-29).

How wonderfully refreshing it must have been to hear Jesus say, "Come to Me, all who are weary and heavy-laden, and I will give you rest. Take My yoke upon you, and learn from Me, for I am gentle and humble in heart; and you shall find rest for your souls. For My yoke is easy, and My load is light" (Matt. 11:28-30). What a contrast those words were from the teaching of the scribes and Pharisees, who added burden upon burden, tradition upon tradition, requirement upon requirement.

Someone has written,

> Let me look on the crowd as my Savior did,
> Till my eyes with tears grow dim;
> Let me view with pity the wandering sheep,
> And love them for the love of Him.

THE COMING CONSUMMATION OF JUDGMENT

Then He said to His disciples, "The harvest is plentiful," (9:37a)

Jesus here changes the metaphor from shepherding to harvesting, but He continues to give His motives for ministry. Jesus ministered not only because it was His nature to have compassion and because the people had a deep need; He also ministered because they faced God's final judgment.

Several interpretations are commonly offered for the meaning of **the harvest.** It is said to represent all the lost, the seekers after God, or those who are elected for salvation. But from other parts of Scripture, including the Old Testament, we discover a different picture of what Jesus doubtlessly meant by the figure of **harvest.**

God declared to Israel through Isaiah, "For you have forgotten the God of your salvation and have not remembered the rock of your refuge. Therefore you plant delightful plants and set them with vine slips of a strange god. In the day that you plant it you carefully fence it in, and in the morning you bring your seed to blossom; but the harvest will be a heap in a day of sickliness and incurable pain" (Isa. 17:10-11). The harvest here was God's judgment.

Through Joel the Lord said, "Hasten and come, all you surrounding nations, and gather yourselves there. Bring down, O Lord, Thy mighty ones. Let the nations be aroused and come up to the valley of Jehoshaphat, for there I will sit to judge all the surrounding nations. Put in the sickle, for the harvest is ripe. Come, tread, for the wine press is full; the vats overflow, for their wickedness is great. Multitudes, multitudes in the valley of decision" (Joel 3:11-14). Again the harvest was God's judgment, and the multitudes faced the decision of their destiny—before they lost the opportunity to decide.

In the parable of the wheat and tares Jesus spoke of the two plants being allowed "to grow together until the harvest," when the tares would be bound into bundles and burned up (Matt. 13:30). In His explanation of that parable Jesus said, "Just as the tares are gathered up and burned with fire, so shall it be at the end of the age. The Son of Man will send forth His angels, and they will gather out of His kingdom all stumbling blocks, and those who commit lawlessness, and will cast them into the furnace of fire; in that place there shall be weeping and gnashing of teeth" (vv. 40-42). The parable includes the truth that the harvest will bring the righteous into eternal blessing (v. 43), but the emphasis is clearly on judgment.

On the island of Patmos, the apostle John saw a vision of the harvest.

And I looked," he said, "and behold, a white cloud, and sitting on the cloud was one like a son of man, having a golden crown on His head, and a sharp sickle in His hand. And another angel came out of the temple, crying out with a loud voice to Him who sat on the cloud, 'Put in your sickle and reap, because the hour to reap has come, because the harvest of the earth is ripe.' And He who sat on the cloud swung His sickle over the earth; and the earth was reaped.

And another angel came out of the temple which is in heaven, and he also had a sharp sickle. And another angel, the one who has power over fire, came out from the altar; and he called with a loud voice to him who had the sharp sickle, saying, "Put in your sharp sickle, and gather the clusters from the vine of the earth, because her grapes are ripe." And the angel swung his sickle to the earth, and gathered the clusters from the vine of the earth, and threw them into the great wine press of the wrath of God. And the wine press was trodden outside the city, and blood came out from the wine press, up to the horses' bridles, for a distance of two hundred miles. (Rev. 14:14-20)

Again, the unmistakable emphasis is one of judgment.

Jesus ministered compassionately and tirelessly because He could see the ultimate consummation of divine judgment toward which every person in the multitudes was headed who did not trust in Him. Paul said, "Therefore knowing the fear of the Lord, we persuade men" (2 Cor. 5:11), and in another letter he reminded his readers of the vengeance of God (Rom. 12:19). In 2 Thessalonians he paints a vivid picture of God's judgment: "The Lord Jesus shall be revealed from heaven with His mighty angels in flaming fire, dealing out retribution to those who do not know God and to those who do not obey the gospel of our Lord Jesus. And these will pay the penalty of eternal destruction, away from the presence of the Lord and from the glory of His power" (1:7-9).

It is easy to lose awareness of the imminence and the inevitability of God's judgment, but the Christian who loses sight of that judgment loses a major portion of his motive for witnessing.

Someone has written,

There is no way to describe hell. Nothing on earth can compare with it. No living person has any real idea of it. No madman in wildest flights of insanity ever beheld its horror. No man in delirium ever pictured a place so utterly terrible as this. No nightmare racing across a fevered mind ever produces a terror to match that of the mildest hell. No murder scene with splashed blood and oozing wound ever suggested a revulsion that could touch the border lands of hell.

Our Lord, however, knew the tragedy and anguish of a destiny of "unquenchable fire, where their worm does not die, and the fire is not quenched" (Mark 9:43-44), and it grieved His heart that even one person should be there, because it is not His will "for any to perish" (2 Pet. 3:9). When He saw the crowds, He taught them and preached to them and healed them—all for the ultimate purpose that they might come to Him and escape **the harvest** of judgment they could not otherwise avoid.

His Method

but the workers are few. Therefore beseech the Lord of the harvest to send out workers into His harvest. (9:37b-38)

The primary problem that hindered Jesus' ministry as He taught, preached, and healed in Palestine is the primary problem that hinders it today: **the workers are few.**

These **workers** should not be confused with the angelic harvesters mentioned in 13:39 and 49. These are rather the *ergatēn,* who are identified by the same term in 10:10 as the twelve. Nor are the *ergatēn* sent into the vineyard (20:2) necessarily identified as harvesters. They work in the field headed for harvest; and that is what our Lord is calling the disciples to do.

Even as the Son of God, Jesus could not reach all the people that lived even in His own country or His own lifetime. The first part of His training method, therefore, was to give His disciples the insight that the need for the gospel to be brought to a world headed for judgment far surpasses the outreach of those who are seeking to minister it.

Who can reach the lost, hell-bound world of sinful, hurting people who need to hear and accept the gospel? Who will tell them of their plight and show them the way of escape? Who will share with them Jesus' love and compassion and power? Who will warn them of the false shepherds that lead them deeper and deeper into darkness and hopelessness?

In his own days on earth Christ's **workers** were **few,** and they are still few today. The first need in His ministry is for **workers,** and one of the most important things those workers must understand is that their numbers *are* few and that they can be increased only by God's provision and power.

After right motives are established in compassionate concern to reach the lost for Christ, God's people need to look at their world as Jesus looked out at the multitudes in Galilee and over the city of Jerusalem. We need to observe the people around us as Ezra observed his fellow Israelites on the way from Babylon to Jerusalem (Ezra 8:15) and the way Nehemiah inspected the walls of Jerusalem before he began to rebuild them (Neh. 2:13).

The next step in Jesus' method is prayer. His disciples are to **beseech the Lord of the harvest to send out workers into His harvest.** Christ's **workers** are to pray for more **workers.**

The Lord of the harvest is a title of God that represents His role as judge. **The Lord of the harvest** is the Judge of the unsaved who will stand before Him in the last day and be condemned to hell, and we are to **beseech** Him to send **workers** to lovingly warn them, so they may be a part of those harvested to eternal glory.

The Christian's first responsibility is not to go out and start working as soon as he sees a need but to come to **the Lord** in prayer. Waiting on the Lord is a crucial part of serving Him. Before the disciples had received the Holy Spirit at Pentecost they were not prepared to witness for Christ, and He therefore instructed them "not to leave

Jerusalem, but to wait for what the Father had promised, 'Which,' He said, 'you heard of from Me'" (Acts 1:4). Before they embarked on their ministry in "Jerusalem, and in all Judea, and Samaria, and even to the uttermost part of the earth," they were to stay where they were for a while. And in the upper room where they were staying, "with one mind [they] were continually devoting themselves to prayer" (v. 14).

It is interesting and significant that Jesus did not command the disciples to pray for the lost, although that is certainly appropriate (cf. 1 Tim. 2:1-8). Their first prayer was to be for **the Lord of the Harvest to send out workers into His harvest.**

It is possible to pray regularly for the salvation of a loved one, a neighbor, a friend, or a fellow employee and to let our concern stop with our prayer. But when we earnestly pray for the Lord to *send* someone to those unsaved people, we cannot help becoming open to being that someone ourselves. It is possible to pray for someone's salvation while keeping them at arm's length. But when we sincerely **beseech the Lord** to send someone to witness to them, we place ourselves at His disposal to become one of His **workers** in that ministry.

BIRDVILLE
BAPTIST CHURCH
LIBRARY

The Messengers of the King (10:1)

And having summoned His twelve disciples, He gave them authority over unclean spirits, to cast them out, and to heal every kind of disease and every kind of sickness. (10:1)

Those whom Jesus had called to pray for workers He then called to become workers. As they began to see the world as He sees it, looking out on lost humanity through their Lord's eyes and with His heart of compassion, they also began to see that they themselves were called to go out and warn that lost world of the coming harvest of judgment and to invite them into the Lord's kingdom.

Vital as it is, prayer is not all that is required. The believer who prays for God to send workers but is unwilling to go himself, prays insincerely and hypocritically. The Christian who genuinely prays for God to send witnesses is also willing to be a witness.

William Barclay reports that when Martin Luther became convinced that the biblical way of salvation was by God's grace working through man's faith in His Son, Jesus Christ, he began earnestly preaching and contending for this doctrine that became the hallmark of the Protestant Reformation. A friend of his was equally convinced of this truth, and the two men agreed that Luther would spend his time out in the world preaching, writing, and debating, while the friend would spend his time alone in a monastery upholding Luther and the cause of the Reformation in prayer. As Luther visited the friend from time to time and reported the difficulties and obstacles of the work, the friend would intensify his praying. One night the friend had a dream in which he saw a gigantic field that stretched over the whole earth. But only one lone figure was working in the field, and when he looked closer the man saw that the lone figure was his dear friend Luther. When he woke up he immediately went to find Luther and tell him that God made clear to him through the dream that it was not enough simply to pray. He, too, must give himself directly to the work of spreading the good news of salvation. He did not forsake praying, but he set aside his pious solitude and began to labor beside Luther in the heat and dirt of battle.

Until this stage of His ministry, Jesus had ministered alone. He had the companionship of the twelve disciples and the company of vast multitudes who followed wherever He went, but none of the twelve, and certainly none in the multitudes, participated in His ministry except as an observer or recipient. After the imprisonment of John the Baptist, Jesus was God's sole worker in the great field of the world. Then He began the preliminary stages of commissioning those twelve to join Him as fellow workers.

The major thrust of Jesus' commissioning process begins in verse 5 of Matthew 10 and continues through the chapter as the Lord sets forth His foundational instructions for ministry. But in the first four verses Matthew gives three essentials of of the commissioning. In verse 1 he tells of Jesus' initiation of the disciples and of the divine impact their ministry was to have on the world. In verses 2-4, which will be discussed in the next several chapters, we are given the disciples' identities.

THEIR INITIATION

And having summoned His twelve disciples, He gave them authority (10:1*a*)

The verb behind **having summoned** is *proskaleō,* a compound of *kaleō* (to call) and *pros* (toward, or to). It is an intense term that means to call someone to oneself in order to confront him face to face. It is used of God's calling the Gentiles to Himself through the gospel (Acts 2:39) and of His calling His chosen men and entrusting them with proclaiming the gospel (Acts 13:2; 16:10).

When Jesus **summoned His twelve disciples,** He was making more than a casual request. The writer's choice of verbs seems to imply that this summoning was connected to an official commissioning to the Lord's service. Here Matthew refers to the **twelve** as **disciples,** whereas in the next verse he calls them apostles. *Mathētēs* (**disciples**) refers to those who learn under the instruction of a master teacher. *Apostoloi* ("apostles," v. 2) refers to qualified representatives who are sent out on a mission. During their training period, the twelve were learners and were primarily called **disciples,** but as they ventured forth themselves in obedience to Christ's commission and in His power, they were most often called apostles. They still had more to learn before they could be fully sent out to represent their Lord, and it is on their further learning that Jesus next concentrated His attention and effort.

There were four general phases in Jesus' training of the disciples to be apostles. The first two, already presented in previous chapters of the gospel, were their conversion and their initial calling to follow Him. From the many who came to trust in Him as Messiah and Lord early in His ministry, Jesus handpicked the **twelve** for special and unique service. He called them away from their former occupations and gave them a completely new vocation.

The third phase of their training could be called an internship, which they experienced as they lived with Jesus constantly for three years, to be taught both by His instruction and by His example. It is this phase that is highlighted in Matthew 10. From Mark's account (Mark 6:7) we learn that this involved their going out in pairs on short-term assignments to practice what their Lord had been teaching them. During this phase they were never far from Jesus, who closely monitored their progress; and the greatest lesson of this phase was that they were totally inadequate without Him. After such short periods of active service, the **twelve disciples** returned to Jesus for further teaching.

The fourth and final phase of the disciples' training began after Jesus' resurrection and ascension, when He returned to heaven and sent the Holy Spirit as the supernatural Helper who would be with them forever (Acts 1:8; 2:4; cf. John 14:16).

It is encouraging to realize that Jesus did not call those **twelve disciples** who became apostles on the basis of their innate worthiness or personal capabilities or faithfulness, but solely on the basis of what He could make of them by His own power working through them. It is a mark of authenticity and honesty that the gospel writers, like all the other Scripture writers, make no effort to mask the faults and shortcomings of God's people, including those of their most outstanding leaders. During the disciples' three years of training under Jesus, we see few signs of maturity and reliability but many signs of pettiness and inadequacy. It is a marvelous insight into the grace of God toward us to see Christ dealing so lovingly and patiently with men who are so weak and unresponsive.

CHOSEN SOVEREIGNLY

Behind Jesus' training of the twelve are several foundational facts. First, these men were chosen sovereignly by God. None of the twelve initiated the idea of following Jesus and becoming His disciples, much less His apostles. It was entirely God's planning and doing. Mark tells us that Jesus "summoned those whom He Himself wanted" (3:13), and near the end of His earthly ministry Jesus reminded them, "You did not choose Me, but I chose you, and appointed you" (John 15:16). The men themselves were not consulted nor were any other men. Jesus' only consultation was with His heavenly Father. Like Abraham, Moses, David, Isaiah, and all the prophets, the **twelve disciples** were chosen by God's sovereign will and for His sovereign purpose, being foreordained to His service before the foundation of the world. That has always been God's way. He divinely chose Israel, He divinely chose His prophets and His apostles, and He divinely chooses those today who become the leaders of His own Body, the church. Acts 13:1-4 and 20:28 clearly teach that the Holy Spirit sovereignly places men in leadership in the church.

CHOSEN AFTER PRAYER

Second, the **twelve** were chosen after prayer. The men were Christ's choice, and His choice was His Father's choice. Jesus sought the Father's will in everything He did, doing absolutely nothing independently or on His own initiative (John 5:19, 30; 8:28). Jesus chose and called those whom He would disciple only after a long vigil of prayer. "And it was at this time that He went off to the mountain to pray," Luke tells us, "and He spent the whole night in prayer to God" (Luke 6:12). It was only after day came that He called "His disciples to Him; and chose twelve of them, whom He also named as apostles" (v. 13). He chose these twelve because they were His Father's choice, the Father's gift to the Son. "I manifested Thy name to the men whom Thou gavest Me out of the world," Jesus later prayed; "Thine they were, and Thou gavest them to Me" (John 17:6). This same pattern of prayer in choosing servants of the Lord can be seen in Acts 13:1-4. Those were very special men, not because of who they were in themselves, but because they had been sovereignly chosen by God the Father to be **disciples** of God the Son.

CHOSEN TO BE PREPARED

Third, the **twelve** were chosen to be prepared. Even though they were converted and called, they were far from ready to serve the Lord. Training is an essential part of any work, including the Lord's. The **disciples** left their nets, their crops, their tax collecting booths, and their other businesses; and for three years they walked with Jesus—watching, listening, observing, learning, and often misunderstanding.

One writer says of them,

They have no occupation, they have given up the pursuits in which they were engaged: their fishing, their tax gathering, and their agriculture. They carry on no business; they simply walk around and behind their leader, talking to each other or to Him, and when He speaks to the people who begin to gather, they listen just like everybody else. The only thing they do is go with Him from place to place. They are idle, and it begins to be a question of whether it is not doing harm and giving rise to reproach that twelve grown men are being kept idle for no apparent purpose and neglecting obvious duties in order to do so. (Herbert Lockyer, *All the Apostles of the Bible* [Grand Rapids: Zondervan, 1972], p. 13)

It must have looked like that to many of those who came to Jesus. It was easy to see what He was doing; but why were the twelve with Him? They did very little to help Him, and on more than one occasion they disagreed with and even tried to interfere with what He was doing.

Yet they were with Jesus for a purpose, and not a moment's time with Him was wasted, regardless of appearances, because their preparation was on a divine schedule. Jesus knew they needed to be taught and trained. They had to be trained before they could be sent. They had to learn as disciples before they could minister as apostles, and theirs was the unimaginable and unparalleled privilege of being trained by the Lord Himself. To every believer Jesus says, "Take My yoke upon you, and learn from Me" (Matt. 11:29). No believer can grow in Christ apart from learning from Him through His Word. But the training of the **twelve disciples** was absolutely unique. In all of history, they alone were taught directly by the incarnate God, as they lived with Him inseparably for those three years.

Much can be learned from the classroom, from good books, and from personal experience. But spiritual growth comes best from close contact with a holy example. A consistently pure life that is patient, loving, reverent, and that has peace of heart and mind is an unmatched tutor for godly living. To hear a godly person talk to others and pray to God, to see him act and react, and to feel his heartbeat for the Lord is to be trained in the best of all schools.

The disciples were a humanly defective and inept group, but their Teacher was unsurpassed. His intention was not to teach them to be the best they could be in their own capacities and strength but to teach them to be what they could be through His provision and power.

One of the most obvious shortcomings of the disciples was their lack of spiritual understanding. They were called to evangelize the world for Christ, yet even far into their training they showed no perception of heavenly truth or of God's unfolding purpose and eternal plan for redeeming the world. They were spiritually alive because they had trusted in Christ, but they had little spiritual perception or sensitivity. They were dense to spiritual things. They struggled to understand Jesus' parables nearly as much as the crowds did. When Jesus asked if they understood what He was teaching, they would often say, "Yes, Lord." But their subsequent words and actions invariably proved they did not understand all that the Lord taught. They were so dull that they did not even understand that they failed to understand. Added to their spiritual dullness were their many prejudices and preconceptions, which they were reluctant to forsake even in light of the Lord's specific teaching to the contrary.

When on one occasion Peter said to Jesus, "Explain the parable to us," Jesus replied, "Are you still lacking in understanding also?" (Matt. 15:15-16). When Jesus gave the disciples an object lesson in humility by personally washing their feet, Peter proudly refused. After Jesus told him that otherwise he would have no part in Him, Peter went to the other extreme, asking to be washed all over (John 13:5-9). By both responses Peter proved he had missed the meaning of what Jesus was doing and teaching.

When Jesus first began to tell the disciples of His coming death in Jerusalem, "Peter took Him aside and began to rebuke Him, saying, 'God forbid it, Lord! This shall never happen to You'"—to which Jesus replied, "Get behind Me, Satan! You are a stumbling block to Me; for you are not setting your mind on God's interests, but man's" (Matt. 16:21-23). When Jesus took His disciples aside to explain His imminent crucifixion—telling them of His predicted arrest, mocking, scourging, death, and resurrection—"they understood none of these things, and this saying was hidden from them, and they did not comprehend the things that were said" (Luke 18:31-34).

After Jesus was crucified, just as He had predicted, the disciples ignored that He had also predicted His resurrection, and they went despondently back to their fishing (John 21). Even after the Lord had appeared to them several times, proving His victory over the grave, they still did not understand the purpose of His suffering or death or resurrection—or what their role in His future ministry was to be.

Yet through all their misunderstandings, contradictions, pettiness, and failures, Jesus patiently continued to teach—repeating many of the essential truths again and again. Even during the time between His resurrection and ascension "He also presented Himself alive, after His suffering, by many convincing proofs, appearing to them over a period of forty days, and speaking of the things concerning the kingdom of God" (Acts 1:3).

Closely related to the disciples' spiritual dullness was their lack of humility. Often they failed to understand what Jesus said simply because they assumed they already knew. They were proud, jealous, and envious men who were frequently more concerned about their own welfare and prestige than about Jesus' teaching or work or about His own human welfare or divine glory.

After Jesus and His disciples arrived in Capernaum one day, He asked them, "What were you discussing on the way? But they kept silent, for on the way they had discussed with one another which of them was the greatest" (Mark 9:33-34). Jesus had just told them again of His coming arrest, crucifixion, and resurrection (v. 31), yet they could think only of their personal rankings in the kingdom! Jesus rebuked them by saying, "If anyone wants to be first, he shall be last of all, and servant of all" (v. 35).

A short while later the contest over greatness became even more intense. Probably at the prompting of her sons, the mother of James and John came to Jesus and asked, "Command that in Your kingdom these two sons of mine may sit, one on Your right and one on Your left" (Matt. 20:20-21). Again Jesus' rebuke was sharp, and it was addressed more to the two disciples than to their mother. He said, "You do not know what you are asking for. Are you able to drink the cup that I am about to drink?" With typical self-confidence they replied, "We are able" (v. 22). Even at this late date in Jesus' ministry they did not fully comprehend that the cup He was about to drink was the crucifixion; but even had they known, their answer would doubtlessly have been the same. As Jesus went on to tell them, their answer was correct, but in a far different way and degree than they imagined. James would be martyred for His Lord, and John would be exiled for life, but not because of their own bravery or strength.

At this point the other ten disciples "became indignant with the two brothers"

(v. 24), but from no better motive. They were simply angered that James and John presumed to claim the high places they themselves coveted. Jesus therefore said to all of them, "You know that the rulers of the Gentiles lord it over them, and their great men exercise authority over them. It is not so among you, but whoever wishes to become great among you shall be your servant, and whoever wishes to be first among you shall be your slave; just as the Son of Man did not come to be served, but to serve, and to give His life a ransom for many" (vv. 25-28).

Jesus not only corrected the disciples' wrong thinking and attitudes by teaching them again the principles of His kingdom, but He gave them object lessons of those principles. On one occasion He picked up a little child and placed it before them as the model of true humility (Mark 9:36), and when He wanted them to comprehend what true servanthood is like, He washed their feet Himself (John 13:5-15).

A third weakness that plagued the disciples was lack of faith. They had trusted Jesus for salvation, but they struggled to trust in His truth, His goodness, or His power. Repeatedly Jesus referred to them—His select inner circle—as men of "little faith." When they became terrified for their lives during the storm at sea, He said, "Why are you so timid? How is it that you have no faith?" (Mark 4:40). Even after His resurrection, "He reproached them for their unbelief and hardness of heart, because they had not believed those who had seen Him after He had risen" (Mark 16:14). The disciples had witnessed virtually every miracle the Lord had performed during His three years of ministry, including at least two miracles of raising the dead. Yet they did not believe the reports of His own resurrection any more than they had believed His predictions of it.

A fourth problem with the disciples was lack of commitment. Their lack of humility and self-understanding made them quick to promise they would never leave or forsake Him, but their lack of faith bred weak commitment, which rendered them just as quick to fail the test of their promises. When the time of real testing came, Judas betrayed Jesus, Peter denied Him, and the other ten were frightened away. In the beginning, when the cost was small, the disciples "left everything and followed Him" (Luke 5:11); but when they faced the swords and clubs of the soldiers in the garden, "they all left Him and fled" (Mark 14:50).

Only a few hours earlier Peter had confidently boasted, "Lord, with You I am ready to go both to prison and to death!" (Luke 22:33), and Matthew reports that "all the disciples said the same thing too" (26:35). But Jesus knew them infinitely better than they knew themselves, and He said to Peter, "The cock will not crow today until you have denied three times that you know Me" (Luke 22:34). Jesus had already warned Peter of Satan's desire to sift him like wheat and assured him He had prayed that his faith would not fail (vv. 31-32).

A fifth frailty of the disciples was lack of power. As with the other problems, however, they themselves were unwilling to admit it. In themselves they were impotent and helpless, yet even after repeated failures they continued to believe they were strong and self-sufficient. When a certain man brought his son to the disciples for healing, they self-confidently tried but "could not cure him" (Matt. 17:16). Before

Jesus Himself healed the boy, He said, "O unbelieving and perverted generation, how long shall I be with you? How long shall I put up with you?" (v. 17). When the disciples asked Jesus privately why they were unsuccessful, He answered, "Because of the littleness of your faith; for truly I say to you, if you have faith as a mustard seed, you shall say to this mountain, 'Move from here to there,' and it shall move; and nothing shall be impossible to you" (vv. 19-20). The day came when the disciples had such power of faith, but it was only after they were filled with the Lord's own Holy Spirit (Acts 1:8; 2:4; cf. John 20:22).

Jesus dealt with His disciples' lack of understanding by continuing patiently to teach them. He dealt with their lack of humility by demonstrating humility. He dealt with their lack of faith by demonstrating the power of God. He dealt with their lack of commitment by praying for them. After He had given them several warnings of the persecutions they would face for His sake (John 15:18-21; 16:1-4, 22, 32-33), He lifted "up His eyes to heaven" and prayed on their behalf the most beautiful prayer ever uttered (17:1-26). And He dealt with their lack of power by sending them His own Holy Spirit as their divine Helper (John 14:16; 16:7, 13-15).

It is therefore not surprising that the Jewish leaders in Jerusalem were amazed at the preaching and healing power of Peter and John, whom they knew to be "uneducated and untrained men." It was at this point the people "began to recognize them as having been with Jesus" (Acts 4:13). They were recognized as Jesus' disciples because they now spoke and acted like Jesus. They had become living mirrors of their Lord, and that is why believers were eventually called Christians, which means "little Christs." The disciples became living illustrations of the axiom that "everyone, after he has been fully trained, will be like his teacher" (Luke 6:40). Jesus had trained them well, and now they went out and lived like their Master. What they had learned by being with Christ and had received from Him through His Spirit not only had transformed their lives but would, through them, transform the world.

For three years they lived with this Man among men who never uttered a word that was not true, who never sinned in thought or deed, who never lost His temper, and who was never angry except in righteous indignation over evil. Though He was the Son of God, He never followed His own will or took glory for Himself. He cared nothing for His own welfare but everything for the welfare of others, literally wearing Himself out with fatigue in their service. He healed the sick, cleansed the demon-possessed, and raised the dead; and He loved anybody and everybody. Now He appointed the "twelve, that they might be with Him" (Mark 3:14) in order that they might become like Him. And they did.

CHOSEN TO BE SENT

Not only were the twelve disciples chosen sovereignly, chosen with prayer, and chosen for training, but they were also chosen to be sent. The disciples ("those who learn") were trained to become apostles ("those who are sent").

Jesus calls all disciples in order to send them out. There were only twelve apostles (Matthias was later added to replace Judas, and Paul was a unique addition beyond the twelve) who were the official "sent ones" of the early church and who one day will "sit upon twelve thrones, judging the twelve tribes of Israel" (Matt. 19:28). But every disciple of Jesus Christ is called to make other disciples (Matt. 28:19-20). We are all trained to be sent.

Their Impact

He gave them authority over unclean spirits, to cast them out, and to heal every kind of disease and every kind of sickness. (10:1b)

Exousia (**authority**) is from a verb that means "it is lawful," and it therefore refers to a right or power that is legitimately delegated. Jesus granted the twelve disciples God's divine **authority** to do exactly what He Himself had been doing (see 4:23; 9:35). To do what He did would demonstrate they were sent by Him, just as what He did demonstrated He was sent by the Father. Throughout the book of Acts we see the disciples doing the very things for which Jesus here gives them **authority.**

The apostles did indeed **cast . . . out** many **unclean spirits** and **heal every kind of disease and every kind of sickness.** Peter and John healed the lame man at the Beautiful Gate of the Temple (Acts 3:2-8). "At the hands of the apostles many signs and wonders were taking place among the people, . . . And also the people from the cities in the vicinity of Jerusalem were coming together, bringing people who were sick or afflicted with unclean spirits; and they were all being healed" (5:12, 16; cf. 8:6-7). To the man in Lystra who was "without strength in his feet, lame from his mother's womb, who had never walked," Paul said, "'Stand upright on your feet.' And he leaped up and began to walk" (14:8-10). While Paul was stranded on the island of Malta, he healed the father of Publius, the leading man of the island, "and after this had happened, the rest of the people on the island who had diseases were coming to him and getting cured" (28:8-9).

The apostles manifested the kind of kingdom power that their Lord had manifested, and by their faithful obedience they turned Jerusalem and then the world upside down (cf. Acts 17:6). Jesus promised that they would do "greater works" (in extent, not power) and His words began to be fulfilled.

The following story fell into my hands from an unknown source:

One night in the East End of London a young doctor was turning out the lights of a mission hall in which he was working. He found a ragged boy hiding in a dark corner, where he begged to be allowed to sleep. The doctor took the homeless boy to his own room, fed him and tried to get his story. He learned that the boy was living in a coal bin with a number of other boys. He persuaded the boy to show him where these boys were. They went through narrow alleys and finally came to a hole in the wall of a factory. "Look in there," he said. The doctor struck a match and looked around, crawling into the cellar. Finally he found thirteen boys with only bits of old burlap to protect them from the cold. One lad was clasping to him a four-year-old brother. All were sound asleep. The doctor caught a vision then and there of service for his Lord. He cared for those boys and started the Bernardo Homes for neglected children. At the time of the death of Dr. Bernardo, the newspapers reported that he had taken, and surrounded with a Christian atmosphere, more than 80,000 homeless boys and girls. Hundreds of them became fine Christian citizens. O that we might have eyes to see the need about us! Thousands will drift into a Christless eternity because Christians do not take Christ to them.

The Master's Men
—part 1
Peter: A Lesson in Leadership (10:2*a*)

12

Now the names of the twelve apostles are these: The first, Simon, who is called Peter, (10:2*a*)

In his book *Quiet Talks on Service,* S. D. Gordon gives an imaginary account of Jesus' return to heaven after His ascension. As the angel Gabriel greets Jesus he asks, "Master, You died for the world, did You not?" to which the Lord replies, "Yes." "You must have suffered much," the angel says; and again Jesus answers, "Yes." "Do they all know that you died for them?" Gabriel continues. "No. Only a few in Palestine know about it so far," Jesus says. "Well, then, what is Your plan for telling the rest of the world that You shed Your blood for them?" Jesus responds, "Well, I asked Peter and James and John and Andrew and a few others if they would make it the business of their lives to tell others. And then the ones that they tell could tell others, and they in turn could tell still others, and finally it would reach the farthest corner of the earth and all would know the thrill and power of the gospel." "But suppose Peter fails? And suppose after a while John just doesn't tell anyone? And what if James and Andrew are ashamed or afraid? Then what?" Gabriel asks. "I have no other plans," Jesus is said to have answered; "I am counting entirely on them" (cited in Herbert Lockyer, *All the Apostles of the Bible* [Grand Rapids: Zondervan, 1972], p. 31).

Though it is a fantasy, that story dramatizes a great truth about the gospel. The only plan the Lord has for reaching the world is for those who know Him to witness about Him to others. The life-changing power of the gospel is in the atoning death of Jesus Christ and can be applied in a life only through the convicting and recreative work of the Holy Spirit. But the declaration of the gospel is in the hands of those who have already experienced the new life and are willing to tell of it to others.

Society routinely sets standards of qualification for a myriad of enterprises. Businesses establish qualifications for their employees, and the more responsible the job, the higher the qualifications. Advertisements for jobs often list requirements such as self-motivation, ability to work under pressure, minimum typing speed, several years' work experience, and willingness to travel. A person must also qualify in order to buy a house or car, get a credit card, enroll in college, or receive a driver's license.

Scripture makes clear that God's standards for His people, especially for the leaders who are to model those standards for His people, are extremely high (1 Tim. 3:1-12; Titus 1:6-9; 2 Pet. 3:14). The standard for every believer, in fact, is nothing less than perfection: "You are to be perfect, as your heavenly Father is perfect," Jesus says (Matt. 5:48). Yet Scripture makes equally clear that no person *in himself* can meet the least of God's standards. Even after he became an apostle, Paul confessed of himself: "I know that nothing good dwells in me, that is, in my flesh" (Rom. 7:18). In the same epistle he says of mankind in general, "There is none righteous, not even one; there is none who understands, there is none who seeks for God; all have turned aside, together they have become useless; there is none who does good, there is not even one" (3:10-12).

The greatness of God's grace is seen in His choosing the undeserving to be His people and the unqualified to do His work. It should be a marvelous encouragement to every believer to know that, just as Elijah (James 5:17), the apostles had a nature like ours. Because there was no other way, God chose to bestow sanctifying grace on those who believe in His Son and by His own power to transform them into men and women of great usefulness.

We are tempted to become discouraged and disheartened when our spiritual life and witness suffer because of our sins and failures. Satan attempts to convince us that those shortcomings render us useless to God; but His use of the apostles testifies to the opposite. They did not lead the church in turning the world upside down because they were extraordinarily talented or naturally gifted, but because—in spite of their human limitations and failures—they surrendered themselves to God, whose power is perfected in man's weakness (2 Cor. 12:9).

That has always been God's way, since He has never had anything but imperfect and sinful men through whom to work. Soon after God delivered Noah and his family through the Flood, Noah became drunk and acted indecently. Abraham, the father of the faithful, doubted God, lied about his wife, and committed adultery with her maid. Isaac told a similar lie about his wife when he thought his life was in danger. Jacob took advantage of his brother Esau's weakness and extorted the birthright from him. Moses was a murderer, and in pride he struck the rock instead of speaking to it as God had instructed. His brother, Aaron, the first high priest, led Israel in erecting and worshiping the golden calf at the very time Moses was on Mount Sinai receiving the law from God. Joshua disobeyed the Lord by making a treaty with the Gibeonites instead of destroying them. Gideon had little confidence in himself and even less in God's plan and power. Samson was repeatedly beguiled by Delilah because of his great lust for her. David committed adultery and murder, was an almost total failure as a father, and was not allowed to build the Temple because he was a man of blood. Elijah stood fearlessly before 850 false prophets but cowered before one woman, Jezebel. Ezekiel was brash, crusty, and quick to speak his mind. Jonah defied God's call to preach to the Ninevites and resented His grace when they were converted through his preaching.

Apart from the brief ministry of His own Son, the history of God's work on earth is the history of His using the unqualified. The twelve disciples who became apostles were no exception. Even from the human standpoint they had few characteristics or abilities that qualified them for leadership and service. Yet God used those men, just as He did Noah, Abraham, and the others, in marvelous ways to do His work.

Writing to the factious, worldly Corinthians, Paul insisted that neither he nor Apollos were anything in themselves. "What then is Apollos?" he asks. "And what is Paul? Servants through whom you believed, even as the Lord gave opportunity to each one. I planted, Apollos watered, but God was causing the growth. So then neither the one who plants nor the one who waters is anything, but God who causes the growth" (1 Cor. 3:5-7).

The New Testament does not teach Christian leaders to follow the individual methods or styles of the apostles. It does not explain their methods or give details of their specific strategies for evangelism or other ministry. The focus of apostolic power in the New Testament is always on the Lord. As with the lowliest believer, the apostles' power and effectiveness were exclusively the work of the Holy Spirit.

The story is told that after a famous artist finished his painting of the Last Supper he asked a friend to comment on the work. When the friend remarked that the cups were the most magnificent parts of the entire painting, the artist was dumbfounded. He picked up his brush and painted over every cup, explaining, "I failed. I wanted you to see Christ, but you only noticed the cups." It is a wonderful thing to be a vessel fit for the Master's use, but the vessel is not the source of spiritual power and should never be the focus of attention.

Emphasizing the methods and practices of famous and visibly successful Christian leaders inevitably weakens the church, and at no time in history has that misguided emphasis been more dominant than it is in much of the church today. When men are elevated, Christ is lowered; and when men's power and resources are relied on, Christ's work is weakened.

Someone has commented that a great writer can take a worthless piece of paper, write a poem on it and instantly make it extremely valuable. A famous artist can take a piece of canvas worth fifty cents and by painting a picture on it make it priceless. A wealthy man can sign his name to a worthless piece of paper and make it worth a million dollars. In an infinitely greater way Jesus Christ can take a worthless, corrupted, and repulsive life and transform it into a righteous child of God and a useful worker in His kingdom.

A church in Strasbourg, France, was severely damaged by bombs during World War II. Although a beloved statue of Christ had survived, a ceiling beam had fallen across the arms and broken them off. A local sculptor offered to restore the statue without charge, but the townspeople decided to leave it as it was. Without hands it would be a continuing reminder to them that God does His work through His people, His earthly hands.

Jesus Christ chooses human hands—and minds and arms and feet—as the instruments of His eternal work of redemption. Those who are not offended by His demands for discipleship and who, like the apostles, give their imperfect and flawed lives to Him as living sacrifices (Rom. 12:1), become His means for drawing all men to Himself.

Jesus did not intend to proclaim the kingdom alone. His own ministry lasted but three years and did not even extend to all of Palestine. From the earliest part of His ministry He began training the twelve who would continue His work. It was in this training of the twelve that the Lord began the process Paul later admonished Timothy to follow: "The things which you have heard from me in the presence of many witnesses, these entrust to faithful men, who will be able to teach others also" (2 Tim. 2:2).

Jesus chose only **twelve** men to be His **apostles**, a seemingly insignificant number for the task ahead. They would be pitted not only against the evil, unbelieving system of the world but against Satan and his demon system.

History is full of amazing exploits by a few men against great odds. Sometimes the few have been victorious, and often they have gone down in tragic defeat. In either case they are remembered and admired for their courage. Against supernatural enemies, however, man can never be successful in his own power, no matter how great his courage. On the other hand, when God empowers His people, no obstacle or enemy can withstand them.

Shamgar, a judge of Israel, killed 600 men with an ox goad. With only 300 men filtered from an original force of 32,000, Gideon, another judge, routed an uncountable number of Midianites and Amalekites, whom the Lord caused to slaughter each other in panic. Still another judge, Samson, slaughtered 1,000 Philistines with only the jawbone of a donkey as a weapon. Jonathan and his armor bearer, who was probably only a boy, killed twenty armed Philistines who were waiting for them at the top of a hill; and that victory led to the defeat of the entire Philistine army by Israelites armed only with farm implements. In one day Elijah singlehandedly slaughtered 850 pagan prophets on Mount Carmel.

The Lord can display His divine power through a handful of men, or even one man, just as surely as through a multitude—so the small number of the apostles was no hindrance to the work of the gospel.

Henry Drummond, the Scottish author and evangelist who wrote the well-known booklet *The Greatest Thing in the World,* was once invited to speak to an exclusive men's club in London. He began his talk with a provocative analogy that those men easily understood: "Gentlemen, the entrance fee into the kingdom of heaven is nothing; however, the annual subscription is everything."

Because Jesus Christ paid the total price for salvation, it costs nothing to *become* His disciple. But to *follow* Him as a faithful disciple costs everything we have. We are not only saved by Christ's blood but are bought with it and therefore belong totally to Him (1 Cor. 6:19-20; 7:23).

The twelve men Jesus called as disciples and transformed into apostles were willing to pay everything. They turned their backs on their occupations, their lifestyles, their homes, their own plans and aspirations. They committed themselves totally to following Jesus Christ, wherever that would lead and whatever that would cost.

They were a committed few among the unbelieving many. From early in His ministry, and especially after He began performing miracles, Jesus never lacked for an audience. The multitudes followed Him wherever He went, so much so that He often had difficulty being alone by Himself or with the twelve. The crowds were attracted by the ring of authority in His voice, by the uniqueness of His message, by the wonder of His miracles, and by His concern for common people and for the sick, diseased, and sinful.

In the broadest sense they were disciples (*mathētēs*), which has the root meaning of follower or learner. But that term does not necessarily carry the idea of commitment, as is clear from several gospel accounts. The morning after Jesus fed the five thousand (plus women and children), many of the people who were fed followed Him back to Capernaum. When He saw them, Jesus said, "Truly, truly, I say to you, you seek Me, not because you saw signs, but because you ate of the loaves, and were filled" (John 6:26). A short while later He said to the same group, "You have seen Me, and yet do not believe" (v. 36). Among this crowd were "many . . . of His disciples" (v. 60) who were disturbed when they heard Jesus say, "He who eats My flesh and drinks My blood has eternal life, and I will raise him up on the last day" (vv. 54). After Jesus further explained what He meant, they were even more offended, and "as a result of this many of His disciples withdrew, and were not walking with Him anymore" (v. 66). Those disciples were only observers and hearers who had no desire to trust and follow the Lord.

Those disciples accepted Jesus as a great teacher and wonder worker, but only on the physical level. They were quite willing for Him to heal their bodies and fill their stomachs, but they did not want Him to cleanse their sins, recreate their hearts, and transform their lives. They gladly came to Him for the "food which perishes," but they had no appetite for "the food which endures to eternal life" (John 6:27).

Jesus' teaching was not "difficult" (v. 60) because it was hard to understand but because it was hard to accept. The people knew that Jesus was not talking of eating and drinking His physical body and blood but of accepting everything that He was, said, and did. His statement was difficult for them to accept for the very reason that they *did* understand it.

As in Jesus' time and throughout history, false disciples today are willing to accept whatever of the gospel fits their personal inclinations and life-styles. They are willing to be identified as Christians, belong to a church, be active in its work, and give money to its support. But they have no intention of giving themselves to Jesus Christ as Lord and Master. When such a demand is made of them, or even suggested, they vanish as quickly and permanently as those disciples at Capernaum.

Jesus' difficult teachings offended them and caused them "to stumble" (John 6:61). "Stumble" translates *skandalizō*, which means to put up a snare or stumbling block, and is the term from which we get *scandal*. The original meaning pertained to a trap held up by a stick. When an animal grabbed food that was attached to the stick, the stick would fall, causing the trap to capture or kill the animal. The offended disciples at Capernaum understood clearly that to accept Christ's demand to eat His flesh and drink His blood in order to receive eternal life meant to give up their old life—which they would not relinquish even for heaven. Consequently, they had nothing more to do with Jesus.

After the crowd left, Jesus asked the disciples, "You do not want to go away also, do you?" (v. 67). He "knew from the beginning who they were who did not believe, and who it was that would betray Him" (v. 64), but He wanted to make sure that the twelve realized in their own minds the cost of true discipleship. Peter replied for the group, saying, "Lord, to whom shall we go? You have words of eternal life. And we have believed and have come to know that You are the Holy One of God" (vv. 68-69).

Except for Judas, the twelve decided to eat Christ's flesh and drink His blood, whatever the cost. They had no idea of the particulars of the cost, but they placed themselves in the Lord's hands, confident that in Him, and only in Him, was eternal life and everything else of any value.

The twelve men Jesus chose as His apostles had in their hands the full responsibility for initially taking the gospel to the rest of the world. The church was "built upon the foundation of the apostles and prophets, Christ Jesus Himself being the corner stone" (Eph. 2:20). Jesus promised them, "But the Helper, the Holy Spirit, whom the Father will send in My name, He will teach you all things, and bring to your remembrance all that I said to you" (John 14:26). Through the Holy Spirit the apostles received God's divine revelation and were the ones responsible for writing most of the New Testament. It was therefore to "the apostles' teaching" to which the true and faithful church has always devoted itself, beginning in Jerusalem immediately after Pentecost (Acts 2:42). Through them the doctrine of the New Covenant was established, explained, and proclaimed.

The apostles not only were the channels of Christian theology and evangelism but were also the first examples of godly, virtuous living for the church to follow. God confirmed their authority as true apostles "by signs and wonders and miracles" (2 Cor. 12:12); and as "His holy apostles" (Eph. 3:5) they received, taught, recorded, and exemplified the gospel of Jesus Christ.

As mentioned in the previous chapter, the third phase of the disciples' training under Jesus was what might be called their internship, which began immediately after their conversion and calling and preceded their final commissioning and sending after

His ascension (Acts 1:8). It is this third phase of training that occupies Matthew in chapter 10. By this time the disciples had been under Jesus' instruction for perhaps eighteen months, but they had not participated directly in the ministry. Until now they had only been observers and learners. Now they began to have direct involvement as the Lord sent them out two by two (see Mark 6:7) to try their wings in the work for which He had given them authority.

The apostles were essential for the future of the Christian faith, because they were the only ones called and empowered to build the foundation of God's only plan for telling the world of redemption through His Son. It was time for them to be more than mere hearers and observers, so they were given "authority over unclean spirits, to cast them out, and to heal every kind of disease and every kind of sickness" (10:1). But their first responsibility was to "preach, saying, 'The kingdom of heaven is at hand'" (v. 7), for which message their miraculous works would be divine authenticating signs. As Nicodemus acknowledged regarding Jesus, "Rabbi, we know that You have come from God as a teacher; for no one can do these signs that You do unless God is with him" (John 3:2).

"How shall we escape if we neglect so great a salvation?" asks the writer of Hebrews. "After it was at the first spoken through the Lord, it was confirmed to us by those who heard, God also bearing witness with them, both by signs and wonders and by various miracles and by gifts of the Holy Spirit according to His own will" (Heb. 2:3-4). The Lord Jesus Christ was the first preacher of the gospel, and the apostles ("those who heard") confirmed what He preached, and God the Father confirmed their testimony by the divinely empowered "signs and wonders . . . various miracles and . . . gifts of the Holy Spirit" that accompanied their preaching. The word of the apostles was miraculously attested as they laid down the foundation for the church.

The apostles were ordinary men. As far as we know, the only one who was materially prosperous was Matthew, who gained his wealth by legally but unethically extorting taxes for Rome. None of the twelve was highly educated or had prominent social, political, or religious status. Details about some of them remain unknown to us today, except for their names, because neither Scripture nor secular history has much to say about them.

Yet there has never been a task in the history of the world equal to that of those common men whom the Lord chose to be His first agents of ministry in setting in motion the advancement of the kingdom of God on earth. They had the monumental assignment of finishing the foundation work of the church that the Lord Himself had begun. Luke mentions this transition of responsibility in the introductory words of Acts: "The first account [i. e., the gospel of Luke] I composed, Theophilus, about all that Jesus began to do and teach, until the day when He was taken up, after He had by the Holy Spirit given orders to the apostles whom He had chosen. To these He also presented Himself alive, after His suffering, by many convincing proofs, appearing to them over a period of forty days, and speaking of the things concerning the kingdom of God" (1:1-3).

A number of truths about the apostles can be learned simply from the scriptural listings of their names. First of all, in the four New Testament lists of the apostles (Matt. 10:2-4; Mark 3:16-19; Luke 6:14-16; and Acts 1:13; cf. v. 26), Peter is always named first. In Matthew 10:2 **the first** does not refer to the order of selection, because Jesus called Andrew, Peter's brother, before He called Peter (John 1:40-42). In this context, *prōtos* (**first**) indicates foremost in rank. The apostles were equal in their divine commission, authority, and power; and one day they will sit on equal thrones as they judge the twelve tribes of Israel (Matt. 19:28). But in terms of *function*, Peter was **the first**, the foremost member of the twelve. *Prōtos* is used with the same meaning in 1 Timothy 1:15, where Paul speaks of himself as the "foremost of all" sinners. In Revelation 1:17, Christ speaks of Himself as "the first [*prōtos*] and the last." No group can function properly without a leader, and **Peter** was the leading member of the twelve from the beginning.

Second, all four lists of the apostles are divided into the same three subgroups. The first group includes Peter, Andrew, James, and John; the second includes Philip, Bartholomew, Thomas, and Matthew; and the third includes James the son of Alphaeus, Thaddaeus, Simon the Zealot, and Judas Iscariot. The names are in different orders within the groups, but they always include the same four names, and the first name in each group is always the same, suggesting that each group had its own identity and leader. The first group includes those Jesus called first (though not in the individual order), the second includes those He called next, and the third group those He called last.

We know a great deal about the men in the first group, much less about those in the second, and almost nothing about those in the third—except for Judas, who betrayed Jesus, committed suicide, and was replaced by Matthias just before Pentecost (Acts 1:26). There is not only a decreasing amount of information about the members of each group but also a decreasing intimacy with Jesus. The first four constituted Jesus' inner circle of disciples; and of those four, Peter, James, and John were especially close to Him. Little is said about His direct instruction or work with the second group, and almost nothing about close contact with the third. He loved all the apostles equally, empowered them equally, and promised them equal glory; but because of the physical limitations common to all men, He was not able to give them equal attention. It is impossible for any leader to be equally close to everyone with whom he works. By necessity he will spend more time with and place more responsibility on certain people who are particularly capable and trustworthy.

The first group included two sets of brothers, Peter and Andrew and James and John, all of whom were fishermen. Matthew was a tax collector, but we know nothing of the occupations of any of the other seven. The two sets of brothers were acquainted even before Jesus called them, because they fished near each other on the Sea of Galilee (see Matt. 4:18-21).

The temperaments of the apostles about whom we know the most were very much different. Peter, for example, was impulsive, a natural leader, and a man of action. Almost invariably he was the first to react to something that was said or done by saying or doing something himself. John, on the other hand, appears to have become quiet and pensive under Christ's tutelage. In the first twelve chapters of Acts we read of Peter and John working closely together during the early days of the church. It must have been a helpful learning experience for both of them, with Peter anxious to charge ahead and John wanting to think things over first. Peter did all the preaching. Men of equal status and office and even of similar giftedness may have different functions relative to the uniqueness of their gifts.

Thomas was clearly the most skeptical of the twelve (John 20:25), and Simon the Zealot's very name indicates he was a radical Jewish revolutionary, dedicated to driving out the Roman oppressor. Before he met Christ he doubtlessly would have willingly plunged a knife into the heart of Matthew, a traitorous collaborator with Rome.

SIMON PETER

The first, Simon, who is called Peter, (10:2*a*)

All of the twelve, including Judas, were integral parts of the Lord's plan. But **Peter** was by far the central figure, both during the three years of Jesus' earthly ministry and during the early years of the church after Pentecost. Jesus spent more time with Peter than with any of the others, partly because Peter was constantly at the Lord's side. He was never far from Jesus and was continually asking Him questions, giving advice, and even giving commands. Apart from that of Jesus, no name is mentioned more often in the New Testament than Peter's. No other person speaks as often or is spoken to as often. No disciple was reproved as often or as severely as Peter, and only he was presumptuous enough to reprove the Lord. No other disciple so boldly confessed Christ or so boldly denied Him. No other disciple was so praised and blessed by Jesus, and yet no other did He call Satan.

How could Jesus take such an ambivalent, inconsistent, and self-centered man and make him into **the first**—the *prōtos*—of the apostles? From the gospel record we can discern at least three instructive elements that were instrumental in the Lord's preparation of Peter: the right raw material, the right experience, and the right lessons.

THE RIGHT RAW MATERIAL

Peter had the right raw material from which Jesus could fashion the sort of leader He intended Peter to be. Peter was a big beginning; he had potential. But while he was in control of his own life, his beginnings never got further than that and his potential was not always easy to see.

But one of Peter's qualifications for leadership is seen in his continually asking questions of Jesus. He always wanted to know the what, when, where, and why of everything the Lord said and did. Many of his questions were superficial and immature, but they reflected a genuine concern about Jesus and His work. A person who does not ask questions has little chance for success as a leader, because he has no desire or willingness to inquire about what he does not understand. When the other disciples failed to understand something, they appear to have been more likely to keep quiet or simply discuss their doubts and questions among themselves. Peter, on the other hand, was never reluctant to ask Jesus about whatever was on his mind.

When Peter did not understand what Jesus meant when He said that it is "not what enters into the mouth [that] defiles the man, but what proceeds out of the mouth," he asked, "Explain the parable to us" (Matt. 15:11, 15). When he was concerned about the reward he and his fellow disciples would get for leaving all and following Jesus, he did not hesitate asking about it (Matt. 19:27). Peter wondered about the fig tree that Jesus caused to wither (Mark 11:21) and, with James, John, and Andrew, he asked Jesus to explain when and how the Temple would be destroyed (Mark 13:4). After Peter was told that he would be a martyr for the Lord, he asked about John's fate: "Lord, and what about this man?" (John 21:21). Peter's questions seldom received the answer he expected, because they usually were self-centered or completely missed the primary truth Jesus was explaining. But the Lord used even his poor questions to patiently train him in leadership. Peter's questions, immature as many of them were, gave the Lord an opportunity to help him grow.

Second, Peter showed initiative, another necessary ingredient of leadership. Just as he was usually the first to ask Jesus questions, he was also usually the first to respond to questions Jesus asked. When the Lord asked the disciples, "Who do you say that I am?" Peter immediately replied, "Thou art the Christ, the Son of the living God" (Matt. 16:15-16). When the soldiers came to arrest Jesus in the Garden of Gethsemane, "Peter therefore having a sword, drew it, and struck the high priest's slave, and cut off his right ear" (John 18:10). Even though his actions were often misguided, Peter was ready to respond in what he thought was Christ's behalf.

Third, Peter positioned himself in the middle of the activity. He was a natural participant, never content to be on the sidelines. He stayed as close to Jesus as possible and wanted to be a part of everything that happened. Even when he denied the Lord, he was at least as near to Jesus as he could be, whereas all the other disciples were nowhere to be found. When they were told of Jesus' resurrection, Peter reached the tomb after John only because John was a better runner (John 20:4). Peter was always there.

The bold fisherman was a native of Bethsaida and later moved to Capernaum, where he and his father, John (or Jonas), and brother, Andrew, carried on their trade. Because he had a mother-in-law, we know that Peter was married when Jesus called him (Matt. 8:14), and from Paul's comments in 1 Corinthians 9:5, it is likely that Peter's wife traveled with him throughout his apostolic ministry.

Even Peter's names give insight into his character. He was given the common name Simon by his parents, but Jesus changed his name to Peter (Cephas in Aramaic) which means stone (Matt. 16:18). By nature Peter was vacillating and unstable, and when the Lord named him Peter, the other disciples doubtlessly had great reservations about the appropriateness of his new name. But the new name was perhaps a gentle and encouraging reminder to Simon of the kind of man Jesus called him to become.

Peter is usually referred to as Simon when the purpose is simply to identify him or something related to him—such as his house or mother-in-law (Mark 1:29-30), his boat (Luke 5:3), or his fishing partners (Luke 5:10). He is also referred to as Simon whenever he is reprimanded for sin or displays special weakness, as when he questioned Jesus' advice to go "out into the deep water and let down your nets for a catch" (Luke 5:4). When Jesus came back from prayer in the garden and found the disciples sleeping, He said, "Simon, are you asleep? Could you not keep watch for one hour?" (Mark 14:37). After the resurrection Peter disobediently returned to his fishing, and when the Lord confronted him three times about his faithfulness, each time He addressed him as Simon (John 21:15-17). He used his old name to point out that he was acting like his old self.

In John's gospel Peter is called by both names together (Simon Peter) some seventeen times. Perhaps because John knew Peter so well he used the two names to depict both the old and the new characteristics of his friend, which were often intermixed and difficult to distinguish.

THE RIGHT EXPERIENCES

A second element in preparing for leadership is having right experiences. The Lord brought into Peter's life all the experiences necessary to develop his leadership ability.

First of all, Jesus gave Peter wondrous revelations. When Peter first confessed that Jesus was "the Christ, the Son of the living God," Jesus explained to him, "Blessed are you, Simon Barjona, because flesh and blood did not reveal this to you, but My Father who is in heaven" (Matt. 16:16-17). When many of Jesus' followers forsook Him because of His teaching about the cost of discipleship, using the figure of eating His flesh and drinking His blood, the Lord asked the twelve, "You do not want to go away also, do you?" Peter's response on that occasion seems also to have been inspired of God as he said, "Lord, to whom shall we go? You have words of eternal life." (John 6:66-68).

Jesus was transforming Peter by letting him know that God wanted to use his mouth to proclaim the great delivering truth of the gospel. One day he would stand up boldly and say, "Men of Judea, and all you who live in Jerusalem, let this be known to you, and give heed to my words" (Acts 2:14). And one day he would take a pen and write God's revelation in the form of two New Testament epistles.

Second, Peter was given great honor and reward. After Jesus explained to Peter that the truth of his confession was revealed to him by the Father, He said, "I also say to you that you are Peter, and upon this rock I will build My church; and the gates of Hades shall not overpower it. I will give you the keys of the kingdom of heaven; and whatever you shall bind on earth shall be bound in heaven, and whatever you shall loose on earth shall be loosed in heaven" (Matt. 16:18). The Lord used Peter to preach the great sermon at Pentecost to the Jews assembled there from all over the world, and He used Peter to bring the gospel to Cornelius, the first Gentile convert. Peter unlocked the doors of the gospel to both the Jews and the Gentiles.

All of the apostles opened the door to the kingdom as they preached the gospel of salvation, and every time any man of God preaches Christ he, too, unlocks those kingdom doors to let men in.

Third, Peter experienced great rebuke. A short while after Jesus honored Peter by the declaration just mentioned above, Peter himself proved that our Lord's reference could not have been to him, since he was then anything but a solid foundation on which Christ could build His church. Perhaps feeling proud and overconfident as the leading disciple, he demonstrated that his mouth could be used by Satan as well as by God. When the Lord "began to show His disciples that He must go to Jerusalem, and suffer many things from the elders and chief priests and scribes, and be killed, and be raised up on the third day, . . . Peter took Him aside and began to rebuke Him, saying, 'God forbid it, Lord! This shall never happen to You'" But his severe rebuke of Jesus brought an even more severe rebuke *from* Jesus: "Get behind Me, Satan! You are a stumbling block to Me; for you are not setting your mind on God's interests, but man's" (Matt. 16:21-23).

A great danger of leadership is not knowing its limits. Many dictators and demagogues were once capable public servants, but great honor and power caused them to believe the right of leadership lay in themselves rather than in their privileged office. When Peter began elevating his own position and understanding, he found himself serving Satan rather than God. Great potential for being used by God also brings great potential for being used by Satan.

Fourth, Peter experienced what might be called great rejection, not *by* Jesus but *of* Him. Peter's extreme self-confidence again caused him to fail Jesus exactly at the point where he thought he was strongest. Just as confidence in his own wisdom resulted in his rebuke by Jesus, his confidence in his own dependability resulted in his rejection of Jesus. When Jesus predicted that all the disciples would fall away when He was arrested, Peter again contradicted Him, asserting, "Even though all may fall away because of You, I will never fall away." When Jesus went on to say that Peter's falling away would occur that very night and would, in fact, happen three times, Peter protested even more strongly: "Even if I have to die with You, I will not deny You." Following his lead, "all the disciples said the same thing too." Jesus, of course, again proved right and Peter again proved wrong. While he warmed himself in the courtyard of the high priest, Peter not only denied the Lord three times, but progressively denied Him more vehemently (Matt. 26:31-35, 69-75).

Fifth, Peter experienced a great recommissioning. When Jesus confronted him with the lack of love, Peter assured the Lord three times that he did indeed love Him, and Jesus three times reinstated him and charged him to care for His flock. Jesus had not given up on Peter. He reassured His faltering disciple that his calling still stood and commanded him again just as He had in the beginning, "Follow Me!" (John 21:15-19).

THE RIGHT ATTITUDES

A third element in Jesus' training of Peter was teaching him the principles of godly leadership. First of all, because leaders can easily become domineering, they have a special need to learn submission. When the Capernaum tax collectors demanded a two-drachma Temple tax from Jesus, He commanded Peter to go and catch a fish, in whose mouth would be a stater, exactly enough to pay the tax for both Jesus and Peter (Matt. 17:24-27). From that experience Peter learned a lesson not only in submitting to Jesus but to human authorities. In his first letter he wrote, "Submit yourselves for the Lord's sake to every human institution, whether to a king as the one in authority, or to governors as sent by him for the punishment of evildoers and the praise of those who do right. For such is the will of God that by doing right you may silence the ignorance of foolish men. . . . Honor all men; love the brotherhood, fear God, honor the king" (1 Pet. 2:13-15, 17).

Second, Peter needed to learn restraint, of which he needed a double portion. As already mentioned, when the Roman soldiers came with the officers of the chief priests and the Pharisees to arrest Jesus in the garden, Peter drew his sword and began to fight—even though the Roman cohort alone may have numbered 500 or more men. Jesus told Peter to put away his sword and to let God's divine plan take its course (John 18:10-11).

Third, Peter needed to learn humility; and again he needed a double portion. Only a few hours after he proudly boasted, "Even though all may fall away because of You, I will never fall away," Peter denied the Lord three times—although he was in little, if any, danger (Matt. 26:33, 69-75). But he eventually learned his lesson, and many years later wrote, "God is opposed to the proud, but gives grace to the humble" (1 Pet. 5:5).

Fourth, Peter needed to learn to sacrifice, and Jesus promised him, "'Truly, truly, I say to you, when you were younger, you used to gird yourself, and walk wherever you wished; but when you grow old, you will stretch out your hands, and someone else will gird you, and bring you where you do not wish to go.' Now this He said, signifying by what kind of death he would glorify God. And when He had spoken this, He said to him, 'Follow Me!'" (John 21:18-19). When Peter became concerned that John might not have to pay such a costly sacrifice, Jesus told him sternly, "If I want him to remain until I come, what is that to you? You follow Me!" (vv. 21-22). For the second time on this occasion Jesus commanded Peter to follow Him, this time using the emphatic *su* ("you").

That was the last time Jesus had to command Peter to follow Him. From then on, Peter obeyed whatever the cost. He even learned to rejoice in his suffering for Christ, and wrote, "To the degree that you share the sufferings of Christ, keep on rejoicing; so that also at the revelation of His glory, you may rejoice with exultation. If you are reviled for the name of Christ, you are blessed, because the Spirit of glory and of God rests upon you. . . . If anyone suffers as a Christian, let him not feel ashamed, but in that name let him glorify God. . . . Therefore, let those also who suffer according to the will of God entrust their souls to a faithful Creator in doing what is right" (1 Pet. 4:13-14, 16, 19).

Fifth, Peter needed to learn love. It was lack of genuine love that caused Peter to deny His Lord, and it was about that love that Jesus pressed him three times. The Holy Spirit led Peter and John to minister together in the early years of the church, and Peter no doubt learned many lessons in true love from the great apostle of love.

Jesus' washing the disciples' feet not only was an example of humility but of the source of humility—love. Service to others, no matter how costly or demeaning, is neither humble nor godly if done from any motive but love (cf. 1 Cor. 13:3). Peter records the lesson he learned: "Above all, keep fervent in your love for one another, because love covers a multitude of sins" (1 Pet. 4:8).

Sixth, Peter needed to learn courage. Because Jesus' prediction of Peter's suffering pointed to great sacrifice, it also pointed to need of great courage. When Peter was brought before the high priest and the Sanhedrin, or Council, for preaching the gospel, he was no longer the fearful coward he had been in the high priest's courtyard the night of Jesus' arrest. Now confident in his Lord rather than in himself, he stood boldly and declared, "Let it be known to all of you, and to all the people of Israel, that by the name of Jesus Christ the Nazarene, whom you crucified, whom God raised from the dead—by this name this man [the one Peter had healed in Solomon's portico] stands here before you in good health. He is the stone which was rejected by you, the builders, but which became the very corner stone" (Acts 4:10-11; cf. 3:1-8). When the Council again charged Peter and John not to continue preaching, the apostles replied, "Whether it is right in the sight of God to give heed to you rather than to God, you be the judge; for we cannot stop speaking what we have seen and heard" (v. 19-20). At the subsequent prayer meeting in Jerusalem they prayed for continued boldness; and "when they had prayed, the place where they had gathered together was shaken, and they were all filled with the Holy Spirit, and began to speak the word of God with boldness" (v. 31).

Peter often learned his lessons slowly, but he learned them well. He took the initiative to seek someone to replace Judas among the apostles (Acts 1:15-17), became the first spokesman of the church at Pentecost (2:14), was the first to defend the gospel before the Sanhedrin (4:8), was the first to enact church discipline (in dealing with the deceit of Ananias and Sapphira, 5:3-9), confronted Simon the magician when he attempted to pervert God's power to his own advantage (8:18-23), healed Aeneas and raised Dorcas from the dead (9:34, 40), was the first to take the gospel to the Gentiles (Acts 10), and wrote two marvelous epistles in which he humbly included all the lessons Jesus had patiently taught him.

Peter was a man God touched with His grace in a special way. As a "wandering heart" that God finally captured and claimed for Himself, Peter would have sung joyfully the words of Robert Robinson's beloved hymn "Come Thou Fount of Every Blessing":

> O to grace how great a debtor
> Daily I'm constrained to be!
> Let Thy goodness, like a fetter,
> Bind my wandering heart to Thee.
> Prone to wander, Lord, I feel it,
> Prone to leave the God I love;
> Take my heart, O take and seal it,
> Seal it for Thy courts above.

Tradition reports that Peter died a cruel death. And before he himself was crucified, he is said to have been forced to witness the crucifixion of his wife. In his *Ecclesiastical History,* the early church Father Eusebius writes that Peter stood at the foot of his wife's cross and kept repeating to her, "Remember the Lord. Remember the

Lord." After she died, it is said he pleaded to be crucified upside down, because he was unworthy to die as his Lord had died.

Peter's life can be summed up in the last words of his second epistle: "Grow in grace, and in the knowledge of our Lord and Savior, Jesus Christ. To Him be glory, both now and forever. Amen" (2 Pet. 3:18).

The Master's Men— part 2

Andrew, James the son of Zebedee, John (10:2b)

and Andrew his brother; and James the son of Zebedee, and John his brother; (10:2b)

Along with Peter, the leading disciple (the foremost, or "first," v. 10:2a), these three men composed Jesus' inner circle of four. Like Peter, they do not appear on the surface to be ideal candidates for becoming apostles and the foundation of the church. Yet from the accounts of these men both in the gospels and the rest of the New Testament, we learn that God is able to use in His service any kind of person who submits to the lordship of Jesus Christ.

The apostles, and especially these four who are the best known of them, are often looked on as "stained glass saints." They have been frequently portrayed with halos above their heads and benign expressions on their faces. Not only children but cathedrals, chapels, cities, and towns are named after them. Their names are often preceded by Saint, adding to the notion that they were on a completely different plane of spiritual existence from other human beings, including other Christians.

But although they had an uncommon calling, the apostles were common men, much like the rest of us. They were saints only in the sense that every believer is a saint, made holy unto God through the imparted righteousness of Jesus Christ and awaiting the full perfection of sainthood in heaven (Rom. 1:7; 1 Cor. 1:2; Phil. 3:12-14;

Heb. 11:40; Jude 14). Until then, they, like all saints, had to live with the weakness of their humanness.

ANDREW

Andrew was Peter's **brother**, and his name means "manly." Like his brother, he was a native of Bethsaida (John 1:44) and was a fisherman on the Sea of Galilee. Even before he met Jesus, Andrew was a godly, dedicated Jew. He and John were disciples of John the Baptist, and when that prophet declared of Jesus, "Behold, the Lamb of God!" they left the Baptist and began to follow Jesus (John 1:36-37). Andrew then "found first his own brother Simon, and said to him, 'We have found the Messiah' (which translated means Christ)" (v. 41). Peter and Andrew lived together (Mark 1:29) and doubtlessly shared everything with each other. It was therefore compelling for Andrew to share with Peter the most important discovery of his life.

Subsequent to his confession of Jesus as the Messiah, however, Andrew had returned to his fishing. A while later, as Jesus was "walking by the Sea of Galilee, He saw two brothers, Simon who was called Peter, and Andrew his brother, casting a net into the sea; for they were fishermen. And He said to them, 'Follow Me, and I will make you fishers of men'" (Matt. 4:18-19). It was at this time that Jesus actually called the two men into discipleship training, and from that point on these two brothers, along with the other two brothers, James and John, became Jesus' most intimate friends. But though he was greatly respected by his fellow disciples and is always spoken of favorably in the few accounts in which he is mentioned, Andrew was apparently never quite as close to the Lord as the other three and is usually referred to as Peter's brother.

In the synoptic gospels (Matthew, Mark, and Luke) Andrew is not mentioned except in the lists of the twelve disciples. And in only three accounts in John's gospel do we find any information about him more than his name.

First, John tells us of Andrew's previous discipleship to John the Baptist, his confession of Jesus as the Messiah, and his reporting to Peter his discovery and introducing him to the Lord (John 1:37-42). From his first encounter with Jesus, Andrew demonstrated an eagerness to introduce others to His Lord, and the desire to witness characterized his entire ministry.

Second, John tells us of Andrew's involvement in Jesus' feeding the five thousand on the far side of the Sea of Galilee. When Philip expressed bewilderment at Jesus' question, "'Where are we to buy bread, that these may eat?' . . . Andrew, Simon Peter's brother, said to Him, 'There is a lad here who has five barley loaves and two fish, but what are these for so many people?'" (John 6:5-9). He, too, was puzzled about Jesus' question, but he did as much as he could in response to it and located some food. The barley loaves were rather small, much like biscuits or large crackers, and were often eaten with fish preserved by pickling so that they could be carried to work as a lunch or on trips away from home. Andrew's bringing the boy to Jesus suggests that he believed his Master could somehow make more of this small amount of food.

Third, John depicts Andrew bringing others to the Lord. When some God-fearing Gentiles came to Philip asking to see Jesus, "Philip came and told Andrew; Andrew and Philip came, and they told Jesus" (John 12:20-22). Although Philip himself was one of the twelve, he apparently felt less than comfortable approaching Jesus alone and asked Andrew to accompany him.

From these three accounts we can discern several insights into the character of Andrew. First of all we see his openness and lack of prejudice. He knew that the disciples' first priority, but not their only task, was to take the gospel to their fellow Jews, "the lost sheep of the house of Israel" (Matt. 10:6). But he also must have known that the person to whom Jesus Himself first revealed His messiahship was a half-breed Samaritan woman, who trusted in Him and, like Andrew, immediately began telling others of Him (John 4:25-29, 40-42).

Andrew was also characterized by simple but strong faith. We do not know what was in his mind when he brought the boy with the loaves and fish to Jesus, but he obviously believed Jesus could make use of the boy and his food. He had seen Jesus make wine, and he probably saw no reason why He could not multiply food as well.

Andrew also appears to have been humble. Throughout his ministry he was known primarily as Peter's brother, and he was never as intimate with Jesus or used by Him as publicly or dramatically as was his brother. And though he was part of the inner circle, Andrew seemed always to be in the shadow of Peter, James, and John. Yet there is no indication that he ever resented his position or function. He was content simply to belong to and serve Jesus, and no doubt to the end of his life was in awe of the fact that he was called to be an apostle at all. He cared more for his Lord and His work than he did for his own welfare or advantage, and he willingly sacrificed his own interests and comfort for the sake of others coming to the Lord. He showed nothing of the self-will and self-interest seen at times in Peter, James, and John.

Andrew is the model for all Christians who labor quietly in humble places and positions. He did not try to please men but God, and had no interest in building a reputation for himself. He would gladly have taken for himself Christina Rossetti's words:

> Give me the lowest place;
> Not that I dare ask for that lowest place,
> But Thou hast died that I might live
> And share Thy glory by Thy side.
> Give me the lowest place;
> Or if for me the lowest place is too high,
> Then make one more low
> Where I may sit and see my God and love Him so.
> (Cited in Herbert Lockyer, *All the Apostles of the Bible* [Grand Rapids: Zondervan, 1972], p. 54.)

Andrew was that rare person who is willing to take second place, who is perfectly content to be in support of the more noticeable and acclaimed ministry of others, if that is where God wants him to be. He does not mind being hidden, so long as the Lord's work is done. Here is the person that all leaders depend on and who are the backbone of every ministry. The cause of Christ is greatly dependent on the self-forgetting souls who are satisfied to occupy a small sphere in an obscure place, free from self-seeking ambition. Andrew was told that one day he would sit on one of the apostolic thrones and judge the twelve tribes of Israel (Matt. 19:28). But for him that unique honor was not cause for boasting but for humble awe and wonder.

The Scotsman Daniel McLean wrote of Andrew, the patron saint of Scotland:

> Gathering together the traces of character found in Scripture [about Andrew], we find neither the writer of an Epistle, nor the founder of a Church, nor a leading figure in the Apostolic Age, but simply . . . an intimate disciple of Jesus Christ, ever anxious that others should know the spring of spiritual joy and share the blessing he so highly prized. A man of very moderate endowment, who scarcely redeemed his early promise, simple minded and sympathetic, without either dramatic power or heroic spirit, yet with that clinging confidence in Christ that brought him into that inner circle of the Twelve; a man of deep religious feeling with little power of expression, magnetic more than electric, better suited for the quiet walks of life than the stirring thoroughfares. Andrew is the apostle of the private life—the disciple of the hearth. (Cited in Lockyer, *All the Apostles,* pp. 55-56)

God uses people like Andrew, and only He can calculate their effectiveness. Sometimes it takes an Andrew to reach a Peter. An obscure Methodist preacher of the eighteenth century named Thomas Mitchell was an Andrew. His obituary read, "Thomas Mitchell, an old soldier of Jesus Christ, a man of slender abilities as a preacher, and who enjoyed only a very defective education." Yet one of his friends wrote of him: "His earnest and loving work caused him to lead many people to Christ." Though a man of "slender abilities" and "defective education," he was nevertheless God's means of bringing to Christ the great preacher Thomas Olivers.

Thomas Mitchell went to a little village in Lincolnshire, where he arose each morning at five o'clock to preach in the open air, as John Wesley often did. His preaching was so fiery that he was arrested and attacked by a mob as he was taken to the public house for a hearing before the village curate. The crowd convinced the curate to let them throw Mitchell into a filthy, slimy pond. Each time he managed to crawl out, the mob threw him back in. He was then painted from head to foot with white paint and taken again to the public house. After a long debate about what to do with him, they decided to drown him. He was thrown into a small lake outside the town, and each time he came to the surface, a man with a long pole would push him under again. Eventually he was taken out, more dead than alive. He was tirelessly cared for by a godly old lady of the village, but when the mob found out that he was recovering, they threatened to rend him limb from limb unless he promised never to preach again. He refused to make such a promise but somehow managed to escape the threatened punishment. He later wrote of the incident, "All the time God kept me in perfect peace and I was able to pray for my enemies." For the rest of his life he continued to minister in obscure faithfulness. But by God's standards and in God's power, he was far from being "a man of slender abilities." So was Andrew.

JAMES THE SON OF ZEBEDEE

The third man named in Matthew's list of the first four disciples is **James the son of Zebedee.** In the gospel accounts, **James** never appears apart from his brother John, and during the three years of training under Jesus they were inseparable. Because James is always mentioned first, he was probably the older and more dynamic of the two. The brothers were fishing partners with their father, **Zebedee,** who was apparently fairly well-to-do, because he employed hired servants in his business (Mark 1:20).

Because so little is said of him, James appears in the gospels more as a silhouette than a detailed portrait. Jesus referred to James and John as "Boanerges, which means, 'Sons of Thunder'" (Mark 3:17), and from that descriptive name alone we can assume James was passionate, zealous, fervent, and aggressive.

As Passion Week approached, Jesus sent several disciples ahead to make arrangements for lodging. Because they were traveling from Galilee, they would need to spend a night in Samaria on the way to Jerusalem. Jews and Samaritans had great religious and racial animosity for one another, and when the Samaritans refused to give accommodations to Jesus "because He was journeying with His face toward Jerusalem," James and John said to Him, "Lord, do You want us to command fire to come down from heaven and consume them?" (Luke 9:52-54). The two brothers may have believed that the repentant Samaritan woman at Sychar and the others there who had trusted in Jesus as the Messiah were barely worthy of salvation (see John 4:25-42). But a Samaritan who refused even to provide the Lord a night's lodging was, in their view, worthy only of instant execution. At that point James and John were hateful and intolerant, and their volatile and vengeful temperaments clouded over what they had heard Jesus teach and seen Him do. He therefore "turned and rebuked them, [and said, 'You do not know what kind of spirit you are of; for the Son of Man did not come to destroy men's lives, but to save them']" (Luke 9:55-56).

James had much zeal but little sensitivity. In his resentment of the Samaritans' rejection of Jesus he reflected a commendable commitment. It is good for God's people to become incensed when He is dishonored and vilified (cf. Ps. 69:9; John 2:13-17). Jesus Himself was angered when His Father's house was profaned (Matt. 21:12-13) and when hardness of heart made His opponents criticize even His healing the diseased and afflicted on the Sabbath (Luke 13:15-16). But Jesus did not return evil for evil (1 Pet. 2:23), and He forbids His followers to do so (Matt. 5:38-42).

When the mother of James and John, doubtlessly at their urging, asked Jesus to grant them seats on either side of His throne in the kingdom, the Lord asked them, "Are you able to drink the cup that I am about to drink?" Without hesitation they replied confidently, "We are able" (Matt. 20:21-22). Whether they instigated their mother's request or not, they obviously thought it was perfectly appropriate. They had no reservations about their deserving the honor or their ability to meet any demands it might make of them.

From a human standpoint James and John displayed more natural reliability than Peter. They were not as vacillating and were not given to compromise or equivocation. But they were brazenly ambitious. The two who vengefully wanted to call down fire on the Samaritans are now seen also as self-serving place seekers, stalking the Lord for His patronage—unashamed of using their mother to gain their personal ends and oblivious of the fact that they were demeaning Christ and His kingdom.

When Herod wanted to attack and destroy the infant church, he singled out James for arrest and execution. The fact that he chose James first suggests that this apostle may have been more publicly noticeable and influential than even Peter or John. It was only after he saw that the murder of James pleased the Jews that Herod "proceeded to arrest Peter also" (Acts 12:1-3). At least in the king's eyes, James seemed to be the most dangerous. He was probably thunderous and unrelenting in his ministry, and because of it became the first apostolic martyr.

Zeal is a great virtue, and the Lord needs those who are fearlessly aggressive. But zeal is also prone to be brash, loveless, insensitive, and lacking in wisdom. Insensitivity can destroy a ministry, and James had to learn to bridle his ambition and to love.

Some pastors who are orthodox in doctrine and morally upstanding are utterly insensitive to their congregations and their own families. The nineteenth-century writer Henrik Ibsen told of a Norwegian pastor who diligently followed the motto "All or nothing." He was stern and uncompromising in everything he said and did. He zealously wanted to advance the kingdom of Christ, but he had no regard for the feelings of fellow believers. He wanted to uphold God's standards of truth and holiness, but he was blind to His standards of love and kindness.

He was especially hard on his own family. When his little girl became seriously ill, he refused to take her out of the cold Norwegian climate to a warmer place, even though the doctor warned that not to do so would cost her life. The pastor responded with his usual "All or nothing," and the girl soon died. Because the mother had found no love in her husband, her life had been completely centered in her little daughter. When the daughter died, the mother was so distraught and shattered that she would sit for hours fondling the clothes of her baby girl, trying to feed her starved heart with the empty garments. After a few days her husband took the clothes away and gave them to a poor woman on the street. The wife had hidden one little bonnet as a last reminder, but her husband soon found that and gave it away—after giving the grieving mother a lecture on "All or nothing." In a few months the mother also died, a victim more of her husband's misguided zeal than of her daughter's untimely death.

The great evangelist Billy Sunday saw thousands of souls converted to Jesus Christ, but every one of his children died in unbelief, because he had had no time for them. Zeal without love is cruel and destructive. A person with flaming passion and enthusiasm for the Lord's work but who tends to be intolerant and impatient is doubtlessly more usable than a lukewarm, uncommitted, and compromising person, who the Lord said is fit only to be spat out of His mouth (Rev. 3:16). But intolerance and insensitivity are a tragic barrier to effective ministry and are never justified. Without love, the most dynamic and dedicated zeal—even in the Lord's own work—is nothing (1 Cor. 13:1-3).

Jesus bridled James's zeal and channeled His servant's energy into fruitful ministry. James and John did indeed drink their Master's cup, as He had predicted (Matt. 20:23). For John the cup was a long life of rejection and a death in exile. For James it was a short bright flame that brought martyrdom.

An ancient Roman coin depicted an ox facing both an altar and a plow, with the inscription "Ready for either." That should be the attitude of every believer. James gave his life for the Lord as a brief and dying sacrifice, whereas John gave his as a long and living sacrifice of service.

JOHN

The last disciple mentioned in the first group is **John,** the **brother** of James. Unlike Andrew and James, John is one of the most prominent disciples in the New Testament. He not only figures prominently in the gospel accounts but wrote one of the gospels himself, as well as three epistles and the book of Revelation.

Because of his eventual gentleness and self-effacing attitude, we are sometimes inclined to think of John as being naturally retiring and mild mannered, perhaps even somewhat effeminate. But in his early years he was fully as much a "Son of Thunder" as James. He joined his brother in wanting to call down fire on the unbelieving Samaritans and in seeking a position next to the Lord in the kingdom. Like James, he was naturally intolerant, ambitious, zealous, and explosive, though perhaps not as much so.

It is interesting that the only time John is mentioned alone in the gospels is in an unfavorable light. On one occasion he came to Jesus and reported, "Teacher, we saw someone casting out demons in Your name, and we tried to hinder him because he was not following us" (Mark 9:38). John appears prejudiced and sectarian, and he did not look favorably on those who were not affiliated with his own group, even if they were faithfully doing the Lord's work.

Christians are justified in breaking fellowship with fellow believers who teach false doctrine and persist in immoral living; in fact are commanded to do so (Rom. 16:17-18; 1 Cor. 5:9-11; Gal. 1:8; 2 Thess. 3:6, 14). But exclusivism or sectarianism based on form, culture, status, race, color, wealth, appearance, or any other such superficiality is anathema to the Lord, in whom "there is neither Jew nor Greek, . . . slave nor free man, . . . male nor female; for [we] are all one in Christ Jesus" (Gal. 3:28).

Throughout his life, John remained uncompromising in doctrine and in standards of morality, but the Holy Spirit developed in him an unparalleled capacity for love, so much so that he is often called the apostle of love. It is apparent from his epistles that he did not slip into the foolish and tolerant sentimentality that often masquerades as love. During the rest of his life, which lasted until near the turn of the second century, he lost none of his intolerance for falsehood and immorality. Love without certain standards or strong convictions is as much a spiritual disaster as zeal without sensitivity. The Lord knew that, as far as the human author was concerned, the apostle who became the most powerful advocate of love would have to be a man who was also uncompromising of truth. Otherwise his love would take him down the road of destructive sentimentalism that is traveled by so many in the name of Christ.

In his five New Testament books John uses forms of the word *love* eighty times and *witness* or its synonyms some seventy times. He was always a witness to the truth and ever a teacher of love. Truth guarded his love, and love surrounded his truth.

John was also a discoverer, a seeker for truth. He was the first to recognize the Lord on the shore of Galilee and was the first disciple to see the risen Christ. It was to him that the Lord entrusted the revelation of future events in the Apocalypse. John did not lean on Jesus' breast (John 13:23) because of maudlin sentimentality but because he had an insatiable hunger for Christ's truth and fellowship. He wanted to gather every word that came from his Master's lips and to bask continually in the warmth of His love.

That John's love was controlled by God's truth is nowhere seen more clearly than in his three epistles, in which his exhortations for love are always balanced by commands for truth and righteousness. He denounced the antichrist and those who sided with him. He rebuked the unloving and the disobedient. It was John that Jesus inspired to record His most sobering distinction between the saved and the unsaved, declaring that the one is the child of God and the other the child of Satan (John 8:41-44). Again and again John appealed to various witnesses to the truth he taught. He spoke of the witness of John the Baptist (John 1:7-8; 3:26), the witness of the miracles (John 5:36), the witness of the apostles (15:27), the witness of the Father (5:37), of the Son (18:37), and of the Holy Spirit and the water and blood (1 John 5:8).

But throughout his teaching John's heart of love and compassion is revealed, and the reflection of his great capacity not only to teach but to exemplify love is manifest. People who love greatly can also be loved greatly, because they are eager to receive it as well as give it. John continually took in the love of Christ and continually gave it out. He so identified with Christ's love that he referred to himself as the disciple whom Jesus loved (John 13:23; 19:26; 20:2; 21:7, 20). John could claim no greater honor for himself than being the apostle whom Jesus loved.

Tradition tells us that John did not leave the city of Jerusalem until Mary the mother of Jesus died, because the Lord had entrusted her into his care (John 19:26). The Lord said to Peter, "Tend My sheep" (John 21:17); but to John He said, in effect, "Take care of My mother." John had a special love that Jesus knew would lead this disciple to treat Mary as his own mother.

John's teaching on love might be summarized in ten truths that run through his writings. He taught that God is a God of love (1 John 4:8, 16), that God loves His Son (John 3:35; 5:20) and is loved by His Son (14:31), that God loved the disciples (16:27; 17:23), that God loves all men (3:16), that Christ loved the disciples (13:34), that He loves all believers (1 John 3:1), that He expects all men to love Him (John 14:15,

21), that believers in Him should love one another (13:34; 1 John 4:11, 21), and that love fulfills all the commandments (14:23; 1 John 5:3).

From the lives of these three men, as from the lives of the other disciples, it becomes obvious that the Lord uses a variety of people. Andrew was humble, gentle, and inconspicuous. He saw the individual more than the crowd. He was not a dynamic evangelist, but he continually brought people to Jesus Christ. James, like Peter, was dynamic, bold, and a natural leader. He initiated, took charge, and moved ahead; but he could also be self-willed, self-assured, prejudiced, and ambitious. John was also a son of thunder, but of a milder sort. He was a truth seeker who was sensitive to those to whom he taught the truth.

Jesus transformed all three into effective fishers of men and foundation layers of His church, and all three suffered for their faithfulness. Tradition says that Andrew led the wife of a provincial governor to Christ and that when she refused to recant her faith the governor had Andrew crucified on an X-shaped cross—which subsequently became his symbol in church lore. He is said to have hung on the cross in agony for two days, preaching the gospel to those who passed by for as long as he was able.

According to tradition, when James had been sentenced to death and was about to be beheaded, the Roman soldier who guarded him was so impressed with his courage and constancy of spirit that he knelt at the apostle's feet, begging forgiveness for the rough treatment he had given him and for his part in the execution. James is said to have lifted the man up, embraced and kissed him, and said, "Peace, my son. Peace to you and the pardon of your faults." The soldier is said to have been so moved by James's compassion that he publicly confessed Christ and was beheaded alongside the apostle.

Scripture reports that John was banished to the small and barren Isle of Patmos in the Aegean Sea, off the west coast of Asia Minor. He died about A.D. 98, during the reign of Emperor Trajan. Some sources suggest that those who knew him well said their reminder of John was the echo of a constant phrase that was on his lips: "My little children, love one another" (cf. 1 John 3:11, 14; 4:7, 11, 20-21).

These were three men with ordinary temperaments, ordinary strengths and weaknesses, and ordinary struggles. Yet in the power of Christ they were transformed into men that turned the world upside down. It was not what they were in themselves but what they were sovereignly and willingly made to become that rendered them such powerful instruments in the Master's hands. The fishermen of Galilee became fishers of men on a vast scale, and in God's power they gathered thousands of souls into the church and played a vital part in the salvation of millions more. Through the testimony of their lives and writings, those fishermen are still casting their nets into the sea of mankind and bringing multitudes into the kingdom.

BIRDVILLE
BAPTIST CHURCH
LIBRARY

The Master's Men— part 3

14

Philip, Bartholomew (Nathanael) (10:3a)

Philip and Bartholomew; (10:3a)

The second group of four disciples begins with **Philip**, as it does in the other listings (Mark 3:18; Luke 6:14; Acts 1:13), probably indicating he was its leader. This Philip is not to be confused with the deacon who became a prominent evangelist in the early days of the church (see Acts 6:5; 8:4-13, 26-40).

All of the twelve were Jews, but many used both Greek and Jewish names. It is not known what this disciple's Jewish name was, because **Philip** (a Greek name meaning "lover of horses") is the only name used of him in the New Testament. It was possibly due to his name that the Greeks who wanted to see Jesus came to Philip first (John 12:20-21).

Philip's hometown was the northern Galilee town of Bethsaida, where Peter and Andrew also lived. Because they were all God-fearing Jews and probably were all fishermen (see John 21:2-3), it seems certain that Peter, Andrew, **Philip and Bartholomew** not only were acquaintances but were close friends even before Jesus called them.

As with Andrew, the first three gospels make no mention of **Philip** except in listings of the apostles, and all that is revealed about him is found in the fourth gospel.

It can be surmised from John's account that Philip was already a devout man.

The day after Jesus called Peter and Andrew, "He purposed to go forth into Galilee, and He found Philip, and Jesus said to him, 'Follow Me'"(John 1:43). Although John, Andrew, and Peter had taken up with Jesus as soon as they realized He was the Messiah (vv. 35-42), Philip was the first person to whom the Lord expressly said, "Follow Me."

God had already given Philip a seeking heart. Salvation is always on the sovereign Lord's initiative, and no one comes to Jesus Christ unless God the Father draws him (John 6:44, 65). But God planted the desire in Philip's heart to find the Messiah even before Jesus called him. Philip therefore said to Nathanael (or Bartholomew), "We have found Him of whom Moses in the Law and also the Prophets wrote, Jesus of Nazareth, the son of Joseph" (1:45). From the perspective of divine sovereignty, the Lord found Philip, but from the perspective of human understanding and volition, Philip had found the Lord. Both the divine and human wills will be in accord when salvation takes place. Jesus came to seek and save the lost (Luke 19:10), and it is those who truly seek Him who find Him (Luke 7:7-8; cf. Jer. 29:13). God seeks and finds the hearts of those who genuinely seek Him.

From his comments to Nathanael, it seems that Philip must have been diligently studying the Scriptures to learn God's will and plan. God's promised Messiah was central on his mind, and when he was introduced to the Messiah, he immediately acknowledged and accepted Him. Using His written Word, God had prepared Philip's heart. From the scriptural record we know of no human agent who was instrumental in Philip's calling or commitment. Jesus simply walked up to Him and said, "Follow Me." Philip's heart and eyes and ears were spiritually attuned, and when he heard Jesus' call he knew it was from God. We can only imagine the excitement and joy that filled his soul at that moment.

The genuineness of Philip's faith is seen not only in the fact the he immediately recognized and accepted the Messiah but in the reality that he also promptly began to serve Christ by telling others of Him. As soon as Jesus called him, Philip found Nathanael and told him he had found the Messiah.

One of the certain marks of genuine conversion is the desire to tell others of the Savior. The new believer who is baptized as a public testimony of his new relationship to Jesus Christ often has a spontaneous desire to use that occasion to witness for the Lord. The believer who has not left his first love for the Lord inevitably has a loving desire to witness to those who do not know Him.

Because Philip already cared about his friend Nathanael, it was natural to communicate to him the most profound and joyous discovery of his life. In every listing of the twelve, Philip and Nathanael are together, and it is likely they had been close friends for many years before they met Jesus.

Second, we learn from John's gospel that Philip had a practical, analytical mind. When Jesus faced the great crowd of people who had followed Him to the far side of the Sea of Galilee, He knew they were tired and hungry and that few of them had made provision for eating. He therefore "said to Philip, 'Where are we to buy bread, that these may eat?'" (John 6:5). Philip had seen Jesus perform many miracles, including the turning of water into wine (John 2:1-11), but at this time his only thoughts were of the practical problems involved in Jesus' suggestion. In addition to the 5,000 men (6:10), it is not unrealistic to assume that there were an equal number of women and several times that many children.

Judging from Philip's response, it may have been that he was normally in charge of getting food for Jesus and his fellow disciples, just as Judas was in charge of the group's money. He therefore would have known how much food they usually ate and how much it cost. But Jesus had a special purpose in asking Philip about the food. "And this He was saying to test him; for He Himself knew what He was intending to do" (v. 6). If Jesus had asked about buying food only for the thirteen men in their own group, the answer would have been simple and practical, and Philip could quickly have given the answer. But he should have realized that, in His asking about feeding the entire multitude, Jesus' question went far beyond the practical and implied the impossible.

But Philip took the question at its practical face value and immediately began to calculate an answer based on his own experience. Making a rough estimate, he concluded that "two hundred denarii worth of bread is not sufficient for them, for everyone to receive a little" (v. 7). A denarii represented the daily wage of an average Palestinian worker, and even if two hundred of them were collected from the crowd or taken from the disciples' treasury, that amount could not buy enough bread even to give the multitude a snack.

Philip's response was sincere, but it revealed a lack of consideration for Jesus' supernatural provision. He was face to face with the Son of God, but he could see no further than the practical, physical dilemma. There was no prospect of a solution from the human standpoint, and that is all he considered. He was so engrossed in the material situation that he completely lost sight of God's power.

It has been noted that the supreme essential of a great leader is a sense of the possible. Like most people, however—including perhaps most believers—Philip only had a sense of the impossible. He did not yet understand that "with God all things are possible" (Matt. 19:26; cf. Mark 9:23).

It would seem that, after having seen Jesus perform so many miracles, Philip's immediate response would have been, "Lord, You made the water into wine, stilled the storm, and have healed every kind of disease. Why bother trying to buy so much food when all You have to do is say the word and create the food necessary to feed all these people?"

Philip failed Jesus' test of faith because he was too taken up with his own understanding and abilities. He was methodical and full of practical common sense; but those virtues, helpful as they often are, can be an obstacle to the immeasurably greater virtue of trusting God for what is impractical. Facts and figures are a poor substitute for faith.

Third, we learn from John's gospel that Philip was not forceful and was inclined to be indecisive. Although he was not a member of the inner circle, Philip had access to Jesus on his own. But when "certain Greeks among those who were going up to worship at the feast . . . came to Philip, who was from Bethsaida of Galilee, and began to ask him, saying, 'Sir, we wish to see Jesus,'" Philip decided to take them first to Andrew (12:20-22).

Philip knew that Jesus healed the Gentile centurion's servant and accepted the half-Gentile Samaritans who came to Him for salvation, yet he seems to have been uncertain about whether it was proper to introduce these Gentiles to the Lord. He may have been thinking of the temporary instruction Jesus gave when He first sent the disciples out on their own: "Do not go in the way of the Gentiles, and do not enter any city of the Samaritans; but rather go to the lost sheep of the house of Israel" (Matt. 10:5-6). Natural Jewish prejudice made that an easy command to obey, and Philip may have thought the restriction was still in effect. But he did not ignore the Greeks' request and at least made the effort to consult Andrew.

Fourth, we discover from John's gospel that Philip lacked spiritual perception. This deficiency was evident in his failing Jesus' test in regard to feeding the multitude, and it was even more pronounced when, almost three years later, he said to Jesus at the Last Supper, "Lord, show us the Father, and it is enough for us" (John 14:8). It must have grieved Jesus deeply to hear such a question, and He replied, "Have I been so long with you, and yet you have not come to know Me, Philip? He who has seen Me has seen the Father; how do you say, 'Show us the Father'? Do you not believe that I am in the Father, and the Father is in Me? The words that I say to you I do not speak on My own initiative, but the Father abiding in Me does His works. Believe Me that I am in the Father, and the Father in Me; otherwise believe on account of the works themselves" (vv. 9-11).

After three years of learning at Jesus' feet, Philip's spiritual perception still seemed almost nil. Neither Jesus' words nor His works had brought Philip to the understanding that Jesus and His Father were one. After gazing for three years into the only face of God men will ever see, he still did not comprehend who he was seeing. He had missed the main truth of Jesus' teaching, that He was God incarnate.

Yet the Lord used that man of limited vision and trust. Philip was slow to understand and slow to trust. He was more at home with physical facts than with spiritual truth. Yet, along with the other apostles, Jesus assured him of a throne from which he would judge the twelve tribes of Israel (Matt. 19:28). Philip was pessimistic, insecure, analytical, and slow to learn; but tradition tells us that he ultimately gave his life as a martyr for the Lord he so often disappointed and who so patiently taught and retaught him. It is reported that he was stripped naked, hung upside down by his feet, and pierced with sharp stakes in his ankles and thighs, causing him slowly to bleed to death. He is said to have asked not to be shrouded with linen after he was dead, because he felt unworthy to be buried as was his Lord.

Bartholomew (Nathanael)

Bartholomew means "son [Aramaic, *bar*] of Tolmai." He was much different from Philip, his close friend and companion with whom he is always paired in the New Testament. The first three gospels refer to him only as Bartholomew, but John always as Nathanael, which may have been his first name. The short account of John 1:45-51 is the only place this apostle is mentioned in the New Testament outside the four listings of the twelve.

Bartholomew came from Cana of Galilee and was brought to the Lord by his friend Philip. As soon as Philip discovered Jesus was the long-awaited Messiah, he "found Nathanael and said to him, 'We have found Him of whom Moses in the Law and also the Prophets wrote, Jesus of Nazareth, the son of Joseph'" (John 1:45).

Philip's words imply that, like himself, Nathanael was a student of Scripture, a seeker after divine truth and well acquainted with the messianic prophecies of the Old Testament. A further implication seems to be that these two men were partners in Scripture study, having examined the Old Testament together for many years. In any case, it is clear from Philip's statement that he knew Nathanael would immediately know whom he was talking about. They both hungered for God's truth and earnestly sought the coming of the anticipated Messiah.

But Nathanael was affected by prejudice. Instead of judging Jesus by what He said and did, Nathanael stumbled over the fact that He was from Nazareth, a town with a notably unsavory reputation. It was an unrefined, rowdy place that hosted many foreign travelers. Nathanael's question, "Can any good thing come out of Nazareth?" (v. 46), was probably a common expression of derision among the Jews of Galilee.

Prejudice is an unwarranted generalization based on feelings of superiority, and it can be a powerful obstacle to the truth. Herbert Lockyer points out that in his allegory *The Holy War*, John Bunyan depicts Christ (called Emmanuel) invading and holding the life of a person (represented as the town Mansoul). During the course of the siege on Mansoul, Emmanuel's forces attack Eargate. But Diabolus (Satan) sets up a formidable guard called "Old Mr. Prejudice, an angry and ill-conditioned fellow who has under his power sixty deaf men" (*All the Apostles of the Bible* [Grand Rapids: Zondervan, 1972], p. 60).

The nature of prejudice is to turn a deaf ear and a blind eye to any truth that does not fit its preconceived and cherished ideas. Consequently, it is a common and powerful weapon of Satan. By appealing to various prejudices he often succeeds in getting a person to reject the gospel even before learning what it is really about. The prejudices of their man-made traditions blinded many Jews to the true teaching of their Scriptures and thereby led them to reject Jesus as the Messiah—despite His clear demonstrations of divine power and fulfillment of Old Testament prophecy.

Fortunately, Nathanael's prejudice was tempered by his genuine desire to know God's truth. He agreed to Philip's suggestion ("Come and see") and went to meet Jesus for himself (v. 46b-47a).

From the mouth of Jesus we learn still other characteristics of Nathanael. As Nathanael approached, Jesus said, "Behold an Israelite indeed, in whom is no guile!" (v. 47b). *Alēthōs* ("indeed") was a word of strong affirmation by which Jesus declared Nathanael to be the kind of man God intended His chosen people to be. He was a Jew in the truest spiritual sense, "a Jew who is one inwardly, . . . [whose] praise is not from men, but from God" (Rom. 2:29). He was not merely a physical descendant of Abraham but, more important, a Jew in the true covenant with God, a spiritual descendant, a child of promise (see Rom. 9:6-8).

Not only was Nathanael a genuine, spiritual Jew, but he was, by the Lord's own testimony, a man "in whom is no guile!" (John 1:47c). He was a genuine Jew and a genuine person. He had no deceit or duplicity, no hypocrisy or phoniness. That characteristic alone set him far apart from most of his countrymen, especially the self-righteous and hypocritical scribes and Pharisees, whose very names Jesus used as synonyms for religious and moral hypocrisy (Matt. 23:13-15, 23, 25, 27).

Nathanael had reflected the common prejudice of the time, but his heart was right and won out over his head. His prejudice was not strong and it quickly withered in the light of truth. What an astoundingly wonderful commendation to be described by the Lord Himself as "an Israelite indeed, in whom is no guile!"

Nathanael's response to Jesus' commendation reflected its appropriateness. He did not swell up with pride at the compliment but wondered how Jesus could speak with such certainty about the inner life of a person He had never met. "How do You know me?" he asked (John 1:48). "How do You know what I am really like on the inside?" he was asking. "How do You know that I truly seek to follow God and that my life is not hypocritical?" Because of his genuine humility, Nathanael may have been inclined to doubt Jesus' judgment and think His comments were mere flattery.

But Jesus' next words removed any doubts Nathanael may have had. When Jesus said, "Before Philip called you, when you were under the fig tree, I saw you," Nathanael knew he stood in the presence of omniscience. He declared, "Rabbi, You are the Son of God; You are the King of Israel" (vv. 48b-49).

Because fig trees of that region could become quite large, they were often planted near a house to provide shade, comfort, and a place of retreat from household activities. Nathanael must have been meditating and praying in the shade of such a tree before Philip came to him.

In any case, Jesus not only saw where Nathanael was sitting but knew what he was thinking. "I saw you in your secret place of retreat," Jesus said, in effect, "and I even saw what was in your heart." Nathanael's prayers were answered and his searching for the Messiah was over. Because his heart was divinely prepared to seek the Messiah, he immediately acknowledged Him when they met, just as the godly Simeon and Anna recognized even the infant Jesus as the Son of God (Luke 2:25-38).

Jesus continued His attestation of Nathanael's faith. "Because I said to you that I saw you under the fig tree, do you believe?" (John 1:50), is better translated as a statement of fact (as in the NIV). Both Jesus and Nathanael knew it was the manifestation of omniscience that convinced Nathanael of Jesus' messiahship. Because of Nathanael's faith, Jesus went on to say, "'You shall see greater things than these.' And He said to him, 'Truly, truly, I say to you, you shall see the heavens opened, and the angels of God ascending and descending on the Son of Man'" (vv. 50b-51). This demonstration of Jesus' omniscience would come to seem small to Nathanael in comparison to the wonders of divine power he would soon begin to witness.

It may be that Nathanael came to understand Jesus' glory as well as any of the other apostles. We know nothing else of the man than what is found in that one brief account. But it seems reasonable to assume that he was among the most dependable and teachable of the twelve. There is no record of his questioning Jesus or arguing with Him or even misunderstanding Him.

The New Testament says nothing of his ministry or his death, and even tradition has little to offer about him. But it is apparent from the Lord's own words that, like David, Nathanael was a man after God's own heart.

The Master's Men—
part 4
Thomas, Matthew (10:3*b*)

15

Thomas and Matthew the tax-gatherer; (10:3*b*)

As in the other lists of disciples, these two men are in the second group of four, although the order of their names varies (see Mark 3:18; Luke 6:15; Acts 1:13).

THOMAS

Probably since the first century, **Thomas** has been known primarily, if not almost exclusively, for his doubt; and "doubting Thomas" has long been an epithet for skeptics. But a careful look at the gospel accounts reveals this disciple was a man of great faith and dedication.

As with several other apostles, all that is known of him besides his name is found in John's gospel. While Jesus was ministering on the other side of the Jordan River near Jericho, the report came that Lazarus had died. On hearing the news, Jesus said to His disciples, "I am glad for your sakes that I was not there, so that you may believe; but let us go to him" (John 11:15). Even after witnessing so many miracles, including the raising of the dead, the twelve were still lacking in faith, and Jesus determined to perform this last great miracle for their benefit. He had already decided to go back to Judea, despite reminders by the disciples that it would cost His life (vv.

7-8). Because Bethany was a near suburb of Jerusalem, for Jesus to go there was almost as dangerous as His going into Jerusalem. Fully realizing the danger for all of them, "Thomas therefore, who is called Didymus, said to his fellow disciples, 'Let us also go, that we may die with Him'" (v. 16).

Thomas, and doubtlessly the other disciples as well, believed that, because of the hostility of the Jewish establishment, going to Jerusalem would be virtual suicide. But he took the initiative to encourage the twelve to go with Jesus and suffer the consequences with Him. He was obviously pessimistic about the outcome of the trip, but the pessimism makes his act all the more courageous. As a pessimist, he expected the worst possible consequences; yet he was willing to go. An optimist would have needed less courage, because he would have expected less danger. Thomas was willing to pay the ultimate price for the sake of His Lord.

Such unreserved willingness to die for Christ was hardly the mark of a doubter. Thomas was willing to die for Christ because he totally believed in Him. Thomas was perhaps equalled only by John in his utter and unwavering devotion to Jesus. He had such an intense love for the Lord that he could not endure existence without Him. If Jesus was determined to go to Jerusalem and certain death, so was Thomas, because the alternative of living without Him was unthinkable.

Herbert Lockyer has commented: "Like those brave knights in attendance upon the blind King John of Bohemia who rode into the battle of Crécy with their bridles intertwined with that of their master, resolved to share his fate, whatever it might be . . . so Thomas, come life, come death, was resolved not to forsake his Lord, seeing he was bound to Him by a deep and enthusiastic love" (*All the Apostles of the Bible* [Grand Rapids: Zondervan, 1972], p. 178).

Thomas had no illusions. He saw the jaws of death and did not flinch. He would rather face death than face disloyalty to Christ.

In the Upper Room following the Last Supper, Jesus urged the disciples not to be troubled in heart and assured them that He was going to prepare a heavenly place for them and would come again and receive them to Himself, in order that they might forever be with Him. He then said, "And you know the way where I am going" (John 14:1-4). Puzzled at this, Thomas asked, "Lord, we do not know where You are going, how do we know the way?" (v. 5).

Only a few days earlier Thomas had declared his determination to die with Christ if necessary. His devotion to Christ was unqualified, but like the other disciples he had almost no understanding of Jesus' death, resurrection, and ascension, for which his Master had been preparing him for three years. Thomas had little comprehension of what Jesus had just said, apparently assuming Jesus was only talking about taking a long journey to a distant country. He was bewildered, saddened, and anxious. Again the disciple's pessimism and also his love are revealed. His pessimism made him fear that he might somehow be permanently separated from his Lord, and his love for his Lord made that fear unbearable. Understanding Thomas's heart as well as his words, Jesus said, "I am the way, and the truth, and the life" (v. 6). "If you know Me," Jesus was saying, "you know the way. And if you are in Me, you are in the way. Your only concern is to be with Me, and I will take you wherever I go."

The third text in which John tells us about Thomas is by far the best known. When Jesus was crucified and buried, all of Thomas's worst fears had seemed to come true. Jesus had been killed, but the disciples were spared. Their Master was gone, and they were left alone, leaderless and helpless. For Thomas it was worse than death, which he had been perfectly willing to accept. He felt forsaken, rejected, and probably even betrayed. From his perspective, his worst pessimism had been vindicated. Jesus' promises had been empty—sincere and well meaning, no doubt, but nevertheless empty. Because he loved Jesus so much, the feeling of rejection was all the more deep and painful. The deepest hurt is potentiated by the greatest love.

When the other disciples told Thomas they had seen the Lord, he probably felt like salt had been poured into his wounds. He was in no mood for fantasies about His departed Lord. It was unbearably painful trying to adjust to Jesus' death, and he had no desire to be shattered by more false hopes. When Thomas heard that Jesus was raised from the dead and alive, he declared, "Unless I shall see in His hands the imprint of the nails, and put my finger into the place of the nails, and put my hand into His side, I will not believe" (John 20:25).

A person who is depressed, especially if he is naturally pessimistic, is hard to convince that anything will ever be right again. Because he is convinced his plight is permanent, the idea of improvement not only seems unrealistic but can be very irritating. To the person confirmed in hopelessness, even the idea of hope can be an offense.

But Thomas's attitude was basically no different from that of the other disciples. They, too, were incredulous when first told of Jesus' resurrection. When Peter and John ran to the tomb and found it empty as Mary had said, "as yet they did not understand the Scripture, that He must rise again from the dead" (John 20:9). Even with evidence of the resurrection, they did not search for a risen Lord but went back home (v. 10). When Christ appeared to the ten disciples (Judas was dead, and Thomas was elsewhere), who huddled behind closed doors "for fear of the Jews," they were not certain that it was the flesh and blood Jesus until after He "showed them both His hands and His side" (vv. 19-20). Nor had the two disciples to whom Jesus appeared on the Emmaus road believed the reports of His resurrection (Luke 24:21-24). None of the disciples believed Jesus was alive until they saw Him in person.

Because they all doubted His promise to rise on the third day, Jesus allowed Thomas to remain in his doubt for another eight days. When He then appeared again to the disciples, He singled out this dear soul who loved him enough to die for Him and who was now utterly shattered in spirit. "Reach here your finger, and see My hands," He said to Thomas, "and reach here your hand, and put it into My side; and be not unbelieving, but believing" (John 20:26-27). In one of the greatest confessions ever made, Thomas exclaimed, "My Lord and my God!" Now all doubt was gone and he knew with full certainty that Jesus was God, that Jesus was Lord, and that Jesus was alive! The Lord then gently rebuked Thomas, saying, "Because you have seen Me, have you believed? Blessed are they who did not see, and yet believed" (vv. 28-29). But His rebuke was fully as much of the other disciples as of Thomas, because his doubt, though openly declared, had been no greater than theirs.

If Jesus is not God and is not alive, the gospel is a foolish and futile deception, the furthest thing from good news. "If Christ has not been raised," Paul told the Corinthian skeptics, "your faith is worthless; you are still in your sins. . . . If we have hoped in Christ in this life only, we are of all men most to be pitied" (1 Cor. 15:17, 19).

Tradition holds that Thomas preached as far away as India, and the Mar Thoma Church, which still exists in southwest India and bears his name, traces its origin to him. He is said to have had died from a spear being thrust through him, a fitting death for the one who insisted on placing his hand in the spear wound of his Lord.)

MATTHEW

Because he wrote the first gospel, **Matthew** is one of the best known apostles. But the New Testament reveals very few details of his life or ministry.

Before his conversion and call to discipleship, **Matthew** collected taxes for Rome (Matt. 9:9). It was not an occupation to be proud of, and one would think he would have wanted to dissociate himself from the stigma as much as possible. Yet when he wrote the gospel some thirty years later, he still referred to himself as **the tax-gatherer.**

As discussed previously in more detail (see chap. 6), tax-gatherers were considered traitors, the most hated members of Jewish society. They were often more despised than the occupying rulers and soldiers, because they betrayed and financially oppressed their own people. They were legal extortioners who extracted as much money as they could from both citizen and foreigner with the full authority and protection of Rome.

They were so despicable and vile that the Jewish Talmud said, "It is righteous to lie and deceive a tax collector." Tax collectors were not permitted to testify in Jewish courts, because they were notorious liars and accepted bribes as a normal part of life. They were cut off from the rest of Jewish life and were forbidden to worship in the Temple or even in a synagogue. In Jesus' parable, the tax collector who came to the Temple to pray stood "some distance away" (Luke 18:13) not only because he felt unworthy but because he was not allowed to enter.

Matthew was hardly proud of what he had been, but he seems to have cherished the description as a reminder of his own great unworthiness and of Christ's great grace. He saw himself as the vilest sinner, saved only by the incomparable mercy of his Lord.

Even from the little information given about him, it is evident Matthew was a man of faith. When he got up from his tax table and began to follow Jesus, he burned his bridges behind him. Tax collecting was a lucrative occupation, and many opportunists were doubtlessly eager to take Matthew's place. And once he forsook his privileged position, the Roman officials would not have granted it to him again. The disciples who were fishermen could always return to fishing, as many of them did after the crucifixion; but there could be no returning to tax collecting for Matthew.

In the eyes of the scribes and Pharisees, Matthew's leaving his tax office to follow Jesus did little to elevate his standing. Casting his lot with Jesus did not increase Matthew's popularity, but it greatly increased his danger. There is little doubt that Matthew faced something of the true cost of discipleship before any of the other apostles.

Matthew was not only faithful but humble. In his own gospel (and even in the other three) he is faceless and absolutely voiceless during his time of training under Jesus. He asks no questions and makes no comments. He appears directly in no narrative. Only from Mark (2:15) and Luke (5:29) do we learn that the banquet Jesus ate with "tax-gatherers and sinners" was in Matthew's house. In his own account, the fact that he was responsible for it is only implied (Matt. 9:10). He was eager and overjoyed for his friends and former associates to meet Jesus, but he calls no attention to his own role in the banquet.

It may be that his humility was born out of his overwhelming sense of sinfulness. He saw God's grace as so superabundant that he felt unworthy to say a word. He was the silent disciple, until the Holy Spirit led him to pick up his pen and write the opening book of the New Testament—twenty-eight powerful chapters on the majesty, might, and glory of the King of kings.

The fact that Matthew is also referred to as Levi indicates his Jewish heritage. We have no idea what his biblical training may have been, but Matthew quotes the Old Testament more often than the other three gospel writers combined—and quotes from all three parts of it (the law, the prophets, and the writings, or Hagiographa). Since it is highly unlikely he studied Scripture while he was a tax collector, he gained his biblical knowledge either in his youth or after he became an apostle.

Matthew had a loving heart for the lost. As soon as he was saved his first concern was to tell others of that great news and invite them to share in it. He was ashamed of his own previous life of sin; but he was not ashamed to be seen eating with his former associates who were despised by society and living under God's judgment, because they needed the Savior just as he had.

He sensed personal sinfulness as perhaps none of his fellow disciples did, because he had been greedily and unashamedly involved in extortion, deception, graft, and probably blasphemy and every form of immorality. But now, like the woman taken in adultery, because he was forgiven much, he loved much (see Luke 7:42-43, 47). The genuineness of his love for the Lord is proved in his concern for the salvation of his friends.

God took that outcast sinner and transformed him into a man of great faith, humility, and compassion. He turned him from a man who extorted to one who gave, from one who destroyed lives to one who brought the way of eternal life.

The Master's Men— part 5
James the son of Alphaeus, Thaddaeus (Judas the son of James), Simon the Zealot
(10:3c-4a)

16

James the son of Alphaeus, and Thaddaeus; Simon the Zealot, (10:3c-4a)

These men are the first three in the third group of four apostles and are the least known of the twelve. Most of what we know of them is inferred from their names or descriptive identities or is gleaned from church tradition. Except for one short question posed to Jesus by Thaddaeus, the Bible tells us nothing about their individual characters, personalities, abilities, or accomplishments, either during their three years of training under Jesus or during their ministry in the early church.

JAMES THE SON OF ALPHAEUS

The first-named of these unknown apostles is **James,** who is distinguished from the other apostle James (the son of Zebedee, v. 2) and from James the half brother of Jesus by being identified as **the son of Alphaeus.** In Mark 15:40 he is referred to as "the Less." *Mikros* ("less") can also mean smaller or younger. Used in the sense of smaller, the name may have been another means of distinguishing him from James the son of Zebedee, who was clearly larger in influence and position and possibly also in physical stature. In the sense of younger, it may have indicated his youthfulness in comparison to the other James.

As just mentioned, this James was considerably less than James the son of Zebedee in the realm of influence. He may have had outstanding traits such as boldness or courage, but, if so, he would likely have been called "the Bold" or something similar, rather than "the Less." He could have been older than the other James; but if that were true, he would probably have been called "the Elder," since that description would have been less confusing and more respectful of his age. It is also possible, of course, that he was smaller in stature. But the most probable meaning of "the Less" would seem to be that of youthfulness, coupled with that of his subordinate position in leadership.

Because Matthew's father was also named Alphaeus (spelled Alpheus in Mark 2:14), James and Matthew may have been brothers. Or this James may have been a cousin of Jesus. Clopas was a form of Alphaeus, and if Jesus' "mother's sister, Mary the wife of Clopas" (John 19:25), was James's mother, he would have been Jesus' first cousin. That possibility is also supported by Mark 15:40, which tells us that the mother of James the Less was named Mary. It is possible that he was both Matthew's brother and Jesus' cousin. In either case or both, this James's low profile testifies to his humility, since there is no indication that he tried to take personal advantage of any such relationship.

James was not distinguished as a gifted leader, either before or after his calling and training. We can assume he faithfully fulfilled the Lord's work during his ministry, and we know that he will one day sit on a heavenly throne and join the other twelve in judging the twelve tribes of Israel (Matt. 19:28). But his apostleship had no relationship to outstanding ability or achievement. He was an unextraordinary man, used in unextraordinary ways to help fulfill the extraordinary task of taking the gospel of Jesus Christ to the world.

After 2,000 years, James the son of Alphaeus remains obscure. We do not know a single word he spoke or a single thing he did. The early church Fathers claimed that he preached in Persia (modern Iran) and was crucified there as a martyr for the gospel. If that is true, one can only wonder what would have happened to that country and to world history had those people responded favorably to the gospel.

THADDAEUS (JUDAS THE SON OF JAMES)

The second apostle listed in the third group is **Thaddaeus**. Based on less reliable Greek manuscripts, the Authorized text reads, "Lebbaeus, whose surname was Thaddaeus." From Luke 6:16 and Acts 1:13 we learn that he was also called Judas the son of James. It is likely that Judas was his original name and that Thaddaeus and Lebbaeus were descriptive names, somewhat like nicknames, added by his family or friends.

Thaddaeus comes from the Hebrew word *shad,* which refers to a female breast. The name means "breast child," and was probably a common colloquialism for the youngest child of a family, the permanent "baby" of the family who was the last to be nursed by his mother.

Although the name Lebbaeus is not found in what are considered the superior

Greek manuscripts, and is therefore not in most modern translations, it may well have been one of this apostle's names. It is based on the Hebrew *leb* ("heart") and means "heart child," which suggests he was known for his generosity, love, and courage.

On the night before His arrest and trial, Jesus said, "He who has My commandments and keeps them, he it is who loves Me; and he who loves Me shall be loved by My Father, and I will love him, and will disclose Myself to him" (John 14:21). At that time Thaddaeus spoke his only words recorded in Scripture: "Judas (not Iscariot) said to Him, 'Lord, what then has happened that You are going to disclose Yourself to us, and not to the world?'" (v. 22).

Judas (Thaddeus) obviously was thinking only of outward, visible disclosure, and he wondered how Jesus could manifest Himself to those who loved Him without also manifesting Himself to everyone else. Like most Jews of his day, he was looking for Christ to establish an earthly kingdom. How, he wondered, could the Messiah sit on the throne of David and rule the entire earth without manifesting Himself to His subjects? Thaddaeus may also have wondered why Jesus would disclose Himself to a small group of insignificant men and not to the great religious leaders in Jerusalem and the powerful political leaders in Rome.

Jesus did not rebuke Thaddaeus for his misunderstanding, which he sincerely and humbly expressed. In light of common Jewish expectations, the question was appropriate and insightful, and it gave Jesus the opportunity to further explain what He meant. He proceeded to reiterate what He had just said and added the negative side of the truth: "If anyone loves Me, he will keep My word; and My Father will love him, and We will come to him, and make Our abode with him. He who does not love Me does not keep My words; and the word which you hear is not Mine, but the Father's who sent Me" (John 14:23-24). Christ was not at that time establishing His earthly kingdom, and the disclosure He was then making was of His divinity and authority as spiritual Lord and Savior. That disclosure can only be recognized by those who trust and love Him, and the genuineness of such trust and love is evidenced by obedience to His Word. Manifestation is limited to reception.

A radio or television broadcast can have a great range, reaching virtually the entire globe by use of satellites. But its programs are only "disclosed" to those who have proper receivers. The rest of the world has no awareness of the broadcast, although its electronic waves completely surround them.

Henry David Thoreau once observed that "it takes two people to speak the truth, the one who says it and the one who hears it." Those who will not listen to the gospel cannot hear it, no matter how clearly and forcefully it may be proclaimed. Jesus Christ was God incarnate, yet "He was in the world, and the world was made through Him, and the world did not know Him. He came to His own, and those who were His own did not receive Him" (John 1:10-11). During His three years of ministry, countless thousands of people—mostly God's chosen people, the Jews—saw and heard Jesus. Yet only a few had more than passing interest in who He really was or in what He said. The god of this world so blinded their minds that when they looked they could not see (2 Cor. 4:4).

Someone has commented that if you tore a beautiful hymn out of a hymnal and threw it down on the sidewalk, you could expect many different reactions from those who saw it. A dog would sniff at it and then go his way. A street cleaner would pick it up and throw it in the trash. A greedy person might pick it up expecting to find a valuable document of some sort. An English teacher might read it and admire its literary quality. But a spiritually-minded believer who picked it up and read it would have his soul blessed. The content would have been the same for all those who came in contact with it, but its meaning and value could only be understood by a person receptive to its godly truth.

Only those whose hearts are purified by love and who walk in obedience to God's Word can perceive Christ's truth, beauty, and glory. Thaddaeus was such a person.

Tradition holds that Thaddaeus was specially blessed with the gift of healing and that through him the Lord healed many hundreds of people in Syria. He is said to have healed the king of that country and won him to the Lord. The supposed conversion threw the land into such turmoil that the king's unbelieving nephew had Thaddaeus bludgeoned to death with a club, which became the symbol for that apostle.

Simon the Zealot

The third name in the third group is **Simon the Zealot**. The King James Version's "Simon the Canaanite" is based on an unfortunate transliteration of *kananaios*, which was derived from the Hebrew *qanna*, meaning "jealous" or "zealous." It is the equivalent of the Greek *zēlōtēs* ("zealot"), a description Luke uses of this Simon (Luke 6:15; Acts 1:13).

Zealot may have signified his membership in the radical party of Zealots whose members were determined to throw off the yoke of Rome by force. The Zealots developed during the Maccabean period, when the Jews, under Judas Maccabaeus, revolted against their Greek conquerors. During the time of Christ, another Judas (a common Jewish name of that period) was the outstanding Zealot leader.

The Zealots were one of four dominant religious parties in Judah (along with the Pharisees, Sadducees, and Essenes) but were for the most part motivated more by politics than religion. They were primarily guerrilla fighters who made surprise attacks on Roman posts and patrols and then escaped to the hills or mountains. Sometimes they resorted to terrorism, and the Jewish historian Josephus called them *sicarii* (Latin, "daggermen") because of their frequent assassinations. The heroic defenders of the great Herodian fortress at Masada were Jewish Zealots led by Eleazar. When that brave group fell to Flavius Silva in A.D. 72 after a seven-month siege, the Zealots disappeared from history.

If **Simon** was that sort of **Zealot**, he was a man of intense dedication and perhaps violent passion. His always being listed next to Judas Iscariot may suggest that those men were somewhat two of a kind, whose primary concern about the Messiah was earthly and material rather than spiritual. But whatever motivations they may originally have had in common soon vanished, as Judas became more confirmed in his rejection of Jesus and Simon more confirmed in his devotion to Him.

Apparently throughout their ministries, James the son of Alphaeus, Thaddaeus, and Simon the Zealot remained unknown even to most of the church. But they joined the ranks of the unnamed Old Testament saints who "experienced mockings and scourgings, yes, also chains and imprisonment. They were stoned, they were sawn in two, they were tempted, they were put to death with the sword; they went about in sheepskins, in goatskins, being destitute, afflicted, ill-treated (men of whom the world was not worthy), wandering in deserts and mountains and caves and holes in the ground. And all these . . . gained approval through their faith" (Heb. 11:36-39).

BIRDVILLE
BAPTIST CHURCH
LIBRARY

The Master's Men— part 6
Judas (10:4*b*)

and Judas Iscariot, the one who betrayed Him. (10:4*b*)

Among the twelve apostles, one stands out against the backdrop of the others as a lonely, tragic misfit, the epitome of human disaster. He is the vilest, most wicked man in Scripture. In the lists of apostles he is always named last and, with the exception of Acts 1:13, is always identified as Jesus' betrayer. For 2,000 years the name **Judas Iscariot** has been a byword for treachery.

Forty verses in the New Testament mention the betrayal of Jesus, and each of them is a reminder of Judas's incredible sin. After the description of his death and his replacement among the twelve in Acts 1, his name is never again mentioned in Scripture. In Dante's *Inferno* Judas occupies the lowest level of hell, which he shares with Lucifer, Satan himself.

His Name

Judas was a common name in New Testament times and was a second name for one of the other apostles, Thaddaeus. It is a personalized form of Judah, the southern kingdom during the Jewish monarchy and the Roman province of Judea during the time of Christ. Some scholars believe the name means "Yahweh (or

Jehovah) leads," and others believe it refers to one who is the object of praise. With either meaning, it was a tragic misnomer in the case of Judas Iscariot. No human being has ever been less directed by the Lord or less worthy of praise.

Iscariot means "man of Kerioth," a small town in Judea, about twenty-three miles south of Jerusalem and some seven miles from Hebron. Judas is the only apostle whose name includes a geographical identification, possibly because he was the only Judean among the twelve. All the others, including Jesus, were from Galilee in the north. Judean Jews generally felt superior to the Jews of Galilee; and although Judas himself was from a rural village, he probably did not fit well into the apostolic band.

HIS CALL

Judas is always listed among the twelve apostles, but his specific call is not recorded in the gospels. He first appears in Matthew's listing, with no indication as to where or how Jesus called him. Obviously he was attracted to Jesus, and he stayed with Him until the end of His ministry, far past the time when many of the other false disciples had left Him (see John 6:66).

There is no evidence that Judas ever had a spiritual interest in Jesus. It is likely that, from the beginning, he expected Jesus to become a powerful religious and political leader and wanted to use the association with Him for selfish reasons. He recognized Jesus' obvious miracle-working power as well as His great influence over the multitudes. But he was not interested in the coming of the kingdom for Christ's sake, or even for the sake of his fellow Jews, but only for the sake of whatever personal gain he might derive from being in the Messiah's inner circle of leadership. Although he was motivated totally by selfishness, he nevertheless followed the Lord in a half-hearted way—until he was finally convinced that Jesus' plans for the kingdom were diametrically opposed to his own.

Christ chose Judas intentionally and specifically, "for Jesus knew from the beginning who they were who did not believe, and who it was that would betray Him" (John 6:64). Although the disciples did not at the time understand what He meant, Jesus alluded to His betrayal a year or more before it occurred. "Did I Myself not choose you, the twelve, and yet one of you is a devil?" Jesus told them soon after the false disciples at Capernaum turned away from Him. John explains that "He meant Judas the son of Simon Iscariot, for he, one of the twelve, was going to betray Him" (vv. 70-71).

David predicted Christ's betrayal a thousand years before the fact. "Even my close friend, in whom I trusted, who ate my bread," he wrote, "has lifted up his heel against me" (Ps. 41:9; cf. 55:12-15, 20-21). Although that passage primarily referred to David, its greater significance applied to Jesus Christ, as He Himself declared (John 13:18).

Zechariah even predicted the exact price of betrayal. "And I said to them, 'If it is good in your sight, give me my wages; but if not, never mind!' So they weighed out thirty shekels of silver as my wages. Then the Lord said to me, 'Throw it to the potter, that magnificent price at which I was valued by them.' So I took the thirty shekels of silver and threw them to the potter in the house of the Lord" (Zech. 11:12-13). At the Lord's command, the prophet had shepherded the Lord's people (vv. 4-11), and the wages they paid Zechariah represented the "magnificent price" at which their descendants would value the Messiah Himself.

In His high priestly prayer, Jesus said to His Father, speaking of the twelve, "While I was with them, I was keeping them in Thy name which Thou hast given Me; and I guarded them, and not one of them perished but the son of perdition, that the Scripture might be fulfilled" (John 17:12). Luther translated "son of perdition" as "lost child," that is, a child whose nature and intention is to be continually wayward and lost. Jesus lost none of the twelve except the one who was confirmed in his sin and refused to be saved. He chose Judas in order to fulfill Scripture, knowing that Judas would reject that choice.

At the Last Supper Jesus said, "Behold, the hand of the one betraying Me is with Me on the table. For indeed, the Son of Man is going as it has been determined; but woe to that man by whom He is betrayed!" (Luke 22:21-22). Although our finite human minds cannot understand it, God had predetermined the betrayal, though, at the same time, Judas was held fully responsible for it, because it was by his own choice.

In Judas's rejection of Christ there is the same apparent paradox of divine sovereignty and human will that exists in the process of salvation. Although a person must receive Jesus Christ as Lord and Savior with an act of his will (John 1:12; 3:16; Rom. 1:16), every believer who does so was chosen to be saved even before the foundation of the world (Eph. 1:4; cf. Acts 13:48). In the same way, Judas had the opportunity to accept or reject Christ in regard to salvation, although Christ planned from the beginning for the disbelief and rejection that would characterize this disciple. Those seemingly conflicting truths—just as others found in Scripture—are resolved only in the mind of God. The Bible is clear that Jesus extended to Judas the opportunity for salvation to the extent that his unbelief was his own choice and fault (cf. Matt. 23:37; John 5:40). Judas *chose* to reject and betray Christ. That is why Christ did not label him as a victim of sovereign decree but "a devil" (John 6:70) and made clear that he did what he did not because God made him do it but rather Satan (John 13:27).

God also predetermined Judas's successor among the twelve from the beginning. Just before Pentecost, the Holy Spirit led Peter to explain to the apostles who remained, "It is therefore necessary that of the men who have accompanied us all the time that the Lord Jesus went in and out among us—beginning with the baptism of John, until the day that He was taken up from us—one of these should become a witness with us of His resurrection" (Acts 1:21-22). Out of the disciples who met that qualification, the eleven then chose "two men, Joseph called Barsabbas (who was also called Justus), and Matthias. And they prayed, and said, 'Thou, Lord, who knowest the hearts of all men, show which one of these two Thou hast chosen to occupy this ministry and apostleship from which Judas turned aside to go to his own place.' And they drew lots for them, and the lot fell to Matthias; and he was numbered with the eleven apostles" (vv. 23-26). Both God's sovereign, predetermined choice and the human choice of the apostles were involved in the selection of Matthias.

A few days later, on the day of Pentecost, Peter said to the crowd in Jerusalem, "Men of Israel, listen to these words: Jesus the Nazarene, a man attested to you by God with miracles and wonders and signs which God performed through Him in your midst, just as you yourselves know—this Man, delivered up by the predetermined plan and foreknowledge of God, you nailed to a cross by the hands of godless men and put Him to death" (2:22-23). God sovereignly predetermined Jesus' crucifixion, but the unbelieving Jews were responsible for sending Him to the cross. It was God's predetermined will to send His Son to die, and it was rebellious man's determined will to put Him to death.

His Character

Judas's outward personality must have been commendable or at least acceptable. Before the actual betrayal, none of the other disciples accused Judas of any wrongdoing or criticized him for any deficiency. When after three years of training them Jesus predicted that one of the twelve would betray Him, the other eleven had no idea who it might be. At first, "being deeply grieved, they each one began to say to Him, 'Surely not I, Lord?'" (Matt. 26:22). Then "they began to discuss among themselves which one of them it might be who was going to do this thing." But they soon lost sight of the betrayal and began to discuss not who was the worst among them but rather "which one of them was regarded to be greatest" (Luke 22:23-24). In any case, Judas was no more suspect than any of the others. In answer to John's question "Lord, who is it?" Jesus replied, "That is the one for whom I shall dip the morsel and give it to him" (John 13:25-26). Jesus then gave the morsel to Judas, saying, "What you do, do quickly." Still the others had no idea the traitor was Judas. "No one of those reclining at the table knew for what purpose He had said this to him," that is, to Judas (vv. 27-28).

Because he was never suspected by the other disciples, Judas must have been a remarkable hypocrite. He had even been selected treasurer of the group and was perfectly trusted (John 13:29). It is probable that, like most of the other disciples, he had led a respectable, religious life before Jesus called him. Perhaps he had not been an extortioner and traitor to his own people like Matthew or a hot-blooded revolutionary and possible assassin like Simon the Zealot, although his coming from Kerioth of Judea might have obscured his background to the other disciples, who were Galileans.

Judas apparently guarded what he said. His only recorded words were spoken near the end of Jesus' ministry, when he objected to Mary's anointing Jesus' feet with expensive ointment. "Why was this perfume not sold for three hundred denarii, and given to poor people?" he asked (John 12:5). "Now he said this," John explains, "not because he was concerned about the poor, but because he was a thief, and as he had the money box, he used to pilfer what was put into it" (v. 6). Under the Holy Spirit's inspiration, John was given that insight which he recorded when writing the gospel decades later; but at the time of the incident he had no awareness of Judas's ulterior motive.

Judas was no more naturally sinful than any other person ever born. He was made of the same stuff as the other apostles, with no less common goodness and no more innate sinfulness. But the same sun that melts the wax hardens the clay, and Judas's choice not to trust in Jesus became more and more hardened and fixed as he continued to resist the Lord's love and Word.

Judas was probably one of the youngest disciples and likely an outwardly devout and patriotic Jew. Though not as radical as Simon the Zealot, he was anxious for the Roman yoke to be thrown off and expected Jesus to usher in the messianic kingdom that would accomplish that. Rome would be overthrown, and God's people would be reestablished in peace and prosperity.

But Judas was first of all a materialist, as his stealing bears witness. He wanted the earthly benefits of a restored Jewish kingdom but had no interest in personal righteousness or regeneration. He was perfectly satisfied with himself and came to Jesus solely for material advantage, not for spiritual blessing. Jesus gave him every opportunity to renounce his self-life and seek God's forgiveness and salvation, but Judas refused. The Lord gave the parables of the unjust steward and the wedding garments, but Judas did not apply the truths to himself. The Lord taught much about the dangers of greed and love of money and even warned the twelve that one of them was a devil, but Judas would not listen. He did not argue with Christ, as Peter and some of the others did and, in fact, probably openly acted as if he agreed with Him. But the response of his heart was continual rejection. Jesus chose Judas because the betrayal was in God's plan and was prophesied in the Old Testament; yet Jesus gave Judas every opportunity not to fulfill that prophecy.

Judas was in the third group of four disciples—with James the son of Alphaeus, Thaddaeus, and Simon the Zealot—indicating he was among the disciples who were least intimate with Jesus. It is likely he was on the fringe even of his own subgroup, participating no more than necessary, and that from the sidelines. It is doubtful he was close to any of the others. He was thought to be honest, but he developed no close friendships or intimate relationships. He was a loner.

In the Orient, a host would always offer an honored guest the first sop, which consisted of a morsel of bread dipped in a syrup-like mixture of fruit and nuts. At the Last Supper Jesus offered the first sop to Judas. Yet at the very moment the Lord extended special honor to Judas, "Satan then entered into him" (John 13:27). To the very end Jesus loved Judas, but he would have none of what He offered him.

HIS PROGRESSIVE REJECTION

Judas did not begin his discipleship intending to betray Jesus. He was in full sympathy with what he thought was Jesus' purpose and plan and was ready to support Him. After each miracle Judas may have expected Jesus to announce His kingship and begin a campaign against Rome, whose vast army, great as it was, would have been no match for Jesus' supernatural power. Judas kept hanging on and hanging on, expecting Jesus to fulfill his dreams of defeating the despised oppressor. Like a gambler who thinks every loss puts him that much closer to winning, Judas perhaps thought that every failure of Jesus to use His power against Rome brought that ultimate and inevitable goal a bit closer.

For three years Judas hoped, and at the triumphal entry into Jerusalem he must have thought the time had finally come. Obviously, Judas reasoned, Jesus had been building up to a grand climax, waiting for the crowds to fully recognize His messiahship and His right to the throne of David. He would ascend His throne by popular demand, and the Lion of Judah would at last expel and destroy the eagle of Rome.

But when Jesus rejected the crowd's crown and instead began to teach even more earnestly about His imminent arrest and death, it was Judas's hopes and expectations that were expelled and destroyed. He was devastated that Jesus could build up to such a perfect opportunity and intentionally let it slip through His hands. He must have thought Jesus mad to willingly allow Himself to be mistreated and even killed, when with one word He could destroy any opponent. Now he knew beyond doubt that, whatever Jesus intended to do, it had no relationship to his own motives and plans.

Judas started at the same place as the other disciples. But they trusted in Jesus and were saved, and as they surrendered more and more to His control, they grew away from their old ways. They, too, were sinful, worldly, selfish, unloving, and materialistic. But they submitted to Jesus, and He changed them. Judas, however, never advanced beyond crass materialism. He refused to trust Jesus and more and more resisted His lordship. Eventually he was confirmed in his own way to the point that he permanently closed the door to God's grace. Like Faust, he irretrievably sold his soul to the devil.

When Jesus turned His back on the crown offered by the multitude, Judas turned his back on Jesus. He could no longer restrain his vile, wretched motives for self-glory and gain. He had given a glimpse of his true self when he showed more concern for the money "wasted" on perfume to anoint Jesus than concern for the Lord's imminent arrest and death, which the disciples by now knew awaited Him in Jerusalem (John 11:16).

Judas's fascination with Jesus had turned first to disappointment and finally to hatred. He had never loved Jesus but only sought to use Him. He had never loved his fellow disciples but rather stole for himself from what small resources they had. Now he turned completely against them.

On the last night Jesus was together with the disciples, He washed their feet with His own hands, to teach them humility and service. As He began He said, "You are clean, but not all of you," referring to Judas (John 13:10-11). After the object lesson He gave another warning that Judas could have heeded: "I do not speak of all of you. I know the ones I have chosen; but it is that the Scripture may be fulfilled, 'He who eats My bread has lifted up his heel against Me'" (John 13:18). Jesus grieved over Judas, being unwilling that even this vile man should perish (cf. 2 Pet. 3:9). As the time for the betrayal came closer, Jesus "became troubled in spirit, and testified, and said, 'Truly, truly, I say to you, that one of you will betray Me'" (v. 21). He did not grieve over the loss of His own life, which He willingly laid down. He grieved over the spiritual death of Judas and, it seems, made one last appeal before it became forever too late. He knew

Judas's unbelief, greed, ingratitude, treachery, duplicity, hypocrisy, and hatred. Still He loved him. The death He was about to die was as much for Judas's sin as for the sins of any person ever born, and it was for Judas that the Lord grieved as only He can grieve. He lamented over Judas in the same way He had lamented over Jerusalem: "How often I wanted to gather your children together, the way a hen gathers her chicks under her wings, and you were unwilling" (Matt. 23:37).

Throughout church history, in the name of love and compassion, some people have tried to attribute a good motive to Judas's betrayal or at least to minimize its evil. But such an attempt flies in the face of Scripture, including Jesus' own specific words. The Lord called Judas a devil and the son of perdition. To make Judas appear better than that is to make God a liar. Every unsaved person is under Satan's control and serves Satan's will. But when Judas accepted the morsel from Jesus' hands without repentance or regret, Satan took possession of him in a way that is frightening to contemplate (John 13:27).

His Betrayal

Judas did not betray Jesus in a sudden fit of anger. We are not told when the idea first came to him, but apparently the incident of Mary's anointing Jesus with the perfume prompted him to pursue it. It was right after this that "one of the twelve, named Judas Iscariot, went to the chief priests, and said, 'What are you willing to give me to deliver Him up to you?'" After accepting the thirty pieces of silver, "from then on he began looking for a good opportunity to betray Him" (Matt. 26:14-16). Luke adds that he sought "a good opportunity to betray Him to them apart from the multitude" (22:6). Judas was a coward, and at that time he assumed the crowds who acclaimed Jesus during the triumphal entry would remain loyal to Him. He wanted no one to know of his treachery, certainly not a hostile multitude. Like the chief priests and scribes who paid him, he was "afraid of the people" (Luke 22:2).

It is difficult to determine the equivalent modern buying power of the thirty pieces of silver Judas received, especially since the specific silver coin is not identified. But at the most generous reckoning, it was a trifling sum for betraying any person to his death, much less the Son of God. The relatively small amount suggests that, in his greed and hatred, Judas was willing to settle for any price. It also suggests the disdain the chief priests and scribes had for Judas. Their hatred for Jesus was public and well known; but Judas was one of Jesus' disciples and friends, and the Jewish leaders doubtlessly had contempt for his treachery even though they used it to their own ends. The small price further suggests the low value all of them placed on Jesus' life.

So that His enemies could recognize Jesus in the darkness of Gethsemane, Judas "had given them a signal, saying, 'Whomever I shall kiss, He is the one'" (Mark 14:44). His contempt for Jesus was such that he used that cherished mark of love and friendship as his sign of betrayal.

Judas not only profaned the Passover by receiving blood money but he also profaned Gethsemane, the private place of worship and solace that He knew Jesus loved. "Judas then, having received the Roman cohort, and officers from the chief priests and the Pharisees, came there with lanterns and torches and weapons" (John 18:3). Unaware that Jesus knew of his wicked plan, Judas thought to deceive Him by the kiss, feigning love and loyalty. But Jesus already knew the soldiers were coming and "went forth, and said to them, 'Whom do you seek?'" (v. 4). When they said, "Jesus the Nazarene," He replied, "I am He" (v. 5). As if to reinforce his hateful determination to betray Jesus, Judas proceeded to kiss Him, although it was no longer necessary to identify Him. His supreme act of hypocrisy was to pretend love for Jesus while giving Him over to His enemies. The Greek text of Matthew 26:49 uses an intensive form that suggests Judas kissed Jesus fervently and repeatedly. Yet even in face of this diabolical sham, Jesus called Judas "friend" as He told him, "Do what you have come for" (v. 50). Jesus' love extended even beyond Judas's point of no return.

The degree of Judas's betrayal was unique but not its nature. Through Ezekiel, God rebuked His people for profaning Him "for handfuls of barley and fragments of bread" (Ezek. 13:19), and through Amos He charged them with selling "the righteous for money and the needy for a pair of sandals" (Amos 2:6). Still today men and women will sell out the Lord for whatever they think is worth more.

> It may not be for silver,
> It may not be for gold;
> But yet by tens of thousands,
> The Prince of life is sold.
> Sold for a godless friendship;
> Sold for a selfish aim;
> Sold for a fleeting trifle;
> Sold for an empty name.
> Sold in the mart of science;
> Sold in the seat of power.
> Sold at the shrine of fortune;
> Sold in pleasure's hour.
> Sold for your awful bargain,
> None but God's eye can see.
> Ponder my soul the question,
> How shall He be sold by thee?
> Sold, O God. What a moment
> Stilled his conscience's voice?
> Sold, unto weeping angels
> Record the fatal choice.
> Sold, but the price accepted
> To a living coal shall turn;
> With the pangs of a late repentance
> Deep in a soul to burn.
> (Author unknown. Cited in Herbert Lockyer, *All the Apostles of the Bible* [Grand Rapids: Zondervan, 1972], p. 110.)

Judas sold Jesus for greed. He was malicious, vengeful, ambitious, and hateful of everything good and righteous. But above all, he was avaricious.

No man could be more like the devil than a perverted apostle. And for the same reason, every false teacher who holds the name of Christ stands in special guilt and is worthy of special disdain.

HIS DEATH

"When lust has conceived, it gives birth to sin," James says, "and when sin is accomplished, it brings forth death" (James 1:15). Judas's sin caused him to sell out Christ, his fellow apostles, and his own soul. When Jesus had been found guilty by the mock trial in the Sanhedrin and was turned over to Pilate, Judas "felt remorse and returned the thirty pieces of silver to the chief priests and elders, saying, 'I have sinned by betraying innocent blood'" (Matt. 27:3-4). But remorse is not repentance. Judas regretted what he had done and recognized something of its horrible sinfulness. But he did not have a change of mind, and he did not ask God to change his heart. He knew he could not undo the damage he had done, but he tried to mollify his conscience by returning the money he had been paid for his wickedness. Because he lived only on the material level, he somehow thought he could resolve his problem by the physical act of giving back the blood money. Then his unforgiven heart turned from vengeance against Christ to vengeance against himself, and he "went away and hanged himself" (v. 5). That did not end the misery of his conscience, however, for his guilt and anguish will last through all eternity.

Apparently Judas failed in his hanging attempt, and Luke reports the consummation of his death. It may have been that the branch to which the rope was tied broke and he fell over a precipice or down a hill, "and falling headlong, he burst open in the middle and all his bowels gushed out" (Acts 1:18).

Although they had no compunction about making false charges against Jesus and of unlawfully condemning Him to death, the chief priests' consciences would not let them put the thirty pieces of silver back into the Temple treasury after Judas threw the money at their feet, "since it is the price of blood" (Matt. 27:6). In perfect fulfillment of the Old Testament prophecy (Zech. 11:12-13), "they counseled together and with the money bought the Potter's Field as a burial place for strangers. For this reason that field has been called the Field of Blood to this day" (Matt. 27:7-8).

God overruled the wickedness of Jesus' betrayer and executioners and used it to fulfill His own Word. Even those who bitterly opposed the Lord's will found themselves unwittingly fulfilling His Word.

LESSONS LEARNED FROM THE LIFE OF JUDAS

Even wickedness and tragedy can teach valuable lessons, and there is great profit from studying the life of Judas. First of all he is the world's greatest example of lost opportunity. Judas was among the original twelve men Jesus called to be His apostles, His gospel ambassadors to the world. He lived and talked and ministered with Jesus for three years, hearing God's Word from the mouth of His own Son and seeing God's power manifested as never before on earth. No human being has every heard a more complete and perfect declaration of the gospel or seen more perfect obedience to it. Judas heard the perfect gospel and saw the perfect life. To none of the apostles did Jesus give more specific warning about sin—and more repeated opportunity to repent of it and to believe—than He did to Judas. Yet Judas turned his back on grace incarnate.

Today many people have heard the gospel clearly and seen genuine though imperfect examples of its transforming power. Yet they, too, reject it and, like Judas, choose instead to stay in the way that leads to destruction.

Second, Judas's life provides the world's greatest example of wasted privilege. He lusted for temporary material possessions and riches when he could have inherited the universe forever. It is a tragically foolish bargain to exchange the riches of God's kingdom for the pittances the world can offer.

Third, Judas's life serves as the clearest illustration of love of money being the root of all kinds of evil (see 1 Tim. 6:10). In the unbelievable extreme of greed, he loved money so much that he sold the Son of God for a trifling amount of it.

Fourth, Judas's life is the supreme object in history of the forbearing, patient love of God. Only God could have known the utter evil of Judas's heart from the beginning and yet never have withdrawn His offer of grace. At the Last Supper Christ presented Judas the dipped morsel as a gesture of love and honor; and even as He was being betrayed by the kiss, He called Judas "friend."

The life of Judas provided an essential qualification in preparing Christ for His high priestly role. Judas's betrayal brought great anguish to Jesus' heart, and through that and other such torment the Son of God was perfected through His suffering (Heb. 2:10). Christ can understand and sympathize with our sufferings partly because Judas helped make Christ's own suffering complete.

Judas was the consummate hypocrite of all time, the supreme illustration of an ungodly life that hides behind Christ while he serves Satan.

Someone has well said,

> Still as of old,
>   Man by himself is priced.
> For thirty pieces of silver
> Judas sold himself, not Christ.

(Author unknown)

Principles for Effective Ministry
(10:5-15)

18

These twelve Jesus sent out after instructing them, saying, "Do not go in the way of the Gentiles, and do not enter any city of the Samaritans; but rather go to the lost sheep of the house of Israel. And as you go, preach, saying, 'The kingdom of heaven is at hand.' Heal the sick, raise the dead, cleanse the lepers, cast out demons; freely you received, freely give. Do not acquire gold, or silver, or copper for your money belts, or a bag for your journey, or even two tunics, or sandals, or a staff; for the worker is worthy of his support. And into whatever city or village you enter, inquire who is worthy in it; and abide there until you go away. And as you enter the house, give it your greeting. And if the house is worthy, let your greeting of peace come upon it; but if it is not worthy, let your greeting of peace return to you. And whoever does not receive you, nor heed your words, as you go out of that house or that city, shake off the dust of your feet. Truly I say to you, it will be more tolerable for the land of Sodom and Gomorrah in the day of judgment, than for that city." (10:5-15)

After the listing of the apostles, chapter 10 may be divided into three parts. The first section (vv. 5-15) deals with the basic task of ministry, the next section (vv.

16-23) with reaction to ministry, and the last section (vv. 24-42) with the cost of ministry.

The apostles were the original missionaries, trained and sent forth to preach the gospel to a world under God's judgment, into a harvest that was plentiful but for which the workers were few (Matt. 9:37; cf. 2 Cor. 5:11). The instruction Jesus gave the apostles at this time was for short-term mission work in their own country; but the basic concepts apply to every believer the Lord sends out into ministry. Some of the specifics were restricted to a given time and situation, whereas the principles are broad and universal.

One of the tragedies of contemporary Christianity, and of the church throughout most of its history, is that many of those who purport to represent Jesus Christ either do not represent Him at all or represent Him poorly. Those whom Christ sends out cannot minister faithfully and effectively for Him if they do not understand and follow the principles for ministry that He Himself taught.

Jesus' purpose for this first apostolic mission was twofold. First, it was for the sake of the lost, to give them opportunity to hear and accept the gospel; and, second, it was for the benefit of the twelve themselves, to give them training in the enterprise of winning souls. Jesus was instructing His disciples how to reproduce disciples.

In Matthew 10:5-15 Jesus articulates eight principles, each of which is a general requirement for effective ministry: a divine commission, a central objective, a clear message, confirming credentials, confident trust, settled commitment, concentration on those who are receptive, and rejection of those who are contemptuous.

A DIVINE COMMISSION

These twelve Jesus sent out after instructing them, saying, (10:5a)

The **twelve** had not volunteered to become disciples and apostles, nor did they volunteer to minister in Christ's behalf. They were sovereignly called, commissioned, and sent out by Him. They were under divine orders. What the Lord said of Jeremiah could be said of each of the twelve: "Before I formed you in the womb I knew you, and before you were born I consecrated you" (Jer. 1:5).

From Mark's parallel passage we learn that Jesus sent the disciples out in pairs (6:7). In that way they would have companionship while beginning a type of work that was new and completely foreign to them. Loneliness is fertile ground for temptation and weakness, and by going out with companions they would be less prone to discouragement, depression, and self-pity. They could encourage one another, hold each other accountable, and take turns ministering, thereby helping to reduce pressure and fatigue. In addition to that, the Old Testament principle of a testimony being confirmed by two or three witnesses (Deut. 19:15) would give added authority to the apostles' preaching.

This particular time of ministry probably lasted only a few weeks, but it was specially significant, because it was the first time kingdom truth was proclaimed by anyone other than Christ Himself. In fulfillment of the purpose for which Christ had said to each of them, "Follow Me!" He now **sent out** each of them on their first assignment in His behalf.

God's calling and sending of His people today is not as direct as that, but it can nevertheless be known. Three criteria can help a believer decide whether or not he is called into the Lord's service. The first criterion is strong desire. God's Word reveals that when we delight in Him, He will give us the desires of our heart (Ps. 37:4). The Christian who loves the Lord and wants above all else to please Him is sensitive to His will in ways that an unfaithful believer cannot be. When one's life is centered on joyous obedience and one's motive is God-honoring, it is perfectly appropriate to seek a place of ministry in the Lord's service. Paul says that if a godly man aspires to the office of bishop, or overseer, "it is a fine work he desires to do" (1 Tim. 3:1). The closer we walk with the Lord, the more certain we can be that our desires are His desires.

A second criterion is the confirmation of the church. When a person feels a strong desire to preach but does not have the encouragement and support of godly believers who know him well, he should reevaluate the source of his feelings. The Lord uses other believers to confirm His call to individuals. The qualifications for church leaders, given in 1 Timothy 3 and Titus 1 are the standards by which the church is to measure the suitability of a person who desires to minister. Such confirmation is illustrated in what Paul told Timothy: "Do not neglect the spiritual gift within you, which was bestowed upon you through prophetic utterance with the laying on of hands by the presbytery [elders]" (1 Tim. 4:14).

A third criterion for determining God's call is that of opportunity. When a person has a strong desire to minister and has the encouragement of the godly believers in the church, God will open a clear door of service, just as he did for Paul at Ephesus (1 Cor. 16:9).

The twelve were called and sent out by the direct spoken command of Jesus. His will for them was specific and unmistakable. *Parangellō,* the verb behind **instructing,** had a number of usages in New Testament times. As a military term it represented the order of an officer to those under his command, an order that required unhesitating and unqualified obedience. As a legal term it was used of an official court summons, the equivalent of a modern subpoena, which to disregard made a person liable to severe punishment. Used ethically, the term represented a moral obligation that was binding on a person of integrity. As a medical term it represented a doctor's prescription or instruction given to a patient. The word was also used to refer to certain accepted standards or techniques, such as those for writing or oratory.

In every dimension of its use, *parangellō* included the idea of binding a person to make the proper response to an instruction. The soldier was bound to obey the orders of his superiors; a person involved in a legal matter was bound by the court's orders; a person of integrity was bound by moral principles; a patient was bound to follow his doctor's instruction if he wanted to get well; and a successful writer or speaker was bound by the standards of his craft. In various forms, the word is used some thirty times in the New Testament.

Jesus used it to direct a leper (Luke 5:14), to command an evil spirit (8:29), to order Jairus and his wife (8:56), and to charge His disciples (9:21). The officers of the Sanhedrin used the term when they commanded Peter and John "not to speak or teach at all in the name of Jesus" (Acts 4:18), as did some of the believing Pharisees in Jerusalem who insisted that it was necessary "to direct [Christians] to observe the Law of Moses" (Acts 15:5). Paul used the term frequently of his own commands as an apostle (1 Thess. 4:11; 2 Thess. 3:4, 6, 10, 12; 1 Tim. 6:13) as well as of instruction by other Christian leaders (1 Tim. 1:3; 6:17).

When one realizes his calling is of the Lord, he has no choice but to respond just as a soldier responds to his superior officer or a person in the courtroom responds to the judge. God sets the standards and gives the orders; our responsibility is to obey. God does not require creativity or innovation in His ministers, but He does require obedience and faithfulness (1 Cor. 4:2). The minister is not a chef but a waiter. He is not called to prepare the meal—because God has already done that—but to serve it just as he has received it. Like Paul, every minister is under God's divine compulsion and should remind himself, "Woe is me if I do not preach the gospel" (1 Cor. 9:16).

In a general sense *every* believer is commissioned by the Lord and is bound to obey His call to go and present Him to the world. Not every believer is called to be a preacher, teacher, pastor, or missionary; but every believer is called to be Christ's witness to the world. Jesus Christ has no followers who are not under His order in the Great Commission to "make disciples of all the nations" (Matt. 28:19).

The first and most essential element for ministry is the unqualified understanding that one is sovereignly called, gifted, and empowered by the Lord to do His work in His way. Children of God do not determine their own destiny or mark out their own patterns or plans. They are under divine orders, and their supreme, overarching concern must be to submit to Christ in all things.

A CENTRAL OBJECTIVE

"Do not go in the way of the Gentiles, and do not enter any city of the Samaritans; but rather go to the lost sheep of the house of Israel." (10:5b-6)

The second principle for ministry that emerges indirectly from this passage is that of having a central objective. A ministry that is not focused on certain priority objectives is a ministry doomed to mediocrity. God gives different objectives to different people, and He often changes objectives from time to time and situation to situation, as He did with the apostles. But He never asks a person to do everything in sight. He is a loving and reasonable God, and when we find ourselves frustrated and overworked, we may be trying to do more than He has called us to do or are seeking to do it in our own power. In spite of the great personal effort required in faithful spiritual service (cf. Phil. 2:30; Col. 1:24), when the yoke and load are truly His, Jesus assures us they will be easy and light (Matt. 11:29).

The Great Commission was Christ's broad, general order to proclaim the gospel to the whole world, but in carrying out that commission the apostles would be given specific gifts and specific ministries. Yet at this particular time in Christ's plan for proclaiming the gospel and for preparing the apostles, His objective was especially narrow and limited.

In the way of and any city of represent two Greek possessive genitives. The apostles were not to go into any **way**, or area, belonging to **Gentiles** or into **any city** that belonged to **Samaritans**. In other words, they were not at this time to proclaim the kingdom message of salvation to non-Jewish people.

That this was a temporary command is seen not only from the clear call of the Great Commission but from the fact that Jesus had already ministered both to **Gentiles** and to **Samaritans**. He had healed the Gentile centurion's servant (Matt. 8:5-13) and had first revealed Himself publicly as the Messiah to the Samaritan woman of Sychar, who believed in Him herself and led other Samaritans to saving faith (John 4:7-42).

The redemption of the whole world had always been in God's plan. He did not call Abraham in order that only he and his descendants, the Hebrew people, would be blessed but that through those descendants "all the families of the earth shall be blessed" (Gen. 12:3). God's chosen people, like His only begotten Son, were called to be a light to the Gentile nations to draw them to His righteousness and to "bring salvation to the end of the earth" (Acts 13:47; cf. Isa. 42:6; 49:6; 60:3; 62:1-2). From the beginning, Israel was not called simply to receive, but also to be the channel of, God's blessing. The covenant people were to be a witnessing people to the rest of the world, that is, to **Gentiles.**

The **Samaritans** were especially despised by Jews, because they were half-breeds, neither true Jews nor true Gentiles. But Jesus always showed kindness to Samaritans, even to the woman from Sychar who was living in adultery. And in His parable of neighborly love, a Samaritan was favorably portrayed as the epitome of godly compassion. In Christ's last words to the apostles before His ascension, He specifically names Samaria as a field of ministry (Acts 1:8).

There are perhaps three reasons that Jesus chose to restrict the apostles' ministry at this time to **the lost sheep of the house of Israel.** First was the Jews' special place in God's plan. They were God's chosen people, the people of the covenants, the promises, and the law. John the Baptist preached primarily to fellow Jews, "saying, 'Repent, for the kingdom of heaven is at hand'" (Matt. 3:1-2), and Jesus began His own ministry with the same declaration to the same people (4:17). As He explained to the Samaritan woman, "Salvation is from the Jews" (John 4:22); that is, it came to the Jews first and, through them, comes to the rest of the world, just as God had promised Abraham. Israel, represented by "Jerusalem, and . . . Judea," was the launching point for taking the gospel to "Samaria, and even to the remotest part of the earth" (Acts 1:8). Even Paul, the apostle to the Gentiles, always began a new ministry in the local synagogue whenever he was able (see Acts 9:20; 13:5; 18:4; 19:8). Jews were the first to hear the gospel and the first to preach the gospel.

Had the apostles gone first to the Samaritans and Gentiles, the Jews would have been very reluctant to listen to them, because they would have perceived the apostles as bearers of a pagan religion. Although they had greatly distorted and disobeyed God's revelation, the Jews were right in their belief that His revelation to them was unique and that they had a unique role in His plan of redemption.

Second, Jesus sent the apostles to preach first to Jews because they were barely up to the task of witnessing effectively to their own people—much less of witnessing to Gentiles and Samaritans, whose cultures and ways they little understood and greatly despised. Even after Pentecost, Peter was not convinced the gospel was for Gentiles. The Lord had to persuade him through a special vision and by firsthand witness of the Spirit's work in Cornelius and his household (Acts 10). Peter's prejudice was so strong that many years later he, along with Barnabas and other Jewish Christians, broke fellowship with their Gentile brothers in Christ, "fearing the party of the circumcision" (Gal. 2:12-13), who taught that Gentiles had to be become Jewish proselytes before they could become Christians.

Except for Cornelius and his household, the Ethiopian eunuch, and a few others, the gospel had little impact on the Gentile world until the Lord raised up Paul. Although a former Pharisee and a "Hebrew of Hebrews" (Phil. 3:5), this apostle had grown up in Tarsus, a Gentile city, and was learned in Gentile literature, religion, and culture.

Third, Jesus probably restricted the apostles' first ministry to the Jews for the practical reason that the twelve needed a special point of attack, a limited and familiar field in which they could concentrate their fledgling efforts. An unfocused ministry is a shallow ministry. The effective worker for Jesus Christ puts his primary energy and effort into the task the Lord has assigned him. He is concerned for all of the Lord's work, but he does not try to do it all himself.

Jesus' own earthly ministry was limited. He did not travel outside Palestine, and His ministry to Gentiles and Samaritans was incidental when compared to His ministry to the Jews. He did not have preaching missions in Gentile territory, and He ministered to Samaritans only as He passed through their land while traveling between the Jewish regions of Judea and Galilee. All of His public teaching and preaching and the vast majority of His miraculous works were done among the Jews. To the Canaanite woman from the district of Tyre and Sidon, Jesus said, "I was sent only to the lost sheep of the house of Israel" (Matt. 15:24). As already pointed out, His personal ministry to others besides Jews and His commands to take the gospel into all the world show that "only to . . . Israel" referred to the primary objective of His work *at that time*. The gospel was not generally taken to non-Jews until it was first fully presented to God's chosen people (cf. Rom. 1:16).

Jesus was now giving a limited command to His apostles that was valid only for that time and place in His divine plan of world redemption. But the command illustrates a principle that is valid for every ministry in every time and place—namely, that God gives His people clear, specific objectives for service and ministry.

Self-styled messiahs are always egotists who expect to win the world immediately. Their ministry often seeks to be so vast that it becomes all breadth and no depth, like a lake a mile across and an inch deep.

A Clear Message

And as you go, preach, saying, "The kingdom of heaven is at hand." (10:7)

The third precept for effective ministry illustrated here is that of having a clear message. Many people fail to understand and receive the gospel because they have not heard it clearly presented.

Some years ago a fellow pastor who was sitting next to me on a plane took a small piece of paper and began writing on it until it was completely covered. When he handed it to me and asked me what it said, I could hardly distinguish a single letter. "Well, what was the first word I wrote?" he asked; and I had to confess again that I had no idea. Then he showed me what he had done. He gave me another small, blank piece of paper and told me to write "Christ" on it. On top of that first word and all over the rest of the paper I was then told to write "Baptist, Presbyterian, Methodist, Episcopal, Pentecostal, dispensational, fundamental, evangelical, liberal, Protestant," and perhaps a dozen more such terms. His point was clear: the simple gospel of Jesus Christ is sometimes so encumbered with secondary matters and human interpretations that the world has no idea what its central message is.

Not only the world but many believers are confused about Christianity because preachers and teachers digress from the gospel of the kingdom into every sort of secondary cause and emphasis. Satan's surest way of making the gospel impotent is simply to keep it from being understood. When the gospel is clouded with political, cultural, social, economic, environmental, ecclesiastical, and other such causes, its message is muddled and its power is diluted.

The message Jesus gave the apostles to **preach** was simply stated: **The kingdom of heaven is at hand.** Obviously they were to elaborate and explain what that meant, but the basic truth was unmistakable.

In Scripture, the kingdom of heaven can be viewed in three aspects. First, it is manifest in conversion, when a person enters the sovereign rule of God by trusting in Christ for salvation (cf. Matt. 18:3). Second, it is manifest in consecration, as believers live out the divine principles of God's revelation by obedience to His Word. "The kingdom of God is . . . righteousness and peace and joy in the Holy Spirit" (Rom. 14:17). Third, the kingdom will be seen in its glorious millennial form when Christ returns to earth to establish and rule it in person and then sets up His eternal kingdom (Matt. 25:31; Acts 3:19-21; Rev. 11:15; 20:4).

The central message of the kingdom is the message about the King. By definition, a kingdom is the domain ruled by a king, its sovereign. But the essence of a kingdom is not the geographical area but the actual *ruling* of the king, the administration of his will over the citizens of the kingdom. **The kingdom of heaven** is above all the domain of God's lordship, where He rules by His divine will. All of Jesus' teaching—from His public instruction of the multitudes in the Sermon on the Mount through His private instruction to the twelve disciples at the Last Supper and for forty days after His resurrection—was teaching the truths and principles of life in God's **kingdom.**

The gospel of the kingdom has many practical ramifications, social as well as personal. But until its central message of God's sovereign provision for man's salvation is clearly understood, accepted, and obeyed, trying to apply it to any other area of life is both disobedient to Christ's command and futile. The gospel transforms society only as it transforms individuals.

Heal the sick, raise the dead, cleanse the lepers, cast out demons; freely you received, freely give. (10:8)

The fourth principle of ministry presented here is that of confirming credentials. Doctors, lawyers, and other professionals prominently display the diplomas and other documents that certify their qualifications and authority to practice. In a far more important way, those who represent Christ must have credentials that confirm their divine mission and message. Jesus gave confirming signs for His own ministry, and now He calls the apostles to demonstrate their authority by performing similar signs and wonders.

Because the twelve had no formal training and were obviously not part of the established Jewish religious leadership, which was dominated by the scribes, Pharisees, Sadducees, and priests; because they were not even itinerant rabbis like Jesus; and because there was no New Testament to confirm their message, and most Jews had a distorted understanding even of their own Scriptures, the Old Testament, they had to have a special means of confirming their preaching and teaching.

"The signs of a true apostle," Paul declared, are "signs and wonders and miracles" (2 Cor. 12:12). It was with those evidential signs that Jesus empowered the apostles as He sent them out on their first mission to preach to "the lost sheep of the house of Israel."

The blind man healed in Jerusalem immediately recognized Jesus' power to heal as proof He was from God. He told the unbelieving Pharisees, "Well, here is an amazing thing, that you do not know where He is from, and yet He opened my eyes. We know that God does not hear sinners; but if anyone is God-fearing, and does His will, He hears him. Since the beginning of time it has never been heard that anyone opened the eyes of a person born blind. If this man were not from God, He could do nothing" (John 9:30-33).

The signs, wonders, and miracles Jesus commanded the apostles to perform were not for the purpose of simply demonstrating raw supernatural power. Jesus did not tell the apostles, for example, to disappear and reappear, to move the Temple from one place to another, or any such thing. The miracles they performed created wonder and demonstrated the character of God and the nature of His kingdom.

The first of the miraculous credential was the ability to **heal the sick** and **cleanse the leper.** Jesus did not want the people simply to know God's power, but to know that He offered His power to *help them*. The miracles were signs pointing to God's compassion and mercy. They demonstrated the sympathetic heart of God, who cares for the suffering, the hurting, the afflicted, and the needy. The future kingdom coming to earth will bring the removal of disease and the restoration of broken bodies, just as God's Word had predicted (Isa. 29:18; 35:5-6; 42:7). Thus these miracles not only revealed the nature of God but predicted the millennium.

When John was imprisoned and sent his disciples to ask Jesus if He were truly the Messiah, Jesus answered, "Go and report to John what you hear and see: the blind receive sight and the lame walk, the lepers are cleansed and the deaf hear, and the dead are raised up, and the poor have the gospel preached to them" (Matt. 11:4-5). Jesus knew John would recognize those miracles as the confirming marks of God's Messiah and God's kingdom.

Though such apostolic miracles ceased with termination of the apostles' work, those who genuinely represent Jesus Christ still give themselves to the sick, the suffering, the downtrodden, and the needy of every sort. The Christian leader who spends all of his time and effort working with those who are healthy and well-to-do either is not sent by God or is not fully faithful to his calling. Every person needs the gospel and every believer continues to need God's help and provision, but God has compassion for those who are in great need.

The Old Testament made that truth clear. "The needy will not always be forgotten, nor the hope of the afflicted perish forever," David wrote (Ps. 9:18). "'Because of the devastation of the afflicted, because of the groaning of the needy, now I will arise,' says the Lord; 'I will set him in the safety for which he longs'" (Ps. 12:5). Again David wrote, "All my bones will say, 'Lord, who is like Thee, who delivers the afflicted from him who is too strong for him, and the afflicted and the needy from him who robs him?'" (Ps. 35:10), and "I know that the Lord will maintain the cause of the afflicted, and justice for the poor" (Ps. 140:12). "The afflicted and needy are seeking water," God declared through Isaiah, "but there is none, and their tongue is parched with thirst; I, the Lord, will answer them Myself, as the God of Israel I will not forsake them" (Isa. 41:17). God is the refuge of the afflicted (Ps. 14:6).

By contrast, the world and its representatives have little compassion. The godless person "oppresses the poor and needy, commits robbery, does not restore a pledge" (Ezek. 18:12). He persecutes the poor (Ps. 10:2), puts heavy burdens on them and defrauds them (Amos 5:11; 8:5-6, grinds them down (Isa. 3:15), and devours them (Hab. 3:14). The world has little use for the afflicted. What concern there is comes as the residual fruit of Christian influence on society.

False prophets have no mercy or compassion but rather use and abuse people to their own selfish advantage. Jesus warned about "the scribes who like to walk around in long robes, and like respectful greetings in the market places, and chief seats in the synagogues, and places of honor at banquets" but "who devour widows' houses" (Mark 12:38-40).

Christians who are thoroughly orthodox in doctrine and sound in moral character often show little compassion for the poor, the sick, and the afflicted. In such cases they are ineffective and inconsistent representatives of Jesus Christ, despite their sound doctrine and high morals, because they lack an important credential that should mark the servant of Christ.

The second apostolic credential was the power to **raise the dead** and **cast out demons.** Here the apostles are enabled to manifest God's power even in bringing the dead back to life and in invading and conquering the unseen demonic kingdom of darkness.

Such gifts of miraculous powers were restricted to the apostolic age, and no believer today manifests such supernatural apostolic credentials. But though it is shown in less dramatic and physically awesome ways, the mark of divine power still validates the work of those God sends out to do His will. The ministry of the true servant of Christ is characterized by God's power in redeeming lives, giving divine spiritual understanding, and bringing spiritual growth. Through the faithful witness even of the least-gifted believer the gospel has unleashed power to raise the spiritually dead to life and to shatter the work of demons and of Satan himself.

The third confirming credential was obedience to Christ's admonition, **freely you received, freely give.** The apostles were given their miraculous power from God, and they were to use it without thought of personal gain or advantage. It was God's power, not theirs, and it was to be used for His glory, not their prosperity. The faithful servant of Jesus Christ is marked by unselfishness.

Exorcists were common among the Jews of Jesus' day, and many of them made a lucrative living purporting to cast out demons. People who were demon possessed or had loved ones who were possessed were willing to pay almost any price for deliverance, and there were plenty of charlatans willing to take advantage of their desperation. People would also pay whatever they could for physical healing, and many became like the woman with the hemorrhage, who "had endured much at the hands of many physicians, and had spent all that she had and was not helped at all" (Mark 5:26).

The apostles could have become immensely wealthy had they charged for healing, raising the dead, and casting out demons. Simon the magician had visions of such wealth as he saw the dramatic miracles being performed in Samaria by Philip. When Peter and John came up there and began laying their hands on the believers that they might receive the Holy Spirit, Simon "offered them money, saying, 'Give this authority to me as well, so that everyone on whom I lay my hands may receive the Holy Spirit.' But Peter said to him, 'May your silver perish with you, because you thought you could obtain the gift of God with money!'" (Acts 8:18-20).

In New Testament times rabbis were bound by Talmudic law to teach for nothing, for the same basic reason Jesus gave the apostles. Moses had been given the law freely by God, and rabbis were not to charge for teaching it. The only exception was for teaching a small child of parents who were shirking their own responsibility for teaching him. The Mishna held that a rabbi was no more to take money for teaching than a judge was to take money for his decision in a court or a witness for his testimony. Rabbi Zedek wrote, "Make not the law a crown wherewith to aggrandize thyself, or a spade wherewith to dig." The famous Hillel said, "He who makes worldly use of the crown of the law shall waste away, hence thou mayest infer that whosoever desires a profit for himself from the words of the law is helping his own destruction."

False teachers, on the other hand, put a price on their ministry, because their motive is not to serve either God or men but themselves. Isaiah spoke of such false shepherds of God's people "who have no understanding; they have all turned to their own way, each one to his unjust gain, to the last one" (Isa. 56:11). Peter says of them that "in their greed they will exploit you with false words"; but, he goes on to say, "their judgment from long ago is not idle, and their destruction is not asleep" (2 Pet. 2:3).

One qualification for elders is that they "shepherd the flock of God . . . not under compulsion, but voluntarily, according to the will of God; and not for sordid gain" (1 Pet. 5:2; cf. Titus 1:7). They are to be "free from the love of money" (1 Tim. 3:3). The pastor who puts a price on his ministry prices himself out of God's blessing.

The present application of this teaching should be that God's ministers are to be supported by God's people, because "the worker is worthy of his support," as Jesus goes on to say (Matt. 10:10: cf. Luke 10:7). But they are not to put their services out for hire to the highest bidder or demand a given amount they feel they deserve to be paid. It is their responsibility to faithfully minister and the people's responsibility to faithfully support them. This balance becomes clear in the next element of our Lord's teaching.

Confident Faith

Do not acquire gold, or silver, or copper for your money belts, or a bag for your journey, or even two tunics, or sandals, or a staff; for the worker is worthy of his support. (10:9-10)

The fifth principle of ministry practically illustrated in this passage is that of confidently trusting God for whatever is needed. The apostles not only were not to demand payment for their services but were not to amass a great amount of money in advance of their mission. They were not to **acquire gold, or silver, or copper for** [their] **money belts.** Those three metals represented the various coinages in use at the time, in descending order of value. They were not to take valuable **gold** or **silver** coins or even less valuable **copper** ones. They were to go out with their **money belts** empty.

The **bag** probably refers to a food sack that was commonly carried on a **journey,** since inns were widely scattered and expensive. The apostles were not even to take a sack lunch.

Nor were they to take extra **tunics, or sandals, or a staff.** The tunic was an important outer garment that served both as overcoat and blanket. **Sandals** were necessary to protect the feet from sharp rocks, thorns, and the hot ground. **A staff** was helpful protection against robbers or wild animals.

The apostles were to go forth with a minimum of clothing and supplies, trusting the Lord to provide whatever else they needed. God Himself established the principle that **the worker is worthy of his support,** and He will see that it is fulfilled.

The rabbis had followed that principle for many years. One ancient rabbi had written, "He who receives a rabbi into his house or as his guest and lets him have his enjoyment from his possessions, the Scripture ascribes to him as if he had offered the continual offerings." They rightly believed that God would bless those who provided food, clothing, shelter, and other aid to the teachers of His Word.

"Let the elders who rule well be considered worthy of double honor," Paul wrote to Timothy, "especially those who work hard at preaching and teaching. For the Scripture says, 'You shall not muzzle the ox while he is threshing,' and, 'The laborer is worthy of his wages'" (1 Tim. 5:17-18). God's people are to do more than simply provide for their ministers' bare needs; they are also to honor them with generosity, especially when they are faithfully proclaiming the Word. It is God's divine plan that those who "proclaim the gospel . . . get their living from the gospel" (1 Cor. 9:14).

Ministers who never demand anything, who never put a price on their work, and who trust the Lord to provide for their needs have the special blessing of knowing that what they do receive is a gift from the Lord, expressive of His loving, generous care.

SETTLED COMMITMENT

And into whatever city or village you enter, inquire who is worthy in it; and abide there until you go away. (10:11)

The sixth principle of ministry Jesus here teaches by implication, and it is in two parts. First, a person is to find a proper place to stay while ministering in a given location, and second, he is to be satisfied to remain there until the work is finished.

Worthy does not mean wealthy or influential but refers to the spiritual and moral character of the host. In **whatever city or village** the apostles would **enter,** they were to seek out someone to stay with who was known to be godly, whose integrity and life-style were beyond question in the community. Otherwise the ungodly association would harm both their own spirituality and the effectiveness of their testimony.

Once they found a satisfactory place to stay, they were to **abide there until** they went **away.** The minister is not to keep his eye out for better accommodations or even to accept a voluntary offer for better lodging and thus offend his original host. His sole focus should be on his ministry, and his contentment with what he has and where he is staying will itself be a testimony to those to whom he ministers.

Such contentment and humble satisfaction will also benefit the minister's own spiritual life, because, Paul assures us, "godliness actually is a means of great gain, when accompanied by contentment" (1 Tim. 6:6). In his own ministry Paul had "learned to be content in whatever circumstances" he was in. He knew "how to get along with humble means, . . . to live in prosperity; in any and every circumstance." He had "learned the secret of being filled and going hungry, both of having abundance and suffering need," because he had learned that he could do all things through Christ, who strengthened him (Phil. 4:11-13).

CONCENTRATION ON THOSE WHO ARE RECEPTIVE

And as you enter the house, give it your greeting. And if the house is worthy, let your greeting of peace come upon it; (10:12-13*a*)

The seventh principle of ministry reflected in our Lord's teaching here is that of concentrating effort on those who are receptive to the gospel.

The house referred to here is not the place where the apostles would lodge but represents the various houses where they would go to minister. A **worthy** house was one where their witness and work were appreciated and accepted as being from God.

The **greeting** was the age-old Jewish greeting *shālom,* which is usually translated simply as **peace** but which carries the much deeper meaning of total well-being and wholeness of body, mind, and spirit.

The household that gladly received the apostles was to have its greeting of peace confirmed **upon it.** The implication is that truly receptive listeners were to be ministered to in the fullest way. Their open hearts to the Lord's work earned them God's richest blessing. "He who receives a prophet in the name of a prophet," Jesus explained a short while later, "shall receive a prophet's reward; and he who receives a righteous man in the name of a righteous man shall receive a righteous man's reward" (Matt. 10:41).

God does not call his servants to minister only where the gospel is immediately and eagerly received. Many fields of service are extremely resistant to the gospel. But the focus of ministry in any area or circumstance should be on those people who are most receptive. Those who hunger and thirst for righteousness are promised satisfaction (Matt. 5:6), and the faithful minister should give of himself fully and freely in feeding them God's Word. God's mandate is that the gospel should be preached first to those who want it most. They not only are the most deserving but are the ones most likely to believe and to win still others to Himself.

REJECTION OF THOSE WHO ARE CONTEMPTUOUS

but if it is not worthy, let your greeting of peace return to you. And whoever does not receive you, nor heed your words, as you go out of that house or that city, shake off the dust of your feet. Truly I say to you, it will be more tolerable for the land of Sodom and Gomorrah in the day of judgment, than for that city.'" (10:13*b*-15)

The last principle for ministry shows the reverse side of the previous one, namely, that of not spending undue time on those who persist in rejecting the gospel.

If a house was **not worthy,** Jesus told the twelve, **let your greeting of peace return to you,** which was an Oriental expression signifying withdrawal of favor or blessing. It is not that such a household would have a blessing and then lose it, but that the *offer* of **peace** was never received and is therefore withdrawn. The greatest blessing of God is worthless for a person who will not accept it. God's gospel is offered to all the world, and it has power to save all the world, but it is powerless to save or help even a single person who will not have Jesus Christ as Lord and Savior (cf. John 5:40).

The same principle applies to false teachers who come to us. "If anyone comes to you," John warns, "and does not bring this teaching, do not receive him into your house, and do not give him a greeting; for the one who gives him a greeting participates in his evil deeds" (2 John 10-11).

When a **house** or a **city** was contemptuous of the apostles and of the **words** they taught, as they left that house or city they were to **shake off the dust of** their **feet.** When they came back into Israel from a Gentile country, many Jews would literally shake as much dust off their feet as possible in order not to bring pagan soil into their homeland. For the apostles to shake the dust off their feet while leaving a Jewish house or town would be to treat the inhabitants like Gentiles—whom most Jews considered to be out of God's reach. When the leaders of the synagogue in Pisidia of Antioch drove Paul and Barnabas out of their district, the two men "shook off the dust of their feet in protest against them and went to Iconium" (Acts 13:51). Of the unbelieving Jews there Paul had declared, "It was necessary that the word of God should be spoken to you first; since you repudiate it, and judge yourselves unworthy of eternal life, behold, we are turning to the Gentiles" (v. 46; cf. Matt. 7:6).

It is not that we are to turn away from those who reject the gospel at first hearing or even after several hearings. Had that practice been followed, many believers would not be in the kingdom today. Through Paul, the Lord Himself entreated unbelieving Corinthians to "be reconciled to God" (2 Cor. 5:20). Were God not marvelously patient and longsuffering with fallen mankind, He would have destroyed the world long ago. He is infinitely patient with sinners, Peter tells us, "not wishing for any to perish but for all to come to repentance" (2 Pet. 3:9).

Jesus was not speaking of those who are slow to understand or believe but of those who, after hearing a clear testimony of the gospel and seeing dramatic and irrefutable signs of confirmation, continue to resist and oppose it. When a person's mind is firmly set against God, we should turn our efforts to others.

When people "have tasted the good word of God and the powers of the age to come, and then have fallen away, it is impossible to renew them again to repentance, since they again crucify to themselves the Son of God, and put Him to open shame" (Heb. 6:5-6). Of such people, Jesus warns, **Truly I say to you, it will be more tolerable for the land of Sodom and Gomorrah in the day of judgment, than for that city.** God utterly destroyed those two ancient cities with brimstone and fire because of their wickedness (Gen. 19:24), and today no certain trace of them has yet been found by archaeologists. But men and women who are contemptuous of the gracious, saving gospel of Jesus Christ face an even worse fate **in the day of judgment** (cf. Matt. 24:50-51; 25:14-46; 2 Thess. 1:5-10).

Sheep Among Wolves (10:16-23)

Behold, I send you out as sheep in the midst of wolves; therefore be shrewd as serpents, and innocent as doves. But beware of men; for they will deliver you up to the courts, and scourge you in their synagogues; and you shall even be brought before governors and kings for My sake, as a testimony to them and to the Gentiles. But when they deliver you up, do not become anxious about how or what you will speak; for it shall be given you in that hour what you are to speak. For it is not you who speak, but it is the Spirit of your Father who speaks in you. And brother will deliver up brother to death, and a father his child; and children will rise up against parents, and cause them to be put to death. And you will be hated by all on account of My name, but it is the one who has endured to the end who will be saved. But whenever they persecute you in this city, flee to the next; for truly I say to you, you shall not finish going through the cities of Israel, until the Son of Man comes. (10:16-23)

As part of their training toward finally being sent on their own after Jesus' resurrection and ascension, the twelve needed to have an idea of the obstacles they would face. As noted in the previous chapter, some of the specifics Jesus taught in Matthew 10:5-42 applied only to the apostles; yet in principle they apply to His witnesses in every generation. In a similar way, some of the instruction applied only to the brief mission on which Jesus now sent the twelve out two by two (Mark 6:7), although the underlying ministry precepts applied to their work even after the Lord Jesus had ascended to heaven and will continue to apply to all His faithful servants throughout the church age and even into the Great Tribulation (Matt. 24:21). Ministry built on divine precepts will not end "until the Son of Man comes" (10:23), the eschatological term Matthew uses to represent the return of Christ to establish His millennial kingdom.

There is a telescoping significance in the passage. Beginning with the limited, dispensational preaching of the kingdom to "the lost sheep of the house of Israel" (vv. 6-7) during this particular mission and until Pentecost, there is a sweep through the entire future of Christ's church—from His first coming to His second. With His omniscient prophetic eye, Jesus pictures the twelve in their full mission, and then He pictures all those who would continue to represent Him throughout redemptive history, including those who will suffer for His sake during the holocaust in the Great Tribulation.

That sort of telescopic prophecy is seen in numerous Old Testament passages, in which a prediction had both immediate and future significance and fulfillment. For example, within three verses, Micah spoke of Jesus' birth in Bethlehem at His first coming and of His ruling Israel and the entire earth at His second coming (Mic. 5:2-4). Yet in that passage the two comings seem to be blended into one.

Apart from understanding Jesus' use of this telescopic method, Matthew 10:5-42 cannot be sensibly interpreted. The apostles did not raise the dead (see v. 8) during this brief mission in Galilee nor at any other time during Jesus' own earthly ministry. Nor did they themselves experience direct persecution or suffering (see vv. 16-23) until after Pentecost.

In Matthew 10:16-23 Jesus first gives an analogy of believers and their opponents (v. 16a) and dual figures illustrating the attitudes they should have as they face those opponents (16b). He then mentions the two primary areas from which direct attack from persecutors will come (vv. 17-18) and promises God's equally direct provision for it (vv. 19-20). Finally, He mentions the two primary areas of indirect attack (vv. 21-22a) and tells His followers how to respond when persecution comes (v. 23).

THE ANALOGY

Behold, I send you out as sheep in the midst of wolves; (10:16a)

In saying, **Behold,** Jesus indicated His desire for the twelve to pay special attention to what He was about to say. He had spoken of the unbelieving multitudes as being like "sheep without a shepherd" (9:36), and He had delegated miraculous powers to the twelve (10:8). Based on such input it could have seemed to the apostles that they were destined to be powerful wolves who would go out with invincibility to conquer the defenseless, unbelieving sheep of the world. But the Lord here made it clear that the world's "sheep" are not really defenseless and that the apostles' powers—divinely endowed and marvelous as they were—would not prevent them from suffering from the hands of men. They, and the rest of His followers until He returns again, would be the real **sheep.** In that paradoxical truth Jesus graphically pointed up the tensions between our vulnerability and our invincibility—between our weakness in ourselves and our strength in Him, between the power of hateful persecution and the power of loving submission, and between the worldly power of the flesh and the supernatural power of the Spirit.

Sheep are perhaps the most dependent, helpless, and stupid of all domesticated animals. They are as often panicked by harmless things as by those that are dangerous. And when real danger does come, they have no natural defense except running, and they are not very good at that.

In *A Shepherd Looks at the Twenty-third Psalm,* Philip Keller gives many insights from his long experience as a shepherd in Canada. He points out that because sheep are so indiscriminate in their choice of vegetation to eat, it is necessary to carefully protect them from eating poisonous weeds. Because they are highly vulnerable to weather extremes and to infections and disease, they must be regularly and individually checked for dangerous symptoms, for cuts and abrasions, and for insects and parasites that can harm them. Flies buzzing around their eyes and ears have been known to so irritate and frighten sheep that they beat their heads against trees or rocks until they are dead. Sometimes flies will lay eggs in a sheep's eyes and ultimately cause blindness. In trying to escape real or imagined danger, sheep will sometimes panic into a blind stampede, and pregnant ewes will lose their lambs from the running and sometimes even their own lives from utter exhaustion.

But the sheep's greatest enemy is predators, the worst of which in Palestine and in many other parts of the world has always been **wolves.** People in Palestine understood the nature of sheep and the danger of wolves. They knew how difficult the task of the shepherd was simply to keep his sheep alive, much less healthy and contented.

Most shepherds did not themselves own the flocks but tended them on behalf of the owners. When a sheep was killed, the shepherd was required to bring back a piece of its torn flesh or some other part of its body to prove it had indeed been killed by a wild animal rather than stolen by a thief or perhaps sold by a dishonest shepherd.

Jesus clearly identifies the **sheep** as **you,** that is, His disciples—the twelve and, by extension, all of His disciples yet to come.

The normal danger for sheep is that wolves come in among *them.* But here Jesus told the twelve, **I send you out as sheep in the midst of wolves.** He called them to go into the wolves' own territory, to walk into the very maw of their enemies. Jesus is the perfect Good Shepherd, who loves His sheep with a divine love, who intimately knows them and is known by them, and who lays down His life for them (John 10:11-15). But in the figure of the **sheep** and **wolves,** Jesus gave a graphic illustration of the rejection and persecution by a God-hating world they would face because of Him. So before the twelve went out into their first brief and relatively undemanding service for the Lord, He set before them the cost of discipleship. Just as

He did not escape opposition and persecution, neither would they (cf. John 15:18-27; 16:33).

The world will continue to make raids on the church just as wolves make raids on flocks of sheep. "I know that after my departure," Paul said, "savage wolves will come in among you, not sparing the flock" (Acts 20:29). In his Romans letter he spoke of believers being looked on by the world as "sheep to be slaughtered" (8:36). Jesus had already warned His followers of "the false prophets, who come to you in sheep's clothing, but inwardly are ravenous wolves" (Matt. 7:15).

It is consistent with their predatory nature for wolves to come into a flock in the field and even into the sheepfold to attack, mutilate, and devour the sheep. But it is *not* natural or consistent with their nature for sheep to voluntarily walk into the wolves' own den. And it is unnatural for a shepherd to send his sheep into such certain peril. Yet that is where Jesus, the Good Shepherd, sends His disciples—into the hostile world of ungodly souls, because that is where they can serve Him best and be most effective in winning others to Him. The apostles, and to various extents every believer after them, would be sent out defenseless in themselves among evil, rapacious, vicious, God-hating mankind.

We do not hear much preaching today of sinners needing to count the cost of salvation and repenting of sin in confessing the lordship of Christ, or of coming to Him humbly, devoid of pride and self-trust, hungering and thirsting for righteousness, and entering the narrow gate and walking the narrow road of righteousness. Rarely are Christians called to take up their crosses and follow Christ in moving out into the world as sheep led to slaughter. The popular appeal is to ease, comfort, riches, advancement, and ambition—and the church often uses that kind of enticement to motivate unbelievers to trust in Christ and to motivate believers to follow Him. But Jesus makes no such offer. To the disciple He promises hardship, suffering, and death.

To present the gospel dishonestly and misleadingly is to be unfaithful to the Lord and to those to whom we present it. Because of false promises, many unredeemed people remain on the broad road that leads to destruction while being under the delusion they are on the road to life. Many believers are confirmed in spiritual mediocrity and unfruitfulness, thinking their health, wealth, and material success is the certain mark of divine approval. Still other believers are disillusioned and embittered because their lives of obedience, faithfulness, and sacrifice for Christ have not been materially rewarded.

After the siege of Rome in 1849, Garibaldi said to his soldiers, "Men, all our efforts against superior forces have been unavailing. I have nothing to offer you but hunger and thirst, hardship and death. But I call on all who love their country to join with me." After the Allies were forced to evacuate Dunkirk in 1940, Churchill said to his fellow Englishmen, "All I can offer you is blood, sweat, and tears."

If those human leaders refused to send out their fellow countrymen to war under false pretenses, how much less would the divine Son of God! Jesus does not send out His followers without warning about the demands and dangers of discipleship. Nor did His apostles mislead the early church about what belonging to Christ would cost. As he wrote to encourage and strengthen Timothy, his son in the faith, Paul also assured him that "all who desire to live godly in Christ Jesus will be persecuted" (2 Tim. 3:12). Godly lives are not marked by continual suffering and hardship inflicted on them by the unbelieving world. Neither the life of Jesus nor the lives of the apostles were characterized by uninterrupted hardship and persecution. But faithfulness to God guarantees that at some times and to some degree Satan and his world system will exact a price for it.

THE ATTITUDE

therefore be shrewd as serpents, and innocent as doves. (10:16*b*)

In Egyptian hieroglyphics, as well as in much ancient lore, **serpents** symbolize wisdom. They were considered to be **shrewd**, smart, cunning, cautious. In that characteristic, at least, Christians are to emulate **serpents.**

Paul advises believers, "Conduct yourselves with wisdom toward outsiders, making the most of the opportunity" (Col. 4:5). Servants of the Lord are to be **shrewd** and cunning in dealing with the unbelieving world around them.

The basic idea is that of saying the right thing at the right time and place, of having a sense of propriety and appropriateness, and of trying to discover the best means to achieve the highest goal. It is neither wise nor loving to be needlessly accusatory or inflammatory. When the Pharisees attempted to trap Jesus into either defending or condemning the Roman government by asking Him about paying taxes to Caesar, He did not take the occasion to vilify Caesar or the Roman government— vile, debauched, unjust, and ungodly as they were. Nor did He condone their wickedness. He replied simply, "Render to Caesar the things that are Caesar's; and to God the things that are God's" (Matt. 22:21). It is neither brave nor wise, and neither spiritual nor loving, to needlessly incite anger or court trouble.

As the most harmless and gentle of birds, **doves** represent being pure, or **innocent,** another characteristic of the faithful disciple of Christ. Being true to God's Word and uncompromising in proclaiming the gospel does not require, and should never include, being abrasive, course, inconsiderate, belligerent, blatant, or blunt.

Wisdom and innocence, cunning and gentleness, are handmaids of discretion. No apostle was more uncompromising of the gospel than Paul; yet he declared,

> I have made myself a slave to all, that I might win the more. And to the Jews I became as a Jew, that I might win Jews; to those who are under the Law, as under the Law, though not being myself under the Law, that I might win those who are under the Law; to those who are without law, as without law, though not being without the law of God but under the law of Christ, that I might win those who are without law. To the weak I became weak, that I might win the weak; I have become all things to all men, that I may by all means save some. (1 Cor. 9:19-22)

Innocence involves more than simply avoiding negative attitudes and approaches. It also involves the positive attribute of purity. Godly wisdom has no part in anything that is impure, deceitful, or defiling. It is always the ally of truth and righteousness. Nothing untruthful or unethical can enhance the gospel or make its witness more effective. Paul assured the Thessalonian believers that his preaching and teaching of the gospel did "not come from error or impurity or by way of deceit" (1 Thess. 2:3). Integrity and honesty are practical manifestations of truthfulness, without which an otherwise orthodox presentation of the gospel is distorted and weakened.

We are to be like our Lord Himself, our great "high priest, holy, innocent, undefiled" (Heb. 7:26). We are to love our enemies and do good to those who hate us (Luke 6:27). Jesus is again our model, because He "committed no sin, nor was any deceit found in His mouth; and while being reviled, He did not revile in return; while suffering, He uttered no threats, but kept entrusting Himself to Him who judges righteously" (1 Pet. 2:23). In following our Lord's example, "when we are reviled, we bless; when we are persecuted, we endure; when we are slandered, we try to conciliate" (1 Cor. 4:12-13).

When Paul was brought before the Sanhedrin in Jerusalem, the high priest Ananias ordered him to be struck in the mouth. In a moment of unguarded anger the apostle replied, "God is going to strike you, you whitewashed wall! And do you sit to try me according to the Law, and in violation of the Law order me to be struck?" (Acts 23:3). When he was rebuked by some bystanders for reviling the high priest, Paul immediately apologized, saying, "I was not aware, brethren, that he was high priest; for it is written, 'You shall not speak evil of a ruler of your people'" (v. 5). What Paul had said to the high priest was perfectly true, and certainly understandable from a human point of view. But it was not appropriate, not only because it was said to the high priest but because it was said in self-defensive anger. It was not the wise and righteous thing to say.

THE PERSECUTION

But beware of men; for they will deliver you up to the courts, and scourge you in their synagogues; and you shall even be brought before governors and kings for My sake, as a testimony to them and to the Gentiles. (10:17-18)

Jesus proceeds to identify the "wolves" and then gives warnings about four areas in which they persecute believers—in religion, government, family, and society in general. Interspersed within the warnings are further instructions about the attitudes His disciples should have and the provision their heavenly Father supplies.

The wolves of whom believers are to **beware** are **men**. The ultimate enemies against whom we struggle are Satan and his demonic hosts, the non flesh-and-blood "rulers, . . . powers, . . . world forces of this darkness, [and] spiritual forces of wickedness in the heavenly places" (Eph. 6:12). But the agents of those supernatural enemies are human beings. It is through **men** that Satan opposes and persecutes the church of Jesus Christ. **Men** are the wolves who malign, oppress, imprison, torture, and kill God's people.

Beware of these opponents, Jesus says—be on guard, be watchful, be perceptive. To be innocent is not to be naive. When well-meaning believers insist on putting the best face on every evil, they are not demonstrating love but foolishness and self-deception. Not to beat an unbeliever over the head with the vileness of his sin is one thing; to minimize his sin and his lostness apart from Christ is quite another. To love our enemies and not return evil for evil is one thing; to deny they are enemies is quite another.

Jesus had already promised blessing for those who are "persecuted for the sake of righteousness" and who have insults and "all kinds of evil" spoken against them falsely for His sake (Matt. 5:10-11). Here He promises the persecution that ultimately brings the blessing.

The disciples themselves had not yet experienced persecution or even opposition. Resistance to Jesus was not yet strong. Some of the scribes had criticized Him for claiming to forgive sins (9:2-3), and some of the Pharisees complained to His disciples that their Teacher ate "with the tax-gatherers and sinners" (v. 11) and later accused Him of casting "out the demons by the ruler of the demons" (v. 34). But these criticisms did not hinder the ministry or pose any danger at that time.

Jesus' purpose in warning about persecution was not to frighten the apostles and make them suspicious of every human being who was not a believer. Their very mission was to convert the unsaved and win them to Christ's kingdom. But they needed to be warned not to expect the world to receive the gospel and its messengers with open arms. Satan's world system, of whom every unbeliever is a part, is diametrically opposed to Christ, His people, and His kingdom. Satan will enlist the support of every unbeliever possible in his fight against God. Jesus' purpose in this text was to caution the apostles, and all of His people, not to be surprised when they are criticized, ostracized, and even imprisoned and put to death for His sake.

PERSECUTION BY RELIGION

for they will deliver you up to the courts, and scourge you in their synagogues; (10:17*b*)

The first source of persecution is religion, to which both **courts** and **synagogues** refer. Even under pagan rulers, the Jews were often allowed to settle most disputes among themselves, including many civil issues. For this purpose they had developed a detailed system of **courts** in which various cases were adjudicated. Every Jewish village and town, as well as every Jewish settlement of any size in Gentile countries, had a synagogue, which simply means a gathering place or a congregation.

Jews would try, convict, and punish (**scourge**) fellow Jews in their own religious **courts**, which were a part of their **synagogues**. A Jew accused of breaking the Mosaic law or a rabbinic tradition would be brought before a tribunal of judges, who decided the verdict, determined the sentence, and meted out punishment, which was often by scourging.

In New Testament times the **scourge** usually consisted of thirty-nine lashes with a whip, one less than the maximum of forty stripes allowed by Mosaic law (Deut. 25:3). One judge would call out the sentence, one would announce the punishment, one or more would do the scourging, and others of them would count the lashes. The Jewish writer Maimonides reported that appropriate Scripture passages were read and sometimes psalms were sung while punishment was being administered.

As the apostles preached and ministered in Christ's name, they could be sure of being brought before and punished by such Jewish courts. Before his conversion, Saul of Tarsus was engaged in just such persecution. Many years later, as an apostle and a persecuted believer himself, he recounted his confession before God that "in one synagogue after another I used to imprison and beat those who believed in Thee" (Acts 22:19). By the time Paul wrote 2 Corinthians he had been scourged by the Jews on five different occasions (2 Cor. 11:24), probably each time in a synagogue.

William Barclay comments that "the man with a message from God has to undergo the hatred and enmity of a fossilized orthodoxy." Jesus Himself was accused, tried, and convicted by religionists. Until the destruction of Jerusalem in A.D. 70—and with it the destruction of the Temple, the priesthood, and the sacrifices—virtually all persecution of Christians was by Jews. Though there remains personal hostility among Jews, after that time Jewish persecution of Christians virtually ceased, and it has never recurred to any significant degree since then.

From Revelation 11, however, we learn that the residual hostility against Christ will cause such persecution to resume during the last days. In the first half of the Tribulation, the beast from the abyss will be aligned with Israel; and in Jerusalem, "where their Lord was crucified," he will kill the two witnesses God sends to preach on earth for twelve hundred and sixty days (vv. 3-8). It is likely that many unbelieving Jews will be party to the martyrdom of those two men and to the worldwide rejoicing over their deaths (v. 10).

In the meanwhile, many other religious groups, some even bearing the name of Christ, will have oppressed, imprisoned, tortured, exiled, and killed countless millions of true believers. During the lifetime of many of the apostles, other religion-related persecution had already begun. Paul was bitterly opposed in Ephesus because the spread of the gospel there had severely cut into the sale of pagan idols, which were the major source of income for the local silversmiths (see Acts 19:24-29). A letter written by Pliny, a first-century Roman governor of Bithynia, indicates he took severe steps to check the rapid growth of Christianity because it threatened the commercial interests of selling idols and sacrificial animals from which pagan temples derived most of their income.

The intimidation, vandalizing, and murder of modern missionaries in primitive societies has, almost without exception, been carried out or instigated by witch doctors, shamans, or other such religious leaders. And the greatest restrictions on Christian ministry and worship outside the atheistic communist world is in Muslim countries.

Religious persecution of believers has frequently been from within Christendom itself. Paul warned the Ephesian elders that "after my departure savage wolves will come in among you, not sparing the flock; and from among your own selves men will arise, speaking perverse things, to draw away the disciples after them" (Acts 20:29).

The final great persecution of God's people will be by the worldwide religious system called "Babylon the great, the mother of harlots and of the abominations of the earth," who will become "drunk with the blood of the saints, and with the blood of the witnesses of Jesus" (Rev. 17:5-6). All false religious systems had their beginnings at Babel, when rebellious mankind determined to storm heaven and establish its own Satan-inspired substitute for the way of God. Man's religions have always opposed and sought to destroy God's truth; and one day they will culminate in an incredibly powerful ecumenical world religion that will relentlessly and mercilessly oppose the gospel of Christ and persecute His people.

PERSECUTION BY GOVERNMENT

and you shall even be brought before governors and kings for My sake, as a testimony to them and to the Gentiles. (10:18)

Persecution will also come from government. **Governors** were Roman procurators, such as were Pilate, Felix, and Festus, but they represent any governmental office or body below the national level. **Kings** (such as the two Agrippas, Herod Antipas, and other monarchs mentioned in the New Testament) represent heads of state.

Here Jesus explains why the wolves are so vicious with the Lord's sheep. It is not because of the sheep themselves but because of their Shepherd. It is **for My sake,** Jesus said, that His disciples would suffer abuse and persecution. The world hates Christians because the world hates Christ. Every person who identifies himself with Christ through salvation becomes a potential target of Satan and his evil forces, including evil men. That it is Christ and not Christians themselves that the world opposes is seen in the fact the more Christ is manifest in us, the more we will be attacked. Conversely, when we do not manifest Christ, we do not incite the world's wrath. The Christian who mimics the world, or simply keeps his faith to himself, is in little danger from the world, because he manifests little of His Lord's nature. The world attacks us only when it sees Christ in us.

Jesus affirmed such reality when He said,

If the world hates you, you know that it has hated Me before it hated you. If you were of the world, the world would love its own; but because you are not of the world, but I chose you out of the world, therefore the world hates you. Remember the word that I said to you, "A slave is not greater than his master." If they persecuted Me, they will also persecute you; if they kept My word, they will keep yours also. But all these things they will do to you for My name's same, because they do not know the One who sent Me. (John 15:18-21)

The stripes, lacerations, bruises, and scars on Paul's body were the "brand-marks of Jesus" (Gal. 6:17). They were made on his body, but they were intended for his Lord. Paul's persecutors did not despise him because of who he was but because Christ worked so powerfully through him. When they eventually took his life, it was because his life was Christ's life. Because the church is Christ's Body, it is faithful believers in the church who, like Paul, fill up "Christ's afflictions" (Col. 1:24). It is for that reason that Paul longed for the privilege of sharing in "the fellowship of His sufferings, being conformed to His death" (Phil. 3:10). "If you are reviled for the name of Christ, you are blessed," Peter says, "because the Spirit of glory and of God rests upon you" (1 Pet. 4:14). It is the "Spirit of glory and of God" in the believer's life that the world hates and seeks to destroy.

When God's kingdom is thriving, Satan causes his people to react against it in proportion to its success. Paul himself had been used of Satan to persecute the church. Under his former name of Saul, he was "breathing threats and murder against the disciples of the Lord." He even asked for letters from the high priest "to the synagogues at Damascus, so that if he found any belonging to the Way, both men and women, he might bring them bound to Jerusalem" (Acts 9:1-2). When the Lord intercepted Saul on his way to Damascus to carry out his wicked plan, His first words to him were, "Saul, Saul, why are you persecuting Me?" and when Saul asked who was speaking to him, the Lord replied, "I am Jesus whom you are persecuting" (vv. 4-5).

Saul had not seen Jesus during His earthly ministry, and Jesus was now in heaven; yet Saul was persecuting Jesus. Although the physical objects of the persecution were Christians (those "belonging to the Way"), the spiritual object was Christ Himself. Jesus' accusation made a deep impression on Paul, and when he testified before the mob in Jerusalem who demanded his arrest and eventually his execution, he quoted the words spoken to him by the Lord on the Damascus road (Acts 22:7). He quoted the same words when he testified before King Agrippa, declaring that he had not been simply a persecutor of Christians but a persecutor of Christ (26:14).

Every antagonistic and injurious unbeliever, no matter how unconsciously, persecutes Christ through His people. Jesus declared unequivocally that "he who is not with Me is against Me; and he who does not gather with Me scatters" (Matt. 12:30).

The phrase **as a testimony to them and to the Gentiles** is not easy to interpret. It could mean that persecuted believers are a living rebuke against their persecutors, **a testimony** *against* **them** and all the unbelieving **Gentiles** (pagans). Others take it to mean **a testimony** *to Christ* that persecuted believers make as His witnesses. The two interpretations are not incompatible, and both seem to be legitimate.

In either case, governments at various levels and to various degrees have been involved in persecution of believers throughout the history of the church. Only a few years after Pentecost, Herod Agrippa I "laid hands on some who belonged to the church, in order to mistreat them. And he had James the brother of John put to death with a sword. And when he saw that it pleased the Jews, he proceeded to arrest Peter also" (Acts 12:1-3). Herod's motivation, even in pleasing the Jews, was not religious but political and personal.

As Christianity began to spread throughout the empire, Rome became especially fearful of its slaves. Because of their great numbers (perhaps as many as 60 million) slaves had long posed the threat of rebellion. They were not permitted to marry free citizens, even free men in the lowest level of society, because slaves were considered less than persons. But when slaves and free Romans alike became Christians, they discovered there was no longer any barrier between them, that they were equal in Christ. Christianity therefore came to be looked on as a threat to the entire Roman social system and economy, and consequently false charges were repeatedly made against Christians. They were accused of cannibalism because they claimed to eat Christ's body and drink His blood during the Lord's Supper. They were accused of immorality in their love feasts and of promoting revolution by preaching about Christ's return to establish His earthly kingdom. Many were martyred.

Throughout church history, various governments have been involved in persecuting the church, sometimes for purely political reasons and sometimes as an enforcer of state-recognized religion. During modern times, communist governments alone have slaughtered millions of Christians and persecuted and imprisoned countless millions more. Because atheism is a central tenet of Communism, it has always sought to suppress and eliminate religion, especially Christianity.

In the end times persecution of the saints will reach its climax, both by religion and by government, and will apparently be wielded as one great powerful arm of the antichrist. The beast that will come "up out of the sea" will shout "blasphemies against God" and will "make war with the saints and to overcome them; and authority over every tribe and people and tongue and nation was given to him" (Rev. 13:1, 6-7).

Although government is established by God to preserve social order, it has also become an instrument of Satan to promote his own work and to oppose the Lord's. Government is ordained by God but manipulated by Satan; and Daniel, Isaiah, and Ezekiel all report demonic forces behind governments that were especially wicked. When its citizens turn away from the Lord and His standards, even the freest and most democratic of governments, including that of our own United States, will eventually inhibit the free expression and practice of the Christian faith in hostility to Christ and His Word.

THE PROVISION

But when they deliver you up, do not become anxious about how or what you will speak; for it shall be given you in that hour what you are to speak. For it is not you who speak, but it is the Spirit of your Father who speaks in you. (10:19-20)

To be maligned, persecuted, arrested, and beaten is traumatic, and while that is being experienced it is extremely difficult not to **become anxious.** When we are charged with a wrongdoing, the natural reaction is to **speak** out in our own defense, to convince our accusers of our innocence.

Paul admonishes us to be at all times "anxious for nothing, but in everything by prayer and supplication with thanksgiving let [our] requests be made known to God" (Phil. 4:6). But in the special circumstance of being brought before a religious or civil court we have the additional promise that **it shall be given** [us] **in that hour what** [we] **are to speak.** Those who suffer for Christ will be defended by Christ.

Many of the most memorable and powerful testimonies of the great martyrs were uttered just before they were put to death. God gave them a special presence of mind and clarity of thought to present a testimony more powerful than they would otherwise have been able to give.

For the apostles, that promise included the added provision of divine inspiration. When Paul, for example, gave testimony while he was on trial, he spoke the Word of God. **For it is not you who speak,** Jesus assured the apostles, **but it is the Spirit of your Father who speaks in you.**

The well-known commentator R. C. H. Lenski writes,

> Without previous thinking, planning, imagining, at the time of their trials in court, the Apostles will receive directly from God just what to utter. It will come into their minds just as it is needed, and thus they will utter it aloud. . . . The apostles, indeed, make utterance, and yet they do not, for their act is due to the Holy Spirit, so that most properly he is the one who does his uttering. Everything that is mechanical, magical, unpsychological is shut out. . . . The apostles will not be like the demoniacs, their organs of speech and their very wills being violated by a demon. Absolutely the contrary: mind, heart, will operate freely, consciously, in joyful, trustful dependence on the Spirit's giving, who enables them to find just what to say and how to say it down to the last word, with no mistake or even a wrong word due to faulty memory or disturbed emotions occurring. This, of course, is Inspiration, Verbal Inspiration. (*The Interpretation of St. Matthew's Gospel* [Minneapolis: Augsburg, 1964], p. 402)

THE HATRED

Persecution of believers is also expressed through the hatred of families who betray their own members and through the hatred of society in general.

BY FAMILY

And brother will deliver up brother to death, and a father his child; and children will rise up against parents, and cause them to be put to death. (10:21)

Believers are promised that they may even be persecuted by their own families. During this same time of instruction, Jesus said, "For I came to set a man against his father, and a daughter against her mother, and a daughter-in-law against her mother-in-law." Then, quoting Micah 7:6, He warned that "a man's enemies will be the members of his household" (Matt. 10:35-36). A year or so later, as He taught about the Tribulation, Jesus repeated the same warning (Mark 13:12).

During Roman persecutions of the second and third centuries an untold number of Christians were betrayed to civil authorities by a **brother** or **father** or **child**. That tragic practice has been repeated many times, and it is not unknown even in our own day.

In certain religious cultures a funeral service is held for a family member who becomes a Christian, because in the eyes of his relatives he is no longer alive. In some instances the converted member has been poisoned to death. Someone has observed that only two things are stronger than natural love; one is born of hell and one is born of heaven. Stronger than natural love are the love that is of God and the hatred that is of Satan.

Speaking of the end times, perhaps the kingdom age, Zechariah prophesied: "And it will come about that if anyone still prophesies, then his father and mother who gave birth to him will say to him, 'You shall not live, for you have spoken falsely in the name of the Lord,' and his father and mother who gave birth to him will pierce him through when he prophesies" (Zech. 13:3). It may be that one day believing parents will kill their children who are false prophets.

BY SOCIETY

And you will be hated by all on account of My name, but it is the one who has endured to the end who will be saved. (10:22)

All is obviously not an absolute term in this context. Believers will not be hated by every single unbeliever on earth. The idea is that of **all** people in general, society as a whole. As verified by the last two thousand years, believers find they are **hated by all** classes, races, and nationalities of mankind.

Some believers live lives of almost constant conflict with the world, while others seem to escape it entirely. Some Christians are not persecuted simply because their testimony is so weak it goes unnoticed by the world. When biblical doctrine and standards are compromised to accommodate fallen human nature, society has little argument with that kind of Christianity and will give little opposition to Christians.

But to confront the world as Paul did with the declaration that "the wrath of God is revealed from heaven against all ungodliness and unrighteousness of men, who suppress the truth in unrighteousness" (Rom. 1:18) is to guarantee society's wrath against the gospel and those who preach it.

Because they were so uncompromising in proclaiming the gospel, Paul declared himself and his fellow apostles to be "men condemned to death; because we have become a spectacle to the world, both to angels and to men. We are fools for Christ's sake, . . . weak, . . . without honor, . . . both hungry and thirsty, and are poorly clothed, and are roughly treated, and are homeless" (1 Cor. 4:9-11).

When a Roman general won a great victory, he would parade his captives through the streets in a grand triumphal procession, purposely making a spectacle of his conquered foes, especially of the military officers and the rulers. That is the sort of spectacle the ancient world figuratively made of the apostles.

In summary, false religion reacts against believers because it is generated by Satan. Government reacts against believers because it is under the control of the prince of the power of the air, the ruler of this world. Ungodly families and society react against believers because they cannot tolerate righteous people in their midst.

Endurance of persecution is the hallmark of genuine salvation: **It is the one who has endured to the end who will be saved.** Endurance does not produce or protect salvation, which is totally the work of God's grace. But endurance is *evidence* of salvation, proof that a person is truly redeemed and a child of God. God gives eternal life "to those who by perseverance in doing good seek for glory and honor and immortality," Paul says (Rom. 2:7). The writer of Hebrews expresses the same truth in these words: "For we have become partakers of Christ, if we hold fast the beginning of our assurance firm until the end" (3:14). We do not earn our salvation by endurance, but prove it. Continuance is a verification of being a real Christian. Theologians call this the perseverance of the saints. The following Scriptures also emphasize perseverance: Matthew 24:13; John 8:31; 1 Corinthians 15:1-2; Colossians 1:21-23; Hebrews 2:1-3; 4:14; 6:11-12; 10:39; 12:14; 2 Peter 1:10.

Persecution quickly burns away chaff in the church. Those who have made only a superficial profession of Christ have no new nature to motivate them to suffer for Christ and no divine power to enable them to endure it if they wanted to. Nothing is more spiritually purifying and strengthening than persecution (cf. James 1:12).

It is because God's Word assures us that absolutely nothing can separate us from Christ that we can count on such unshakable endurance. "Who shall separate us from the love of Christ?" Paul asks rhetorically. "Shall tribulation, or distress, or persecution, or famine, or nakedness, or peril, or sword?" He then answers his own question. "But in all these things we overwhelmingly conquer through Him who loved us. For I am convinced that neither death, nor life, nor angels, nor principalities, nor things present, nor things to come, nor powers, nor height, nor depth, nor any other created thing, shall be able to separate us from the love of God, which is in Christ Jesus our Lord" (Rom. 8:35, 37-39).

THE RESPONSE

But whenever they persecute you in this city, flee to the next; for truly I say to you, you shall not finish going through the cities of Israel, until the Son of Man comes. (10:23)

Persecution is never to be sought or endured for its own sake; nor should we intentionally bring it on ourselves, supposedly for Christ's sake. We have no right to provoke animosity or ridicule. And Christ here urges escaping persecution when doing so is expedient and possible. We are not obligated to stay in a place of opposition and danger until we are killed, or even imprisoned. **Whenever they persecute you in this city,** Jesus says, **flee to the next.**

That is the pattern Paul followed throughout his ministry (see Acts 12-14, 17). When persecution became so severe in one place that he could no longer minister effectively, he left and went to another. He was not afraid of persecution, and many times he was severely beaten before he left a city. At least once he was stoned and left for dead. But he did not try to test the limits of the opposition. He endured whatever ridicule, reviling, beatings, and imprisonment were necessary while he ministered. But he left a place when his effectiveness there ceased.

That is the pattern that every faithful minister and missionary is to follow **until the Son of Man comes.** Even during the Great Tribulation, Christ's faithful 144,000 Jewish people will preach all over the world and keep moving from place to place as they are persecuted and afflicted.

Despite their many misunderstandings, shortcomings, failures, and boastings, the disciples knew that Jesus was their only resource, that without Him they could do nothing (John 15:5). They hung close to Him and huddled around Him whenever there were problems or difficulties. He continually turned nature into one grand parable of God's sovereignty, power, and love. Every field, mountain, tree, flower, animal, leaf, and threshing floor became a picture of spiritual truth. He not only taught them, but He cared for them, loved them, and provided for them. When they finally realized He was actually going to leave them, they panicked.

The Lord would indeed send the twelve out among wolves into dangers they could never have imagined while they were with Him. But just as He promised to send them out among wolves, He also promised to send His own Spirit to indwell, empower, and encourage them. If the world persecuted the Master, it would certainly persecute His servants (John 15:20), and a time would soon come when those who killed His followers would actually think they were "offering service to God" (16:2). It was therefore both advantageous and necessary that Jesus go away, in order that the Holy Spirit, the divine Helper and Comforter, could come to them (v. 7). "These things I have spoken to you," Jesus told them, "that in Me you may have peace. In the world you have tribulation, but take courage; I have overcome the world" (v. 33).

BIRDVILLE
BAPTIST CHURCH
LIBRARY

The Hallmarks of Discipleship—part 1
(10:24-31)

20

A disciple is not above his teacher, nor a slave above his master. It is enough for the disciple that he become as his teacher, and the slave as his master. If they have called the head of the house Beelzebul, how much more the members of his household! Therefore do not fear them, for there is nothing covered that will not be revealed, and hidden that will not be known. What I tell you in the darkness, speak in the light; and what you hear whispered in your ear, proclaim upon the housetops. And do not fear those who kill the body, but are unable to kill the soul; but rather fear Him who is able to destroy both soul and body in hell. Are not two sparrows sold for a cent? And yet not one of them will fall to the ground apart from your Father. But the very hairs of your head are all numbered. Therefore do not fear; you are of more value than many sparrows. (10:24-31)

Jesus' most crucial and definitive teaching about discipleship, setting forth its true nature and its real demands, is presented in the remainder of this chapter. The call of the Great Commission is the call to "make disciples of all the nations" (Matt. 28:19). Disciple-making is the central work of the people of Christ's church, the work of bringing men and women to a saving relationship to Jesus Christ and of helping them grow in His knowledge and likeness. It is what Paul calls "the equipping of the saints for the work of service, to the building up of the body of Christ" (Eph. 4:12).

When Jesus called the twelve to Himself, He carefully instructed them about what they would be expected to do and to endure. In so doing, He excluded the half-hearted people who wanted the benefits of the kingdom but not its commitments. He elected to Himself only those who were willing to enter the narrow gate and walk the narrow road.

In Matthew 10:24-42 Jesus sets forth the essence of this Christian dedication and consecration. The truths He teaches here were obviously of great importance to Him, because He repeated them frequently throughout His ministry. Like every effective teacher, He understood the importance of emphasizing and reemphasizing basic truths. Each area of study has a core of information that is absolutely founda-tional, and the good teacher continually goes back to that information and reinforces it.

As an aside, it should be noted that redaction criticism fails largely at that very point. Because certain biblical analysts do not recognize the validity and importance of repetitive teaching, they assume that the gospel writers pulled together various sayings of Jesus and arbitrarily decided to insert them at different places in His ministry. They maintain that we therefore cannot be sure of what Jesus actually spoke on any given occasion. But to accept the redaction critic's view is to reject the integrity of the gospel writers and therefore of Scripture itself.

Like every good teacher, Jesus taught the same truths with many formats, in various circumstances and with various applications. The Lord is here providing the twelve apostles with the body of His basic teaching on discipleship. Using a variety of phrases and illustrations throughout His ministry, He would repeat these truths over and over again to the disciples and to the multitudes.

Because the truths of Matthew 10 are so foundational and so profound, believers who have wholeheartedly lived out these truths are the men and women who have made great marks on the world for Jesus Christ. They are the ones with total dedication, total commitment, and total obedience.

Florence Nightingale wrote in her diary: "I am thirty years of age, the age at which Christ began His mission. Now, no more childish things, no more vain things." Years later, near the end of her heroic life of service, she was asked the secret of her ability to accomplish so much for the Lord. She replied, "I can give only one explanation, and that is this: I have kept nothing back from God." That is exactly what Jesus is talking about in this passage—keeping nothing back from Him.

When the famous surgeon Howard A. Kelly graduated from medical school he wrote in his diary: "Today I dedicate myself, my time, my capabilities, my ambition, everything to Him. Blessed Lord, sanctify me to Thy uses; give me no worldly success which may not lead me nearer to my Saviour."

Soon after graduating from college, Jim Elliot wrote in his diary: "God, I pray Thee, light these idle sticks of my life that I may burn for Thee. Consume my life, my God, for it is Thine. I seek not a long life but a full one like You, Lord Jesus." God answered that prayer, and in the flower of young manhood Jim Elliot's life was cut short by the spear of an Auca Indian as he and several other young men sought to take the gospel deep into the jungles of Ecuador.

Jonathan Edwards, the great preacher and theologian whom God used to bring revival to colonial America, wrote:

> I claim no right to myself, no right to this understanding, this will, these affections that are in me. Neither do I have any right to this body or its members, no right to this tongue, to these hands, feet, ears or eyes. I have given myself clear away and not retained anything of my own. I have been to God this morning and told Him I have given myself wholly to Him, I have given every power so that for the future I claim no right to myself in any respect. I have expressly promised Him, for by His grace I will not fail. I take Him as my whole portion and felicity, looking upon nothing else as any part of my happiness. His law is the constant rule of my obedience. I will fight with all my might against the world, the flesh and the devil to the end of my life. I will adhere to the faith of the gospel however hazardous and difficult the profession and practice of it may be. I pray God for the sake of others to look on this as self-dedication. Henceforth, I am not to act in any respect as my own. I shall act as my own if I ever make use of any of my powers to do anything that is not to the glory of God or to fail to make the glorifying of Him my whole and entire business. If I murmur in the least at affliction, if I am in any way uncharitable, if I revenge my own case, if I do anything purely to please myself or omit anything because it is a great denial, if I trust myself, if I take any praise for any good which Christ does by me, or if I am in any way proud, I shall act as my own and not God's. But I purpose to be absolutely His.

The instruction of Matthew 10 was first of all to the twelve, not only because they were the only ones present with Jesus on this occasion but also because some of the instruction (preaching only to Israel, v. 6) was temporary and because some of it involved use of powers (healing, raising the dead, and casting out demons, v. 8) that were delegated only to them. Much of the teaching, however, applies to every disciple of Jesus Christ in every age. In verse 24 Jesus begins using the indefinite third person ("a disciple," "a slave," "everyone," "whoever") in addition to the second person "you"—clearly indicating that He is speaking about every believer, every true disciple. Jesus here teaches with the widest possible perspective. "For every person who would be My disciple," He says, in effect, "here is what I ask. For all who follow Me, this is the cost of discipleship."

Because Jesus refused to disguise or minimize the cost of discipleship, many would-be disciples left Him. When He made clear that to participate in the kingdom and to follow Him demanded complete identification with Him—pictured by the eating of His flesh and the drinking of His blood—"many of His disciples withdrew, and were not walking with Him anymore" (John 6:53-66). When "a certain scribe came and said to Him, 'Teacher, I will follow You wherever You go,'" and Jesus replied, "The foxes have holes, and the birds of the air have nests; but the Son of Man has nowhere to lay His head," that scribe disappeared (Matt. 8:19-20). When Jesus called two other men to follow Him, one gave the excuse of having to bury his father, meaning he wanted to wait until his father died in order to receive the inheritance. The other man wanted "to say good-bye to those at home," meaning he wanted to take care of all his family responsibilities before following Jesus. To both of them Jesus said, "No one, after putting his hand to the plow and looking back, is fit for the kingdom of God" (Luke 9:59-62). The kingdom is entered and served on God's terms, not man's.

Jesus' instructions in Matthew 10:5-15 led to His warning of the dangers of discipleship (vv. 16-23), which led to His teaching about the characteristics and benefits of discipleship (vv. 24-42). He first gave instruction on how to minister and then described the reaction of the world to faithful ministry. Finally, He presented the characteristics of the faithful disciple, gave additional warnings about the cost of discipleship, and mentioned provisions God promises to make for His true disciples.

Jesus' teaching and the gospel writers' presentation of it are always logical and clear. Only the person who doubts either the intelligence or the integrity of Jesus and those writers can miss the purpose and progression of His instruction when it is carefully studied. Jesus was not teaching only for scholars, and the writers were not writing only for scholars. They were teaching and writing for the common man, and their purpose was not to obscure and complicate the message but to make it clear enough for the simplest believer to grasp. Only the blindness of willing unbelief can prevent a person's understanding the way of salvation and the path of obedience.

In the remainder of the chapter (10:24-42) Jesus identifies a comprehensive definition of discipleship, in which He lists some six hallmarks. The true disciple of Jesus Christ emulates His Master; he fears God rather than the world; he confesses the Lord; he forsakes family; he follows his call; and he receives a reward.

A Disciple Emulates His Master

A disciple is not above his teacher, nor a slave above his master. It is enough for the disciple that he become as his teacher, and the slave as his master. If they have called the head of the house Beelzebul, how much more the members of his household! (10:24-25)

Jesus first presents the negative aspect of the truth (v. 24), then the positive (v. 25a), and then the consequence (v. 25b).

First, it is axiomatic that **a disciple is not above his teacher, nor a slave above his master.** By definition, **a disciple** (learner) is beneath **his teacher** in knowledge and wisdom and **a slave** is beneath **his master** in social and economic standing. Also by definition, a disciple who is genuinely a disciple learns from his teacher, and a slave who genuinely is a slave obeys his master.

Man's volition is represented by the figure of disciple and teacher, and God's sovereignty is represented by that of slave and master. The two illustrations unite to emphasize that the first and most obvious principle of discipleship is submission.

From the beginning to the end of his gospel, Matthew's purpose is to reveal Jesus as the divine King of kings, the Messiah and Son of God who came to redeem and to eventually rule the world. He is the only King, the only Messiah, the only Son of God, the only Savior and Lord. In all of those roles He demands and is deserving of total submission.

After David finally became king of Israel, there was still scattered loyalty to the family of Saul, despite that king's poor showing as a ruler. Abner, the commander of Saul's army, refused to recognize David as king and managed to temporarily establish Ish-bosheth, Saul's son, as ruler over part of the kingdom for a period of two years. But when Ish-bosheth made a foolish and ill-founded accusation against Abner, the commander came to his senses, finally realizing how unqualified Ish-bosheth was to rule and how foolish his own thinking had been in opposing David, God's chosen and anointed man for leadership (see 2 Sam. 2:8-3:21).

Matthew calls the Abners of the world, as it were, to abandon their foolish allegiances to false leaders and false gods and to become subjects of Jesus Christ, God's anointed Savior and Lord.

Second, as Jesus goes on to point out, it is also axiomatic that the purpose of a true disciple is to learn from his teacher in order to **become as his teacher** and that the purpose of a faithful **slave** is to serve and become **as his master.** When teaching the same truth on another occasion, Jesus said, "Everyone, after he has been fully trained, will be like his teacher" (Luke 6:40). A disciple's single, overriding purpose is to emulate his **teacher. It is enough** for him to **become as his teacher,** not only in the teacher's wisdom and character but also in the teacher's treatment. The disciple desires nothing more and settles for nothing less.

"The one who says he abides in [Christ]," John informs us, "ought himself to walk in the same manner as He walked" (1 John 2:6). The function of discipleship is clearly stated in the Great Commission: "to observe all that I commanded you" (Matt. 28:20). A disciple becomes like his Christ, his Teacher, when he learns and obeys Scripture. He is one in whom the Word of Christ richly dwells (Col. 3:16). To grow in discipleship is to grow in Christlikeness, looking forward to the day when "we shall be like Him, because we shall see Him just as He is" (1 John 3:2).

The logical result of being like Christ is being treated like Christ. **If they have called the head of the house Beelzebul, how much more the members of his household.** Jesus continues to develop the same truth but changes the figure from those of disciple/teacher and slave/master to that of **head of the house/members of his household.** Family **members** and servants should not expect to be treated better than **the head** of the family is treated.

Paul knew that to truly know Christ and the power of His resurrection involves "the fellowship of His sufferings, being conformed to His death," and that apostle desired all of those things, knowing they are inseparable (Phil. 3:10). The true disciple does not demand to be accepted and loved by the world, when His Lord was rejected and crucified by the world. He does not expect his commitment to the Lord to cause him to become famous and respected, when His Lord was considered infamous and was despised.

Beelzebul (sometimes found as "Beelzebub" or "Baalzebub") was originally the name of a pagan Canaanite deity. The name *Baalzebub* probably meant "lord of the flies," and it was later changed to Baalzebul, "lord of the dwelling." Because he was an especially despicable deity, his name had long been used by Jews as an epithet for Satan.

Jesus' point was that, if people called Him Satan, they would surely call His disciples the same thing. The Pharisees had already done precisely that when they accused Jesus of casting "out the demons by the ruler of the demons" (Matt. 9:34), who was often referred to as **Beelzebul** (Mark 3:22; cf. Matt. 12:24).

Jesus repeated this general warning to the disciples many times. As noted earlier, in one of His last discourses He told them, "If the world hates you, you know that it has hated Me before it hated you. If you were of the world, the world would love its own; but because you are not of the world, but I chose you out of the world, therefore the world hates you" (John 15:18-19; cf. v. 20; 13:16). The day would come when the one who persecuted the disciples would actually "think that he is offering service to God" (16:2). But in reality, those who oppose and persecute Jesus' disciples do so "because they have not known the Father" or the Lord Jesus Christ (v. 3). As Jesus had already explained, His disciples are not hated because of who they are in themselves but "on account of My name" (Matt. 10:22).

Thus the call to discipleship is the call to be like Christ, including being treated like Christ. To people who are truly seeking God, the lives of His faithful saints are beautiful and attractive. It is often the Christlike qualities of love, joy, peace, and kindness in Christians that attract unbelievers to the Lord. The more we emulate Christ, the more attractive we will become to those God is calling to Himself. But at the same time we will become more unattractive to those who reject God. Because they want nothing of Him, they will want nothing of us.

A DISCIPLE DOES NOT FEAR THE WORLD

Therefore do not fear them, for there is nothing covered that will not be revealed, and hidden that will not be known. What I tell you in the darkness, speak in the light; and what you hear whispered in your ear, proclaim upon the housetops. And do not fear those who kill the body, but are unable to kill the soul; but rather fear Him who is able to destroy both soul and body in hell. Are not two sparrows sold for a cent? And yet not one of them will fall to the ground apart from your Father. But the very hairs of your head are all numbered. Therefore do not fear; you are of more value than many sparrows. (10:26-31)

The true disciple of Jesus Christ not only emulates his Master but is also not afraid of the world. Three times in these six verses Jesus says, **do not fear**. In light of what He had just promised, His exhortation not to be afraid was in order. He had told the disciples He was sending them out as sheep in the midst of wolves, that they would be tried and scourged in Jewish courts, "brought before governors and kings" for His sake, delivered up in various ways, betrayed by their families, hated and persecuted by the world in general, and called satanic (vv. 16-25).

We are warned in Proverbs that "the fear of man brings a snare" (29:25). Fear of what people may think, say, or do has strangled many testimonies and hindered much service in the Lord's name. Human nature wants to avoid problems and conflicts, especially if they might bring ridicule and hardship. People do not naturally want to be thought little of or mistreated, and even less to suffer or die. Christians who have fallen prey to today's great emphasis on self-preservation find it especially difficult to confront sinful society with the demands and standards of the gospel. Our culture has produced an unacceptable "softness" among evangelicals.

Continued refusal to confront the world gives strong evidence that a professed believer may not belong to Christ at all. "If anyone loves the world, the love of the Father is not in him," John says. "For all that is in the world, the lust of the flesh and the lust of the eyes and the boastful pride of life, is not from the Father, but is from the world" (1 John 2:15-16).

But every believer, like Peter warming himself in the courtyard while Jesus was on trial, at times finds it difficult to speak out for the Lord for fear of being considered foolish, backward, extremist, unsophisticated, obtrusive, or strange.

Because criticism, abuse, and danger would become frequent companions of the apostles, Jesus repeatedly exhorted them not to be afraid (see, e. g., Matt. 14:27; 28:10; Luke 12:32; John 14:27). At this time Jesus gave three reasons for His followers not to be afraid: their vindication by God, their veneration of God, and their valuation by God.

VINDICATION BY GOD

Therefore do not fear them, for there is nothing covered that will not be revealed, and hidden that will not be known. What I tell you in the darkness, speak in the light; and what you hear whispered in your ear, proclaim upon the housetops. (10:26-27)

First, believers should never be afraid of the world because they know God will one day vindicate them. **Therefore** looks back to what Jesus had said in verse 25. Although God's children will be mistreated and accused of being wicked and even demonic, Jesus says, **do not fear them,** that is, those who cause you trouble. **For** looks forward, introducing the promise that in the end God will make everything right. All truth and goodness and all falsehood and wickedness will be seen for what they really are.

The world is highly successful at illusion and deception. It can make an impressive and convincing case for sin by covering it over with seemingly good motives and helpful benefits. The world puts the best face on wickedness and the worst face on righteousness. But the Lord has decreed that **there is nothing covered**

that will not be revealed, and hidden that will not be known. The world's wickedness will be shown for what it is, and believers' righteousness will be shown for what it is. God has bound Himself to vindicate His children.

We should not be concerned about what the world says now but about what God will say at the final day. When the Lord returns, He "will both bring to light the things hidden in the darkness and disclose the motives of men's hearts; and then each man's praise will come to him from God" (1 Cor. 4:5). What greater motive could we have for faithfully serving the Lord and fearlessly facing the world? Why should we worry about unpopularity in this life when we know we will be fully vindicated in the next? Paul calls this great coming event "the revealing of the sons of God" (Rom. 8:19) and "the freedom of the glory of the sons of God" (8:21; cf. 1 Tim. 5:24-25).

"Now no one after lighting a lamp covers it over with a container, or puts it under a bed," Jesus said; "but he puts it on a lampstand, in order that those who come in may see the light" (Luke 8:16). When God gives truth to declare, the business of Christians is to make it known, not to hide it—just as one day God Himself will instantly and perfectly make every truth known. In view of what is coming, it is both faithless and shortsighted to hide the light now in order to avoid criticism and persecution.

With mock encouragement Solomon wrote, "Rejoice, young man, during your childhood, and let your heart be pleasant during the days of young manhood. And follow the impulses of your heart and the desires of your eyes." He then added, "Yet know that God will bring you to judgment for all these things" (Eccles. 11:9). "The conclusion, when all has been heard, is: fear God and keep His commandments, because this applies to every person" (12:13).

The disciple's perspective should be God's perspective. In His eternal view He already sees the final outcome of every life. Those in the world's eyes who now look like winners will turn out to be losers, and those who seem to be losers will be winners.

There are to be no secrets in Christianity. What the Lord has, in effect, revealed to us **in the darkness** we are to **speak in the light**; and what has been **whispered in** [our] **ear** we are to **proclaim upon the housetops.**

Fraternal orders and lodges that have secret rites and ceremonies have no part in the work of Christ's kingdom, no matter how much they may try to defend their religious purposes and standards. All spiritual and moral truth that man needs to know and can know, God has already fully made known; and His desire is for that truth to be proclaimed, not hidden. Christians are not elite defenders of man-made secrets but bold proclaimers of God-given truth. Secrecy has no part in the gospel.

As His followers study, meditate, and pray over God's Word in solitude and in the company of fellow believers, God opens up His truth to their hearts and minds. But what is learned in those places of figurative **darkness,** hidden from the world, the child of God is then to **speak in the light** of open proclamation. What we figuratively **hear whispered in** [our] **ear** we are then to **proclaim upon the housetops.**

During New Testament times Jewish rabbis would often train their students to speak by standing beside them and whispering in their ears. What the student heard whispered he would then speak aloud. What the Lord has, in effect, whispered in our ears through His Word we are to speak aloud to the world, holding nothing back. What the Lord has made known to us, we are to make known to others.

In Jesus' day a person shouting from **housetops** could be heard for a great distance. Both official and personal announcements were often publicized by that means. The objective of shouting from the housetop was to be heard by as many people as possible. The Talmud tells of rabbis blowing trumpets from housetops to announce the beginning of religious holidays. A modern remnant of that practice is the announcement of Muslim prayer times from high in a minaret.

Making God's truth known includes teaching the so-called hard sayings of Scripture. We are not to be needlessly offensive, and never offensive in our approach or attitude. But when the fullness of God's revelation is taught, the world will invariably be offended, because it will stand accused. Fallen man does not like to hear that he is fallen; sinful man does not like to face the reality that he is sinful; rebellious man does not like to be told that he is God's enemy. Those are truths that Jesus and the apostles never refused to proclaim, and it was because they boldly taught such truths that the world rejected and persecuted them.

The world shows little objection to a gospel that is only "positive," that only mentions God's offers of peace, joy, and blessing. An unbeliever is not offended by those elements of the gospel, true as they are. But he is terribly offended when he is told that he is a sinner under God's judgment and destined for hell.

John 3:16-17 is often only partially preached and taught. That God loves the world, sent His Son to save the world rather than judge the world, and saves everyone who believes in the Son is not the total truth of the passage. Implicit in verse 16 and explicit in verse 18 is the truth that apart from such faith a person will perish, because "he who does not believe has been judged already, because he has not believed in the ¬ame of the only begotten Son of God."

VENERATION OF GOD

And do not fear those who kill the body, but are unable to kill the soul; but rather fear Him who is able to destroy both soul and body in hell. (10:28)

The second **do not fear** has to do with **those who kill the body.** The harm they do is only temporary. We should instead **fear Him who is able to destroy both soul and body in hell. Fear** is used here in two senses. The first has to do with fright and terror, while the second has to do with awe and veneration.

There may be a price to pay for speaking God's truth in the light and proclaiming it from the housetops. As Paul determined to go to Jerusalem despite many warnings from his friends, "a certain prophet named Agabus came down from Judea. And coming to us," Luke reports, "he took Paul's belt and bound his own feet and hands, and said, 'This is what the Holy Spirit says: "In this way the Jews at Jerusalem will bind the man who owns this belt and deliver him into the hands of the Gentiles"'" (Acts 21:10-11). When his friends began crying at the news, Paul said,

"What are you doing, weeping and breaking my heart? For I am ready not only to be bound, but even to die at Jerusalem for the name of the Lord Jesus" (v. 13). Paul had no fear of those who could only **kill the body.** He had already said, "Neither count I my life dear unto myself" (Acts 20:24, KJV).

Such people, however, and even Satan himself, **are unable to kill the soul.** Physical death is the full extent of the harm they can bring us; they cannot touch the **soul,** the eternal person. Even the bodies they destroy will one day be resurrected and become imperishable (1 Cor. 15:42).

It should be made clear that **destroy** does not here mean annihilation. The lost will not cease to exist, but in their resurrected bodies "will go away into eternal punishment," just as the saved in their resurrected bodies will go into "eternal life" (Matt. 25:46). The word behind **destroy** (*appolumi*) does not convey the notion of extinction but of great loss or ruin. Paul uses the same term in 2 Thessalonians 1:9, where he speaks of "eternal destruction"—a phrase that would not make sense if "destruction" meant annihilation, which by definition cannot be eternal. That which is annihilated ceases to exist.

Jesus' point here is that the only **fear** a believer should have is of **Him who is able to destroy both soul and body in hell;** and only God can do that. In the last days Satan himself will be cast into hell, which is the Lord's domain, not Satan's.

But this **fear** is not that of terror or fright, but of reverential awe and honor. It is not that a believer is in danger of having his soul and body cast into hell, because his eternal destiny is heaven. God's ability to **destroy both soul and body in hell** is mentioned here only to contrast His unlimited and permanent power with Satan's limited and temporary power. God is the only One who can determine and bring to pass the destiny of souls and bodies.

Reverence of God in His sovereign majesty is a powerful motivation for Christians to serve Him and to be fearless of any earthly, physical consequences that service may bring. The power of human threats seems rather puny in comparison to the power of God's promises.

When Hugh Latimer was preaching one day in the presence of King Henry VIII, he reports that he said to himself, "Latimer! Latimer! Remember that the king is here; be careful what you say." Then he said to himself, "Latimer! Latimer! Remember that the King of kings is here; be careful what you do not say." For such unflinching faithfulness Latimer was eventually burned at the stake. But He feared failing God more than he feared offending men.

Over a period of some 300 years of terrible persecution, ten generations of Christians dug nearly 600 miles of catacombs beneath and around the city of Rome. Archaeologists estimate that perhaps a total of 4 million bodies were buried there. A common inscription found in the catacombs is the sign of the fish, the Greek word for which (*ichthus*) was used as an acrostic for "Jesus Christ, God's Son, Savior." Another common inscription found there is "The Word of God is not bound." During the most prolonged period of persecution in the history of the church, those believers revered God more than they feared man.

Since that day, many more millions have given their lives for the cause of Christ. Perhaps as many as 50 million believers were martyred during the Dark Ages, and millions more have been martyred in our own century, largely by communist regimes in Europe, Asia, and Africa. As is said of Lord Lawrence on his memorial in Westminster Abbey, they feared man so little because they feared God so much. In many other countries, state religions prohibit Christian missionary and evangelistic work and seriously restrict worship by those who are already Christians.

The faithful disciple values his **soul** immeasurably more than he values his **body,** and he will gladly sacrifice that which is only physical and corruptible for the sake of that which is spiritual and incorruptible. Jim Elliot, mentioned earlier in the chapter, wrote, "He is no fool who gives up what he cannot keep to gain what he cannot lose."

Jesus' warning in verse 28 may have been specially directed at Judas, as an early appeal for him to consider that the God he rejected was **able to destroy both** his **soul and** his **body in hell.** Beyond that, it stands as a continuing warning to the unbelieving Judases of all time.

VALUATION BY GOD

Are not two sparrows sold for a cent? And yet not one of them will fall to the ground apart from your Father. But the very hairs of your head are all numbered. Therefore do not fear; you are of more value than many sparrows. (10:29-31)

Jesus assures the twelve, and every person who would ever trust in Him, that they are dear to their heavenly Father. With divine intimacy and intensity the Lord loves and cherishes those who belong to Him, and He will not allow any permanent harm come to them.

An *assarion* (**cent**) was the smallest coin in circulation in Jesus' day and was worth one-sixteenth of a denarius, the average daily wage for a laborer. One such **cent** would buy **two sparrows,** which were as common and relatively valueless in New Testament times as they are today. Roasted **sparrows** were often served as cheap finger food, as a type of appetizer or hors d'oeuvre.

Yet not one sparrow **will fall to the ground apart from your Father,** Jesus says. This most insignificant of little birds cannot even fall without God's knowledge. In some Greek usages, the word for **fall** is translated as "hop"—in which case a little sparrow cannot even hop on the ground without God's knowledge!

God's knowledge of us is so detailed and His interest in us is so keen that **the very hairs of** [our] **head are all numbered.** The average hair count on the human head is said to be about 140,000, which means that some people have many more hairs even than that. God, who has all knowledge of every person, illustrates that omniscience by this mundane and spiritually inconsequential bit of information pertaining to the number of **hairs** on a person's **head**. If He takes notice of such things as that, how much more is He concerned about spiritual matters of far greater consequence?

Jesus then gives a third exhortation to **not fear** (cf. vv. 26, 28) and another reason *why* we should not fear: we **are of more value than many sparrows.** The obvious understatement illustrates how very dear God's children are to Him. In a similar promise Jesus said, "If God so arrays the grass of the field, which is alive today and tomorrow is thrown into the furnace, will He not much more do so for you, O men of little faith?" (Matt. 6:30). How can we be anxious and fearful, knowing of such care and protection by our heavenly Father?

From among the finest athletes in the Roman Empire, Nero selected a group called The Emperor's Wrestlers. Their motto was: "We, the wrestlers, wrestling for thee, O Emperor, to win for thee the victory and from thee, the victor's crown." The wrestlers were also soldiers and were often sent out on special military campaigns. On a certain mission in Gaul (modern France), many of the wrestlers were converted to Christ. Upon hearing the news, Nero ordered the commander, Vespasian, to execute any wrestler who refused to renounce Christ and swear religious as well as military allegiance to the emperor. The emperor's orders were received in the dead of winter, as the men were encamped on the shore of a frozen lake. When Vespasian assembled the soldiers and asked how many were Christians, forty men stepped forward. Hoping not to lose any of these fine men, many of whom were his friends, he gave them until sundown the next day to reconsider. But at the given hour, all of them still refused to renounce Christ. In order that they not die at the hands of their comrades, the commander ordered the forty men to disrobe and walk naked out onto the ice. Throughout the night the soldiers on shore could hear the forty sentenced men singing triumphantly, "Forty wrestlers, wrestling for Thee, O Christ, to win for Thee the victory, and from Thee, the victor's crown." The singing grew fainter as morning neared, and at dawn a lone figure walked back and approached the fire. He confessed that his faith was not strong enough to face death. When Vespasian then heard the faint strains of "Thirty-nine wrestlers, wrestling for Thee, O Christ," he was so moved that he threw off his armor and clothes and marched out to join the others, shouting as he went, "*Forty* wrestlers, wrestling for Thee, O Christ, to win for Thee the victory, and from Thee, the victor's crown."

The Hallmarks of Discipleship—part 2
(10:32-42)

21

Everyone therefore who shall confess Me before men, I will also confess him before My Father who is in heaven. But whoever shall deny Me before men, I will also deny him before My Father who is in heaven.

Do not think that I came to bring peace on the earth; I did not come to bring peace, but a sword. For I came to set a man against his father, and a daughter against her mother, and a daughter-in-law against her mother-in-law; and a man's enemies will be the members of his household. He who loves father or mother more than Me is not worthy of Me; and he who loves son or daughter more than Me is not worthy of Me. And he who does not take his cross and follow after Me is not worthy of Me. He who has found his life shall lose it, and he who has lost his life for My sake shall find it.

He who receives you receives Me, and he who receives Me receives Him who sent Me. He who receives a prophet in the name of a prophet shall receive a prophet's reward; and he who receives a righteous man in the name of a righteous man shall receive a righteous man's reward. And whoever in the name of a disciple gives to one of these little ones even a cup of cold water to drink, truly I say to you he shall not lose his reward. (10:32-42)

After Henry Martyn spent virtually a lifetime of ministry in India, he announced that God had laid a burden on his heart to go to Persia (modern Iran) and translate the New Testament and Psalms into the Persian language. Doctors had already told him that he would die because of the heat if he stayed in India. He went to Persia, studied the language, and eventually finished the translation work in 1812. He then learned, however, that he could not print and distribute the Scriptures without the shah's permission. He traveled 600 miles to Teheran but was denied permission to see the shah. He took another 400-mile trip to visit the British ambassador, who gave him proper papers of introduction. Riding a mule at night and resting during the heat of the day, he came back to Teheran and managed to obtain the needed permission. Ten days later he died. Shortly before his death he had written in his diary, "I sat and thought with sweet comfort and peace of my God. In solitude my Companion, my Friend, and Comforter."

Bound up in the spirit of Henry Martyn was the key to genuine discipleship: being so utterly consumed with the cause of Christ that you take no thought for your own life or welfare.

A Disciple Confesses the Lord

Everyone therefore who shall confess Me before men, I will also confess him before My Father who is in heaven. But whoever shall deny Me before men, I will also deny him before My Father who is in heaven. (10:32-33)

In addition to emulating his Lord and not fearing the world (see chap. 20, on Matt. 10:24-31), a true disciple openly confesses Christ before the world.

In his book *I Love Idi Amin* ([Westwood, N.J.: Revell, 1977], p. 112) Festo Kivengere, a leading evangelical minister in Uganda, tells the history of persecution and martyrdom of Christians in that country. In 1885 three Christian boys, ranging in age from eleven to fifteen, were forced to give their lives for Christ because they would not renounce their faith in Him. The king was adamantly opposed to Christianity and ordered the boys' execution if they did not recant. At the place of execution the boys asked that the following message be given to the king: "Tell his majesty that he has put our bodies in the fire but we won't be long in the fire. Soon we will be with Jesus, which is much better. But ask him to repent and change his mind or he will land in a place of eternal fire." As they stood bound and awaiting death they sang a song that soon became greatly loved by Christians in that country as "The Martyrs' Song." One verse testifies,

O that I had wings like the angels,
I would fly away and be with Jesus.

The youngest of the boys, named Yusufu, said, "Please don't cut off my arms. I will not struggle in the fire that takes me to Jesus." Because of the boys' testimony that day, forty adults trusted in Jesus Christ for salvation, and indirectly countless more converts were won to the Lord over a period of many years. By 1887 a large number of other Christians were martyred, many of them inspired by the fearless, loving testimony of those three boys. None of those martyrs knew much theology or much about the Bible, because most of them were illiterate and all of them were relatively new believers. But they had a deep love for Jesus that they refused to hide, no matter what the cost. As is nearly always the case, those who died were replaced severalfold by new converts who came to Christ because of their testimony.

Everyone is an inclusive term that gives a sober warning to all would-be and all professing believers for careful self-examination. A person's willingness to **confess** Christ before men determines Christ's willingness to claim that person before His Father. Paul eagerly confessed, "For I am not ashamed of the gospel, for it is the power of God for salvation to everyone who believes" (Rom. 1:16). He was not ashamed to acknowledge the person and work of Christ because His is the only message that offers salvation and hope to a corrupt and dying world.

Throughout the history of the church, believers who have been unashamed to **confess** Jesus **before men** are those the Lord uses to bring others to Himself. Whether it is through preaching, teaching, personal witnessing, or the courage of martyrdom, those who **confess** Him boldly and unapologetically before the world not only are the Lord's most faithful disciples but also His most effective disciple makers.

Confess means to affirm and agree with. It is not simply to recognize a truth but to identify with it. Even the demons, for example, recognize that God is one (James 2:19), but they by no means confess God, because they are His implacable enemies. We do not **confess** Christ simply by acknowledging that He is Lord and Savior but by acknowledging and receiving Him as *our* Lord and Savior. "If you confess with your mouth Jesus as Lord," Paul says, "and believe in your heart that God raised Him from the dead, you shall be saved; for with the heart man believes, resulting in righteousness, and with the mouth he confesses, resulting in salvation" (Rom. 10:9-10). Outward confession with the mouth is a reflection of genuine belief in the heart.

Men, like **everyone**, is universal. A true disciple is willing to openly identify with Christ wherever he is, whether before a fellowship of other believers, a group of serious inquirers, or a hostile crowd of unbelievers. "Whoever confesses that Jesus is the Son of God, God abides in him, and he in God" (1 John 4:15). To the faithful church at Pergamum, the Lord said, "I know where you dwell, where Satan's throne is; and you hold fast My name, and did not deny My faith, even in the days of Antipas, My witness, My faithful one, who was killed among you, where Satan dwells" (Rev. 2:13).

Near the end of his life Paul wrote to his beloved Timothy, "For I am already being poured out as a drink offering, and the time of my departure has come. I have fought the good fight, I have finished the course, I have kept the faith" (2 Tim. 4:6-7). But a few verses later he spoke of Demas, who "loved this present world, [and] has deserted me and gone to Thessalonica" (v. 10). Demas had been a faithful helper of Paul's, but when persecution became severe, he held the things of the world too dear to give them up (cf. Matt. 13:22). Hard times are the test of faith. The church does not lack for supporters when it is popular and respected; but when the world turns against it, its fair-weather friends are not to be found.

Believers can be silenced by much less than persecution. Simple embarrassment or friendly ridicule has closed many Christian mouths. It is sometimes easier to stand up to vicious physical injury by a hostile government than to stand up to unbelieving family and friends who would never do us physical harm.

Every believer has lapses of faithfulness, which is why the Lord's promise of 1 John 1:9 is so dear: "If we confess our sins, He is faithful and righteous to forgive us our sins and to cleanse us from all unrighteousness." Peter denied the Lord, but he could not live with his denial and he went out and wept bitterly. His heart was broken because he had so terribly failed and grieved His Lord. Timothy was Paul's most promising protegé, yet years after he had himself become a leader in the church, Timothy apparently had become reticent about openly proclaiming the gospel. Paul therefore admonished him, "Do not be ashamed of the testimony of our Lord" (2 Tim. 1:8).

Peter and Timothy had lapses of faithfulness, but feeling shame of the gospel and of the Lord was not their normal attitude. Those whose lives are characterized by confessing Christ, in name and in obedience, are those whom Jesus **will also confess . . . before** [His] **Father who is in heaven.** What an incredibly wonderful thought, to know that all Christians will stand before the **Father . . . in heaven** and hear Jesus tell Him that they are His, that He claims them because they have claimed Him!

When Pliny was governor of the province of Bithynia, in northern Asia Minor, he wrote a letter to the emperor Trajan trying to explain why he had been unsuccessful in stamping out the sect called Christians. He had tried arrest, fines, imprisonment, beatings, torture, and various forms of execution in order to get them to renounce Christ and to burn incense to Caesar as an act of worship, but to no avail. In trying to excuse himself before the emperor, he said, "None of these acts, those who are really Christians can be compelled to do." Even a pagan ruler knew that a person with such unflinching conviction must be a true believer.

The negative side of Jesus' warning is sobering: **But whoever shall deny Me before men, I will also deny him before My Father who is in heaven.** This warning applies to a person who makes an outward profession of Christianity but turns away when hard testing comes.

It is possible to **deny** Christ **before men** by silence, by failing to witness for Him and trying to be an unnoticed Christian—whose friends and neighbors, and perhaps even family, would never suspect of being a believer. It is also possible to deny Christ by actions, living like the rest of the world lives, with no higher standards or values. It is possible to deny Christ by words, using the world's profanity, vulgarity, and blasphemy. It is possible to deny Christ in many ways that are short of verbally and publicly renouncing Him.

The future tenses in verses 32-33 tell us that Jesus is speaking of future judgment. In that day, those who confess Him, He **will also confess,** and those who deny Him, He **will also deny.**

The difference between true and false discipleship is a much-repeated theme in Matthew. Near the beginning of the Sermon on the Mount Jesus said, "Unless your righteousness surpasses that of the scribes and Pharisees, you shall not enter the kingdom of heaven" (5:20). Later during the sermon He distinguished between false disciples, who go in the wide gate and travel the broad way, and true disciples, who enter by the narrow gate and walk in the narrow way (7:13-14).

He spoke of those who bear good fruit and those who bear bad fruit (7:16-20) and then said, "Not everyone who says to Me, 'Lord, Lord,' will enter the kingdom of heaven; but he who does the will of My Father who is in heaven. Many will say to Me on that day, 'Lord, Lord, did we not prophesy in Your name, and in Your name cast out demons, and in Your name perform many miracles?' And then I will declare to them, 'I never knew you; depart from Me, you who practice lawlessness'" (vv. 21-23). Immediately after that He distinguished between the person who builds his religious house on the sand of man's wisdom and is destroyed and the person who builds on the rock of His Word and is saved (vv. 24-27).

In chapter 13 Jesus gives the parables of the sower, of the wheat and tares, and of the dragnet (vv. 1-30, 47-50), all three of which illustrate distinctions between true and false faith. He pictured the judgment of the nations at the end of the Tribulation as the separation of believing sheep to His right and unbelieving goats to His left. "Then the King will say to those on His right, 'Come, you who are blessed of My Father, inherit the kingdom prepared for you from the foundation of the world'" (Matt. 25:34).

The sheep are those who not only identify themselves with Him but who, by their public confession of Him and their daily obedience to His will, reflect His own love and compassion by serving others in His name (vv. 35-36, 40). They confess Christ by their words and their actions, by loving as He loved, reaching out as He reached out, caring as He cared. The all-essential hallmark of being a true disciple of Christ—and therefore of truly confessing Christ—is to be like Christ, our Teacher and Master (10:25).

In the story of the sheep and goats Jesus went on to say, "Then He [the King] will also say to those on His left, 'Depart from Me, accursed ones, into the eternal fire which has been prepared for the devil and his angels'" (Matt. 25:41). Although pagans, agnostics, atheists, and every other kind of unbeliever will face the same eternal fire, Jesus was not talking about such people in this illustration. He was speaking of those who claimed to be His followers and who will say to Him on the day of judgment, "Lord, when did we see You hungry, or thirsty, or a stranger, or naked, or sick, or in prison, and did not take care of You?" (v. 44). Like Judas, they professed Him but they did not genuinely confess Him. They claimed Him as Lord but they never belonged to Him; they had not trusted in Him or obeyed Him.

I believe that Jesus was continually concerned about Judas, whom He knew did not believe and whom He therefore could not confess before the Father. Judas is the classic example of a professor who is not a confessor.

Every conscientious pastor at times becomes anxious that some people in his congregation may not truly know the Lord and will wake up in eternal damnation, although they may be active in church activities and live moral and seemingly selfless lives.

A DISCIPLE FORSAKES HIS FAMILY

Do not think that I came to bring peace on the earth; I did not come to bring peace, but a sword. For I came to set a man against his father, and a daughter against her mother, and a daughter-in-law against her mother-in-law; and a man's enemies will be the members of his household. He who loves father or mother more than Me is not worthy of Me; and he who loves son or daughter more than Me is not worthy of Me. (10:34-37)

A fourth hallmark of discipleship is willingness to forsake everything, including one's own family if necessary, for Christ's sake. Jesus introduces this point by using the figure of war and peace. As far as many human relationships are concerned, He did not come **to bring peace on the earth, . . . but a sword.**

The Jews of Jesus' day for the most part expected the Messiah to bring political deliverance for Israel and to usher in an eternal kingdom of righteousness and peace. The Old Testament spoke of the Messiah's peace-making. Isaiah called Him the Prince of Peace (Isa. 9:6) and spoke of His reign of perfect justice and peace (2:4). Solomon wrote of the Messiah's worldwide rule of peace and abundance (Ps. 72).

Jesus' disciples had already experienced inner peace and bliss that they had never known before, and they no doubt expected that experience to grow in intensity and extent the longer they were with Jesus. They may have expected the world to fall at their feet as they preached the good news of the kingdom and offered lost mankind the way of salvation and happiness.

Therefore, lest they misunderstand the true nature of His first coming and of their own ministry, Jesus began early to prepare them for His own rejection and suffering and also theirs. The gospel is indeed a gospel of peace, because it offers the way to bring peace between a holy God and sinful man, and it shows the only way for having truly peaceful relationships between men and other men. But because the world system is evil and man's fallen nature is sinful, God's offer of peace continues to be rejected and to be offensive to most of the world's people. This brings conflict into the most intimate of human relations, so that **a man's enemies will be the members of his household.**

Using another figure of destruction, Jesus said, "I have come to cast fire upon the earth; and how I wish it were already kindled! . . . Do you suppose that I came to grant peace on earth? I tell you, no, but rather division; for from now on five members in one household will be divided, three against two, and two against three" (Luke 12:49, 51-52; cf. v. 53).

The Old Testament also spoke of that aspect of the Messiah's coming. Micah predicted a time when "son treats father contemptuously, daughter rises up against her mother, daughter-in-law against her mother-in-law; [and] a man's enemies are the men of his own household" (Mic. 7:6)—the passage Jesus here quotes. In the ancient rabbinical writings we find a paraphrase of that passage, which indicates clearly that they recognized the messianic age would involve conflict even within the family: "In the period when the Son of David shall come, daughter will rise up against her mother, a daughter-in-law against her mother-in-law. The son despises his father, the daughter rebels against the mother, the daughter-in-law against the mother-in-law, and a man's enemies are they of his own household."

Against is from *dixazō,* which means to cut in two, to rend asunder, and is used only here in the New Testament. It denoted complete and often permanent separation. Sometimes the rift between believers and unbelieving relatives is lifelong and irreconcilable. Yet a true disciple must be willing to pay that price. The gospels report at least two would-be disciples who did not accept Jesus' call to follow Him because they were unwilling to sacrifice their family ties. One wanted to wait for his inheritance before following the Lord, and the other wanted to delay obedience until he had settled everything with his family. Of such half-hearted, divided commitment Jesus said, "No one, after putting his hand to the plow and looking back, is fit for the kingdom of God" (Luke 9:57-62).

Husbands or wives will sometimes not come to Christ because of fear of separation from their spouses. Children will sometimes not come because of possibly offending their parents, and vice versa. Such fears are often ungrounded, because one member of a family coming to Christ sometimes leads to the whole family being converted. But the conversion of one member often leads instead to bitterness and permanent disruption of family relationships. No one can be sure in advance what other people's reactions to his conversion will be, not even the reactions of his own family. Jesus' point is that the concern for saving one's own soul and yielding to Christ's absolute lordship must be paramount, whatever the cost in relationships may be. The phrase **is not worthy of Me** identifies the person who will not come to Christ because of other intimate and meaningful relationships that might be affected.

I once talked to a young girl at a Christian conference who told me she had been raised in a pagan family and that since her conversion her father had refused to speak to her. She said, "I can understand why he objects to my decision, because he knows nothing of the gospel and believes all religion is superstition. But you would think he would at least be happy that I am not an alcoholic, drug addict, prostitute, criminal, or a cripple. I have never had such joy in my life, and I have never loved my father so much; yet he has cut me out of his life." Like many others, she had experienced the sword and fire the gospel sometimes brings.

In marriages where one partner is a believer and the other is not, Paul says that "the unbelieving husband is sanctified through his wife, and the unbelieving wife is sanctified through her believing husband. . . . Yet if the unbelieving one leaves, let him leave; the brother or the sister is not under bondage in such cases, but God has called us to peace" (1 Cor. 7:14-15). If the sword of division causes an unbeliever to sever a marriage, the separation is to be accepted for the sake of the believer's peace.

Through Zacharias the Holy Spirit proclaimed John the Baptist as the forerunner of "the Sunrise from on high," who would "guide our feet into the way of peace" (Luke 1:78-79). At Jesus' birth the angels sang, "Glory to God in the highest, and on earth peace among men with whom He is pleased" (2:14). Shortly before His

crucifixion Jesus assured the twelve, "Peace I leave with you; My peace I give to you;
. . . Let not your heart be troubled, nor let it be fearful" (John 14:27); and again, "These
things I have spoken to you, that in Me you may have peace" (16:33). But He qualified
both of those promises, explaining in the first instance, "not as the world gives, do I
give [peace] to you" (14:27b), and in the second, "In the world you have tribulation,
but take courage; I have overcome the world" (16:33b).

At the second coming of Christ a perfect kingdom of peace on earth will be
established, ushered in and sovereignly sustained by the Prince of Peace. But for now,
during the interval between His two comings, the gospel that brings inner peace to
those who believe will also be the cause of their being misunderstood, maligned, and
mistreated by those who do not believe—including those nearest and dearest to them.
The most heart-rending divisions are always among those who are closest to us.
Nowhere can feelings be hurt more deeply than in the home.

Because the intervention in history by the Son of God was going to split and
fracture human relationships, Jesus determined that His disciples be prepared for that
experience. Martin Luther said, "If our gospel were received in peace, it would not be
the true gospel." Luther's preaching and teaching produced the greatest rift in the
history of religion, challenging the unbiblical teachings and practices of the Catholic
Church and shattering its millennium of complacency and political power.

Becoming a Christian requires affirming the lordship of Christ to the point
where you are willing to forsake everything else. It is not simply raising a hand,
signing a card, or walking down an aisle and declaring love for Jesus. Salvation is by
faith alone, apart from any works at all; but faith that is genuine will be manifested in a
commitment that cannot be swayed by any influence. The Christian is to love his
family with self-sacrificing love. Christian husbands and wives are to love each other
and their children with unreserved devotion. Christian children are to love, respect,
and care for their parents as unto the Lord. But a believer's commitment to Christ is so
profound and far-reaching that any relationship that endangers *that* relationship must
be sacrificed if necessary.

John Bunyan was told to quit preaching or be thrown in prison. He knew that
if he went to prison his wife and children would be left destitute. They had little
enough to eat and wear when he was free; but if he were imprisoned they would be
totally impoverished. Yet he knew he must preach the gospel God had called him to
preach. Because he refused to stop preaching, he was imprisoned; and from his cell he
wrote,

> The parting with my wife and poor children hath often been to me in this
> place as the pulling of the flesh from my bones; and that not only because I am
> somewhat too fond of these great mercies, but also because I would have often
> brought to my mind the many hardships, miseries, and wants that my poor
> family was like to meet with, should I be taken from them, especially my poor
> blind child, who lay nearer my heart than all I have besides. Oh, the thought
> of the hardship I thought my blind one might go under would break my heart

to pieces. . . . But yet, recalling myself, thought I, I must venture all with God, though it goeth to the quick to leave you. Oh, I saw in this condition, I was a man who was pulling down his house upon the head of his wife and children; yet thought I, I must do it. I must do it.

A Disciple Offers His Own Life

And he who does not take his cross and follow after Me is not worthy of Me. He who has found his life shall lose it, and he who has lost his life for My sake shall find it. (10:38-39)

Love of one's own life is often the greatest hindrance to full commitment to Christ. Yet Jesus calls His disciples to total self-denial, including, if necessary, sacrifice to the point of death.

No one in the Roman Empire in New Testament times, and certainly no one in Palestine, could have missed Jesus' point when He said, **He who does not take his cross and follow Me is not worthy of Me.** The **cross** symbolized the extremes of both excruciating pain and heartless cruelty; but above all it symbolized death. Only a few years before Jesus spoke those words, a zealot named Judas had gathered together a band of rebels to fight the Roman occupation forces. The insurrection was easily quelled, and in order to teach the Jews a lesson, the Roman general Varus ordered the crucifixion of over 2,000 Jews. Their crosses lined the roads of Galilee from one end to the other.

The twelve knew immediately that to **take** their **cross and follow after Me** meant to abandon themselves without reservation to Jesus' lordship, with no consideration of cost—even of life itself.

No matter how terrible they may be, the hardships and tragedies of human living that often befall Christians are not the crosses of which Jesus speaks. Such things as a cruel spouse, a rebellious child, a debilitating or terminal illness, the loss of a job, or destruction of a house by a tornado or flood, may strongly test a believer's faith; but those are not crosses.

The **cross** of a believer is not a mystical or spiritual identification with the cross of Christ or some "crucified life" idea. Such concepts are foreign to the context, and the cross of Christ was yet future when Jesus spoke here. The disciples would hear **cross** and think only of physical death.

A **cross** is the willing sacrifice of everything one has, including life, for the sake of Christ. It is something that, like the Lord Himself, a believer must **take** on himself when it is thrust upon him by the unbelieving world because of his relationship to God.

But as the Lord goes on to explain, no sacrifice for Him compares with what is received from Christ. The person who thinks he **has found his life** in the things of the world **shall lose it.** Earthly life is temporary, and the person who holds on to it above all else holds on to something that he cannot possibly keep—and in the process he forfeits the eternal life that he cannot lose.

On the other hand, the person who **has lost his life for My sake,** Jesus says, **shall find it.** The Lord is not isolating martyrdom, because no human sacrifice can merit salvation. But the willingness to forsake everything, including physical life if necessary, for the sake of Christ indicates the spirit of true discipleship, and therefore the spirit of a person who is destined for heaven and eternal life in God's presence.

When John Bunyan was brought before the magistrate to be sentenced to prison, he said, "Sir, the law of Christ hath provided two ways of obeying: the one to do that which I in my conscience do believe I am bound to do actively; and where I cannot obey it actively, there I am willing to lie down and suffer what they shall do unto me."

A Disciple Receives His Reward

He who receives you receives Me, and he who receives Me receives Him who sent Me. He who receives a prophet in the name of a prophet shall receive a prophet's reward; and he who receives a righteous man in the name of a righteous man shall receive a righteous man's reward. And whoever in the name of a disciple gives to one of these little ones even a cup of cold water to drink, truly I say to you he shall not lose his reward. (10:40-42)

The sixth hallmark of a true disciple is not what he does or is but what he receives. This mark is the most positive one but is also the most invisible. It is not experienced fully—sometimes very little—in this life, but is primarily reserved for heaven and is enjoyed now by faith and hope.

Although many people reject the gospel, many also believe. Those who accept the gospel will accept the one who brings them the gospel. The true disciple and minister of Jesus Christ is an agent of God. Not even the apostles had within themselves the power to forgive sin or reconcile men to God. But *every* Christian whose witness brings another person to Christ is God's instrument of salvation. In that sense, Jesus said, **He who receives you receives Me.** A person who receives us and our testimony also receives Christ, because we are His ambassadors.

The person who receives the Son also receives the Father: **and he who receives Me receives Him who sent Me.** There is no such thing as believing in God the Father without believing in God the Son. Jesus told the unbelieving Jews in Jerusalem, "You know neither Me, nor My Father; if you knew Me, you would know My Father also." A short while later he said to the same group, "If God were your Father, you would love Me; for I proceeded forth and have come from God, for I have not even come on My own initiative, but He sent Me" (John 8:19, 42).

In His limitless grace God not only rewards a prophet for his faithfulness but also rewards anyone else **who receives a prophet in the name of a prophet,** even giving them **a prophet's reward.** The same principle, in fact, applies to *every* believer who is accepted for Christ's sake. **He who receives a righteous man shall receive a righteous man's reward.** In an incomprehensible sharing of blessing, God showers His rewards on every person who receives His people because they are His people.

Extending the promise of God's grace still further, Jesus said, **And whoever in the name of a disciple gives to one of these little ones even a cup of cold water to drink, truly I say to you he shall not lose his reward.**

Little ones are believers who seem insignificant and unimportant (cf. Matt. 18:3-1; 25:31-46). They might be new believers who are untaught and are stumbling in their new life; or they might be lifelong believers whose devoted years of service have attracted little attention. Jesus' point is that *any* service done to *any* of His people in His name amounts to service to Him and will be rewarded. The simplest help given to the simplest disciple will not go unnoticed or unrewarded by God.

While a young boy in a country village in England struggled hard to study for the ministry, an old cobbler helped him in whatever ways he could. The godly man encouraged the boy spiritually and helped support him with what little money he could spare. When the young man was finally licensed to preach, the cobbler said to him, "I always had in my heart the desire to be a minister of the gospel; but circumstances never made it possible. You are doing what was always my dream but never a reality. I want you to let me make your shoes for nothing, and I want you to wear them in the pulpit when you preach. In that way I will feel you are preaching the gospel I always wanted to preach, standing in my shoes."

Whenever we become the source of blessing for others, we are blessed; and whenever other believers become a source of blessing to us, they are blessed. In God's magnificent economy of grace, the least believer can share the blessings of the greatest, and no one's good work will go unrewarded.

John Calvin was banished from Geneva by ungrateful citizens who resented his giving them the full truth of God's Word. In response to the disappointing news he said, "Most assuredly, if I had merely served man, this would have been a poor recompense. But it is my happiness that I have served Him who never fails to reward His servants to the full extent of His promise."

Overcoming Doubt
(11:1-6)

And it came about that when Jesus had finished giving instructions to His twelve disciples, He departed from there to teach and preach in their cities.

Now when John in prison heard of the works of Christ, he sent word by his disciples, and said to Him, "Are You the Expected One, or shall we look for someone else?" And Jesus answered and said to them, "Go and report to John what you hear and see: the blind receive sight and the lame walk, the lepers are cleansed and the deaf hear, and the dead are raised up, and the poor have the gospel preached to them. And blessed is he who keeps from stumbling over Me." (11:1-6)

The first ten chapters of Matthew are, in general, a series of testimonies that prove who Jesus is. He presents the testimony of history (1:1-17), of the miraculous birth (1:18-25), of fulfilled prophecy (2:1-23), of Christ's forerunner (3:1-12), of God the Father (3:13-17), of Jesus' power (4:1-11), of His words (5:1–7:29), of His works (8:1–9:38), and of His disciples (10:1-42). Matthew marshals all of that evidence in the courtroom, as it were, to testify that Jesus is the Christ, the promised Messiah and Son of God.

In chapters 11-12 Matthew focuses on the reactions of various individuals and groups to that evidence, organized into several general categories of response. In each chapter there is a series of negative responses followed by a positive appeal. Chapter 11 looks at the negative responses of doubt (vv. 1-15), criticism (16-19), and indifference (20-24), followed by a positive appeal to faith (25-30). Chapter 12 looks at the negative responses of rejection (vv. 1-21), amazement (22-23), blasphemy (24-27), and curious fascination (38-45), followed by another positive appeal to faith (46-50).

In the opening six verses of this section, Matthew first mentions Jesus' brief tour of ministering alone (v. 1; see 10:5) and then presents John's negative response of doubt (vv. 2-3) and Jesus' response to that doubt (vv. 4-6).

JESUS MINISTERS ALONE

And it came about that when Jesus had finished giving instructions to His twelve disciples, He departed from there to teach and preach in their cities. (11:1)

Although the text does not say so explicitly, it can be assumed that, after **Jesus had finished giving instructions to His twelve disciples,** they went out preaching and healing among the Jews of Galilee as He had told them to do (see 10:5). While they were gone, Jesus **departed from there** (the place of instruction; see 10:1) and began Himself **to teach and preach in their cities,** that is, the cities of Galilee. For a relatively brief period of time Jesus ministered alone while the disciples were out on their first mission.

His twofold ministry was **to teach** and to **preach,** to explain and to proclaim the good news. Most of His teaching would have been done in the streets of the cities, but since the synagogues were the normal place where Scripture was taught among the Jews, some of His teaching was probably done there as well. The Jewish historian Philo reports that the main purpose of synagogue services was to read and expound Scripture. Visiting rabbis and scholars were always welcome to teach in the local synagogues, and Jesus availed Himself of that privilege many times (see Matt. 4:23; 9:35; 12:9; Mark 6:2; Luke 6:6; John 18:20).

JOHN DOUBTS JESUS

Now when John in prison heard of the works of Christ, he sent word by his disciples, and said to Him, "Are You the Expected One, or shall we look for someone else?" (11:2-3)

In the case of John the Baptist, and of countless believers since his time, doubt might better be described as perplexity or confusion. The perplexity dealt with in these verses is the perplexity of a believer, a true child of God and citizen of His kingdom. John was not questioning the truthfulness of God's Word as revealed in the Old Testament or as revealed to him at the baptism of Jesus. He was rather uncertain about his understanding of those truths. Virtually all the gospel references to doubt pertain to believers rather than to unbelievers; and the kind of questioning John the Baptist experienced concerning Jesus' identity can only occur in the life of a believer. In that transitional time, before the written revelation of the New Testament, there were many things that seemed unclear and needed explanation and confirmation.

Jesus Himself testified of John that "among those born of women there has not arisen anyone greater than John the Baptist" (Matt. 11:11). He was the greatest man who had lived until his time, and, when they are confused, all believers can take comfort in his perplexity. It is also encouraging to remember that it was to His true disciples, primarily the twelve, that Jesus repeatedly said such words as "O you of little faith" and "How long will you doubt?" (Matt. 8:26; 14:31; 21:21; cf. 28:17; Mark 11:23; 16:11; Luke 12:28).

Though the Lord understands the doubts of His children, He is never pleased with their doubt, because it reflects against Him. While Peter was pondering the vision of the unclean animals, the messengers from Cornelius arrived at the house where he was staying, and the Holy Spirit said to Peter, "Behold, three men are looking for you. But arise, go downstairs, and accompany them without misgivings," that is, without doubt (Acts 10:19-20). James warns believers that "the one who doubts is like the surf of the sea driven and tossed by the wind" (James 1:6; cf. Eph. 4:14). But the doubt of which John the Baptist was guilty was the result of weakness rather than sin.

By the time Jesus began this time of ministering alone in Galilee, **John** the Baptist had been put in **prison** by Herod for denouncing the king's adulterous marriage to his brother's wife (Matt. 14:3-4). John had already announced Jesus' coming as the Messiah, addressed Him as the Lamb of God, baptized Him in the Jordan River, and declared in humility that "He must increase, but I must decrease" (John 3:30). He had already acknowledged Jesus as the Christ and trusted Him as his own Lord and Savior. Yet he was now perplexed, and **he sent word by his disciples, and said to Him, "Are You the Expected One, or shall we look for someone else?"**

The fact that John sent his disciples to Jesus is a strong testimony to his faith. In his heart he believed that Jesus truly was the Messiah and trusted Him as his Lord; but the events or lack of them caused his mind or emotions to put a cloud of doubt over his assurance. He was saying, in effect, "I have firmly believed You are the Messiah; but have I been wrong?" He was not asking for information but for confirmation. He believed, but his faith had become weakened. John came to Jesus through his disciples, saying, like the father of the boy Jesus cleansed of an evil spirit, "I do believe; help my unbelief" (Mark 9:24).

A number of John's disciples had already been observing Jesus for some time, probably on John's instruction. Shortly after the banquet Matthew gave in honor of Jesus and to which he invited fellow "tax-gatherers and sinners," the "disciples of John came to Him, saying, 'Why do we and the Pharisees fast, but Your disciples do not fast?'" (Matt. 9:10, 14). And after Jesus raised the son of the widow of Nain, "the disciples of John reported to him about all these things" (Luke 7:18).

Obviously John's disciples had some access to him while he was in prison, and apparently he sent them out on various assignments, primarily to observe and report on Jesus' ministry. After being imprisoned for many months, unable to preach or to have any contact with the outside world except for occasional visits by his disciples, John was plagued with misgivings and doubts about Jesus—the One he had announced, baptized, and declared to be the Christ.

He therefore told two of his disciples (see Luke 7:19) to ask Jesus specifically, **Are You the Expected One?** Along with the Branch, Son of David, King of kings, and other such titles, **the Expected One** (*ho erchomenos*) was a common designation for the Messiah. The title is first found in Psalms 40:7 and 118:26 and is frequently used or alluded to by the gospel writers (see Matt. 3:11; Mark 1:7; 11:9; Luke 3:16; 13:35; 19:38; John 1:27). Every Jew of Jesus' day would have known that to ask if He were **the Expected One** was to ask if He were the Messiah.

It should be reassuring to us that even a man of John's spiritual stature and gifts was subject to doubt. From the text and from John's situation at least four reasons for his doubt can be seen—reasons that also cause many Christians today to doubt. Those reasons are difficult circumstances, worldly influence, incomplete revelation, and unfulfilled expectations.

DIFFICULT CIRCUMSTANCES

Humanly speaking the career of **John** the Baptist had ended in disaster. He had been the fiery, independent, dramatic, confrontational, courageous man who preached exactly what needed to be preached, to whom it needed to be preached, and when it needed to be preached. He was fearless, aggressive, and faithful to the Lord in every way. He called sin sin and sinners sinners. And now he was **in prison** because of his faithfulness.

On a trip to Rome, Herod Antipas, governor of Galilee, had taken a liking to Herodias, the wife of his brother Philip, and had seduced her. After returning to Galilee, Herod divorced his own wife and married Herodias. When John the Baptist heard of it, he publicly confronted Herod with his sin and was promptly thrown into prison. Only Herod's fear of the multitudes kept John from being killed immediately (Matt. 14:5).

John was imprisoned at an old fort at Machaerus, located in a hot and desolate region five miles east and fifteen miles south of the northern end of the Dead Sea. He was placed in a dark, stifling dungeon that was little more than a pit. After some eighteen months in the limelight, this free spirit of the wilderness was confined and isolated. He had been in prison for perhaps a year when he sent the two disciples to Jesus.

William Barclay captures much of the significance of John's situation:

He was the child of the desert; all his life he had lived in the wide open spaces, with the clean wind on his face and the spacious vault of the sky for his roof. And now he was confined within the four narrow walls of an underground dungeon. For a man like John, who had probably never lived in a house, this must have been an agony. In Carlisle Castle there is a little cell. Once long ago they had put a border chieftain in that cell and had left him for years. In that cell there is one little window, which is placed too high for a man to look out of it when he is standing on the floor. On the ledge of the window, in the stone, there are two depressions worn away. They are the marks of the hands of the border chieftain, the places where, day after day, he had lifted himself up by placing his hands on the ledge that he might look out on the green dales across which he would never ride again. John must have been like that; and there is nothing to wonder at, and still less to criticize, in the fact that questions began to form themselves in John's mind. (*The Gospel of Matthew*, vol. 2 [Philadelphia: Westminster, 1958], p. 2)

John was a true saint and a true prophet of God—holy, loyal, selfless, and unreserved in His service to the Lord. He had done exactly what God told him to do. He had been filled with the Spirit from the time he was in his mother's womb, and all his life had lived under the Nazirite vow, the highest vow of dedication a Jewish man could take. But now he could not help wondering if prison, shame, hunger, physical torment, perplexity, and loneliness were his rewards.

John knew the Old Testament well, and he could hardly have kept from wondering where the God of comfort (Ps. 119:50; Isa. 51:12) was now. And if Jesus were truly the Messiah, why did He let his forerunner and servant suffer in prison? Where was God's love and compassion, not to mention His justice? Where was God's promise that the Messiah would "bind up the brokenhearted, . . . proclaim liberty to captives, and freedom to prisoners; . . . proclaim the favorable year of the Lord, and the day of vengeance of our God; to comfort all who mourn, to grant those who mourn in Zion, giving them a garland instead of ashes, the oil of gladness instead of mourning" (Isa. 61:1-3)?

When a believer has faithfully and sacrificially served the Lord for many years and then experiences tragedy, perhaps even a series of tragedies, it is difficult not to wonder about God's love and justice. When a child is lost to death or to unbelief, a husband or wife dies or leaves, cancer strikes us or a loved one, we are tempted to ask, "God, where are You now when I really need You? Why have You let this happen to Me. Why don't You help?" But if we dwell on such thoughts, Satan magnifies them and tries to use them to undermine our trust and confidence in God. Except for when we willingly continue in sin, we are never so vulnerable to doubting God's goodness and truth and believing Satan's lies as when we are suffering.

John knew where to go to find the answers to his questions and the resolution of his doubts. He had indeed begun to have doubts about Jesus' identity as the Christ; but it was to Jesus that he sent his disciples for confirmation. In his mind he had perhaps been crying, "Lord, why don't You help me?" Now, through his disciples, he was pleading, "Lord, please help me!"

In His great love and mercy, Jesus was glad to respond, performing miracles especially for John's sake and promising him spiritual blessing if he did not waver in trust even in the midst of mystifying circumstances.

Paul was himself in prison, probably in Rome, when he wrote, "Rejoice in the Lord always; again I will say, rejoice! Let your forbearing spirit be known to all men. The Lord is near. Be anxious for nothing, but in everything by prayer and supplication with thanksgiving let your requests be made known to God. And the peace of God, which surpasses all comprehension, shall guard your hearts and your minds in Christ Jesus" (Phil. 4:4-7). He went on to say, "I have learned to be content in whatever circumstances I am. I know how to get along with humble means, and I also know how to live in prosperity; in any and every circumstance I have learned the secret of being filled and going hungry, both of having abundance and suffering need. I can do all things through Him who strengthens me. . . . And my God shall supply all your needs according to His riches in glory in Christ Jesus" (vv. 11-13, 19).

Negative circumstances are painful and trying, but our response should be same as John's—going to the Lord and asking Him to quell our doubts, anxieties, and fears (cf. James 1:2-12).

INCOMPLETE REVELATION

A second major cause of doubt is incomplete revelation. Although John had **heard of the works of Christ**, his information was secondhand and not complete. He had been in prison for a year; but even while he was preaching, He had no direct contact with Jesus after the baptism. If Jesus' own disciples failed to understand Him fully and demonstrated "little faith" after being with Him intimately for three years, it is easy to understand why John had doubts. He was not an "eyewitness of His majesty," as were Peter, James, and John (2 Pet. 1:16-18; cf. Matt. 17:2), nor did he have the opportunity to see with his own eyes or handle with his own hands the Son of God as He taught, preached, and healed, as had the twelve and many others besides (see 1 John 1:1).

John did not experience the full truth about the Messiah he was sent to proclaim. He was in a position not unlike that of the Old Testament prophets. "As to this salvation," Peter explains, "the prophets who prophesied of the grace that would come to you made careful search and inquiry, seeking to know what person or time the Spirit of Christ within them was indicating as He predicted the sufferings of Christ and the glories to follow" (1 Pet. 1:10-11).

The information that John's **disciples** brought back to him was still not firsthand, but their report was based on confirming demonstrations of divine power that Jesus performed specifically for John's benefit.

Many believers today also doubt certain truths about God because of incomplete information, because they have inadequate knowledge or understanding of His Word. The Christian who is immersed in Scripture has no reason to stumble. When God is allowed to speak through His Word, doubt vanishes like mist in the sunlight.

Jesus responded to the doubts of the two disciples on the Emmaus road by first rebuking them for being "slow of heart to believe in all that the prophets have spoken." Then, "beginning with Moses and with all the prophets, He explained to them the things concerning Himself in all the Scripture" (Luke 24:25, 27). After Jesus revealed to them who He was and "vanished from their sight, . . . they said to one another, 'Were not our hearts burning within us while He was speaking to us on the road, while He was explaining the Scriptures to us?'" (vv. 31-32). Even before they knew it was Jesus who was speaking to them, the truth of His Word began dispelling their doubts and building up their faith.

We all need the continual truth of His Word to protect us from doubt and to dispel doubt when it comes. The Bereans were noble-minded and "received the word with great eagerness" because they examined "the Scriptures daily, to see whether" the things Paul preached were true (Acts 17:11).

WORLDLY INFLUENCE

A third cause of doubt is worldly influence, from which not even the godly John was completely insulated. What Jesus was preaching and doing did not square with what most Jews thought the Messiah, **the Expected One,** would do, and John probably shared some of those misconceptions. The Messiah was expected first of all to free Israel from her bondage, which at the time was under Rome. He obviously could not establish His own kingdom of justice and righteousness without first dealing with the pagan, unjust, and cruel Romans. But Jesus had done nothing to oppose Rome, either in words or actions.

The Jewish people also thought the Messiah would eliminate all suffering— all disease, affliction, hunger, and pain. Yet Jesus' miracles, marvelous and extensive as they were, had not fully banished those things from Israel, much less from all the world. Many Jews also probably envisioned a type of welfare state, in which all their material needs would be provided for them. They expected health, wealth, and instant happiness, and when Jesus fed the multitude on the far side of the Sea of Galilee, they were ready to immediately crown Him king (John 6:15, 26).

John the Baptist knew Jesus refused to be made king, and that He had done nothing to change either the pagan and brutal political and military systems of Rome or the worldly and corrupt religious system in Israel. Sin was still rampant, injustice was still the rule, political and religious corruption were the norm, and the world was essentially the same as it had been for thousands of years—except for a few cleansed lives and healed bodies. No visible kingdom was in sight, and no radical changes could be seen.

A common misconception about the Messiah was that His coming would be preceded by the coming of a number of other men. First Elijah would return, then Jeremiah, then a group of other prophets. Therefore when Jesus asked His disciples, "'Who do people say that the Son of Man is?' . . . they said, 'Some say John the Baptist [who by that time had been killed]; and others, Elijah; but still others, Jeremiah, or one of the prophets" (Matt. 16:13-14). It is possible that John the Baptist thought that perhaps Jesus was not the Messiah after all but only one of those forerunners, as he himself was.

Jesus' own disciples had some of those misconceptions concerning the Messiah. They were continually fighting doubts about Jesus because He did not fit their preconceived ideas. Even after the resurrection they still expected Him to establish His earthly kingdom. "Lord, is it at this time You are restoring the kingdom to Israel?" they asked (Acts 1:6). He had repeatedly told them about the nature of His mission and plan, but the ideas they had formed from the world around them clouded and distorted their understanding. What Jesus said to Philip shortly before His crucifixion applied to all the disciples: "Have I been so long with you, and yet you have not come to know Me?" (John 14:9). Even after Peter confessed that Jesus was "the Christ, the Son of the living God," he could not accept the truth that the Christ would have to die, even though he heard that truth from Jesus' own lips (Matt. 16:16, 21-22). The disciples on the road to Emmaus were puzzled for the same reason (Luke 24:19-24). All of them had been victimized by what people around them thought the Messiah should be and do.

The people's ideas about the Messiah were so distorted and ingrained that they disregarded or misconstrued whatever Jesus said or did that did not fit those ideas. When some of the Jewish leaders said to Jesus, "How long will You keep us in suspense? If You are the Christ, tell us plainly," Jesus answered, "I told you, and you do not believe" (John 10:24-25).

People today, including some believers, are confused and perplexed about the plan of God for the same reason. Their minds are so full of the ideas of people around them that they fail to understand God's plan even when they read it in Scripture. We continually hear people ask, "If Christ loves everybody so much, why do children die and people starve and get diseased and become crippled? If God is a God of justice, why is there so much corruption and injustice in the world? Why do so many good people have it so bad and so many bad people have it so good? If God is so loving and merciful, why does He send people to hell? If God is so powerful and false religions are so evil, why doesn't He just wipe out those false systems?" Because the Lord does not fit their preconceived ideas of what He should be like, people are perplexed, often indignant, and sometimes even blasphemous.

The world does not know God or understand His nature or His plan. "A natural man does not accept the things of the Spirit of God; for they are foolishness to him, and he cannot understand them, because they are spiritually appraised" (1 Cor. 2:14). The Jews who would not believe Jesus' claim to messiahship even when He told them plainly of it, did so because they did not belong to Him. "You do not believe," Jesus said, "because you are not of My sheep" (John 10:26).

To the unbelieving Pharisees who asked Jesus about "when the kingdom of God was coming, He answered them and said, 'The kingdom of God is not coming with signs to be observed; nor will they say, "Look, here it is!" or, "There it is!" For behold, the kingdom of God is in your midst'" (Luke 17:20-21). Ignorance and unbelief always blind the eyes of men to the realities of the kingdom that are all around them.

UNFULFILLED EXPECTATIONS

The fact that John instructed his disciples to ask, **or shall we look for someone else?** seems to indicate that John's expectations about the Messiah were unfulfilled. Under the Spirit's direction, John had been boldly proclaiming, "He who is coming after me is mightier than I, and I am not fit to remove His sandals; He will baptize you with the Holy Spirit and fire. And His winnowing fork is in His hand, and He will thoroughly clear His threshing floor; and He will gather His wheat into the barn, but He will burn up the chaff with unquenchable fire" (Matt. 3:11-12). John knew that what he preached was true, and he knew that Jesus was the one about whom he preached; yet Jesus had done none of those things. The Messiah was to come in judgment, and John therefore expected Jesus to take "His winnowing fork in His hand" and start clearing the threshing floor and burning up the chaff. He expected Jesus to display the blazing power of absolute, complete, and worldwide judgment.

But instead of executing judgment, Jesus assembled a group of twelve nondescript followers and began teaching them in the same manner as many other rabbis had done for centuries before Him. He demonstrated miracle-working power, but He used it only to save and heal, never to judge. Especially now that he was imprisoned, John no doubt wanted to cry out with David, "When my enemies turn back, they stumble and perish before Thee. For Thou hast maintained my just cause; Thou dost sit on the throne judging righteously" (Ps. 9:3-4); and, "Surely there is a reward for the righteous; surely there is a God who judges on earth!" (Ps. 58:11: cf. 35:1-9; 52:1-5). John wanted to cry out like the saints under the altar who said, "How long, O Lord, holy and true, wilt Thou refrain from judging and avenging our blood on those who dwell on the earth?" (Rev. 6:10). But John saw no divine intervention, no judgment, no execution of justice. Jesus did not avenge the righteous. He did not even defend Himself against His accusers.

It has always been hard for believers to understand why God allows so many of His children to suffer and allows so many wicked, ungodly people to prosper. It was doubly hard for John the Baptist. For one thing, he had a deep devotion to righteousness and was called by God to preach repentance and judgment. More than that, he was called to proclaim the coming of **the Expected One** who would execute that judgment—which he thought would begin shortly, if not immediately, after the Messiah appeared on the scene.

Christians today sometimes get excited about the Lord's imminent return; but when many years pass and He does not come, their hope, along with their dedication, often fades. They do not stop expecting Him to return some day, but they stop thinking about it and hoping for it as much as they once did. Some scoffers will even say, "Where is the promise of His coming? For ever since the fathers fell asleep, all continues just as it was from the beginning of creation" (2 Pet. 3:4).

JESUS REASSURES JOHN

And Jesus answered and said to them, "Go and report to John what you hear and see: the blind receive sight and the lame walk, the lepers are cleansed and the deaf hear, and the dead are raised up, and the poor have the gospel preached to them. And blessed is he who keeps from stumbling over Me." (11:4-6)

Jesus did not answer with a simple yes or no, because He knew that would not have satisfied John. He rather told John's disciples to present their teacher the evidence. **Go and report to John what you hear and see: the blind receive sight**

and the lame walk, the lepers are cleansed and the deaf hear, and the dead are raised up, and the poor have the gospel preached to them.

Because many of John's disciples had already been with Jesus and heard Him teach and seen Him perform miracles, part of the **report to John** would be a reminder of what they had reported earlier. In addition to having heard accounts from his disciples, John doubtlessly had heard from other sources as well, because people from all over Palestine—from Syria, "from Galilee and Decapolis and Jerusalem and Judea and from beyond the Jordan"—had followed Jesus from early in His ministry, largely on account of His miraculous works (Matt. 4:23-25). After Jesus cleansed a man in Capernaum of an unclean spirit, "immediately the news about Him went out everywhere into all the surrounding district of Galilee" (Mark 1:28); after He raised Jairus's daughter from the dead, "this news went out into all that land" (Matt. 9:26; cf. Luke 4:14, 37); and after He healed the Galilean man of leprosy, "the news about Him was spreading even farther" (Luke 5:15).

John was a great man of God and beloved by Jesus. As His faithful forerunner languished in prison facing imminent death, the Lord Jesus determined to give him a more direct and personal report of evidence. Luke tells us that when John's disciples asked Jesus if He was "the Expected One," that "at that very time He cured many people of diseases and afflictions and evil spirits; and He granted sight to many who were blind" (7:20-21). Right on the spot and before their eyes, Jesus put on a display of miracles expressly for the personal benefit of John's disciples and even more for the benefit of John himself. How it must have thrilled John's heart not only to receive fresh confirming evidence of Jesus' messiahship but to know that the Lord had performed that plethora of miracles specifically to reassure him in his time of loneliness and perplexity.

Although Jesus did nothing to relieve John's physical confinement and suffering, He did send back to him special confirmation that He was indeed performing messianic works: **the blind receive sight and the lame walk, the lepers are cleansed and the deaf hear, and the dead are raised up, and the poor have the gospel preached to them**—just as Isaiah had prophesied (Isa. 35:5; 61:1). Jesus said, in effect, "This, John, is but a preview, a taste, a picture of the coming kingdom. You can see by what I am doing now that I care, that I heal, and that I have power over all things."

John's circumstances did not improve; in fact, he was soon beheaded at the cruel request of Herodias. But it is safe to assume that Jesus' response was more than enough to encourage John and renew his faith and confidence.

Jesus' closing beatitude was primarily for the sake of John: **And blessed is he who keeps from stumbling over Me.** It was a gentle warning, a tender rebuke. "Don't doubt," He said to John, "if you want to have the blessing of My joy and peace." The warning did not take away from Jesus' esteem for John, as his testimony immediately afterward shows (vv. 7-11).

Stumbling is from *skandalizō*, which originally referred to the trapping or snaring of an animal. It was used metaphorically to signify an entrapment or stumbling block and carried the derived meaning of causing offense. Jesus' divine messiahship and the gospel of deliverance from sin through faith in Him are great stumbling blocks to sinful, unbelieving man, and Jesus did not want John to be affected by the world's skepticism and unbelief.

Matthew does not tell of the end to John's doubt until later. After John was beheaded by Herod, "his disciples came and took away the body and buried it; and they went and reported to Jesus" (Matt. 14:12). They went to Jesus because He was the most important Person in John's life and apparently had become the most important Person in their lives as well. When he died, John did not have all his questions answered, and he must have still wondered when Jesus would establish His kingdom, judge the wicked, and usher in the long-awaited kingdom of righteousness. John must have regretted not being able to witness those marvelous events about which he had so earnestly preached. But he no longer had doubts about who Jesus was or about His goodness and justice or His sovereignty and wisdom. He was content to leave in the Lord's hands the many things he did not yet understand—and that is the secret of being **blessed** and of not **stumbling**.

"If we are faithless, He remains faithful," Paul assures us; "for He cannot deny Himself" (2 Tim. 2:13). Even when we doubt Him, God is faithful to us. Doubt does not cause a believer to lose his relationship to the Lord, because God cannot deny His own promises to keep those whom He had saved. And because of His faithfulness, we can go to Him even when we doubt Him. In fact, *only* by going to Him as John did can our doubts be relieved.

John the Baptist would have loudly affirmed the apostle John's declaration, "Beloved, now we are children of God, and it has not appeared as yet what we shall be. We know that, when He appears, we shall be like Him, because we shall see Him just as He is. And everyone who has this hope fixed on Him purifies himself, just as He is pure" (1 John 3:2-3).

True Greatness
(11:7-15)

And as these were going away, Jesus began to speak to the multitudes about John, "What did you go out into the wilderness to look at? A reed shaken by the wind? But what did you go out to see? A man dressed in soft clothing? Behold, those who wear soft clothing are in kings' palaces. But why did you go out? To see a prophet? Yes, I say to you, and one who is more than a prophet. This is the one about whom it is written, 'Behold, I send My messenger before Your face, who will prepare Your way before You.' Truly, I say to you, among those born of women there has not arisen anyone greater than John the Baptist; yet he who is least in the kingdom of heaven is greater than he. And from the days of John the Baptist until now the kingdom of heaven suffers violence, and violent men take it by force. For all the prophets and the Law prophesied until John. And if you care to accept it, he himself is Elijah, who was to come. He who has ears to hear, let him hear." (11:7-15)

The world has many standards by which it measures greatness. These standards include intellectual achievement, political and military leadership, scientific and medical discoveries, wealth and power, and athletic, dramatic, literary, and musical skill.

Jesus here sets forth *God's* measure of greatness, first in the human, historical

249

dimension as seen in the life and ministry of John the Baptist. He then briefly contrasts John's greatness with the superior greatness of kingdom citizens.

From verses 7-14 three marks of John's greatness can be discerned: his personal character, his privileged calling, and his powerful culmination.

JOHN'S PERSONAL CHARACTER

And as these were going away, Jesus began to speak to the multitudes about John, "What did you go out into the wilderness to look at? A reed shaken by the wind? But what did you go out to see? A man dressed in soft clothing? Behold, those who wear soft clothing are in kings' palaces." (11:7-8)

HE OVERCAME WEAKNESS

The first characteristic of John's personal greatness demands reflection on two preceding verses (2-3) that demonstrate his ability to recognize and overcome his weaknesses.

Many people cannot rise above their difficulties and circumstances. Everyone has problems; it is overcoming them that separates great people from others. Great people fight through, refusing to give in to their ignorance, handicaps, laziness, indifference, or whatever other obstacles may be in their way. John the Baptist had that characteristic of greatness in full measure.

As discussed in the previous chapter of this volume, John was filled with the Holy Spirit from his mother's womb and had been set apart by God to announce the Messiah and to prepare Israel for His coming. He had seen the Holy Spirit descend on Jesus at His baptism and had heard God the Father declare Jesus to be His beloved Son. From many sources, including some of his own disciples, he had heard of Jesus' miraculous powers. Yet—because of difficult circumstances, incomplete revelation, the influence of popular misconceptions, and unfulfilled expectations—John had misgivings about Jesus' identity as the Messiah. Consequently he sent two of disciples to Jesus to question what had previously been unquestioned (vv. 2-3; cf. Luke 7:19).

John was deeply perplexed by his lingering doubts and probably felt he was betraying the very One he was sent to announce. But because he could not dispel the doubts, he acknowledged them to his disciples and asked two of them to seek out Jesus and confirm the truth from His own lips.

Above all other considerations, John wanted to know the truth about Jesus. He was not concerned about protecting himself by not admitting his doubts to his own disciples, to Jesus' disciples, or to the multitudes among whom he had become so popular. John had no desire to play the hypocrite. He had no interest in religious pretense, illusion, or self-deception. His assurance about certain truths had become clouded, but his humility and his underlying faith protected him from skepticism and denial.

John had no resentment of Jesus' popularity when it began to overshadow his own and had in fact declared of Jesus that "He must increase, but I must decrease" (John 3:30). He confessed publicly that he was unworthy even to remove Jesus' sandals; and when Jesus asked to be baptized by John, John replied, "I have need to be baptized by You, and do You come to me?" (Matt. 3:11, 14).

Pride curses true greatness, and the person who proudly refuses to admit and deal with personal weaknesses is doomed to hypocrisy and mediocrity.

General Douglas MacArthur prayed on behalf of his son:

> Build me a son, O Lord, who will be strong enough to know when he is weak, and brave enough to face himself when he is afraid; one who will be proud and unbending in honest defeat, and humble and gentle in victory. . . .
>
> Build me a son whose heart will be clear, whose goal will be high; a son who will master himself before he seeks to master other men; one who will learn to laugh, yet never forget how to weep; one who will reach into the future, yet never forget the past.
>
> And after all these things are his, add, I pray, enough of a sense of humor, so that he may always be serious, yet never take himself too seriously. Give him humility, so that he may always remember the simplicity of true greatness, the open mind of true wisdom and the meekness of true strength.
>
> Then I, his father, will dare to whisper, "I have not lived in vain."

STRONG IN CONVICTION

And as these were going away, Jesus began to speak to the multitudes about John, "What did you go out into the wilderness to look at? A reed shaken by the wind? (11:7)

A second characteristic of John's personal greatness was strong conviction, which made the first characteristic even more remarkable. A person with weak convictions is seldom reluctant to face doubts or change his beliefs. To him, vacillation is no cause for embarrassment or shame. But the very strength of John's convictions made his admission of doubt all the more admirable.

John's disciples did not question Jesus privately, which is apparent from the fact that, **as these were going away, Jesus began to speak to the multitudes about John.** The crowds, as well as Jesus' own disciples, surely were perplexed when they heard that **John,** the symbol of boldness and certainty, would publicly admit to misgivings about the very Person he had been proclaiming. John had had a large and loyal following, and many people recognized him as a prophet with a divine message (Matt. 14:5; 21:26). Was John not as trustworthy as they thought, and was his message not reliable?

To answer the questions in the minds of **the multitudes,** Jesus asked them a question: **What did you go out into the wilderness to look at? A reed shaken by the wind?** He appealed to their own experiences, asking, in effect, "Was the man you saw preaching and baptizing in **the wilderness** uncertain and vacillating, **a reed shaken by the wind?** Did you ever hear John change his message or compromise his standards?" He asked.

The **reed** to which Jesus referred was common along Near Eastern river banks, including those of the Jordan where John baptized. They were light and flexible, waving back and forth with every breeze. The people knew that John was not swayed like those reeds. If ever there had been a man with unswerving convictions, it was John. He stood up to the scribes, the Pharisees, the Sadducees, and even to Herod himself—for which boldness he was now in prison. The people knew John was as far as possible from being spineless or irresolute. As John Bunyan points out in his *Pilgrim's Progress*, Mr. Pliable does not go to prison to be martyred for the truth.

John had many opportunities to play the crowd and win approval of the authorities. He was such a powerful and commanding figure that many people thought he might himself be the Messiah (Luke 3:15). By being less direct and honest he could have gained the support of the hypocritical Pharisees and Sadducees who came to him for baptism. Instead, he confronted them with their sin and hypocrisy, saying, "You brood of vipers, who warned you to flee from the wrath to come? Therefore bring forth fruit in keeping with repentance; and do not suppose that you can say to yourselves, 'We have Abraham for our father'; for I say to you, that God is able from these stones to raise up children to Abraham. And the axe is already laid at the root of the trees; every tree therefore that does not bear good fruit is cut down and thrown into the fire" (Matt. 3:7-10). Then, speaking of Jesus, he continued, "And His winnowing fork is in His hand, and He will thoroughly clear His threshing floor; and He will gather His wheat into the barn, but He will burn up the chaff with unquenchable fire" (v. 12). Like William Penn, John believed that "right is right, even if everyone is against it, and wrong is wrong, even if everyone is for it."

The following incident is reported about John Chrysostom, the famous fourth-century Christian leader:

> When the great Chrysostom was arrested by the Roman Emperor, the latter sought to make the Greek Christian recant, but without success. So the Emperor discussed with his advisors what could be done to the prisoner. "Shall I put him in a dungeon?" the Emperor asked.
>
> "No," one of his counsellors replied, "for he will be glad to go. He longs for the quietness wherein he can delight in the mercies of his God."
>
> "Then he shall be executed!" said the Emperor.
>
> "No," was the answer; "For he will also be glad to die. He declares that in the event of death he will be in the presence of his God."
>
> "What shall we do then?" the ruler asked.
>
> "There is only one thing that will give Chrysostom pain," the counsellor said. "To cause him to suffer, make him sin. He is afraid of nothing except sin."

"A double-minded man [is] unstable in all his ways," James says (James 1:8). He is the man Paul describes as "tossed here and there by waves, and carried about by every wind of doctrine" (Eph. 4:14). Like Chrysostom, however, John the Baptist was far from being double-minded.

HIS SELF-DENIAL

But what did you go out to see? A man dressed in soft clothing? Behold, those who wear soft clothing are in kings' palaces. (11:8)

Jesus continues to challenge the crowd by asking them another question about John. In doing so He reminds them of a third characteristic of John's greatness: his self-denial.

Great generals put their lives on the line with their troops. Great athletes train their bodies mercilessly, denying themselves pleasures most people take for granted. Great scientists often risk their health to make an important discovery. Great inventors sacrifice social life in order to develop and perfect an invention. Great medical researchers risk exposure to deadly disease in order to save thousands of lives. The easy way is never the way of success.

The self-indulgent **man dressed in soft clothing** does not live in the wilderness as John did. He wore "a garment of camel's hair, and a leather belt about his waist; and his food was locusts and wild honey" (Matt. 3:4). His life-style was a living, visual protest against self-indulgence and self-centeredness.

Historians report that in order to court the king's favor, some scribes of Jesus' day forsook the rather drab garments they usually wore and donned the ornate, luxurious robes of the king's court. Because it served to silence possible criticism from those religious leaders, the king gladly encouraged the practice.

But John the Baptist was not a self-seeker or self-server. Both physically and symbolically he dressed, ate, and lived far apart from the hypocritical and corrupt religious and political systems. He was not interested in the ease or approval of the world. He had no penchant for gaining the favor of those who could advance his career or promote his welfare. He was so consumed by the cause God gave him that he was not attracted to the world and its standards. His devotion to his ministry completely superceded any personal interests and comforts.

As predicted before his birth, John had taken a life-long Nazirite vow. John "will be great in the sight of the Lord," the angel told his father, Zacharias, "and he will drink no wine or liquor" (Luke 1:15). Along with not drinking wine or liquor, the vow also involved never cutting the hair or touching anything, such as a dead body, that was ceremonially unclean. Many Jews, both men and women, took a Nazirite vow for a few months or years. But along with Samson (Judg. 13:7; 16:17) and Samuel (1 Sam. 1:11), John the Baptist is one of only three persons mentioned in Scripture who took the vow for life. His was a life-long, voluntary commitment to self-denial as an act of devotion to God.

John did not think his self-denial had meritorious blessing in itself. He was not like the many ascetics throughout church history who have sought to win God's favor by feats of self-inflicted poverty, pain, and humiliation. Ascepsimas wore heavy chains about his neck that forced him to crawl on his hands and knees. For forty years the monk Besarion slept only while sitting in a chair. Macarius the Younger lived without clothes in a swamp for six months and was so severely bitten by mosquitos that his body looked leprous. Simeon Stylites, the most famous of the ancient ascetics, died at the age of seventy-two, after having spent thirty-seven years sitting atop various pillars, the last of which was 66 feet high.

When in 1403 the father of the beautiful, respected, and wealthy Agnes de Rocher died, she decided to become a religious recluse. From the age of eighteen until the age of eighty, when she died, Agnes spent her life sealed in a small chamber specially built into the wall of a Paris cathedral. A small opening enabled her to hear the mass, receive communion, and accept gifts of food from friends.

John the Baptist knew nothing of such misguided piety. His self-denial was purposeful; it was for the sake of his ministry and it aided his own physical and spiritual discipline.

JOHN'S PRIVILEGED CALLING

But why did you go out? To see a prophet? Yes, I say to you, and one who is more than a prophet. This is the one about whom it is written, 'Behold, I send My messenger before Your face, who will prepare Your way before You.' Truly, I say to you, among those born of women there has not arisen anyone greater than John the Baptist; yet he who is least in the kingdom of heaven is greater than he. (11:9-11)

John's second mark of greatness was his privileged calling. Until Christ's own ministry began, no human being had been called to a task as high and sacred as that of John the Baptist. In many ways his privilege overshadowed that of Mary, who gave Jesus birth. John was chosen to announce and prepare the way for the Messiah, the Son of God, the King of kings.

Jesus now asked the crowd a third question: **But why did you go out? To see a prophet?** The answer to that question is clearly yes. As already mentioned, John the Baptist had developed a large and dedicated following in addition to his disciples, and most of the people did indeed consider him to be **a prophet** (Matt. 14:5; 21:26).

The prophetic office began with Moses and extended until the Babylonian captivity, after which for 400 years Israel had no prophet until John the Baptist. He was the valedictorian of the prophets, the most dynamic, articulate, confrontational, and powerful spokesman God had ever called. As the last prophet, he would not only announce that the Messiah was coming but that He had arrived.

In true greatness, the right person is always matched to the right position. A person with much potential will accomplish little if his talents are not channeled into work that takes full advantage of those abilities. No person can fulfill his human potential like a Christian can, because God omnisciently matches our talents, gifts, and calling. In John the Baptist the greatest man and the greatest human mission came together by God's sovereign and providential direction.

Jesus assured the people that John not only was a prophet but **more than a** prophet. Quoting Malachi 3:1, He said, **This is the one about whom it is written, "Behold, I send My messenger before Your face, who will prepare Your way before You."** The expression **before Your face** means to be in front of, or to precede. An expanded translation, as interpreted here by Jesus, would read, "Behold, I, Jehovah, send My messenger John the Baptist to be the forerunner of You, the Messiah, and to prepare the people for Your coming."

John was both prophet and fulfillment of prophecy. He was the Lord's **messenger** who was to **prepare** [the] **way** for Messiah and who would even baptize Him. He announced the Messiah and ministered to the Messiah with his own hands— as no other prophet had done or would ever again do. After thousands of years of God's preparation and prediction, John was given the unequalled privilege of being the Messiah's personal herald.

Continuing His praise of John, Jesus said, **Truly, I say to you, among those born of women there has not arisen anyone greater than John the Baptist.** To emphasize the unquestionable truthfulness of what He said, Jesus prefaced His words with **verily** (*amēn*), a term of strong affirmation often simply transliterated as "Amen."

Born of women was a common ancient expression that simply referred to basic humanness, to identification with the human race (see Job 14:1; 15:14). Jesus' point was that, as far as mankind is concerned, **there has not arisen anyone greater than John the Baptist.** He was the greatest human being who had lived until that time. From an earthly perspective, John's character and calling made him the greatest man yet born besides Jesus Himself. In superior qualities as a human being, John was unequalled.

Arisen is from *egeirō*, which means to rise up or to appear on the stage of history and was often used of prophets, both true and false (see, e.g., Matt. 24:11, 24). Not only as a human being but as a prophet, no one had **arisen** to equal John, because he was sent on the very threshold of the kingdom of the Lord Jesus.

But lest the people misunderstand the nature of John's greatness, Jesus added, **yet he who is least in the kingdom of heaven is greater than he.** Although he was a spiritual giant among men, John's unique greatness was in his role in human history, not in his spiritual inheritance, in which he would be equal to every believer. Therefore, **the least in the kingdom of heaven,** the spiritual dimension, **is greater than he,** that is, than anyone in the human dimension, including John.

JOHN'S POWERFUL CULMINATION

And from the days of John the Baptist until now the kingdom of heaven suffers violence, and violent men take it by force. For all the prophets and the Law prophesied until John. And if you care to accept it, he himself is Elijah, who was to come. (11:12-14)

Even if a man has outstanding character and an outstanding calling, he must also have opportunity in order to reach the potential of his greatness. **John the**

Baptist entered the scene of history at precisely the right time—according to God's own plan, prediction, and provision. After 400 years with no word from the Lord, Israel was expectant; and until Jesus began His own ministry, John was the focal point of redemptive history. He was the culmination of Old Testament history and prophecy.

But John generated conflict wherever he went, because his message upset the status quo. With his call for repentance, he stirred up a hornet's nest among the religious leaders and even with the king. Everywhere he moved there was reaction, and often even **violence**, which eventuated in his being arrested, imprisoned, and finally executed.

From the days of John the Baptist until now (which had been a relatively brief period of time, perhaps eighteen months), **the kingdom of heaven suffers violence, and violent men take it by force.** Everywhere he went, John evoked strong reaction.

The kingdom of heaven refers to God's general rule, His will for and His work with mankind, especially His chosen people, the Jews. It represents His purpose, message, principles, laws, and activities relating to mankind—all of which had been associated with some form of **violence** since John began preaching.

The form of *biazō* (from which **suffers violence** comes) can be read as either a Greek passive or middle voice. As a passive, it would carry the idea of *being* oppressed or treated violently, which would indicate that **violence** is brought on **the kingdom of heaven** by those outside of it. The Pharisees and scribes had attacked John verbally, and Herod had attacked him physically. The **kingdom** was being violently denied and rejected; and because it was being rejected in its spiritual dimension, the kingdom would not come in its earthly, millennial dimension. Soon the enemies of the kingdom would kill not only **John** but even the Messiah Himself. They would destroy both the herald and the King.

In the middle voice the verb carries the active idea of applying force or of entering forcibly—in which case the translation would be, "The kingdom of heaven is vigorously pressing itself forward, and people are forcefully entering it." With its focus in John the Baptist, the kingdom moved relentlessly through the godless, sin-darkened human system that opposed it.

The first of those two interpretations is negative and the second is positive; but both are true. As already seen, the negative is illustrated by the persecution of John. The positive is illustrated by the many people that John's preaching led to the Lord, just as the angel predicted: "He will turn back many of the sons of Israel to the Lord their God. And it is he who will go as a forerunner before Him in the spirit and power of Elijah, to turn the hearts of the fathers back to the children, and the disobedient to the attitude of the righteous; so as to make ready a people prepared for the Lord" (Luke 1:16-17).

Although both interpretations are possible and true, the second seems preferable in the context. Jesus had already taught that the few who enter the kingdom do so by first finding and then entering the narrow gate and walking the narrow way (Matt. 7:13-14). He also said that citizenship in His kingdom requires denying self, taking up one's cross, and following Him (Matt. 16:24; cf. 10:38). Following the Lord demands earnest endeavor, untiring energy, and the utmost exertion. To be a Christian is to swim against the flow of the world, to go against its grain, because the adversary—Satan, his demons, and the world system—are extremely powerful. Those who enter the kingdom of grace through faith in Christ do so with great effort through the sovereign power of the convicting and converting Holy Spirit.

All of God's previous revelation culminated in John the Baptist, **for all the prophets and the Law prophesied until John.** Everything from Genesis to Malachi to John pointed to and moved toward Christ, the Messiah. Their common theme—sometimes explicit and sometimes implicit—was, "The Messiah is coming!"

And if you care to accept it, Jesus continued, **he himself is Elijah, who was to come.** Through the last words of the last prophet, God had said, "Behold, I am going to send you Elijah the prophet before the coming of the great and terrible day of the Lord. And he will restore the hearts of the fathers to their children, and the hearts of the children to their fathers, lest I come and smite the land with a curse" (Mal. 4:5-6).

This man would not be a reincarnated Elijah but another prophet much like Elijah. That Malachi's prophecy referred to John the Baptist and not to a literally-returned Elijah is made clear by the angel's message to Zechariah about John: "It is he who will go as a forerunner before Him in the spirit and power of Elijah" (Luke 1:17); and John himself denied that he was actually Elijah (John 1:21). John was *like* Elijah—internally in "spirit and power" and externally in rugged independence and nonconformity.

Jesus' point was that if the Jews received John's message as God's message and received the Messiah he proclaimed, he would indeed be the Elijah spoken of by Malachi. But if they refused the King and His kingdom, another Elijah-like prophet would be sent in the future.

Because Israel did *not* accept the message of John the Baptist, John could not be Elijah and the kingdom could not be established. Another prophet like Elijah is therefore still yet to come, perhaps as one of the two witnesses of Revelation 11:1-19.

Because most Jews did not accept John or the Messiah he heralded, Jesus gave a final admonition and warning: **He who has ears to hear, let him hear.** "John is indeed the forerunner of the Messiah," Jesus was saying; "and I am indeed the Messiah, as John has testified to you. I am the King, and I am offering you the kingdom—individually as you turn to Me in personal faith and nationally if you come to Me as God's chosen nation."

John was the greatest man to live before Christ, but the highest greatness God offers is not like John's. John was a unique man and greatly used by God in the redemptive scheme before the New Covenant. But his greatness pales, Jesus says, besides those who enter His spiritual kingdom through trust in Him as Lord and Savior in the New Covenant. True greatness is not being like John the Baptist but being like Christ. That is the "one pearl of great value" for which it is worth sacrificing everything else (Matt. 13:46).

Responding to Christ with Criticism or Indifference (11:16-24)

"But to what shall I compare this generation? It is like children sitting in the market places, who call out to the other children, and say, 'We played the flute for you, and you did not dance; we sang a dirge, and you did not mourn.' For John came neither eating nor drinking, and they say, 'He has a demon!' The Son of Man came eating and drinking, and they say, 'Behold, a gluttonous man and a drunkard, a friend of tax-gatherers and sinners!' Yet wisdom is vindicated by her deeds."

Then He began to reproach the cities in which most of His miracles were done, because they did not repent. "Woe to you, Chorazin! Woe to you, Bethsaida! For if the miracles had occurred in Tyre and Sidon which occurred in you, they would have repented long ago in sackcloth and ashes. Nevertheless I say to you, it shall be more tolerable for Tyre and Sidon in the day of judgment, than for you. And you, Capernaum, will not be exalted to heaven, will you? You shall descend to Hades; for if the miracles had occurred in Sodom which occurred in you, it would have remained to this day. Nevertheless I say to you that it shall be more tolerable for the land of Sodom in the day of judgment, than for you." (11:16-24)

Jesus' words in verse 15 were a warning to the people to take seriously what He had just said about responding to John the Baptist: "He who has ears to hear, let him hear." A fundamental teaching of Scripture is that God's truth demands response.

In the present passage Jesus continues to deal with various responses of men to Himself. John's questioning had reflected honest doubt. For the various reasons already discussed, he came to have some misgivings; but his primary attitude was not doubt but faith, because even when doubts came he looked to Jesus to resolve them.

Now Jesus mentions two negative responses—criticism and indifference—that were much more serious than John's, because they reflect basic rejection of Christ. As is John's case, honest doubt can come even to a believer. But the criticism and indifference Jesus mentions here came from unbelief.

THE RESPONSE OF CRITICISM

"But to what shall I compare this generation? It is like children sitting in the market places, who call out to the other children, and say, 'We played the flute for you, and you did not dance; we sang a dirge, and you did not mourn.' For John came neither eating nor drinking, and they say, 'He has a demon!' The Son of Man came eating and drinking, and they say, 'Behold, a gluttonous man and a drunkard, a friend of tax-gatherers and sinners!' Yet wisdom is vindicated by her deeds." (11:16-19)

Although Jesus' miracles had already established His messianic credentials beyond any legitimate question, most of the Jewish people who witnessed those miracles refused to recognize the facts or accept Him as the Messiah.

But to what shall I compare this generation reflects a common oriental expression used to introduce a parable or other illustration. The Midrash, an ancient compilation of Jewish traditional teaching, contains many expressions (such as "To what is the matter like?" or "How can I illustrate this point?") used by rabbis to introduce illustrative metaphors, analogies, and stories. In this tradition Jesus was saying, "How can I illustrate the responses of **this generation** of God's people to His truth and work? To what do they **compare?**"

Some of those who refused to believe the gospel covered their unbelief with criticism. Jesus compared them to foolish **children sitting in the market place** who objected to everything the other children did. They were like many people today who find fault with whatever the preacher and other church leaders do. No matter what is said or done, such people pick it apart and use the objection—whether real or imagined, justified or unjustified—as an excuse for rejection. Because they have no saving relationship to Christ, they refuse to receive His truth or serve in His church. But they love to harp against both.

The *agora* (**market place**) was a central area of cities and towns where people went to do business and to socialize. On certain days of the week, farmers, craftsmen, and merchants of all sorts would bring their produce or wares to sell from stalls, tents, carts, or simply from a cleared place on the ground.

Children played with each other **in the market place** while their parents sold, bought, or visited. Two games, "Wedding" and "Funeral," were particularly popular. Weddings and funerals were the two major social events, and children liked to mimic their elders by performing mock weddings and mock funerals. Weddings involved festive music and dancing, and when children played the wedding game they expected everyone to **dance** when the imaginary **flute** was played, just like grownups did in the real ceremony. Likewise, when they played the funeral game they expected everyone to **mourn** and wail when the imaginary **dirge** was played, just like the paid mourners did when a person actually died.

There were always holdouts, however, who refused to go along with the rest of the children. If the game was "Wedding," they wanted to play "Funeral," and vice versa. Nothing the other children did satisfied them. They were peevish, perpetual spoilsports who threw a wet blanket on everything their friends did.

Jesus applied the first illustration to the response of the people to John the Baptist. When **John came neither eating nor drinking**, the people said, **He has a demon!** The phrase **neither eating nor drinking** was a figurative description of John's austere life-style. He ate a Spartan diet of locusts and wild honey, and he lived in the desert and dressed in uncomfortable garments of camel's hair (Matt. 3:4). His message was serious and severe as he cried out for repentance and for corresponding good works.

John's message and way of life were in the funeral mode, so to speak. Some people became so resentful of his continual emphasis on repentance and judgment that they charged him with having **a demon.** He grated against their immoral and unspiritual nerves, and they railed out against him. They tolerated him for a short while, enjoying the novelty and excitement of his preaching. But he would not let them be neutral bystanders, uncommitted onlookers who heard and observed without decision or commitment. When they saw they had to choose, they chose not to believe or follow him. Instead of accepting John's rebuke of their wickedness, they rebuked his righteousness. They charged the prophet who had no equal, who was greater than any other person "born of woman" (11:11), with being demon possessed.

Jesus applied the second illustration to the response of the people to Himself: **The Son of Man came eating and drinking, and they say, "Behold, a gluttonous man and a drunkard, a friend of tax-gatherers and sinners!"** Jesus lived basically in the normal pattern of Jewish life, **eating and drinking** like everyone else. In contrast to John's ascetic life-style, Jesus participated in all the normal social activities. He traveled throughout most of Israel, going from city to city, village to village, synagogue to synagogue. He had individual, intimate contact with many hundreds of people as He talked with them, healed their diseases, forgave their sins, and called them to follow Him.

Just as John lived in the funeral mode Jesus lived in the wedding mode. That fact did not escape the notice of John's disciples, who had already asked Jesus, "Why do we and the Pharisees fast, but Your disciples do not fast?" (Matt. 9:14). In reply, Jesus used the figure of a wedding: "The attendants of the bridegroom cannot mourn as long as the bridegroom is with them, can they?" (v. 15). But Jesus' critics ridiculously exaggerated His normal activities, charging Him with being **a gluttonous man and a drunkard.**

The wine Jesus and most other Jews drank was *oinos,* a drink made by boiling or evaporating fresh grape juice down to a heavy syrup or paste in order to prevent spoilage and simplify storage. To make a beverage, water would be added as needed to a small quantity of the syrup. That mixture was nonalcoholic, and even when allowed to ferment it was not intoxicating, because it was mostly water. Perhaps Jesus miraculously made wine from water for the wedding at Cana by creating the paste.

The second charge, that Jesus was **a friend of tax-gatherers and sinners,** was true, but not in the sense His critics meant. In identifying Jesus with those social and moral outcasts the critics also intended to identify Him with the outcasts' sin and wickedness. But when Jesus associated with sinful people, He not only did not participate in their sin but offered deliverance from it—because that is why He came to earth (see Matt. 9:12-13).

As William Barclay points out,

> The plain fact is that when people do not want to listen to the truth, they will easily enough find an excuse for not listening. They do not even try to be consistent in their criticism. They will criticize the same person and the same institution from quite opposite grounds and reasons. If people are determined to make no response, they will remain stubbornly and sullenly unresponsive no matter what invitation is made to them. (*The Gospel of Matthew* [Philadelphia: Westminster, 1958], 2:10)

Jesus' unnamed critics were not interested in truth or justice but in condemnation. John the Baptist and Jesus were enemies of traditional religion, with its elevation of human wisdom and disregard for divine. Because John and Jesus could not be reasoned down they would be shouted down; and if no truth could be found against them, falsehood would be eagerly used.

Yet wisdom is vindicated by her deeds, Jesus said. Corrupt human **wisdom** produces corrupt human **deeds,** such as the false accusations against John and Jesus. On the other hand, the righteous, divinely empowered **wisdom** of John and Jesus produced righteous **deeds** that resulted in repentance, forgiven sin, and redeemed lives.

Through the centuries the church's detractors have found it easy to criticize its people and its work. Yet they are hard pressed to explain how so many lives have been changed from wickedness to righteousness, from despair to hope, from anger to love, from sadness to happiness, and from selfishness to self-giving by the power of Christ.

Jesus' rebuke of His critics was serious, but it contained a certain restraint, a restraint not seen in the brief series of withering rebukes He proceeded to give those who treated Him with indifference.

The Response of Unbelieving Indifference

Then He began to reproach the cities in which most of His miracles were done, because they did not repent. "Woe to you, Chorazin! Woe to you, Bethsaida! For if the miracles had occurred in Tyre and Sidon which occurred

in you, they would have repented long ago in sackcloth and ashes. Nevertheless I say to you, it shall be more tolerable for Tyre and Sidon in the day of judgment, than for you. And you, Capernaum, will not be exalted to heaven, will you? You shall descend to Hades; for if the miracles had occurred in Sodom which occurred in you, it would have remained to this day. Nevertheless I say to you that it shall be more tolerable for the land of Sodom in the day of judgment, than for you." (11:20-24)

Jesus' harsh **reproach** against **the cities in which most of His miracles were done** seems on the surface to be less justified than His comparatively mild rebuke of those who openly criticized Him. For the most part, the three **cities** mentioned here—which typified all the places where **His miracles were done**—did not take any direct action against Jesus. They simply ignored Him. While the Son of God preached, taught, and performed unprecedented **miracles** in their midst, they carried on their business and their lives as usual, seemingly unaffected. From the human perspective, their indifference appears foolish but it does not appear to be terribly sinful.

But indifference is a heinous form of unbelief. It so completely disregards God that He is not even an issue worth arguing about. He is not taken seriously enough to criticize.

As the young King Josiah declared, the great sin of Israel in that day was that the people had "not listened to the words of this book, to do according to all that is written concerning us." And for that disregard of God's Word the king said, "the wrath of the Lord . . . burns against us" (2 Kings 22:13).

In the parable of the royal wedding feast, the guests who were first invited "paid no attention and went their way, one to his own farm, another to his business" (Matt. 22:5). They did not mistreat and kill the king's slaves as some of the other citizens did (v. 6), but they were equally excluded from the feast. They picture the many people Christ calls but whose indifference excludes them from being among the few who are chosen (v. 14).

Indifference to the Lord will continue in the world until He returns. "Just as it happened in the days of Noah, so it shall be also in the days of the Son of Man," Jesus said; "they were eating, they were drinking, they were marrying, they were being given in marriage, until the day that Noah entered the ark, and the flood came and destroyed them all. It was the same as happened in the days of Lot: they were eating, they were drinking, they were buying, they were selling, they were planting, they were building; . . . It will be just the same on the day that the Son of Man is revealed" (Luke 17:26-28, 30). Some of the people in Noah's day doubtlessly criticized him abusively for building a ship in the middle of the desert; and some of the worst inhabitants of Sodom tried to homosexually attack the angels who came to rescue Lot. But most of the people in the days of Noah and of Lot paid no attention to the Lord or to His servants. Yet they, too, were totally destroyed, because they rejected God just as totally as those who actively expressed their unbelief.

Jesus' righteous anger boiled against the privileged **cities** who witnessed the awesome evidence of His divine power and goodness yet **did not repent.** In His holy fury He declared to them, **Woe to you, Chorazin! Woe to you, Bethsaida!**

The interjection **woe** is sometimes used in Scripture to represent grief (see, e.g., Rev. 18:10), but most often it represents denunciation, as it clearly does here.

Probably most inhabitants of **Chorazin** and **Bethsaida** had personally witnessed Jesus' **miracles,** and everyone else knew about His mighty works from the reports of friends and relatives. But the number who responded in faith was small (cf. Matt. 7:13-14).

When people have great opportunity to hear God's Word, and even to see it miraculously demonstrated, their guilt for rejection is intensified immeasurably. It is far better to have heard nothing of Christ than to hear the truth about Him and yet reject Him. "For if we go on sinning willfully after receiving the knowledge of the truth, there no longer remains a sacrifice for sins, but a certain terrifying expectation of judgment, and the fury of a fire which will consume the adversaries" (Heb. 10:26-27). The greater the privilege, the greater the responsibility; and the greater the light, the greater the punishment for not receiving it.

Jesus' marvelous works should have shaken to the foundation every Jew in Galilee, even more than the preaching of Jonah shook every person in pagan Nineveh, from the king down to the least servant (Jonah 3:5). But most Galileans did not respond to Christ at all, much less **repent.**

Chorazin was a small village nestled in the hills some two and a half miles north of Capernaum. It has long ceased to exist, and its ruins are known today as Charaza, a variation of Chorazin. **Bethsaida,** the home town of Philip, Andrew, and Peter, was located still farther north and to the west, in the plain of Gennesaret. These were two of the many towns and villages Jesus visited as He ministered out of His headquarters in Capernaum.

To Galilean Jews, **Tyre and Sidon** epitomized pagan, Gentile corruption and worthlessness. The people in those cities were descendants of the ancient Phoenicians, the renowned seafaring merchants and colonizers of the Mediterranean. Both cities were typical seaports, noted for their immorality and godlessness (even by pagan standards) and were deeply involved in the licentious Baal worship. A certain king of **Tyre** was so proud and evil that Ezekiel used him as a picture of Satan (Ezek. 28:11-15). The city's violence, profanity, pride, injustice, greed, and immorality were so excessive that the Lord destroyed it (vv. 16-19; cf. Jer. 25:22; 47:4). It had even sold many of God's own people into slavery (Amos 1:9).

Yet those two wicked cities **would have repented long ago in sackcloth and ashes,** Jesus said, if they had had the privileges of Chorazin and Bethsaida. The self-righteous, traditional religion of Galilean Jews blinded them more to God than the heathen religions did the Gentiles of Tyre and Sidon. Those chosen people had so long rejected God and His Word that they were totally indifferent to His Messiah when He came to them.

Few things Jesus might have said could have stunned Jews more than to be unfavorably compared to Gentiles. **Nevertheless, I say to you,** Jesus continued, **it shall be more tolerable for Tyre and Sidon in the day of judgment, than for**

you. At the great white throne judgment, the dead of all the ages will be brought before the throne of God to be judged and sentenced to eternal punishment. And at that judgment the unbelieving Gentiles of Tyre and Sidon will fare better than the unbelieving Jews of Chorazin and Bethsaida.

Jesus here makes two truths clear: there will be degrees of punishment in hell, and among those given the severest punishment will be those who have received the divine revelation and been the most religious and outwardly upright. Those who thought they were eternally safe—because they were Abraham's physical descendants and because they kept the religious traditions of their forefathers—looked with contempt on all Gentiles. Yet in hell many Gentiles will look down on those Jews.

But another city of Galilee was guiltier still. **And you, Capernaum, will not be exalted to heaven, will you? You shall descend to Hades.** Jesus made His headquarters in this beautiful, prosperous fishing village on the northern shore of the Sea of Galilee. He performed more miracles and preached more sermons in and around **Capernaum** than at any other place during His entire ministry. It was there that He raised Jairus's daughter from the dead and healed the nobleman's son. It was here that He healed the demoniac, Peter's mother-in-law, the woman with the hemorrhage, the two blind men, the centurion's servant, the dumb demoniac, and the paralytic who was lowered through the roof by his friends.

Yet those marvels had little impact on most citizens of **Capernaum**; and because of their indifference they would not **be exalted to heaven** as they thought they deserved but would rather **descend to Hades.**

Although **Hades** is sometimes used in Scripture to represent the place of all the departed dead, it is often used, as here, to represent hell, the place of eternal punishment for the unsaved.

Jesus said that the **miracles** He performed in Capernaum were so amazing that, had they **occurred in Sodom, . . . it would have remained to this day.** Its people would have repented of their sin, turned to God, and been spared destruction.

Even in the secular world, **Sodom** is a synonym for moral depravity and has the infamous distinction of lending its name (in sodomy) to the most extreme forms of homosexuality and sexual bestiality. When a group of Sodom's worst perverts tried to rape the angels at Lot's house, they were struck blind. But their homosexual enslavement was so intense that even after being blinded "they wearied themselves trying to find the doorway" in order to satisfy their perverted lust (Gen. 19:11).

As far as is known, the people of **Capernaum** had no homosexual problem or any other apparent moral deficiency. Most of them were upright, law-abiding, and decent. Yet because they ignored and rejected the Son of God, their fate on the day of judgment will be worse than that of **Sodom.**

Capernaum exceeded Chorazin and Bethsaida in privilege, and Sodom exceeded Tyre and Sidon in wickedness. In these striking and sobering contrasts, Jesus makes plain that people who are the most blessed by God will receive the worst punishment if they reject Him. Judgment against the moral abominations of Sodom will be exceeded by judgment against the spiritual indifference of Capernaum. For the respectable and upright unbelievers of Capernaum, **Hades** will be hotter than for the crude and immoral unbelievers of Sodom. The self-righteous orthodox person is even more repulsive in God's sight than the idolatrous and immoral pagan.

The people of **Capernaum** never persecuted Jesus, and few of them even criticized Him. They never mocked Him, ridiculed Him, ran Him out of town, or threatened His life. Yet their sin was worse than if they had done those things. Theirs was not the sin of violence or of immorality but of indifference. As G. A. Studdert-Kennedy has written in his poem "Indifference," "They only just passed down the street, and left Him in the rain."

Jesus' teaching perhaps mildly interested them, and His miracles entertained them, but nothing more. His grace never rent their hearts, His truth never changed their minds, His warning about sin never provoked repentance, and His offer of salvation never induced faith. And because of their indifferent unbelief, Jesus said to them, **I say to you that it shall be more tolerable for the land of Sodom in the day of judgment than for you.**

The eighteenth-century commentator Johann Bengel wrote, "Every hearer of the New Testament truth is either much happier or much more wretched than the men who lived before Christ's coming." Such a hearer is also either more secure or more condemned.

Jesus' Personal Invitation (11:25-30)

At that time Jesus answered and said, "I praise Thee, O Father, Lord of heaven and earth, that Thou didst hide these things from the wise and intelligent and didst reveal them to babes. Yes, Father, for thus it was well-pleasing in Thy sight. All things have been handed over to Me by My Father; and no one knows the Son, except the Father; nor does anyone know the Father, except the Son, and anyone to whom the Son wills to reveal Him. Come to Me, all who are weary and heavy-laden, and I will give you rest. Take My yoke upon you, and learn from Me, for I am gentle and humble in heart; and you shall find rest for your souls. For My yoke is easy, and My load is light." (11:25-30)

The heart of the gospel is that "Christ Jesus came into the world to save sinners" (1 Tim. 1:15). Jesus said that He came "to seek and to save that which was lost" (Luke 19:10). He tells men that because He is the Bread of Life, those who come to Him will never hunger and those who believe in Him will never thirst (John 6:35; cf. 7:37). Because He is the Light of the World, those who follow Him will "not walk in the darkness, but shall have the light of life" (8:12). Because He is "the resurrection and the life," those who believe in Him will live even if they die (11:25).

The message of salvation is the theme of all Scripture. God's promise to Adam and Eve after the Fall was that their descendant one day would bruise the serpent's head (Gen. 3:15)—a figure of Christ's conquest of Satan. Through Isaiah, the Lord pleaded, "Turn to Me, and be saved, all the ends of the earth; for I am God, and there is no other" (Isa. 45:22); and again, "Ho! Every one who thirsts, come to the waters; and you who have no money come, buy and eat. Come, buy wine and milk without money and without cost. . . . Incline your ear and come to Me. Listen, that you may live" (55:1, 3). Among the last words of Scripture is a final invitation to mankind to be saved: "The Spirit and the bride say, 'Come.' And let the one who hears say, 'Come.' And let the one who is thirsty come; let the one who wishes take the water of life without cost" (Rev. 22:17).

As the hymn writer F. W. Faber reminds us,

> There's a wideness in God's mercy
> Like the wideness of the sea.
> There's a kindness in His justice
> That is more than liberty.
> For the love of God is broader
> Than the measure of man's mind;
> And the heart of the Eternal
> Is most wonderfully kind.

THE CONTEXT

At that time Jesus answered and said, "I praise Thee, O Father, Lord of heaven and earth," (11:25a)

At that time could mean that Jesus' invitation was given immediately after His upbraiding of Chorazin, Bethsaida, and Capernaum, in order to take advantage of any interest in salvation those sobering words may have evoked.

It is also possible that Jesus was repeating an invitation He had given on other occasions and would continue to give throughout His ministry. In that case, Matthew here calls attention to what may have been Jesus' last invitation during His first and major Galilean ministry—as He offered the people one final appeal to be saved.

After Jesus' performing countless miracles to attest His divinity and His messianic credentials (4:23-24), after His preaching in detail the message of the gospel and the Christian life (5-7), and after His having sent out the twelve (10:5-15) and then the seventy (see Luke 10:1-16), the people of Galilee had the greatest opportunity to learn of God and of His way of salvation than any people in history, before or since. Yet in spite of that great opportunity, the majority willfully rejected Christ and His message, either by hostility or by indifference.

Though the nation had turned its back on the Messiah, He continued to call to Himself that remnant who were weary of carrying their heavy spiritual burdens and who sought rest in God's grace.

Jesus' early period of popularity was ending, and opposition was growing in amount and in intensity. As Jesus would soon make clear, the only possible alternatives are acceptance or rejection. A person is either for Christ or against Him (Matt. 12:30; cf. Mark 9:40). Consequently, Jesus' teaching became more and more specifically directed either to those who accepted or those who rejected Him. Side by side are messages of judgment and of compassion, of warning and of encouragement, just as we see here. Jesus had just presented the God of judgment and wrath (Matt. 11:20-24), and now He presents the God of love and mercy.

Answered and said is a Hebrew idiom that means to speak out openly, as opposed to privately or confidentially. Jesus' invitation to follow Him was universal and open to everyone who would come on God's terms.

Jesus' prayer to His Father was meant to be heard by prospective believers. As He prayed, **I praise Thee, O Father, Lord of heaven and earth,** Jesus called attention both to His unique relationship to the **Father** and to the Father's sovereign control over salvation. Salvation is a provision of the **Lord of heaven and earth,** and is not a result of man's wisdom, plans, purposes, or power; and for that truth Jesus gives **praise** to the **Father.**

Every faithful pastor, evangelist, and witness is sometimes disappointed that more people do not respond. He asks himself, "What more can I do? What new approach can I take? How can I make the message clearer and more persuasive?" Yet he also knows that some people will reject Christ no matter how clear, loving, and powerful the presentation of the gospel may be. If men could reject salvation from the very lips of the Lord Himself—and in the midst of awesome, authenticating miracles—we can hardly expect every person who hears our imperfect witness to fall at Christ's feet.

We weep over those who refuse to be saved, just as our Lord wept over Jerusalem when it would not receive Him. But also like Christ, we should **praise** our heavenly **Father** that all things are under His divine control and that His sovereign plan for the world and for His own people cannot be frustrated. Men's rejection of Christ proves their failure, not God's.

God's sovereignty should be the foremost thought in the mind of every witnessing believer. We should remember with confidence that His plan is always on course and that even the most unrepentant, wicked, vindictive, and cynical rejection of our testimony does not alter God's timetable or thwart His purpose. Our responsibility is simply to make our witness faithful (1 Cor. 4:2); it is God's responsibility alone to make it effective.

Because Jesus had an unyielding trust in His Father's perfect will, He could rest in that will and give Him **praise** no matter what responses people made to Him.

As Jesus compassionately invited His hearers to come to Him and be saved, He set forth the five essential elements that constitute a genuine invitation to salvation.

HUMILITY AND DEPENDENCE

that Thou didst hide these things from the wise and intelligent and didst reveal them to babes. Yes, Father, for thus it was well-pleasing in Thy sight. (11:25*b*-26)

Jesus' specific cause for praise is God's sovereign wisdom in hiding **these things from the wise and intelligent and** instead revealing them **to babes.** He thanks His Father that the first step to salvation is humility, coming to God in utter despair of one's own merit or resources. It is not by accident that the first beatitude is "Blessed are the poor in spirit, for theirs is the kingdom of heaven" (Matt. 5:3). The kingdom belongs only to the humble.

These things refers to the kingdom, on which Jesus' entire ministry focused. Even during the forty days between His resurrection and ascension Jesus was "speaking of the things concerning the kingdom of God" (Acts 1:3). His teachings about His messiahship, lordship, and saviorhood, and about salvation, submission, and discipleship all centered in the kingdom of God—the realm where He is sovereign, where His people dwell by grace through faith, and where His righteous will is done.

The wise and intelligent sarcastically refers to those who are intelligent in their own eyes and who rely on human wisdom and disregard God's. The Lord does not exclude smart people from His kingdom but rather those who trust in their smartness. Paul was a brilliant, highly educated scholar, and he did not forsake his intelligence when he became a Christian. But he stopped relying on his intelligence to discern and understand spiritual and divine matters. It is not intelligence but intellectual pride that shuts people out of the kingdom. Intelligence is a gift of God, but when it is perverted by pride it becomes a barrier to God, because trust is in the gift rather than in the Giver. "For though the Lord is exalted, yet He regards the lowly; but the haughty He knows from afar" (Ps. 138:6).

The **wise and intelligent** include both religious and nonreligious people, who in their love of human wisdom are much more alike than different. Whether religious or irreligious, the proud person will not submit to God's wisdom and truth and therefore excludes himself from the kingdom. The religious man who relies on tradition or good works to please God is just as far from God as the atheist.

The means God uses to **hide these things** from such people is the darkness of their proud, unregenerate hearts, which prevent them from seeing what God desires them to know and to accept. Paul said, "Just as it is written, 'Things which eye has not seen and ear has not heard, and which have not entered the heart of man, all that God has prepared for those who love Him.' For to us God revealed them through the Spirit; for the Spirit searches all things, even the depths of God" (1 Cor. 2:9-10). God's spiritual truth is not empirically, objectively knowable. It cannot be externally discovered, but must be willingly received through man's heart as God reveals it. As someone has said, "The heart and not the head is the home of the gospel." No amount of human reasoning or speculation can discover or explain God's saving truth, because, as Paul continues to say, "a natural man does not accept the things of the Spirit of God; for they are foolishness to him, and he cannot understand them, because they are spiritually appraised" (v. 14).

No amount of evidence is sufficient to convince the confirmed unbeliever. John says of such people that, though Jesus "had performed so many signs before them, yet they were not believing in Him; that the word of Isaiah the prophet might be fulfilled, which he spoke, 'Lord, who has believed our report? And to whom has the arm of the Lord been revealed?' For this cause they could not believe, for Isaiah said again, 'He has blinded their eyes, and He hardened their heart; lest they see with their eyes, and perceive with their heart, and be converted, and I heal them'" (John 12:37-40). Those who hear God's Word and refuse to receive it are subject to God's judicial confirmation of that choice.

Just as **wise and intelligent** does not refer to mental ability but to a *proud* spiritual attitude, **babes** does not refer to physical age or capability but to a *humble* spiritual attitude.

A baby is totally dependent on others to provide everything it needs. It has no abilities, no knowledge, no skills, no resources at all to help itself. *Nēpios* (**babes**) is used in 1 Corinthians 3:1 and Hebrews 5:13 of infants who cannot eat solid food but only milk. In 1 Corinthians 13:11 it is used of those who have not yet learned to speak and in Ephesians 4:14 of those who are helpless.

During a question and answer period in a meeting one time, a young girl, perhaps 9 or 10 years old, came up to me and asked, "What happens to babies and retarded children when they die?" She was obviously very serious, and I did my best to answer her from Scripture. Beginning with David's comment about his infant son who had died, "I shall go to him, but he will not return to me" (2 Sam. 12:23), I explained that God takes to Himself all of those, such as babies and retarded people, who are not *able* to choose Him. Afterward her mother explained that a younger brother was seriously retarded and understood almost nothing of what went on around him. His sister, young as she was, knew the way of salvation and was deeply concerned that her little brother might not go to heaven because he was not able to understand how to receive Christ as Savior. I reminded her that Jesus said, "Unless you are converted and become like children, you shall not enter the kingdom of heaven" (Matt. 18:3). She was greatly relieved when I said that her little brother was a living illustration of the kind of person Jesus came to save and to receive into heaven—the utterly helpless.

It is to spiritual **babes**, those who acknowledge their utter helplessness in themselves, to whom God has sovereignly chosen to **reveal** the truths of His kingdom. It is to the "poor in spirit" who humbly confess their dependency that God makes the way of salvation clear and understandable. By the Holy Spirit they recognize they are spiritually empty and bankrupt and they abandon all dependence on their own resources. They are the cringing spiritual beggars to whom Jesus refers in the first beatitude—the absolutely destitute who are ashamed to lift up their head as they hold out their hands for help.

Babes are the exact opposite of the kind of person the scribes, Pharisees, and rabbis taught was pleasing to God. They are also the exact opposite of the imagined ideal Christian touted by many popular preachers and writers who glorify self-assertion and self-worth.

The contrast between **wise and intelligent** and **babes** is not between the knowledgeable and the ignorant, the educated and the uneducated, the brilliant and the simpleminded. It is a contrast between those who think they can save themselves by their own human wisdom, resources, and achievement and those who know they cannot. It is a comparison between those who rely on themselves and those who rely on God.

People who are famous, highly educated, wealthy, powerful, or talented are often difficult to reach for Christ, simply because human accomplishments easily lead to pride and pride leads to self-sufficiency and self-satisfaction.

Yes, Father, Jesus continues, **for thus it was well-pleasing in Thy sight.** God is well-pleased with the gospel of grace because it brings glory to Him, which is the supreme purpose in the universe. "For thus says the high and exalted One who lives forever, whose name is Holy, 'I dwell on a high and holy place, and also with the contrite and lowly of spirit in order to revive the spirit of the lowly and to revive the heart of the contrite'" (Isa. 57:15). God loves to help the humble and the repentant, because they know they are helpless. He is pleased when they come to Him for help, because that honors His grace and gives Him glory (cf. Luke 18:9-14).

> Still to the lowly soul
> He doth Himself depart,
> And for His dwelling and His throne
> He chooses the humble heart.
>
> (Author unknown)

"For consider your calling, brethren" Paul reminded the Corinthian believers, "that there were not many wise according to the flesh, not many mighty, not many noble; but God has chosen the foolish things of the world to shame the wise, and God has chosen the weak things of the world to shame the things which are strong" (1 Cor. 1:26-27).

Jesus referred to Nicodemus as *the* "teacher of Israel," suggesting that he was perhaps the most highly respected rabbi in the land. He was a student of the Old Testament and of the many traditional writings of Judaism. Yet with all his religious training and knowledge he could not grasp Jesus' teaching that "unless one is born again, he cannot see the kingdom of God." Even after Jesus explained, Nicodemus did not understand, and Jesus said to him: "Truly, truly, I say to you, we speak that which we know, and bear witness of that which we have seen; and you do not receive our witness. If I told you earthly things and you do not believe, how shall you believe if I tell you heavenly things?" (John 3:3-12). Before he could comprehend or receive the gospel, Nicodemus had to go all the way back and start over as a spiritual babe, putting aside his human knowledge and achievements and coming to Christ with no merit of his own.

Revelation

All things have been handed over to Me by My Father; and no one knows the Son, except the Father; nor does anyone know the Father, except the Son, and anyone to whom the Son wills to reveal Him. (11:27)

These words of Jesus are basically a commentary on verse 25, expanding on the truth that God has chosen to reveal His will to babes, the spiritually humble and helpless, rather than to those who are proud and self-reliant. A genuine invitation to salvation must consider God's revelation, because no person, even the most determined or sincere, could know the way to Him unless the Lord had already made it known. The way of salvation is disclosed only through the sovereign revelation of God.

The first important truth of this verse is not so much taught as taken for granted. Jesus unequivocally equates Himself with God, calling Him **My Father** in a way that Jews would never do except when referring to His corporate fatherhood of Israel. Here is one of Jesus' clearest statements of His deity, disclosing the intimate and absolutely unique relationship of the **Father** and the **Son**. In essence they are one and are inseparable.

There was no doubt in the minds of Jesus' hearers that His referring to God as **My Father** was a claim to deity. The Jews had earlier accused Jesus of making Himself "equal with God" and sought to kill Him (John 5:18). When on another occasion He said, "I and the Father are one," the crowd wanted to stone Him to death for blasphemy (John 10:30-31; cf. vv. 15, 17-18, 25, 29, 32-38).

That Jesus is Himself God is the heart of the gospel, because apart from His deity He could not save a single soul. No heresy so corrupts the gospel and robs it of its power as the teaching that Jesus is not God. Apart from His deity, there is no gospel and no salvation.

The second truth of this verse is explicit. In His deity Jesus not only was intimate with His Father but had received **all things**—all authority, sovereignty, truth, and power—from the **Father**. At some time in preexistent eternity the Father committed these **things** to the Son (cf. John 5:21-24).

It was because all authority had been given to Him "in heaven and on earth" that Jesus had the right to send out His followers to "make disciples of all the nations, baptizing them in the name of the Father and the Son and the Holy Spirit" (Matt. 28:18-19). The underlying purpose of Jesus' miracles was to demonstrate His authority over illness, disease, demons, nature, life, death, and sin. He had authority to forgive sins, to save from divine judgment, and to sovereignly control everything on earth and in heaven. **All things** in the universe and pertaining to the universe are under His divine sovereignty. His power displayed during His ministry was a preview of the full display in the coming earthly Millennium, when He will reign over the earth.

The third truth of this verse is that **no one knows the Son except the Father.** Man has no way in himself of discovering what God is like, because his finite mind cannot grasp God's infinite nature. Because **the Son** is divine, Jesus says, only the divine Father truly **knows** Him. The obverse is equally true: **nor does anyone know the Father, except the Son, and anyone to whom the Son wills to reveal Him.** Divine truth can only be divinely perceived and divinely imparted (cf. 1 Cor. 2:9-16).

Philosophy and religion are utterly incapable of reasoning out God or His truth because they are of a finite, lower order. Human ideas and concepts are earthbound and totally fruitless in producing spiritual truth or guidance. God must break into the darkness and emptiness of man's human understanding and show Himself before man can know Him.

What Jesus teaches here about God's revelation of Himself is at once simple and utterly profound. It is to the person who sets aside all human knowledge and wisdom and becomes as an unlearned, helpless infant, that God chooses to **reveal** Himself. "No man has seen God at any time; the only begotten God, who is in the bosom of the Father, He has explained Him" (John 1:18). Only the person emptied of human wisdom can be filled with divine truth.

Martin Luther said, "Here the bottom falls out of all merit, all powers and abilities of reason or the free will men dream of, and it all counts nothing before God. Christ must do and must give everything."

FAITH

Come to Me, (11:28a)

Just as man's part in salvation is to come humbly, it is also to **come** in faith. Although finite minds cannot fully comprehend the truth, divine grace and human faith are inseparable in salvation. God sovereignly provides salvation, which includes the fact that man must give himself to the Lord Jesus Christ in commitment before it becomes effective. Jesus said, "All that the Father gives Me shall come to Me," and then immediately added, "and the one who comes to Me I will certainly not cast out" (John 6:37).

Salvation is not through a creed, a church, a ritual, a pastor, a priest, or any other such human means—but through Jesus Christ, who said, **Come to Me.** To **come** is to believe to the point of submitting to His lordship. "I am the bread of life," Jesus declared; "he who comes to Me shall not hunger, and he who believes in Me shall never thirst" (John 6:35). *Comes* and *believes* are parallel just as are *hunger* and *thirst.* Coming to Christ is believing in Him, which results in no longer hungering and thirsting. Other biblical synonyms for believing in Christ include confessing Him, receiving Him, eating and drinking Him, and hearing Him.

Peter declared, "Of Him [Jesus Christ] all the prophets bear witness that through His name everyone who believes in Him receives forgiveness of sins" (Acts 10:43). And the Lord Himself said, "As Moses lifted up the serpent in the wilderness, even so must the Son of Man be lifted up; that whoever believes may in Him have eternal life. For God so loved the world, that He gave His only begotten Son, that whoever believes in Him should not perish, but have eternal life" (John 3:14-16).

REPENTANCE AND REST

all who are weary and heavy-laden, and I will give you rest. (11:28:b)

All who are indicates a condition that already exists. Those whom Jesus invites to Himself are those who already **are weary and heavy-laden.** Although this aspect of Jesus' invitation is mentioned after faith ("Come to Me"), chronologically it precedes faith, referring to the repentance that drives the humble, seeking person to Christ for salvation.

Kopiaō (to grow **weary**, or "to labor") carries the idea of working to the point of utter exhaustion. John uses the term to describe Jesus' fatigue when He and the disciples reached Sychar after a long, hot journey from Jerusalem (John 4:6).

Weary translates a present active participle and refers figuratively to arduous toil in seeking to please God and know the way of salvation. Jesus calls to Himself everyone who is exhausted from trying to find and please God in his own resources. Jesus invites the person who is wearied from his vain search for truth through human wisdom, who is exhausted from trying to earn salvation, and who has despaired of achieving God's standard of righteousness by his own efforts.

Heavy-laden translates a perfect passive participle, indicating that at some time in the past a great load was dumped on the wearied person. Whereas **weary** refers to the internal exhaustion caused by seeking divine truth through human wisdom, **heavy-laden** suggests the external burdens caused by the futile efforts of works righteousness.

In Jesus' day, the rabbinical teachings had become so massive, demanding, and all-encompassing that they prescribed standards and formulas for virtually every human activity. It was all but impossible even to learn all the traditions, and was completely impossible to keep them all. Jesus spoke of the heavy loads of religious tradition that the scribes and Pharisees laid on the people's shoulders (Matt. 23:4); and at the Jerusalem Council, Peter noted that the Judaizers were trying to saddle Christianity with the same man-made "yoke which neither our fathers nor we have been able to bear" (Acts 15:10).

Although the term itself is not used in the text, Jesus gives a call to repent, to turn away from the self-centered and works-centered life and come to Him. The person who is **weary and heavy-laden** despairs of his own ability to please God. He comes to the end of his own resources and turns to Christ. Desperation is a part of true salvation, because a person does not come to Christ as long as he has confidence in himself. To repent is to make a 180-degree turn from the burden of the old life to the restfulness of the new.

Repentance was the theme of John the Baptist's preaching (Matt. 3:2) and the starting point of the preaching of Jesus (4:17), Peter (Acts 2:38; 3:19; cf. 5:31), and Paul (17:30; 20:21; cf. 2 Tim. 2:25). The person who humbly receives God's revelation of Himself and His way of salvation, who turns from the unbearable burden of his sin and self-effort, and who comes to Christ empty-handed is the only person God will save.

Anapauō (to **give . . . rest**) means to refresh or revive, as from labor or a long journey. Jesus promises spiritual **rest** to everyone who comes to Him in repentance and humble faith.

God's **rest** is a common Old Testament theme. The Lord warned Israel, "Do not harden your hearts, as at Meribah, as in the day of Massah in the wilderness; when your fathers tested Me, they tried Me, though they had seen My work. . . . Therefore I swore in My anger, truly they shall not enter into My rest" (Ps. 95:7-9, 11). After quoting that passage, the writer of Hebrews warns those who make a pretense of faith in Christ but have not really trusted Him: "Take care, brethren, lest there should be in any one of you an evil, unbelieving heart, in falling away from the living God" (Heb. 3:12). To intellectually acknowledge Christ's deity and lordship is a dangerous thing if it does not lead to true faith, because it gives a person the false confidence of belonging to Christ.

In the time of the early church many Jews were attracted to the gospel and outwardly identified themselves with the church. But for fear of being unsynagogued, ostracized from the worship and ceremonies of Judaism, some of them did not truly receive Christ as saving Lord. They went part way to Him but stopped before full commitment. "As a result" of such superficial allegiance, John says, "many of His disciples withdrew, and were not walking with Him anymore" (John 6:66). Consequently they would not enter God's rest, that is, His salvation, because they still possessed "an evil, unbelieving heart" (Heb. 3:11-12).

Just as those Israelites who rebelled against Moses in the wilderness were denied entrance into the Promised Land because of unbelief, so those who refuse to fully trust in Christ are denied entrance into God's kingdom rest of salvation for the same reason (v. 19). "Therefore, let us fear lest, while a promise remains of entering His rest, any one of you should seem to have come short of it. For indeed we have had good news preached to us, just as they also; but the word they heard did not profit them, because it was not united by faith in those who heard. For we who have believed enter that rest, just as He has said, 'As I swore in My wrath, they shall not enter My rest'" (4:1-3).

The dictionary gives several definitions of rest that remarkably parallel the spiritual **rest** God offers those who trust in His Son. First, the dictionary describes rest as cessation from action, motion, labor, or exertion. In a similar way, to enter God's rest is to cease from all efforts at self-help in trying to earn salvation. Second, rest is described as freedom from that which wearies or disturbs. Again we see the spiritual parallel of God's giving His children freedom from the cares and burdens that rob them of peace and joy.

Third, the dictionary defines rest as something that is fixed and settled. Similarly, to be in God's rest is to have the wonderful assurance that our eternal destiny is secure in Jesus Christ, our Lord and Savior. It is to be freed from the uncertainties of running from philosophy to philosophy, from religion to religion, from guru to guru, hoping somehow and somewhere to discover truth, peace, happiness, and eternal life.

Fourth, rest is defined as being confident and trustful. When we enter God's rest we are given the assurance that "He who began a good work in [us] will perfect it until the day of Christ Jesus" (Phil. 1:6). Finally, the dictionary describes rest as leaning, reposing, or depending on. As children of God, we can depend with utter certainty that our heavenly Father will "supply all [our] needs according to His riches in glory in Christ Jesus" (Phil. 4:19).

SUBMISSION

Take My yoke upon you, and learn from Me, for I am gentle and humble in heart; and you shall find rest for your souls. For My yoke is easy, and My load is light." (11:29-30)

Salvation involves submission, because it is impossible for Christ to exercise lordship over those who refuse to obey Him. Jesus' invitation therefore includes the call to submission, symbolized by a **yoke**.

A **yoke** was made of wood, hand-hewn to fit the neck and shoulders of the particular animal that was to wear it in order to prevent chafing. For obvious reasons, the term was widely used in the ancient world as a metaphor for submission. The **yoke** was part of the harness used to pull a cart, plow, or mill beam and was the means by which the animal's master kept it under control and guided it in useful work. A student was often spoken of as being under the yoke of his teacher, and an ancient Jewish writing contains the advice: "Put your neck under the yoke and let your soul receive instruction."

That is the particular meaning Jesus seems to have had in mind here, because He adds, **and learn from Me.** *Manthanō* (to **learn**) is closely related to *mathētēs* (disciple, or learner) and reinforces the truth that Christ's disciples are His submissive learners. They submit to Christ's lordship for many reasons, among the most important of which is to be taught by Him through His Word. A yoke symbolizes obedience, and Christian obedience includes learning from Christ.

The power of salvation is entirely of grace and nothing of works. An unbeliever has neither the understanding nor the ability to save himself, just as a babe has neither the understanding nor the ability to help itself. But although good works do not produce salvation, salvation does produce good works. Believers are, in fact, "created in Christ Jesus for good works, which God prepared beforehand, that we should walk in them" (Eph. 2:10).

But because Jesus is **gentle and humble in heart,** He gives **rest,** not weariness, to the **souls** of those who submit to Him and do His work. His **yoke is easy, and** His **load is light.** His burden is not like that of Pharaoh, who bitterly oppressed the children of Israel, or like that of the scribes and Pharisees, who burdened the Jews of Jesus' day with a grievous legalism.

Christ will never oppress us or give us a burden too heavy to carry. His **yoke** has nothing to do with the demands of works or law, much less those of human tradition. The Christian's work of obedience to Christ is joyful and happy. "For," as John explains, "this is the love of God, that we keep His commandments; and His commandments are not burdensome" (1 John 5:3).

Submission to Jesus Christ brings the greatest liberation a person can experience—actually the *only* true liberation he can experience, because only through Christ is he freed to become what God created him to be.

Thy precious will, O conquering Saviour,
    Doth now embrace and compass me;
All discords hushed, my peace a river,
    My soul a prisoned bird set free.
Sweet will of God still fold me closer,
    Till I am wholly lost in Thee.

                           (William E. Blackstone)

BIRDVILLE
BAPTIST CHURCH
LIBRARY

The Lord of the Sabbath (12:1-14)

26

At that time Jesus went on the Sabbath through the grainfields, and His disciples became hungry and began to pick the heads of grain and eat. But when the Pharisees saw it, they said to Him, "Behold, Your disciples do what is not lawful to do on a Sabbath." But He said to them, "Have you not read what David did, when he became hungry, he and his companions; how he entered the house of God, and they ate the consecrated bread, which was not lawful for him to eat, nor for those with him, but for the priests alone? Or have you not read in the Law, that on the Sabbath the priests in the temple break the Sabbath, and are innocent? But I say to you, that something greater than the temple is here. But if you had known what this means, 'I desire compassion, and not a sacrifice,' you would not have condemned the innocent. For the Son of Man is Lord of the Sabbath."

And departing from there, He went into their synagogue. And behold, there was a man with a withered hand. And they questioned Him, saying, "Is it lawful to heal on the Sabbath?"—in order that they might accuse Him. And He said to them, "What man shall there be among you, who shall have one sheep, and if it falls into a pit on the Sabbath, will he not take hold of it, and lift it out? Of how much more value then is a man than a sheep! So then, it is lawful to do good on the Sabbath." Then He said to the man, "Stretch out your hand!" And he stretched it out, and it was restored to normal, like the other. But the Pharisees went out, and counseled together against Him, as to how they might destroy Him. (12:1-14)

The events recorded in Matthew 12 mark a major turning point in Jesus' ministry, focusing on the rejection of the Messiah by His own people. Verses 1-21 depict the mounting unbelief of Israel crystalizing into conscious rejection, and verses 22-50 depict the blasphemy that follows the rejection. After the King was presented and attested, He was then rejected and blasphemed before finally being put to death on the cross.

Herod's wicked plan to destroy the prophesied King of the Jews by killing all the male babies in Judah was the first evidence that the Messiah would not be accepted. When His forerunner, John the Baptist, confronted the Pharisees and Sadducees by calling them a generation of vipers and warning them to flee from the wrath to come, the rejection became still more evident. From the beginning of Jesus' own ministry the Jewish leaders were skeptical of Him, and that skepticism rapidly escalated into criticism, open hostility, and direct opposition.

As Jesus increasingly attacked the man-made religion of rabbinical tradition, the leaders of that religion increasingly attacked Him. They accused Him of blasphemy (9:3) and of fellowshipping with tax-collectors and sinners (v. 11). They even accused Him of being demon possessed (v. 34). The more directly Jesus confronted the Jewish leaders with their internal sinfulness and their external emptiness, the more they hardened their antagonism to Him. Criticism and indifference grew into sharp rebuke and then into furious rage.

One of the primary causes for opposition centered on observance of the Sabbath, the problem with which the present text (12:1-14) deals. It deals with the incident that prompted the opposition, then Jesus' indictment, instruction, and illustration, and finally the insurrection against Him.

THE INCIDENT

At that time Jesus went on the Sabbath through the grainfields, and His disciples became hungry and began to pick the heads of grain and eat. (12:1)

Sabbath observance was the heart of the Jewish legalistic system, and when Jesus violated the traditions as to how that day should be honored, He struck a raw nerve.

Both the English Sabbath and the Greek *sabbaton* transliterate the Hebrew *shabbāt*, which has the basic meaning of ceasing, rest, and inactivity. At the end of creation "God blessed the seventh day and sanctified it, because in it He rested from all His work which God had created and made" (Gen. 2:3). In honor of that day, the Lord declared it to be a special time of rest and remembrance for His people and incorporated its observance into the requirements of the Ten Commandments (Ex. 20:9-11).

But that law is the only one of the Ten Commandments that is nonmoral and purely ceremonial; and it was unique to the Old Covenant and to Israel. The other nine commandments, on the other hand, pertain to moral and spiritual absolutes and are repeated and expanded upon many places in the New Testament. But Sabbath observance is never recommended to Christians, much less given as a command in the New Testament.

When Jesus began His ministry, the Old Covenant was still in effect and all of its requirements were binding on Jews, the special people of that covenant. Jesus observed every demand and met every condition of Scripture, because it was His own Word, which He came to fulfill and not destroy (Matt. 5:17). But for several hundred years the various schools of rabbis had added regulation after regulation, going far beyond the teaching of Scripture and in many instances actually contradicting it (see Matt. 15:6, 9). In no area were those additions more extensive and extreme than in regard to Sabbath observance.

Keeping the Sabbath was still a binding ceremonial obligation for Israel, but most Jews had little idea of the original purpose of the Sabbath or of how God intended it to be honored. Instead of being a day of rest it had become a day of incredible burden. Because of the thousands of man-made restrictions regarding it, the Sabbath was more tiresome than the six days devoted to one's occupation. It was harder to "rest" than to earn a living.

Jewish tradition had even caused the Sabbath to be dangerous. The apocryphal book of 1 Maccabees (2:31-38) tells of an incident during the time of Judas Maccabaeus when a group of Jews refused to defend themselves on the Sabbath against the Greek army led by Antiochus Epiphanes. As the soldiers of Antiochus attacked, the Jews "answered them not, neither cast they a stone at them, nor stopped the places where they lay hid; but said: 'Let us die in our innocency: heaven and earth shall testify for us, that ye put us to death wrongfully.' So they rose up against them in battle on the Sabbath, and they slew them with their wives and children and cattle, to the number of a thousand people."

In his *Antiquities,* the Jewish historian Josephus reports that it was also because Jews would not defend themselves on the Sabbath that the Roman general Pompey was able to capture Jerusalem. As was the custom in ancient Roman warfare, Pompey began building a high mound from which his troops could bombard the city. Aware that the Jews defending Jerusalem would not oppose him then, the general did all construction work on the Sabbath. "Had it not been for that practice, from the days of our forefathers, to rest on the seventh day," Josephus wrote, "this bank could never have been perfected, by reason of the opposition the Jews would have made; for though our Law gave us leave then to defend ourselves against those that begin to fight with us and assault us (this was a concession), yet it does not permit us to meddle with our enemies while they do anything else."

One section alone of the Talmud, the major compilation of Jewish tradition, has twenty-four chapters listing Sabbath laws. One law specified that the basic limit for travel was 3,000 feet from one's house; but various exceptions were provided. If you had placed some food within 3,000 feet of your house, you could go there to eat it; and because the food was considered an extension of the house, you could then go another 3,000 feet beyond the food. If a rope were placed across an adjoining street or alley, the building on the other side, as well as the alley between, could be considered part of your house.

Certain objects could be lifted up and put down only from and to certain places. Other things could be lifted up from a public place and set down in a private one, and vice versa. Still others could be picked up in a wide place and put down in a legally free place—but rabbis could not agree about the meanings of *wide* and *free*!

Under Sabbath regulations, a Jew could not carry a load heavier than a dried fig; but if an object weighed half that amount he could carry it twice. Eating restrictions were among the most detailed and extensive. You could eat nothing larger than an olive; and even if you tasted half an olive, found it to be rotten and spit it out, that half was considered to have been eaten as far as the allowance was concerned.

Throwing an object into the air with one hand and catching it with the other was prohibited. If the Sabbath overtook you as you reached for some food, the food was to be dropped before drawing your arm back, lest you be guilty of carrying a burden.

Tailors did not carry a needle with them on the Sabbath for fear they might be tempted to mend a garment and thereby perform work. Nothing could be bought or sold, and clothing could not be dyed or washed. A letter could not be dispatched, even if by the hand of a Gentile. No fire could be lit or extinguished—including fire for a lamp—although a fire already lit could be used within certain limits. For that reason, some orthodox Jews today use automatic timers to turn on lights in their homes well before the Sabbath begins. Otherwise they might forget to turn them on in time and have to spend the night in the dark.

Baths could not be taken for fear some of the water might spill onto the floor and "wash" it. Chairs could not be moved because dragging them might make a furrow in the ground, and a woman was not to look in a mirror lest she see a gray hair and be tempted to pull it out. You could carry ink enough to draw only two letters of the alphabet, and false teeth could not be worn because they exceeded the weight limit for burdens.

According to those hair-splitting regulations, a Jew could not pull off even a handful of grain to eat on the Sabbath unless he were starving—which, of course, is often a difficult thing to determine and would be cause for considerable differences of opinion. If a person became ill on the Sabbath, only enough treatment could be given to keep him alive. Treatment to make him improve was declared to be work, and therefore forbidden. To determine just how much food, medicine, or bandaging would be necessary to keep a person alive—and no more—was itself an impossible burden.

Among the many other forbidden Sabbath activities were: sewing, plowing, reaping, grinding, baking, threshing, binding sheaves, winnowing, sifting, dying, shearing, spinning, kneading, separating or weaving two threads, tying or untying a knot, and sewing two stitches.

The Sabbath was anything but a time of rest. It had become a time of oppressive frustration and anxiety. The people were sick to death of this system that had been imposed on them by ungodly, worldly legalists, and they were indeed "weary and heavy-laden" (Matt. 11:28).

At that time (cf. 11:25) does not necessarily indicate that the events about to be described occurred directly after those just mentioned, but rather that they occurred in the same general period of **time** (from *kairos,* season).

That **Jesus went on the Sabbath through the grainfields** with **His disciples** was itself a violation of Jewish tradition, though not of Scripture. And the fact that they **became hungry** shows that they were not in the fields for the purpose of finding something to eat. They were simply passing **through.** Because they would have eaten only ripened grain, the time was probably late March or early April (when grain normally ripened in the Jordan valley) and therefore near Passover.

Roads as we know them today were few, and much travel was done on wide paths that went from town to town and passed through many pastures and **grainfields.** As travelers walked along, they passed within an arm's length of the crops on either side. Inns were rare even in small towns and villages and were nonexistent between them. If a traveler did not take enough food with him or found his trip extended for some reason, he had to live off the land. The Lord recognized such need in a provision of the Mosaic law: "When you enter your neighbor's vineyard, then you may eat grapes until you are fully satisfied, but you shall not put any in your basket. When you enter your neighbor's standing grain, then you may pluck the heads with your hand, but you shall not wield a sickle in your neighbor's standing grain" (Deut. 23:24-25).

The disciples were not reaping on the Sabbath, which was forbidden by Mosaic law (Ex. 34:21), but simply satisfying their hunger according to the provision of Deuteronomy 23. Rabbinic tradition, however, had ridiculously interpreted the rubbing of grain together in the hands (which the disciples were doing; see Luke 6:1) as a form of threshing; and they regarded blowing away the chaff as a form of winnowing. The Talmud said, "If a person rolls wheat to remove the husks, it is sifting. If he rubs the heads of wheat, it is threshing. If he cleans off the side adherences, it is sifting. If he bruises the ears, it is grinding. And if he throws it up in his hand, it is winnowing."

The disciples had left everything to follow Jesus and had no source of income other than occasional gifts from their families and fellow believers. When they **became hungry and began to pick the heads of grain and eat,** they were perfectly within their scriptural and social rights. They lived by faith, and the divine law of the land provided for just such sustenance. Jesus did nothing to discourage the disciples and probably joined them in eating the grain.

THE INDICTMENT

But when the Pharisees saw it, they said to Him, "Behold, Your disciples do what is not lawful to do on a Sabbath." (12:2)

One wonders what the Pharisees were doing out in the grainfields themselves or what the vantage point was from which they **saw** Jesus and His disciples. It may be that certain exceptions were made for these self-appointed guardians of tradition, just as policemen have the right to temporarily break certain laws while performing their duty.

The charge that Jesus' **disciples** were doing **what is not lawful to do on a Sabbath** was itself sinful, because it put human tradition on a par with God's own Word. Rabbinic tradition was not legitimate Jewish law, but many centuries of observance had given it that status in the minds of most Jews, especially the legalistic scribes and **Pharisees.** God's Word was honored in name and was the supposed basis for the traditions. But Scripture was not studied and obeyed directly; it was rather used as a means to justify the traditions, many of which actually contradicted and "invalidated the word of God" (Matt. 15:6).

The **Pharisees** indicted the Lord and His disciples for disobeying their distorted, man-made traditions, thus perverting God's intention for the **Sabbath,** which was to provide man with a special day of rest, not a painful day of burdens.

THE INSTRUCTION

But He said to them, "Have you not read what David did, when he became hungry, he and his companions; how he entered the house of God, and they ate the consecrated bread, which was not lawful for him to eat, nor for those with him, but for the priests alone? Or have you not read in the Law, that on the Sabbath the priests in the temple break the Sabbath, and are innocent? But I say to you, that something greater than the temple is here. But if you had known what this means, 'I desire compassion, and not a sacrifice,' you would not have condemned the innocent. For the Son of Man is Lord of the Sabbath." (12:3-8)

Have you not read what David did . . . ? was deep-cutting sarcasm, because the account of **David** to which Jesus referred was, of course, from Scripture, about which the Pharisees considered themselves the supreme experts and custodians. They must have winced in anger as Jesus said to them, in effect, "Don't you teachers of Scripture know what it says?"

In responding to the Pharisees' false charge, Jesus instructed them about God's purposes for the Sabbath, particularly about three things it was *not* designed to do.

Like the other nine Commandments, the one to observe the Sabbath was given to promote love toward God and love toward one's fellow man. The first three pertain to showing love of God through reverence, faithfulness, and holiness. The other seven pertain to love of other people through personal purity, unselfishness, truthfulness, and contentment and through respect for their possessions, rights, and well-being.

The scribes and Pharisees, however, knew nothing of love—for God or for men. They were legalistic functionaries, trapped in their own system of endless, futile traditions. Instead of fulfilling the law by loving their neighbors as themselves (Lev. 19:18; cf. Rom. 13:8-10), they attempted to fulfill it through loveless and lifeless traditions.

Jesus here reaffirms that the Sabbath was given for God's glory and for man's welfare. It was never intended to restrict the expression of love through deeds of necessity, service to God, or acts of mercy.

THE SABBATH DOES NOT RESTRICT DEEDS OF NECESSITY

But He said to them, "Have you not read what David did, when he became hungry, he and his companions; how he entered the house of God, and they ate the consecrated bread, which was not lawful for him to eat, nor for those with him, but for the priests alone? (12:3-4)

David was the supreme hero of Judaism, loved and honored even above the patriarchs and prophets. He was the great king, poet, and warrior. Jesus reminded the Pharisees of a familiar story about David and **his companions** as they fled for their lives south of Gibeah to escape the jealous and vengeful Saul. When they came to Nob, where the Tabernacle was then located, they asked for food. Ahimelech the priest gave them **the consecrated bread** of the Presence, **which was not lawful for him to eat, nor for those with him, but for the priests alone**, because there was "no ordinary bread on hand" in the Tabernacle (1 Sam. 21:4).

The bread of the Presence was baked weekly, and each Sabbath twelve fresh loaves (representing the twelve tribes) replaced the previous ones, which could be eaten only by the priests. On that particular occasion, however, an exception was made on behalf of David and his men, who were weak from hunger. God was not offended by that act, and He did not discipline either Ahimelech or David. The Lord was willing for a ceremonial regulation to be violated when doing so was necessary to meet the needs of His beloved people.

If God makes allowances for His *own* law to be broken under certain circumstances for the welfare of His people, Jesus said, He surely permits purposeless and foolish man-made traditions to be broken for that purpose.

THE SABBATH DOES NOT RESTRICT SERVICE TO GOD

Or have you not read in the Law, that on the Sabbath the priests in the temple break the Sabbath, and are innocent? But I say to you, that something greater than the temple is here. (12:5-6)

Jesus did not have to explain what He meant by saying **that on the Sabbath the priests in the temple break the Sabbath.** The Pharisees had often **read in the**

Law that priests not only were allowed but required to do many things on the Sabbath that otherwise would have violated God's **Law** of rest, not to mention rabbinic tradition.

In the performance of their duties in the Tabernacle and then the **temple**, the ministering **priests** had to light the altar fires, kill the sacrificial animals, and then lift up the carcasses and place them on the altar. Sacrifices on **the Sabbath** were, in fact, double sacrifices, requiring twice the work of the normal daily sacrifice (Num. 28:9-10; cf. Lev. 24:8-9).

The most legalistic Pharisee considered **the priests** who ministered **in the temple** as **innocent** of breaking **the Sabbath**, despite the fact that they worked twice as hard as they did on other days. Similarly, even the most legalistic Christian does not consider preaching, teaching Sunday school, leading a youth group, or any other such work as profaning the Lord's Day, despite the fact that those activities require a great deal of effort.

Jesus embarrassed and angered the Pharisees by pointing out the inconsistency of their legalistic thinking. But their anger turned to rage when Jesus then said, **But I say to you, that something greater than the temple is here.** Even if the Pharisees did not immediately understand that Jesus was referring to Himself, they were horrified—because *nothing,* other than God Himself, was greater than **the temple.** In our day it is difficult even for Jews, much less Gentiles, to grasp how highly the Jews of Jesus' day revered the Temple.

Because of His previous claims to deity (see, e.g., 9:2-6; 11:3-5, 25-27), the Pharisees probably realized Jesus was referring to Himself as being **greater than the temple** and therefore claiming to be God. A few moments later He removed all doubt in their minds about what He meant (12:8).

The Lord's immediate purpose, however, was not to *prove* His deity but to point out that, in light of that deity, He had the right to abrogate Sabbath regulations as He saw fit—immeasurably more than David had the right to violate the Tabernacle laws or the priests had to violate the Sabbath laws in serving in the Temple.

THE SABBATH DOES NOT RESTRICT ACTS OF MERCY

But if you had known what this means, "I desire compassion, and not a sacrifice," you would not have condemned the innocent. For the Son of Man is Lord of the Sabbath. (12:7-8)

Jesus' third point regarding the Sabbath was that its observance was never meant to restrict acts of mercy, as the Pharisees would have known had they understood and honored Scripture as they claimed.

If they **had known what** the Lord meant when He said, **I desire compassion, and not a sacrifice,** they **would not have condemned the innocent** for supposed Sabbath breaking. That one truth alone—a quotation of but one half of one verse from the book of Hosea (6:6a)—would have been sufficient to teach the Pharisees, and any sincere Jew, what God's primary desire was for His people.

Sacrifice here represents the entire Mosaic system of ritual and ceremony, which was always of secondary and temporary importance in God's plan. **Sacrifice** was never more than symbolic, a means pointing to God's gracious and future provision of what no man, and certainly no animal, could provide.

Observing the Sabbath was a kind of **sacrifice**, a symbolic service to the Lord in obedience to His command. It was a reminder of God's completion of creation and a shadow of the perfect rest His redeemed people look forward to in salvation and in heaven.

Even under the Old Covenant that required it, Sabbath observance was not a substitute for the heart righteousness and **compassion** that characterize God's faithful children. God is merciful, and He commands His people to be merciful.

God sometimes sets aside His laws for the sake of mercy. If He did not, none of us would be saved—or even born—because Adam and Eve would have been destroyed the moment they sinned. Not only that, but God has always shown mercy in enforcing the temporal penalties for breaking His laws.

The Lord's desire is not to condemn men for sin but to save them from it. He only condemns those who will not have His mercy (cf. 2 Pet. 3:9). And if righteous, holy God is supremely characterized by love and mercy—even to the extent of graciously setting aside the penalty for breaking some of His own laws for man's benefit—how much more are His still-sinful children obligated to reflect His **compassion?**

Because the Sabbath was the Lord's special day under the Old Covenant, a faithful Jew should have been especially concerned to follow his Lord's example of **compassion** on that day. But because the Pharisees and most other Jews were far from God, they were also far from understanding His nature and His will. Jesus' instruction about God's purpose for the Sabbath further indicted the Pharisees' unbelief and hardness of heart. *They* were the true violators of the Sabbath, because they "invalidated the word of God for the sake of [their] tradition" (Matt. 15:6). Those who **condemned the innocent** stood condemned themselves. They did not refuse to do acts of mercy because of devotion to God's law but because of lack of compassion.

To substantiate His authority for saying what He had just said, Jesus added, **For the Son of Man is Lord of the Sabbath.** That statement must have rendered the Pharisees speechless. What He had implied by "something greater than the temple" (12:6), He now made unambiguous. Jesus stood before them and claimed He was greater than God's Temple and greater than God's Sabbath. He was God, the **Son of Man,** the divine Messiah whom the Temple honored and the **Sabbath** served.

Because the **Lord of the Sabbath** had come, the shadow of His Sabbath rest was no longer needed or valid. The New Testament does not require Sabbath observance, but rather allows freedom as to whether or not *any* day is honored above others. The only requirement is that, whatever position is taken, it is taken for the purpose of glorifying the Lord (Rom. 14:5-6); and no believer has the right to impose his views in this regard on anyone else (Gal. 4:9-10; Col. 2:16).

From the days of the early church (Acts 20:7; 1 Cor. 16:2), Christians have set aside Sunday, the first day of the week, as a special day of worship, fellowship, and giving offerings, because that is the day our Lord was raised from the dead. But the Lord's Day is not the "Christian Sabbath," as it was considered to be for many centuries and still is in some groups today.

THE ILLUSTRATION

And departing from there, He went into their synagogue. And behold, there was a man with a withered hand. And they questioned Him, saying, "Is it lawful to heal on the Sabbath?"—in order that they might accuse Him. And He said to them, "What man shall there be among you, who shall have one sheep, and if it falls into a pit on the Sabbath, will he not take hold of it, and lift it out? Of how much more value then is a man than a sheep! So then, it is lawful to do good on the Sabbath." Then He said to the man, "Stretch out your hand!" And he stretched it out, and it was restored to normal, like the other. (12:9-13)

Without waiting for a response from the Pharisees, Jesus immediately **went to their synagogue**, into their very lair as it were, and gave them a living illustration of the true meaning of Sabbath observance and of His authority over both man and the Sabbath.

Although what happened in the **synagogue** was planned by Jesus for the purposes just mentioned, when the Pharisees saw **a man with a withered hand** there, they thought they had the perfect trap for Jesus. Completely unaffected by Jesus' reminder from Scripture that God desires "compassion, and not a sacrifice" (v. 7), **they questioned Him, saying, "Is it lawful to heal on the Sabbath?"** Their only purpose in listening to anything Jesus said or in watching anything He did was **that they might accuse Him.** They were not looking for the truth but for a way to dispose of this upstart young rabbi who dared to make a sacrilege of their revered traditions and blaspheme God with His claims.

The fact that they asked Jesus this question indicates they acknowledged His power to heal. Because His miraculous power was so indisputable, Jesus' opponents tried to undercut the significance of it by such means as accusing Him of casting out demons by Satan's power (Matt. 9:34; 12:24). His miracles made them all the more determined to destroy Him (Matt. 12:14). The same signs that convinced the humble of Jesus' divinity and messiahship confirmed the proud in their unbelief and rejection.

The Pharisees chose the **man with a withered hand** to test Jesus because the man's healing was not a life-or-death issue, which according to their tradition was the only justification for giving medical help on the Sabbath. They reasoned that, if Jesus were truly of God, He would respect that tradition and wait until the next day to heal the man.

The illustration of the **sheep** that **falls into a pit on the Sabbath** dealt with an economic justification for breaking the Sabbath that was probably provided for in the traditions. The commentator William Hendriksen says, "It is safe to infer, perhaps, that the question asked by Jesus at the moment indicates to us that there was a particular legislation permitting this." In any case, Jesus' question was rhetorical, and the answer was obvious and assumed: Any Jew, including a Pharisee, would find some way to rescue his sheep in such a situation. If there were a regulation permitting him to do such a thing, he would certainly take advantage of it. If there were not, he would find some way of circumventing or bending the law in order to save his sheep. Either within the tradition or in spite of it, he would find a way to **take hold of** the sheep **and lift it out**. The Pharisees did not argue the point with Jesus, proving the assumed answer was correct.

The Lord therefore declared, **Of how much more value then is a man than a sheep!** No Pharisee would have contended that sheep were as valuable as men, who they knew were created in God's image. But in practice, the Pharisees treated other men with less respect than they treated their animals, because in their hearts they did not respect, much less love, their fellow men, including their fellow Jews. They contemptuously subjugated human life and welfare to religious tradition.

One of the most obvious tragedies of Hinduism is its disregard for human welfare in the name of human welfare. A beggar is not given food because it would interfere with his karma and prevent him from suffering his way to the next highest level of existence. A fly is not killed because it is the reincarnation of some unfortunate human being of past ages. Rats are not killed for the same reason and are allowed to eat and contaminate food supplies without any interference. Cows are considered sacred and are given what food is available, while human beings are allowed to starve.

In a similar way the Pharisees despised other human beings, showing more compassion for **a sheep** than for a crippled **man** who was even a fellow Jew. Mark reports that Jesus then asked the Pharisees, "'Is it lawful on the Sabbath to do good or to do harm, to save a life or to kill?' But they kept silent" (Mark 3:4). Had they approved doing good and saving a life, they would have contradicted tradition; and, on the other hand, they obviously would not have advocated doing evil or killing. They were trapped in the illogic of their heartless, unscriptural traditions. Their only outward recourse was to keep silent; but inwardly they "were filled with rage" (Luke 6:11).

The Lord therefore answered the question Himself: **It is lawful to do good on the Sabbath**—no doubt putting strong emphasis on **is**. At that point Jesus' righteous anger confronted the Pharisees' unrighteous anger. "And after looking around at them with anger" (Mark 3:5), Jesus **said to the man, "Stretch out your hand!" And he stretched it out, and it was restored, like the other.** Jesus not only *approved* doing good on the Sabbath but *did* good on the Sabbath. As Lord of the Sabbath He demonstrated that, if anything, the Sabbath was the supreme day for doing good.

THE INSURRECTION

But the Pharisees went out, and counseled together against Him, as to how they might destroy Him. (12:14)

Neither the power of Jesus' argument nor the power of His miracles moved the Pharisees. They refused to be convinced. Jesus had indisputably connected the heart of God with benevolence, kindness, mercy, goodness, and compassion; and He had connected those virtues with Sabbath observance. But the Pharisees would have none of it, because they "loved the darkness rather than the light; for their deeds were evil" (John 3:19). Their trust was in tradition and in their own works, and neither God's Word nor God's Son would change them.

Because they could not disprove the truth of what Jesus said or the power of what He did, **the Pharisees went out, and counseled together against Him, as to how they might destroy Him.** True to the nature of their spiritual father, the devil (John 8:44), the Pharisees sought to **destroy** what they could not subvert.

The Pharisees would have killed Jesus on the spot had not Rome restricted them from inflicting capital punishment and had they not been afraid of the many people who followed and admired Him. The Greek term from which **counseled** is translated includes the idea of carrying out a decision already made. Jesus' enemies were already determined to **destroy Him;** the only remaining decision had to do with **how.**

From Mark we learn that the Pharisees were so determined to destroy Jesus at any cost that they enlisted the help of their usual archenemies, the Herodians (3:6)— the irreligious and worldly political party who supported Herod, the half-Jew Idumean king who had bought his title from Rome. The Herodians were the antithesis of the Pharisees in almost every way, and the fact that the Pharisees sought to join forces with them reveals how desperate they were to do away with Jesus. The religious legalists joined forces with the secular libertarians to destroy an enemy they considered to be even more dangerous than each other.

Despite their differences, those two groups had the same spiritual orientation. They both disregarded God's Word in favor of their own ideas; they both rejected His Son; and their mutual unwitting allegiance was to Satan, the spiritual leader of the present world system (cf. John 8:44). Neither the Gentile world nor the Jewish nation recognized or received the divine Visitor who had made them and had come to redeem them (John 1:10-11).

As Donald Grey Barnhouse observed, "It is at this point in history that Israel's clock stopped." Because Israel, God's chosen and specially blessed people, rejected her Messiah, God placed her on the shelf as a nation "until the fulness of the Gentiles has come in" (Rom. 11:25; cf. Acts 15:14-18).

Legalism is the implacable enemy of grace. Even the Mosaic law, demanding as it was, was a reflection of God's grace, a means of guiding men toward Jesus Christ, the one true and only hope of coming to God. As Paul explains, the law was a "tutor to lead us to Christ, that we may be justified by faith" (Gal. 3:24). If God's own law was only a shadow, how much less spiritual substance does human tradition have? If even divine law cannot save, of how much less value is human tradition?

Just as trust in tradition and good works is a barrier to salvation, it is also a barrier to faithful living after salvation. "Having begun by the Spirit, are you now being perfected by the flesh?" Paul asked Galatian believers who were being misled by the legalistic Judaizers (Gal. 3:3). "Does He then, who provides you with the Spirit and works miracles among you, do it by the works of the Law, or by hearing with faith? . . . Christ redeemed us from the curse of the Law, having become a curse for us—for it is written, 'Cursed is everyone who hangs on a tree'—in order that in Christ Jesus the blessing of Abraham might come to the Gentiles, so that we might receive the promise of the Spirit through faith" (vv. 5, 13-14).

God's Beloved Servant (12:15-21)

27

But Jesus, aware of this, withdrew from there. And many followed Him, and He healed them all, and warned them not to make Him known, in order that what was spoken through Isaiah the prophet, might be fulfilled, saying, "Behold, My Servant whom I have chosen; My Beloved in whom My soul is well-pleased; I will put My Spirit upon Him, and He shall proclaim justice to the Gentiles. He will not quarrel, nor cry out; nor will anyone hear His voice in the streets. A battered reed He will not break off, and a smoldering wick He will not put out, until He leads justice to victory. And in His name the Gentiles will hope." (12:15-21)

Scripture ascribes many titles to Christ [Messiah], and none is more fitting or lovely than My Servant, a title first used by Isaiah (42:1). Just as the prophet predicted of the Messiah, Jesus came in wonder, beauty, and majesty as the divine Servant, serving the Father and serving mankind in the Father's name.

This brief passage is an oasis of refreshing beauty in the desert of chapters 11 and 12—which chronicle the first major rejection of Christ, led by the scribes and Pharisees. After Jesus put them to shame by showing that their Sabbath traditions were hardhearted, illogical, and unscriptural, "the Pharisees went out, and counseled together against Him, as to how they might destroy Him" (12:14). Those ungodly leaders believed the very opposite of the truth about Jesus, even to the point of accusing Him of doing His work by the power of Satan.

In the midst of his account of that mounting antagonism, Matthew here presents some of the outstanding characteristics of this Servant whom the world despises but God dearly loves.

CONFORMED TO GOD'S PLAN

But Jesus, aware of this, withdrew from there. And many followed Him, and He healed them all, and warned them not to make Him known, in order that what was spoken through Isaiah the prophet, might be fulfilled, saying, (12:15-17)

In His omniscience **Jesus** was **aware** of the Pharisees' plan to destroy Him, and He therefore **withdrew from there.** Jesus had not come to do His own will but His Father's (Matt. 26:29; John 6:38), and it was not yet the Father's time for the Son's ministry and life to be ended. When that time came, Jesus accepted His arrest, trial, and crucifixion without complaint or resistance—although at any time He could easily have saved Himself and destroyed those who sought to destroy Him. When the soldiers came to arrest Him in the Garden of Gethsemane, they fell down in awe simply at hearing Him say, "I am He" (John 18:6). When, a few moments later, Peter drew his sword and cut off the ear of the high priest's slave, Jesus said, "Put your sword back into its place; for all those who take up the sword shall perish by the sword. Or do you think that I cannot appeal to My Father, and He will at once put at My disposal more than twelve legions of angels?" (Matt. 26:52-53).

Until the time of the events described in the Matthew 21, Jesus' ministry was a continual cycle that consisted of going to a particular city or region; of preaching, teaching, and healing; of acceptance by some and rejection by others, particularly the religious leaders; and then of withdrawal to another place. As His ministry progressed, the cycles became shorter because opposition came more quickly and more intensely.

Yet Jesus was never forced away from a place of ministry, but always **withdrew** of His own volition. Had He been willing to use His power for that purpose, He could have continued at any place doing entirely as He pleased—because no force, including the crack troops of Rome, could have hindered Him in the least way. But the Father's plan was not to shed Roman blood but His Son's blood, because only His Son's blood could atone for the sins of mankind and open the way to heaven.

The essence of Jesus' life, His very food, was to do His Father's will and "to accomplish His work" (John 4:34). Jesus had the true heart of a servant, and He was submissive to His Father and wholly given to redeeming a lost world. There was never a servant like this Servant, "who, although He existed in the form of God, did not regard equality with God a thing to be grasped, but emptied Himself, taking the form of a bond-servant, and being made in the likeness of men. And being found in appearance as a man, He humbled Himself by becoming obedient to the point of death, even death on a cross" (Phil. 2:6-8).

After Jesus left the synagogue, **many followed Him, and He healed them all.** The Lord **healed** many people who did not believe in Him to salvation. Of the ten lepers He cleansed on one occasion, only one showed evidence of faith by returning to give thanks. Jesus' words "Your faith has made you well" refer to the man's spiritual healing through salvation, not to his physical healing, which had already taken place. All ten lepers were physically healed, but only one was healed spiritually (Luke 17:11-19).

Jesus' miracles of healing demonstrated His divine power, but they also demonstrated His divine love and compassion for suffering people. He healed in order to reveal the loving heart of God, which continually goes out to those who are hurting, burdened, and persecuted. The people Jesus healed were despised and neglected by the scribes and Pharisees, as well as by the priesthood, which God had established as a means for bringing His people nearer to Himself. The religious leaders were interested in the rich and influential, not the sick, the poor, and the outcast. As in the case of the man with the withered hand, their only interest in his affliction was to use it as a means of inducing Jesus to break a Sabbath tradition in order to accuse and convict Him (Matt. 12:10).

Jesus, on the other hand, always had time for those who were suffering and in need. When He looked out over "the multitudes, He felt compassion for them, because they were distressed and downcast like sheep without a shepherd" (9:36). Not only were they oppressed by the Romans but by their own religious leaders, those who should have been their shepherds. Those leaders were wolves dressed like shepherds, and instead of feeding the sheep they devoured them (Matt. 7:15; 23:14). They were like the wicked shepherd spoken of by Zechariah who devoured the flesh of the fat sheep and tore off their hooves (Zech. 11:16).

But when the true Shepherd came to Israel, He had great compassion for His suffering people and He lovingly healed them of every kind of disease and affliction. He called out to them saying, "Come to Me, all who are weary and heavy-laden, and I will give you rest. Take My yoke upon you, and learn from Me, for I am gentle and humble in heart; and you shall find rest for your souls. For My yoke is easy, and My load is light" (Matt. 11:28-30). False shepherds impose burdens, but the true Shepherd lifts them. That is why Peter tells us to cast our burdens and anxieties on the "Chief Shepherd," because He cares for us (1 Pet. 5:4, 7).

Christ feels the pain that hurts us and the weight of burdens that grind us down; and in His gracious lovingkindness He heals our hurts and lifts our burdens.

After Jesus healed **all** the afflicted among those who had followed Him, He **warned** them **not to make Him known,** just as He had told the leper, "See that you tell no one" (Matt. 8:4), and the two blind men, "See here, let no one know about this!" (9:30).

There are probably several reasons why Jesus gave such instructions on certain occasions. In the case of the leper, Jesus prescribed the Old Testament procedure for going to the priests to have a cleansing verified (Lev. 14:2-32). The testimony of the priests would give official recognition of the man's healing and therefore give more dramatic evidence of Jesus' messianic credentials.

It may also have been that Jesus sometimes commanded that His miracles not be publicized so that He could confront in person as many people as possible with the initial wonder of His miraculous power. When John the Baptist sent his disciples to ask Jesus if He were really the Messiah, Jesus did not simply tell them about what He had been doing but performed miracles especially for their sakes, giving them direct proof of His divine power. "At that very time," Luke tells us, Jesus "cured many people of diseases and afflictions and evil spirits; and He granted sight to many who were blind" (Luke 7:21).

Jesus also may not have wanted His miracles to become too widely known in order to keep them in perspective. The miracles were evidence of His divine power and His rightful claim to messiahship. He did not perform them to become famous or to build up a popular base of power and influence—as many of His followers expected Him to do. And although He had great compassion for the physical afflictions of the people, His primary work was to save souls, not bodies. Not only that, but continual demonstrations of power could easily have inflamed zealous enthusiasm for Him as a military and political deliverer, which most Jews expected the Messiah to be but which Jesus refused to be. It was for that reason that He withdrew from the crowds after the feeding of the five thousand. "Jesus therefore perceiving that they were intending to come and take Him by force, to make Him king, withdrew again to the mountain by Himself alone" (John 6:15).

Jesus' miracles also served to further incite the rage of the scribes and Pharisees; and if His fame had spread too widely and quickly it would have prematurely increased the fatal opposition against Him.

But perhaps the most important reason Jesus did not want His miracle power to be too highly acclaimed was that this was not the time of His exaltation but of His humiliation.

Many of the people must have wondered why, if Jesus really was the Messiah, He was not accepted by the religious leaders and why He kept withdrawing from the multitudes and why He spent so much time with the poor and needy instead of the powerful and influential. How could such a person overthrow Rome and restore Israel?

But Matthew assures His readers that Jesus is indeed the Messiah, just as foretold by **Isaiah the prophet.** Jesus did not come to fulfill the confused and unscriptural expectations of the people but to fulfill His divine mission as predicted in His own Word. He was therefore determined that every divine prediction about Him **might be fulfilled.**

Matthew 12:18-21 is a modified quotation of Isaiah 42:1-4 and is one of the most strikingly beautiful descriptions of Jesus Christ anywhere in Scripture. Here we see that Jesus was commended by the Father and commissioned by the Holy Spirit, that He communicated His Father's message, that He was committed to meekness and to comforting the weak, and that He would consummate the victory over sin and Satan.

COMMENDED BY THE FATHER

Behold, My Servant whom I have chosen; My Beloved in whom My soul is well-pleased; (12:18a)

Pais (**Servant**) is not the usual word for "servant" and is often translated "son." In secular Greek it was used of an especially intimate servant who was trusted and loved like a son. In the ancient Greek edition of the Old Testament (the Septuagint), *pais* is used of Abraham's chief servant (Gen. 24:2), of Pharaoh's royal servants (41:10, 38), and of angels as the Lord's supernatural servants (Job 4:18).

Jesus Christ is God's supreme **Servant,** His only Son whom He has **chosen** to redeem the world. The Greek phrase translated **I have chosen** (from *hairetizō*) indicates a firm and determined decision and is used nowhere else in the New Testament. It was used in secular Greek of irrevocably adopting a child into the family as an heir who could never be disenfranchised. The Father had irrevocably **chosen** His **beloved** Son to be His divine **Servant,** the only One qualified for the task of redemption.

Because the prophets frequently spoke of God's choosing the Messiah, He was often referred to as "The Chosen One." At Jesus' crucifixion, "the rulers were sneering at Him, saying, 'He saved others; let Him save Himself if this is the Christ [Messiah] of God, His Chosen One'" (Luke 23:35). The fact that they knew so much truth about the Messiah made them all the more culpable for rejecting Him.

Jesus is the Father's **beloved, in whom** His **soul is well-pleased.** It is through the grace of God "which He freely bestowed on us in the Beloved," that "we have redemption through His blood, the forgiveness of our trespasses" (Eph. 1:6-7). The One who is hated and rejected by the world, including His own people, is **beloved** by God, who **is well-pleased.** Against the testimony of Israel and of the world is the testimony of the Father. Jesus said, "If I alone bear witness of Myself, My testimony is not true. There is another who bears witness of Me, and I know that the testimony which He bears of Me is true. . . . the witness which I have is greater than that of John; for the works which the Father has given Me to accomplish, the very works that I do, bear witness of Me, that the Father has sent Me. And the Father who sent Me, He has borne witness of Me" (John 5:31-32, 36-37).

At Jesus' baptism the Father declared, "This is My beloved Son, in whom I am well-pleased" (Matt. 3:17), and at the transfiguration He declared again, "This is My beloved Son, with whom I am well-pleased; listen to Him" (17:5).

It is not possible for men to be well-pleasing to God unless they come to Him through His Son, with whom He *is* **well-pleased.** "Those who are in the flesh cannot please God," Paul tells us. "However, you are not in the flesh but in the Spirit, if indeed the Spirit of God dwells in you" (Rom. 8:8-9). God is well-pleased with believers because He sees them as He sees His own Son.

COMMISSIONED BY THE HOLY SPIRIT

I will put My Spirit upon Him, (12:18*b*)

Through Isaiah, God promised that He would **put** His **Spirit upon** the Messiah in a unique way, and at Jesus' baptism the Holy Spirit descended upon Him as a dove (Matt. 3:16). But that was not when He was indwelt by the Spirit. Unique to all mankind, Jesus was conceived by the Holy Spirit (Matt. 1:20); and if John the Baptist was filled with the Spirit from His mother's womb (Luke 1:15), how much more so was Jesus.

Yet, if Jesus was the preexistent Son, eternally one with the Father and the Holy Spirit, in what way could the **Spirit** have come **upon Him** during His humanity? First of all, the coming of the Spirit upon Jesus was a bestowing of power to His human nature. His divine nature was already one with the **Spirit** and did not require special assistance, but His human nature did. Jesus was fully human, even to the point of being tempted in the same ways every human being is, yet without sinning (Heb. 4:15). As a child, He grew in wisdom, stature, and in favor with God and man (Luke 2:52). He had human feelings and human emotions. He was hungry and thirsty, and He became tired and felt pain and sorrow. His humanness received the indwelling power of the Holy Spirit in order for it to function in concert with His deity. Therefore "God anointed Him with the Holy Spirit and with power" (Acts 10:38).

Second, Jesus required the anointing of the Spirit in order to attest to His royal service as the Messiah. For thirty years He had lived in obscurity, but when His ministry began He was given a special attestation of authority and approval by the Father. A prophecy of the Messiah was quoted by Jesus and applied to Himself as He taught in the synagogue at Nazareth: "The Spirit of the Lord is upon Me, because He anointed Me to preach the gospel to the poor. He has sent Me to proclaim release to the captives, and recovery of sight to the blind, to set free those who are downtrodden, to proclaim the favorable year of the Lord" (Luke 4:18-19). After He sat down, Jesus explained, "Today this Scripture has been fulfilled in your hearing" (v. 21).

As the perfect submissive Servant, Jesus functioned not only in the Father's will and by the Father's commendation but in the power of the Father's **Spirit.**

COMMUNICATING THE MESSAGE

and He shall proclaim justice to the Gentiles. (12:18*c*)

Isaiah prophesied that the Lord's beloved Servant would **proclaim** a message of truth and **justice** even to the **Gentiles**; and that is what Jesus did. Contrary to the thinking and expectations of most Jews, the Messiah was to be the Redeemer of the whole world, not just of Israel. Israel was, in fact, to be the channel of God's grace to the rest of the world. In His first great promise to Abraham, God declared, "And in you all the families of the earth shall be blessed" (Gen. 12:3). Israel was called to be God's agency for reaching the world for Himself; and when the Jews as a nation rejected God, He had to raise up a new agent, the church, to accomplish that purpose.

The first woman to whom Jesus revealed His messiahship was a Samaritan, half Jew and half Gentile (John 4:26). Early in His ministry He had Gentile followers from Idumea, the Trans-Jordan, and the region around Tyre and Sidon (Mark 3:8). Of the Gentile centurion whose servant He healed, Jesus said, "Truly I say to you, I have not found such great faith with anyone in Israel" (Matt. 8:10).

But the Jews resented Jesus' giving any attention to Gentiles, and especially His treating them equally with Jews. And the idea of the Messiah coming to *redeem* Gentiles was anathema. When Paul was defending himself before a large group of Jews in Jerusalem, he managed to keep their attention as he recounted his former life, his conversion experience, and his vision in the Temple. But when he reported that God told him, "'Go! For I will send you far away to the Gentiles,' . . . they listened to him up to this statement, and then they raised their voices and said, 'Away with such a fellow from the earth, for he should not be allowed to live!'" They were so uncontrollably incensed that "they were crying out and throwing off their cloaks and tossing dust into the air" (Acts 22:21-23). Almost no truth of the gospel was as hard for Jews to accept as the truth that salvation and fellowship with God were for Gentiles as well as Jews. The notion was utterly inconceivable to them, and, as is clear from the account just mentioned, they considered it a form of blasphemy.

But God's plan for redemption had always included the **Gentiles,** and to them the Messiah was to **proclaim justice** and deliverance from sin just as to the Jews.

COMMITTED TO MEEKNESS

He will not quarrel, nor cry out; nor will anyone hear His voice in the streets.
(12:19)

Epizō (to **quarrel**) carries the idea of wrangling, hassling, or even brawling. *Kraugazō* (to **cry out**) means to shout or scream excitedly. The term was sometimes used of a dog's barking, a raven's squawking, and even a drunk's bawling.

Jesus did not come to harangue and cajole people with the gospel like a rabble-rousing zealot who inflames his hearers by appealing to their emotions and prejudices. He spoke with dignity and control, and He used no means of persuasion but the truth. He never organized a mob or resorted to trickery, lies, or scheming, as His opponents routinely did against Him. His was the way of gentleness, meekness, and lowliness. Although He was the Son of God, the divine Messiah, and the rightful King of kings, Jesus never tried to secure a hearing, much less a following, by political power, physical force, or emotional agitation.

Even the wisdom of man knows that no real persuasion can be made by force or intimidation. As Solomon reminds us, "The words of the wise heard in quietness are better than the shouting of a ruler among fools" (Eccles. 9:17; cf. 1 Cor. 2:1-4).

COMFORTING THE WEAK

A battered reed He will not break off, and a smoldering wick He will not put out, (12:20*a*)

In ancient times reeds were used for many purposes, but once a **reed** was bent or **battered** it was useless. A shepherd would often make a flute-like instrument from a reed and play soft music on it to while away the hours and to calm the sheep. When the reed became soft or cracked, it would no longer make music and the shepherd would **break** it and throw it away.

When a lamp burned down to the end of the wick, it would only smolder and smoke without making any light. Since such a **smoldering wick** was useless, it was **put out** and thrown away, just like a broken reed.

The **battered reed** and the **smoldering wick** represent people whose lives are broken and worn out, ready to be discarded and replaced by the world. Because they can no longer "make music" or "give light," society casts off the weak and the helpless, the suffering and the burdened. Those were the kind of people the Romans ignored as useless and the Pharisees despised as worthless.

One of the most obvious legacies of the Fall is man's natural tendency to destroy. Small children will often step on a bug just for the sake of killing it, or snap off a beautiful bud just before it flowers. A tree branch is broken for the sake of breaking it, and a stone is thrown at a bird just to see it fly away or fall to the ground. On a more destructive scale, adults devour and undercut each other in business, society, politics, and even in the family.

The nature of sinful man is to destroy, but the nature of the holy God is to restore. The Lord will **not break off** or **put out** even the least of those who come to Him, and He gives dire warning to those who would do so. "Whoever causes one of these little ones who believe in Me to stumble," Jesus said, "it is better for him that a heavy millstone be hung around his neck, and that he be drowned in the depth of the sea" (Matt. 18:6).

In the hands of the Savior, the **battered reed** is not discarded but restored, and the **smoldering wick** is not put out but rekindled.

CONSUMMATING THE VICTORY

until He leads justice to victory. And in His name the Gentiles will hope. (12:20*b*-21)

Ultimately right will win. In spite of oppression, persecution, and rejection, Jesus was destined to be be victorious. As **He leads justice to victory,** He will bring with Him all who belong to Him and who have themselves been oppressed, persecuted, and rejected by the world. When Christ takes His rightful place as Lord and King, justice will "roll down like waters and righteousness like an ever-flowing stream" (Amos 5:24).

> Down in the human heart,
>   Crushed by the tempter,
> Feelings lie buried
>   That grace can restore,
> Touched by a loving heart,
>   Wakened by kindness,
> Chords that were broken
>   Will vibrate once more.
>
> ("Rescue the Perishing," Fanny J. Crosby)

BIRDVILLE
BAPTIST CHURCH
LIBRARY

Blaspheming the Holy Spirit (12:22-32)

28

Then there was brought to Him a demon-possessed man who was blind and dumb, and He healed him, so that the dumb man spoke and saw. And all the multitudes were amazed, and began to say, "This man cannot be the Son of David, can he?" But when the Pharisees heard it, they said, "This man casts out demons only by Beelzebul the ruler of the demons." And knowing their thoughts He said to them, "Any kingdom divided against itself is laid waste; and any city or house divided against itself shall not stand. And if Satan casts out Satan, he is divided against himself; how then shall his kingdom stand? And if I by Beelzebul cast out demons, by whom do your sons cast them out? Consequently they shall be your judges. But if I cast out demons by the Spirit of God, then the kingdom of God has come upon you. Or how can anyone enter the strong man's house and carry off his property, unless he first binds the strong man? And then he will plunder his house. He who is not with Me is against Me; and he who does not gather with Me scatters. Therefore I say to you, any sin and blasphemy shall be forgiven men, but blasphemy against the Spirit shall not be forgiven. And whoever shall speak a word against the Son of Man, it shall be forgiven him; but whoever shall speak against the Holy Spirit, it shall not be forgiven him, either in this age, or in the age to come. (12:22-32)

By nature God is forgiving. The Old Testament abounds with teachings about His forgiveness. David declared, "For Thou, Lord, art good, and ready to forgive, and abundant in lovingkindness to all who call upon Thee" (Ps. 86:5). In another psalm he reminds us that God pardons all our iniquities (Ps. 103:3). Daniel said, "To the Lord our God belong compassion and forgiveness" (Dan. 9:9). God described Himself to Moses as, "the Lord, the Lord God, compassionate and gracious, slow to anger, and abounding in lovingkindness and truth; who keeps lovingkindness for thousands, who forgives iniquity, transgression and sin" (Ex. 34:6-7). Micah extolled the Lord, saying, "Who is a God like Thee, who pardons iniquity and passes over the rebellious act of the remnant of His possession? He does not retain His anger forever, because He delights in unchanging love. He will again have compassion on us; He will tread our iniquities under foot. Yes, Thou wilt cast all their sins into the depths of the sea" (Mic. 7:18-19).

The Old Testament also abounds with examples of His forgiveness. When Adam and Eve committed sin, God forgave them. When Abraham, Isaac, and Jacob sinned, God forgave them. When Moses sinned God forgave him. When Israel under the judges and under the kings repeatedly sinned, God forgave her. Israel's history is a history of God's forgiveness.

Likewise the New Testament pictures God as supremely the God of forgiveness. That is the essence of the gospel: God's divine and gracious provision for the forgiveness of man's sin. In Christ, Paul says, "we have redemption through His blood, the forgiveness of our trespasses, according to the riches of His grace" (Eph. 1:7; cf. Col. 1:14). John assures us that, "If we confess our sins, He is faithful and righteous to forgive us our sins and to cleanse us from all unrighteousness" and that our "sins are forgiven [us] for His name's sake" (1 John 1:9; 2:12).

No matter how severe the sin, God can forgive it. The worst conceivable sin would be to kill God's own Son—and that while He was on earth for the very purpose of providing salvation from sin and the way to everlasting life. Nothing could possibly be more heinous, vicious, and wicked than that. And, of course, killing Him is exactly what men did to the Son of God. Yet, while hanging on the cross and about to die, Jesus prayed and affirmed the forgiving mercy available to His executioners, "Father, forgive them; for they do not know what they are doing" (Luke 23:34). The *degree* of sin does not forfeit forgiveness, because even killing the Son of God was forgivable.

Nor does the *volume* of sin end the possibility of mercy. A seventy-year-old profligate who has lived a life of debauchery, stealing, lying, profanity, blasphemy, and immorality is just as forgivable as a seven-year-old who has done nothing worse than normal childhood naughtiness.

Nor does the particular *kind* of sin cancel grace. In Scripture we find God forgiving idolatry, murder, gluttony, fornication, adultery, cheating, lying, homosexuality, covenant breaking, blasphemy, drunkenness, extortion, and every other kind of sin imaginable. He forgives self-righteousness, which is the deceiving sin of thinking that one has no sin. He even forgives the sin of rejecting Christ; otherwise no one could be saved, because before salvation *everyone,* to some degree, is a Christ rejecter. There is no forgiveness of even the smallest sin unless it is confessed and repented of; but there is forgiveness of even the greatest sin if those divine conditions are met.

The rejection of Jesus as Messiah and King gradually escalated as His ministry continued. As we have seen, first there was doubt, then criticism, then indifference, culminating in open rejection. The religious leaders of Israel then added blasphemy against the Holy Spirit to their rejection of Christ. Although their animosity would continue to spread and intensify, this blasphemy was the epitome of its expression.

For centuries God's people had longed for the Messiah, their divine Deliverer. The hope of every godly prophet and teacher of Israel was to live to see Him; and every Jewish girl dreamed of being His mother. Yet when He arrived He was denied and rejected. In 12:22-32, Matthew details five features of the climax of that rejection: the activity of Jesus in healing a seriously afflicted man; the amazement of the crowd over the miracle; the accusation against Jesus because of the miracle; Jesus' answer to His accusers; and the anathema His accusers brought on themselves.

THE ACTIVITY

Then there was brought to Him a demon-possessed man who was blind and dumb, and He healed him, so that the dumb man spoke and saw. (12:22)

The **man** had multiple problems. He was **demon-possessed . . . blind and dumb,** and possibly also suffered deafness, so often associated with inability to speak. But the fact that Jesus **healed him** was not unique. He had healed hundreds, perhaps even thousands, of people who were demon-possessed, blind, dumb, and deaf; and many of those had more than one affliction, just as this man did.

As was often the case, this healing demonstrated in one act Jesus' dominion over both the spirit world of demons and the physical world of disease. He undeniably possessed the power to heal every kind of disease, to cast out any kind and any number of demons, and even to restore life to the dead. He had performed thousands of instantaneous, total, permanent, and verifiable healings. His supernatural powers could no longer be questioned, either by the common multitudes or by the more educated and skeptical religious leaders.

Yet most of the sin-blinded people remained ambivalent about Jesus' identity and the source of His great power. They knew that miracles would be proof signs of the Messiah; but they also expected Him to come with royal fanfare and with military might. But instead of regal robes, sovereign authority, a throne, trumpets, swords, horses, chariots, and a mighty army, they saw a Man of compassion, gentleness, and humility—with a following of twelve nondescript disciples and a multitude of hangers-on whose loyalty could hardly be counted on. Because Jesus did not appear to be a conqueror or a king by their definition, the people would not accept His being the Messiah. They had chosen to be selective about the Old Testament predictions of the Messiah. His predicted coming in power and glory to defeat the foes of Israel and set His people free was easy for them to be excited about. His predicted coming in meekness and humility was not.

The scribes and Pharisees had been dogging Jesus' footsteps for some time and were already convinced He was an enemy of Judaism—so much so that they even collaborated against Him with the Herodians, who normally were their arch foes (Mark 3:6). The religious leaders were no longer merely skeptical and resentful but had become adamantly hostile to Jesus. It would be over a year before Jesus would be crucified, but the irrevocable decision to destroy Him had already been made (Matt. 12:14).

Jesus therefore seems to have performed the particular healing on this occasion especially for the benefit of the Pharisees, forcing them to make their verdict concerning Him public. Before their eyes they saw a man become immediately and dramatically delivered of three great afflictions, and he now stood before them in sound mind and spirit and both **spoke and saw**. The miracle was incontestable.

THE AMAZEMENT

And all the multitudes were amazed, and began to say, "This man cannot be the Son of David, can he?" (12:23)

Although many people among **the multitudes** present that day had doubtlessly seen Jesus perform many miracles of healing, they were especially **amazed** by this one. *Existēmi* (to be **amazed**) means to be totally astounded, beside oneself with amazement and wonder. One writer suggests that "it means to be literally knocked out of your senses," and another that "it means to be out of your mind with amazement." In ways that we may not fully see from the narrative, this particular miracle was unusually overwhelming, as if Jesus meant to intensify its demonstration of supernaturalness.

Although it comes down on the negative side of probability in their minds, the very question the people **began** to ask among themselves—**This man cannot be the Son of David, can he?**—reveals that they recognized such miracles as possible messianic signs. **Son of David** was one of many scriptural titles for the Messiah (see 2 Sam. 7:12-16; Ps. 89:3; Isa. 9:6-7), and for the people to consider whether Jesus could be **the Son of David** was a query related to His being the Messiah. That was the title later ascribed to Jesus by the crowds who welcomed Him into Jerusalem as their Messiah and King (Matt. 21:9; cf. v. 5).

THE ACCUSATION

But when the Pharisees heard it, they said, "This man casts out demons only by Beelzebul the ruler of the demons." (12:24)

The fact that the multitudes were seriously wondering if Jesus might be the Messiah drove **the Pharisees** to panic, and they unwittingly reacted with the foolish accusation that Jesus cast **out demons only by Beelzebul the ruler of the demons**. These Jewish religious leaders, of whom the Pharisees were always the most zealous and vocal, could not tolerate the thought that this man who denounced them as unrighteous hypocrites and trampled on their human system of traditions could be the prophesied and long-awaited Deliverer of Israel.

Matthew's telling us that Jesus knew their thoughts (v. 25) indicates that the Pharisees were some distance from Jesus, perhaps on the fringe of the crowd or standing outside as Jesus ministered within a house. Their intent was to poison the minds of the people against Jesus by answering their question about Him with a resounding no. They said, in effect, that He was the antithesis of the Son of David. He was the servant of **Beelzebul the ruler of the demons.**

They had only one option. Because Jesus' power was indisputably supernatural, because the only two sources of supernatural power are God and Satan, and because they refused to recognize Jesus as being from God, they were forced to conclude that He was an agent of Satan. He must serve **the ruler of the demons,** for whom Beelzebul (or Beelzebub) was a popular title, derived from the name of an ancient Canaanite deity. (See chapter 9 of this volume for a discussion of the name *Beelzebul.*)

THE ANSWER

And knowing their thoughts He said to them, "Any kingdom divided against itself is laid waste; and any city or house divided against itself shall not stand. And if Satan casts out Satan, he is divided against himself; how then shall his kingdom stand? And if I by Beelzebul cast out demons, by whom do your sons cast them out? Consequently they shall be your judges. But if I cast out demons by the Spirit of God, then the kingdom of God has come upon you. Or how can anyone enter the strong man's house and carry off his property, unless he first binds the strong man? And then he will plunder his house. He who is not with Me is against Me; and he who does not gather with Me scatters. (12:25-30)

Although the Pharisees were speaking to the crowd beyond Jesus' hearing, He nevertheless knew **their thoughts.** Mark tells us that some scribes from Jerusalem joined the Pharisees in accusing Jesus of casting out demons by the power of Beelzebul, and that Jesus "called them to Himself and began speaking to them in parables" (3:22-23). They would not confront Him directly with their accusation, but He confronted them directly with its absurdity, its prejudice, and its rebelliousness.

THE ACCUSATION WAS ABSURD

"Any kingdom divided against itself is laid waste; and any city or house divided against itself shall not stand. And if Satan casts out Satan, he is divided against himself; how then shall his kingdom stand?" (12:25b-26)

Jesus first showed His accusers that their charge was a logical absurdity. It is axiomatic that a **kingdom divided against itself** would soon be **laid waste** by self-destruction. The truism also applies to **any city** or **any house.** If one or the other becomes **divided against itself,** it obviously **shall not stand.**

Applied to the spirit world, the principle is just as clear: **If Satan casts out Satan, he is divided against himself; how shall his kingdom stand?** Outside of the Trinity, Satan is the most intelligent being in existence, and he certainly does not assign his forces to fight against each other and internally destroy his own program.

It is true, of course, that evil is destructive by nature, and that destruction often includes self-destruction. Satan is the father of hatred and lies, and where such things rule there is confusion and inconsistency. There can be no true harmony within or among evil beings. Just as God is the Lord of order and harmony, Satan is the lord of disorder and chaos, whether he chooses to be or not.

It is also true that although Satan is brilliant, powerful, and able to move from place to place with seemingly instantaneous speed, he is nevertheless not omniscient, omnipotent, or omnipresent. And the supreme deceiver is supremely self-deceived, especially in thinking he can overpower God and usurp His kingdom.

And it is further true that Satan often disguises himself as an angel of light (2 Cor. 11:14). In that role he may pretend to cast out a demon by restricting its power over the possessed person in order to give the impression of a cleansing. That sort of supposed exorcism has been common throughout the history of the church and is practiced today by various cults, false healers, and exorcists.

Even Satan's demons may on occasion act inconsistently and in conflict with him and each other. But despite the disorder of his kingdom, his creaturely limits, his false exorcisms, and demon confusion, **Satan** does not cast **out Satan,** and **he is** not **divided against himself.** There is no harmony, trust, or loyalty in his **kingdom,** but he tolerates no disobedience or division. It was therefore preposterous to accuse Jesus of casting out demons by the power of the ruler of demons.

THE ACCUSATION WAS PREJUDICED

And if I by Beelzebul cast out demons, by whom do your sons cast them out? Consequently they shall be your judges. (12:27)

Second, Jesus showed that the Pharisees' accusation was also prejudiced, revealing the corrupt, wicked bias of their hearts. **Sons** was often used as an epithet for disciples or followers, as in the common Old Testament expression "sons of the prophets" (see, e.g., 2 Kings 2:3). Certain followers or **sons** of the Pharisees **cast out demons,** and the Jewish historian Josephus reports that they used many strange, exotic incantations and cultic formulas in their rites.

Luke tells of a group of seven brothers, sons of a chief priest named Sceva, who practiced exorcism. When they and other Jewish exorcists heard of the apostles' great success in casting out evil spirits, they decided to try a new formula—exorcising in "the name of the Lord Jesus, saying, 'I adjure you by Jesus whom Paul preaches'" (Acts 19:13-14). The fact that they thought the mere use of certain words and names would accomplish the exorcism proves their magical orientation. The demon, however, was not the least affected, and he responded by saying to the seven men, "'I recognize Jesus, and I know about Paul, but who are you?' And the man, in whom was the evil spirit, leaped on them and subdued all of them and overpowered them, so that they fled out of that house naked and wounded" (vv. 15-16).

Jesus pointed out the Pharisees' extreme prejudice by showing that they approved the exorcisms attempted by the **sons** who were part of their religious establishment. They would never have claimed that those activities were ungodly, much less satanic. Yet when Jesus not only cast out every sort of demon but also healed every sort of disease, they accused Him of being in league with the devil.

The Pharisees' response reflects the basic response of every person who intentionally rejects Jesus Christ. They did not reject Him for lack of evidence but because they were biased against Him. Their own deeds were evil and they could not handle the intimidating reality of Jesus' righteousness; they were children of darkness and could not tolerate His light (John 3:19). They were not looking for truth but for ways to justify their own wickedness and to destroy anyone who dared expose them.

To put His opponents further on the spot, Jesus suggested that the Pharisees let their exorcist **sons** be their **judges**. The implied suggestion was that they ask those practitioners by whose power they cast out evil spirits. If they said, "By Satan's power," they would condemn themselves and the religious leaders who supported them. But if they said, "By God's power," they would undercut the Pharisees' accusation against Jesus.

THE ACCUSATION WAS REBELLIOUS

But if I cast out demons by the Spirit of God, then the kingdom of God has come upon you. Or how can anyone enter the strong man's house and carry off his property, unless he first binds the strong man? And then he will plunder his house. He who is not with Me is against Me; and he who does not gather with Me scatters. (12:28-30)

The third, and basic, reason behind the Pharisees' accusation was their rebelliousness against God. Jesus had dispelled the foolish charge that He worked under Satan's power, and the only remaining possibility was that He **cast out demons by the Spirit of God.**

If He did His work **by the Spirit of God,** then His miracles were of God and He had to be the Messiah, "the Son of David," just as the multitudes had considered (v. 23). Every religiously literate Jew knew that the prophets predicted that just such signs would accompany the Messiah's coming (Isa. 29:18; 35:5-6). They also knew that the Messiah was to be Israel's supreme and eternal King (Ps. 2:6; Jer. 23:5; Zech. 9:9). "Therefore," Jesus was saying, "if I am the Messiah, I am also the coming King, and if I am the King, **then the kingdom of God has come upon you.**"

Jesus will not reign on earth in His full glory and divine prerogatives until the millennial kingdom, and after that in the eternal kingdom of the new heavens and new earth. But in widest sense, Christ's **kingdom** is the sphere of His rule in any place or age. In that sense He is King wherever He may be, and those who love Him are His subjects; therefore His **kingdom** was always with Him during His earthly ministry. In a similar way it exists now on earth wherever He is served as Lord. "For [God] delivered us from the domain of darkness," Paul says, "and transferred us to the kingdom of His beloved Son" (Col. 1:13). It is in that **kingdom** that every believer begins to live the moment he receives the King as His Lord and Savior.

Or how can anyone enter the strong man's house and carry off his property, Jesus continued, **unless he first binds the strong man? And then he will plunder the house.** Could not the Pharisees see that everything Jesus said and did was opposed to Satan? Jesus healed sickness and disease, which were brought upon mankind by sin, which, in turn, was brought and promoted by Satan. Jesus raised people from death, which was also a consequence of sin and indirectly the work of Satan (cf. Heb. 2:14-17). Jesus cast out demons, which, as He had just pointed out, was in obvious opposition to Satan. He even forgave sins—something Satan neither would nor could do—and verified His authority to forgive sins by His power to perform miracles (Matt. 9:5-6). Every detail of what He taught and did corresponded to the teaching of Old Testament Scripture. And although the scribes and Pharisees often charged Jesus with opposing and violating their man-made traditions, they could never convict Him of committing sin or of teaching falsehood (John 8:46).

Jesus used the figure of a thief who planned to rob a **strong man's house** while **the strong man** was there. The thief knows that **unless he first binds the strong man** he has no chance of being successful and, in fact, risks being arrested and seriously beaten in the process.

Jesus' point was this: "Haven't I demonstrated before you and all of Israel My power over Satan and his kingdom of evil, darkness, and destruction? Haven't I demonstrated beyond all doubt that My authority is higher than Satan's? Haven't I cleansed people of every kind of disease and freed them from every kind of demonic control and oppression? Haven't I demonstrated My authority over both sin and death? Haven't I rescued souls from hell? Who could have such power and authority but God Himself? Who but God could **enter** the very **house** of Satan and successfully bind him **and carry off his property?** I have shown you that I can defeat Satan and a legion of his demonic hosts at will. How could I be any other than your divine Messiah?"

The death blow to Satan was inflicted at the cross and will be actualized in the future; but even before that ultimate victory Christ repeatedly demonstrated His unlimited and unhindered power to thwart and bind Satan. Christ also committed that power to His disciples, and when the seventy returned from their mission, Jesus "said to them, 'I was watching Satan fall from heaven like lightning'" (Luke 10:18). Satan is presently still powerful, but His power is limited, his doom is sealed, and his time is short.

Jesus next made clear to the Pharisees that there is no neutral ground as far as relationship to Him is concerned. **He who is not with Me is against Me; and he who does not gather with Me scatters.** It is not necessary to oppose Christ in order to be **against** Him; it is only necessary **not** to be **with** Him. Nor is it necessary to actively interfere with His work in order to be one who **scatters;** it is only necessary to **not gather with** Him. The person who does not belong to God is the enemy of God (Rom. 5:10); the person who is not a child of God through Christ is a rebel against God.

There are only two possible relationships to Jesus Christ, and therefore to God: **with** or **against.** It is both spiritually and rationally impossible to accept Jesus as a kind man, a good teacher, and a great man of God—and nothing more. Only God has the right to claim for Himself the honor and authority Jesus claimed for Himself; and only God has the power over disease, sin, demons, Satan, and death that Jesus both claimed and demonstrated.

The Anathema

Therefore I say to you, any sin and blasphemy shall be forgiven men, but blasphemy against the Spirit shall not be forgiven. And whoever shall speak a word against the Son of Man, it shall be forgiven him; but whoever shall speak against the Holy Spirit, it shall not be forgiven him, either in this age, or in the age to come. (12:31-32)

Few passages of Scripture have been more misinterpreted and misunderstood than these two verses. Because of their extreme seriousness and finality, it is critical to understand them correctly.

Jesus first stated that **any sin and blasphemy shall be forgiven men.** Although **blasphemy** is a form of **sin,** in this passage and context the two are treated separately—with blasphemy representing the most extreme form of sin. **Sin** here represents the full gamut of immoral and ungodly thoughts and actions, whereas **blasphemy** represents conscious denouncing and rejection of God. **Blasphemy** is defiant irreverence, the uniquely terrible sin of intentionally and openly speaking evil against holy God or defaming or mocking Him (cf. Mark. 2:7). The Old Testament penalty for such blasphemy was death by stoning (Lev. 24:16). In the last days blasphemy will be an outstanding characteristic of those who rebelliously and insolently oppose God (Rev. 13:5-6; 16:9; 17:3).

But even **blasphemy,** Jesus says, is **forgiven,** just as any other **sin** is forgiven when it is confessed and repented of. An unbeliever who blasphemes God can be forgiven. Paul confessed that, "even though [he] was formerly a blasphemer and a persecutor and a violent aggressor," he was nevertheless "shown mercy, because [he] acted ignorantly in unbelief; and the grace of our Lord was more than abundant, with the faith and love which are found in Christ Jesus" (1 Tim. 1:13-14). "Christ Jesus came into the world," the apostle continues, "to save sinners, among whom I am foremost of all" (v. 15). Peter blasphemed Christ with curses (Mark 14:71) and was forgiven and restored.

Even a believer can blaspheme, since any thought or word that sullies or defames the Lord's name constitutes blasphemy. To question God's goodness, wisdom, fairness, truthfulness, love, or faithfulness is a form of blasphemy. All of that is forgivable by grace. Speaking to believers, John said, "If we confess our sins, He is faithful and righteous to forgive us our sins and to cleanse us from all unrighteousness" (1 John 1:9).

There is one exception, however: **blasphemy against the Spirit shall not be forgiven.** Even the person who blasphemes Jesus, who dares to **speak a word against the Son of Man . . . shall be forgiven. Son of Man** designates the Lord's humanity, which He experienced in His time of humiliation and servitude during the incarnation. A person's perception may not allow him to see more than the Lord's humanity, and if he only misjudges at that level and speaks against Him in His humanness, such **a word against the Son of Man** can **be forgiven.** When a person rejects Christ with less than full exposure to the evidence of His deity, he may yet be forgiven of that sin if, after gaining fuller light, he then believes.

It was hard even for the disciples to keep clearly in mind that their Teacher was indeed the Son of God. He ate, drank, slept, and became tired just as they did. Not only that, but many of the things He did simply did not seem to reflect God's glory and majesty. Jesus continually humbled Himself and served others. He took no earthly glory for Himself, and when others tried to thrust it on Him, He refused to receive it— as when the crowd wanted to make Him king after He miraculously fed the five thousand (John 6:15). It was even more difficult for those outside Jesus' inner circle to appreciate His deity. Even when He performed His greatest miracles, He did so without fanfare or flare. Jesus did not always look or act like even a human lord, much less like the divine Lord.

But to misjudge, belittle, and discredit Jesus from the vantage point of incomplete revelation or inadequate perception was forgivable, wrong as it was. As already mentioned, the apostle Paul had himself been an ignorant blasphemer of the Lord Jesus Christ of the worst sort and a fierce persecutor of His church. And many of those who had denied and rejected Christ during His earthly ministry later saw the truth of who He was and asked forgiveness and were saved.

But **the blasphemy against the Spirit** was something more serious and irremediable. It not only reflected unbelief, but determined unbelief—the refusal, after having seen all the evidence necessary to complete understanding, even to consider believing in Christ. This was **blasphemy** against Jesus in His deity, **against the Spirit** of God who uniquely indwelt and empowered Him. It reflected determined rejection of Jesus as the Messiah against every evidence and argument. It reflected seeing the truth incarnate and then knowingly rejecting Him and condemning Him. It demonstrated an absolute and permanent refusal to believe, which resulted in loss of opportunity *ever* to **be forgiven . . . either in this age, or in the age to come.** Through **this age** (all of human history), such rejection is unforgivable. **The age to come** implies that through all of eternity there will be no forgiveness. In the age of human history and in the age of divine consummation, no forgiveness.

Scripture is clear that during His ministry on earth our Lord was submissive to the Father (John 4:34; 5:19-30) and empowered by the Spirit (Matt. 4:1; Mark 1:12; Luke 4:1, 18; John 3:34; Acts 1:2; Rom. 1:4). Peter said that God anointed Jesus of Nazareth "with the Holy Spirit and with power" (Acts 10:38).

Those who spoke **against the Holy Spirit** were those who saw His divine power working in and through Jesus but willfully refused to accept the implications of that revelation and, in some cases, attributed that power to Satan. Many people had heard Jesus teach and preach God's truth, as no man had ever taught before (Matt. 7:28-29), yet they refused to believe Him. They had seen him heal every kind of disease, cast out every kind of demon, and forgive every kind of sin, yet they charged Him with deceit, falsehood, and demonism. In the face of every possible evidence of Jesus' messiahship and deity, they said no. God could do nothing more for them, and they would therefore remain eternally unforgiven.

> For penitence they substitute hardening, for confession plotting. Thus, by means of their own criminal and completely inexcusable callousness, they are dooming themselves. Their sin is unpardonable because they are unwilling to tread the path that leads to pardon. For a thief, an adulterer, and a murderer there is hope. The message of the gospel may cause him to cry out, "O God be merciful to me, the sinner." But when a man has become hardened, so that he has made up his mind not to pay any attention to the . . . Spirit, . . . he has placed himself on the road that leads to perdition. (William Hendriksen, *The Exposition of the Gospel According to Matthew* [Grand Rapids: Baker, 1973], p. 529)

Through Isaiah, the Lord pictured Israel as a vineyard He had carefully planted, cultivated, and tended. He built a tower in the middle of it, representing Jerusalem, and a wine vat in it, representing the sacrificial system. "Then He expected it to produce good grapes, but it produced only worthless ones." "What more was there to do for My vineyard that I have not done in it?" God asked. "So now let Me tell you what I am going to do to My vineyard: I will remove its hedge and it will be consumed; I will break down its wall and it will become trampled ground. And I will lay it waste; it will not be pruned or hoed, but briars and thorns will come up. I will also charge the clouds to rain no rain on it" (Isa. 5:1-6). After the people had been blessed with every blessing and had every opportunity but still turned their backs on God, there was nothing left for Him to do but turn His back on them.

During Jesus' earthly ministry, the unbelieving Pharisees and all the others who blasphemed **the Spirit** cut themselves off from God's mercy, not because it was not offered but because it was abundantly offered yet rebelliously and permanently rejected and ridiculed as satanic.

Within forty years, God would destroy Jerusalem, the Temple, the priesthood, the sacrifices, and the nation of Israel. In 70 A.D. the Romans razed Jerusalem, utterly destroyed the Temple, slaughtered over a million of its inhabitants, and all but obliterated nearly a thousand other towns and villages in Judea. His own chosen people had said no to Him, and He said no to them. Until He returns and regathers a remnant of His people to Himself in the last days, except for a few faithful, they are as a nation totally apart from God.

To unsaved Jews who had heard the full gospel message and had seen its evidence in supernatural power, and to all who would come after them with similar exposure to the truth and the biblical record of miraculous evidence, the writer of the book of Hebrews gave a stern warning: "How shall we escape if we neglect so great a salvation? After it was at the first spoken through the Lord, it was confirmed to us by those who heard [that is, the apostles], God also bearing witness with them, both by signs and wonders and by various miracles and by gifts of the Holy Spirit according to His own will" (Heb. 2:3-4). Later in the letter an even more severe warning to those who reject with full revelation is given: "For in the case of those who have once been enlightened and have tasted of the heavenly gift and have been made partakers of the Holy Spirit, and have tasted the good word of God and the powers of the age to come, and then have fallen away, it is impossible to renew them again to repentance, since they again crucify to themselves the Son of God, and put Him to open shame" (Heb. 6:4-6). (For a detailed discussion of that important passage, see the author's commentary in this series on Hebrews.)

The generation immediately after Christ was on earth was ministered to by the apostles, enlightened by their teaching, and given proof of the truth of the gospel by their miracles. That generation had evidence equivalent to that of those who heard and saw Jesus in person. They had the highest possible revelation from God, and if they refused to believe in the face of such overwhelming evidence, there was nothing more God could do for them. They did not blaspheme; they simply turned away. The guilt of the Pharisees who added blasphemy to unbelief was greater than that of those who saw the same evidence and disbelieved but did not **speak against the Holy Spirit**. But the rebels in both groups left themselves no future but hell.

In a similar way, people today can so totally turn their backs on God's revelation that they permanently cut themselves off from salvation. "We must work the works of Him who sent Me, as long as it is day," Jesus said; "night is coming, when no man can work" (John 9:4).

During World War II, an American naval force in the North Atlantic was engaged in heavy battle with enemy ships and submarines on an exceptionally dark night. Six planes took off from the carrier to search out those targets, but while they were in the air a total blackout was ordered for the carrier in order to protect it from attack. Without lights on the carrier's deck the six planes could not possibly land, and they made a radio request for the lights to be turned on just long enough for them to come in. But because the entire carrier, with its several thousand men as well as all the other planes and equipment, would have been put in jeopardy, no lights were permitted. When the six planes ran out of fuel, they had to ditch in the freezing water and all crew members perished into eternity.

There comes a time when God turns out the lights, when further opportunity for salvation is forever lost. That is why Paul told the Corinthians, "Now is 'the acceptable time,' behold, now is 'the day of salvation'" (2 Cor. 6:2). One who rejects full light can have no more light—and no forgiveness.

Exposing the Truth About Man's Heart

(12:33-37)

29

Either make the tree good, and its fruit good; or make the tree bad, and its fruit bad; for the tree is known by its fruit. You brood of vipers, how can you, being evil, speak what is good? For the mouth speaks out of that which fills the heart. The good man out of his good treasure brings forth what is good; and the evil man out of his evil treasure brings forth what is evil. And I say to you, that every careless word that men shall speak, they shall render account for it in the day of judgment. For by your words you shall be justified, and by your words you shall be condemned. (12:33-37)

It has been estimated that from the first "Good morning" to the last "Good night," the average person engages in thirty conversations a day. Each day, his words could make a book of 50-60 pages—the equivalent of more than one hundred books a year of 200 pages each.

Someone in the last century wrote the following about the incessant talker:

> He shakes a man by the ear as a dog does a pig, and never loosens his hold till he has tired himself as well as his patient. He is a walking pillory, and punishes more ears than a dozen standing ones. He will hold any argument rather than

his tongue, and maintain both sides at his own charge; for he will tell you what you will say, though perhaps he does not intend to give you leave. His tongue is always in motion, though very seldom to the purpose: like a barber's scissors, which are kept snipping as well when they do not cut as when they do. He is so full of words that they run over, and are thrown away to no purpose; and so empty of things, or sense, that his dryness has made his leaks so wide, whatsoever is put in him runs out immediately. He is so long delivering himself, that those that hear him desire to be delivered too, or dispatched out of their pain.

It is not surprising that, immediately after Jesus excoriated the Pharisees for their unforgivable blasphemy against the Holy Spirit, He then began to speak about the importance of the tongue. The most self-damning words ever spoken had just been uttered by the religious leaders who accused Jesus of casting out demons by the power of Satan (v. 24). Now the Lord gives one of His most sobering warnings, and in the process He exposes the truth about the nature of man's heart.

THE PARABLE

Either make the tree good, and its fruit good; or make the tree bad, and its fruit bad; for the tree is known by its fruit. (12:33)

Jesus initiates the warning with a short parable to illustrate an obvious maxim: a tree and its fruit correspond. A good tree produces good fruit, and a bad tree produces bad fruit (cf. 7:17, 20; Luke 6:43-44).

Poieō (to **make**) is used here in a figurative sense. As in English, the term can refer physically to creating or constructing—as in making a clay pot or a chair. Also as in English, it can refer metaphorically to considering, evaluating, or judging—as in making up one's mind about something.

Jesus' general point was: "You must make up your minds about Me and My work. Either I am evil and do evil work, or else I am good and do good work. I cannot be evil and do good work or be good and do evil work. If I do good works, it is by God's power; and if I do evil works, it is by Satan's. God empowers nothing evil, and Satan empowers nothing good."

His specific point was: "Sickness and death are the result of sin, as you yourselves recognize. Demon possession is obviously Satan's doing and an evil thing. Therefore, healing the sick, raising the dead, and casting out demons could not be other than good things—the deliverance of men from the destructive work of sin. Consequently, My casting out demons must be by God's power, not Satan's. Because you accuse Me of doing good by Satan's power, you attribute to Satan the work of the Holy Spirit, and that is the supreme and unforgivable blasphemy."

Jesus again trapped the self-righteous Pharisees in their perverted thinking, publicly exposing their hard-heartedness and absurd illogic. As He pointed out to them on other occasions, no matter what they thought of Him personally, His works indisputably testified to His goodness and to His divine power (John 5:36; 10:25, 37-38; 14:11; cf. Matt. 11:4-5).

THE PERSONALIZATION

You brood of vipers, how can you, being evil, speak what is good? (12:34a)

Changing the metaphor, Jesus applies the parable of the good and bad trees directly to the Pharisees, saying, in effect, "**You** are immeasurably worse than a group of bad trees; you are a veritable **brood of vipers.**" That is the same epithet John the Baptist used of the hypocritical Pharisees and Sadducees who came to him for baptism (3:7) and that Jesus used during His long series of "Woes" against the scribes and Pharisees in the Temple (Matt. 23:33).

Those who preach falsehood or practice immorality are invariably offended when they are exposed; but fear of offending should not keep believers from exposing their evil. When, in the name of love and humility, we fail to expose religions, cults, and philosophies that give men false spiritual hope or we fail to challenge those who promote irreverence and moral filth, we serve neither love nor humility but sin.

Jesus did not shy away from condemning men to their faces, especially when their sin was cruel, hypocritical, self-righteous, or blasphemous. He came to save people from their sin, not help confirm them in it by underplaying its seriousness or their guilt. He was not in a popularity contest, and it was His concern to please His Father, not men. It is never to God's glory or to man's good to encourage in any way those who do evil or to minimize their sin.

Calling the Pharisees a **brood of vipers** was a fierce denunciation that everyone understood. **Vipers** was a general name for a variety of poisonous snakes common to Palestine and the Mediterranean area. A deadly viper bit Paul on the hand as he gathered firewood on the island of Malta after a shipwreck, and the native islanders were amazed that he did not "swell up or suddenly fall down dead" (Acts 28:3, 6).

Vipers not only are deadly but deceptive. Because most of them blend into surrounding rocks or sticks, they can often attack their victims with total surprise, as the one on Malta did Paul. The mother viper normally lays a large number of eggs, and when they hatch the **brood** of little potential killers scurry around like insects.

The Pharisees were the epitome of religious and moral corruption and danger. Like a **brood of vipers,** they traveled from place to place, usually in groups, teaching and promoting their man-made traditions. "Woe to you, scribes and Pharisees, hypocrites," Jesus later said to them, "because you travel about on sea and land to make one proselyte; and when he becomes one, you make him twice as much a son of hell as yourselves" (Matt. 23:15). Their unbiblical, legalistic traditions poisoned the minds of fellow Jews against the pure and redeeming truth of God's Word, and their hypocritical self-righteousness led countless others into that same evil attitude. When someone reached into the woodpile of religion, thinking to pick up a stick of truth, he could be bitten to death by those soul-damning liars.

How can you, Jesus continued, **being evil, speak what is good?** "In light of your **being evil** by nature, how could anything but blasphemy and other ungodliness be expected of you? How could you possibly **speak what is good?**" **Being evil** expresses the depravity of the natural human heart, which can *produce* only evil because it *is* only **evil.** That is the legacy of fallen man because of Adam's sin. As Paul explained to the Roman church, "Both Jews and Greeks are all under sin; as it is written, 'There is none righteous, not even one; . . . there is none who does good, there is not even one,' . . . for all have sinned and fall short of the glory of God" (Rom. 3:9-10, 12, 23). He explained to the Ephesians that every person is "dead in [his] trespasses and sin" until he trusts in Jesus Christ for salvation (Eph. 2:1).

The Old Testament also clearly chronicles the evil heart of man. From the time of Adam's sin mankind was henceforth characterized by hatred, corruption, murder, lying, and every other form of wickedness. David knew that he inherited a sin nature the moment he was conceived (Ps. 51:5), and Jeremiah declared that the human "heart is more deceitful than all else and is desperately sick" (Jer. 17:9).

THE PRINCIPLE

For the mouth speaks out of that which fills the heart. The good man out of his good treasure brings forth what is good; and the evil man out of his evil treasure brings forth what is evil. (12:34b-35)

Here is one of the most basic principles of Scripture regarding man: **the mouth speaks** what is in **the heart.** What a person is on the inside, his mouth will give evidence of on the outside. In fact, James says that one who did not sin with his mouth would be "a perfect man" (James 3:2). The most immediate illustration of that principle showed that it was the evil hearts of the Pharisees that made them blaspheme the Holy Spirit by accusing Jesus of casting out demons by Satan's power. They spoke evil because their hearts were filled with evil, and by their own words they condemned themselves as they sought to condemn Jesus.

In Scripture **the heart** represents the seat of thought and will, rather than the seat of emotions (represented by the bowels, or stomach area, as indicated in the KJV renderings of Song of Sol. 5:4; Jer. 31:20; Phil. 1:8; 2:1; Col. 3:12; Philem. 7, 12, 20; and 1 John 3:17). **The heart** represents the character of a person, and therefore to say that words reveal what the heart is like is to say they reveal what the person is like. When it **speaks,** the **mouth** simply reproduces verbally what is in **the heart.** Using the same figure, Jesus explained on a later occasion that "the things that proceed out of the mouth come from the heart, and those defile the man. For out of the heart come evil thoughts, murders, adulteries, fornications, thefts, false witness, slanders" (Matt. 15:18-19).

That which fills translates the Greek noun *perisseuma,* which means great abundance, fullness, or overflow. It carries the idea of excess, which, in the terms of Jesus' figure, spills over from the heart and out of the mouth in the form of words. What the heart is full of, will overflow from the mouth.

The person who harbors ill will against someone will eventually express those feelings. The person who is filled with lustful thoughts will eventually express those thoughts in crude or suggestive remarks. The person who is persistently angry and hateful will sooner or later put those feelings into words. In the same way, the person who is genuinely loving, kind, and considerate cannot help expressing those feelings in words as well as actions.

After Elihu waited long and impatiently for three older friends to convince Job of his sin, he could hold back no longer. He had to say what was on his heart. "For I am full of words," he said; "the spirit within me constrains me. Behold, my belly is like unvented wine, like new wineskins it is about to burst. Let me speak that I may get relief; let me open my lips and answer" (Job 32:18-20).

What the heart, or the mind, dwells on and feeds on is what it is full of; and **that which fills the heart** it is that which **the mouth** inevitably **speaks.** A person may carefully monitor his words most of the time, but the pressure of evil thoughts, anger, stress, pain, or the association with vulgar friends will sometimes force his real thoughts and attitudes to the surface in the form of words.

James understood that principle and gave several powerful warnings about the tongue. "If anyone thinks himself to be religious," he said, "and yet does not bridle his tongue but deceives his own heart, this man's religion is worthless" (James 1:26). Later in the same letter he said, "But no one can tame the tongue; it is a restless evil and full of deadly poison" (3:8). In summing up his description of men's depraved nature, Paul said, "Their throat is an open grave, with their tongues they keep deceiving, the poison of asps is under their lips; whose mouth is full of cursing and bitterness" (Rom. 3:13-14). The mouth is the ultimate expression of the heart. As the writer of Proverbs declared, "For as [a person] thinks within himself, so he is" (23:7).

Expanding on the principle He has just stated, Jesus then gives the positive and the negative aspects of it. **The good man out of his good treasure brings forth what is good; and the evil man out of his evil treasure brings forth what is evil.**

Treasure is from *thēsauros,* which means storehouse or treasury and is the term from which we get the English *thesaurus,* a treasury of words. A person's heart is the treasury of his thoughts, ambitions, desires, loves, attitudes, and loyalties. It is the reservoir from which the mouth draws its expressions. It is axiomatic that a **good treasure brings forth what is good** and an **evil treasure brings forth what is evil.** "Does a fountain send out from the same opening both fresh and bitter water?" James asked (James 3:11).

A common expression in the computer world is GIGO, which stands for "Garbage in, garbage out." In other words, the quality of data entered determines the quality of the results produced from that data. In exactly the same way, the quality of what is in a person's heart determines the quality of speech his mouth produces.

THE PUNISHMENT

And I say to you, that every careless word that men shall speak, they shall render account for it in the day of judgment. For by your words you shall be justified, and by your words you shall be condemned. (12:36-37)

Because men's words are an accurate gauge of their hearts, **they shall render account for** their words **in the day of judgment.** It is by his **words** that a person is either **justified** or **condemned.** Salvation and condemnation are not produced by words or deeds, but they are manifested by them. Words and deeds are objective, observable evidence of a person's spiritual condition. **In the day of judgment,** that future general time when the Lord evaluates who belongs in and out of His eternal kingdom, the criteria will include the speech of every person.

The consistent teaching of both Old and New Testaments is that the only way of salvation is by God's grace working through man's faith. Jesus' point is not that words are the *basis* of salvation or condemnation but that they are reliable evidence of the reality of salvation. The speech of a redeemed person will be different, because it comes from his renewed heart. Pure, wholesome, praising speech shows a new heart.

We are not saved *by* good works, but we are saved *for* "good works, which God prepared beforehand, that we should walk in them" (Eph. 2:10). In the same way, we are saved for good **words.** "With the heart man believes, resulting in righteousness, and with the mouth he confesses, resulting in salvation" (Rom. 10:10), which, in turn, results in "obedience . . . by word and deed" (15:18). Salvation *will* produce good words, and it is for that reason and in that sense that **words** bring justification or condemnation.

The ungodly will be eternally condemned for their speech. Apart from what they did, what they said is enough evidence of their unregenerate heart to send them to hell. Jesus does not limit this warning to extremes such as blasphemy, but makes explicit that men will **render account** for **every careless word that** they **speak**—whether or not it is immoral, vulgar, cruel, or blasphemous. They will have to **render account** even for words that are **careless.**

The basic meaning of *argos* (**careless**) is useless, barren, unproductive, or otherwise worthless. Such words include those that are flippant, irresponsible, or in any way inappropriate. Hypocritical words are among the most **careless** and worthless that men speak and are, unfortunately, among the most common. When men self-consciously keep their vocabulary orthodox, moral, and evangelically acceptable while among fellow Christians—for the sake of impressing them or to keep from embarrassing ourselves—those words are **careless** and worthless in God's sight, and He will **render** them against their **account.** The calculated hypocrisy of such "holy talk" is a stench in His nostrils.

The Christian's speech will reflect God's transforming work in the heart; but because of our unredeemed humanness, it still needs constant care if it is to be increasingly spiritual, wholesome, fitting, kind, sensitive, loving, purposeful, edifying, and truthful. With the Psalmist he should pray, "Set a guard, O Lord, over my mouth; keep watch over the door of my lips" (Ps. 141:3).

But for the unbeliever, *all* the words of his unredeemed heart are worthless as far as spiritual value is concerned. His evil words are obviously worthless. Among the most common evil words are those that express *lust* (Prov. 5:3-4); *deceit* (Jer. 9:8); *cursing* and *oppression* (Ps. 10:7); *lying* (Prov. 6:12; 12:22); *destruction* (Prov. 11:11); *vanity* (2 Pet. 2:18); *flattery* (Prov. 26:28); *foolishness* (Prov. 15:2); *verbosity* (Eccles. 10:14); *falsehood* (Titus 1:11); *pride* (Job 35:12); *vulgarity* (Col. 3:8); *hatred* (Ps. 109:3); and *gossip* (Prov. 26:20).

For the unbeliever, **careless** and worthless words also include those that are otherwise good. Although his words of love, encouragement, comfort, and kindness may be sincere and greatly helpful to others, they are of no spiritual value to him because they do not come from a redeemed and righteous heart. No spiritually good thing can come from a heart that is spiritually evil—as Jesus has just pointed out.

A person can get a good indication of his spiritual condition by listening to his own words. A Christian can fall into evil words just as he can fall into evil deeds, but his customary speaking will be pure just as his customary activities will be righteous.

Although this passage has application to both the saved and the unsaved—to the "good man" and the "evil man"—Jesus' thrust here is directed to unbelievers, represented in the extreme by the blaspheming Pharisees.

The day of judgment for unbelievers culminates at the great white throne judgment, the ultimate and eternal judgment at which all unbelievers **shall be condemned.** Christians' sins will have all been dealt with at Calvary, dismissed by the atoning blood of Christ applied on behalf of their faith. Every Christian has sinned with his tongue after salvation, but Christ's sacrifice is sufficient to cover that and every other sin he commits. The evil words and deeds of unbelievers, however, will remain to stand in evidence against them. Like the unfaithful slave in Jesus' parable, unbelievers will be judged by their own words (Luke 19:22).

In his vision of the great white throne judgment John saw "the great and the small, standing before the throne, and books were opened; and another book was opened, which is the book of life; and the dead were judged from the things which were written in the books, according to their deeds. . . . And if anyone's name was not found written in the book of life, he was thrown into the lake of fire" (Rev. 20:12, 15). When the record books are scanned, no good deeds will be listed by the names of unbelievers; and when the book of life is scanned, not even their names will appear. The books that report deeds and the book that reports faith will alike testify against them.

Scientists theorize that sound waves are never completely lost but gradually fade beyond detection. With sufficiently sensitive instruments, every word ever spoken in the history of mankind presumably could be retrieved. How much more certain can we be that in God's infallible records every word and deed of mankind is perfectly preserved for use as evidence in the coming judgment!

Judgment on Christ Rejecters (12:38-42)

Then some of the scribes and Pharisees answered Him, saying, "Teacher, we want to see a sign from You." But He answered and said to them, "An evil and adulterous generation craves for a sign; and yet no sign shall be given to it but the sign of Jonah the prophet; for just as Jonah was three days and three nights in the belly of the sea monster, so shall the Son of Man be three days and three nights in the heart of the earth. The men of Nineveh shall stand up with this generation at the judgment, and shall condemn it because they repented at the preaching of Jonah; and behold, something greater than Jonah is here. The Queen of the South shall rise up with this generation at the judgment and shall condemn it, because she came from the ends of the earth to hear the wisdom of Solomon; and behold, something greater than Solomon is here. (12:38-42)

Man's natural sinfulness and lostness are not always apparent. Many outwardly religious, moral, and decent people say they believe in God and are kind and helpful to others. Even completely irreligious people sometimes live law-abiding lives and behave as good neighbors. Sometimes the kindly attitude and good works of unbelievers even put the behavior of some Christians to shame. From the human perspective it can be difficult to see how such people could be inherently sinful and alienated from God. Many of them speak well of God, have high behavioral standards, are loving husbands and wives, caring parents, fair employers or employees, good citizens, and faithful friends. They may even go to church regularly, give generously to its support, serve on its boards and committees, and teach in Sunday school. How, it is often asked, could such obviously "good" people be spiritually depraved and lost?

Although truly righteous people will manifest the godly evidence of that righteousness, some people appear to be righteous who are not, because man's basic sinfulness is not most fully revealed by what he does or says—despite the importance of those evidences, as Jesus has just made clear (vv. 33-37). Sin is most clearly and indisputably manifested by how a person responds to Jesus Christ. No matter what a person's outward life is like, his innate spiritual nature and his true attitude toward God are seen with absolute certainty in his attitude toward Jesus Christ. The person who rejects Christ is dead spiritually and an enemy of God, no matter what religious profession he may make or how morally and selflessly he may appear to live. The issue of sin becomes perfectly focused when a person confronts Christ, and the crux of damning sin is rejection of Him. Men are convicted of "sin because they do not believe in Me," Jesus said (John 16:9).

When Jesus met with His disciples in the Upper Room to celebrate the last Passover meal with them, Israel's unbelief and rejection had reached their climax. Plans for Jesus' death were already set in motion; and that was the night of His betrayal, arrest, and mock trials that led to His crucifixion.

As Jesus spoke to the disciples on that occasion, He revealed many deep insights into His divine plan and gave wonderful promises of encouragement and strength for the time after He was gone. In addition to such positive and appealing promises as the Holy Spirit's being with them to teach and empower, He gave the less appealing but just as certain promise that the world would hate them just at it hated Him. "Remember the word that I said to you," He said; "'A slave is not greater than his master.' If they persecuted Me, they will also persecute you; if they kept My word, they will keep yours also" (John 15:20). Then He gave the reason behind the persecution: "But all these things they will do to you for My name's sake, because they do not know the One who sent Me. If I had not come and spoken to them, they would not have sin, but now they have no excuse for their sin. He who hates Me hates My Father also. If I had not done among them the works which no one else did, they would not have sin; but now they have both seen and hated Me and My Father as well" (vv. 21-24).

Jesus' words on that occasion applied to everyone who had seen and rejected Him, but they applied with direct force to the Jewish religious leaders, those who represented the nation of Israel, God's specially chosen, blessed, and enlightened people. On the surface, those leaders appeared to be righteous men of God, dedicated to His service and to His Word. They wore their religion on their sleeves for all men to see as a supposed testimony to their devotion to God. But when Jesus confronted them, their masks of godliness were ripped off and their real spiritual condition and their devotion to self were laid bare. Despite religious and moral pretensions, their hatred and rejection of Jesus proved their hatred and rejection of God. Both spiritually and morally they were "whitewashed tombs which on the outside appear beautiful, but inside they are full of dead men's bones and all uncleanness. Even so you too outwardly appear righteous to men, but inwardly you are full of hypocrisy and lawlessness" (Matt. 23:27-28). They were a brood of spiritual vipers (12:34).

Had Jesus not come into their midst and declared to them God's truth and demonstrated God's power, their true evil natures would not have surfaced so dramatically. But Jesus left them no out as He confronted them with truth and righteousness incarnate. To reject Him is to reject truth, and to despise Him is to despise righteousness. To hate Jesus is to hate God; to hate the Son is to hate the Father (John 15:23).

A person may successfully hide his sin for a long time (cf. 1 Tim. 5:24), but when he rejects Jesus Christ, he reveals his true corrupt nature. No matter how good his life appears to be on the surface, and no matter what reasons or rationalizations may be given, the person who refuses to accept the lordship and saviorhood of Christ proves himself to be the most damnable of sinners and in the most literal and absolute sense a hater of God.

Until the present point in Jesus' ministry, the scribes and Pharisees had generally managed to keep a facade of tolerance regarding Jesus. Because of His popularity and obvious supernatural power, they had kept their opposition largely to themselves. Much of their thinking and planning would be lost to us were it not that Jesus read their minds and openly exposed their wicked schemes. He continually pulled away their masks of false piety and refused to let them hide their evil character. It is for that perhaps more than for anything else that they hated him so intensely.

The attitude of the scribes and Pharisees is generally characteristic of any person who maintains an appearance of godliness but who does not have saving trust in Jesus Christ. It is especially true of members of denominations, cults, or other religious groups who purport to be followers of Christ. They have a false and distorted view of Jesus, just as the scribes and Pharisees had a false and distorted view of the Messiah. They may verbally praise God, honor Jesus, extol Scripture, and often hold high standards of morality—but when they are confronted with Jesus' own claims of unique divine sonship and unique sacrifice for sin, they cannot hide their rejection of the true gospel and the true God. Like the scribes and Pharisees, they are deeply offended at the suggestion that their religion and their works, not to mention their hearts, are not acceptable to God and that they can be made right with Him only through humble and obedient trust in His Son to remove their sin. Their refusal to accept Christ as He declared Himself to be proves their rejection of God, because God's only true and perfect revelation of Himself is through the Son. They do not love God, but hate and despise Him, because they hate and despise the Son and the way of salvation He provides.

By the time the scribes and Pharisees asked Jesus to show them a special sign, their opposition to Him had already hardened into implacable hatred. Even before Jesus accused them of blaspheming the Holy Spirit and of thereby eternally forfeiting God's forgiveness, they had been planning "how they might destroy Him" (12:14). He then told them they were corrupt trees bearing corrupt fruit, were a brood of spiritual vipers, and that the evil of their words proved the evil of their hearts, for which they faced God's condemnation (vv. 33-37). Jesus had castigated them as strongly and unequivocally as was possible.

The more the Jewish leaders verbally attacked Jesus and sought to entrap Him, the more He exposed the foolishness, insensitivity, and ungodliness of their traditions and attitudes. They had failed to show that He had broken any scriptural commandment, that He had profaned the Sabbath, or that He cast out demons by the power of Satan. Because of their repeated embarrassment in failing to prove Jesus was either teaching or doing anything unscriptural, the Pharisees were concerned about losing their reputation with the people. They wanted to be sure the next attempt to discredit Him would succeed, and they believed that demanding a special sign from Him would be certain to prove that He was an imposter and deceiver and would save their own reputations.

THE LAST SIGN

Then some of the scribes and Pharisees answered Him, saying, "Teacher, we want to see a sign from You." But He answered and said to them, "An evil and adulterous generation craves for a sign; and yet no sign shall be given to it but the sign of Jonah the prophet; for just as Jonah was three days and three nights in the belly of the sea monster, so shall the Son of Man be three days and three nights in the heart of the earth. (12:38-40)

Some of the scribes and Pharisees probably refers to a special committee delegated to present this final challenge to Jesus. **Scribes** had to be at least thirty years old and had to have spent many years in intensive study of the Hebrew scriptures, especially the Torah, or law, and of the rabbinic traditions as set forth in the Talmud. They were known as the supreme interpreters and teachers of the law (see Matt. 22:35; Luke 10:25). Although some **scribes** belonged to the party of the Sadducees, most of them were **Pharisees,** which explains their frequently being mentioned together in the gospels. They were the authorized interpretive scholars and lawyers of Judaism and were generally held in great honor.

That they **answered** Jesus' scathing accusations by asking Him a seemingly forthright and nondefensive question indicates they were biting their tongues, as it were, determined to give the impression of civility and patience until the appropriate moment to condemn Him.

THE CHALLENGE

"Teacher, we want to see a sign from You." (12:38b)

That group of scholars and religious leaders considered no person outside their own ranks to be qualified to teach them the least truth about Jewish law and tradition. Their addressing Jesus as **Teacher** was therefore both sarcastic and hypocritical. It was sarcastic in that they considered Jesus to be a heretic and blasphemer, and it was their intention here, as on previous occasions, to expose Him as a *false* teacher. It was hypocritical in that they used the title to show mock respect for Him in front of the crowd and possibly to try to put Him off guard by flattery.

The request **we want to see a sign from You** amounted to an official demand for Jesus to prove Himself to be the Messiah. For the sake of the people, the question was posed in a seemingly courteous and respectful form, but its purpose was to prove that Jesus was *not* the Messiah but a blasphemous imposter. Because the scribes and Pharisees were the uncontested experts on the law, the people would expect them to know how to properly test the claims of anyone who posed as the Messiah. The implication of the question was that, if Jesus truly was the Messiah, He would have no trouble performing an appropriate **sign** to validate His identity.

The kind of **sign** they wanted is not specified, but it must have been an absolutely extraordinary one and of perhaps worldwide magnitude—such as causing the sun to stand still or a constellation to change its configuration or the moon to race across the sky. Jesus had already performed thousands of public miracles of healing, casting out demons, and raising the dead. The additional **sign** now demanded was therefore obviously meant to be on an even grander scale.

From a parallel passage in Matthew 16 we learn that "the Pharisees and Sadducees came up, and testing Him asked Him to show them a sign from heaven" (v. 1). "A sign from heaven" would be a vast and spectacular sign, one that came from heaven and perhaps could be seen in the heavens, such as those just mentioned relating to the sun, moon, and stars.

In his first letter to the church at Corinth, Paul noted the commonly known fact that "Jews ask for signs" (1:22). Although the great majority of the Old Testament prophets did not perform miracles or confirm their God-given messages by anything but the truth of what they said, the Jews had come to expect miraculous signs to accompany *every* true prophet or great man of God, especially the Messiah.

According to fallacious Jewish tradition, a certain Rabbi Eliezar was challenged in regard to the authority of his teaching. To prove his genuineness, he is said to have made a locust tree move 300 cubits and a stream of water flow backwards. When he caused the wall of a building to lean forward, it was returned upright only by the bidding of another rabbi. Finally Eliezar exclaimed, "If the law is as I teach, let it be proved from heaven." At that moment, the story goes, a voice came out of the sky saying, "What have you to do with Rabbi Eliezar? The instruction is as he teaches."

No doubt **the scribes and Pharisees** wanted just such a celestial **sign** from Jesus—a spectacular, sensational demonstration of supernatural power. They perhaps expected Him to fulfill Joel's prophecy of turning the moon into blood (Joel 2:31) or to paint the sky a rainbow of colors with a wave of His hand. Or perhaps He would cause a great procession of angels to descend a heavenly stairway into the Temple, heralding Him with anthems of praise as they came.

It is not that the Jewish leaders expected Jesus to perform any such **sign**, because their very purpose was to prove He could *not* do such a thing and thereby to discredit Him in the eyes of the people. Although no Old Testament prophecy

327

predicted that the Messiah would perform **a sign** of the type they demanded, the leaders gave the impression to the people that such was the case.

But He answered and said to them, "An evil and adulterous generation craves for a sign; and yet no sign shall be given to it but the sign of Jonah the prophet; for just as Jonah was three days and three nights in the belly of the sea monster, so shall the Son of Man be three days and three nights in the heart of the earth. (12:39-40)

Jesus responded to the hypocritical challenge by first declaring that the very *request* **for a sign** reflected the wicked expectations of **an evil and adulterous generation.** The scribes and Pharisees represented the nation of Israel, which had wandered far from God's Word and fellowship and which had become enmeshed in the superficial, self-righteous, and legalistic religion those leaders epitomized.

The unbelieving Jews were not only physically and mentally but spiritually **adulterous** because they had breached the vows of their unique covenant relationship with God, a relationship the Old Testament frequently speaks of in terms of marriage (see Ps. 73:27; Isa. 50:1; Jer. 3:6-10; 13:27; Hos. 9:1). Their idolatry, immorality, unbiblical traditions, and hardness of heart marked them as **an evil** people. During the Babylonian captivity Jews had forsaken formal idolatry, in the sense of worshiping physical objects carved from wood, stone, or metal. But in its place they erected idols of man-made tradition in which they trusted and put their hope. They had abandoned the Canaanite gods for ones of their own making and in doing so were just as much in rebellion against the true God as when they offered sacrifices to Baal or Molech.

A Jew who faithfully served God under the covenant given to Moses would accept His Son when He came, because anyone rightly related to the Father could not fail to recognize the Son—just as did the godly Simeon and Anna (Luke 2:25-38), John the Baptist (Matt. 3:14), and the twelve disciples, except Judas (4:20-22; Mark 3:13; Luke 5:27-28; John 1:41, 49). Because they knew the Father, they knew the Son and did not need **a sign** to verify His identity.

Consequently, Jesus continued, **no such sign shall be given.** It was not possible for Jesus to perform a miracle of the sort the scribes and Pharisees wanted— not because He did not have the power to do it, but because it was utterly contrary to God's nature and plan. Jesus could easily have performed it from the standpoint of His omnipotence, but not from the standpoint of His moral nature—because God is not in the business of bending Himself to satisfy the whims of evil people who have no relationship to Him.

On the other hand, He said, another kind of sign *would* be given: **the sign of Jonah the prophet.** When Jonah refused to obey God's call to preach to Nineveh and fled to Tarshish on a ship, the Lord sent a great storm and Jonah was thrown into the sea to save the rest of the men on board. God then caused him to be swallowed by "a great fish," or **sea monster,** in whose stomach he remained unharmed for three days and nights (Jonah 1:17).

And **just as Jonah was three days and three nights in the belly of the sea monster,** Jesus said, **so shall the Son of Man be three days and three nights in the heart of the earth.**

The Old Testament contains two kinds of prophecy regarding Christ. One is what may be called the verbally predictive, in which specific and sometimes detailed predictions are given. Such prophecies include those that the Christ would be born of a virgin (Isa. 7:14), that He would be a descendant of David who would rule the entire earth with justice and righteousness (Jer. 23:5), and that He would be born in Bethlehem (Mic. 5:2).

The second type of messianic prophecy is typical, in which an Old Testament person or event foreshadowed the person or work of Christ. We can be certain of typical predictions only if they are specifically identified as such in the New Testament. Here Jesus Himself tells us that **Jonah's** spending **three days and three nights in the belly of the sea monster** before he was vomited up on the shore typified the burial of **the Son of Man,** for **three days and three nights in the heart of the earth** before His resurrection. It was a predictive prophecy in picture rather than in specific word. Just as Jonah was buried in the depths of the sea, Jesus was buried in the depths of the earth; and just as Jonah came out of the great fish after three days, Jesus came out of the grave after three days.

Jesus obviously believed in the full literalness of the biblical account of Jonah. If Jonah had not been literally swallowed and miraculously protected while submerged for **three days and three nights in the belly of the sea monster,** that event could not have typified Jesus' literal burial and resurrection. In light of Jonah's hardhearted stubbornness, it is not difficult to believe that he would lie about his experience; but it is difficult indeed to believe that Jesus would join Jonah in such duplicity or be mistaken about the historicity of the story. In declaring Jonah's experience to be a type of His own burial and resurrection, Jesus also verified the authenticity of Jonah's account of himself.

The matter **of three days and three nights** is often used either to prove Jesus was mistaken about the time He would actually spend in the tomb or that He could not have been crucified on Friday afternoon and raised early on Sunday, the first day of the week. But as in modern usage, the phrase "day and night" can mean not only a full 24-hour day but any representative part of a day. To spend a day, or a day and night, visiting in a neighboring city does not require spending 24 hours there. It could refer to arriving in the late morning and leaving a few hours after dark. In the same way, Jesus' use of **three days and three nights** does not have to be interpreted as 72 hours, three full 24-hour days. The Jewish Talmud held that "any part of a day is as the whole." Jesus was simply using a common, well-understood generalization.

Jesus' resurrection after three days was not the kind of **sign** the unbelieving religious leaders expected and demanded, but it was infinitely more miraculous and wonderful. It was the final sign Jesus directly gave to the world of His messianic credentials and saving power. In His glorified body He appeared miraculously to His disciples on numerous occasions after the resurrection and then dramatically ascended before their eyes into heaven. He also continued to work miracles through the apostles as verification of their unique authority in His behalf. But the resurrection was the last sign given *to the world* that involved Jesus directly. His own resurrection, Jesus told the unbelieving scribes and Pharisees, would be the only **sign** from heaven they would receive.

But the Jewish leaders, and most of the Jewish people, did not believe *that* **sign** either. Because they did not "listen to Moses and the Prophets, neither [would] they be persuaded if someone rises from the dead" (Luke 16:31). The Jewish leaders not only rejected the truth of Jesus' resurrection but paid the soldiers who guarded the tomb to spread the false story that His disciples had stolen His body to create the illusion of a resurrection (Matt. 28:11-15).

When a person is confronted with the living Christ and with His atoning death and resurrection, the matter of that person's eternal destiny is determined. To turn your back on Jesus Christ and His sacrifice for your sins is to show yourself to be the vilest of sinners, no matter how superficially religious and moral you might otherwise be.

THE LAST SENTENCE

The men of Nineveh shall stand up with this generation at the judgment, and shall condemn it because they repented at the preaching of Jonah; and behold, something greater than Jonah is here. The Queen of the South shall rise up with this generation at the judgment and shall condemn it, because she came from the ends of the earth to hear the wisdom of Solomon; and behold, something greater than Solomon is here. (12:41-42)

Continuing with His illustration from the life of Jonah, Jesus contrasts the response of the pagan Ninevites to Jonah's message with the response of the Jewish leaders to His. In one of His most scathing denunciations, the Lord tells the self-righteous scribes and Pharisees, those who thought they were the best of God's favored people, that **the men of Nineveh shall stand up with this generation at the judgment, and shall condemn it because they repented at the preaching of Jonah.**

Despite Jonah's reluctance to preach God's message to the wicked, corrupt, idolatrous Assyrians of Nineveh, when the prophet finally began to preach, God effected an unprecedented awakening. "Then the people of Nineveh believed in God; and they called a fast and put on sackcloth from the greatest to the least of them. When the word reached the king of Nineveh, he arose from his throne, laid aside his robe from him, covered himself with sackcloth, and sat on the ashes" (Jonah 3:5-6). Covering oneself with sackcloth and sitting in ashes was an oriental way of showing genuine repentance and sorrow for wrongdoing. Because of their sincere repentance and belief, "God relented concerning the calamity which He had declared He would bring upon them. And He did not do it" (v. 10).

The men of Nineveh not only were Gentiles, and therefore apart from God's covenant and law, but they were especially wicked and brutal, even by pagan standards. They had no previous knowledge of the true God or of His will, yet their repentance of sin and their belief in God brought them spiritual salvation and spared them physical destruction. Jonah did not preach a message of hope but of judgment: "Yet forty days and Nineveh will be overthrown" (Jonah 3:4). The prophet despised the Ninevites and preached to them only under the Lord's compulsion. He performed no miracles and gave no promise of deliverance, but on the basis of that brief, direct, and confrontative message of doom from a loveless prophet, the people of Nineveh threw themselves on God's mercy and were saved.

Israel, on the other hand, was the chosen covenant people of God, privileged to have been given His law, His promises, His leading, His protection, and His special blessings in ways too numerous to list. Yet her people would not repent and turn from their sin even when God's own Son, **something greater than Jonah,** preached to them in gentle humility and gracious love, performed thousands of miracles as attesting signs of His divine authority, and offered God's gracious forgiveness and eternal life with Him in heaven. God's own chosen and uniquely blessed people turned their backs on Him—and for that they would stand under the condemnation of former pagans at **the judgment.**

Not only that, Jesus continued, but **the Queen of the South shall rise up with this generation at the judgment and shall condemn it.** The Queen of ancient Sheba, the country of the Sabeans, was often called **the Queen of the South,** because her country was in lower Arabia, some 1,200 miles to the southeast of Israel. The Sabeans were an extremely prosperous people, having earned their wealth from highly productive agriculture and from the lucrative Mediterranean to India trade routes that passed through their land. Yet the wealthy and prominent **Queen of the South**—who was a Gentile, a woman, a pagan, and an Arab—came to visit Solomon, the king of Israel, to learn God's wisdom from him and to pay him homage (1 Kings 10:1-13).

To the people of ancient Palestine, the land **of the South** seemed to be at **the ends of the earth.** Joel referred to it as "a distant nation" (Joel 3:8), and Jeremiah spoke of it as "a distant land" (Jer. 6:20). Yet **the Queen** and her large entourage made the long and arduous trip across the Arabian desert **to hear the wisdom of Solomon,** a man of God. She brought treasure upon treasure to the king, who was already wealthy beyond description, as a testimony of honor and gratitude for the godly **wisdom** he taught.

Again Jesus makes a comparison to the rebellious Jews who rejected Him. "That pagan woman," He said, in effect, "brought great treasures to Solomon and sat at his feet to glean **wisdom** from his lips. Yet **behold,** when I, **something greater than Solomon,** came **here** to you, preaching not only wisdom but salvation from sin and the way of eternal life, you refused to come. Therefore, that pagan **Queen** will **rise up with this generation at the judgment and shall condemn it.** That Gentile woman, with no advantage and no invitation, came on her own initiative to learn God's truth from Solomon. But you Jews of **this generation**—who have had countless centuries of divine advantage and blessing and who have the invitation of God's own Son to come to Him and be saved—have rejected the Son and thereby rejected forgiveness and eternal life. One day you will stand condemned even by the faith of Gentiles."

Reformation Versus Relationship (12:43-50)

Now when the unclean spirit goes out of a man, it passes through waterless places, seeking rest, and does not find it. Then it says, 'I will return to my house from which I came'; and when it comes, it finds it unoccupied, swept, and put in order. Then it goes, and takes along with it seven other spirits more wicked than itself, and they go in and live there; and the last state that man becomes worse than the first. That is the way it will also be with this evil generation.

While He was still speaking to the multitudes, behold, His mother and brothers were standing outside, seeking to speak to Him. And someone said to Him, 'Behold, Your mother and Your brothers are standing outside seeking to speak to You.' But He answered the one who was telling Him and said, 'Who is My mother and who are My brothers?' And stretching out His hand toward His disciples, He said, 'Behold, My mother and My brothers! For whoever does the will of My Father who is in heaven, he is My brother and sister and mother.'" (12:43-50)

In recent years there has been a great resurgence of interest in morality and ethics, of returning this nation to the religious and moral standards of its founding fathers. Many denominations, cults, and special interest groups have become highly visible and vocal in their national, and sometimes international, efforts to promote or oppose certain customs, laws, or practices—ranging from civil rights and capital punishment to abortion and divorce.

Some evangelicals have become active in preaching morality, patriotism, and loyalty to traditional American values. Much effort is spent trying to influence legislators and political leaders to assist in returning America to its former standards of more biblical behavior and integrity.

Christians cannot but be concerned about moral and ethical issues, because God's Word is unequivocal and unmatched in its standards of righteous living, justice, and social responsibility. But Scripture also makes clear that morality by itself, without a right relationship to God, is in many ways more dangerous than immorality. In the Sermon on the Mount, Jesus repeatedly emphasizes that mere outward righteousness is one of the greatest hindrances to the gospel.

The Pharisees were classic moralists. No other Jews, and certainly no Gentiles, were committed to such rigid standards of religion, morality, ethics, and daily living. They lived by a complex and demanding code, a system of laws that regulated virtually every aspect of life. But those man-made standards, purportedly based on God's Word, had led them further and further from God. They were so self-sufficient and self-righteous that when God Himself came among them in human form they rejected, vilified, and finally crucified Him. They had so thoroughly convinced themselves of their righteousness that when the very Source of righteousness stood in their midst they accused Him of being in league with Satan. Under the illusion of their own goodness they became unreachable with the saving message of the gospel. When Jesus came preaching deliverance from sin, they were not interested, because they could not imagine such a message having relevance for them. And when Jesus declared that their self-righteousness was, in fact, the most insidious form of unrighteousness (Matt. 5:20), they were infuriated.

Jesus had little trouble reaching prostitutes, thieves, extortioners, murderers, and the outcasts of society. But He had an almost impossible time reaching religious and moral people who were under the delusion that outward propriety made them acceptable to God. Because they refused to recognize their sin, they recognized no need for a Savior. Their strict standards of morality gave an illusion of safety and prevented them from seeing that trust in themselves was their greatest spiritual danger and a massive barrier between them and God.

In His series of woes against the scribes and Pharisees in Matthew 23, Jesus repeatedly called them hypocrites and charged them with possessing only spurious righteousness.

> For you clean the outside of the cup and of the dish, but inside they are full of robbery and self-indulgence. You blind Pharisee, first clean the inside of the cup and of the dish, so that the outside of it may become clean also. . . . For you are like whitewashed tombs which on the outside appear beautiful, but inside they are full of dead men's bones and all uncleanness. Even so you too outwardly appear righteous to men, but inwardly you are full of hypocrisy

and lawlessness. . . . For you build the tombs of the prophets and adorn the monuments of the righteous, and say, "If we had been living in the days of our fathers, we would not have been partners with them in shedding the blood of the prophets." Consequently you bear witness against yourselves, that you are sons of those who murdered the prophets. Fill up then the measure of the guilt of your fathers. You serpents, you brood of vipers, how shall you escape the sentence of hell. (Matt. 23:25-32)

There has never been a group of men more committed to a demanding religious and moral code than the Pharisees and never a group of men so far from God.

By itself, morality leads to self-righteousness and is a damning thing. A person is better off being grossly immoral and recognizing his need than being highly moral and admitting no need. There is nothing God can do for the person who, like the Pharisee in Jesus' parable, prays confidently, "God, I thank Thee that I am not like other people: swindlers, unjust, adulterers, or even like this tax-gatherer. I fast twice a week; I pay tithes of all that I get" (Luke 18:11-12). In his own eyes he is already right with God and needs nothing from God (cf. Matt. 19:20). But God can do a great deal for the person who, like the tax-gatherer in that same parable, cries out, "God, be merciful to me, the sinner!" He is the person who goes "down to his house justified rather than the other; for everyone who exalts himself shall be humbled, but he who humbles himself shall be exalted" (vv. 13b-14).

Matthew 12:43-50 presents another of Jesus' many warnings to the people not to listen to or follow the example of their moralistic but ungodly religious leaders but to come to Him. Their need was not for the outer reformation offered by the scribes and Pharisees but the inner transformation that could be theirs only as they gained a right relationship to God the Father by trusting in His Son for salvation from sin.

THE DANGER OF REFORMATION

Now when the unclean spirit goes out of a man, it passes through waterless places, seeking rest, and does not find it. Then it says, 'I will return to my house from which I came'; and when it comes, it finds it unoccupied, swept, and put in order. Then it goes, and takes along with it seven other spirits more wicked than itself, and they go in and live there; and the last state of that man becomes worse than the first. That is the way it will also be with this evil generation. (12:43-45)

In this parable Jesus vividly and frighteningly pictures the consequence of religious and moral reformation apart from a right relationship to Him. Morality apart from the living Christ can never be more than a sham, and the more it is relied on the more dangerous it becomes.

The main character in this illustration is an **unclean spirit,** whose specific evil characteristics are not identified. He is a demon, a fallen angel and a member of

Satan's host of supernatural, evil coworkers. **Unclean** represents the wicked, vile nature of all demon spirits; but this particular **spirit** was not as evil as he could have been, because, as we learn later in the parable, he had demon friends who were worse than himself.

We are not told by what means this **unclean spirit** went **out of a man**. It may be that the **man** made a moral decision to forsake the sin in which this demon had entrapped him and that the demon no longer had control over the **man**. It may be that the man had been cleansed of the demon but, just as many people whom Jesus cleansed and healed, did not trust in Him for salvation. For whatever reason or by whatever means, the **man** was temporarily freed from the demon's presence and influence.

After he left the man, this demon passed **through waterless places, seeking rest, and** [did] **not find it.** Being spirits, demons do not need food and water as human beings do, and therefore **waterless places** here figuratively represents desolation, barrenness, and extreme discomfort. In its own corrupt way the demon was **seeking rest,** some place of greater satisfaction. From this and many other passages in the New Testament, it seems evident that demons prefer to indwell bodily creatures, preferably human beings but secondarily even animals (see Matt. 8:31), rather than exist as unattached beings in Satan's evil realm. Perhaps this particular demon was restless because it could not express its evil nature through inanimate, lifeless things. It was most at home in a human being, because it is through human beings that Satan and his demons can most successfully work their evil and oppose God.

When it could find no other satisfactory place to dwell, the demon decided to go back to its former residence: **I will return to my house from which I came.** Whether the spirit was simply being presumptuous or whether it had some continuing access to and control over the man's life, its reference to **my house** indicates a strong sense of ownership and possessiveness. And the fact that it was able to regain entrance so easily proves the boast was not vain. When it returned and found its former **house** was **unoccupied, swept, and put in order,** the first spirit took **along . . . seven other spirits more wicked than itself, and they** [went] **in and** [lived] **there.**

That the man's **house** was **unoccupied** (that is, by another demon), **swept, and put in order** suggests that a genuine moral reformation had taken place. Whether by the power of his own will or by the cleansing of God, he was temporarily free of that sin and its related demon and from any other.

Through fear of imprisonment, disease, social stigma, financial ruin, and many other such motivations, a person can manage to rid himself of certain sinful habits. Sometimes the motive is more positive and the person determines to change because of love for wife, husband, or children. But such self-cleansing—no matter how thorough and extensive and no matter what the motivation—is never permanent. Even if the cleansing is by the Lord, it is not permanent if not accompanied by saving faith in Him. Surely many of the people whom Jesus cleansed of demons died and joined those demons in hell, because they did not also accept the Lord's forgiveness and offer of salvation. The vast majority of those to whom Jesus ministered accepted only temporary healing from disease and temporary relief from demonic control. They surrendered the symptoms and consequences of sin to Him, but not sin itself. Of the ten lepers Jesus cleansed on one occasion, only one received the true wholeness of salvation (Luke 17:11-19).

When the basic sin nature is not dealt with through the miracle of repentance and trust in Christ, the removal of a particular sin or even a demon leaves a person's spiritual **house . . . unoccupied, swept, and put in order,** but subject to reoccupation by **seven other spirits more wicked than** the first. **And they go in and live there; and the last state of that man becomes worse than the first.**

A religious, self-righteous, reformed person is subject to Satan in a way that a guilt-ridden immoral person is not, because his very morality blinds him to his basic sinful condition and need. He is perfectly satisfied with his empty house, thinking that freedom from outward manifestation of sin is freedom from its presence, power, and damnation.

Katoikeō (to **live**) carries the idea of dwelling and settling down. It is the same verb Paul used as he prayed for the Ephesians, "that Christ may dwell in your hearts through faith" (Eph. 3:17). Where Christ does not live, demons are free to **live.** Satan's emissaries can **go in and live** in a reformed but Christless life in a settled and secure way, because in his religious delusion their host may be oblivious to their presence. **The last state of that man becomes worse than the first,** but he does not know it. He is like a leper who rubs off his fingers and toes because he feels no pain. In an infinitely more tragic way, self-righteousness desensitizes a person to sin to the point that he is not aware that his very soul is rotting away under demonic corruption.

One of the worst aspects of religious legalism is that it tends to get progressively more ungodly from generation to generation. "Woe to you, scribes and Pharisees, hypocrites," Jesus said, "because you travel about on sea and land to make one proselyte; and when he becomes one, you make him twice as much a son of hell as yourselves" (Matt. 23:15). A person who is discipled into legalism often becomes more zealous and self-righteous than his teacher.

To preach morality, even according to biblical standards of behavior, but not salvation through Christ promotes a religion that drives men further from God than they were before they reformed. It is much easier to reach someone who is overwhelmed with a true sense of His sin than someone who is overwhelmed with a false sense of his righteousness. That is what Jesus meant when He said, "I did not come to call the righteous, but sinners" (Matt. 9:13). It was not the immoral and irreligious people of Israel who put Jesus to death but the religious leaders who prided themselves in their goodness. Christ could not reach them, because they thought they had no need of any spiritual help, least of all salvation from sin.

Peter says of such persons that "after they have escaped the defilements of the world by the knowledge of the Lord and Savior Jesus Christ, they are again entangled in them and are overcome, the last state has become worse for them than the first. For it would be better for them not to have known the way of righteousness, than having known it, to turn away from the holy commandment delivered to them. It has happened to them according to the true proverb, 'A dog returns to its own vomit,' and, 'A sow, after washing, returns to wallowing in the mire'" (2 Pet. 2:20-22). The reformed but unconverted person will eventually revert to sinful ways for the same reason that the dog returns to its vomit and the washed sow returns to the mud wallow—because in each case the original nature has not been changed.

Jesus' parable applied to Israel as a nation, to **this evil generation,** as well as to individual Jews. During the Babylonian Captivity the Jews forsook idolatry, and in the more than two thousand years since then they have never, as a people, fallen back into it. But by the time their Messiah came, they had become so satisfied with their reformation and with their religious ceremonies and moral traditions, that they saw no need for a Savior. Consequently, in the end times, that people will find themselves in league with the antichrist during the Great Tribulation.

Whether in the broad range of history or in an individual life, the same principle applies: outer reformation without inner transformation brings susceptibility to even worse evil than that from which one turned away.

The Power of Relationship

While He was still speaking to the multitudes, behold, His mother and brothers were standing outside, seeking to speak to Him. And someone said to Him, 'Behold, Your mother and Your brothers are standing outside seeking to speak to You.' But He answered the one who was telling Him and said, 'Who is My mother and who are My brothers?' And stretching out His hand toward His disciples, He said, 'Behold, My mother and My brothers! For whoever does the will of My Father who is in heaven, he is My brother and sister and mother.'" (12:46-50)

Reformation is not salvation, regeneration, or redemption. It may, in fact, work toward the very opposite by entrenching a person in self-satisfaction and blinding him to his need for God's mercy. In order to have salvation there must be a new and right relationship to God, which comes only as a sinner humbly confesses and turns from his sin and receives Jesus Christ as Lord and Savior.

The arrival of Jesus' family gave Him the perfect opportunity to give a graphic illustration of the need for personal relationship to Him. **While He was still speaking to the multitudes** in a house (see 13:1), **His mother and brothers were standing outside, seeking to speak to Him.** When Jesus was informed of this, **He answered the one who was telling Him and said, "Who is My mother and who are My brothers?"**

By this time Joseph had probably been dead for many years, and Jesus' immediate family consisted of His **mother,** Mary, his half **brothers** (James, Joseph, Simon, and Judas), and His half sisters, who are not named (Matt. 13:55-56).

After the resurrection, Jesus' **brothers** eventually came to believe in Him, His brother James becoming the head of the Jerusalem church (see Acts 15:13-22) and author of the epistle that bears his name. But during Jesus' preaching and teaching ministry there is no clear evidence that any member of His family other than Mary fully understood who He really was or trusted in Him as Savior. We are told specifically that His **brothers** did not believe in Him (John 7:5), and it may be that even His **mother**—despite the revelations to her before and after Jesus' birth and her magnificent confession at that time (see Luke 1:26–2:38)—did not yet personally trust in Jesus as her own Lord and Savior.

We are not told (cf. Mark 3:31-32; Luke 8:19-20) why Jesus' **mother and brothers were . . . seeking to speak to Him,** but it seems reasonable to assume that they were greatly concerned about His welfare and perhaps even feared with some of His home town friends that He had "lost His senses" (Mark 3:21). His condemnation of the scribes and Pharisees continued to grow in intensity and seriousness, and those leaders, in turn, were accusing Him of doing His work by Satan's power. Their plan to destroy Jesus (Matt. 12:14) was probably already rumored among the people. Jesus' **mother and brothers** were therefore hoping to dissuade Him from continuing His work and perhaps hoped He would flee to a safe place until the religious leaders forgot about Him or lost interest. His family was on a rescue mission to save Him from imminent death.

For most men such an incident would have been embarrassing in the extreme, but Jesus was neither embarrassed nor resentful. He loved and cared for His family, and He understood their concern, misguided as it was. He did not, in fact, respond directly to the request of His family but rather used the occasion to teach an important truth: **And stretching out His hand toward His disciples, He said, "Behold, My mother and My brothers!"**

Jesus was not renouncing His family. He loved them even more than they loved Him. His last request from the cross was for John to care for His mother (John 19:26-27), and through His gracious love His brothers eventually came to believe in Him as their Lord and Savior (Acts 1:14).

The Lord's purpose in referring to **His disciples** as His **mother** and **brothers** was to teach that He invites the entire world into His intimate and divine family. Anyone can enter His spiritual family by trusting in Him, and the family of God is the only family that ultimately matters.

Even being a member of Jesus' own earthly family did not merit salvation by virtue of that relationship. Jesus' invitation therefore extended to His natural **mother** and half **brothers,** because they, too, needed to be saved from sin. Apart from personal faith, they were no more spiritually related to Him than any other human being. "All of those, and only those, who believe in Me are spiritually related to Me," He was saying. **For whoever does the will of My Father who is in heaven, he is My brother and sister and mother.**

The **whoever** indicates the universality of the invitation. No one who believes is excluded. And, on the other hand, no one who does *not* believe will be included. God's first and most absolute desire and requirement for mankind is belief in His Son. "This is the work of God," Jesus said, "that you believe in Him whom He has sent"

(John 6:29). Until a person believes in Christ, God cannot give him any spiritual help, and that person cannot give God any spiritual service.

At Jesus' baptism God declared, "This is My beloved Son, in whom I am well-pleased" (Matt. 3:17), and at the transfiguration He spoke the same words to Peter, James, and John, adding, "Listen to Him" (17:5). God's supreme will for mankind is for them to be well-pleased with the Son, just as He is—and to trust in Him, listen to Him, follow Him, and obey His Word.

After declaring, "For the Son of Man has come to save that which was lost" (Matt. 18:11), Jesus told a parable explaining the Father's great love for mankind and His desire that they be saved. "What do you think?" He asked rhetorically. "If any man has a hundred sheep, and one of them has gone astray, does he not leave the ninety-nine on the mountains and go and search for the one that is straying? And if it turns out that he finds it, truly I say to you, he rejoices over it more than over the ninety-nine which have not gone astray. Thus it is not the will of your Father who is in heaven that one of these little ones perish" (vv. 12-14). Many years later the apostles echoed that truth. Paul wrote, "God our Savior . . . desires all men to be saved and to come to the knowledge of the truth" (1 Tim. 2:3-4), and Peter declared that the Lord does not wish "for any to perish but for all to come to repentance" (2 Pet. 3:9).

Being rightly related to Christ, however, requires more than a mere verbal declaration of loyalty. "Not everyone who says to Me, 'Lord, Lord,' will enter the kingdom of heaven," Jesus warned; "but he who does the will of My Father who is heaven. Many will say to Me on that day, 'Lord, Lord, did we not prophesy in Your name, and in Your name cast out demons, and in Your name perform many miracles?' And then I will declare to them, 'I never knew you; depart from Me, you who practice lawlessness'" (Matt. 7:21-23). Saving relationship to Jesus Christ comes only from submissively believing in Him and receiving the gift of salvation He offers. "There is salvation in no one else; for there is no other name under heaven that has been given among men, by which we must be saved" (Acts 4:12).

At best, reformation changes only the outside of a person; at worst it becomes a barrier to his being changed on the inside. A right relationship to Christ, however, brings completely new life, both inside and outside. All the rest of Scripture surrounds the central truth that Jesus Christ came into the world to save sinners—to transform them, not reform them. Until a person claims that truth, no other can be of any benefit.

The great message of the gospel, and therefore of the church, is not a call to morality but a call to deliverance from sin through the Lord Jesus Christ.

The Kingdom and the Gospel—part 1
(13:1-17)

32

On that day Jesus went out of the house, and was sitting by the sea. And great multitudes gathered to Him, so that He got into a boat and sat down, and the whole multitude was standing on the beach. And He spoke many things to them in parables, saying, "Behold, the sower went out to sow; and as he sowed, some seeds fell beside the road, and the birds came and ate them up. And others fell upon the rocky places, where they did not have much soil; and immediately they sprang up, because they had no depth of soil. But when the sun had risen, they were scorched; and because they had no root, they withered away. And others fell among the thorns, and the thorns came up and choked them out. And others fell on the good soil, and yielded a crop, some a hundredfold, some sixty, and some thirty. He who has ears, let him hear."

And the disciples came and said to Him, "Why do You speak to them in parables?" And He answered and said to them, "To you it has been granted to know the mysteries of the kingdom of heaven, but to them it has not been granted. For whoever has, to him shall more be given, and he shall have an abundance; but whoever does not have, even what he has shall be taken away from him. Therefore I speak to them in parables; because while seeing they do not see, and while hearing they do not hear, nor do they understand. And in their case the prophecy of Isaiah is being fulfilled, which says, 'You will keep on hearing, but will not understand; and you will keep on seeing, but will not perceive; for the heart of this people has become dull, and with their ears they scarcely hear, and they have closed their eyes lest they should see with their eyes, and hear with their ears, and understand with their heart and return, and I should heal them.' But blessed are your eyes, because they see; and your ears, because they hear. For truly I say to you, that many prophets and righteous men desired to see what you see, and did not see it; and to hear what you hear, and did not hear it. (13:1-17)

There seems to be no end of the books being written today on the mission of the church. From many sources and from almost every possible viewpoint, the church and its task in the world are being studied, scrutinized, analyzed, praised, blamed, exalted, damned, criticized, and shored up. Every sort of program, principle, method, and scheme is being applied to its operation. With high visibility, the church is being discussed everywhere from the back room to the boardroom, from the kitchen to the seminary class, and by pastors, theologians, laymen, and even the people of the world. Yet with all that study and concern, in few times of its history has more of the church been less certain about what it is, what it should be, and what it should do.

Some foundational truths for understanding the mission of the church are found in the thirteenth chapter of Matthew's gospel. The Lord of the church reveals the nature of the church and the spiritual characteristics of the period of time often referred to as the church age. In this marvelously prophetic chapter Jesus describes the character of the era between His first and second comings.

By His authoritative teaching and His indisputable miracles our Lord had early in His ministry proved Himself to be Israel's long-awaited Messiah and King. He had pronounced judgment on the nation and on individuals because of their unbelief, and He had offered an invitation into God's kingdom and family to any who would believe in Him.

But because Israel had rejected her King, He would not establish the earthly kingdom. For centuries the Jewish people had awaited their Messiah and Deliverer and the kingdom on earth He would establish. They had longed for the promised times of refreshing and restoration, for the throne of David to once again and forever be established. But when the King came, He did not please them and they rejected Him and His kingdom. That most spiritually blessed and enlightened of all generations of mankind turned its back on its King, the Son of God.

In his commentary on Matthew, Stanley Toussaint says, "Not seeing the Messiahship of Jesus in His words and works, they separated the fruit from the tree." None of the people denied Jesus' miracles, and most of them recognized that He performed them by God's power. While acknowledging the divine source of Jesus' miracles, they refused to recognize that He was Himself that divine Source. The scribes and Pharisees who charged Jesus with casting out demons by Satan's power (12:24) did not represent the majority of the common people. But even those who admired Jesus and were awed by His power would not connect the evidence with what it clearly was—proof of His divinity and messiahship.

The questions that come to the thoughtful reader are, "If Jesus came to offer the kingdom to Israel and to establish and rule it as prophesied in Scripture, and it was rejected, was God's plan totally frustrated? Did His own predictions fail to come true? What, then, is to be the character of the present time? What is to be the nature of the message and mission of the disciples and of all believers? And throughout this time, what response is to be expected from people?" It is those questions that Jesus addresses in Matthew 13 with a series of eight parables. The underlying truth was that the kingdom in its final fulfillment would be postponed until the time that Israel *would* believe in and receive her King. That time will be at the second coming of Christ, when He will establish His earthly kingdom for a thousand years. God cannot forsake His promise, and in His grace He will send His Son again to offer the kingdom. On that day, the Lord promised, "I will pour out on the house of David and on the inhabitants of Jerusalem, the Spirit of grace and of supplication, so that they will look on Me whom they have pierced; and they will mourn for Him, as one mourns for an only son, and they will weep bitterly over Him, like the bitter weeping over a first-born. . . . And it will come about in that day that living waters will flow out of Jerusalem, half of them toward the eastern sea and the other half toward the western sea; it will be in summer as well as in winter. And the Lord will be king over all the earth; in that day the Lord will be the only one, and His name the only one" (Zech. 12:10; 14:8-9).

But Zechariah tells us nothing of what would happen between Israel's piercing of the Messiah and her subsequent mourning over Him. The prophet does not even hint that such an intermediate period would occur—although it has now lasted for almost 2,000 years. It was a mystery until revealed here and more fully throughout the New Testament.

In the end "all Israel will be saved," Paul declares; "just as it is written, 'The Deliverer will come from Zion, He will remove ungodliness from Jacob.' 'And this is My covenant with them, when I take away their sins'" (Rom. 11:26-27). But the day of that fulfilled kingdom had to be postponed, because when the King first "came to His own, . . . those who were His own did not receive Him" (John 1:11).

But an *internal* kingdom *was* established, because "as many as received Him, to them He gave the right to become children of God, even to those who believe in His name" (John 1:12). Christ's external, visible kingdom was postponed, but the internal, spiritual kingdom of His saints was established, and in their hearts the Lord reigns and through their lives and testimony He now expresses His will on earth.

The period between Christ's first and second comings has been called the parenthesis, the interim, the interregnum, and many other such terms. It is a period that was not revealed in the Old Testament, a period to which Jesus refers as "the mysteries of the kingdom of heaven" (13:11). Those mysteries will be discussed below as that verse is expounded. In the eight parables of chapter 13 and in His explanations of them Jesus describes the interim period, the period that began with His rejection and crucifixion and which has continued until the present time. An understanding of this period was essential for the disciples as they set out to evangelize.

THE PLACE: THE SEASHORE

On that day Jesus went out of the house, and was sitting by the sea. And great multitudes gathered to Him, so that He got into a boat and sat down, and the whole multitude was standing on the beach. (13:1-2)

That day refers to the day on which Jesus' mother and brothers came looking for Him (12:46-47), probably to persuade Him to stop the preaching and teaching they knew could cost Him His life. On **that day** He had healed many people of various unnamed diseases, explained the true character of the promised Messiah, healed and cleansed the blind and dumb demoniac, charged the unbelieving Pharisees of committing the unpardonable sin by accusing Him of casting out demons by Satan's power, declared that unbelieving Jews would be condemned by believing Gentiles on the day of judgment, and warned against the deceptive danger of moral reform without spiritual rebirth (12:15-45).

It is also interesting to note that, during His earlier ministry, Jesus seemed to spend more time inside, in houses and synagogues. As His ministry progressed, however, and He was more and more rejected by the Jews, He spent more time ministering outdoors—on the seashore and mountainside and in the countryside, highways, and streets.

Although the religious leaders had rejected Him, Jesus remained immensely popular with the common people, and **great multitudes** still **gathered to Him** in fascination to hear Him speak and see Him heal, and some to be healed themselves.

Perhaps pushed by the crowd to the water's edge and seeking to put some distance between the people and Himself in order to address the crowd better, Jesus **got into a boat and sat down, and the whole multitude was standing on the beach.** The fact that He **sat down** in typical rabbinic fashion was necessary because of the moving of the boat in the water; and because the **beach** sloped sharply upward from the water, the people were enabled to see and hear Him best while He was seated in the boat.

THE PLAN: TO SPEAK IN PARABLES

And He spoke many things to them in parables, (13:3a)

On this occasion, and on most future occasions, Jesus **spoke many things to them** [the multitudes, v. 2] **in parables,** and only in parables (v. 34). He did not explain their meaning to the multitudes but only to His disciples (vv. 10-11, 18, 36; Mark 4:34).

Parabolē (**parable**) is a compound word made up of a form of the verb *ballō* (to throw, lay, or place) and the prefix *para* (meaning alongside of). The idea is that of placing, or laying, something alongside of something else for the purpose of comparison. A spiritual or moral truth would often be expressed by laying it alongside, so to speak, a physical example that could be more easily understood. A common, observable object or practice was used to illustrate a subjective truth or principle. That which was well known was laid alongside that which was not known or understood in order to explain it. The known elucidated the unknown. The parable was a common form of Jewish teaching, and the term is found some 45 times in the Septuagint, the Greek Old Testament.

In His earlier teaching, Jesus used many graphic analogies to illustrate divine truth. He had spoken of believers as salt and light in the world (Matt. 5:13-16), of their following the example of the birds and lilies in not being anxious about the necessities of life (6:26-30), and of building their lives on the solid rock of God's Word rather than the insecure sand of man's philosophy (7:24-27). Although those and other such figures were embryonic parables, their meaning was clear in the context of Jesus' teaching.

Teaching through **parables** and other figurative means is effective because it helps make abstract truth more concrete, more interesting, easier to remember, and easier to apply to life. When a truth is externalized in the figures of a parable, the internalizing of moral and spiritual meaning is much easier.

In the series of parables in chapter 13, Jesus uses such familiar figures as soil, seed, birds, thorns, rocks, sun, wheat, tares, mustard seed, leaven, hidden treasure, and a pearl. But in these particular **parables** themselves the truth is *not* made clear, because the basic story tells nothing but the literal account, without presenting the moral or spiritual truth. It was only to His disciples that Jesus explained what the soil, the seed, the thorns, and the other figures represent. And an *unexplained* parable was nothing but an impossible riddle, whose meaning could only be guessed at.

THE PARABLE: THE SOWER

saying, "Behold, the sower went out to sow; and as he sowed, some seeds fell beside the road, and the birds came and ate them up. And others fell upon the rocky places, where they did not have much soil; and immediately they sprang up, because they had no depth of soil. But when the sun had risen, they were scorched; and because they had no root, they withered away. And others fell among the thorns, and the thorns came up and choked them out. And others fell on the good soil, and yielded a crop, some a hundredfold, some sixty, and some thirty. He who has ears, let him hear." (13:3b-9)

As Jesus told the story of the **sower**, His hearers perhaps could have looked around and seen a man actually sowing seed. In any case, the scene was familiar to them, whether they were farmers or not. A man with his seed bag slung over his shoulder as he **went out to sow** was a common and vivid image. As he walked up and down the furrows of his field, **he sowed** as he went, repeatedly reaching into his bag for a handful of seed to cast on either side.

The various kinds of ground on which the seed could fall in a field were also familiar. When broadcasting seed by hand it was impossible to control accurately where all the seed fell, and **some seeds** were bound to fall **beside the road.** Palestine, especially the highly productive Galilee region, was crisscrossed with fields, and **road** here refers primarily to the narrow paths that separated one field from another. Farmers used the paths to walk between the fields, and travelers walked on them as they went from one part of the country to another. It was along such a **road** through a grainfield that Jesus and His disciples were traveling one Sabbath as they picked grain to eat (Matt. 12:1).

The soil on and **beside the road** would, of course, be untilled and packed down hard by the walking, which prevented any **seeds** that happened to fall on it from penetrating and taking root. Because those **seeds** were exposed and easily accessible, **the birds came and ate them up** as soon as the farmer got a safe distance down the path. What was not eaten by birds "was trampled under foot" (Luke 8:5). Undoubtedly, birds followed closely after a sower.

The second type of ground on which some of the seeds **fell** Jesus refers to as **the rocky places, where they did not have much soil. Rocky** does not refer to loose rocks, because the farmer always removed all rocks, sticks, and other such objects from his field before planting. It rather refers to underlying beds of solid rock deeper than the plow reached, mostly limestone, which **did not have much soil** covering them. The seeds that fell on such ground **immediately . . . sprang up, because they had no depth of soil.** When the seed began to germinate, its roots could not penetrate the rock that was just below the surface, and the little plant would instead start to **spring up** above ground much faster than it normally would.

For a brief period these plants would look healthier and hardier than those in good soil, because more of them showed above ground and they grew faster. **But when the sun had risen, they were scorched; and because they had no root, they withered away.** Lack of roots prevented the plants from reaching and absorbing moisture or nourishment. After **the sun had risen** in the morning, the plants that looked so promising **were scorched** and quickly **withered away.**

The third type of ground on which some of the seeds **fell** was infested with **thorns.** After this ground had been cultivated, it looked perfectly good, but when the grain began to sprout, so did the thorns. These tough, thistle-bearing weeds **came up and choked . . . out** the good plants by taking most of the space, moisture, nourishment, and sunlight for themselves.

The fourth type of ground on which some of the seeds **fell** was **good soil.** It was away from the path and was loose and soft. It had sufficient depth to support the good plants and it was free of weeds. Because of those favorable conditions, it **yielded a crop, some a hundredfold, some sixty, and some thirty.**

In Palestine during New Testament times, the average ratio of harvested grain seeds to those that were planted is said to have been less than eight to one. Even a tenfold crop would have been well above average; and the yields of which Jesus speaks were truly phenomenal.

At the end of this unexplained parable Jesus said, **He who has ears, let him hear.** That is to say, "If you can understand it, then understand it." Jesus was not mocking His hearers but was rather pointing out to them that they would need more than their own human understanding to interpret the meaning. He may have been giving an invitation to those in the multitudes who were serious about following Him to come to Him and ask for an explanation, as the disciples were about to do. Otherwise, they would not have **ears** to **hear** what He was really saying.

Only those who accept the King can understand the King and profit from His teaching and lordship. To all others His teaching is meaningless riddles.

THE PURPOSE: TO REVEAL AND TO CONCEAL

And the disciples came and said to Him, "Why do You speak to them in parables?" And He answered and said to them, "To you it has been granted to know the mysteries of the kingdom of heaven, but to them it has not been granted. For whoever has, to him shall more be given, and he shall have an abundance; but whoever does not have, even what he has shall be taken away from him. Therefore I speak to them in parables; because while seeing they do not see, and while hearing they do not hear, nor do they understand. And in their case the prophecy of Isaiah is being fulfilled, which says, 'You will keep on hearing, but will not understand; and you will keep on seeing, but will not perceive; for the heart of this people has become dull, and with their ears they scarcely hear, and they have closed their eyes lest they should see with their eyes, and hear with their ears, and understand with their heart and return, and I should heal them.' But blessed are your eyes, because they see; and your ears, because they hear. For truly I say to you, that many prophets and righteous men desired to see what you see, and did not see it; and to hear what you hear, and did not hear it. (13:10-17)

When **the disciples came** to Jesus **and said to Him, "Why do You speak to them** [the multitudes] **in parables?"** it was the fact that the **parables** were *unexplained* that puzzled them. They were asking, in effect, "Why do you bother saying anything to them at all, if they can't understand it?"

At this point Jesus gives the twofold reason for His speaking in **parables:** to reveal meaning to those who receive Him and to conceal meaning from those who do not. **He answered and said to them, "To you** [who believe in Me] **it has been granted to know the mysteries of the kingdom of heaven, but to them** [who do not believe in Me] **it has not been granted."**

Mysteries does not refer to stories such as those found in modern mystery novels, whose complex plot and unexpected situations pique the curiosity of the reader. In the ancient world a mystery was a sacred secret known only to initiates and sometimes only to upper level religionists. The system of mystery religions began in ancient Babylon and spread in various forms to every part of the civilized world. A influential Greek philosophical system of New Testament times was called gnosticism, a name derived from *gnōsis,* which means knowledge. Gnostics considered themselves the ones "in the know" as far as philosophical matters were concerned.

In ancient Egypt a popular religious mystery involved the mythical god Osiris and his goddess wife Isis. Osiris was a wise and benevolent king who was persuaded by his wicked brother Seth to come to a banquet, where, with the help of seventy-two co-conspirators, Seth placed the king in a coffin and threw him into the Nile River to drown. Osiris was rescued by Isis and brought home; but when Seth discovered his brother was alive, he went to the palace and cut Osiris into fourteen pieces, which he shipped to fourteen far-separated locations throughout Egypt. After Isis managed to collect all the pieces of his body, Osiris miraculously restored himself to life; and from the time of his "resurrection" he became the immortal king of both the living and the dead.

Although the story itself was fascinating to anyone who heard it, its deeper meanings were known only to initiates of the Osiris and Isis cults. For them each person and incident in the story had special significance. For example, Osiris represented all good and was attacked by Seth, who represented all evil. The unrelenting devotion of Isis represented the redemptive and triumphal power of love. The ultimate secret, or mystery, was the formula, "I am thou, and thou art I," which, when spoken to Osiris, would place the worshiper in eternal union with that god.

Similar attitudes of exclusiveness and concepts of mystery are seen in modern secret societies, whose most important rituals and principles are known only to members, and sometimes only to the highest ranking leaders.

In Scripture, however, **mysteries** refers to the revelation of something previously hidden and unknown. New Testament **mysteries** are therefore revelations and explanations of divine truths that were not revealed to saints under the Old Covenant.

The particular **mysteries** about which Jesus teaches here have to do with **the kingdom of heaven** (see also vv. 24, 31, 33, 44, 45, 47, 52)—which from parallel passages in Mark (4:11, 30) and Luke (8:10; 13:18) is seen to be the same as the kingdom of God (cf. Matt. 19:23-24). One title emphasizes the King (God) and the other emphasizes the sphere of His reign (heaven). Of this kingdom the Old Testament gives only limited and incomplete glimpses. Most messianic prophecies in the Old Testament point to Christ's second coming and the establishment of His earthly millennial kingdom and His subsequent eternal kingdom. Only hints are given about His present earthly **kingdom,** that began with His rejection and crucifixion and will continue until He returns. This is the **kingdom** that exists spiritually in the hearts of His people while the King is physically absent from the earth. He is present with believers, but He is not visible or evident to the world, except as revealed through their lives and testimony.

Some interpreters insist that no present **kingdom of heaven** of any sort can exist because the King is absent. But David's reign over Israel while he was fleeing from his rebellious son Absalom is a classic instance of a king having full rights and authority over his realm while temporarily being unable to exercise those rights because of certain circumstances. During the period of usurpation, David is repeatedly referred to as King David, although he was unable to sit on his throne or even to live in his capital city of Jerusalem (see 2 Sam. 15-17). David's kingship was acknowledged and respected only by those Israelites who remained faithful to him, but his rejection by the followers of Absalom did not make him any less the rightful king. He was the only legitimate monarch, and every faithful citizen of his kingdom recognized it.

In much the same way, Jesus Christ, the promised Messiah of the Old Testament, now rules in the hearts of His people, although He is physically absent from earth and rules them from His heavenly dwelling through His Spirit—while the usurper Satan temporarily is the spiritual ruler of this world (John 12:31).

The **kingdom of heaven** has two important but distinct aspects. First is the universal kingdom, which includes every created thing in every time and place. God is the Creator and absolute Sovereign of the universe, and will be eternally. Nothing exists or occurs without His divine provision or permission.

David reminds us that "The Lord sat as King at the flood; yes, the Lord sits as King forever" (Ps. 29:10). He ruled the earth even when it was so wickedly rebellious that He destroyed every human being except Noah and his family in the Flood. Again David tells us, "The Lord has established His throne in the heavens; and His sovereignty rules over all" (Ps. 103:19). God is sovereign "over all," even over Satan and his demons, whom He has allowed certain freedoms for a limited period of time. Their final and certain destiny is hell, which God rules just as surely as He rules heaven. The Lord has prepared that place for the specific purpose of their punishment along with every unbelieving human being (Matt. 25:41). "Thine, O Lord, is the greatness and the power and the glory and the victory and the majesty," declares the writer of the Chronicles; "indeed everything that is in the heavens and the earth; Thine is the dominion, O Lord, and Thou dost exalt Thyself as head over all" (1 Chron. 29:11).

The second aspect of God's **kingdom** is what Alva McClain has appropriately called mediatorial, because His rule is mediated through others. Both the universal and the mediatorial aspects of the **kingdom** are seen in the Lord's Prayer, as Jesus commands us to pray, "Thy kingdom come. Thy will be done, on earth as it is in heaven" (Matt. 6:10). "In heaven" refers to God's universal and direct reign, whereas "on earth" refers to the present kingdom, in which only His saints are His subjects in the fullest sense.

From the beginning of creation God intended the earth to be ruled by human instruments in His behalf. After everything had been created except man, "God said, 'Let Us make man in Our image, according to Our likeness; and let them rule over the fish of the sea and over the birds of the sky and over the cattle and over all the earth, and over every creeping thing that creeps on the earth" (Gen. 1:26). When Satan succeeded in leading Adam and Eve into the rebellion he had begun in heaven, he became the temporary ruler and prince of earth (John 12:31; 14:30; 16:11). But, like Absalom, he is a usurper, and his rule is both illegitimate and doomed to end.

Even after the Fall, God maintained certain dominion over the earth through human mediators, and since that time every person who has trusted in Him has been a channel for expressing His will and power on earth. Abel, Seth, Noah, Abraham, Sarah, Isaac, Rebekah, Jacob, Rachel, Joseph, Moses, David, and countless others mediated the Lord's rule on earth. Through select individuals God gave His holy Word, which was written down for all men to know and obey. In that Word He revealed His nature, His will, His moral and spiritual standards for mankind, and His promises of redemption and restoration. He called out a special people, the nation of Israel, to be "a kingdom of priests and a holy nation" (Ex. 19:6) before the world, to be the forerunners of His Son as "a light of the nations so that My salvation may reach to the end of the earth" (Isa. 49:6). He raised up prophets, priests, and kings to give special leadership on His behalf.

When the Son of God became incarnate, He was God's unique Mediator, the divine/human instrument of rule, who in His own right deserved to establish and reign over God's earthly kingdom. When the Son was rejected, God continued to rule through those who belonged to Christ, those who were now empowered within by His own indwelling Holy Spirit. From Pentecost through the present day and until Christ returns, Christians are God's mediatorial rulers on earth.

Even during the Tribulation, God will raise up 144,000 faithful believers from among the twelve tribes of Israel, and an innumerable host of Gentiles, "a great multitude, which no one could count, from every nation and all tribes and peoples and tongues," will also be converted and stand "before the throne and before the Lamb, clothed in white robes" (Rev. 7:4, 9).

Throughout its history the mediatorial kingdom has attracted both true and false citizens; and it will remain so until its end. Failure to understand that truth has caused untold confusion in interpreting many Bible passages. Among other things, it has caused many sincere Christians to believe that salvation can be lost.

Careful study of Scripture shows that, although the true subjects of God's kingdom are only those who belong to Him by saving faith, those true citizens can be infallibly distinguished from false ones only by God Himself. God's chosen people, Israel, was always composed of both the true and the false. Jesus spoke of certain "sons of the kingdom" who would "be cast out into the outer darkness; in that place there shall be weeping and gnashing of teeth" (Matt. 8:12). Those "sons of the kingdom" obviously were not true subjects of the King. As Jesus makes clear in His explanation of the parable of the wheat and tares, from the human perspective the true sons of the kingdom and the sons of the evil one are often not distinguishable (Matt. 13:38). In the figure of the vine and branches, Jesus illustrates the truth that many branches that seem to belong to the vine really do not. Jesus even spoke of the spurious branches as being "in Me," but those branches will be pruned away, dry up, and be thrown into the fire to be burned (John 15:2, 6). The people represented by those unfruitful branches were closely, but superficially, identified with Christ. Condemned "sons of the kingdom" are never part of God's spiritual kingdom, and unproductive "branches" are never a part of Christ. They only appear to be from man's imperfect view.

Paul says, "They are not all Israel who are descended from Israel; neither are they all children because they are Abraham's descendants" (Rom. 9:6-7). As the apostle had declared earlier in the same letter, only "he is a Jew who is one inwardly" (2:29). Yet in Scripture such terms as *Israel, God's people,* and *disciples* are frequently used in ways that include both nominal and real believers.

The gospels frequently speak of the twelve disciples, or apostles—a group that included Judas, an unbelieving traitor. Throughout its history, the visible church has always included adherents who have not trusted in Christ and who therefore do not belong to Him and are not a part of His spiritual body.

Even during the Millennium, when Christ perfectly and directly rules His kingdom on earth, there will be disloyal citizens of the kingdom. It is from among those false subjects that Satan will gather together his rebellious army in a last futile attempt to defeat Christ (Rev. 20:7-8).

God's universal kingdom over heaven and earth has no conditions. To exist is to be in that kingdom. To be in His mediatorial kingdom, however, requires intentional identity with Him. For the false citizen the identity is hypocritical and superficial. For the true citizen the identity is genuine, being based on repentance, faith in Christ, and the new life that faith in Him brings (Mark 1:15).

When Christ bodily returns to earth, His indirect rule in the mediatorial kingdom will become His direct rule in the millennial kingdom and then in the eternal kingdom of the new heavens and new earth.

God's kingdom and the church are distinct in that the kingdom preceded the church and will continue eternally after the church as such has ceased to exist. But during the present mediatorial period, often called the church age, the kingdom and the church are identical. That truth is part of the mystery "which in other generations was not made known to the sons of men, as it has now been revealed to His holy apostles and prophets in the Spirit; to be specific, that the Gentiles are fellow heirs and fellow members of the body, and fellow partakers of the promise in Christ Jesus through the gospel" (Eph. 3:5-6).

Expanding on the truth that His parables were given to reveal and conceal, Jesus continued, **For whoever has, to him shall more be given, and he shall have an abundance; but whoever does not have, even what he has shall be taken away from him.**

Whoever has refers to those who believe, those who have been sovereignly given the gift of eternal life, received by trust in Jesus Christ. These are the true citizens of the kingdom who have received the King. And whoever accepts salvation from God, **to him shall more be given.** The person who accepts the true Light (John 1:9) will receive still further light as he grows in obedience and maturity in the Lord. To the believer who lives up to the light he has in Christ, more and more light will continually be given until **he shall have an abundance.**

But the fate of the unbeliever is just the opposite. Because of his unbelief, he **does not have** salvation, and therefore **even what** light of God's truth **he has shall be taken away from him.** Many thousands of people heard Jesus teach and saw Him perform miraculous signs as evidence of His divine messiahship; but most of them did not recognize Him as Lord or receive Him as Savior. They were exposed to God incarnate, and yet they rejected Him—either by direct opposition or by indifferent neglect. They said no to the King, and because they refused to receive the divine light that shined on them, they drifted deeper and deeper into spiritual darkness.

To this day, no people on earth are more religiously disoriented than Jews. They were called to be God's people, given His promises, His covenants, His laws, and His immeasurable blessings. They were even sent His only Son as one of their own people—to teach, heal, comfort, redeem, and deliver them—but they would not have Him rule over them (Luke 19:14). Because they rejected God's perfect Light, even the light they had went out, and everything in their religion lost its true meaning. The Temple was destroyed by the Romans in A.D. 70, and with it the priesthood and the sacrifices. The ceremonial and sacrificial requirements of their covenant with God could no longer be met; but since that time Jews have continued to follow various aspects of their ancient religion—without prophets, priests, kings, Temple, or sacrifices. Even those who call themselves orthodox believe and practice only a small part of what their own Scripture teaches and commands. The conservative and reformed branches of Judaism believe and practice even less. Most Jews do not even try to make sense out of most of the Old Testament. For most, all that is left is a nonreligious tradition.

All men are either progressing or regressing spiritually. No person remains static in his relationship to God. The longer a person knows and is faithful to Christ, the more his Lord is faithful to reveal His truth and power. The longer a person rejects the knowledge of God he has, whether much or little, the less of God's truth he will understand. Willful human rejection leads to divine judicial rejection. When a man says no to God, God says no to that person. God confirms men in their stubbornness, and binds them with their own chains of unbelief.

TO CONCEAL

Therefore I speak to them in parables; because while seeing they do not see, and while hearing they do not hear, nor do they understand. And in their case the prophecy of Isaiah is being fulfilled, which says, "You will keep on hearing, but will not understand; and you will keep on seeing, but will not perceive; for the heart of this people has become dull, and with their ears they scarcely hear, and they have closed their eyes lest they should see with their eyes, and hear with their ears, and understand with their heart and return, and I should heal them." (13:13-15)

Those verses from Isaiah 6:9-10 perfectly describe the unbelieving Jews of Jesus' day. Isaiah wrote during a time of sweeping judgment on Judah. He had just pronounced a series of curses on the people for their drunkenness, debauchery, immorality, dishonesty, injustice, and hypocrisy. While Isaiah was preaching his message of doom, King Uzziah died (6:1) and the nation was plunged into some of its darkest days. They were on the verge of captivity by Babylon as part of God's judgment; yet they refused to turn to Him for mercy and help.

The people kept **on hearing, but** they did **not understand; and** they kept **on seeing, but** they did **not perceive,** because they had intentionally **closed their eyes** and **their ears** to God and refused to **understand with their heart and return** to Him in order for Him to **heal them.** Because they chose to ignore God and His word, God judicially locked them up in their unbelief so that they would fear His judgment.

The first fulfillment of Isaiah's warning came in the judgment of the Babylonian Captivity, just as the prophet promised. The second fulfillment, Jesus declared, was about to be accomplished as Israel once again turned her back on the Lord and faced the judgment of centuries of darkness and despair.

Jesus' parables were a similar form of judgment on unbelief. Those who would not accept His clear and simple teachings—such as those in the Sermon on the Mount—not only would not be able to understand His deeper teachings but would lose the benefit of the teaching and miraculous witness they had been given.

The gift of languages in the early church was still another form of judgment on unbelievers. Quoting from Isaiah 28:11, Paul wrote, "In the law it is written, 'By men of strange tongues and by the lips of strangers I will speak to this people, and even so they will not listen to Me,' says the Lord. So then tongues are for a sign, not to those who believe, but to unbelievers" (1 Cor. 14:21-22). Tongues were manifested in an astounding and dramatic way on the day of Pentecost and continued to be manifested from time to time during the apostolic age as a form of testimony against those who refused to believe. The Lord first gave His truth to Israel in simple, clear teaching; and when that was ignored, He spoke to them in parables, which, without explanation, were no more than meaningless riddles. Finally He spoke in unintelligible languages that could not be understood at all without translation.

TO REVEAL

But blessed are your eyes, because they see; and your ears, because they hear. For truly I say to you, that many prophets and righteous men desired to see what you see, and did not see it; and to hear what you hear, and did not hear it. (13:16-17)

When men choose to believe God's Word and trust in His grace, He gives them salvation and more and more truth by which to walk and to worship. **Blessed are your eyes,** Jesus said to His disciples, **because they see; and your ears, because they hear.**

Christians can understand even the deep things of God's Word, because they have them written in the New Testament and illumined by the indwelling Holy Spirit (cf. 1 Cor. 2:9-10). When Jesus finished explaining the parables to His disciples and asked, "Have you understood all these things?" they could honestly answer, "Yes" (Matt. 13:51). It was not that they were smarter than the unbelieving Jews. The scribes and Pharisees were highly educated and had studied the Scriptures diligently since their youth. But their eyes were blinded to the truth of Jesus' teaching because of their unbelief. The **eyes** of the disciples, on the other hand, were able to **see** and their **ears** were able to **hear,** because they *did* believe.

Part of the Lord's ministry was to give understanding of His Word to those who trusted in Him. In his account of this occasion, Mark says Jesus "was explaining everything privately to His own disciples" (4:34). During perhaps His last appearance to the disciples after His resurrection, Jesus "opened their minds to understand the Scriptures" (Luke 24:45). The psalmist knew he could not comprehend God's Word in his own intellect, and he prayed, "Open my eyes, that I may behold wonderful things from Thy law" (Ps. 119:18).

Not even the most faithful and enlightened saints of the Old Testament were given the insights that the apostles and every believer since have been given the privilege of having. **For truly I say to you,** Jesus continued, **that many prophets and righteous men desired to see what you see, and did not see it; and to hear what you hear, and did not hear it.** "As to this salvation, the prophets who prophesied of the grace that would come to you made careful search and inquiry, seeking to know what person and time the Spirit of Christ within them was indicating as He predicted the sufferings of Christ and the glories to follow. It was revealed to them that they were not serving themselves, but you, in these things which now have been announced to you through those who preached the gospel to you by the Holy Spirit sent from heaven—things into which angels long to look" (1 Pet. 1:10-12).

Even for believers there must be divine illumination, and that is promised to every Christian who searches God's Word and relies on the Holy Spirit within him (see 1 Cor. 2:9-16; 1 John 2:20, 27). As Christians, we not only have God's completed revelation in Scripture but the very author of that Scripture living within us—to explain, interpret, and apply its truths.

The Kingdom and the Gospel—part 2 The Interpretation of the Parable (13:18-23)

Hear then the parable of the sower. When anyone hears the word of the kingdom, and does not understand it, the evil one comes and snatches away what has been sown in his heart. This is the one on whom seed was sown beside the road. And the one on whom seed was sown on the rocky places, this is the man who hears the word, and immediately receives it with joy; yet he has no firm root in himself, but is only temporary, and when affliction or persecution arises because of the word, immediately he falls away. And the one on whom seed was sown among the thorns, this is the man who hears the word, and the worry of the world, and the deceitfulness of riches choke the word, and it becomes unfruitful. And the one on whom seed was sown on the good soil, this is the man who hears the word and understands it; who indeed bears fruit, and brings forth, some a hundredfold, some sixty, and some thirty." (13:18-23)

Privately to the twelve and a few other genuine followers (v. 10; Mark 4:10), Jesus began to explain the meaning of **the parable of the sower**. For them, to **hear** was to understand, because, as the Lord had just told them, their faith allowed their eyes to see and their ears to hear what unbelievers could not (Matt. 13:11-12, 16-17).

Jesus does not here identify **the sower**, but in the parable of the wheat and tares He says, "The one who sows the good seed is the Son of Man" (v. 37). In the present passage He takes for granted that the disciples understand the identity of the seed, which is made explicit in Luke's account: "The seed is the word of God" (8:11; cf. Mark 4:14). In particular, **the sower** sows the **word of the kingdom,** the good news of entrance into the kingdom by grace through faith.

In a broader sense, of course, any believer who preaches or testifies to the gospel is a **sower** who sows Christ's **word** in his Lord's behalf. The parable therefore applies to any true presentation of the gospel.

The nineteenth-century commentator William Arnot wrote of sowers: "As every leaf of the forest and every ripple on the lake, which itself receives a sunbeam on its breast, may throw the sunbeam off again, and so spread the light around; in like manner, everyone, old or young, who receives Christ into his heart may and will publish with his life and lips that blessed name."

The most faithful and dedicated Christian cannot create **the word of the kingdom** any more than a farmer or a scientist can create the simplest seed. Just as only God creates seeds that reproduce themselves, only God creates **the word** of the gospel that brings the life of His Son to a believer. The work of Christ's witnesses is not to manufacture a message to create a synthetic seed, or to modify the seed given to them, but to sow God's revelation by proclaiming it exactly as He has given it. The power of new spiritual life is in **the word,** just as the power of plant life is in the seed. The seeds in the parable are all of the same nature, sown from the same bag by the same sower. The only variables are in what happens to those seeds when they are sown on the different types of soil.

The Bible is the written **word,** but Jesus Christ is the living **word** who gives it life. The Bible, as it were, is the husk and Jesus is the kernel. "You search the Scriptures, because you think that in them you have eternal life," Jesus told a group of unbelieving Jewish leaders in Jerusalem; "and it is these that bear witness of Me" (John 5:39).

The parable of the sower revolves around proclaiming the saving gospel, heralding **the word** about the King and His **kingdom.** But the main teaching has to do with the heart soils on which the truth of that **word** falls as it is preached. Jesus mentions four different soils onto which the seed falls as it is sown, representing four kinds of hearts that hear the gospel.

The soils themselves are basically the same—dirt that, given the right conditions, could support the growth of crops. Although every human heart is naturally sinful and hostile toward God (Rom. 8:7; Eph. 2:15-16), every human heart is also capable of being redeemed. There is no such thing as a naturally unredeemable heart. If a person is not saved it is because he does not want to be saved. "The one who comes to Me," Jesus says categorically, "I will certainly not cast out" (John 6:37). Every person *could* receive the seed of the gospel and participate in its life if he believed. The differences in the soils, and in the hearts to which they correspond, are not in their composition but their condition.

Jesus was preparing the apostles, and every other proclaimer of the gospel, to understand the four basic kinds of hearers they could expect to encounter: the unresponsive, the superficial, the worldly, and the receptive.

THE UNRESPONSIVE HEARER

When anyone hears the word of the kingdom, and does not understand it, the evil one comes and snatches away what has been sown in his heart. This is the one on whom seed was sown beside the road. (13:19)

The hard-packed soil beside the road (v. 4) represents the person who **hears the word of the kingdom, and does not understand it.** The reason he **does not understand** is not due to any deficiency in the message but to his own hardheartedness. He is the person often referred to in the Old Testament as stiff-necked. He is unconcerned with the things of God, completely indifferent to anything spiritual. The word makes no penetration into his mind or heart. He does not give the gospel the least consideration, thinking it to be total foolishness. He has so continually and consistently resisted anything that smacks of spirituality, that the soil of his heart has become pounded down until it is impervious and insensitive.

Because it makes no penetration, the seed of God's word is fully exposed to the enemy of the soul, and **the evil one comes and snatches away what has been sown in** the person's **heart.** His lack of repentance or of any sense of guilt and shame insulates him from God's help and leaves him utterly exposed to Satan's attack. **His heart** has never been softened by remorse, never broken up by conviction of sin, never cultivated by the smallest desire for anything good, pure, and holy.

That person is the fool who hates wisdom and instruction (Prov. 1:7) and who says there is no God (Ps. 14:1). He is self-sufficient, self-satisfied, and often self-righteous. On such a person the gospel has no effect, because it is veiled to determined unbelievers, "in whose case the god of this world has blinded the minds of the unbelieving, that they might not see the light of the gospel of the glory of Christ, who is the image of God" (2 Cor. 4:4).

The evil one uses many means as he **snatches away what has been sown.** Luke adds that some seed was trampled under the feet of those who walk the hard path (8:5; cf. Heb. 10:29). Satan uses false teachers, who promote spiritual lies and contradict God's truth. He uses fear of what other people might think about a person's becoming a Christian. Satan constantly uses pride to blind people to their sinful condition and need of salvation. He makes them believe they are not really so bad, or that, if they do need improvement, they can improve themselves. He uses doubt, prejudice, stubbornness, procrastination, love of the world, love of sin, and every combination of those ploys.

THE SUPERFICIAL HEARER

And the one on whom seed was sown on the rocky places, this is the man who hears the word, and immediately receives it with joy; yet he has no firm root

in himself, but is only temporary, and when affliction or persecution arises because of the word, immediately he falls away. (13:20-21)

The second patch of soil covers unseen **rocky places** and has no depth. This soil represents **the man who hears the word, and immediately receives it with joy.** By his quick response to the gospel it seems as if he has been waiting eagerly to hear it and cannot embrace it soon enough. In contrast to the person with the hardened, unresponsive heart, this **man** offers no resistance at all, but rather manifests emotional excitement in his response to the message.

Sometimes shallow acceptance of the gospel is encouraged by shallow evangelism that holds out the blessings of salvation but hides the costs—such as repenting from sin, dying to self, and turning from the old life. When people are encouraged to walk down the aisle, raise their hand, or sign a card without coming to grips with the full claims of Christ, they are in great danger of becoming further from Christ than they were before they heard the message. They may become insulated from true salvation by a false profession of faith.

In any case, the superficial convert accepts the message of salvation with open arms and is overcome with **joy** and enthusiasm. He cannot say enough good about the gospel, the preacher, the church, and the Lord. He is on an emotional high, in a state of grand euphoria. He is certain he has found the answer to his felt needs. He has been accepted with those who believe and cannot wait to tell everyone of the new meaning, purpose, and happiness in his life.

Because his emotional response to the gospel is so immediate and positive, this sort of convert stands out above most others. He is often more vocal in talking about his experience and may even be zealous in church attendance, Bible study, and prayer for a while.

But because the soil of his heart is shallow, **he has no firm root in himself.** The gospel prompts an immediate positive reaction, but it is **temporary,** and all the change is on the surface, rather than in the depths of his heart. His feelings were changed but not his soul. God's life-giving **word** cannot take **root** because just below the surface of his heart is a **rocky** base that is even harder to penetrate than the soil beside the road. There is no repentance, no remorse over sin, no recognition of lostness, no contrition, no brokenness. And there is no humility, which is the first mark of true conversion (Matt. 5:3).

When this person hears the gospel it brings a religious experience but it does not bring salvation—evidenced by the fact that **when affliction or persecution arises because of the word, immediately he falls away.** The gospel truth has not penetrated his heart but only the edge of his mind, and it is therefore as **immediately** renounced as it was immediately received. He has come to Christ for what he thought he would get in the way of personal benefit, but when confronted with the high cost of salvation, he will not pay the price. He has built his religious house on the sand of emotional experience, and when the storms of **affliction or persecution** beat on his house, it crumbles and washes away (Matt. 7:26-27). He has the foliage of a religious experience, but he has no root in spiritual reality and therefore cannot produce spiritual fruit, which, as Jesus goes on to say (13:22-23), is the only reliable evidence of true conversion.

The falling away comes **immediately** after the **affliction and persecution because of the word,** but it may be many years before that severe testing comes. The superficial believer may be baptized, serve in the church, and apparently function as a model member for a long time. But testing will eventually come that will expose his lifelessness.

The **affliction and persecution** Jesus is talking about does not have to do with the ordinary hardships and troubles of life, but specifically with problems that result **because of the word.** When the cost of discipleship becomes too high, this person **falls away** and becomes lost to the visible church just as he was always lost to the spiritual.

Falls away is from *skandalizō,* which means to cause to stumble or fall and is the term from which we get *scandalize.* It is sometimes translated with the idea of causing offense—as in the Authorized Version of this verse. All of those meanings are appropriate here, because the superficial Christian is scandalized, offended, stumbles, and **falls away** when his faith is put to the test (cf. John 8:31; 1 John 2:19).

When friends, family, fellow students, co-workers, or employers begin to criticize him for his faith or pressure him to compromise or even renounce it, he cannot resist. He becomes ashamed of the gospel and of the One he had so joyously proclaimed as Lord. Because his profession had no conviction or sincerity, he never experienced the new birth and the new life that Christ gives—and his sham faith soon withers.

William Arnot again has a helpful comment: "If the law of God has never rent the 'stony heart' and made it 'contrite,' that is, bruised it small, you may, by receiving the Gospel on some temporary, superficial softness of nature, obtain your religion more easily and quickly than others who have been more deeply exercised; but you may perhaps not be able to hold it so fast or retain it so long. . . . He that endureth to the end shall be saved; but he that falls away in the middle shall not."

If a person's profession of Christ does not involve a deep conviction of sin, a genuine sense of lostness, a strong desire for the Lord to cleanse and purify, a hungering and thirsting for righteousness and a love of His Word, along with a genuine willingness to suffer for His sake, there is no root to his spiritual life and it will be only a matter of time before his religious house falls.

It is encouraging, however, that the same persecution that makes the false believer wither will make the true believer stronger. "All who desire to live godly in Christ Jesus will be persecuted" (2 Tim. 3:12); but "after you have suffered for a little while," Peter assures us, "the God of all grace, who called you to His eternal glory in Christ, will Himself perfect, confirm, strengthen and establish you" (1 Pet. 5:10).

THE WORLDLY HEARER

And the one on whom seed was sown among the thorns, this is the man who

hears the word, and the worry of the world, and the deceitfulness of riches choke the word, and it becomes unfruitful. (13:22)

The third patch of soil is infested with **thorns** and represents **the man who hears the word** but who is too worldly for it to take root and grow in his heart. This person **hears the word** of the gospel and may make a token profession of faith. But his first love is for the things of **the world**, and his **worry** about or preoccupation with those things blinds him to the importance of the gospel or anything else spiritual and eternal. He loves **riches** and lives as if they are the answer to all his needs and desires. He is oblivious to their **deceitfulness**, to their utter inability to satisfy the heart or bring lasting happiness. He does not notice his deceiving worldliness **chokes the word**, because his attention is on his **riches**, possessions, prestige, position, and other things of **the world**. He is not even aware that he has lost what knowledge of **the word** he once had or that his spiritual life is totally **unfruitful**—because he has no real interest in such things.

There are few barriers to the gospel greater than love of **riches** and of **the world** in general. Paul warns that "the love of money is a root of all sorts of evil, and some by longing for it have wandered away from the faith, and pierced themselves with many a pang" (1 Tim. 6:10). And John warns, "Do not love the world, nor the things in the world. If anyone loves the world, the love of the Father is not in him. For all that is in the world, the lust of the flesh and the lust of the eyes and the boastful pride of life, is not from the Father, but is from the world" (1 John 2:15-16).

Some years ago the U. S. Department of Agriculture developed a soil treatment that contains 6 percent ethyl alcohol. When the solution is applied to a field in the proper amount, it reportedly causes all the weeds to sprout and grow vigorously. Once they are grown, the weeds can then be mechanically removed before they have a chance to develop seeds. The field becomes virtually free of weeds for up to five years.

That is something of a picture of true conversion. Christ's cleansing is complete and thorough. The preaching of the law of God makes sin flourish (cf. Rom. 7:7-12), and in salvation He removes all the weeds of sin in order to cleanse the field of the heart and prepare it for the pure seed of His Word. Subsequent sin requires subsequent cleansing; and that sin, too, when confessed, Christ is also "faithful and righteous to forgive" (1 John 1:9). The Lord's desire is to keep His people free from all sin at all times.

A professing believer who is unconcerned about sin in his life and does not hate evil and love righteousness gives strong evidence that the soil of his heart is weedy. He will eventually discover that his love of the **world** and his identification with Christ's **word** cannot coexist. If his faith is genuine, he will forsake the **world**; if it is not, his sin will **choke** out what knowledge of the **word** he has.

A person who comes to church but never becomes committed to serving, who is continually preoccupied with money, career, fashions, sports, and everything but the Lord's work is a person with a weed-infested heart. A person who claims to love

Christ but who cannot remain faithful in marriage has a weedy heart. The person who refuses to let go of his worldliness is a person in whom the seed of God's saving gospel has not found root and is in danger of being choked out altogether.

THE RECEPTIVE HEARER

And the one on whom seed was sown on the good soil, this is the man who hears the word and understands it; who indeed bears fruit, and brings forth, some a hundredfold, some sixty, and some thirty." (13:23)

The fourth patch of ground **on whom seed was sown** is **good soil**. It is **good** not because it has a different basic composition than the other kinds of soil, but because it is rightly prepared. Because his heart is prepared by the Spirit and receptive to God (cf. John 16:8-11), the person this soil represents **hears the word and understands it**. Before salvation, the person who receives Christ had the same basic nature as those who reject Him. He is not necessarily any less sinful or more perceptive than they. A person who is saved may have lived a life of debauchery and utter wickedness, whereas many who do not believe are humanly moral and respectable. A person who is saved may have little education and a low IQ, whereas many who do not believe are highly intelligent and trained.

The only barrier to salvation is unbelief, and anyone who is willing to accept Jesus Christ on His terms is **good soil**. He **hears the word** of the gospel because God honors his humility and opens his spiritual ears; and he **understands** the gospel because God honors his faith and opens his spiritual mind and heart.

Jesus told of this kind of hearer in order to encourage His disciples and all other believers who witness in His name. Despite the hardness, shallowness, and worldliness of most human hearts, there are *always* those who are **good soil,** in which the gospel can take root and flourish. There will always be people whom the Spirit has prepared to receive **the word** with sincere, surrendered hearts.

The ultimate mark of the genuine believer, **the good soil,** is fruitbearing. He not only **hears** and **understands** but also **indeed bears fruit.** Spiritual **fruit** is the inevitable product of spiritual life.

The spiritual fruit of attitude is described by Paul in Galatians: "love, joy, peace, patience, kindness, goodness, faithfulness, gentleness, self-control" (5:22-23). The genuine believer also bears fruit of behavior, which Paul refers to as "the fruit of righteousness which comes through Jesus Christ, to the glory and praise of God" (Phil. 1:11). Fruit is the spiritual reality that God produces in the lives of His children. The Spirit-filled life of the believer "is constantly bearing fruit" (Col. 1:6).

The psalmist rejoiced that the believer who delights in God's Word and meditates on it day and night is "like a tree firmly planted by streams of water, which yields its fruit in its season. And its leaf does not wither; and in whatever he does, he prospers" (Ps. 1:2-3). Jesus declared that true and false branches—those who are genuinely related to Him and those who only seem to be—are distinguished by their bearing or not bearing fruit (John 15:2-5). We are not saved *by* bearing fruit or by any other good work, because we cannot bear spiritual fruit or do any truly good work until after we are saved. But we are saved *for* fruitbearing. "We are His workmanship," Paul says, "created in Christ Jesus for good works, which God prepared beforehand, that we should walk in them" (Eph. 2:10).

Not only does Jesus assure us that true believers bear fruit but that they bear it in great abundance: **one a hundredfold, some sixty, and some thirty.** Those figures represent phenomenal yields of 10,000 percent, 6,000 percent, and 3,000 percent. Believers differ in fruitbearing because they differ in commitment to obedience, but all are profusely fruitful.

As mentioned above (under v. 8), the average yield ratio of grain crops in Palestine was less than eight to one. Therefore even the least productive **thirty** to one was almost four times the average. It is not that a believer produces a hundred, sixty, or thirty times the amount of fruit that an unbeliever produces—because an unbeliever can produce no spiritual fruit at all. Jesus simply used these figures to represent the great productivity He gives to the faithful proclamation of His Word. That is the point of the entire parable: *true believers produce fruit.*

To His witnesses Jesus is saying, "Go and preach, and realize as you go that some people will reject your message outright. Because they want nothing to do with God, Satan will not allow the gospel to have any impact on them whatsoever. Others will seem to accept it gladly but will soon fall away, because they only had a superficial religious experience and were not born again. These are the ones who live by the flesh, whose lives are controlled by emotion, feeling, and sentiment. Others will seem to accept the gospel while holding on to the old life and its ways; and their faith will also prove vain and will eventually disappear as it is choked out by the world. But others will truly believe. In humility they will confess and repent of their sins, look to Me for help, and be given new life. You will know these true believers from the others by the evidence of fruit in their lives."

He is also saying to His witnesses that they should not lose heart. God alone can plow up the heart that is hard and resistant. In His sovereign will He gives the shallow heart depth, and the cluttered heart cleansing. The Lord guarantees that His faithful witnesses will produce fruit and will do so abundantly. It is impossible for a faithful sower of the Word to fail, because the Lord of the harvest will not permit it. So we anticipate the wrong and right responses. What marvelously helpful insight for those who sow!

The Lord is teaching His people that anyone who belongs to Him can and should be a witness for Him. The responsibility of the one who sows the gospel in His name is not to produce the seed, the soil, or the fruit. His only responsibility is to faithfully spread the seed as far and wide as he is able. When they fall on good soil, the seeds that a little child throws here and there as he follows his father through the field will produce fruitful plants just as genuine and productive as those the experienced father plants. And the untrained Christian who faithfully scatters his few seeds will produce a greater harvest than the most learned and experienced believer who never bothers to sow at all.

To those who are considering His claims or have made a perfunctory decision for Him, Jesus gives an appeal to think about the kind of soil that represents their heart. If it is hardpacked and beaten down by continual neglect of God, or perhaps even by conscious opposition, He calls that person to allow His Spirit to break up the ground and make it receptive to His Word. If the soil of his heart is shallow and superficial, He calls that person to allow the Spirit to remove the rocky resistance that lies beneath the surface of his seeming acceptance of the gospel and give him true faith. If the soil of his heart is infested with the weedy cares and concerns of the world, He asks that person to allow the Spirit to cleanse him of his worldliness and to receive Him with no reservations or competing loyalties.

BIRDVILLE
BAPTIST CHURCH
LIBRARY

The Kingdom and the World (13:24-43)

34

He presented another parable to them, saying, "The kingdom of heaven may be compared to a man who sowed good seed in his field. But while men were sleeping, his enemy came and sowed tares also among the wheat, and went away. But when the wheat sprang up and bore grain, then the tares became evident also. And the slaves of the landowner came and said to him, 'Sir, did you not sow good seed in your field? How then does it have tares?' And he said to them, 'An enemy has done this!' And the slaves said to him, 'Do you want us, then, to go and gather them up?' But he said, 'No; lest while you are gathering up the tares, you may root up the wheat with them. Allow both to grow together until the harvest; and in the time of the harvest I will say to the reapers, "First gather up the tares and bind them in bundles to burn them up; but gather the wheat into my barn.""

He presented another parable to them, saying, "The kingdom of heaven is like a mustard seed, which a man took and sowed in his field; and this is smaller than all other seeds; but when it is full grown, it is larger than the garden plants, and becomes a tree, so that the birds of the air come and nest in its branches."

He spoke another parable to them, "The kingdom of heaven is like leaven, which a woman took, and hid in three pecks of meal, until it was all leavened."

All these things Jesus spoke to the multitudes in parables, and He did not speak to them without a parable, so that what was spoken through the prophet might be fulfilled, saying, "I will open My mouth in parables; I will utter things hidden since the foundation of the world."

Then He left the multitudes, and went into the house. And His disciples came to Him, saying, "Explain to us the parable of the tares of the field." And He answered and said, "The one who sows the good seed is the Son of Man, and the field is the world; and as for the good seed, these are the sons of the kingdom; and the tares are the sons of the evil one; and the enemy who sowed them is the devil, and the harvest is the end of the age; and the reapers are angels. Therefore just as the tares are gathered up and burned with fire, so shall it be at the end of the age. The Son of Man will send forth His angels, and they will gather out of His kingdom all stumbling blocks, and those who commit lawlessness, and will cast them into the furnace of fire; in that place there shall be weeping and gnashing of teeth. Then the righteous will shine forth as the sun in the kingdom of their Father. He who has ears, let him hear." (13:24-43)

In the first of the eight parables in Matthew 13, Jesus explained the four kinds of responses—three negative and one positive—that people would make to the gospel during the mystery form of the kingdom of heaven that is the church age, the period between His first and second comings (vv. 3-8, 18-23), as well as through the Millennium. In the second parable the Lord explains what happens to unbelievers during these periods of the kingdom.

THE PARABLE OF THE WHEAT AND TARES

He presented another parable to them, saying, "The kingdom of heaven may be compared to a man who sowed good seed in his field. But while men were sleeping, his enemy came and sowed tares also among the wheat, and went away. But when the wheat sprang up and bore grain, then the tares became evident also. And the slaves of the landowner came and said to him, 'Sir, did you not sow good seed in your field? How then does it have tares?' And he said to them, 'An enemy has done this!' And the slaves said to him, 'Do you want us, then, to go and gather them up?' But he said, 'No; lest while you are gathering up the tares, you may root up the wheat with them. Allow both to grow together until the harvest; and in the time of the harvest I will say to the reapers, "First gather up the tares and bind them in bundles to burn them up; but gather the wheat into my barn."'" (13:24-30)

This **parable** also uses the figure of a farmer sowing seed in his field; but here the emphasis is not on what happens to the **good seed** (as in the first parable) but rather on what happens to the bad seed that **his enemy came and sowed** alongside the good seed.

This **good seed** is assumed to fall on fertile ground, take root, and grow into healthy and productive grain, identified here as **wheat**. The **man who sowed the good seed** is the landowner (v. 27) who is planting **in his field**.

The phrase **while men were sleeping** does not imply neglect or laziness but simply refers to the nighttime, when the farmer and his **men** were home **sleeping** and were therefore oblivious to what was happening in the newly-planted field. While they slept, the farmer's **enemy came and sowed tares also among the wheat, and went away.**

Tares is from *zizanion,* a variety of darnel weed that closely resembles **wheat** and is almost impossible to distinguish from it until the **wheat** ripens and bears **grain.** Because of this resemblance, sowing **tares . . . among the wheat** was sometimes done in ancient times out of spite or revenge by an **enemy** who wanted to destroy or at least greatly reduce the value of someone's crop. It was a common enough crime for the Romans to have had a specific law against it.

It was not until many weeks later, **when the wheat sprang up and bore grain,** that **the tares became evident also.** When they saw so many **tares** among the wheat, **the slaves of the landowner** asked him how this could have happened. It was not uncommon, of course, for a few weeds, including some **tares,** to grow up among the good plants; but the great quantity of **tares** in this field made it obvious that their crop was intentionally sabotaged. The landowner explained the obvious: **An enemy has done this!**

Realizing the seriousness of the devastating crime, **the slaves said to** their master, **Do you want us, then, to go and gather them up? No,** he replied, **lest while you are gathering up the tares, you may root up the wheat with them.** The **slaves** were rightly concerned, fearing **the tares** would weaken and possibly completely ruin **the wheat** harvest. But the experienced landowner knew that more damage would be done to the good crop by pulling out the weeds at that time than by leaving them alone. Pulling out **the tares** would result in rooting up much of **the wheat with them.** For one reason, the plant roots would have become closely intertwined, and even if all the good and bad plants could be distinguished from each other, uprooting **the tares** would also uproot some the of **the wheat.** Not only that, but wheat that was planted or that germinated later would mature later, and some of **the wheat** that had not yet produced heads of grain would be mistaken for **tares.**

Allow both to grow together until the harvest, the farmer instructed, **and in the time of the harvest I will say to the reapers, "First gather up the tares and bind them in bundles to burn them up.** Only at the time of **harvest** could the good and bad plants be distinguished with certainty. **The reapers** were more experienced than the slaves and were qualified to weed out **the tares** and **burn** them. After that was done, they would proceed with **the harvest** and **gather the wheat into** the landowner's **barn,** where it would be stored and protected for future use.

Two Parables About Influence

He presented another parable to them, saying, "The kingdom of heaven is like a mustard seed, which a man took and sowed in his field; and this is smaller than all other seeds; but when it is full grown, it is larger than the garden plants, and becomes a tree, so that the birds of the air come and nest in its branches."

He spoke another parable to them, "The kingdom of heaven is like leaven, which a woman took and hid in three pecks of meal, until it was all leavened." (13:31-33)

After hearing the parables of the sower and of the wheat and tares, the disciples no doubt wondered how Christ's kingdom could survive if so many people rejected Him and were then allowed to stay on earth with contaminating influence. How could God's people survive, much less thrive, in the midst of such unfavorable circumstances? Would not the great power of Satan and his evil forces, both demonic and human, utterly overwhelm and stifle the few (cf. 7:13-14) of God's saints on earth?

Long before Jesus' arrest, trial, and crucifixion it was evident that the Jewish leaders rejected His claims of messiahship. It was also obvious that the multitudes who praised and followed Him did not understand His true nature or mission and were only superficially attracted to Him. His true disciples were a handful against the whole nation of Israel, not to mention the vast and ungodly Roman empire and the regions beyond. In response to that unspoken concern, Jesus used these two parables to emphasize that small things can have far-reaching effects.

Western music is commonly composed of only twelve notes—the seven basic notes and their five sharps/flats. Every symphony, hymn, love song, oratorio, and other piece of music is made up of various combinations and octaves of those same few notes. Similarly, every poem, essay, novel, letter, and other piece of English literature is composed of combinations of the same twenty-six letters.

Lord Kelvin once suspended a large piece of metal from a cord in his laboratory. He then proceeded to wad up small pieces of paper into balls about the size of a pea and systematically throw them at the metal weight. At first the almost imperceptible impact of paper hitting metal seemed to have no effect. But eventually the steel weight was swaying rhythmically back and forth due to the cumulative force patiently applied against it.

In an immeasurably more dramatic and important way, God would demonstrate through the church how a handful of believers, totally weak and inept in themselves, would in His power turn the world upside down. The kingdom of heaven would grow and prosper in spite of Satan's opposition and would ultimately permeate and influence the whole world in Jesus' name.

THE PARABLE OF THE MUSTARD SEED

He presented another parable to them, saying, "The kingdom of heaven is

like a mustard seed, which a man took and sowed in his field; and this is smaller than all other seeds; but when it is full grown, it is larger than the garden plants, and becomes a tree, so that the birds of the air come and nest in its branches." (13:31-32)

In this **parable** Jesus again uses the figure of planting and compares **the kingdom of heaven** to **a mustard seed** and its growth into a full-grown plant.

Mustard has long been a widely-used herb throughout much of the world, and in modern times it has found additional commercial value in the manufacture of film. Amazingly, years ago it was discovered that cows whose feed was supplemented with mustard seed developed bones that had a superior quality for use in making the silver compounds used in photographic film.

Jesus' referring to the **mustard seed** as being **smaller than all other seeds** has often been cited as proof that Scripture is errant—that Jesus was either fallible and made a mistake or that He accommodated His teaching to the ignorance of His hearers and knowingly distorted the truth. But He was not comparing this seed to all other seeds in existence but only to the seeds of **garden plants** in Palestine. Many seeds, such as those of the wild orchid, are much smaller than the seed of the mustard plant. But of the many plants grown at that time in the gardens and fields of Palestine, the mustard plant has the smallest seeds, just as Jesus said.

When *sperma* (**seed**) is used in the New Testament in reference to plants, it is always used of agricultural plants, those intentionally grown for food. And of those **plants,** the mustard had seeds that were **smaller than all other seeds.**

Dr. L. H. Shinners, director of the herbarium at Southern Methodist University in Dallas and lecturer at the Smithsonian Institution, stated in a converstation that

the mustard seed would indeed have been the smallest of those to have been noticed by the people at the time of Christ. The principal field crops (barley, wheat, lentils, and beans) have much larger seeds, as do other plants which might have been present as weeds and so forth. There are various weeds and wild flowers belonging to the mustard, amaranth, pigweed, or chickweed families with seeds that are as small as or smaller than mustard; but they would not have been known or noticed by the inhabitants. They are wild and they certainly would not have been planted as a crop. . . . The only modern crop plant in existence with smaller seeds than mustard is tobacco, and this plant of American origin was not grown in the old world until the sixteenth century or later.

This parable is also criticized for supposedly exaggerating the size of the mustard plant, referring to it as **a tree,** in which **the birds of the air come and nest in its branches.** Many varieties of mustard plants are rather small bushes whose **branches** are too flimsy for **birds** to **nest** in. But the mustard plant of Palestine often grows to a height of twelve or fifteen feet. Just as Jesus said, **when it is full grown, it**

is larger than the garden plants, and, from a comparative viewpoint, **becomes a tree.** At certain times of the year the branches become rigid enough to easily support a bird's nest.

But, even though the omniscient Jesus was speaking literally and accurately in this parable, His purpose was proverbial, not technical or scientific. Because of its tiny size, the mustard seed was commonly used in the ancient Near East to represent things that were extremely small. Ancient Jewish literature contains references to a drop of blood or a blemish on an animal that was the size of a mustard seed. To this day Arabs sometimes speak of faith weighing as little as a mustard seed, in much the same way Jesus did (Matt. 17:20).

If Jesus explained this parable to the disciples, we have no record of it, and in the context of His teaching about the kingdom it would not have been necessary. Its meaning was self-evident. As just mentioned, the idea of a small mustard seed growing into a large plant was proverbial, and the disciples would have immediately understood Jesus' point: the kingdom of heaven, though now very small and seemingly insignificant, would one day grow into a large body of believers. That is the central lesson of this parable.

During Jesus' earthly ministry, the kingdom was almost imperceptible, both because of its few citizens and because it was spiritual and invisible. It did not come "with signs to be observed," Jesus explained on another occasion; "nor will they say, 'Look, here it is!' or, 'There it is!' For behold, the kingdom of God is in your midst" (Luke 17:20-21).

When He was born, Jesus was placed in a manger, in the midst of cows, sheep, goats, donkeys, and other animals. The region of Judea, in which He was born, and of Galilee, where He grew up, were insignificant backwaters of the Roman empire. In the region of Galilee, Nazareth was among the least promising towns—a fact that prompted Nathanael to ask Philip, "Can any good thing come out of Nazareth?" (John 1:46). None of the twelve disciples came from the Jewish religious leadership or from the economic and social aristocracy. They were few in number, uneducated, fearful, weak, slow to understand and believe, and generally unqualified to be the leaders of any significant earthly kingdom. The group of believers who gathered for prayer in Jerusalem just before Pentecost numbered only about 120 (Acts 1:15). A modern church of that size is thought to be quite small, yet that was the nucleus of the early church. When Jesus ascended to heaven, His kingdom on earth was, figuratively and relatively speaking, much smaller even than a mustard seed.

But the kingdom that started very small would one day become very large. Although the Old Testament writers were not aware that the Messiah would come to earth twice or of the intermediate kingdom that would separate those two comings, they knew that ultimately the Lord would "rule from sea to sea, and from the River to the ends of the earth" (Ps. 72:8). The desert nomads would bow before Him, the kings of Tarshish and of the islands would bring Him presents, the kings of Sheba and Seba would offer gifts, all kings would bow down before Him, and all nations would serve Him (vv. 9-11). In the end, "the kingdom of the world [will] become the kingdom of our Lord, and of His Christ; and He will reign forever and ever" (Rev. 11:15).

Another lesson of the parable of the mustard seed is that the kingdom of heaven will be a blessing to the rest of the world. The **tree** that grows from the small **mustard seed** represents the kingdom of heaven, which in the present age corresponds to the church.

Some interpreters have held that the **birds of the air** represent demons or other evil forces, as they do in the parable of the sower (Matt. 13:19). But there is no reason to expect a given figure to always represent the same thing, and the idea of evil is alien to the context of this parable.

The figure of **birds** making nests normally calls to mind that which is positive and helpful. Nesting carries the idea of protection, safety, refuge, and sanctuary, which the mother bird provides for her young.

In Nebuchadnezzar's dream he beheld "a tree in the midst of the earth, and its height was great. The tree grew large and became strong, and its height reached to the sky, and it was visible to the end of the whole earth. Its foliage was beautiful and its fruit abundant, and in it was food for all. The beasts of the field found shade under it, and the birds of the sky dwelt in its branches, and all living creatures fed themselves from it" (Dan. 4:10-12). In his interpretation of the king's vision Daniel explains that "the tree that you saw . . . is you, O king; for you have become great and grown strong, and your majesty has become great and reached to the sky and your dominion to the end of the earth" (vv. 20, 22). Under Nebuchadnezzar the Babylonian empire had brought unparalleled advancement in almost every field of endeavor—agriculture, architecture, education, the arts, literature, economics, and many others. Despite the cost in lives and slave labor, it had brought prosperity to a large part of the known world at that time. In the king's vision, the birds and animals who benefited from the tree's shade and food were the other nations of the world.

In a revelation to Ezekiel, the Lord described Assyria as "a cedar in Lebanon with beautiful branches and forest shade, and very high; and its top was among the clouds. The waters made it grow, the deep made it high. . . . Therefore its height was loftier than all the trees of the field and its boughs became many and its branches long because of many waters as it spread them out. All the birds of the heavens nested in its boughs, and under its branches all the beasts of the field gave birth, and all great nations lived under its shade" (Ezek. 31:3-6).

Both Jesus and the disciples were familiar with those accounts, and the parallel to the parable of the mustard seed seems obvious. The kingdom of heaven would grow from tiny beginnings to a great **tree** and would ultimately provide shelter, protection, and benefit to the entire world.

When Christians live in obedience to the Lord, they are a blessing to those around them. Individual believers become the source of benediction to nations. And with all their faults, those nations of the world who have been so influenced and who have recognized God's sovereignty and have sought to build their laws and standards of living on His Word have proved a blessing to the rest of the world in economic, legal, cultural, and social ways as well as spiritual and moral. It is from the teachings of Scripture through Christian witness that high standards of education, justice, the dignity of women, the rights of children, prison reform, and countless other such social benefits have come. Whenever the gospel of the kingdom of God is faithfully preached and practiced, all the world benefits.

What the church is to the world is a macrocosm of what a believing spouse is to an unbelieving husband or wife. Just as the unbelieving partner is sanctified through the one who believes (1 Cor. 7:14), the unbelieving world is to a degree sanctified by the presence of the true church.

Jesus' point is that, in spite of great opposition, represented by the three bad soils and the tares, His kingdom will start small and spread in power and influence to become victorious.

THE PARABLE OF THE LEAVEN

He spoke another parable to them, "The kingdom of heaven is like leaven, which a woman took, and hid in three pecks of meal, until it was all leavened." (13:33)

As always, Jesus constructed the parable out of the common experiences of His hearers. In every household the **woman** responsible for baking would save a piece of leavened dough from a risen batch just before it was baked. When the next batch of dough was mixed, she **took** the saved piece from the previous batch and **hid** it in the new, in order that its **leaven,** or yeast, could ferment the new batch of dough and make it rise.

Three pecks of meal was about the equivalent of a modern bushel. But such a large batch of dough was not uncommon in most households of the day, because bread was the major item of food. That was about the same amount of bread that Abraham asked Sarah to bake for the Lord and the two angelic visitors (Gen. 18:6) and that Gideon prepared before the angel of the Lord at Ophrah (Judg. 6:19).

The first point in this parable is that small things can have great influence, in the way that a small piece of leavened dough can permeate a large piece of unleavened dough to make it rise. The power of **the kingdom of heaven** is great, far greater than its initial size and appearance would suggest. The smallest part of **the kingdom** that is placed in the world is sure to have influence, because it contains the power of God's own Spirit. The influence of **the kingdom** is the influence of the King, of His Word, and of His faithful people.

The second point of the parable is that the influence is positive. Leavened bread has always been considered tastier and more enjoyable than unleavened. To symbolize the break with their former life in Egypt, God commanded His people to eat only unleavened bread during the Feast of the Unleavened Bread, which began on Passover evening. They were not even allowed to have leaven of any sort in the house during the seven days of the feast (Ex. 12:15, 18-19). But the bread they ate the rest of the year was leavened and perfectly acceptable to the Lord. To the average person of Jesus' day, Jew or Gentile, there is no evidence that **leaven** carried any connotation of evil or corruption.

The ancient rabbis often referred to leaven in a favorable way. One of them wrote, "Great is peace, in that peace is to the earth as leaven is to the dough." When a Jewish girl was married, her mother would give her a small piece of leavened dough from a batch baked just before the wedding. From that gift of leaven the bride would bake bread for her own household throughout her married life. That gift, simple as it was, was among the most cherished that the bride received, because it represented the love and blessedness of the household in which she grew up and that would be carried into the household she was about to establish.

William Arnot writes insightfully:

> Boldly as a sovereign may, this teacher seizes a proverb which was current as an exponent of the adversary's successful strategems and stamps the metal with the image and superscription of the rightful King. The evil spreads like leaven; you tremble before its stealthy advance and relentless grasp: but be of good cheer, disciples of Jesus, greater is He that is for you than all that are against you; the word of life which has been hidden in the world, hidden in believing hearts, is a leaven too. The unction of the Holy One is more subtle and penetrating and subduing than sin and Satan. Where sin abounded, grace shall much more abound.

Because leaven causes fermentation, some interpreters insist that in Scripture it always signifies that which is evil and corrupting when it is used figuratively. But such a restrictive view is arbitrary and certainly does not fit the present text. Jesus specifically says that **the kingdom of heaven,** the most positive of all influences imaginable, **is like leaven.** To take this **leaven** as representing evil that permeates the kingdom is to twist the obvious meaning and construction of words—whether in the Greek or English texts. Nor does that interpretation fit Jesus' development of this group of parables, in which this one parallels that of the mustard seed. They both illustrate the power of the kingdom to overcome the resistance and opposition illustrated in the parables of the sower and of the wheat and tares.

Even when leaven is used in relation to something evil, as in Jesus' warning about "the leaven of the Pharisees, which is hypocrisy" (Luke 12:1), the point is not that leaven and hypocrisy are both inherently evil but that they both are inherently pervasive and powerful in their influence. In his letter to the Galatians, Paul uses leaven in the same way—not to illustrate the evil of legalism (which is great) but rather to point up its great influence: "A little leaven leavens the whole lump of dough" (5:9).

As Paul indicts the Corinthians for arrogant indifference to the gross immorality of some of the church members, he states the same well-known proverb that he uses in Galatians and that Jesus had in mind in this parable: "Do you not know that a little leaven leavens the whole lump of dough?" (1 Cor. 5:6). He is speaking in the context of demanding that believers remove immoral members from their midst, in order that the evil conduct might not contaminate the rest of the church (vv. 2-5). Here again, the figure of leaven is used in regard to something evil, but the focus of the

373

analogy is not on common evil but on common permeation.

As Paul continues his warning to the Corinthians, he also uses leaven to represent discontinuation. Israel under Moses was commanded not to take any leaven from bread in Egypt as they prepared to leave that land of captivity and oppression and journey toward the Promised Land. In the same way, Christians are commanded to "clean out the old leaven" of "malice and wickedness" that characterized their unsaved lives and take nothing of it into their new life in Christ (1 Cor. 5:7-8a). The bread of their new life in Christ is then called "the unleavened bread of sincerity and truth" (v. 8b).

But no analogy can be pressed too far. In this instance Paul uses leaven to illustrate the discontinuity that should be evident between an unsaved and a saved life. The relationship of leaven to the evil of the old life and of no leaven to the righteousness of the new life is incidental. The focus is on discontinuity, just as in the parable it is on permeation and influence.

In following out the story of the Exodus it becomes clear that, after the seven restricted days, the Israelites were again allowed to make leavened bread—though not from *Egyptian* leaven. At the Feast of Pentecost, in fact, the bread offered to the Lord *had* to be "baked with leaven" (Lev. 23:17), which He would hardly have required had leaven intrinsically represented evil. Otherwise that feast would have been a perpetual reminder of God's tolerance of evil rather than of His holiness and goodness (v. 21).

The term *leaven* can incidentally represent something that is good, evil, or morally and spiritually neutral, depending on how it is used. But the primary analogy pertains to pervasive influence, which is leaven's most obvious and distinctive characteristic.

A third lesson of this parable is that the positive influence of the kingdom comes from within. The **leaven** must be **hid** in order to have any impact. The idea here is not that of hiding so as not to be seen but rather of hiding in the sense of penetrating deeply, completely permeating the world as leaven completely permeates the dough. Christians are not to be *of* the world, but we are to be *in* the world, because that is the only way the gospel can reach and affect the world (John 17:14-16). Christ sends His people into the world just as the Father sent Him into the world (v. 18). The supreme purpose of the church is to "go into all the world and preach the gospel to all creation" (Mark 16:15).

When **the kingdom of heaven** is faithfully reflected in the lives of believers, its influence in the world is both pervasive and positive. The life of Christ within believers is spiritual and moral leavening in the world. A Christian does not have to be a national leader, a famous entertainer, or a sports figure to influence the world for his Lord. It is the power of God's kingdom within a believer that makes his witness effective, and that is the influence on the world that Christians should seek to have.

That the meaning of these two parables was immediately clear to the disciples is seen in the fact that afterward they did not ask Jesus to explain them. Instead they asked Him to explain the parable of the wheat and tares (Matt. 13:36). The obvious purpose of the mustard seed and leaven parables was to encourage the disciples and all subsequent believers.

Each week, hundreds of new churches are started throughout the world. In China—which is still closed to missionary work, overt evangelism, and free worship—it is estimated that there are perhaps 50 million or more Christians! Most of the world's people have the Scriptures printed in their own language, and more and more languages are added to the list each year. Through radio and literature, many millions are being reached with the gospel who could never personally hear it preached or taught.

But evangelism and other work and witness of the church often seem to have little immediate or noticeable effect. Even with the great growth and impact of the church in the world today, from the human perspective the world seems to be winning the contest for men's souls by a wide gap. As the church grows in numbers, so does world population; and, by comparison, God's people are still a remnant. As thousands of new converts are won daily in some countries, in others the church is losing membership and influence.

How much more reason did the disciples have for being discouraged and perplexed about the prospects of Christ's kingdom on earth? The Messiah Himself was daily meeting more and more opposition and receiving more and severer threats against His life. The twelve knew that they themselves were totally unprepared to win the world for the Lord. If the Son of God Himself was rejected and put to death, what could a handful of His weak, insignificant followers hope to accomplish after He was gone?

But Jesus' purpose in these two parables, as in many others teachings, was to assure the apostles, the early church, and every believer in every age that ultimately His kingdom not only would not fail but would prosper and grow. Christianity will win, evil will be destroyed, and Jesus will reign. Christ Himself is building His church, and the very "gates of Hades [death itself] shall not overpower it" (Matt. 16:18).

THE INTERPRETATION OF THE PARABLE OF THE WHEAT AND TARES

All these things Jesus spoke to the multitudes in parables, and He did not speak to them without a parable, so that what was spoken through the prophet might be fulfilled, saying, "I will open My mouth in parables; I will utter things hidden since the foundation of the world."

Then He left the multitudes, and went into the house. And His disciples came to Him, saying, "Explain to us the parable of the tares of the field." And He answered and said, "The one who sows the good seed is the Son of Man, and the field is the world; and as for the good seed, these are the sons of the kingdom; and the tares are the sons of the evil one; and the enemy who sowed them is the devil, and the harvest is the end of the age; and the reapers are angels. Therefore just as the tares are gathered up and burned with fire, so shall it be at the end of the age. The Son of Man will send forth His angels, and they will gather out of His kingdom all stumbling blocks, and those who commit lawlessness, and will cast them into the furnace of fire; in that place there shall be weeping and gnashing of teeth. Then the righteous

will shine forth as the sun in the kingdom of their Father. He who has ears, let him hear." (13:34-43)

Before he presents the interpretation of the parable of the wheat and tares, Matthew explains that Jesus' speaking in parables was not an afterthought but had been prophesied in God's Word hundreds of years earlier. **To the multitudes** Jesus **did not speak . . . without a parable,** Matthew says, **so that what was spoken through the prophet might be fulfilled.**

Asaph, a **prophet** and seer (2 Chron. 29:30), wrote Psalm 78, from which Matthew here quotes: **I will open My mouth in parables; I will utter things hidden since the foundation of the world.** The rejection of His messiahship did not catch the Lord by surprise, and the postponement of the kingdom was not a backup plan. The **things hidden since the foundation of the world** pertained to "the mysteries of the kingdom of heaven," which Jesus explained to His disciples but not the unbelieving multitudes and religious leaders (Matt. 13:11-16). To those who rejected Him, He spoke "in parables; because while seeing they [did] not see, and while hearing they [did] not hear, nor [did] they understand" (v. 13). God made no alterations of His plan of redemption. Everything was exactly on schedule and according to the predictions of His Word.

After telling the parables of the mustard seed and leaven, **He left the multitudes, and went** back **into the house** where He had been staying (see 13:1). As soon as they were all inside, **His disciples came to Him, saying, "Explain to us the parable of the tares of the field."**

Although they did not fully understand that parable, the fact that they called it **the parable of the tares** shows they realized the major emphasis was on the **tares** rather than the wheat. The parable was obviously about judgment, and **the tares** obviously represented unbelievers. The disciples' question may have reflected the same attitude as that of the slaves in the parable—"Do you want us, then, to go and gather them up?" (v. 28). James and John demonstrated their attitude toward unbelievers when they asked Jesus' permission "to command fire to come down from heaven and consume" the Samaritans who refused to receive Him (Luke 9:54).

All the disciples were doubtlessly wondering why the wicked **tares** would be allowed to coexist with the good wheat. Had the landowner done as the slaves suggested and had all the tares immediately been pulled out and destroyed, the disciples would have readily understood. But as it was, they were perplexed about the landowner's reaction, because they still did not understand the greatness of God's grace or His plan of redemption for the intermediate and millennial periods of the kingdom before Christ would judge the world.

The one who sows the good seed is the Son of Man, Jesus began, **and the field is the world.** The disciples knew that by **the Son of Man** Jesus referred to Himself. Because it focused on His humility and humanity in the incarnation, it was the title He most commonly used of Himself. It beautifully identified Him as He fully participated in human life as the perfect Man, the second Adam, and the sinless representative of the human race. It was also a title clearly understood by Jews as referring to the Messiah (Luke 22:69; cf. Dan. 7:13). The title is used of Jesus by others only twice in the New Testament, once by Paul (Acts 7:56) and once by John (Rev. 14:14).

The one who sows is Jesus Christ, **the Son of Man**, and He is sowing in His own **field**, which **is the world**. It is difficult to understand why so many interpreters maintain that **the field** in this parable represents the church, and that Jesus' point is that true and false believers, represented by the wheat and tares, will exist together in the church throughout the present age. The Lord could not have identified **the field** more explicitly. It is **the world**, not the church. This is a picture of the church in the world, not of the world in the church.

Although Satan is temporarily the ruler of this **world**, it still belongs to God, who created it and will one day redeem and restore it. God's "creation itself also will be set free from its slavery to corruption into the freedom of the glory of the children of God. For we know that the whole creation groans and suffers the pains of childbirth together until now" (Rom. 8:21-22).

In the parable of the sower Jesus speaks of **the good seed** as "the word of the kingdom" (13:19); but here it represents **the sons of the kingdom**, whom the Lord scatters throughout **the world**. The Lord plants His people in the world as His witnesses, to grow and become fruitful plants of righteousness. **The sons of the kingdom** are faithful to the King and reflect His will and His standards before a wicked, corrupt, unbelieving **world**. Christians are not left in the world by accident but are placed there on divine assignment from their Lord.

The tares, on the other hand, **are the sons of the evil one**, who is Satan. All human beings are either spiritual children of God and **sons of the kingdom** through faith in His Son or they are spiritual **sons of the evil one**, simply by virtue of their sinful nature and unbelief (John 8:44; Eph. 2:2-3; 1 John 3:10; 5:19).

Jesus does not make the point in this parable, because it would not fit the analogy, but all **good seeds** were once **tares**; all **the sons of the kingdom** were once **sons of the evil one**. To go beyond the scope of this parable, while still using some of its figures, it could be said that the primary purpose of the "good seeds" in the world is to make converts of "tares," that they might also become **sons of the kingdom**.

The enemy who sowed the tares **is the devil**, the evil one. As is evident from the wording of the parable itself (see v. 25), **sowed** here carries the idea of thoroughness. Throughout history the tares have outnumbered the wheat by enormous percentages; and some parts of the world seem to be totally sown with the seed of **the enemy**.

The harvest represents God's judgment at **the end of the age**, when **the reapers**, who **are angels**, will execute judgment on unbelievers, just as the human reapers in the parable separated out **the tares**, which were then **gathered up and burned with fire**.

So shall it be at the end of the age, Jesus explains. The disciples were doubtlessly ready to put the sickle to the unbelieving tares right away, just as the landowner's slaves were prepared to do (v. 28). This was revealed as the attitude of James and John toward the unbelieving Samaritans when they said, "Lord, do You want us to command fire to come down from heaven and consume them?" (Luke (9:54).

377

In the parable we are told that "the wheat sprang up and bore grain, [and] the tares became evident also" (v. 26). Jesus does not elaborate on that statement, but in light of His other parable explanations, that aspect of the parable would seem to teach that most true believers can be identified by their spiritual and practical fruit (grain) and unbelievers by their lack of it.

The only reason given in the parable for not having the slaves pull out the obvious tares was that, in doing so, they might "root up the wheat with them" (v. 29). As observed above under the discussion of that verse, damage could be done to some of the good crop either because some plants matured late and would be mistaken for tares because they did not yet have grain or because the roots were so intermingled that some good plants would be uprooted with the tares.

In addition to the fact that the church age is for evangelism and not judgment, Christians are not qualified to infallibly distinguish between true and false believers. Every time the church has presumed to do that it has produced an ungodly bloodbath. When the fourth-century Roman emperor Constantine required every person to make a profession of faith in Christ on pain of death, he succeeded in killing many true believers who refused to submit to his spurious brand of Christianity. During the Crusades of the Middle Ages, unbelievable brutality was committed against non-Christians, especially Muslims and Jews, in the name of the Prince of Peace. During the inquisitions in reaction to the Protestant Reformation, countless thousands of Christians who did not submit to the dogma and authority of Roman Catholicism were imprisoned, tortured, and executed.

This is not the age of God's judgment, and certainly not of judgment and execution by the church. While on earth, the Lord Himself would not lift a finger against His enemies. To Judas, who betrayed Him to His death, He offered the first sop at the Last Supper as a gesture of love and a final appeal for belief (John 13:26). For those who falsely accused Him and sent Him to the cross, He asked forgiveness (Luke 23:34). How, then, can His followers consider themselves ever justified in taking the role of judge or avenger and executioner? In the present age, believers are not God's instruments of judgment and destruction but of truth and grace. Toward unbelievers we are not to have hearts of condemnation but of compassion.

The church is called to preach and teach against sin and all unrighteousness, but, in doing that, its purpose is not to judge but to win souls, not to punish but to convert sons of the evil one into sons of the kingdom.

In any case, the Lord makes clear that the separation of the wheat and tares, of the sons of the kingdom and the sons of the evil one, would be only **at the end of the age.** In the meanwhile they exist side by side, breathing the same air, enjoying the same sunshine and rain, eating the same food, attending the same schools, working in the same factories and offices, living in the same neighborhoods, and sometimes attending the same churches.

The **angels** whom **the Son of Man will send forth . . . will gather out of His kingdom all stumbling blocks, and those who commit lawlessness, and will cast them into the furnace of fire.** The whole earth is seen here as the Lord's **kingdom,** and truly He is the rightful monarch. Out of His world the **angels** collect **all stumbling**

blocks—the devil's sons who work against God and seek to cause many to fall into hell and **those who commit lawlessness** by disobeying God's Word.

When Jesus returns, He will "come in the glory of His Father with His angels; and will then recompense every man according to his deeds" (Matt. 16:27). The **angels** will deal "out retribution to those who do not know God and to those who do not obey the gospel of our Lord Jesus. And these will pay the penalty of eternal destruction, away from the presence of the Lord and from the glory of His power" (2 Thess. 1:8-9).

Fire causes the greatest pain known to man, and **the furnace of fire** into which the sinners are **cast** represents the excruciating torment of hell, which is the destiny of every unbeliever. This **fire** of hell is unquenchable (Mark 9:44), eternal (Matt. 25:41), and is pictured finally as a great "lake of fire which burns with brimstone" (Rev. 19:20). The punishment is so fearsome that **in that place there shall be weeping and gnashing of teeth.**

Hell will not be a place, as some jokingly envision, where the ungodly will continue to do their thing while the godly do theirs in heaven. Hell will have no friendships, no fellowship, no camaraderie, no comfort. It will not even have the debauched pleasures in which the ungodly love to revel on earth. There will be no pleasure in hell of any kind or degree—only torment, "day and night forever and ever" (Rev. 20:10).

Jesus' last word of explanation is positive, beautiful, and hopeful: **Then the righteous will shine forth as the sun in the kingdom of their Father.** When the Son of Man returns with His angels, they will not only perfectly separate out the wicked for eternal punishment but also the righteous for eternal blessing. The Lord "will send forth His angels with a great trumpet and they will gather together His elect from the four winds, from one end of the sky to the other" (Matt. 24:31). Then comes the long-anticipated and long-postponed kingdom of righteousness, in which there will be no evil people and no evil deeds or even thoughts. This is the fulfilled, eternal **kingdom of** our heavenly **Father,** where, with all **the righteous** of all ages, we **will shine forth as the sun.** There we "will shine brightly like the brightness of the expanse of heaven, and those who lead the many to righteousness, like the stars forever and ever" (Dan. 12:3).

Lest anyone fail to take seriously these truths that are both fearsome and wonderful, Jesus added, **He who has ears, let him hear.** Every person who is uncertain about his relationship to God should ask himself if he is wheat or merely a tare that looks like wheat, if he is a child of God or of the evil one. If he does not belong to God, he can come to God, because God is in the business of making wheat out of tares, saints out of sinners.

Those who are sure they are sons of the kingdom should **hear** what Jesus says here in order that their attitude toward the world might be the loving, merciful, compassionate attitude of their Lord—who has called them to witness rather than condemn, to love rather than hate, to show mercy rather than judgment. In that way we prove ourselves "blameless and innocent, children of God above reproach in the midst of a crooked and perverse generation, among whom [we will] appear as lights in the world" (Phil 2:15).

Entering the Kingdom (13:44-46)

The Kingdom of heaven is like a treasure hidden in the field, which a man found and hid; and from joy over it he goes and sells all that he has, and buys that field.

Again, the kingdom of heaven is like a merchant seeking fine pearls, and upon finding one pearl of great value, he went and sold all that he had, and bought it. (13:44-46)

In the first four of the eight kingdom parables in Matthew 13, Jesus focuses on men's various responses to God's kingdom, on its present coexistence with Satan's kingdom, and on its power and influence in the world.

A basic question that would naturally have arisen in the minds of Jesus' hearers was, "How does one become a part of God's kingdom?" "Are people simply born into it, like they are born into citizenship of their country?" they wondered. "Or is it like being a Jew? Are we, as Jews, automatically citizens of the kingdom because we are descendants of Abraham, or must we do something else?"

In this third couplet of parables the Lord teaches about appropriating salvation and thereby becoming a citizen of God's kingdom and a member of His family.

THE PARABLE OF THE HIDDEN TREASURE

The kingdom of heaven is like a treasure hidden in the field, which a man found and hid; and from joy over it he goes and sells all that he has, and buys that field. (13:44)

As He does in the other parables, Jesus builds this simple story around an experience or situation familiar to His hearers. Few, if any, would themselves have found such a treasure; but the practice of hiding valuables in the ground was common. Because there were no banks or other public depositories, most people protected their valuables in a secret spot in the ground. When they needed money or decided to sell or trade a piece of jewelry, for instance, they would go to the place at night, uncover the jar or storage box, take out what was desired, and rebury the rest.

Because Palestine had been a battleground for hundreds of years, families would often even bury food, clothing, and various household objects to protect them from plundering enemy soldiers. The famed Jewish historian Josephus wrote, "The gold and the silver and the rest of that most precious furniture which the Jews had and which the owners treasured underground was done to withstand the fortunes of war."

Over the years, the ground of Palestine became a veritable treasure house. When the owner of buried treasure died or was forcefully driven from the land—sometimes deported to a foreign land such as Assyria or Babylon—the treasure would be forever lost unless someone accidentally discovered it, as occasionally happened.

No doubt that was the fate of the **treasure hidden in the field, which a man found and hid** again. The man may have stumbled over part of the **treasure** or seen some of it protruding above ground as he happened to pass through the **field**. Or he may have been a hired hand who inadvertently dug it up while plowing or cultivating. In any case, the **field** did not belong to him, because, **from joy over it he goes and sells all that he has, and buys that field.**

Many Christians are embarrassed by this story, thinking Jesus used an unethical act to illustrate a spiritual truth. It seems to them that the **man** was obligated to tell the owner of the **field** about the **treasure**, since it was on his property and therefore rightfully belonged to him.

The point of the parable does not involve the ethics of what the **man** did, but rather his willingness to sacrifice everything he had in order to possess the **treasure.** But what he did was not unethical or dishonest.

In the first place, it is obvious that the treasure was not hidden by the present owner of the field and was unknown to him. Otherwise, he would have retrieved it before he sold the field. The **man** who bought the field obviously knew the owner was not aware of the **treasure** or he would not have offered to buy the field, knowing the treasure would not be included in the deal.

In the second place, rabbinic law provided that "if a man finds scattered fruit or money, it belongs to the finder." If a person came across money or other valuables that were obviously lost and whose owner was dead or unknown, the finder had the right to keep what was found.

In the third place, the basic honesty of the **man** is testified to by the fact that, had he been dishonest, he would simply have taken the **treasure** without any thought of buying the field. But he did not even use part of the **treasure** to buy the field; rather, he **sells all that he has, and buys that field.**

THE PARABLE OF THE PEARL OF GREAT VALUE

Again, the kingdom of heaven is like a merchant seeking fine pearls, and upon finding one pearl of great value, he went and sold all that he had, and bought it. (13:45-46)

An *emporos* (**merchant**) was a wholesale dealer, whose business was to buy and resell merchandise. He would travel about the country, perhaps to many countries, looking for items to buy and then sell for a profit. This particular **merchant** spent his time **seeking fine pearls.** He probably made regular visits to the various coastal areas where pearls were harvested and haggled with the divers or their employers over prices. Diving for pearls was extremely hazardous, and many divers lost their lives or ruined their health in obtaining the oysters that contained the beautiful gems. That fact, in addition to their scarcity and natural beauty, made **pearls** extremely precious.

Pearls were the most highly valued gems in the ancient world and were often bought as investments, much as diamonds are today. In the form of **pearls,** a great amount of wealth could be kept in a small space—concealed in one's clothing while traveling or buried in a field for safekeeping, as was the treasure of the previous parable.

The Jewish Talmud spoke of pearls as being beyond price, and some Egyptians and Romans held the pearl in such awe that they worshiped it. Adorning their heads with "gold or pearls" apparently was a common practice among both Jewish and Gentile women (see 1 Tim. 2:9). When Jesus warned against believers' casting their pearls before swine (Matt. 7:6), He was emphasizing the priceless value of the gospel and its attendant truths, which unbelievers disdain as worthless. In John's vision of the New Jerusalem, the city had twelve pearl gates, and "each one of the gates was a single pearl" (Rev. 21:21).

It was reported that the wife of the Roman emperor Caligula often wore a vast fortune in pearls in her hair and on her ears, neck, wrists, and fingers. Cleopatra is said to have owned two extremely valuable pearls, each of which would be worth several million dollars in today's market. When an extravagant ruler wanted to flaunt his wealth, he would sometimes dissolve a pearl in vinegar and drink it in his wine.

When the **merchant** came across **one pearl of great value, he went and sold all that he had, and bought it.** Obviously the **merchant** considered that particular **pearl** to have been worth more than all his other pearls together, because they would have been included in the sale of **all that he had.**

Because the emphasis of these parables is personal appropriation of **the**

kingdom of heaven, the message is obviously one of salvation. In this context, **the kingdom of heaven** represents the saving knowledge of God through trust in His Son and all the benefits and glory that relationship brings.

LESSONS FROM THE PARABLES

From the parables of the hidden treasure and the pearl of great price we can learn at least six valuable lessons about **the kingdom,** and therefore about salvation: it must be personally appropriated, it is priceless, it is not superficially visible, it is the source of true joy, it may be entered from different circumstances, and it is made personal by a transaction.

THE KINGDOM MUST BE PERSONALLY APPROPRIATED

The central truth of these two parables is that the kingdom of heaven must be personally appropriated. It is not obtained by natural inheritance, as one automatically becomes a member of his parents' race or a citizen of their country. Both parables center around a single individual who sacrifices all that he has in order to personally obtain that which has become immeasurably valuable to him.

Every human being is under God's dominion in the sense that he lives on the earth—which is under the Lord's ultimate control, despite Satan's temporary and limited power over it. And an unbeliever who associates with believers can benefit from many blessings of the kingdom because of that association. Nevertheless, although an unbeliever may attend an evangelical church, enjoy biblical preaching, and be a professing and baptized member of a church, he is not a citizen of the kingdom. Such superficial and nongenuine "sons of the kingdom shall be cast out into the outer darkness," where "there shall be weeping and gnashing of teeth" (Matt. 8:12).

As Paul reminded his Jewish brethren, "They are not all Israel who are descended from Israel; neither are they all children because they are Abraham's descendants" (Rom. 9:6-7). Even under the Old Covenant a person could be a Jew racially, nationally, and religiously—fully identified with God's chosen people in those outward ways—and yet have no part in the true, spiritual Israel. In the same way, a person can be born into a family who traces its church membership back for many generations, and yet have no part in Christ's true church. Although it gives many advantages, even being born into a family of godly believers does not make a person a Christian. To be saved, he must make his own decision to receive Jesus Christ as Lord and Savior.

THE KINGDOM IS PRICELESS

The parables express the value of salvation through the idea that it is worth selling all one possesses in order to receive it.

A major diamond mining company in South Africa specializes in mining certain coastal areas where the rough gems have been deposited below some fifty or so feet of stone, gravel, and sand. After giant earth movers remove the cover layers, the diamond-bearing conglomerate is dynamited and then excavated by hydraulic water pressure. Using large nylon brushes, workers sweep out all the crevices and hollows to be sure nothing is lost. The loosened conglomerate is then pounded, crushed, washed, and sifted to discover every possible diamond. It is estimated that some 180 million parts of earth are processed to yield one part diamond.

Though written at least 3,000 years ago, Job's description of man's tireless quest for riches sounds amazingly contemporary:

> Surely there is a mine for silver, and a place where they refine gold. . . . Man puts an end to darkness, and to the farthest limit he searches out the rock in gloom and deep shadow. He sinks a shaft far from habitation, forgotten by the foot; they hang and swing to and fro far from men. . . . Its rocks are the source of sapphires, and its dust contains gold. The path no bird of prey knows, nor has the falcon's eye caught sight of it. . . . He hews out channels through the rocks; and his eye sees anything precious. He dams up the streams from flowing; and what is hidden he brings out to the light." (Job 28:1, 3-4, 6-7, 10-11)

For all the efforts taken to find, mine, refine, cut, polish, mount, sell, and buy precious stones and metals, none of them offers anything truly worthwhile or lasting. They cannot heal a broken relationship, give peace to a troubled mind, or forgive a sinful heart. They offer little for the present and nothing for the future.

"But where can wisdom be found?" Job asks. "And where is the place of understanding? Man does not know its value, nor is it found in the land of the living. The deep says, 'It is not in me'; and the sea says, 'It is not with me.' Pure gold cannot be given in exchange for it, nor can silver be weighed as its price. . . . Thus it is hidden from the eyes of all living. . . . God understands its way; and He knows its place. . . . And to man He said, 'Behold, the fear of the Lord, that is wisdom; and to depart from evil is understanding'" (Job 28:12-15, 21, 23, 28).

On the immeasurable worth of the kingdom of heaven, the nineteenth-century Scottish preacher Thomas Guthrie wrote, "In the blood of Christ to wash out sin's darkest stains, in the grace of God to purify the foulest heart, in peace to calm life's roughest storms, in hopes to cheer guilt's darkest hour, in a courage that defies death and descends calmly into the tomb, in that which makes the poorest rich and without which the richest are poor indeed, the gospel 'has treasures greater far than east or west unfold, and its rewards more precious are than all the stores of gold'" (Thomas Guthrie, The Parables [London: Alexander Strahan, 1866], p. 213).

The blessing of being a child of God through faith in Christ is utterly priceless, more valuable than all the possessions the richest man could acquire. There is absolutely nothing to compare to it in worth and beauty, because it is "an inheritance which is imperishable and undefiled and will not fade away" (1 Pet. 1:4). It is forgiveness, love, peace, happiness, virtue, purity, righteousness, eternal life, glory, and more.

When Robert Herbert Thompson—who owned 180 newspapers, controlled 290 other companies, and was personally worth more than 300 million dollars—was asked how much he would give to buy the *New York Times* newspaper, he is said to have replied, "I'd mortgage my soul." If they could, many people would do just that in order to achieve the possessions, fame, or power for which they lust.

The value of God's kingdom far exceeds that of all earthly riches and advantages together—and would still exceed them in worth even if they brought the satisfaction they promise. Yet God offers His priceless kingdom to any person, no matter how poor, how insignificant, how sinful, who trusts in Christ. The price is the same for everyone—all they have. For those whose hearts are genuinely turned to Christ, whatever values they have clung to in the past will be exchanged eagerly for this priceless treasure.

THE KINGDOM IS NOT SUPERFICIALLY VISIBLE

When Jesus was "questioned by the Pharisees as to when the kingdom of God was coming, He answered them and said, 'The kingdom of God is not coming with signs to be observed; nor will they say, "Look, here it is!" or "There it is!"'" (Luke 17:20-21). The kingdom will not be observable until Jesus returns and establishes His millennial rule over the earth. At that time He "is going to come in the glory of His Father with His angels," and men will "see the Son of Man coming in His kingdom" (Matt. 16:27-28). But the present kingdom "is not of this world" (John 18:36).

"A natural man does not accept the things of the Spirit of God," Paul tells us; "for they are foolishness to him, and he cannot understand them, because they are spiritually appraised" (1 Cor. 2:14). In his next letter to Corinth the apostle further explains that "the god of this world has blinded the minds of the unbelieving, that they might not see the light of the gospel of the glory of Christ, who is the image of God" (2 Cor. 4:4). Even when the truth of the gospel is clearly presented to him, the natural man cannot see it. As long as he resists the moving of God's Spirit on his heart, he cannot see past the spiritual blinders Satan has placed over his eyes. He is completely content to seek his ephemeral pleasures and the things which can never satisfy, considering the trinkets of the world to be of great value and the gospel of salvation to be worthless.

One writer expresses the truth in these words: "Under the form of a man, under the privacy and poverty of a Nazarene, was the fullness of the Godhead hidden that day from the wise and prudent of the world. The light was near them and yet they did not see it. The riches of divine grace were brought to their door and yet they continued poor and miserable."

The treasure of salvation is not obvious to men, and it is therefore not something they naturally seek. They do not understand why it is so prized by Christians and why some people give up so much—their self-dependency, sinful pleasures, and sometimes even their social, political, and economic freedom and welfare—to gain what seems to be so little. They cannot understand why believers willingly live by standards of ethics and morality that go against man's deepest drives and lusts. The way of the kingdom is narrow and unattractive to the natural man, and that is why so few find it or desire to walk in it once it is found (Matt. 7:14).

The full value of a pearl may not be evident to the average person, who may admire its beauty yet be unaware of its pricelessness. Many people have passing admiration for Jesus and the gospel but are totally unaware of the supreme and priceless gift that could be theirs in belonging to Him. They see the pearl in plain view, but to their worldly eyes it has little worth. Jesus "was the true light which, coming into the world, enlightens every man. He was in the world, and the world was made through Him, and the world did not know Him. He came to His own, and those who were His own did not receive Him" (John 1:9-11).

THE KINGDOM IS THE SOURCE OF TRUE JOY

It was from joy that the man sold all he had in order to buy the field that held the priceless treasure. Joy is a basic desire in every human being and is the desire that all the others either directly or indirectly serve. We like to eat because food brings joy and satisfaction to our palate and a good feeling and health to our bodies. The desire for money is primarily based in the joy we hope to find in the things money can buy. Fame, power, knowledge, and all other things we long after are desired for the joy it is hoped they will bring. Even the miser, who seems to love money for its own sake, hordes his possessions for the joy the hording brings. Some people thrive on misery, because they find joy in feeling sorry for themselves.

Yet all of those joys are temporary and disappointing. The only true and eternal joy is the joy found in Christ and His kingdom, because man was made by God for Himself. Human satisfaction can be found only in God's divine provision.

After Jesus exhorted the twelve to abide in Him and to have His words abide in them, to prove their true discipleship by bearing much fruit, and to keep His commandments and so abide in His love, He said, "These things I have spoken to you, that My joy may be in you, and that your joy may be made full" (John 15:1-11). A short while later in the same discourse He said, "Until now you have asked for nothing in My name; ask, and you will receive, that your joy may be made full" (16:24).

The apostle John declares in the opening of his first letter, "These things we write, so that our joy may be made complete" (1 John 1:4). Paul tells us that "the kingdom of God is . . . peace and joy in the Holy Spirit" (Rom. 14:17); and in the beautiful benediction of that letter he prays for his readers, "Now may the God of hope fill you with all joy and peace in believing, that you may abound in hope by the power of the Holy Spirit" (15:13). True joy comes only in the discovery and appropriation of Christ and His kingdom through trust in Him.

THE KINGDOM MAY BE ENTERED FROM DIFFERENT CIRCUMSTANCES

A fifth principle found in these two parables is that a person may come into the kingdom out of different circumstances. There is no precondition for turning from sin and turning to Christ in faith. A person does not have to become anything else before he becomes a Christian, and he can come from wherever he may be.

The two parables are much alike in that the main character in each is a man who discovers something of extreme value and sacrifices everything he owns to buy it. But the ways in which they come across their precious treasures are vastly different, almost opposite. In the first parable the man comes upon the treasure completely by accident. As far as we are told, he was not looking for anything and certainly not a priceless treasure. In the second parable, however, the man was diligently looking for the very thing he eventually found and bought.

In the course of going about his normal business of earning a living, the first man was working in the field or perhaps passing through it on a journey. Finding a treasure was the last thing on his mind.

In a similar way, many people come across the gospel while pursuing the activities of their daily life, with no expectation or concern for salvation or anything else spiritual. While busily occupied with earning a living, caring for a family, getting an education, or building a career, they hear a sermon, read a book, listen to a tape, or have a conversation that presents the gracious claims and promises of Christ. By the Spirit's gracious power they recognize the priceless value of the message, and they believe, are saved, and inherit the kingdom.

That is what happened to Paul. His experience was unique in that it was a dramatic, awesome, and audible encounter with the risen Christ and in that he was called to be an apostle. But it was not unique in the fact that trusting Christ as Lord and Savior was not his intention. He was, in fact, in the midst of zealously persecuting those who trusted in Christ. In the nearly two millennia since then, millions of others have been convicted and converted by the power of God while in the midst of a life of denying and opposing Him. Some have come to church or to an evangelistic meeting to mock the preacher or ridicule the gospel and left a child of the kingdom.

The woman at the well near Sychar had come there simply to draw water and go on about her chores, but she encountered the Source of living water, went home redeemed, and led many others to redemption (John 4:5-42). The blind beggar in Jerusalem whom Jesus healed by applying clay to the man's eyes and having him wash in the Pool of Siloam did not even know who Jesus was—much less ask Him for healing and still less for salvation. But he was healed immediately and eventually received salvation as well (John 9:1-38).

Charles Haddon Spurgeon grew up in a Christian home, but as a boy he attended church only because it was the proper thing to do. He was not immoral or rebellious but was basically satisfied with his life and was not seeking any more religion than he had. One New Year's morning, when he was fifteen years old, he decided he ought to attend the service at his church. When the snow and cold wind became too fierce for him, he ducked into a little storefront type of church, as much to get out of the cold as anything.

"When I could go no further," he writes of the event, "I turned down a court and came to a little Primitive Methodist church. The preacher who was to have conducted the service never got there because he was held up by the weather, and quickly one of the officers had to be brought forward to conduct the service with the congregation of perhaps fifteen people. The man was really stupid. His text was, 'Look unto Me and be ye saved, all the ends of the earth.' And he just kept repeating it because he had nothing else to say." But something about Spurgeon caught the man's eye, and he said, "Young man, you look very miserable. And miserable in life and miserable in death you will be if you don't obey my text." He then shouted, "Young man, look to Jesus! Look, look, look!" "I looked," said Spurgeon; "and then and there the cloud was gone and the darkness rolled away and that moment I saw the Son."

Like Paul, the woman of Sychar, the beggar in Jerusalem, and countless others, Spurgeon was looking for nothing but found everything.

The second parable, on the other hand, depicts a man whose life business was searching for the thing he eventually found. He represents the seeker after God who for years looks everywhere for meaning and purpose in life, trying one religion or philosophy and then another. He finds nothing that satisfies but believes that the true way is out there if he can only find it, and he never stops looking.

That was the experience of the Ethiopian eunuch whom the Holy Spirit led Philip to intercept on the road to Gaza. The man was a Gentile proselyte who had come to Jerusalem to worship, and as he returned home he was reading from Isaiah but understanding nothing of what he read. After all his seeking and study, he was still confused and unsatisfied. But when Philip explained that Isaiah was writing about Christ, the Savior, the Ethiopian immediately believed. His long quest was ended, and he "went on his way rejoicing" (Acts 8:26-39).

Another Gentile, Cornelius, was also a God-fearing proselyte, who "gave many alms to the Jewish people, and prayed to God continually." God honored his sincere seeking by sending Peter to explain the gospel and lead him and his household to salvation (Acts 10). In similar ways, the Gentile Lydia (Acts 16:14-15) and both Jewish and Greek worshipers in the synagogue at Berea (17:10-12) sought and found the Lord.

Several years ago I met a couple attending our church who were celebrating their fiftieth wedding anniversary. The husband had been blind for a number of years, and they were visiting from a distant state. They told me they had sought God all of their married lives, trying one religion after another and finally ending up in the Unity cult. They soon came to realize that that religion was just as empty as their lives, and they went home from a service one day in utter despair. They turned on the radio and came across one of my broadcasts. After listening intently during the first half of the message, they both broke down in tears and said to each other, "This is the truth for which we've been searching for fifty years. At last we've found it!"

All of those men and women were looking for spiritual pearls and found the one that was priceless beyond their greatest hopes.

THE KINGDOM IS MADE PERSONAL BY A TRANSACTION

In both parables the priceless object was bought at the expense of every possession the finder owned. For that reason some Christians feel uncomfortable about these parables, because they seem to teach that salvation can be bought. But from beginning to end, Scripture makes abundantly clear that salvation is totally the free gift of God. Yet interpreted in the right way, salvation is bought in the sense that the person who accepts Jesus Christ as Lord and Savior surrenders everything he has to Him.

In all parables, the physical and earthly is used to illustrate the spiritual and heavenly. In these two parables the economic transaction of buying represents the spiritual transaction of surrender. There is an exchange in salvation. The old is exchanged for the new.

A familiar Old Testament passage that speaks of salvation as the free gift of God uses the expression "come, buy" twice in one verse. "Ho! Every one who thirsts, come to the waters," Isaiah wrote, "and you who have no money come, buy and eat. Come, buy wine and milk without money and without cost" (Isa. 55:1). The buying is not with money or any other possessions, material or otherwise. But in this passage, just as in the parables of the hidden treasure and the pearl of great price, a transaction is clear. The sinner gives up all the worthless things he has while freely receiving all the priceless things God has to give in Christ. What we give up in no way pays for salvation. To the contrary, what we give up not only is worthless but worse than worthless. Even the "righteous deeds" of an unbeliever "are like a filthy garment" (Isa. 64:6).

In eagerness to defend one truth of the gospel, it is possible to contradict or compromise another. In order to defend the freeness of the gospel, some interpreters deny or underplay the cost of salvation to believers as well as to Christ. Only Christ's payment *purchases* salvation, but the true believer will also be willing to pay whatever cost salvation involves. Apart from the willingness to yield all he has, a person's profession of faith is hollow and worthless. The rich young ruler of Matthew 19:16-22 is the classic example of one who saw the value of the pearl but refused to submit all he was and had to the lordship of Jesus Christ.

It must be noted that such surrender is not a human work to gain salvation but a part of the saving work of God wrought in the soul by the Holy Spirit.

Several other men who declared their intention to follow Jesus made various excuses for not doing so, proving their insincerity by their unwillingness to do what Jesus required. Of one man He demanded the sacrifice of comfort by joining "the Son of Man [who] has nowhere to lay His head" (Matt. 8:20); and of another He demanded the sacrifice of an inheritance the man wanted to receive when his father died (v. 21). Of another He demanded the sacrifice of family ties (Luke 9:61-62), and of still another He demanded surrender of wealth already possessed (Luke 18:22).

Surrender of possessions, whether great or small, present or prospective, cannot buy salvation. They have no spiritual merit and are of no value to God. Surrender is necessary not because it can buy anything but because it is inevitable when salvation is truly sought. Salvation that is not desired above everything else is not truly desired. Salvation costs nothing in the sense of payment but everything in the sense of surrender. "He who loves father or mother more than Me is not worthy of Me," Jesus said, "and he who loves son or daughter more than Me is not worthy of Me. And he who does not take his cross and follow after Me is not worthy of Me. He who has found his life shall lose it, and he who has lost his life for My sake shall find it" (Matt. 10:37-39). On another occasion the Lord said, "If anyone wishes to come after Me, let him deny himself, and take up his cross, and follow Me" (Matt. 16:24). To take up the cross is to forfeit everything, including physical life.

Speaking of coming to Him for salvation, Jesus said,

> For which one of you, when he wants to build a tower, does not first sit down and calculate the cost, to see if he has enough to complete it? Otherwise, when he has laid a foundation, and is not able to finish, all who observe it begin to ridicule him, saying, "This man began to build and was not able to finish." Or what king, when he sets out to meet another king in battle, will not first sit down and take counsel whether he is strong enough with ten thousand men to encounter the one coming against him with twenty thousand? Or else, while the other is still far away, he sends a delegation and asks terms of peace. So therefore, no one of you can be My disciple who does not give up all his own possessions. (Luke 14:28-33)

Jesus could not have made clearer the truth that the person who will not surrender his old life will never have the new.

Most people who consider receiving Christ as Savior and Lord do not consciously inventory all their material, social, and other possessions to see if He is worth sacrificing those things for. When they discover the infinite value of salvation, they simply yield to Christ. Their focus is not on what they give up but on what they receive. But if their redemption is genuine, their lives will evidence a willingness to surrender whatever stands between them and faithfulness to their Lord.

Some of men's most cherished possessions are their sins; and these must certainly be surrendered, because it is from sin that Christ saves us. No one can come to Christ by stopping his stealing, cursing, immorality, lying, or a dozen such sins. But the one who truly belongs to Him will long to give up those sins and every other. This is the attitude taught by Jesus in the Beatitudes—poverty of spirit that recognizes the bankruptcy of all human resources, mourning over sin, meekness in the presence of God, and hunger and thirst for righteousness in exchange for sin and guilt. God's sovereign, saving work incorporates that response.

In his letter to the church at Philippi, Paul recounts his many personal advantages and achievements before he was saved. I was "circumcised the eighth day," he says, "of the nation of Israel, of the tribe of Benjamin, a Hebrew of Hebrews; as to the Law, a Pharisee; as to zeal, a persecutor of the church; as to the righteousness which is in the Law, found blameless. But whatever things were gain to me," he continues to explain, "I have counted as loss for the sake of Christ" (Phil. 3:5-7). No New Testament writer more staunchly defends the freeness of salvation than does Paul. Yet he testifies that, in coming to Christ, he counted as loss—that is, he willingly surrendered as worthless—everything he was and had. Like the men who bought the treasure in the field and the pearl of great value, he liquidated everything he had for the priceless Treasure he had discovered.

BIRDVILLE
BAPTIST CHURCH
LIBRARY

Judgment and Proclamation

(13:47-52)

"Again, the kingdom of heaven is like a dragnet cast into the sea, and gathering fish of every kind; and when it was filled, they drew it up on the beach; and they sat down, and gathered the good fish into containers, but the bad they threw away. So it will be at the end of the age; the angels shall come forth, and take out the wicked from among the righteous, and will cast them into the furnace of fire; there shall be weeping and gnashing of teeth.

"Have you understood all these things?" They said to Him, "Yes." And He said to them, "Therefore every scribe who has become a disciple of the kingdom of heaven is like a head of a household, who brings forth out of his treasure things new and old." (13:47-52)

The last two of the eight parables on the kingdom found in Matthew 13 illustrate the separation and judgment of unbelievers and the preaching and teaching of God's ministers. The first gives a warning, and the second gives a call to proclaim that warning to a condemned world.

THE PARABLE OF THE DRAGNET—JUDGMENT

"Again, the kingdom of heaven is like a dragnet cast into the sea, and gathering fish of every kind; and when it was filled, they drew it up on the beach; and they sat down, and gathered the good fish into containers, but the bad they threw away. So it will be at the end of the age; the angels shall come forth, and take out the wicked from among the righteous, and will cast them into the furnace of fire; there shall be weeping and gnashing of teeth." (13:47-50)

In the previous parables Jesus illustrated the nature of the kingdom, the power and influence of the kingdom, and the personal appropriation of the kingdom. Now He focuses again (see v. 42) on the judgment connected with the kingdom.

The parable of the dragnet is a frightening warning about what happens to the wicked when they are separated from the righteous in the last days. Here Jesus gives a vivid picture of judgment, a brief explanation of the principle of judgment, and a sobering warning about the peril of judgment.

THE PICTURE

"Again, the kingdom of heaven is like a dragnet cast into the sea, and gathering fish of every kind; and when it was filled, they drew it up on the beach; and they sat down, and gathered the good fish into containers, but the bad they threw away." (13:47-48)

The activity Jesus uses to illustrate God's judgment on unbelievers was a common one to His hearers. It was especially familiar to those who lived near the Sea of Galilee, and most especially to those, including several of the disciples, who were fisherman.

On the Sea of Galilee three basic methods of fishing were employed, all of which are still used there today. The first was with a line and hook, which was used to catch one fish at a time. That was the type of fishing the Lord instructed Peter to do when they needed money to pay the two-drachma tax (Matt. 17:24-27).

The other two types of fishing involved nets. One net was a small, one-man casting net called an *amphiblēstron*. Peter and his brother Andrew were taking turns casting an *amphiblēstron* when Jesus called them to become "fishers of men" (Matt. 4:18-19). The folded net was carried over the fisherman's shoulder as he waded in shallow water looking for a school of fish. When the fish were near enough, he would hold the center cord in one hand and with the other hand throw the net so that it opened into a large circle and came down over the fish. Weights around the perimeter of the net caused it to sink and trap the fish. The fisherman then pulled on the cord, which was attached to the center of the net and drew it around the fish like a sack. When the net had been pulled closed, the fisherman would haul his catch to shore.

A second type of net was the *sagēnē*, a very large **dragnet**, or seine, that required a team of fishermen to operate and sometimes covered as much as a half square mile. It was pulled into a giant circle around the fish, between two boats out in deep water or by one boat when working from the shore. In the latter case, one end of the net would be firmly moored on shore while the other was attached to the boat, which would make a large circle out into the water and come back to the starting place. Floats were attached to the top of the net and weights to the bottom, forming a wall of net from the surface to the bottom of the lake.

Because the net permitted nothing to escape, all sorts of things besides the desirable fish were caught. It swept everything in its path—weeds, objects dropped overboard from boats, all manner of sea life, and **fish of every kind.**

When the net **was filled,** it would take a large number of men several hours just to drag **it up on the beach.** Then **they sat down, and gathered the good fish into containers, but the bad they threw away.** The **fish** to be carried to a distant market would be put in **containers** with water to keep the fish alive, and those that were to be sold nearby were placed in dry **containers,** usually baskets.

THE PRINCIPLE

So it will be at the end of the age; the angels shall come forth, and take out the wicked from among the righteous, (13:49)

Jesus begins His interpretation of the parable by explaining that the separation of the good and bad fish represents God's judgment **at the end of the age.** The parable of the wheat and tares illustrates the coexistence of believers and unbelievers in the present form of the kingdom, and this parable illustrates their separation as the form of the kingdom changes.

In His interpretation of the parable of the wheat and tares Jesus stated the same truth He gives here: **At the end of the age** [His] **angels shall come forth, and take out the wicked from among the righteous** (cf. vv. 39-41). During the present era, which is the church age, God permits unbelief and unrighteousness. But the time is coming when His toleration will end and His judgment begin. The first phase of judgment will be the separation of **the wicked from among the righteous,** the tares from among the wheat. The dragnet of God's judgment moves silently through the sea of mankind and draws all men to the shores of eternity for final separation to their ultimate destiny—believers to eternal life and unbelievers to eternal damnation.

Men move about within that net as if they were forever free. It may touch them from time to time, as it were, startling them. But they quickly swim away, thinking they have escaped, not realizing they are completely and inescapably encompassed in God's sovereign plan. The invisible web of God's judgment encroaches on every human being just as that of the dragnet encroaches on the fish. Most men do not perceive the kingdom, and they do not see God working in the world. They may be briefly moved by the grace of the gospel or frightened by the threat of judgment; but they soon return to their old ways of thinking and living, oblivious to the things of eternity. But when man's day is over and Christ returns to set up His glorious kingdom, then judgment will come.

Jesus is not giving a full description of the last days, but is concentrating on the judgment of unbelievers. He is speaking of judgment in general, with special focus on what is referred to as the final judgment at the great white throne (Rev. 20:11-15). There "the dead, the great and the small" will be "judged, everyone of them" (vv. 12-13).

As already mentioned in the interpretation of the wheat and tares parable (v. 41) and declared in many other New Testament passages (e. g., Matt. 24:31; 25:31-32; Rev. 14:19; 15:5–16:21), **angels** are the Lord's instruments of separation and execution of sentence. The separation will include all persons who are then living and all who have died—"those who did the good deeds to a resurrection of life, those who committed the evil deeds to a resurrection of judgment" (John 5:29).

Some people wonder why Jesus repeated the teaching about the angelic separation in this parable, when it is almost word for word what He had just said at the end of His explanation of the wheat and tares (Matt. 13:41). For one thing, the emphasis here is exclusively on the aspect of separation of believers from unbelievers, whereas in the other parable the major emphasis is on their coexistence. For another, it is such a vitally important truth that it bears frequent repetition.

Over and over Jesus warns about the horrors of hell and pleads with men to avoid it by coming to Him for salvation. He warned that, just as in the days of Noah before the flood, people will be "eating and drinking, . . . marrying and giving in marriage. . . . Then there shall be two men in the field; one will be taken, and one will be left. Two women will be grinding at the mill; one will be taken, and one will be left" (Matt. 24:38, 40-41).

God takes no pleasure in the death of the wicked (Ezek. 18:23) and does not desire that anyone perish (2 Pet. 3:9). The Lord wept over Jerusalem because the people would not come to Him and be saved (Luke 19:41). He warned about hell not to put people in agony but to save them from it. Hell was not even created for men but for the devil and his fallen angels (Matt. 25:41).

THE PERIL

and will cast them into the furnace of fire; there shall be weeping and gnashing of teeth. (13:50)

Perhaps no doctrine is harder to accept emotionally than the doctrine of hell. Yet it is too clear and too often mentioned in Scripture either to deny or to ignore. Jesus spoke more of hell than any of the prophets or apostles did—perhaps for the reason that its horrible truth would be all but impossible to accept had not the Son of God Himself absolutely affirmed it. It had special emphasis in Jesus' teaching from the beginning to the end of His earthly ministry. He said more about hell than about love. More than all other teachers in the Bible combined, He warned men of hell, promising no escape for those who refused His gracious, loving offer of salvation.

In the Sermon on the Mount alone, the Lord gives several specific and direct warnings about hell: "Whoever shall say, 'You fool,' shall be guilty enough to go into the fiery hell" (Matt. 5:22), and, "It is better for you that one of the parts of your body perish, than for your whole body to be thrown into hell" (v. 29; cf. v. 30; 18:8-9; Mark 9:43).

Jesus declares that the wicked "sons of the kingdom shall be cast out into the outer darkness; in that place there shall be weeping and gnashing of teeth" (Matt. 8:12) and that unbelieving Capernaum would "descend to Hades" (11:23; cf. Luke 10:15). He asked the evil and hypocritical scribes and Pharisees, "How shall you escape the sentence of hell?" (Matt. 23:33). On many other occasions Jesus alludes to hell and warns about damnation (5:20; 7:13, 19, 23, 27; 10:28; 12:36; 16:18; 18:8-9; 21:43-44; 23:14-15; 24:40-41, 51; 25:30, 46; Mark 3:29; Luke 12:9-10, 46; 16:23; John 5:29; 15:6).

Hell is not merely the fate of forever reliving bad memories or of going out into nothingness, as many people believe and teach. Nor is it a place where sinners will continue their sinning, unrestrained and unrebuked. There will be no pleasure at all in hell, not even the perverted pleasure of sin—only its punishment.

When an interviewer asked a young punk rock singer what she was looking forward to at the end of her career, she replied, "Death. I'm looking forward to death." When asked why, she said, "I want to go to hell, because hell will be fun."

Such deception is tragic beyond words. Nothing could less describe hell than fun. The human mind cannot begin to conceive of the eternal horror that is hell. Even the biblical figures related to hell are only suggestive, because the finite mind cannot comprehend infinite pain and torment any more than it can comprehend infinite joy and bliss. But from God's Word we learn four basic truths about **the furnace of fire** that will help us to partially grasp its terror.

First, hell is a place of constant torment, misery, pain. The torment is often described as darkness (Matt. 22:13), where no light can penetrate, and nothing can be seen. Throughout the numberless eons of eternity the damned will never again see light or anything that light illumines. Hell's torment is also described as fire that will never go out and cannot be extinguished (Mark 9:43) and from which the damned will never find relief. Hell could not be other than a place where **there shall be weeping and gnashing of teeth.**

Second, hell will involve the torment of both body and soul. Neither the soul nor the body is annihilated at death; nor will they ever be. When an unsaved person dies, his soul goes out from the presence of God into everlasting torment. At the resurrection of all the dead, the bodies of the unsaved will be raised, and those resurrected bodies will join the soul in hell's torment (Matt. 10:28; cf. John 5:29; Acts 24:15; Rev. 20:11-15). Just as believers will be fitted with resurrected bodies so they can enjoy the glories of heaven forever, unbelievers will be fitted with resurrected bodies so they can endure the torments of hell without being destroyed.

Jesus spoke of hell as a place "where their worm does not die" (Mark 9:44). When physical bodies are buried and begin to decay, the worms can attack them only as long as the flesh lasts. Once consumed, the body can experience no more harm. But the resurrected bodies of unbelievers will never be consumed, and the hellish "worms" that feed on them will themselves never die.

Third, the torments of hell will be experienced in varying degrees. For everyone in hell the suffering will be intense and permanent, but some will experience greater torment than others. "Anyone who has set aside the Law of Moses dies without mercy on the testimony of two or three witnesses," says the writer of Hebrews. "How much severer punishment do you think he will deserve who has trampled under foot the Son of God, and has regarded as unclean the blood of the covenant by which he was sanctified, and has insulted the Spirit of grace?" (Heb. 10:28-29). Those who willfully reject Jesus Christ and trample, as it were, on the sacrifice He made for them with His own blood will receive much greater punishment than those who had only the light of the Old Covenant. And on the day of judgment it will be more tolerable for the pagan cities of Tyre, Sidon, and Sodom than for the Jewish cities of Chorazin, Bethsaida, and Capernaum—who not only had the light of the Old Covenant but the opportunity to see and hear the Son of God in person and to witness His miraculous works (Matt. 11:22-23).

In the parable of the slaves who awaited their master's return from the wedding feast, Jesus explains that "that slave who knew his master's will and did not get ready or act in accord with his will, shall receive many lashes, but the one who did not know it, and committed deeds worthy of flogging, will receive but few" (Luke 12:47-48).

"Hell will have such severe degrees," writes John Gerstner, "that a sinner, were he able, would give the whole world if his sins could be one less."

Fourth, the torment of hell will be everlasting. Nothing will be so horrible about hell as its endlessness. Jesus uses the same word to describe the duration of hell as the duration of heaven: "These will go away into eternal punishment, but the righteous into eternal life" (Matt. 25:46). People in hell will experience the total absence of hope.

Although God originally designed hell for the devil and his fallen angels, men who choose to follow Satan's way instead of God's will also suffer Satan's fate.

The great Puritan writer and preacher John Bunyan describes hell with his customary vivid imagery:

> [In hell] thou shalt have none but a company of damned souls with an innumerable company of devils to keep company with thee. While thou art in this world, the very thought of the devil's appearing to thee makes thy flesh to tremble and thine hair ready to stand upright on thy head. But oh, what wilt thou do when not only the supposition of the devil's appearing but the real society of all the devils of hell will be with thee—howling, roaring and screeching in such a hideous manner that thou wilt be even at thy wit's end and ready to run stark mad again for anguish and torment. If after ten thousand years, an end should come, there would be comfort. But here is thy misery: here thou must be forever. When thou seest what an innumerable company of howling devils thou art amongst, thou shalt think this again— this is my portion forever. When thou hast been in hell so many thousand years as there are stars in the firmament or drops in the sea or sands on the

seashore, yet thou hast to lie there forever. Oh, this one word—ever—how will it torment thy soul. (*New Cyclopedia of Prose Illustrations,* ed. Elon Foster [New York: T. Y. Crowell, 1877], p. 450)

THE PARABLE OF THE HOUSEHOLDER: PROCLAMATION

"Have you understood all these things?" They said to Him, "Yes." And He said to them, "Therefore every scribe who has become a disciple of the kingdom of heaven is like a head of a household, who brings forth out of his treasure things new and old." (13:51-52)

Understood comes from *suniēmi,* which has the literal meaning of bringing or putting together. "Have you rightly put **all these things** together?" Jesus was asking. **"Have you understood** what I have been saying about the kingdom in these parables? Do you comprehend the truth that the present form of the kingdom will continue to have good and evil in it? Do you realize that believers will continue to grow in numbers and to permeate and influence the world? Do you know that entering the kingdom involves the recognition of the worthlessness of everything a person has apart from salvation in Jesus Christ? Do you see that the final separation of the righteous and wicked is inexorable and inescapable, and that the fate of both is eternal—the righteous to everlasting life and the wicked to everlasting punishment?"

In answer, the disciples **said to Him, "Yes."** But from what they later said and did, we know their understanding was far from perfect. But Jesus accepted their response as genuine; otherwise He would not have said to them the words of verse 52. On the level at which they were able to understand at that time, they **understood.**

Jesus had instructed the disciples to "beseech the Lord of the harvest to send out workers into His harvest" (Matt. 9:38)—to proclaim the coming harvest of judgment and to warn men of it and tell them how to escape it while they could. In the following four chapters we see Him specifically call them to this ministry and begin teaching, training, and in every way preparing them for it.

Based on their affirmative response, Jesus then **said to them, "Therefore every scribe who has become a disciple of the kingdom of heaven is like a head of a household.** A *grammateus* (**scribe**) literally referred to one who wrote. But among Jews the term had long carried the distinctive connotation of a man who was a learner, interpreter, and teacher of the law, God's revealed Word that we now call the Old Testament. Although the scribes and rabbis had added so much tradition that it subordinated and often contradicted God's true Word (Matt. 15:6), their purported task was to study and interpret Scripture. They were the theologians of Judaism, and many were members of the high Jewish council, the Sanhedrin.

Under Jesus' instruction, each of the twelve was becoming a genuinely learned **scribe** and a true **disciple of the kingdom of heaven.** They had become **like a head of a household, who brings forth out of his treasure things new**

and old. The **head of a household** was responsible for the entire welfare of the family, and a major part of his duty was to maintain ample supplies of food, clothing, and all other **things** the members of the **household** might need. He kept these supplies in a storehouse, or **treasure,** from which he would dispense items as they were needed.

The wise householder was frugal and was careful not to waste the supplies. When they were reusable, food that was uneaten and clothing that was no longer worn were returned to the **treasure** to be used again. When further need arose, economy demanded that these **old** supplies would be dispensed first, before any **things new** were issued.

The twelve disciples (learners) would become the twelve apostles (sent ones), Judas being replaced by Matthias (Acts 1:23). Through these twelve, along with Paul, the apostle appointed "last of all" (1 Cor. 15:8), the Lord entrusted the continued revelation of His Word and the founding of His church. They knew the **old** truths of His previous revelation and were being given additional truths that were **new.** They would proclaim the significance of both.

Brings forth is from *ekballō* and carries the idea of casting out, scattering, or distributing widely. In this context it also connotes generosity, giving out the truth of God both wisely and liberally. Apart from the Lord Himself, the apostles were the supreme Bible scholars, preachers, teachers, and theologians of all time—scribes and disciples without equal (cf. Matt. 11:11).

As is clear from the parables of the sower, the wheat and tares, and the dragnet, the message of the gospel is not simply the offer of heaven but a warning about hell. What makes the gospel such *good* news is its power to save men from the indescribably *bad* destiny toward which every person without Christ is headed. A person does not have to choose hell to go there. He only has to refuse the claims of Jesus Christ—or do nothing at all.

Though not with the same degree of authority, Jesus' charge to the twelve is given to every believer, and in particular to those He has called to teach and preach His Word. It is an awesome responsibility to warn the unsaved about hell and to offer them the way of escape through our precious Lord. "Therefore knowing the fear [or terror] of the Lord," Paul says, "we persuade men" (2 Cor. 5:11). The Christian's heart is cold indeed who is not deeply concerned and exercised about those around him who are destined for the eternity of hell. To have the gift of eternal life but not to share it with those who now have only the prospect of eternal death is the epitome of selfishness and lovelessness.

Yet some who call themselves Christian refuse, in the name of love, to proclaim anything that is fearful or uncomfortable. I recently read that the purpose of a certain "Christian" broadcasting organization is "to be a good neighbor to a variety of listeners." The policy statement given to prospective broadcasters includes the instruction: "When you are preparing your program for these stations, please avoid using the following: criticism of other religions and references to conversion, missionaries, believers, unbelievers, old covenant, new covenant, church, the cross, crucifixion, Calvary, Christ, the blood of Christ, salvation through Christ, redemption through Christ, the Son of God, Jehovah or the Christian life. These people listening are hungering for words of comfort," the statement continues. "We ask you to adhere to these restrictions so that God's Word can continue to go forth. Please help us maintain our position of bringing comfort to suffering people."

How tragic that an organization dedicated to bringing comfort refuses to so much as mention the elements essential to the only message that can bring true peace and comfort to a troubled soul! Whatever message of comfort would be left after complying with the restrictions of that network would be the false comfort that damns people by leaving them content in their sins. Whatever the foolish motivation for such thinking, it could not be the love of Christ—who loved the world and its people too much not to warn of the imminent and eternal danger that faces every person apart from Him.

The Power of Unbelief (13:53-58)

37

And it came about that when Jesus had finished these parables, He departed from there. And coming to His home town He began teaching them in their synagogue, so that they became astonished, and said, "Where did this man get this wisdom, and these miraculous powers? Is not this the carpenter's son? Is not His mother called Mary, and His brothers, James and Joseph and Simon and Judas? And His sisters, are they not all with us? Where then did this man get all these things?" And they took offense at Him. But Jesus said to them, "A prophet is not without honor except in his home town, and in his own household." And He did not do many miracles there because of their unbelief. (13:53-58)

Although Jesus continued to teach many additional truths and to reinforce and illustrate those already taught, the eight parables of Matthew 13 mark the end of the disciples' basic instruction. As noted earlier, Jesus' use of parables was primarily in response to His rejection by the Jews. The same stories that clarified truth for His true followers obscured truth for those who refused to trust in Him. "All these things Jesus spoke to the multitudes in parables, and He did not speak to them without a parable" (Matt. 13:34), because, as He had earlier explained to the disciples, "To you it has been granted to know the mysteries of the kingdom of heaven, but to them it has not been granted. . . . Therefore I speak to them in parables; because while seeing they do not see, and while hearing they do not hear, nor do they understand" (vv. 11, 13).

As far as preparation of the disciples was concerned, the two most important parables of Matthew 13 were those of the sower and of the wheat and tares. The story of the sower made clear that some people would believe the gospel but many would not; and it prepared them to anticipate the four basic responses men would make to the gospel. The vivid story of the wheat and tares made clear that, for the present period of Christ's kingdom, the saved and the unsaved would coexist side by side. The twelve— and all succeeding witnesses of Christ—would carry on their ministry in a time of both belief and unbelief and of both good and evil.

Beginning with 13:53 and continuing through the first part of chapter 16, Matthew records eight incidents in the life of the Lord that correspond to and demonstrate the truths presented in the two parables just mentioned.

The first incident involved the offense taken against Jesus by His hometown of Nazareth (13:54-58). To them Jesus was a stumbling block, and the soil of their hearts was obviously hard.

The second incident involved Herod (14:1-12), whose heart was also hard but who rejected the Lord more out of indifference than hatred.

The third incident had two parts and centered first on the large multitude whom Jesus miraculously fed and then around the people of Gennesaret (14:13-21, 34-36). In both instances, the initial fascination with Jesus was positive but superficial. The first group followed Him because they were fed and the second because they were healed. Their interest eventually withered, just like plants in shallow soil do when the sun comes out.

The fourth incident occurred between the two parts of the third and involved the twelve disciples, whose "good soil" was evidenced by their worshiping Jesus after He walked on the water and calmed the storm (14:22-33).

The fifth incident involved the scribes and Pharisees who tried to find an excuse to condemn Jesus (15:1-20), and it illustrates again the hard and stony ground of unbelieving rejection.

The sixth incident centered on the Canaanite woman who immediately confessed Jesus as Lord and begged Him to deliver her demon-possessed daughter (15:21-28). The soil of her heart was soft and fertile, and the seed of the Word took firm root.

The seventh incident involved the Galileans who brought their sick and afflicted to Jesus for healing but made no genuine commitment (Luke 15:29-39). Here was a mixture of shallow and thorny soils, in which the gospel was partially but not permanently received.

The eighth and last incident involved the Pharisees and Sadducees who sought to test and entrap Jesus by asking for a special sign (16:1-4). The soil of their hearts was obviously hard.

In these eight accounts there is exactly the ratio of belief to unbelief (one out of four) found in the parable of the sower. By the marvelous wisdom and provision of the Lord, the twelve, through these incidents, witnessed living demonstrations of the principles He had just taught them about men's response to the gospel in the present age. In these situations both the power of belief and the power of unbelief are revealed.

The power of belief is attested throughout Scripture. Abraham believed God and became the father of a great nation and of God's chosen people. Israel believed God and walked through the Red Sea on dry land. David believed God and was enabled to slay Goliath. Naaman believed God and was healed of his leprosy. Daniel believed God, and the lions could not harm him. A Roman centurion believed God, and his servant was healed. Two blind men believed God and received their sight and their salvation. Jairus believed God, and his daughter was brought back to life. The Philippian jailer and his household believed God and received eternal life. The list could go on and on.

But the list of accounts showing the power of unbelief is also long. Adam and Eve failed to believe God, and the whole world was cursed. The world itself refused to believe God's warning preached through Noah, and it was destroyed in the Flood, except for eight people. Pharaoh refused to believe God, and he lost his firstborn son, his entire army, and his own life. Israel refused to believe God and wandered forty years in the wilderness; and as a kingdom the people again refused to believe and were scattered for centuries among foreign nations. Aaron refused to believe God's command about worship and led the people into idolatry, resulting in the loss of 3,000 lives. Moses refused to believe God, and it cost him the privilege of entering the Promised Land. Nebuchadnezzar refused to believe God and became a senseless beast. Many would-be disciples refused to believe God because they were offended by Christ's teaching, and they entered into eternity without hope. The rich young ruler refused to believe God and forfeited eternal life. Most of the scribes, Pharisees, and Sadducees refused to believe God and were condemned to the eternal torment of hell. Although he lived for three years with Jesus, in the presence of the living Truth and Light, Judas refused to believe God and was condemned to hell, which Jesus said was Judas's own place. Felix, Festus, and Agrippa refused to believe God through the witness of Paul, and they were lost forever.

Just as faith has the power to bring forgiveness of sins and eternal life, unbelief has the power to hold a person in his sins and under the condemnation of eternal hell. Just as belief has the power to bring eternal happiness, joy, peace, and glory in God's presence, unbelief has the power to bring eternal sorrow, pain, and anguish in God's absence.

As the parable of the sower illustrates, most of the response Jesus faced and the disciples would face was that of unbelief. Whether unbelief comes from the heart beaten hard by sin, from the rocky heart covered by a shallow layer of superficial belief, or from the thorny heart whose worldliness chokes out the truth of the gospel—all unbelief is a matter of will. Unbelief is a choice; it is saying no to God in spite of the evidence.

Matthew's account of the first incident illustrating the parable of the sower is preceded by the brief mention of Jesus' departure from Capernaum.

LEAVING CAPERNAUM

And it came about that when Jesus had finished these parables, He departed from there. (13:53)

Jesus had been ministering in and around Capernaum for about a year, using it as His home base (see 4:13; 8:5). But the majority of the people who saw and heard Him in that region eventually fell away, manifesting their rejection either by blasé indifference or direct opposition. Because of that rejection, His last teaching there was done entirely in **parables**, in order that, "while seeing they [would] not see, and while hearing they [would] not hear, nor . . . understand" (13:13). After Jesus finished the **parables** on the kingdom, **He departed from there.**

Because the Lord had spent more time there than anywhere else thus far in His ministry, Capernaum was especially guilty for rejecting Him. Earlier, Jesus had scorchingly rebuked them, saying, "And you, Capernaum, will not be exalted to heaven, will you? You shall descend to Hades; for if the miracles had occurred in Sodom which occurred in you, it would have remained to this day" (11:23).

Jesus had, in effect, pronounced a curse on Capernaum, and when **He departed from there,** that city's doom was imminent. Jesus never went there again except as He passed through to minister elsewhere. He had come into the city and demonstrated power that could only have been from God. Yet the people would not have Him as Lord. Many marveled and some criticized, but few believed. Now Capernaum's opportunity was passed, and she entered a decline into oblivion from which she never recovered. Today the city is in virtually the same state of ruin—without houses or people—that it was a few centuries after Jesus was there. Apparently the town and the synagogue enjoyed a period of worldly prosperity for a while, but archaeological excavations show increasing pagan influence on the Jews there. The last synagogue built in Capernaum, erected over the floor of the one where Jesus taught, was decorated with various animals and mythological figures. Having rejected the true God, the people were at the mercy of false ones.

RETURNING TO NAZARETH

And coming to His home town He began teaching them in their synagogue, so that they became astonished, and said, "Where did this man get this wisdom, and these miraculous powers? Is not this the carpenter's son? Is not His mother called Mary, and His brothers, James and Joseph and Simon and Judas? And His sisters, are they not all with us? Where then did this man get all these things?" And they took offense at Him. But Jesus said to them, "A prophet is not without honor except in his home town, and in his own household." And He did not do many miracles there because of their unbelief. (13:54-58)

Jesus' **home town** was Nazareth, where Joseph and Mary went to live after returning from Egypt with their infant Son (2:23). It was to Nazareth that Jesus returned after His baptism and temptations (4:12-13); and we learn from Luke that the response to Him then was the same as it was on this occasion.

Luke reports that, after the wilderness temptations, "Jesus returned to Galilee in the power of the Spirit; . . . And He came to Nazareth, where He had been brought up; and as was His custom, He entered the synagogue on the Sabbath, and stood up to read" (Luke 4:14a, 16).

Jesus had been away only a short while and was still a familiar figure in the synagogue, where it was "His custom" to be every Sabbath. The crowd assembled on this particular Sabbath was essentially the same as it had been for many years; but Jesus was not the same. During the intervening time He had begun His ministry and suddenly become famous, because from the onset of His work the "news about Him spread through all the surrounding district, . . . and [He] was praised by all" (vv. 14b, 15b).

After Jesus stood and read the familiar messianic text of Isaiah 61:1-2, He handed the scroll to the synagogue attendant and sat down to comment on the reading. (The reader always stood to read the Scripture and then sat down as he gave an interpretation, lest he give the impression that his comments were equal in authority to God's Word.) As He began to interpret, Jesus said, "Today this Scripture has been fulfilled in your hearing"; and He probably made other comments as well. At first the people did not understand that Jesus was referring to Himself, because their initial response was quite favorable: "All were speaking well of Him, and wondering at the gracious words which were falling from His lips; and they were saying, 'Is this not Joseph's son?'" (Luke 4:17-22).

Knowing that the people's praise was based merely on faithless recognition of His popularity and power, Jesus began to expose their real motives. He knew they wanted Him to duplicate in Nazareth the miracles He had performed in Capernaum. And He knew that if He complied with their demand they still would not accept Him as the Messiah, because "no prophet is welcome in his home town." In further rebuke of their hypocrisy and faithlessness, He reminded them that in the days of Elijah God had shut up the rain in Israel for three-and-a-half years and caused a great famine. During that time the Lord showed mercy on none of the many suffering widows in Israel but showed great mercy on a Gentile widow of Zarephath. He also reminded them that during the time of Elisha, God cleansed no lepers in Israel but did cleanse the leprosy of the Gentile Naaman of Syria (vv. 23-27). They could not have missed Jesus' powerful, rebuking point that a believing Gentile is dearer to God than an unbelieving Jew.

When Jesus made clear that He understood their wicked motives and would not bend to their hardhearted provincial desire to have their own display of miracles, "all in the synagogue were filled with rage as they heard these things"; and they rose up and cast Him out of the city, and led Him to the brow of the hill on which their city had been built, in order to throw Him down the cliff" (vv. 28-29). In their attempt to kill

Jesus, their evil character and unbelief became apparent. They wanted entertainment by Jesus and benefit for themselves from the miracle worker, not conviction of sin and a message of salvation by Jesus the Messiah.

From Jesus' second, and similar, encounter with His former neighbors in Nazareth we can learn four important truths about unbelief: it blurs the obvious, builds up the irrelevant, blinds to the truth, and blocks the supernatural.

UNBELIEF BLURS THE OBVIOUS

And coming to His home town He began teaching them in their synagogue, so that they became astonished, and said, "Where did this man get this wisdom, and these miraculous powers?" (13:54)

The people at the **synagogue** in Jesus' **home town** of Nazareth immediately recognized Him as the person they had known as a boy and young man. They also remembered that less than a year earlier He had worked miracles in other parts of Galilee, had impressed them with His great wisdom, and had so angered them by exposing their hypocrisy and unbelief that they tried to throw Him over the cliff to His death. It soon became evident on this trip to Nazareth that their basic attitude about Him had not changed. They were still **astonished** at His **wisdom** and His **miraculous powers,** and they still refused to recognize the obvious, asking again, **Where then did this man get all these things?**

How could the people for the second time reject Jesus as the Messiah, when it was so obvious that **these things,** at which they marveled, could only have come by God's power? In less than a year He had demonstrated profound wisdom and authority beyond anything the people had ever witnessed, or even heard of. He taught profoundly on virtually every subject related to life and death, time and eternity, truth and falsehood, righteousness and sin, God and man, heaven and hell. He taught about regeneration, worship, evangelism, sin, salvation, morality, divorce, murder, service, servanthood, pride, hate, love, anger, jealousy, hypocrisy, prayer, fasting, true and false doctrine, true and false teachers, the Sabbath, the law, discipleship, grace, blasphemy, signs and wonders, repentance, humility, dying to self, obedience to God, and countless other subjects. He taught the truth about everything that pertained to spiritual life and godliness (cf. 2 Pet. 1:3).

Jesus had not studied in any of the famous rabbinical schools and had no more formal training in the Scriptures than the average Jewish man. Consequently, when He taught in the Temple during the feast of booths, the Jewish leaders in Jerusalem marveled at Him, "saying, 'How has this man become learned, having never been educated?'" (John 7:15). Despite the absence of traditional credentials, His spiritual and moral wisdom was so true and profound that it could not be refuted even by His severest critics.

In addition to teaching with great wisdom, Jesus had displayed supernatural power that all but banished sickness and disease from Palestine and had performed miracles of nature that astonished the most hardened skeptics. At the very least, it should have been clear that Jesus was a prophet of God unequalled by any of the Old Testament era. How could the people not believe Jesus was from God, when only divine power and wisdom could explain the greatness of what He said and did?

When Nicodemus came to Jesus at night, he immediately acknowledged that Jesus had "come from God as a teacher; for no one can do these signs that You do unless God is with him" (John 3:2). Even the antagonistic Jewish leaders recognized His power was real, although they illogically and blasphemously attributed it to Satan. One of the greatest apologetics for Jesus' divinity is the clear testimony even of His enemies that He had miraculous powers that no other man had ever had. As Jesus reminded the unbelieving Jews in Jerusalem, "The works which the Father has given Me to accomplish, the very works that I do, bear witness of Me, that the Father has sent Me" (John 5:36). Later in Jerusalem He told another group of Jews who wanted to stone Him, "If I do not do the works of My Father, do not believe Me; but if I do them, though you do not believe Me, believe the works, that you may know and understand that the Father is in Me, and I in the Father" (John 10:37-38). At the end of his gospel John declares, "And there are also many other things which Jesus did, which if they were written in detail, I suppose even the world itself would not contain the books which were written" (21:25).

Like the scribes and Pharisees, the people of Jesus' hometown synagogue refused to make the logical and obvious connection between His power and His divinity because they were willfully unbelieving. The seed of the gospel fell on the hard-packed soil of sin-loving hearts into which God's truth could not make the slightest penetration. As Jesus explained to Nicodemus, "He who believes in Him is not judged; he who does not believe has been judged already, because he has not believed in the name of the only begotten Son of God. And this is the judgment, that the light is come into the world, and men loved the darkness rather than the light; for their deeds were evil. For everyone who does evil hates the light, and does not come to the light, lest his deeds should exposed" (John 3:18-20).

Those who heard and saw Jesus did not reject Him for lack of evidence but in spite of overwhelming evidence. They did not reject Him because they lacked the truth but because they rejected the truth. They refused forgiveness because they wanted to keep their sins. They denied the light because they preferred darkness. The reason for rejecting the Lord has always been that men prefer their own way to His.

The Jewish leaders in Jerusalem marveled at the obvious wisdom and power of Peter and John, knowing "that they were uneducated and untrained men" (Acts 4:13). But just as they had done with Peter's and John's Master, they did not judge the message on its scriptural merits but on its relation to their human traditions—which derived from and appealed to their works-oriented self-righteousness.

When a person willfully rejects the Lord, even the most compelling evidence will not convince Him of divine truth. Cultists and liberal theologians who refuse to acknowledge Jesus as the divine Son of God can find countless ways to discount or explain away the most obvious truths of Scripture. They then congratulate themselves for their intellectualism in explaining Scripture without accepting its truths, for seeming to honor Christ without believing in Him or in what He taught, and for calling themselves by His name while denying His divine nature and power. To such false disciples Jesus continues to say, "Not everyone who says to Me, 'Lord, Lord,' will enter the kingdom of heaven; but he who does the will of My Father who is in heaven" (Matt. 7:21; Luke 6:46).

The person who has heard many clear presentations of the gospel but continually asks for more evidence of its truth simply reveals the obstinacy of his unbelief. As Jesus explained in the story of the rich man and Lazarus, "If they do not listen to Moses and the Prophets, neither will they be persuaded if someone rises from the dead" (Luke 16:31). The person who does not accept the light from God he already has will not believe no matter how much more light he is given.

UNBELIEF BUILDS UP THE IRRELEVANT

"Is not this the carpenter's son? Is not His mother called Mary, and His brothers, James and Joseph and Simon and Judas? And His sisters, are they not all with us? Where then did this man get all these things?" (13:55-56)

Instead of accepting the obvious and overwhelming evidence that Jesus was the Messiah, the people of Nazareth focused their attention on the irrelevant. It was indeed surprising to see someone they had watched grow up and with whom they had gone to synagogue all His life suddenly come on the scene as a great leader—with no formal training and no recognition by the accepted religious hierarchy.

The facts that Jesus was **the carpenter's son** and the Son of **Mary**, that He had **brothers** named **James and Joseph and Simon and Judas** who everyone in Nazareth knew, and that He had **sisters** who still lived there were irrelevant to the issues of His being the Messiah or not. Although the Jews had many incomplete and false notions about the Messiah, they knew He was to come to earth as a man and that He would have to be born into *some* family and live in *some* community. But instead of feeling highly honored that God chose to place His Son in Nazareth to grow up into manhood—as **Mary** felt highly honored to be His mother (Luke 1:48)—the people were skeptical, jealous, and resentful.

From this text and numerous others (see, e. g., Matt. 12:46-47; Luke 2:7; John 7:10; Acts 1:14), it is clear that **Mary** did not live in perpetual virginity, as Roman Catholic heresy claims. After Jesus' birth, Joseph began normal marital relations with his wife, and she bore at least four sons and two daughters by him. **Mary** was a woman of extraordinary godliness, but she was no more divine than any other woman ever born, and certainly was not the mother of God, as Catholic dogma maintains. She even referred to the Lord as "God my Savior" (Luke 1:47), affirming her own sinfulness and need of salvation.

Joseph had been a *tektōn* (**carpenter**), which was the general term for a craftsman who worked with hard material, including wood. He may also have worked with bricks and stones. In any case, he had surely built many houses, windows, doors, yokes, and other things for his neighbors in Nazareth; and many products of his workmanship were probably still being used in the village. Joseph was an ordinary laborer like most other men of the village, and Jesus learned carpentry under him and no doubt took over the business after Joseph died (see Mark 6:3).

The fact that the citizens of Nazareth did not regard Jesus and His family as being out of the ordinary completely undercuts myths that attribute bizarre miracles to Him when He was a child. One story maintains that whenever He found a bird with a broken wing, He would stroke it gently and send it flying on its way healed and healthy. This text completely mitigates against such fabrications.

When He came to earth, Jesus emptied Himself of certain divine prerogatives, "taking the form of a bond-servant, and being made in the likeness of men" (Phil. 2:7). And although He was sinless and morally perfect during every minute of His life, His perfection was clearly not of the sort that called attention to itself or set Him apart as strange or peculiar. To those who knew Him as a child and young man, Jesus was simply a carpenter and a **carpenter's son.** It was partly over the commonness of Jesus and His family that the people of Nazareth stumbled. They found it impossible to accept Him even as a great human teacher, much less as the divine Messiah.

It is tragic that small issues can be used as great excuses for not believing. The people of Nazareth were like people throughout the history of the church who can find every foolish reason to justify their rejection of the gospel. They don't like the attitude of the one who witnesses to them; they think most church people are hypocrites; they think the preacher is too loud or too soft, too stuffy or too overbearing; and the services are too formal or too informal. They are offended at the slightest things Christians do and construe the insignificant as being all important. They put up one smoke screen after another to excuse their unwillingness to believe the clear and demanding claims and promises of Christ.

As a means of escape or self-justification, unbelief diverts attention away from the truth. The genuine seeker may have many questions about the gospel before he is ready to commit himself to Christ. But his sincerity is proven by his willingness to accept the truth once it is explained. Each new ray of light leads him closer to belief. For the confirmed unbeliever, on the other hand, each new truth prompts him to raise another objection, and his argument against that truth pushes him still further from salvation.

It is characteristic of unbelief to disguise itself, and in order to hide their self-satisfaction and refusal to accept the clear evidence about Jesus, the people of Nazareth dismissed Him on the basis of having known Him since He was a child and of knowing His family as ordinary citizens of the community. They allowed pride, jealousy, resentment, embarrassment, and a host of other wicked and petty feelings to fill their hearts and become barriers to salvation.

UNBELIEF BLINDS TO THE TRUTH

And they took offense at Him. But Jesus said to them, "A prophet is not without honor except in his home town, and in his own household." (13:57)

Took offense is from *skandalizō*, which has the basic idea of causing to stumble or trip up and is the term from which our English scandalize is derived. Jesus' friends and former neighbors were offended by His claims. They were offended by His ordinary background, by the commonness of His family, the limits of His formal training, His lack of official religious status, and many other irrelevant or secondary issues.

We have no full account of what Jesus taught on either occasion in that Nazareth synagogue; but both times He offended the people by what He said. He unmasked their hypocrisy by exposing their wicked desire to see Him perform miracles for miracles' sake (Luke 4:23); and He probably talked to them about their sinfulness and need to repent. In any case, they became antagonistic and **took offense at Him,** because their unbelief blinded them to the truth He taught. "While seeing they [did] not see, and while hearing they [did] not hear, nor [did] they understand" (Matt. 13:13). As Paul declared to the Corinthian believers, Christ is "to Jews a stumbling block, and to Gentiles foolishness" (1 Cor. 1:23).

Until a person is willing to have the hard ground of his heart plowed up by God's truth and to confess and forsake his sin, he will be offended by the gospel. Until a person faces his sin in penitence, the truth of the gospel is hidden from him, and the blessing of the gospel is lost to him.

Again (see Luke 4:24) Jesus reminded the people of Nazareth of the well-known proverb that **a prophet is not without honor except in his home town, and in his own household.** It is often difficult for those who have watched a child grow up as a neighborhood kid to later accept him as a community leader, government official, pastor, or such—to say nothing of accepting him as the divine Son of God! Even when the man is personally liked, it is not easy for him to gain the respect that an outsider of the same capabilities would enjoy. Jesus' brothers eventually came to believe in Him as their Savior (Acts 1:14), but for several years after He began His ministry they did not (John 7:5).

UNBELIEF BLOCKS THE SUPERNATURAL

And He did not do many miracles there because of their unbelief. (13:58)

Some of Jesus' miracles were done in direct response to personal faith; but many others, perhaps most of them, were done regardless of any specific expression of an individual's faith. All of the miracles were done to strengthen the faith of those who believed in Him; but although God can perform miracles where there is no belief, He chose not to perform them where there was hard and willful unbelief. Unbelief, then, became a barrier to divine blessing, and because of the **unbelief** of the people of Nazareth, Jesus **did not do many miracles there.** Mark reports that "He could do no miracles there except that He laid His hands upon a few sick people and healed them" (Mark 6:5). It was not that Jesus lacked supernatural power while He was in Nazareth but that He chose to operate only in response to faith, with the result that the people's unbelief prevented Him from fully exercising that power.

Just as believing saves the soul and enables the power of God to work in its fullness, so unbelief blocked the release of His power and dammed up the flood of His blessing.

Jesus warned, "Do not give what is holy to dogs, and do not throw your pearls before swine, lest they trample them under their feet, and turn and tear you to pieces" (Matt. 7:6). The hardened unbeliever despises the precious truths and blessings of God and will even use them against the Lord and His people if he can. Jesus refused to bend to the request of the hypocritical scribes and Pharisees who wanted to see a sign from Him (Matt. 12:38). "He answered and said to them, 'An evil and adulterous generation craves for a sign; and yet no sign shall be given to it but the sign of Jonah the prophet'" (v. 39). Jesus' miracles were of spiritual benefit only as they led to faith in Him or strengthened those who already believed. For those who refused to believe, His miracles had no spiritual value at all, and He would not perform them in order to entertain or to satisfy ungodly curiosity.

When Jesus and His disciples came upon the man in Jerusalem who had been blind from birth, the "disciples asked Him, saying, 'Rabbi, who sinned, this man or his parents, that he should be born blind?' Jesus answered, 'It was neither that this man sinned, nor his parents; but it was in order that the works of God might be displayed in him'" (John 9:2-3). The man was born blind, Jesus explained, so that his healing could glorify God.

After the man's sight was restored while he was washing in the pool of Siloam as Jesus had commanded, his neighbors could hardly believe he was the same person whom they had known from infancy as totally blind and helpless. He was brought before the Pharisees, who took the occasion to express various opinions about the godliness of Jesus. Because He dared to "work" on the Sabbath by performing a miracle, some of them were certain Jesus could not be from God. Others argued that a person who was not from God could never do such things.

Some of the leaders did not even believe the man had ever been blind, and they called in his parents to testify. When asked to explain what happened to their son, the parents said, "We know that this is our son, and that he was born blind; but how he now sees, we do not know." When the man was called back the second time, the leaders said to him, "Give glory to God; we know that this man is a sinner," referring to Jesus. The man responded that, although he could not be certain about Jesus' sin, he was certain that it was Jesus who had healed him. And he did not believe a sinful man could do such marvelous things as Jesus had undeniably done for him. "If this man were not from God," he insisted, "He could do nothing."

But as the man's testimony became more and more favorable to Jesus, the Pharisees' unbelief only became more and more hardened. They finally said to the man, "'You were born entirely in sins, and are you teaching us?' And they put him out."

After they dismissed the man, Jesus came to him and asked, "Do you believe in the Son of Man?" When he discovered that Jesus was Himself the Son of Man, the former blind man confessed, "'Lord, I believe.' And he worshiped Him." Then Jesus said, "For judgment I came into this world, that those who do not see may see; and that those who see may become blind." In reply to some of the Pharisees who asked Him, "'We are not blind too, are we?' Jesus said to them, 'If you were blind, you would have no sin; but since you say, "We see," your sin remains'" (see John 9:6-41).

As those Pharisees perfectly illustrate, when unbelief investigates the supernatural work of God, it comes up empty. It meets a dead end when it tries to probe divine things. It cannot recognize the works of God because it will not recognize the truth of God.

Fear That Forfeits Christ (14:1-13)

At that time Herod the tetrarch heard the news about Jesus, and said to his servants, "This is John the Baptist; he has risen from the dead; and that is why miraculous powers are at work in him." For when Herod had John arrested, he bound him, and put him in prison on account of Herodias, the wife of his brother Philip. For John had been saying to him, "It is not lawful for you to have her." And although he wanted to put him to death, he feared the multitude, because they regarded him as a prophet. But when Herod's birthday came, the daughter of Herodias danced before them and pleased Herod. Thereupon he promised with an oath to give her whatever she asked. And having been prompted by her mother, she said, "Give me here on a platter the head of John the Baptist." And although he was grieved, the king commanded it to be given because of his oaths, and because of his dinner guests. And he sent and had John beheaded in the prison. And his head was brought on a platter and given to the girl; and she brought it to her mother. And his disciples came and took away the body and buried it; and they went and reported to Jesus.

Now when Jesus heard it, He withdrew from there in a boat, and to a lonely place by Himself; and when the multitudes heard of this, they followed Him on foot from the cities. (14:1-13)

C. I. Scofield appropriately referred to the events of Matthew 14-23 as "The Ministry of the Rejected King." Christ the King had been rejected by His own people; but, with His disciples, He continued to preach the kingdom. During the early part of this period the disciples witnessed remarkable incidents that illustrated the four basic responses to the gospel portrayed in the parable of the sower.

In this account of John the Baptist's murder we see the second of the eight incidents Matthew records. The first portrayed Jesus' rejection by the resentful people of His hometown of Nazareth, who were deeply offended that a man they had known as merely a carpenter's son would presume to confront them and even to proclaim Himself the Messiah (Matt. 13:53-58).

The second incident, recorded in this text, links Herod the tetrarch's rejection of Jesus with the execution of John the Baptist. Like the first incident, this one illustrates the gospel's falling on hard and stony soil that God's saving truth cannot penetrate. The first story deals with a town that rejected Christ; this one deals with a man who rejects Him. The first deals with the common people; this one deals with an earthly king who opposes the divine King. The first deals with the treatment of the Messiah Himself; this one deals with the treatment of the Messiah's forerunner. The first deals with rejection based on jealous resentment; this one deals with rejection based on fear. Behind both rejections was the common selfish pride of the unbelieving human heart.

This true account is more incredible than the most bizarre soap opera. It is a story of infidelity, divorce, remarriage, incest, political intrigue, jealously, spite, revenge, lewdness, lust, cold-heartedness, cruelty, brutality, violence, ungodly remorse, and godly mourning. But above all, it is the story of godless fear and the power of such fear to confuse, deceive, corrupt, destroy, and damn. Nowhere in Scripture is the truth "The fear of man brings a snare" (Prov. 29:25) more vividly illustrated than here. It is one of the most tragic yet triumphant texts in the Word of God.

The focal point of this brief episode is Herod's reaction to Jesus. Then, in a flashback to previous events, the reason for Herod's reaction is given and is followed by Jesus' response to the atrocity behind that reason.

HEROD'S REACTION

At that time Herod the tetrarch heard the news about Jesus, and said to his servants, "This is John the Baptist; he has risen from the dead; and that is why miraculous powers are at work in him." (14:1-2)

Kairos (**time**) refers to a special season or period of time and in this context indicates the general season when Jesus was facing increasing hostility and rejection. He had been ministering for about a year, teaching, preaching, and performing many signs and wonders— healing every kind of disease, raising the dead, and casting out demons. The exact chronology is difficult to determine, but **that time** likely covered the year and a half to two years directly after Jesus' baptism.

Although **Herod the tetrarch** was not a Jew and had little interest in them or their religion, he eventually **heard the news about Jesus**. The term **tetrarch** technically referred to a "ruler of a fourth part," but it came to be used as a general title for any subordinate ruler of a Roman province or region. He was not a true king in the sense that his father, Herod the Great, was; but he coveted the title and was often called by it (cf. v. 9). He would later ask the emperor Caligula to proclaim him king, but was refused. He was a relatively minor potentate in Palestine who had little power or influence outside his own jurisdiction.

Herod the tetrarch was a son of Herod the Great by his fourth wife, Malthake, a Samaritan, and was a half brother of Herod Philip, the son of his father's third wife, Mariamne the Boethusian. Herod the Great was an Idumean; and because he not only was a Gentile but was a descendant of Esau and had married a Samaritan, he had been especially despised by the Jews. His cold-blooded atrocities—such as his having all the members of the Sanhedrin put to death for daring to challenge his authority, his having at least one of his wives and two of his sons executed, and his slaying all the male babies of Bethlehem in an unsuccessful attempt to try to destroy the Messiah—made him more hated still.

In secular history **Herod the tetrarch** was known as Herod Antipas, and after the death of his father, Herod the Great, the Romans divided the kingdom (which comprised most of Palestine) among three of his many sons. The two besides Antipas were his brother Archelaus (see Matt. 2:22) and his half brother Philip (see 14:3). Archelaus was given the southern provinces of Judea and Samaria, Philip was given the northern provinces of Trachonitis and Iturea, and **Herod** Antipas was given the area in between, which included Galilee and Perea.

At the time **Herod the tetrarch heard the news about Jesus,** Herod the Great had long been dead, and this **Herod** was in his thirty-second year of rule. He spent most of the year at his palace in Tiberias, on the southwest shore of the Sea of Galilee. But he also spent considerable time at the massive fortress palace his father had built at Machaerus, seven miles east of the northern tip of the Dead Sea.

It is interesting that, although Jesus ministered in Galilee more than in any other region, there is no evidence that He visited or even passed through Tiberias. It was within walking distance of Capernaum, Nazareth, Cana, and many other places Jesus went, but, as far as we know, He never set foot in that city. The Lord may have avoided Tiberias in order not to prematurely arouse Herod's attention. And it may have been for that reason, along with the pagan king's general disdain for the Jews and his preoccupation with luxurious living, that **Herod** seemed to be so long in hearing **the news about Jesus.**

When he finally heard **about Jesus,** Herod was greatly distressed. As he explained **to his servants,** he thought **Jesus** was **John the Baptist,** who had **risen from the dead.** Because of haunting guilt for having murdered John, Herod was afraid he had come back **from the dead** to seek revenge.

We learn from Luke that this notion did not originate with Herod but that he had "heard of all that was happening; and he was greatly perplexed, because it was said by some that John had risen from the dead, and by some that Elijah had appeared, and by others, that one of the prophets of old had risen again" (Luke 9:7-8; cf. Matt. 16:14). Herod confessed, "I myself had John beheaded"; and out of morbid curiosity "he kept trying to see Him" (Luke 9:9). In his guilt-ridden mind he had decided that this **Jesus** was none other than **John the Baptist . . . risen from the dead.**

The angel of the Lord told John's father, Zacharias, that his son would "go as a forerunner before [Jesus] in the spirit and power of Elijah" (Luke 1:17). Elijah had been endowed with great miraculous powers, and it may be that John the Baptist performed miracles of which we are not told. In any case, Herod obviously believed John had such gifts and was convinced that the **miraculous powers** that were **at work in** Jesus proved He was John returned from the dead.

HEROD'S REASON

For when Herod had John arrested, he bound him, and put him in prison on account of Herodias, the wife of his brother Philip. For John had been saying to him, "It is not lawful for you to have her." And although he wanted to put him to death, he feared the multitude, because they regarded him as a prophet. But when Herod's birthday came, the daughter of Herodias danced before them and pleased Herod. Thereupon he promised with an oath to give her whatever she asked. And having been prompted by her mother, she said, "Give me here on a platter the head of John the Baptist." And although he was grieved, the king commanded it to be given because of his oaths, and because of his dinner guests. And he sent and had John beheaded in the prison. And his head was brought on a platter and given to the girl; and she brought it to her mother. (14:3-11)

These verses are a flashback to events that began a year or more earlier, just before Jesus started His ministry—to the time **when Herod had John arrested, . . . bound him, and put him in prison** (see Matt. 4:12).

Before John's birth, the angel declared that he would "be great in the sight of the Lord, and . . . be filled with the Holy Spirit, while yet in his mother's womb" (Luke 1:15). Jesus testified that "among those born of women there has not arisen anyone greater than John the Baptist" (Matt. 11:11). The forerunner of the Messiah was a remarkable man, single-mindedly dedicated to fulfilling his divine mission of paving the way for his Lord and Master. In genuine humility he was happy to have his own fame and influence decrease as that of Jesus increased (John 3:30).

The almost single theme of John's preaching was, "Repent, for the kingdom of heaven is at hand" (Matt. 3:2). As hundreds came and confessed their sins in preparation for the Messiah, John would baptize them as a symbol of their desire for a cleansed heart. He confronted sin and called for holiness; yet despite his somber message and ascetic life-style, he was amazingly popular and respected by the people. "Jerusalem was going out to him, and all Judea, and all the district around the Jordan" (Matt. 3:5).

By extreme contrast, **Herod** Antipas was evil, debauched, shameless, henpecked, lustful, and given to every kind of sinful excess. He had more of a conscience than his bestial father, but he did not have the courage to follow it. It could be said that to the extent John was admired and honored, Herod was despised and feared.

Instead of putting John to death, as he wanted to do (v. 5), **Herod had John arrested, . . . bound** and put **in prison,** probably in the dungeon at his palace at Machaerus. The palace was located on a mountain higher even than the city of Jerusalem and offered a beautiful and dramatic view. But the dungeon was dug deep into the earth beneath, and archaeologists have discovered the many places where prisoners were chained to the walls. There was no natural light and only dank, foul air to breathe. Here John the Baptist was incarcerated for about a year until his execution.

Herod had imprisoned **John . . . on account of Herodias, the wife of his brother Philip. For John had been saying to him, "It is not lawful for you to have her."** The tetrarch had taken **Herodias** as his own wife after seducing her away from his half **brother Philip** while on a visit to Rome. In order to marry her, he had to divorce his present wife, the daughter of king Aretas, with whom the marriage of his daughter had sealed a political and military alliance. Aretas ruled Nabatean Arabia, whose capital was the famed fortress city of Petra, located about fifty miles southeast of the Dead Sea. Aretas was so angered by the treatment of his daughter that he destroyed most of Herod's army and would have slain the tetrarch as well, had not the Roman army intervened.

Herodias is one of the most wicked and perverse women mentioned in Scripture, perhaps second only to Jezebel. Although she was at first beguiled by **Herod,** it was not long until he was being manipulated by her. Because both **Herod** and **Herodias** were already married, their marriage to each other was doubly **not lawful.** The Holy Spirit refused to recognize her as Herod's wife and directed Matthew to refer to her as **the wife of his brother Philip,** although she had been divorced from **Philip** for a number of years. The new marriage not only was unlawful but incestuous, because **Herodias** was the daughter of Aristobulus, another half brother of **Herod,** making her Herod's niece.

It is not known exactly where and how **John** the Baptist first confronted **Herod** about his unlawful marriage. It is possible the tetrarch had summoned **John** to his palace, hoping to have some astounding miracle performed on his behalf, just as He later expected of Jesus (Luke 23:8). But regardless of who initiated the meeting, John presented the king with a scathing rebuke rather than a miraculous sign. From the wording, **John had been saying to him** (cf. Mark 6:18), it seems that **John** had rebuked the king and his wife on more than one occasion.

Both **Herod** and **Herodias** were incensed at the prophet's presumption, and she, more than he, **wanted to put him to death.** Had it not been that Herod **feared the multitude, because they regarded him as a prophet,** John would have been executed immediately.

John was neither a compromiser nor a diplomat. His only fear was of the Lord, and he no more hesitated confronting Herod and Herodias with their wickedness than he had hesitated confronting the unrepentant Pharisees and Sadducees whom he called a brood of vipers (Matt. 3:7).

Such godly boldness, which does not consider the consequences, is the hallmark of prophetic greatness. The faithful man of God confronts sin wherever it is and by whomever it is committed, regardless of the power they might have over him—including power over his life. That holy boldness was the mark of Stephen, of Paul, of Peter, and of innumerable other saints of God who, throughout the nineteen centuries of the church, have forfeited their lives rather than their message. The great New Testament scholar A. T. Robertson wrote, "It cost him his head; but it is better to have a head like John the Baptist and lose it than to have an ordinary head and keep it."

Josephus said of John: "Now when many others came in crowds about him, for they were greatly moved by hearing his words, Herod, who feared lest the great influence John had over the people might put it into his power and inclination to raise a rebellion, thought it best by putting him to death to prevent any mischief he might cause."

Just as John was fearful of nothing and no one except God, Herod feared almost everything and everyone but God. He not only **feared the multitude,** but also feared John the Baptist, his wife, and his peers (v. 9). He feared another attack by Aretas, and, as Josephus reported, he feared a rebellion by his own people—inspired by, and perhaps even led by, John the Baptist. And Herod feared the emperor might replace him with someone more in favor with Rome. That fear was well grounded, because some years after this, his jealous and scheming nephew, Agrippa (the brother of Herodias), convinced the emperor Caligula that Herod was planning a rebellion. Perhaps because Caligula did not fully trust Agrippa's word, Herod and Herodias suffered exile to Gaul (modern France) rather than execution, which was the normal penalty for treason.

Herod's feelings about John were ambivalent; he was both fearful and fascinated. Mark reports that "Herod was afraid of John, knowing that he was a righteous and holy man, and kept him safe. And when he heard him, he was very perplexed; but he used to enjoy listening to him" (Mark 6:20). The king enjoyed listening to the man he wanted to put to death! These audiences with Herod no doubt were John's only respite from the torments of prison; but to John they were not an escape but opportunities to witness for his Lord and to try to bring his persecutor to repentance and salvation.

From the passage in Mark 6, as well as from the fact that Herod was grieved at Herodias's request for the head of John (Matt. 14:9), it seems that the king had developed a certain fondness for John, or at least a more respectful fear. But his feelings for John were no match for his fear of his wife and his friends.

Herodias had few equals in immorality, evil cunning, or vindictiveness. From the time of John's first rebuke she had been scheming to rid herself of this meddlesome prophet who rankled her own feelings and also fueled the loathing her Jewish subjects already had for her. She was biding her time, waiting for the right opportunity—which presented itself **when Herod's birthday came** and **the**

daughter of Herodias danced before them and pleased Herod.

From Josephus we learn that the name of this **daughter** was Salome, whose father was Philip, her mother's first husband and Herod's half brother. **Herodias** was so hate-filled, vengeful, and immoral that she had no compunction about involving her **daughter** both in a lewd dance before her stepfather and his guests and in the ploy to have John murdered.

In the ancient world, **birthday** celebrations were entirely Gentile and pagan, and the Jews, with good reason, considered them shameful. Roman nobles frequently held stag birthday parties in which gluttony, excessive drinking, erotic dancing, and sexual indulgence were common. The phrase *Herodes dies* (Latin for "Herod's birthday") became an epithet for such orgiastic festivals.

Pleased was a euphemism for "sexually aroused," and the drunken king was so enamored of his stepdaughter that he rashly **promised with an oath to give her whatever she asked,** even up to half his kingdom (Mark 6:23). This was the chance Herodias had been waiting for, and, **prompted by her mother,** Salome asked Herod, **"Give me here on a platter the head of John the Baptist."** It is obvious that the provocative dance was planned by Herodias for the purpose of evoking just such a promise from her drunken, leering, lecherous husband. And lest Herod change his mind after sobering up, Herodias told her daughter to ask for John's head **here on a platter** "right away" (Mark 6:25).

In his gluttonous, lustful stupor the king had been easily taken in by his scheming wife and her seductive daughter. He had lost all dignity, all sensibility, and what little desire for the right that he may have had. Wanting to appear the magnanimous benefactor before his guests, he had boxed himself in and was now completely vulnerable to his conniving wife.

And although he was grieved, the king commanded it to be given because of his oaths, and because of his dinner guests. It was not that the word of **the king** was respected and that to break **his oaths** would tarnish his reputation, because he was noted for his dishonor and duplicity. But in the ancient Near East a promise made with an oath was considered sacred and inviolable (cf. Matt. 5:33), especially when made by a ruler. And although Herod had no concern for principle, he had great concern for appearance. By breaking his word so soon after giving it, he would have been embarrassed in front of **his dinner guests,** who doubtlessly included many political and military dignitaries.

Herod **was grieved,** but his grief had nothing to do with remorse for sin or with genuine repentance. Like Pilate—who knew Jesus was innocent and would have freed Him except for continued pressure by the Jewish leaders (Luke 23:4, 14-16, 20, 22-25; cf. John 19:12)—Herod cowardly capitulated to what he knew was unjust and vindictive. Even drunk, he knew he had been tricked; but his pride would not let him do what was right. Instead of admitting the foolish excess of his promise, the king allowed himself to be used to commit an enormous crime—all to save a reputation he did not have. With the help of his wicked wife and unprincipled stepdaughter, his cup of iniquity was filled.

Quickly and coldly John was decapitated in his cell **and his head was brought on a platter and given to the girl; and she brought it to her mother.** Gruesome and ghoulish as that act was, such things were not uncommon in those days. Potentates had life and death power over their subjects and prisoners, and that power was frequently exercised and seldom questioned. Herodias had an ancestor named Alexander Junius, who held a feast at which he had eight hundred rebels crucified before the assembled guests. While the men were hanging on their crosses, their wives and children were slain in front of their eyes.

One writer comments, "When the dish was brought in with the bleeding head on it, no doubt [Salome] took it daintily in her hands lest a drop of it should stain her, and she tripped away to her mother as if bearing her some choice dish of food from the king's table. It was not uncommon to bring the head of one who had been slain to the person who ordered it, as a sure proof that the command had been obeyed." It is reported that when the head of Cicero was brought to Fulvia, the wife of Antony, that she spat on it, pulled its tongue out and drove her hairpin through it. The early church Father Jerome believed that is what Herodias did with the head of John. That particular barbarism cannot be verified, but it would not have been the least out of character for Herodias to have done such a ghastly thing.

Herod's morbid fascination with John and with the miraculous and supernatural had nothing to do with genuine seeking after the truth and certainly nothing to do with seeking salvation. It was the religious curiosity of unbelief that is impregnable to God's truth, love, or grace.

After Herod had John beheaded, he inquired about Jesus and "kept trying to see Him" (Luke 9:9). But Jesus made no effort to see Herod and would not allow Herod to see Him until it was His Father's time. Jesus once sent a message to the king when it was reported that Herod wanted to kill Him, saying, "Go and tell that fox, 'Behold, I cast out demons and perform cures today and tomorrow, and the third day I reach My goal'" (Luke 13:32). Jesus went about His mission and left the king to his unresolved fear, to his unrelenting sin, and to his doom of damnation. After His appearance before the Sanhedrin and Pilate, Jesus was sent to Herod and they saw each other for the first time. "Now Herod was very glad when he saw Jesus; for he had wanted to see Him for a long time, because he had been hearing about Him and was hoping to see some sign performed by Him. And he questioned Him at some length; but He answered him nothing. . . . And Herod with his soldiers, after treating Him with contempt and mocking Him, dressed Him in a gorgeous robe and sent Him back to Pilate" (Luke 23:8-9, 11).

In the greatest of irony, "Herod and Pilate became friends with one another that very day; for before they had been at enmity with each other" (23:12). Two ruthless men and former enemies now built a friendship around the common bond of crucifying the Son of God!

Herod rejected Christ, and Christ rejected Herod. For fear of a woman, for fear of his reputation, for fear of his peers, for fear of his throne—and for *lack* of fear for God—he damned his soul forever.

JESUS' RESPONSE

And his disciples came and took away the body and buried it; and they went and reported to Jesus.

Now when Jesus heard it, He withdrew from there in a boat, and to a lonely place by Himself; and when the multitudes heard of this, they followed Him on foot from the cities. (14:12-13)

In a beautiful ending to an ugly scene, John's **disciples came and took away the body and buried it**. It is hard to imagine the pain they must have experienced in carrying the decapitated **body** of the one they dearly loved and had faithfully followed. He was a great and godly man, who had been their friend and teacher, the one under whose fiery preaching they had confessed and forsaken their own sins and under whose inspiration and direction they had perhaps led others to repentance.

Possibly following John's previous instruction, the **disciples** then **went and reported to Jesus** what had happened. John was deeply loved by **Jesus, and when Jesus heard it, He withdrew from there in a boat, to a lonely place by Himself.** As Mark explains in more detail, Jesus was **by Himself** with His disciples, whom he asked to go with Him "'to a lonely place and rest a while' (For there were many people coming and going, and they did not even have time to eat)" (Mark 6:31).

Some commentators suggest that Jesus left the area for fear of meeting the same fate as John; but if John was not afraid of Herod, surely Jesus was not. And why would Jesus have wanted to escape a threat that was only potential, when He knew that, not many months later, He would walk willingly to certain death? If Jesus left to escape possible arrest by Herod, it was only because that was not in the Father's plan or timetable for the Son.

John the Baptist was the first martyr to die for Christ, and it seems certain that Jesus took this opportunity to further prepare His disciples for what lay ahead for them. Christ Himself would be the next to die; and all the other twelve (including Matthias, Judas's replacement) apparently suffered martyrdom, except for John, who died in exile.

Although Christians in most parts of the world today have relative freedom to practice and propagate their faith, many believers are suffering a fate like John's. When they convert to Christianity, their families disown them, declare them to be dead, and sometimes even murder them. Countless thousands forfeit their jobs, their freedom to worship, and even the right to teach their faith to their own children. Many are imprisoned, tortured, exiled, and publicly maligned. But like John the Baptist, they will not deny their Lord to save their rights, their freedom, or their lives.

The Miraculous
Feeding (14:14-21)

And when He went ashore, He saw a great multitude, and felt compassion for
them, and healed their sick. And when it was evening, the disciples came to
Him, saying, "The place is desolate, and the time is already past; so send the
multitudes away, that they may go into the villages and buy food for
themselves." But Jesus said to them, "They do not need to go away; you give
them something to eat!" And they said to Him, "We have here only five loaves
and two fish." And He said, "Bring them here to Me." And ordering the
multitudes to recline on the grass, He took the five loaves and the two fish,
and looking up toward heaven, He blessed the food, and breaking the loaves
He gave them to the disciples, and the disciples gave to the multitudes, and
they all ate, and were satisfied. And they picked up what was left over of the
broken pieces, twelve full baskets. And there were about five thousand men
who ate, aside from women and children. (14:14-21)

The fact that the feeding of the five thousand is the only one of Jesus' many
miracles recorded in all four gospels, testifies to its unique importance. In each gospel
account this miracle is placed at the climax of the Lord's ministry.

When Jesus began His extensive Galilean ministry, it was almost completely
public. The Lord sought out the crowds, going from town to town and city to city,

proclaiming the gospel of the kingdom to all who would listen. The King openly manifested Himself before the people of Israel and offered them the opportunity to receive Him as their Lord.

But from the earliest days, the religious leaders were skeptical; and soon they became unfriendly and ultimately hostile. The clearer Jesus' message became, the higher the flames of their opposition flared. With the death of John the Baptist and Herod's fear that Jesus was John returned from the dead, the political antagonism was also becoming manifest. Herod felt threatened by Jesus just as he had been by John the Baptist; and he would not have hesitated doing to Jesus what he had done to John.

The reaction of the people was mixed and fickle. Although the citizens of Nazareth had twice rejected Jesus because of their familiarity with Him as a boy and young man, most of the people were still fascinated by His miracles. With the miracle of creating food for feeding the crowd of five thousand, Jesus' popularity reached its pinnacle as the people tried to take Him by force to be their king and deliverer (John 6:15).

As the religious and political opposition became more intense and the allegiance of the crowds more vacillating, Jesus began to spend less time in public and more time in private with His disciples. During the last year of His life, He devoted the majority of His attention to the twelve, preparing them for what was soon to happen to Him in the crucifixion and for what would soon after that happen to them as they embarked on their task of laying the foundation for His church.

When the disciples of John the Baptist brought the news of John's death to Jesus, He withdrew from the area of Capernaum so that He could be alone with His own disciples (Matt. 14:13a; cf. Mark 6:31). Jesus was not afraid for His life, because He knew no one could take it from Him unless He permitted it (John 10:18). He withdrew to avoid premature confrontation with Herod, to be alone with His Father, and to explain the significance of John's death to His disciples.

Jesus also needed refreshment. Even if all the reaction to Him had been positive, He would have been physically drained after such a rigorous schedule of teaching and healing. The growing opposition of His enemies, the fickleness of the multitudes, and the continued misunderstanding and immaturity of His disciples made the drain immeasurably worse.

But when the multitudes heard that Jesus had gone to the other side of the Sea of Galilee, "they followed Him on foot from the cities" (Matt. 14:13b). Some of the people even arrived before Jesus and the disciples did (Mark 6:33), while the lame and sick obviously took much longer. But almost all of them came out of selfish motives, "because they were seeing the signs which He was performing on those who were sick" (John 6:2). They came to be healed or to watch the healings. Few came for what Jesus could do for them spiritually.

The majority of the multitude were thrill seekers, whose ranks at this time were probably swelled by Jews passing through Galilee on their way to the annual Passover celebration in Jerusalem (John 6:4). Their perspective was self-centered and self-indulgent. In addition to wanting to be healed or entertained, many no doubt hoped this great miracle worker would prove Himself to be the political Messiah who would use His power to overthrow the hated Roman oppressors and their puppet Herod.

But the expectations of the people neither determined nor undermined the importance of the occasion. As He often does, God chose to accomplish His purposes in the very face of ungodly human motives and desires. In Matthew 14:14-21 the Lord's plan continues to unfold flawlessly according to His perfect divine will.

THE DEEDS OF PIETY

And when He went ashore, He saw a great multitude, and felt compassion for them, and healed their sick. (14:14)

As Jesus **went ashore, He saw a great multitude,** whose men alone numbered five thousand, "aside from women and children" (v. 21). Because women seemed especially drawn to Jesus, it is likely many of them came together in groups or with their fathers or brothers—in addition to those who came with their husbands and children. Children were considered a great blessing from the Lord, and most families in those days were large. It is therefore not unreasonable to estimate that the total crowd exceeded twenty-five thousand.

The normal inclination would have been to ignore the people and keep going or to have dismissed the **multitude,** telling them that no healings or other signs would be performed. It would have been easy to go so far into the hills that most of the people could not have followed or to go back into the boat and head for a location where they would not be discovered.

But Jesus did not follow the usual human inclinations and, although He was exhausted and in great need of rest, He was drawn to them because He **felt compassion for them.** *Splanchnizomai* (to have **compassion**) means literally to be moved in one's bowels, or viscera, where the ancients considered the emotions and feelings to reside. The Son of God was not remote or coldly calculating and analytical concerning men's needs but was deeply moved by the suffering, confusion, despair, and spiritual lostness of those around Him. Jesus felt pain, experiencing genuine anguish for the suffering of others, whether they were believer or unbeliever, Jew or Gentile, man or woman, young or old, wealthy or poor. He must have felt much as He did when He approached Lazarus's grave and wept (John 11:35) and when He looked out over Jerusalem through tears and said, "If you had known in this day, even you, the things which make for peace! But now they have been hidden from your eyes" (Luke 19:42). He represented the compassionate heart of God even more fully than had Jeremiah, who declared to rebellious Judah, "But if you will not listen to [God's warning], my soul will sob in secret for such pride; and my eyes will bitterly weep and flow down with tears" (Jer. 13:17).

In His great mercy, Christ extended His **compassion** even to the shallow, self-centered thrill seekers. He again revealed the loving heart of God toward those who would not understand or believe and who He knew would ultimately reject Him. The

Lord likewise empowered the apostles to cure disease, cast out demons, and heal the crippled and afflicted—with no restrictions or qualifications (Matt. 10:1)—rather than to demonstrate God's power by moving buildings from one place to another or by doing other such dazzling but impersonal wonders. That kind of miracle would have demonstrated the Lord's power, but it would have shown nothing of His compassion and mercy.

Jesus also **felt compassion** because of His perfect perception of hell and the torment those would face who did not receive Him. Even as He lovingly healed their bodies, He had infinitely greater concern to heal their souls. Even after Jesus healed a body, it could become sick or crippled again. But when He heals a sin-diseased soul, it is forever freed from sin's dominion and penalty.

Arrhōstos (**sick**) means to be weak, without strength. These afflicted ones whom Jesus **healed** obviously made a special effort to follow Him around the northern end of the Sea of Galilee. Most of them probably had to be carried or helped along by relatives or friends, and they arrived many hours after the rest of the crowd. Above all else they wanted to be healed by this Man who had such compassionate power.

Jesus postponed His rest, His privacy, His time alone with the disciples, and even His time with His Father in order to meet the needs of those helpless people who suffered.

THE DULLNESS OF PERSPECTIVE

And when it was evening, the disciples came to Him, saying, "The place is desolate, and the time is already past; so send the multitudes away, that they may go into the villages and buy food for themselves." But Jesus said to them, "They do not need to go away; you give them something to eat!" And they said to Him, "We have here only five loaves and two fish." (14:15-17)

The Jews had two periods of **evening**, one from three to six and the other from six to nine. This was the first **evening**, which was just prior to sunset. Because of the lateness in the day, **the disciples** were concerned about what the crowd would have to eat. **The place was desolate**, many miles from the nearest town, which, in any case, could not have provided food for such a vast horde of people. Not only was it near the end of the day, but the long trip had doubtlessly made the people hungrier than usual.

From John's account we learn that Jesus had brought up the matter of feeding the multitude much earlier in the day. Even while the "great multitude was coming to Him," Jesus had said to Philip, "Where are we to buy bread, that these may eat?" (John 6:5). Jesus did not ask Philip the question in order to get advice but "to test him; for He Himself knew what He was intending to do" (v. 6). Philip was from that area and would most likely have known what food would have been available; but Jesus was hoping Philip would look to Him rather than to human and earthly resources. Unfortunately, Philip was more awed at the magnitude of the crowd than the magnitude of Jesus' power, and he responded incredulously, "Two hundred denarii worth of bread is not sufficient for them, for everyone to receive a little" (v. 7). A denarius was the normal day's wage for a common laborer, but it was obvious that nearly six month's of such wages would not be enough to feed the thousands of people that were assembled. Philip knew they did not have a fraction of the money needed to buy enough food, even if they bought the cheapest bread available.

Either at this point or later in the day, Andrew discovered a small boy who had "five barley loaves and two fish"; but, like Philip, he was quick to express his despair: "but what are these for so many people?" (John 6:8-9). Apparently the Lord let Philip and Andrew continue to think about His request during the rest of the day, while He was healing the multitudes and also "speaking to them about the kingdom of God" (Luke 9:11). He provided a day-long test of the disciples' faith.

As we look back on the scene from our two-thousand-year vantage point, it seems impossible that even when **Jesus said to them, "They do not need to go away; you give them something to eat!"** the idea of His feeding the people miraculously did not enter the disciples' minds. Seeing no further than their own resources, they replied, **We have here only five loaves and two fish.** It would seem to have required so little faith and to have been so natural for the disciples to expect Jesus to feed the crowd. But they were like a person who stands in front of Niagara Falls and asks where he can find a drink. They were face to face with the supreme power in the universe and yet were spiritually blind. They knew it, but they did not know it. Had anyone asked them if Jesus could do such a thing, their answer would have been an unhesitating and unanimous, "Of course He can!" But even when prompted by Jesus' suggestion, they saw their own lack instead of His sufficiency.

We are tempted to think that, had we been there, our first thought would have been to ask Jesus to feed the multitudes, as He had proved Himself capable of doing hundreds of times. What could have been a more obvious solution than to have the Son of God create food to feed this crowd, just as He had created wine for the wedding guests at Cana? That would hardly have been an impossible challenge to the One who healed every sort of disease, raised the dead, cast out demons, walked on water, and instantaneously calmed a fierce storm. Yet, how many times has every believer faced a crisis that seemed overwhelming and insurmountable and failed to consider the Lord's power?

Despite two years of walking with the Lord, hearing Him teach God's truth and seeing Him demonstrate miraculous power, the twelve were too spiritually dull to see the obvious. They were looking only with their human eyes and only at human resources.

THE DISPLAY OF POWER

And He said, "Bring them here to Me." And ordering the multitudes to recline on the grass, He took the five loaves and the two fish, and looking up toward heaven, He blessed the food, and breaking the loaves He gave them to the disciples, and the disciples gave to the multitudes, and they all ate, and were satisfied. And they picked up what was left over of the broken pieces, twelve

full baskets. And there were about five thousand men who ate, aside from women and children. (14:18-21)

Here is the primary focus of the story, in which the disciples' dullness of perspective is overruled by Jesus' display of power.

No doubt with sadness in His eyes, Jesus **said, "Bring them here to Me,"** referring to the loaves and fish. He had to tell the disciples to do what, by this time, should have been second nature to them. He was saying, in effect, "I knew that you did not have sufficient food or money to feed the people, and I knew that you had no way of getting it. I never expected you to feed them from your own resources or by your own power. In asking you to feed them I was asking you to trust Me. Without having to tell you, I was giving you the opportunity to bring to Me what little you had and trust Me for the rest."

The northeastern shore of the Sea of Galilee is often beautiful and green with grass in the spring of the year. But instead of sitting, the people had been standing up in order to see and hear and Jesus better. He therefore ordered **the multitudes to recline on the grass,** to make themselves more comfortable and to make distribution of the food easier. He sat them *prasiai prasiai* (which literally means "garden bed by garden bed"), in groups of hundreds and fifties (Mark 6:40), allowing paths between the groups for the disciples to walk while serving. In their brightly-colored garments the crowd must have resembled an enormous mosaic of flower beds or a gigantic quilt spread across the hillside.

The people probably had little if any idea why they were so carefully seated in groups. The disciples may have guessed why, but they still did not know how. When the people were seated, Jesus **took the five loaves and the two fish;** but before He performed the miracle He had planned all along, **looking up toward heaven, He blessed the food,** giving thanks to His heavenly Father (John 6:6, 11; cf. 1 Tim. 4:3-5).

Then the Lord broke **the loaves** and **gave them to the disciples,** who, in turn, **gave to the multitudes, and they all ate.** We are not told exactly at what moment the miracle took place. Apparently it was a continuous multiplication that occurred as the disciples walked among the groups distributing the food. The men could not possibly have carried containers large enough to hold all the food, even with it divided into twelve parts. There was no fanfare and no dramatic change from little to much. The miracle was all but invisible, its magnitude being evident only as the thousands of people **all ate.**

Chortazō (to be **satisfied**) was used of animals who stayed at the feed trough until they wanted nothing more to eat. Jesus uses the same term in the Beatitudes when He promises that those who hunger and thirst for righteousness "shall be satisfied" (Matt. 5:6). Because the multiplied barley **loaves** and **fish** were divinely created, the satisfaction the people experienced must have been like no other in their lives. This food was perfect, not tainted by the Fall and its consequent corruption of all the earth through sin.

There was more than enough food to satisfy the multitudes, and a considerable amount **was left over of the broken pieces, twelve full baskets.** After the food had been distributed among the groups, each disciple had a basket of food left for himself, out of which he could share with Jesus! In the great economy of God, there was neither too little nor too much.

As already noted, the fact that **there were about five thousand men who ate, aside from women and children,** indicates the total crowd could have been as large as twenty-five thousand.

Although Matthew does not mention it, at this point the people were so awed at Jesus' power that they tried "to come and take Him by force, to make Him king" (John 6:15). Here was a Man who not only could heal all their diseases but could deliver them from the constant work and preparation needed to put food in all their stomachs—all with but a word, and sometimes even without a word. They were convinced beyond doubt that Jesus was their kind of Messiah, and they were determined to crown Him king. They were right that He was the Messiah; but they were wrong about the kind of Messiah He was. He was not the political deliver or food supplier they were expecting, and His coronation was not in their power to perform. During the present age, as Jesus later declared, His "kingdom is not of this world" (John 18:36).

The great multitude that day was composed of three groups: the twelve disciples, the believing remnant among the multitudes, and the vast majority of unbelievers. In regard to each group we can discern many spiritual lessons.

The twelve were established. The twelve disciples were the constant object of Jesus' concern, instruction, and training. It was upon their shoulders that the establishing of His church would soon fall, and He knew the time of their training for this task was short. From this one incident alone, He taught them a number of important principles and truths.

First, He gave them the example of withdrawing from needless danger. Martyrdom or any other type of suffering that is sought as a form of self-glory is not endured for the sake of the Lord. The disciples also learned the importance of rest and solitude, even when in the midst of serving the Lord. Sometimes, as here, rest cannot be attained in the way or at the time we prefer; but even the Lord in His humanity did not escape the need for rest, solace, and refreshment. The twelve learned the importance of spending time away from work with those with whom one labors. Co-workers need special time together to support one another and to share needs and feelings.

Jesus also confirmed the disciples' need to show compassion for those in need, even when the needy are fickle and undeserving. The Son of God selflessly met the needs of the multitude that day, although He knew that most of them would soon lose interest in Him and fall away. He taught them that, as important as rest and leisure are, these must sometimes be sacrificed to meet the even more important needs of others. The believer has no inalienable rights to personal freedom and benefits. Everything we have, including our own needs and rights, should be expendable in serving others in Christ's name (see 1 Cor. 9).

Jesus taught the disciples that, in meeting the physical needs of others, they were also to minister the truth of the kingdom. A "social gospel" that does not witness to men's need for spiritual salvation through Christ is no gospel at all (see Gal. 1:6-9).

Jesus taught the disciples to do things in an orderly and careful manner, just as God does (1 Cor. 14:33, 40). Along with the lesson of orderliness was the even more important lesson of obeying the Lord even when the reason cannot be seen. The twelve were told to divide the multitude into groups of fifties and hundreds (Mark 6:40) before they knew the purpose for doing it. And after Jesus blessed the loaves and fish and handed them to the disciples, the food probably did not begin to multiply until it was distributed. The miracle became effective only as the disciples obeyed Jesus' command.

Jesus also demonstrated God's great generosity in providing enough food for every person to be fully satisfied, yet with an economy of stewardship that allowed no waste. Ours is a God of abundant providence, who does not give stingily. The ministry of God's servants should also be characterized by giving without reserve or measure, considering the needs of others before our own. Before the disciples knew that food would be left for them, they obediently gave all they had to the multitudes. Just as the food did not begin to multiply until after the disciples started to distribute it, their own needs were not met until they had met the needs of others. The little bit of food Jesus handed to the disciples was far short of enough to feed even twelve men. It was one little boy's lunch. But in obedience to Jesus, they gave away even what little they had.

The supreme lesson for the disciples was to learn to trust God to supply what seems impossible. Even after pondering all day over Jesus' instruction for them to feed the crowd themselves, the thought of turning to Him did not enter their heads. Like most of us, they were still inclined to look everywhere but to Him, even after having experienced so many previous miracles. And within that lesson was the lesson that, although God is perfectly able to do His work without us and without what we have, He chooses to use us and our meager resources to magnify His goodness and His power.

God's plan of redemption involves the witness, the work, and the means of those who belong to Him. In His infinite wisdom, the Lord most fully manifests His power through our weakness and His abundance through our poverty (1 Cor. 1:26-29). God often uses the small things to greater effectiveness than the things that are thought to be the greatest and most promising.

As the song goes, "Little becomes much in the Master's hand." God used a baby's cry to move the heart of Pharaoh's daughter and a shepherd's crook to work mighty miracles in Egypt. He used a boy and his slingshot to slay Goliath and rout the Philistine army. He used a poverty-stricken widow to sustain Elijah and a young girl to lead the leprous Naaman to Elisha. He used Balaam's donkey to teach His truth and the jawbone of another donkey to slay a thousand men. He used a little child to teach His disciples humility, and He used one boy's lunch to feed twenty-five thousand people.

The faithful remnant was confirmed. Among the huge multitude were a few who had already trusted in Christ for salvation and who followed Him to the other side of the lake not to be healed or entertained but to be spiritually blessed. There were also those who sought and received salvation. The next day some of them asked Jesus, "What shall we do, that we may work the works of God?" and begged, "Lord, evermore give us this bread" (John 6:28, 34). That elect remnant saw God's divine power at work in Jesus and glorified Him. With their spiritual eyes they not only saw the crowds being fed but the Lord's compassion being manifested. They saw Jesus' great integrity and stewardship. He did not resort to spectacular demonstrations that mesmerized His audience, like so many charlatans and false healers have done and continue to do. They also saw a manifestation of the kingdom of God, because they saw the King Himself at work. They saw the King graciously minister to His subjects and even to those who would not have Him as their sovereign.

The unbelieving rejecters were revealed. By far the greatest amount of soil on which the gospel of the kingdom fell that day was hard and thorny. Most of the people saw nothing more than what seemed an amazing feat of magic. They saw the human Jesus plainly, but they could not see the divine Son of God at all. They had their stomachs filled to a satisfaction they had never before experienced; but they did not have so much as a taste of the Bread of Life. They left physically filled but spiritually empty. Because they had received great light from God but preferred darkness, they went home further from Him and in greater sin than when they came. They came there for what Jesus could give them; but their self-indulgent, unbelieving hearts prevented them from receiving His greatest gift of all.

BIRDVILLE
BAPTIST CHURCH
LIBRARY

Worshiping the Son of God (14:22-33)

40

And immediately He made the disciples get into the boat, and go ahead of Him to the other side, while He sent the multitudes away. And after He had sent the multitudes away, He went up to the mountain by Himself to pray; and when it was evening, He was there alone. But the boat was already many stadia away from the land, battered by the waves; for the wind was contrary. And in the fourth watch of the night He came to them, walking on the sea. And when the disciples saw Him walking on the sea, they were frightened, saying, "It is a ghost!" And they cried out for fear. But immediately Jesus spoke to them, saying, "Take courage, it is I; do not be afraid." And Peter answered Him and said, "Lord, if it is You, command me to come to You on the water." And He said, "Come!" And Peter got out of the boat, and walked on the water and came toward Jesus. But seeing the wind, he became afraid, and beginning to sink, he cried out, saying, "Lord, save me!" And immediately Jesus stretched out His hand and took hold of him, and said to him, "O you of little faith, why did you doubt?" And when they got into the boat, the wind stopped. And those who were in the boat worshiped Him, saying, "You are certainly God's Son!" (14:22-33)

The pinnacle of this passage is the disciples' worship of Jesus as they confessed, "You are certainly God's Son" (v. 33). Though the Father had said this of

Jesus at His baptism (3:17) and even the demons at Gadara addressed Him as the Son of God (8:29), but this was the first time the twelve unequivocally declared their Master to be God's Son.

Within the events of Matthew 14:22-33 are five demonstrations, or proofs, of Jesus' deity that led to the disciples' confession. Within the period of but a few hours they received unmistakable verifications of Jesus' divine authority, divine knowledge, divine protection, divine love, and divine power.

PROOF OF HIS DIVINE AUTHORITY

And immediately He made the disciples get into the boat, and go ahead of Him to the other side, while He sent the multitudes away. And after He had sent the multitudes away, He went up to the mountain by Himself to pray; and when it was evening, He was there alone. (14:22-23)

The first affirmation of Jesus' deity on this occasion was His demonstration of divine authority. The fact that Jesus **made the disciples get into the boat** strongly suggests they were reluctant to leave Him and perhaps had argued with Him about it. As soon as the five thousand men, along with the women and children, had been fed and the twelve baskets of leftovers picked up, the multitude said, "This is of a truth the Prophet who is to come into the world" and "they were intending to come and take Him by force, to make Him king" (John 6:14-15a). To prevent that from happening, Jesus "withdrew again to the mountain by Himself alone" (v. 15b). He was indeed the predicted King, but He would not establish His earthly kingdom at that time. In any case, it was not the crowd's prerogative to crown Him.

The disciples no doubt thought the recognition of the crowd was long overdue and rejoiced that Jesus was at last being acknowledged as the Messiah, the coming King who would overthrow the Herods and Rome and establish Israel in her rightful place of world leadership. Jesus Himself had taught them to pray for the kingdom to come (Matt. 6:10), and this seemed an opportune time for Him to begin making the answer to that prayer a reality.

The disciples were also probably thinking of the high positions they would have as Jesus' chief administrators in the kingdom and of the prestige and power those offices would bring. They had suffered indifference and indignities with the Lord for some two years, while living from hand to mouth. Now that the crowd was at fever pitch in support of Jesus, what better time could there be to make His first public move toward the throne? It seems certain that the worldly, self-centered, and ambitious Judas, in particular, would have strongly fostered such thinking among his fellow disciples.

Knowing their thoughts and the growing influence of the crowd on them, Jesus removed them from the evil solicitation by commanding them to **get into the boat, and go ahead of Him to the other side.** At least in part because of their susceptibility to the political plans of the people, He **made** the disciples leave.

John identifies the specific destination on **the other side** as Capernaum (6:24) and Mark as Gennesaret (6:53), a small, fertile plain on the western shore of the Sea of Galilee between Capernaum and Magdala. It was a short trip across the northern tip of the sea, one that most of the disciples had made many times. But they resisted leaving now, not only because of the enthusiasm of the crowd to make Jesus king but also because they did not want to be separated from Jesus. Although they were weak in faith and easily influenced, they nevertheless were deeply devoted to the Lord and felt incomplete and vulnerable when He was not with them. They may also have not wanted to leave then because they could feel the wind starting to blow and were cautious about making even that short trip after dark in bad weather.

But regardless of the reasons for their reluctance, the disciples got **into the boat** and departed. They were under the Lord's authority, but He did not have to use supernatural force to make them leave. His firm word was enough, and it is to their credit that they obeyed. When He told them to cross over **ahead of Him to the other side,** that is what they did.

Jesus also demonstrated His divine authority over the multitudes, who, despite their great numbers (probably twenty-five thousand or more), could not make Jesus do anything contrary to His Father's plan and will. After He sent the disciples on their way to Capernaum, He **sent the multitudes away** as well. They were determined to make Him king in their own way and for their own purposes, but they could not. Without argument or fanfare, He simply dispersed **the multitudes,** and they bedded down for the night wherever they could near Bethsaida Julias, a few miles inland from the northeast shore of the lake.

Jesus has authority over the destinies of all men, including their final judgment (John 5:22). He has authority over all the supernatural world, including the evil world of Satan and his demonic fallen angels (Mark 1:27). He has authority over the holy angels, whom He could at any time have summoned to His aid (Matt. 26:53). The crowds who heard Him deliver the Sermon on the Mount recognized that "He was teaching them as one having authority" (Matt. 7:29). When He sent the twelve out on their first mission, He delegated to them part of His own "authority over unclean spirits, to cast them out, and to heal every kind of disease and every kind of sickness" (Matt. 10:1). And in His Great Commission He declared to the eleven who remained, "All authority has been given to Me in heaven and on earth" (Matt. 28:18).

Jesus has sovereign control over everything in heaven and on earth. He commands and controls men; He commands and controls angels, fallen and holy; and He commands and controls nature.

And after He had sent the multitudes away, He went up to the mountain by Himself to pray; and when it was evening He was there alone. Jesus had little time to rest or to spend unhurried hours with the disciples. He only had time **to pray,** after which He would miraculously encounter the disciples in the middle of the furious wind at sea.

Jesus' temptations neither began nor ended with the three in the wilderness immediately after His baptism. At the end of that session, the devil only "departed from Him until an opportune time" (Luke 4:13). The enthusiasm of the crowds and the disciples to make Him king was very much like the third temptation in the wilderness, in which Satan offered Jesus "all the kingdoms of the world, and their glory" (Matt. 4:8-9). "What better time to establish your kingdom than the Passover season, and in what better way than by marching triumphantly into Jerusalem at the head of thousands of faithful, enthusiastic supporters?" the devil may have asked. Jesus would surely gather many more thousands on the way to the Holy City, and His supernatural power would guarantee victory against any opposition. He could easily conquer the Herods, and even mighty Rome would be no match for the Son of God. He could bypass the cross and avoid the agony of having to take the sin of the world upon Himself.

Whatever thoughts Satan may have tried to put into His mind, Jesus turned His back on that evil just as He did on all other. He then came before His heavenly Father **to pray.** In a sense He did celebrate a victory, but it was over temptation, not Rome; and He turned His attention to His heavenly Father, whom He joined in intimate, refreshing communion. As in the Garden, He doubtlessly longed to be restored to the glorious fellowship He had had with His Father before the world even came into existence (John 17:5). But He had other things yet to do.

At the close of His earthly ministry, Jesus told Peter, "Behold, Satan has demanded permission to sift you like wheat; but I have prayed for you, that your faith may not fail" (Luke 22:32). Many times before He did it in His high priestly prayer (John 17:6-26), Jesus prayed for His disciples, and it is likely that He prayed for them on this occasion.

By this time it was the second **evening** of the day, which lasted from six to nine o'clock. The multitudes had been fed during the earlier evening (Matt. 14:15), which was from three to six. And as it became dark, Jesus was **there alone** in the mountain.

Proof of His Divine Knowledge

But the boat was already many stadia away from the land, battered by the waves; for the wind was contrary. And in the fourth watch of the night He came to them, walking on the sea. (14:24-25)

The second proof of Jesus' deity was His demonstration of divine knowledge. In obedience to His command the disciples had entered the boat and headed for the other side of the Sea of Galilee. Soon after they left, however, a violent wind erupted, and they were caught **many stadia away from the land.** A **stadia** was about an eighth of a mile, and John informs us that the **many stadia** amounted to twenty-five or thirty (in the Greek text), or "about three or four miles" (John 6:19).

Because in a normal trip across the northern end of the Sea of Galilee **the boat** would not have traveled more than a mile or two from shore at any point, the storm had obviously carried it several miles south, out into the middle of the lake. The disciples and their little craft were being **battered by the waves,** and **the wind was**

contrary, pushing them farther and farther away from their destination and closer and closer to disaster. Whether or not the boat had a sail, it would have been useless in the high winds and tossing waves. The only means of movement was rowing, and they were desperately "straining at the oars" (Mark 6:48) for their very lives.

The disciples were already confused, frustrated, disillusioned, and disappointed that Jesus had sent them away. Though they must have wondered why He sent them to certain death, the twelve are to be admired for their obedience and perseverance. Although the night was dark, the sea stormy, and the situation apparently hopeless, they were doing their best to do what the Lord commanded. The worst part was that Jesus was not with them. During a similar storm, they had awakened Him and He "rebuked the winds and the sea; and it became perfectly calm" (Matt. 8:26). But now He was miles away. He probably heard the storm and was aware of their plight; but there seemed no way He could get to them. If all the disciples together could not row against the wind and waves, one man could never do it.

Jesus knew of their situation long before it happened, and He did not have to rush away from prayer in order to be on time to help. The storm and the disciples were equally in His hands, and He knew in advance exactly what He would do with both.

The night was divided into four watches, or shifts. The first was from six to nine, the second from nine to twelve, the third from twelve to three, and the fourth from three to six. **The fourth watch of the night** therefore included the time just before dawn, indicating the disciples had been at sea for at least nine hours, most of the time battling the wind storm.

Jesus waited a long time before **He came to them,** just as He waited until Lazarus had been dead for several days before He came to Bethany. In both instances, He could have come much sooner than He did and in both instances He could have performed the ensuing miracle without being present—just as He had done in healing the centurion's servant (Matt. 8:13). He could, of course, have prevented the death of Lazarus and the rising of the wind in the first place. But in His infinite wisdom Jesus purposely allowed Mary and Martha and the disciples to reach the extremity of need before He intervened. He knew everything about all of them, and had known it since before they were born. And He knew infinitely better than they did what was best for their welfare and for God's glory.

The disciples should have been rejoicing with David that, "If I make my bed in Sheol, behold, Thou art there. If I take the wings of the dawn, if I dwell in the remotest part of the sea, even there Thy hand will lead Me, and Thy right hand will lay hold of me" (Ps. 139:8-10). The twelve should have remembered that "the Lord also will be a stronghold for the oppressed, a stronghold in times of trouble" (Ps. 9:9), that the Lord was their fortress and deliverer and their rock of refuge (Ps. 18:2), and that He would keep them safe even as they walked "through the valley of the shadow of death" (Ps. 23:4). They should have remembered God's word to Moses out of the burning bush: "I have surely seen the affliction of My people who are in Egypt, and have given heed to their cry because of their taskmasters, for I am aware of their sufferings" (Ex. 3:7). They should have remembered that, just before Abraham would have plunged the knife into Isaac's heart, the Lord provided a ram to take Isaac's place (Gen. 22:13).

But in the exigencies of the night, the twelve had forgotten those psalms and the Lord's power in which they exult. They had little confidence that the Lord, who had known all about the suffering of His people in Egypt and did not forsake them, was relevant in that storm. They saw no relation between their plight and the fact that God had provided a substitute for Isaac when he faced death.

The disciples had even forgotten Jesus' own assurance that their heavenly Father knew all their needs before they asked Him (Matt. 6:32) and that not even a single sparrow "will fall to the ground apart from your Father" and that "the very hairs of your head are all numbered" (10:29-30). All they could think of was their danger and all they could feel was fear.

But Jesus had not forgotten the disciples, and He came to them through the very danger that threatened to destroy them, **walking on the sea.** He used the trial as His footpath. He could not physically see them from the mountain or through the stormy darkness, but He knew exactly where they were. God's vision is not like ours, because "The eyes of the Lord are in every place, watching the evil and the good" (Prov. 15:3). "There is no creature hidden from His sight, but all things are open and laid bare to the eyes of Him with whom we have to do" (Heb. 4:13).

PROOF OF HIS DIVINE PROTECTION

And when the disciples saw Him walking on the sea, they were frightened, saying, "It is a ghost!" And they cried out for fear. But immediately Jesus spoke to them, saying, "Take courage, it is I; do not be afraid." (14:26-27)

The third proof of Jesus' deity was manifested in His protection of the disciples. As He first approached them, they thought they were getting anything but help, because, **when the disciples saw Him walking on the sea, they were frightened, saying, "It is a ghost!" And they cried out for fear.** *Theōreō* (from which **saw** is derived) means to look intently, indicating that the disciples' gaze was transfixed on the apparition before them. At first Jesus did not walk directly toward the boat but appeared to be passing by (Mark 6:48); but that made little difference to the disciples. For **a ghost** to be anywhere near them was enough to make them **frightened** almost out of their senses. The term **ghost** is the Greek *phantasma*, which refers to an apparition, a creature of the imagination, and is the word from which come the English *phantom* and *phantasm.*

Many liberal interpreters insist that the disciples only *thought* they saw Jesus walking across the water as their tired and frightened minds played tricks on them. But it would have been quite impossible for all twelve of them to simultaneously experience the same imagined apparition. And such an explanation hardly accounts for the fact that Jesus somehow got into the boat with them, and that as soon as He did the storm instantly ceased. The writers make a point of the fact that the boat was a great distance from the shore. Neither, as some suggest, could the disciples have seen Jesus walking along the beach while appearing to be walking on the water—even in broad daylight. Either they lied in reporting the event or it occurred as they say it did.

Because of the darkness, the mist from the wind and waves, the fatigue from rowing, and the fear that already gripped them because of the storm, they did not recognize Jesus when He appeared to them. Mark reports that "they all saw Him" (Mark 6:50), but none of them suspected it was Jesus. And their fear instantly turned into abject terror as they beheld the form they thought was **a ghost** come to add to their torment. In the dark before the dawn, hopelessness turned to utter horror and despair. In their panic they could not help but **cry out for fear.**

Although Jesus was testing the disciples' faith, He understood their frailty. He calmed their fear by saying simply, **Take courage, it is I; do not be afraid.** In spite of the raging winds, the waves battering against the boat, and their fear-stricken minds, they immediately recognized their Master's voice.

It was not the time for an explanation of why He was there, of what He planned to do next, or of why He had not come sooner. It was time to give **courage,** to still the storm that raged within the disciples, even before stilling the one that raged without.

Jesus did not walk on the water to teach the disciples how to do it. Peter tried and failed; and there is no record of any of the others ever doing it at all. The Lord's purpose was to demonstrate His loving willingness to do whatever is necessary to rescue His children. He did not have to walk on the water to save them, but His doing so gave them an unforgettable reminder of the power and extent of His divine protection. It was not to teach them to walk on water but to teach them that God can and will act on behalf of His own.

We will never find ourselves in a place where Christ cannot find us; and no storm is too severe for Him to save us from it. He protects His own, whom He will never fail or forsake (Josh. 1:5; Heb. 13:5). The lesson for the disciples is the lesson for us: There is no reason for God's people to fear. There is no reason for anxiety, no matter how hopeless and threatening our problems seem to be. Life is often stormy and painful, often threatening and frightening. Some believers suffer more than others, but all suffer at some time and in some way. In spite of that, the storm is never so severe, the night never so black, and the boat never so frail that we risk danger beyond our Father's care.

When Paul was on the ship taking him to Rome to appear before Caesar, it encountered an exceptionally violent storm in the Mediterranean Sea near the island of Crete. After the crew had thrown all the cargo, tackle, supplies, and food overboard, the ship was still in danger of foundering on the rocks. Paul had warned they should remain in the safety of the port at Fair Havens through the winter, but his advice was not heeded by the centurion or the pilot of the ship. When everyone else on board had despaired of reaching land alive, an angel appeared to Paul assuring him that, although the ship would be lost, no lives would be. Yet even before the angel's message, Paul, unlike the fearful disciples, was at perfect peace and offered encouragement to those on the ship with him, saying, "Keep up your courage, men, for I believe God, that it will turn out exactly as I have been told" (Acts 27:25).

So the disciples who were reluctant to leave Jesus and go to Capernaum obeyed by rowing out into the storm they knew was coming, and Jesus honored their faithfulness. When believers are in the place of obedience they are in the place of safety, no matter what the circumstances. The place of security is not the place of favorable circumstance but the place of obedience to God's will.

PROOF OF HIS DIVINE LOVE

And Peter answered Him and said, "Lord, if it is You, command me to come to You on the water." And He said, "Come!" And Peter got out of the boat, and walked on the water and came toward Jesus. But seeing the wind, he became afraid, and beginning to sink, he cried out, saying, "Lord, save me!" And immediately Jesus stretched out His hand and took hold of him, and said to him, "O you of little faith, why did you doubt?" (14:28-31)

The fourth proof of Jesus' deity was His demonstration of divine love. Although Mark and John report Jesus' walking on the water, only Matthew tells of this incident concerning Peter.

Peter's **if** did not reflect doubt that it was actually his Lord, because going out onto the water to join an unidentified ghost was the last thing Peter would have done. He was naturally impetuous and brash, and more than once his overconfidence got him into trouble—including trouble with the Lord. But it would have taken more than brashness for this life-long fisherman to have ventured out on the water without benefit of a boat, because no one on board better knew the dangers of Galilee storms than Peter. He had probably been thrown into the water at times by high winds or waves and had seen others experience the same trauma. He was no fool, and it is highly unlikely that impetuosity would have so easily overridden his reason and instinctive caution.

It seems much more probable that Peter was overjoyed to see Jesus and that his supreme concern was to be safely with Him. Mere impetuosity might have caused him to jump out of the boat, expecting Jesus somehow to come to his rescue. But he knew better, and he therefore asked the Lord, **Command me to come to You on the water.** He knew Jesus had the power to enable him to walk **on the water,** but he did not presume to attempt the feat without His express instruction. Peter's request was an act of affection built on confident faith. He did not ask to walk on water for the sake of doing something spectacular, but because it was the way to get to Jesus.

Peter did many things for which he can be faulted. But he is sometimes faulted for things that reflect love, courage, and faith as much as brashness or cowardice. For instance, although he denied the Lord while in the courtyard during Jesus' trial, he was nevertheless there, as close to Him as he could get. The rest of the disciples were nowhere to be found. On the Mount of Transfiguration, Peter's suggestion was unwise but it was prompted by sincere devotion: "Lord, it is good for us to be here; if You wish, I will make three tabernacles here, one for You, and one for Moses, and one for Elijah" (Matt. 17:4). He genuinely loved Jesus and sincerely wanted to serve and please

Him. Peter did not resist Jesus' washing his feet because of pride, but because, in his deep humility, he could not conceive of His Lord washing the feet of anyone so unworthy. And when Jesus explained the significance of what He was doing, Peter said, "Lord, not my feet only, but also my hands and my head" (John 13:9).

Peter was continually in the Lord's shadow and footsteps. By reading between the lines of the gospel accounts it is not difficult to imagine that Peter sometimes followed so closely behind Jesus that he bumped into Him when He stopped. Peter sensed in Jesus' presence a wonderful safety and comfort, and that is where Peter now wanted to be. It was safer to be with Jesus **on the water** than to be without Him in the boat.

Peter's love for Jesus was imperfect and weak, but it was real. Three times Jesus asked Peter if he loved Him, and each time Peter responded affirmatively. Jesus did not contradict Peter's answer but reminded him of his obligation to care for his Master's sheep and warned him of the great cost his love would demand (John 21:15-18). Tradition has it that when Peter was about to be crucified, he requested being put on the cross upside down, not feeling worthy to die in the same way as his Lord.

Jesus' telling Peter to **come** confirms the disciple's right motive. Jesus never invites, much less commands, a person to do anything sinful. Nor is He ever a party to pride or presumption. With the greatest of compassion, Jesus told Peter to **come,** highly pleased that he wanted to be with his Lord.

As much as anything else, it was Peter's great love for Christ that made him the leader of the disciples. He appears to have been the closest to Christ, and is always named first in lists of the twelve. Just as the Lord never rejects weak faith, but accepts it and builds on it, He also never rejects weak and imperfect love. With great patience and care He takes the love of His children and, through trials and hardships as well as successes and victories, builds that love into greater conformity to His own love.

Jesus' telling Peter, **"Come!"** was an act of love. John declared, "We have come to know and have believed the love which God has for us." In fact, he goes on to say, "God is love" (1 John 4:16; cf. v. 8). It is God's nature to be loving, just as it is water's nature to be wet and the sun's to be bright and hot. He loves his own with an infinite, uninfluenced, unqualified, unchanging, unending, and perfect love.

Christians most perfectly reflect their heavenly Father when they are loving, especially to each other. "If someone says, 'I love God,' and hates his brother, he is a liar," John continues to explain; "for the one who does not love his brother whom he has seen, cannot love God whom he has not seen" (1 John 4:20).

Although Peter was sincere, he did not comprehend the reality or the extremity of what he was asking to do. From the relative safety of the boat the feat did not seem so terrifying; but once **Peter got out of the boat, and walked on the water and came toward Jesus,** the situation appeared radically different. Peter temporarily took His eyes off the Lord and, **seeing the wind, he became afraid, and beginning to sink, he cried out, saying, "Lord, save me!"** His faith was enough to get him out of the boat, but it was not enough to carry him across the water.

Faith is strengthened by its being taken to extremities it has never faced before. Such strengthening is basic to Christian growth and maturity. "Blessed is a man who perseveres under trial," James says; "for once he has been approved, he will receive the crown of life, which the Lord has promised to those who love Him" (James 1:12). The Lord takes us as far as our faith will go, and when it ends we begin to sink. It is then that we call out to Him and He again demonstrates His faithfulness and His power, and our faith learns to extend that much further. As we trust God in the faith we have, we discover its limitations; but we also discover what it can yet become.

When Peter was **beginning to sink,** he was probably fully clothed and would have had great difficulty swimming through the high waves. And in his fright he could think of nothing but drowning. But as soon as **he cried out . . . "Lord, save me,"** he was safe, because **immediately Jesus stretched out His hand and took hold of him.**

When Jesus rebuked him, saying, **O you of little faith, why did you doubt?** Peter must have wondered at the question. The reason for his doubt seemed obvious. He was bone weary from rowing most of the night, scared to death by the storm and then by what he thought was a ghost, and now it seemed he was about to drown before he could reach the Lord. He had never been in such a situation before, and it may be that his actually walking a few feet on the water added to his shock.

But Peter's weak faith was better than no faith; and, as in the courtyard when he denied the Lord, at least he was there and not holding back like the rest. He at least started toward Jesus, and when he faltered, the Lord took him the rest of the way.

Jesus had been interceding for Peter and the others while He was on the mountain, and now He came directly to their aid in the midst of the storm. The Lord goes before us and He goes with us. When we get frustrated, anxious, bewildered, and frightened, Satan tempts us to wonder why God allows such things to happen to his children. And if we keep our attention on those things we will begin to sink just as surely as Peter did. But if we cry out to the Lord for help, He will come to our rescue just as surely as He did to Peter's.

Peter would one day write, "In this you greatly rejoice, even though now for a little while, if necessary, you have been distressed by various trials, that the proof of your faith, being more precious than gold which is perishable, even though tested by fire, may be found to result in praise and glory and honor at the revelation of Jesus Christ" (1 Pet. 1:6-7).

PROOF OF HIS DIVINE POWER

And when they got into the boat, the wind stopped. (14:32)

The most spectacular miracle was accomplished without Jesus saying a word or raising a hand. The moment He and Peter **got into the boat** with the other disciples, **the wind stopped.** It was as if **the wind** was simply waiting for the miracle to be finished; and when it had served its purpose, it **stopped.**

Just as instantaneously, "the boat was at the land to which they were going"

(John 6:21). They had been three or four miles out to sea and the storm was still raging as fiercely as ever; but in an instant it stopped and the boat was at its destination. On the basis of normal human experience it is hardly surprising that the disciples "were greatly astonished" (Mark 6:51). But the disciples had been having astounding displays of Jesus' miraculous power for two years, and for them these remarkable events should not have been astonishing. We learn from Mark that their amazement resulted from their not having "gained any insight from the incident of the loaves"—or from Jesus' earlier stilling of the storm or from any other great work He had done—because "their heart was hardened" (Mark 6:52).

Yet in that moment those same hearts were softened and those eyes opened as they had never been before; **and those who were in the boat worshiped Him, saying, "You are certainly God's Son!"** They were now more than simply amazed, as the crowds and they themselves had always been. They were taken past amazement to worship, which is what Jesus' signs and miracles were intended to produce. At last they were beginning to see Jesus as the One whom God highly exalted and on whom He bestowed the name which is above every name, and at whose name "every knee should bow, of those who are in heaven, and on earth, and under the earth, and that every tongue should confess that Jesus Christ is Lord, to the glory of God the Father" (Phil. 2:9-11).

BIRDVILLE
BAPTIST CHURCH
LIBRARY

Empty Worship: Confusing the Traditions of Men with the Doctrine of God (14:34–15:20)

And when they had crossed over, they came to land at Gennesaret. And when the men of that place recognized Him, they sent into all that surrounding district and brought to Him all who were sick; and they began to entreat Him that they might just touch the fringe of His cloak; and as many as touched it were cured.

Then some Pharisees and scribes came to Jesus from Jerusalem, saying, "Why do Your disciples transgress the tradition of the elders? For they do not wash their hands when they eat bread." And He answered and said to them, "And why do you yourselves transgress the commandment of God for the sake of your tradition? For God said, 'Honor your father and mother,' and 'He who speaks evil of father or mother, let him be put to death.' But you say, 'Whoever shall say to his father or mother, "Anything of mine you might have been helped by has been given to God," he is not to honor his father or his mother.' And thus you invalidated the word of God for the sake of your tradition. You hypocrites, rightly did Isaiah prophesy of you, saying, 'This people honors Me with their lips, but their heart is far away from Me. But in vain do they worship Me, teaching as doctrines the precepts of men.'" And after He called the multitude to Him, He said to them, "Hear, and understand. Not what enters into the mouth defiles the man, but what proceeds out of the mouth, this defiles the man." Then the disciples came and said to Him, "Do You know that the Pharisees were offended when they heard this statement?" But He answered and said, "Every plant which My heavenly Father did not plant shall be rooted up. Let them alone; they are blind guides of the blind. And if a blind man guides a blind man, both will fall into a pit." And Peter answered and said to Him, "Explain the parable to us." And He said, "Are you still lacking in understanding also? Do you not understand that everything that goes into the mouth passes into the stomach, and is eliminated? But the things that proceed out of the mouth come from the heart, and those defile the man. For out of the heart come evil thoughts, murders, adulteries, fornications, thefts, false witness, slanders. These are the things which defile the man; but to eat with unwashed hands does not defile the man." (14:34–15:20)

One of God's supreme commands is: "You shall not take the name of the Lord your God in vain" (Ex. 20:7). That command obviously prohibits profanity or vulgarity in which the Lord's name is used. It also obviously prohibits flippant, irreverent use of His name. But more than those obvious things, it also forbids any use of God's name that is superficial, indifferent, insincere, or hypocritical.

It has been said that God's name is taken in vain more often inside the church than outside. His name is taken in vain whenever it is mechanically used in repetitious prayers and liturgies, in singing His praise while having no thought of Him, and in praying thoughtlessly and without genuine devotion. His name is taken in vain through empty worship perhaps more than in any other way.

Hypocritical worship was among the worst offenses of ancient Israel. The Lord declared through Isaiah, "Bring your worthless offerings no longer, incense is an abomination to Me. New moon and sabbath, the calling of assemblies—I cannot endure iniquity and the solemn assembly. I hate your new moon festivals and your appointed feasts, they have become a burden to Me. I am weary of bearing them. So when you spread out your hands in prayer, I will hide My eyes from you, yes, even though you multiply prayers, I will not listen. Your hands are covered with blood" (Isa. 1:13-15).

Even the ceremonies and observances God Himself had ordained became unacceptable, because they were offered hypocritically and without meaning. Isaiah continued: " 'Wash yourselves, make yourselves clean; remove the evil of your deeds from My sight. Cease to do evil, learn to do good; seek justice, reprove the ruthless; defend the orphan, plead for the widow. Come now, and let us reason together,' says the Lord, 'Though your sins are as scarlet, they will be as white as snow; though they are red like crimson, they will be like wool' " (vv. 16-17).

Unless the heart of the worshiper is cleansed and purified, he cannot worship God acceptably, because he cannot worship God honestly and sincerely. The person with a sinful heart is opposed to God and it is not possible for him to worship rightly. Isaiah ends his prophecy with much the same warning as he begins it: "To this one I will look, to him who is humble and contrite of spirit, and who trembles at My word.

But he who kills an ox is like one who slays a man; he who sacrifices a lamb is like the one who breaks a dog's neck; he who offers a grain offering is like one who offers swine's blood; he who burns incense is like the one who blesses an idol" (Isa. 66:2-3; cf. Prov. 21:27). As they went through the pretensions of offering sacrifices, the people were no better than criminals and pagans, because their hearts were not humble and contrite, but proud and rebellious.

Through Amos, the Lord proclaimed the same message: "I hate, I reject your festivals, nor do I delight in your solemn assemblies. Even though you offer up to Me burnt offerings and your grain offerings, I will not accept them; and I will not even look at the peace offerings of your fatlings. Take away from Me the noise of your songs; I will not even listen to the sound of your harps. But let justice roll down like waters and righteousness like an ever-flowing stream" (Amos 5:21-24). Malachi declared that to offer blemished and unworthy sacrifices was to despise God's name (Mal. 1:6-7).

In Matthew 14:34–15:20 Jesus preaches the same message as those prophets: Hearts that are not right with God cannot worship Him. Jesus was still popular with the multitudes of common people, but it was not because they trusted in Him as their Messiah-Savior but because He fed and healed them. Their interest in Him was selfish and their devotion to Him was superficial. They had no desire to follow Him as Lord but only to get from Him what they wanted. They did not want to serve Him but rather wanted Him to serve their every whim.

Most of the religious leaders were already openly hostile to Jesus and had been plotting for some time how to kill Him (12:14). But to keep from antagonizing the common people who still followed Jesus, the leaders tried first to discredit Him before they openly attacked Him.

In the present passage Jesus confronts the Jewish religious system of His day head on, showing, above all, the emptiness and worthlessness of its worship. In doing so, He further crystallizes the irreconcilable conflict between His gospel and that system. As the conflict unfolds, Jesus is first seen as the compassionate Healer (14:34-36), then as the condemning Judge (15:1-9), and finally as the correcting Teacher (vv. 10-20).

THE COMPASSIONATE HEALER

And when they had crossed over, they came to land at Gennesaret. And when the men of that place recognized Him, they sent into all that surrounding district and brought to Him all who were sick; and they began to entreat Him that they might just touch the fringe of His cloak; and as many as touched it were cured. (14:34-36)

After Jesus stepped into the boat with Peter, the storm immediately stopped (Matt. 14:32) and the boat immediately arrived "at the land to which they were going" (John 6:21). The land was **Gennesaret,** a small but very beautiful plain located between Capernaum and Magdala. According to Josephus it was a lush and extremely fertile area that produced a wide variety of crops. The fields and vineyards were irrigated from no less than four large springs, enabling farmers to produce three crops a year. Because the soil was so rich, it was all devoted to farming, and the area contained no towns or villages. It was therefore a quiet, peaceful region, inhabited by many kinds of birds and offering a good place for retreat and rest.

Jesus probably intended to spend some time there alone with His disciples; but again His plans were interrupted, because **when the men of that place recognized Him, they sent into all that surrounding district and brought to Him all who were sick.** Although Jesus had previously healed thousands of people in that general area, there were obviously still many others who were **sick** with various afflictions.

The people's confidence in Jesus' miraculous powers was now so firmly established that **they began to entreat Him that they might just touch the fringe of His cloak.** They may have heard of the woman with the hemorrhage who had been healed by that act (Matt. 9:20) and assumed that anyone could be healed in the same way. Whatever their thinking and motives may have been, Jesus had compassion on them and honored their expression of faith, because **as many as touched it were cured.**

But Jesus wanted to do much more for them. Above all, He wanted to heal their sin-diseased hearts. That same day He offered Himself to them as the Bread of life which came down from heaven, which to eat would cause them never to hunger or thirst again and would give them eternal life (John 6:33-35, 48-51). But when they realized what it meant to eat that heavenly food and drink that heavenly drink, many of the shallow followers were offended and left Him (vv. 52-60, 66). Like so many people today who look to God only for what they want and care nothing for what He wants, most of the multitude had little to do with Jesus after He healed them.

Although He did not withhold it from them, Jesus was grieved that the people sought no more from Him than physical healing. Because they did not ask for a full meal, He did not refuse them a piece of bread. Because they did not ask for spiritual help, He did not refuse them physical. In spite of their superficiality, ingratitude, and self-centeredness, He mercifully healed them in order to reveal the compassionate heart of God.

THE CONDEMNING JUDGE

Then some Pharisees and scribes came to Jesus from Jerusalem, saying, "Why do Your disciples transgress the tradition of the elders? For they do not wash their hands when they eat bread." And He answered and said to them, "And why do you yourselves transgress the commandment of God for the sake of your tradition? For God said, 'Honor your father and mother,' and 'He who speaks evil of father or mother, let him be put to death.' But you say, 'Whoever shall say to his father or mother, "Anything of mine you might have been helped by has been given to God," he is not to honor his father or his mother.' And thus you invalidated the word of God for the sake of your

tradition. You hypocrites, rightly did Isaiah prophesy of you, saying, 'This people honors Me with their lips, but their heart is far away from Me. But in vain do they worship Me, teaching as doctrines the precepts of men.'" (15:1-9)

Just as Jesus offered compassion for the fickle crowds who wanted only food and healing from Him, He offered condemnation for the self-righteous, hypocritical religious leaders who wanted *nothing* from Him. They wanted nothing at all to do with Him, except what was necessary to discredit and destroy Him.

In this crucial passage we see the antithetical nature of the gospel message in Jesus' teaching: The God of compassion is also the God of condemnation. Just as He heals those who come to Him, He condemns those who reject Him. In these nine verses we first see Jesus' confrontation and then His condemnation of the unbelieving and rebellious scribes and Pharisees.

THE CONFRONTATION

Then some Pharisees and scribes came to Jesus from Jerusalem, saying, "Why do Your disciples transgress the tradition of the elders? For they do not wash their hands when they eat bread." (15:1-2)

Then is indefinite and does not precisely indicate the time sequence between the healings and the approach of the **Pharisees and scribes.** It is possible that this confrontation occurred several days after the healings. From John 6:4 we know it was the Passover season and that many Jews were traveling through Galilee on their way to Jerusalem for the feast. It was the third Passover of Jesus' ministry, a year before His final celebration of it with the disciples in the upper room.

Since **Pharisees and scribes** from **Jerusalem** would not normally carry on their work in Galilee, it is likely their fellow religionists there had requested help in confronting Jesus, possibly channeling their request through the Sanhedrin, the high Jewish council. **Jerusalem** was the location of the Temple and of the most eminent schools of Judaism; and therefore this delegation doubtlessly carried heavy ecclesiastical weight. And because these **Pharisees and scribes** had prestige and learning superior to that of their counterparts in Galilee, Jesus treated them with greater severity.

These men were familiar with Jesus' teaching and ministry and came to Him with the specific purpose of proving Him to be an offender against their tradition. As soon as Jesus had begun to preach and teach, the leaders of the religious establishment realized He posed a severe threat to their legalistic system. Their religion was intentionally external and superficial, because it could be outwardly practiced with great zeal and diligence no matter what the condition of the heart or soul. It was a religion of ceremony and tradition that the most hardened unbeliever could follow. It was concerned with covering up sin, not exposing and cleansing it, with appearing righteous, not being righteous. Even before Jesus unequivocally proclaimed the truth in the Sermon on the Mount (Matt. 5:20), the Jewish leaders sensed that His kind of righteousness and theirs were diametrically opposed. The conflict ultimately resulted in the crucifixion—which they considered to be the victory of their way, whereas it was really its death knell.

The visiting leaders first asked Jesus, **Why do Your disciples transgress the tradition of the elders? For they do not wash their hands when they eat bread.** They did not try to hide the fact that Jesus' offense was against **the tradition of the elders** rather than God's law. In their minds **the tradition of the elders** was superior to Scripture, in the sense that it was the only reliable interpretation of God's Word. Just as Roman Catholics look to church dogma to discover what Scripture "really means," most Jews of Jesus' day looked to **the tradition of the elders.** In much the same way, many Protestants give more authority to the pronouncements of their denomination than to the Bible.

The Talmud, which is the repository of Jewish tradition, teaches that God gave the oral law to Moses and then told Moses to pass it on to great men of Israel. These men were then to do three things with the law they had received. First, they were to deliberate on it and properly apply it. Second, they were to train disciples in order that the next generation would have teachers of the law. Third, they were to build a wall around the law in order to protect it.

Because their hearts were not right with God, the rabbis' wall-building "protection" of His law actually undermined and contradicted it. Their purpose was not to lead the people to worship and serve God from pure hearts made clean by Him, but to worship and serve Him by human means and from unchanged hearts. To provide the means for superficially keeping God's commandments, regulation after regulation and ceremony after ceremony were added, until God's own Word was utterly hidden behind the wall of tradition. Instead of protecting God's Word, **the tradition** obscured and perverted it.

When the northern kingdom of Israel and then the southern kingdom of Judah were taken into captivity, the Jewish people felt as if God had abandoned them. The real reason for their captivity, of course, was that they had abandoned Him. They were suffering God's judgment, just as Isaiah, Jeremiah, and other prophets had repeatedly and vividly warned they would.

While the Jews were in exile, scribes (the first of whom was Ezra) began to assemble and copy the various books of Scripture written to that time. They also began to make comments on various passages that seemed unclear; and gradually a larger and larger accumulation of interpretations was developed until there was more interpretation than Scripture. The distinction between Scripture and the traditions based on interpretations of Scripture gradually became less and less distinct, and before long **tradition** was more familiar and more revered than God's own Word.

By Jesus' day, **the tradition of the elders** had for many years supplanted Scripture as the supreme religious authority in the minds of Jewish leaders and of most of the people. The traditions even affirmed that "the words of scribes are more lovely than the words of the law," and it became a greater offense in Judaism to transgress the teaching of some rabbi such as the revered Hillel than to trangress the teaching of Scripture.

In the thinking of the Pharisees and scribes who approached Jesus on this occasion, it was therefore an extremely serious matter that His **disciples** would **transgress the tradition of the elders.** Jesus and His disciples disregarded all the rabbinical traditions, and the particular infraction cited here was simply representative of many others that could have been mentioned. But the disciples' failing to **wash their hands when they** ate was considered to be an especially serious offense.

Wash had nothing to do with physical hygiene but referred to ceremonial rinsing. The purpose was to remove the ritual defilement caused by having touched something unclean, such as a dead body or a Gentile. Some of the rabbis even taught that a certain demon named Shibtah attached itself to people's hands while they slept and that, if he were not ceremonially washed away, he would actually enter the body through the food handled by defiled hands.

The value of ceremonial rinsing was held so high that one rabbi insisted that "whosoever has his abode in the land of Israel and eats his common food with rinsed hands may rest assured that he shall obtain eternal life." Another rabbi taught that it would be better to walk four miles out of the way to get water than to eat with unwashed hands. A certain rabbi who was imprisoned and given a small ration of water used it to wash his hands before eating rather than to drink, claiming he would rather die than transgress the tradition.

God had instituted certain prescribed ceremonial washings as part of the covenant given through Moses, but those were never more than outward symbols or pictures of spiritual truths. The Old Testament nowhere holds them up as having any merit, value, or blessing in themselves.

Water jars were kept ready to be used before every meal. The minimum amount of water to be used was a quarter of a log, enough to fill one and a half egg shells. The water was first poured on both hands, held with the fingers pointed upward; and it must run down the arm as far as the wrist and drop off from the wrist, for the water was now itself unclean, having touched the unclean hands. And if it ran down the fingers again it would render them unclean. The process was repeated with hands held in the downward direction, the fingers pointing down. And finally each hand was cleansed by being rubbed with the fist of the other. A strict Jew would do this before every meal and between every course in every meal. (For a fuller discussion read Alfred Edersheim's *The Life and Times of Jesus the Messiah,* vol. 2, pp. 10-13.)

Throughout history, man-made religion has attached great significance and benefit to ceremonies and ritualistic acts. Commenting on this universal tendency of man, Charles Spurgeon is reported to have facetiously asked his congregation, "If there were no Sunday morning service at eleven, how many of you would be Christians?"

THE CONDEMNATION

And He answered and said to them, "And why do you yourselves transgress the commandment of God for the sake of your tradition? For God said, 'Honor your father and mother,' and 'He who speaks evil of father or mother, let him be put to death.' But you say, 'Whoever shall say to his father or

mother, "Anything of mine you might have been helped by has been given to God," he is not to honor his father or his mother.' And thus you invalidated the word of God for the sake of your tradition. You hypocrites, rightly did Isaiah prophesy of you, saying, 'This people honors Me with their lips, but their heart is far away from Me. But in vain do they worship Me, teaching as doctrines the precepts of men.'" (15:3-9)

Before answering the Pharisees' charge, Jesus gave a counter charge. He did not deny that His disciples disregarded the rabbinical traditions; and He later explained to the multitudes (v. 11) and then to the disciples (vv. 17-18) why this particular tradition was worthless and meaningless. But He gave no answer or explanation to the accusing Pharisees and scribes, dismissing their question as irrelevant. Instead, He asked them the immeasurably more important question, **Why do you yourselves transgress the commandment of God for the sake of your tradition?**

Just as the Pharisees mentioned failure to wash their hands ceremonially before eating as an example of the disciples' breaking **tradition,** Jesus mentioned the Pharisees' overturning the fifth commandment, **honor your father and mother** (see Ex. 20:12), as an example of their breaking **the commandment of God.** He also reminded them of God's penalty for breaking that command: **He who speaks evil of father or mother, let him be put to death** (see Ex. 21:17).

Bound up in honoring **father and mother** is the responsibility to show them respect and love and to help meet their needs. One tradition taught that "a son is bound to support his father even if he has to beg for him." But another tradition had come to supersede that one as well as the fifth commandment. It taught that **whoever shall say to his father or mother, "Anything of mine you might have been helped by has been given to God," he is not to honor his father or his mother.**

The scribes and Pharisees knew the Ten Commandments well and could recite them easily from memory. They were the most educated of all Jewish men and were considered the supreme authorities on Scripture as well as tradition. They could not possibly have failed to see that this tradition directly violated God's commandment **to honor** one's **father and mother.** They knowingly replaced God's specific command with their own contradicting tradition.

Anything of mine translates *dōron,* which means gift. Mark uses the more technical term *korban* (7:11), which refers to a gift or sacrifice specifically offered to God. Sometime in the past, a tradition had developed that allowed a person to call all his possessions *korban,* thereby dedicating them to God. And because Scripture taught that a vow to God must not be violated (Num. 30:2), those possessions could not be used for anything but service to God. Therefore, if a man's **father or mother** asked for financial assistance, he could tell them, **Anything of mine you might have been helped by has been given to God.** The Greek text of the next phrase is more emphatic than the English suggests. **He is not to honor** might better be rendered, "He *must not* honor." The vow did not simply allow withholding help from **father or . . . mother** but actually forbade it.

Except for what may have been actually given to the Temple or synagogue, however, the *korban* possessions remained in the person's hands. And when he decided to use them for his *own* purposes, tradition permitted him to do so simply by saying *korban* over them again. In other words, the tradition was not designed to serve either God or the family but the selfish interests of the person making the hypocritical vow. To avoid giving up his possessions in order to support his parents, he could declare those possessions sacred and unusable; but as soon as he wanted to use them for himself he could just as easily reverse the vow. The covert purpose of that tradition was to invalidate **the word of God** by circumventing the fifth commandment.

Angered by the callous selfishness of that tradition, Jesus said, **You hypocrites, rightly did Isaiah prophesy of you, saying, "This people honors Me with their lips, but their heart is far away from Me"** (see Isa. 29:13). What Isaiah said of the **people** of his own day applied to the **hypocrites** of Jesus' day as well, and to those of our own.

An ancient rabbi said, "There are ten parts of hypocrisy in the world, nine at Jerusalem and one everywhere else." The same might be said of much of the church. Satan has no greater allies than **hypocrites** who go under the guise of God's people. And hypocrites have no greater ally than tradition, because tradition can be followed mechanically and thoughtlessly, without conviction, sincerity, or purity of heart. Because traditions are made by men, they can be accomplished by men. They require no faith, no trust, no dependence on God. Not only that, but they appeal to the flesh by feeding pride and self-righteousness. Often, as in this case, they also serve self-interest.

Because traditions require no integrity of heart, they are easily substituted for true worship and obedience. That is why it is easy for people to honor God with **their lips** while **their heart is far away from** Him. And that is why ritual, ceremony, and other religious traditions are more likely to take worshipers further from God than bring them closer. And the further a person is from God, the more **vain** his **worship** becomes.

The only heart that can worship God in spirit and in truth (John 4:24) is the heart that belongs to Him; and the only heart that belongs to Him is the heart cleansed from sin and made righteous by Him. It is this divine cleansing that God has always offered to those who trust in Him. "I will give you a new heart and put a new spirit within you," He said through Ezekiel, "and I will remove the heart of stone from your flesh and give you a heart of flesh. And I will put My Spirit within you and cause you to walk in My statutes, and you will be careful to observe My ordinances" (Ezek. 36:26-27). Unless that transformation happens within a person, his righteousness cannot exceed the hypocritical and superficial righteousness of the scribes and Pharisees—in which case he can never enter the kingdom of God (Matt. 5:20).

Jesus was condemned and crucified because He exposed the vileness of religious hypocrites who rejected God's holy **doctrines** of grace in favor of their own sinful **precepts** of self-righteous works.

There is, of course, nothing wrong with tradition as such. Many traditions help us to remember, cherish, and honor things that are noble and beautiful. But when traditions are substituted for, or in any way distort or distract from God's Word, they are an offense against God and a barrier to right worship and living. When **the**

precepts of men are taught **as doctrines,** man's wisdom is elevated above God's—which is the very root of all sin. It was Satan's inducing Eve to trust her own wisdom above God's that led to the Fall and to every subsequent sin and evil in the world.

THE CORRECTING TEACHER

And after He called the multitude to Him, He said to them, "Hear, and understand. Not what enters into the mouth defiles the man, but what proceeds out of the mouth, this defiles the man." Then the disciples came and said to Him, "Do You know that the Pharisees were offended when they heard this statement?" But He answered and said, "Every plant which My heavenly Father did not plant shall be rooted up. Let them alone; they are blind guides of the blind. And if a blind man guides a blind man, both will fall into a pit." And Peter answered and said to Him, "Explain the parable to us." And He said, "Are you still lacking in understanding also? Do you not understand that everything that goes into the mouth passes into the stomach, and is eliminated? But the things that proceed out of the mouth come from the heart, and those defile the man. For out of the heart come evil thoughts, murders, adulteries, fornications, thefts, false witness, slanders. These are the things which defile the man; but to eat with unwashed hands does not defile the man." (15:10-20)

Pollution has become a major problem in the modern world, and we read and hear much about it. The air, the soil, the rivers and lakes, and even the oceans have become polluted to a degree thought impossible a generation ago.

The Bible also has much to say about pollution, but this pollution has plagued mankind from its beginning. It is a pollution that cannot be seen, smelled, tasted, or measured. Yet it is more lethal than anything modern environmentalists oppose. The New Testament uses five different verbs, three nouns, and one adjective to represent the idea of pollution, or defilement, and various forms of those terms are used dozens of times. The five uses in the present text of **defile** and **defiles** (vv. 11, 18, 20) are all from the verb *koinoō*, which means to make common, unclean, or polluted.

God is concerned about the defilement of all of His creation, but especially about the defilement of man, who is made in His image, and most especially about the defilement of His own redeemed children. James admonishes Christians to hold to "pure and undefiled religion" (James 1:27), and Paul warns against consciences that are weak and defiled (1 Cor. 8:7). It is a terribly serious matter for Christians to defile themselves, because their bodies are temples of the Holy Spirit (1 Cor. 3:16-17). The Lord commends the church at Sardis for not having soiled, or defiled, its garments (Rev. 3:4), and in the eternal heavenly kingdom there will be no object or person who is defiled (Rev. 14:4; 21:27). But even in our present earthly life, we are commanded to grow into the likeness of our Lord Jesus Christ (Eph. 4:13), who is "holy, innocent, undefiled" (Heb. 7:26). Like His Son, God's people are to be clean, pure, holy, spotless, unpolluted, and undefiled (2 Cor. 11:2; Eph. 5:27; 2 Pet. 3:14).

In Matthew 15:1-20, Jesus first states the principle of spiritual defilement, then describes the violation of the principle, and finally elucidates the meaning of the principle.

THE PRINCIPLE STATED

And after He called the multitude to Him, He said to them, "Hear, and understand. Not what enters into the mouth defiles the man, but what proceeds out of the mouth, this defiles the man." (15:10-11)

Because the time sequence between chapters 14 and 15 is not clear, we cannot be certain about the identity of this **multitude**; but it is probably the group described in 14:34-36 who had come to Jesus for healing.

This period of healing and teaching (see John 6:26-71) apparently lasted for many days, because it carried Jesus to numerous villages, cities, and countrysides (Mark 6:56). Sometime during this period the delegation of scribes and Pharisees from Jerusalem had come to Galilee to discredit Jesus and had instead been discredited by Him.

The multitude had been standing on the sidelines, listening to Jesus condemn the religious leaders. Now **He called** them **to Him** in order to explain what He had just said about unscriptural traditions and empty worship.

Hear, and understand was a common idiom that meant, "Listen carefully and pay close attention," and was used to precede a message of great importance. It was not that what Jesus said would be hard to understand but that it would be hard to accept. The greatest stumbling block to salvation has always been lack of acceptance and belief of the gospel, not lack of understanding it. It is precisely when the gospel is clearest—as when it was taught by Jesus Himself—that it is also likely to be the most unacceptable.

As usual, Jesus' illustration was simple and based on the common knowledge and everyday experiences of the people. **Not what enters into the mouth defiles the man,** He explained, **but what proceeds out of the mouth, this defiles the man.** Spiritual defilement is a matter of the inside, not the outside. No spiritual or moral contamination can result from what we eat. The physical has no way of defiling the spiritual. "Don't be deceived and misled by the foolish traditions you have been taught," Jesus was saying. "The practice of washing your hands before you eat has nothing to do with making you undefiled. What matters is what is in your heart. It is the evil in the heart, which eventually **proceeds out of the mouth, that defiles the man.**"

No Jew *should* have been shocked at what Jesus was saying. Just as in the Sermon on the Mount, He was not teaching new truths but was simply reinforcing truths that God's Word had always taught. Even the most unlearned among the crowd had doubtlessly heard the story of the Lord's choosing David to be Israel's king in place of Saul. When Jesse brought his sons before Samuel, the prophet thought that Eliab, the eldest, was "'surely the Lord's anointed.' . . . But the Lord said to Samuel, 'Do not look at his appearance or at the height of his stature, because I have rejected him; for God sees not as man sees, for man looks at the outward appearance, but the Lord looks at the heart'" (1 Sam. 16:6-7).

Circumcision was the mark of the covenant given to Abraham, and it was looked on with the greatest possible reverence by Jews. But even before Israel entered the Promised Land, God declared through Moses, "And now, Israel, what does the Lord your God require from you, but to fear the Lord your God, to walk in all His ways and love Him, and to serve the Lord your God with all your heart and with all your soul, and to keep the Lord's commandments and His statutes which I am commanding you today for your good? . . . Circumcise then your heart" (Deut. 10:12-13, 16). The Old Testament repeatedly declares that the only religious ceremony or activity that pleases God is that which comes from a contrite, pure, and loving heart (Josh. 24:23; 1 Kings 8:23; 2 Chron. 11:16; Isa. 51:7; 57:15).

The expression **proceeds out of the mouth** ties in closely with the idea of not eating with unwashed hands. But Jesus was referring not simply to what a person says but also to what he thinks and does. In the parallel passage in Mark's gospel, Jesus says, "The things which proceed out of the *man* are what defile the man" (Mark 7:15, emphasis added). A person's defiled heart is expressed both in what he says and in what he does; but the **mouth** is the more dominant revealer of internal pollution, because it is through our words that hatred, deception, cruelty, blasphemy, and most other evils are most clearly manifest.

Mark also tells us that, in overturning this superficial, unscriptural tradition of hand washing, Jesus "declared all foods clean" (Mark 7:19). Jesus' teaching that **not what enters into the mouth defiles the man** may therefore have been the most astounding thing the people had ever heard, because few things were more sacred to the Jews of that day than their dietary laws. Form was everything. Following the teaching and example their religious leaders, orthodox Jews lived entirely by externals—which are the marks of every false religion.

Jewish traditions had multiplied so much by Jesus' time that it became impossible for anyone, even full-time religionists such as the scribes and Pharisees, to keep all of them. The rabbis had therefore developed "the law of intention." If a person arose in the morning and said, "I intend to be pure all day," he could waive the ceremonies and consider them fulfilled because of his good intention. The intention, of course, was not good at all, because its purpose was to evade rather than fulfill the tradition—showing that the Jews were hypocritical even about their own man-made standards.

In fairness to the Jews, many ceremonies and restrictions had been given to them by God as expressions of their covenant relation to Him. The book of Leviticus is filled with prescribed rituals and procedures for the priesthood in regard to the sacrificial system. God also declared certain animals unclean for any Jew to eat; and even many acceptable foods had to be prepared in carefully prescribed ways before they could be eaten. Many things were forbidden even to be touched; and certain diseases, such as leprosy, and some physical conditions, such as menstruation, were considered ceremonially defiling. But none of those ceremonially or symbolically unclean things or conditions are ever in themselves called sinful. They were to act as vivid pictures representing sin. Under the Old Covenant, being involved in or having contact with a ceremonially unclean thing rendered a person unfit to participate in certain worship ceremonies or certain social activities. But that external unfitness is never called sin. It needed ceremonial cleansing but not divine forgiveness. Yet it illustrated in a practical way the spiritual defilement of sin, as circumcision illustrated the need for a heart to have the sin "cut away."

If those ceremonial requirements and restrictions were entirely external, we might ask, why did God require them? God gave those outward signs in the early days of the Old Covenant, immediately after His people had spent four hundred years among the pagan, idolatrous, and morally corrupt Egyptians. The Ten Commandments were Israel's first written communication from God, and before that time they had only limited knowledge of His character and will. After He called Abraham to be the head of His chosen people, the Lord gave specific instructions and directions to select leaders of His people from time to time, but He had not revealed Himself in any detail. And just as parents use pictures to help teach their young children, God used those symbols and pictures to help teach His truth to the children of Israel, who were then young in His ways.

God's forbidding a person to sacrifice while ceremonially unclean was a picture of not coming to worship Him when not spiritually clean from sin. Outward cleanliness was a picture of inward cleanliness. The Old Testament nowhere teaches that circumcision, ceremonial cleansing, refraining from certain foods, or any such outward act—even though prescribed by God—could save a person and make him right with the Lord. As Paul makes clear, Abraham was counted righteous on the basis of his faith—before the rite of circumcision, or any other rite, was established. Circumcision was but "a seal of the righteousness of the faith which he had while uncircumcised" (Rom. 4:1-12). That is why, even from the earliest days of the nation Israel, God's command was to "circumcise . . . your heart" (Deut. 10:16; cf. Jer. 4:4).

The book of Hebrews is a commentary on the book of Leviticus, and neither can be properly understood without the other. The writer of Hebrews continually reminds his Jewish readers that the Old Testament sacrifices were but pictures of the real, true, perfect, and complete sacrifice that Christ made on the cross. The Old Testament priests were "a copy and shadow of the heavenly things" (Heb. 8:5). The Tabernacle and its Holy Place were "a symbol for the present time. Accordingly both gifts and sacrifices are offered which cannot make the worshiper perfect in conscience, since they relate only to food and drink and various washings, regulations for the body imposed until a time of reformation" (9:9). The time of reformation was the time of the ministry and sacrifice of the Messiah, God's Son. The Old Testament law—holy, righteous, and good as it was (Rom. 7:12)—nevertheless was "only a shadow of the good things to come and not the very form of things" (Heb. 10:1). It was always God's desire and intention that His people "draw near with a sincere heart in full assurance of faith, having [their] hearts sprinkled clean from an evil conscience and [their] bodies washed with pure water" (10:22).

Hebrews 5:12 through 6:8 is devoted entirely to appealing to Jews who were considering the gospel, and perhaps had taken some tentative steps toward acceptance, to leave behind their symbolic ceremonies and sacrifices and come all the way to the living Reality to whom those symbols pointed. (See the author's commentary on Hebrews.)

From the time the Old Covenant was first given to them, God's people were more concerned with outside ritual than with inside righteousness. Ritual requires no change of heart, no forsaking of sin, no repentance before God. It allows a person to display symbols of religion while holding on to his sins. It is religion of form rather than faith, and is therefore empty and hypocritical.

The people of Israel not only failed to appreciate the spiritual truths pictured by God's prescribed ceremonies and restrictions but they also added their own pictures to God's. And the more they multiplied the pictures, the more they trusted in the pictures and the less they trusted in God. Instead of pointing them to God, the traditions led them further from Him. Instead of enhancing faith, the traditions stifled faith and enhanced self-reliance and self-righteousness. Therefore, when God's perfect Reality came to earth, His people were so enmeshed in their traditions and so far from His Word, that they crucified God incarnate.

The matter of externals was so deeply ingrained in Jewish thinking that even Jewish believers in the early church often had great difficulty forsaking them. Several years after Pentecost, Peter still could not accept the idea that all foods were now clean. It required a special vision from God, instruction repeated three times, and a special demonstration of the work of the Holy Spirit to convince Him that both all foods and all people cleansed by God are acceptable to Him (see Acts 10:1-33). Even years after that experience, Peter slipped back into his old mind-set and for a while "began to withdraw and hold himself aloof [from Gentiles], fearing the party of the circumcision" (Gal. 2:12).

Paul warns that

> the Spirit explicitly says that in later times some will fall away from the faith, paying attention to deceitful spirits and doctrines of demons, by means of the hypocrisy of liars seared in their own conscience as with a branding iron, men who forbid marriage and advocate abstaining from foods, which God has created to be gratefully shared in by those who believe and know the truth. For everything created by God is good, and nothing is to be rejected, if it is received with gratitude; for it is sanctified by means of the word of God and prayer. (1 Tim. 4:1-5)

THE PRINCIPLE VIOLATED

Then the disciples came and said to Him, "Do You know that the Pharisees were offended when they heard this statement?" But He answered and said,

"Every plant which My heavenly Father did not plant shall be rooted up. Let them alone; they are blind guides of the blind. And if a blind man guides a blind man, both will fall into a pit." (15:12-14)

From Mark we learn that Jesus and His disciples "entered the house" (Mark 7:17), probably the home where they had been staying in Capernaum. They were now away from the crowd and the Jewish leaders from Jerusalem, and the disciples said to Jesus, **Do you know that the Pharisees were offended when they heard this statement?** Jesus knew very well that His **statement** about ceremonial washings undercut the very foundation of the legalistic system **of the Pharisees** and that they would be greatly **offended** by it. He *meant* to offend them.

Just as their opposition to Jesus would continue to increase until they finally put Him to death, so would His accusations against them. He would accuse them of not entering the kingdom and of preventing others from entering, of devouring widow's houses while making a pretense of prayer, of making their converts twice as much sons of hell as themselves, of carefully tithing their smallest herbs but of neglecting justice, mercy, and faithfulness, of appearing clean on the outside but of being full of robbery and self-indulgence, of being whitewashed tombs that contained filthy bones of dead men, of being full of hypocrisy and lawlessness, and of being of the same character as their forefathers who killed God's prophets (Matt. 23:13-30).

The **Pharisees** so idolized their system of tradition that they actually taught that God spent all day studying His own law and all night studying the Mishna that interpreted the law. Some believed God presided over the heavenly Sanhedrin, that the rabbis sat next to God according to their holiness, and that together they studied the Halakah (the legal part of the Talmud) and made decisions. They taught that, after God had spent such hard work studying the law and the Mishna, He spent three hours each evening playing with leviathan. The Lord was so distraught at the destruction of the Temple, they claimed, that in each of the three watches of the night He roared like a lion; and when He cried, His tears fell into the ocean and caused earthquakes. They even taught that, like themselves, God wore a prayer shawl and phylacteries. Worst of all, they taught that when Moses died, God touched his body and was therefore Himself defiled and had to be cleansed by Aaron, the first high priest. They had carefully boxed the Creator of the universe within their imaginative, petty, foolish, and wicked system.

The first truth about hypocrites that is evident from this passage is that they are **offended** by the truth. People who live in spiritual and moral darkness cannot stand to be exposed to the light and be shown for what they really are. The truth tears off their masks and reveals the sinful, ugly reality behind it.

Second, hypocrites are destined for judgment, because, Jesus said, **every plant which My heavenly Father did not plant shall be rooted up.** Those plants are the ungodly tares, which God now allows to grow alongside the godly wheat. But at the end of the age, the tares will be "gathered up and burned with fire" as God's angels "will gather out of His kingdom all stumbling blocks, and those who commit lawlessness, and will cast them into the furnace of fire" (Matt. 13:40-42).

Hypocrisy is so reprehensible in God's eyes that Jesus condemns the sinner along with the sin. Jesus' most constant and repeated charge against the scribes and Pharisees was their hypocrisy. They were so far from the kingdom and such intransigent enemies of the kingdom that the King said, **Leave them alone,** which could also be translated, "Keep away from them and have nothing to do with them." In a similar way, when Ephraim had joined itself to idols, God said, "Let him alone" (Hos. 4:17), as if that people were abandoned to judgment.

It is spiritually dangerous to stay around apostates and others who steadfastly reject and oppose the gospel of Christ. If there is opportunity to witness to them, it should be done with the greatest of caution, "snatching them out of the fire," as it were, and being careful not to get burned ourselves in the process (Jude 23). We should not even listen to "the opposing arguments of what is falsely called knowledge" (1 Tim. 6:20). Exposing ourselves to such people and such teaching risks spiritual disaster (cf. 2 John 8-11).

Even Jesus did not debate the ungodly scribes and Pharisees. When He responded to their questions or accusations, it was always in the form of correcting their doctrinal error and of condemning their spiritual and moral wickedness.

Perhaps the disciples were told to **leave them alone** also in the sense of not trying to judge men in order to weed out those who seem to be tares. Human judgment is imperfect and would inevitably uproot some good plants with the bad (Matt. 13:29). Concern for the purity of God's church sometimes makes believers want to take judgment into their own hands; but the Lord forbids that. In the first place, believers are not qualified for it; and in the second, it is not yet the time.

Third, hypocrites always lead others to disaster. It is bad enough that they themselves cannot and will not see the truth; it is even worse that they recruit others to their ungodliness. They are not only blind but **blind guides of the blind. And if a blind man guides a blind man, both will fall into a pit.**

The **pit** physically referred to holes that were dug in a field or pasture and filled with water for use as drinking troughs for animals. **A blind man** walking through a field would eventually **fall into a pit.** But the spiritual meaning of **pit** is hell. The **blind guides** are the Pharisees themselves, and the other **blind** are their converts, who become twice the sons of hell as their teachers (Matt. 23:15).

Jesus' calling the Pharisees **blind guides** was a play on their own description of themselves as "leaders of the blind." Jesus was saying, "Yes, you *are* leaders of the blind; but you are in the same condition as those you lead. You yourselves are blind."

THE PRINCIPLE ELUCIDATED

And Peter answered and said to Him, "Explain the parable to us." And He said, "Are you still lacking in understanding also? Do you not understand that everything that goes into the mouth passes into the stomach, and is eliminated? But the things that proceed out of the mouth come from the heart, and those defile the man. For out of the heart come evil thoughts,

murders, adulteries, fornications, thefts, false witness, slanders. These are the things which defile the man; but to eat with unwashed hands does not defile the man." (15:15-20)

The parable that **Peter** wanted Jesus to **explain** refers to the illustration of verse 11. It was not so much that the disciples did not understand what Jesus meant as that they found it hard to accept—just as had the crowd and the scribes and Pharisees. As already mentioned, even years after Pentecost, **Peter** was not able to accept fully the idea that all foods were clean (Acts 10:14; Gal. 2:11-12).

In what must have been a tone of grief, Jesus replied, **Are you still lacking in understanding?** "With all I have taught during the last two years," the Lord was saying, "are you still like the multitudes who do not know what I am talking about? Do you still fail to comprehend the absolute superiority of spirituality over formality, of the internal over the external, of reality over the shadow?"

Continuing with the figure of eating, Jesus said, **Do you not understand that everything that goes into the mouth passes into the stomach, and is eliminated?** In Mark's account, Jesus' adds, "because it does not go into his heart" (7:19). Because food is only physical, it can only affect the physical. It cannot defile the inner person, represented by the heart, because the physical and the spiritual are of two different orders. Physical pollution, no matter how corrupt, cannot cause spiritual or moral pollution. Ceremonies, rituals, and other external practices cannot cleanse a person spiritually, and failure to observe them cannot defile a person spiritually. Ceremonial cleansing, even under the Old Covenant, never did more than *picture* spiritual cleansing.

Rather, Jesus said, it is **the things that proceed out of the mouth** and **come from the heart** that **defile the man.** The **heart** represents the inner person, his thoughts, attitudes, desires, loyalties, and motives. When the **heart** is filled with **evil thoughts, murders, adulteries, fornications, thefts, false witness, slanders,** and other such ungodliness, **these are the things which defile.**

It was the Pharisees' inner unrighteousness—shown in the extreme by their **evil thoughts** to destroy Jesus—that corrupted them. The central moral thrust of the Sermon on the Mount is that the basis of all sin is the inner thought, not the outward act. A person commits the sin when he *wants* to do it, whether or not he ever carries it out in action. **Murders, adulteries, fornications, thefts, false witness, slanders,** and all other sins begin in the heart (see Matt. 5:21-37).

The things that **defile the man** come from an unwashed **heart,** not from **unwashed hands.** The need is for God to cleanse men's hearts, not for men to wash their hands.

Paul warned Titus that "rebellious men, empty talkers and deceivers, especially those of the circumcision, . . . must be silenced because they are upsetting whole families, teaching things they should not teach. . . . For this cause reprove them severely that they may be sound in the faith, not paying attention to Jewish myths and commandments of men who turn away from the truth" (Titus 1:10-11, 13-14). The apostle then goes on to say, "To the pure, all things are pure, but to those who are defiled and unbelieving, nothing is pure, but both their mind and their conscience are defiled. They profess to know God, but by their deeds they deny Him, being detestable and disobedient, and worthless for any good deed" (vv. 15-16).

When a person is defiled on the inside, what he does on the outside is also defiled. But when a person is pure in heart—undefiled on the inside—he will see God (Matt. 5:8).

BIRDVILLE
BAPTIST CHURCH
LIBRARY

The Quality of
Great Faith (15:21-28)

42

And Jesus went away from there, and withdrew into the district of Tyre and Sidon. And behold, a Canaanite woman came out from that region, and began to cry out, saying, "Have mercy on me, O Lord, Son of David; my daughter is cruelly demon-possessed." But He did not answer her a word. And His disciples came to Him and kept asking Him, saying, "Send her away, for she is shouting out after us." But He answered and said, "I was sent only to the lost sheep of the house of Israel." But she came and began to bow down before Him, saying, "Lord, help me!" And He answered and said, "It is not good to take the children's bread and throw it to the dogs." But she said, "Yes, Lord; but even the dogs feed on the crumbs which fall from their master's table." Then Jesus answered and said to her, "O woman, your faith is great; be it done for you as you wish." And her daughter was healed at once. (15:21-28)

The Bible has much to say about faith. It speaks of weak faith, strong faith, bold faith, rich faith, abiding faith, steadfast faith, dead faith, precious faith, common faith, unfeigned faith, working faith, obedient faith, and many other kinds.

It also speaks of little faith and great faith, and this text contains the second reference in Matthew's gospel in which Jesus speaks of great faith. Of the Roman centurion who asked for his servant to be healed Jesus said, "I have not found such great faith with anyone in Israel" (8:10). In both cases the person expressing great faith was a Gentile; and in this second instance the context seems to imply that the woman's faith not only was for the deliverance of her daughter but was also for personal salvation.

THE SETTING

And Jesus went away from there, and withdrew into the district of Tyre and Sidon. (15:21)

Until this time **Jesus** had carried on most of His ministry in Galilee; but now He **went away** because of the rapidly mounting pressures that faced Him **there.**

He was under pressure first of all from the multitudes who followed Him from place to place and were convinced He was the long-predicted Messiah. They were right in recognizing that His miraculous powers marked Him as the true Messiah, but they were wrong about the kind of Messiah He had come to be. They expected Him to deliver them from the oppressive Romans and their Herodian lackeys and to usher in an unending period of political freedom and material prosperity. After His feeding of the five thousand, they even intended "to come and take Him by force, to make Him king" (John 6:15).

Second, Jesus was under the pressure of possible arrest and execution by Herod Antipas, who thought Jesus was John the Baptist come back from the dead (Matt. 14:2). The king's jealous hatred of anyone who threatened his throne would have led him to murder Jesus just as coldly as he had John.

The greatest pressure, however, was from the Jewish religious leaders. The scribes and Pharisees of Galilee had already determined to destroy Jesus (12:14), and after He rebuked and embarrassed the delegation from Jerusalem by showing the ungodliness of their man-made traditions (15:1-9), the danger from the religious establishment escalated. As Alfred Edersheim commented, Jesus "was saying distinctly un-Jewish things," and even the enthusiasm of the multitudes cooled rapidly when He began to make clear what allegiance to Him demanded (John 6:60-66).

Besides His need for physical refreshment and time to be alone with the twelve, Jesus therefore had those additional reasons to find a place of temporary retreat. He had moved away by going across the Sea of Galilee to Bethsaida Julias, only to be followed by a massive crowd whom He miraculously fed. And after crossing back over to the Plain of Gennesaret just south of Capernaum, He was immediately recognized and was again surrounded by the sick, crippled, and diseased who wanted healing.

Jesus therefore **withdrew** from the frenzy of Galilee and traveled northwest **into the district of Tyre and Sidon,** out of the land of Israel and beyond the jurisdiction of both Herod and the Jewish religious leaders. **The district of Tyre and Sidon** was the Gentile territory of ancient Phoenicia, an area now in southern

Lebanon, on the eastern coast of the Mediterranean Sea. It is possible that He and the disciples spent most of their time in the foothills of the mountains, which would have been a refreshing change in climate from the hot and arid region of Galilee.

More importantly, Jesus would gain time to be alone with the disciples and to further prepare them for His coming crucifixion and their apostolic ministry. Palestine afforded no privacy and numerous dangers, but Jesus did not withdraw out of fear. When the time came for Him to face the cross, "He resolutely set His face to go to Jerusalem" (Luke 9:51; cf. 19:28).

Some interpreters believe that Jesus' statement "I was sent only to the lost sheep of the house of Israel" (Matt. 15:24) indicates that He could not have actually gone into a Gentile area and that this woman must have come down into Galilee to see Jesus just as many others had done. But Mark makes clear that Jesus not only went to the "region of Tyre" but that He "came through Sidon to the Sea of Galilee" (7:24, 31). It is true, however, that the Lord did not go to this area to minister but to rest, just as centuries earlier the Lord had sent Elijah to that same region to rest at the home of the widow at "Zarephath, which belongs to Sidon" (1 Kings 17:9).

When Jesus went to the house near Tyre, "He wanted no one to know of it; yet He could not escape notice" (Mark 7:24*b*). As Archbishop Trench commented, "Like perfume betrays itself, so He whose name is perfume poured out cannot be hid." Jesus did not purposely expand His ministry into Gentile territory, but many people of that area had heard of Him and already had gone into Galilee to see and hear Him and to be healed (Matt. 4:24-25; Mark 3:8).

In His omniscience Jesus was not surprised at being discovered or of being drawn into ministry. Many Gentiles, illustrated by the Roman centurion, were more humbly receptive than the Jewish multitudes, who often took Jesus' healings as a matter of their rightful heritage. In their thinking, the Messiah belonged exclusively to Israel, and He was obligated to serve, heal, and liberate His fellow Jews. It was that proud and self-righteous attitude that drove the multitude to try to force a crown on Him (John 6:15).

But most of the native Gentiles in and near Palestine were less religiously and intellectually proud than their Jewish neighbors. They had long since lost their military and commercial power as well as much of their religious and cultural heritage. Their pagan religious systems had repeatedly failed them and now had little influence on their living. They were empty, in need, and open to help. Jesus had told the Jews of Chorazin, Bethsaida, and Capernaum that if Tyre, Sidon, and Sodom had experienced a revelation of God's power such as they had been witnessing, those Gentile cities would have repented and been spared judgment (Matt. 11:21-23).

Jesus' first priority was to minister to God's people Israel, to reveal Himself as their Messiah and to offer them the kingdom; but He always extended Himself to open hearts and never refused a person of any race or culture who came to Him in faith. The Lord's going to the Gentile region of Tyre and Sidon must have been refreshing because of the people as well as the climate. They were deep in darkness, but many anxiously sought for light (cf. John 1:9-11).

Whether Jew or Gentile, the person who approached Jesus with true faith and humility was always received. The person who came with an empty but open heart left with a filled heart, while the person who came with a filled and closed heart left with nothing. Jesus declared, "Come to Me, all who are weary and heavy-laden, and I will give you rest" (Matt. 11:28); and He promised, "The one who comes to Me I will certainly not cast out" (John 6:37).

The gospel came through the Jews (John 4:22) and first to the Jews, but it was never intended to be only for them. The gospel "is the power of God for salvation to everyone who believes, to the Jew first and also to the Greek" (Rom. 1:16). The Great Commission was to "make disciples of all the nations" (Matt. 28:19), beginning with Jerusalem but reaching "even to the remotest part of the earth" (Acts 1:8). Israel was the channel through which the gospel would be carried to the entire world.

THE QUALITIES OF GREAT FAITH

And behold, a Canaanite woman came out from that region, and began to cry out, saying, "Have mercy on me, O Lord, Son of David; my daughter is cruelly demon-possessed." But He did not answer her a word. And His disciples came to Him and kept asking Him, saying, "Send her away, for she is shouting out after us." But He answered and said, "I was sent only to the lost sheep of the house of Israel." But she came and began to bow down before Him, saying, "Lord, help me!" And He answered and said, "It is not good to take the children's bread and throw it to the dogs." But she said, "Yes, Lord; but even the dogs feed on the crumbs which fall from their master's table." (15:22-27)

Jesus' encounter with the **Canaanite woman** is the story of a faith Jesus called great (v. 28). Great faith is, of course, a relative term. This woman's faith was not great because it was stronger or more sincere or mature than the faith of many Jews who believed in Christ but because it was based on so little light. When Peter's faith faltered and he began to sink into the water, Jesus referred to it as "little faith" (Matt. 14:31). In general character it was greater than this woman's faith and surely greater than the faith of the other eleven disciples, who did not even attempt to walk on the water, but it was not as strong as it should have been for that situation. Peter was a Jew and therefore had the heritage of God's Word and special blessing. More than that, he had lived for nearly two years in intimate fellowship with the Son of God. He had seen virtually every miracle Jesus performed and heard virtually every word He preached and taught. He had saving faith in Jesus as his Lord and Savior and had left everything to follow Him; but his great privilege and advantage was no guarantee that, under severe testing, his faith might not be reduced to relatively little.

The **Canaanite woman,** on the other hand, had been raised in a pagan culture that had been renowned for its wickedness and vileness. She was a descendant of a people God had commanded Israel to conquer and "utterly destroy" (Deut. 7:2). She had no heritage of God's Word, God's blessing, or of His Tabernacle, Temple, priesthood, or sacrifices. Therefore, because she believed so much relative to so little revelation, Jesus called her faith great (Matt. 15:28). And from her story we can propose five general qualities that mark all great faith: It is repentant, properly directed, reverent, persistent, and humble.

REPENTANT

And behold, a Canaanite woman came out from that region, and began to cry out, saying, "Have mercy on me, (15:22*a*)

Because this **woman** was **a Canaanite,** "of the Syrophoenician race" (Mark 7:26), she was probably a worshiper of Astarte and other pagan deities that were popular in **that region.** The fact that she came to Jesus, a Jewish teacher and healer, indicates she was disillusioned with the idolatry and immoral debauchery that characterized her religion. In turning to Jesus, she turned from the way of Satan and sin to the way of God, and that is the essence of repentance.

The woman's plea is further proof of her penitence. She knew she did not deserve Jesus' help, that she was unworthy of Him, and that her only hope for undeserved forgiveness was in His gracious **mercy.** By definition, the person who asks for **mercy** asks for something undeserved. This woman did not come demanding but pleading. She did not ask Jesus' help on the basis of her own goodness but on the basis of His.

Mercy is integral to God's redemptive work for man. From the time of the Fall, man has had no way back to God except through His merciful grace. It is not surprising, therefore, that in the New Testament and the Greek Old Testament (Septuagint) various forms of the verb *eleeō* (to **have mercy**) are used some five hundred times.

When the Sinai covenant was renewed with the people of Israel, God declared Himself to Moses as "The Lord, the Lord God, compassionate and gracious, slow to anger, and abounding in lovingkindness and truth; who keeps lovingkindness for thousands, who forgives iniquity, transgression and sin" (Ex. 34:6-7). In his reply Moses said, "If now I have found favor in Thy sight, O Lord, I pray, let the Lord go along in our midst, even though the people are so obstinate; and do Thou pardon our iniquity and our sin, and take us as Thine own possession" (v. 9). In his profound penitential psalm written after he confessed his sin with Bathsheba, David pleaded for nothing but **mercy:** "Be gracious to me, O God, according to Thy lovingkindness; according to the greatness of Thy compassion blot out my transgressions" (Ps. 51:1).

Faith that apprehends the blessings of Christ involves repentance that comes from a deep and sincere sense of unworthiness. In his book *All of Grace* (Chicago: Moody, pp. 97-100) Charles Spurgeon wrote:

> Repentance is the inseparable companion of faith. All the while that we walk by faith and not by sight, the tear of repentance glitters in the eye of faith. That

is not true repentance which does not come of faith in Jesus, and that is not true faith in Jesus which is not tinctured with repentance. Faith and repentance, like Siamese twins, are vitally joined together. . . . Faith and repentance are but two spokes in the same wheel, two handles of the same plow. Repentance has been well described as a heart broken *for* sin and *from* sin, and it may equally well be spoken of as turning and returning. It is a change of mind of the most thorough and radical sort, and it is attended with sorrow for the past and a resolve of amendment in the future. . . . Repentance of sin and faith in divine pardon are the warp and woof of the fabric of real conversion.

Repentance adds nothing to faith but is rather an integral part of it. Saving faith is repentant faith. "Repentance toward God and faith in [the] Lord Jesus Christ" are inseparable (Acts 20:21). Because they are inseparable, Scripture sometimes refers to salvation as repentance. Paul declares that "the kindness of God leads you to repentance" (Rom. 2:4), and Peter that God does not desire "for any to perish but for all to come to repentance" (2 Pet. 3:9).

RIGHTLY DIRECTED AND REVERENT

O Lord, Son of David; my daughter is cruelly demon-possessed." (15:22b)

Great faith must, of course, be directed at the right object. Those who believe that somehow, in some way, by some means everything will ultimately work out for the good have faith in an illusion. To declare, "Somewhere there's somebody who hears every prayer" or "I believe in the darkest night a candle glows," is to believe in nothing more trustworthy than your own imagination and wishful thinking. It is unbelievably foolish to put ultimate trust in something or someone you know nothing about. When John Greenleaf Whittier wrote, "The steps of faith fall on the seeming void and find the rock beneath," he proved himself a better poet than theologian.

That sort of faith is essentially faith in faith, which is to say no faith at all. To jump out of an airplane with a parachute is an act of faith. To jump without a parachute while exclaiming, "I believe," is an act of stupidity. To say no more than, "I believe in love," "I believe in believing," or, "I believe it will all work out," is contentless faith and therefore pointless and powerless. It shows no more sense than to go on vacation and leave your three-year-old child behind with instructions to look after the house and pay all the bills while you are gone.

For faith to make sense and to have power it must be placed in a trustworthy object; and as the Canaanite woman turned her back on her idols she placed her faith in the **Lord**, the **Son of David**. Despite her pagan background, she had heard of the Jews' coming Messiah, who was called the **Son of David**; and she reverently addressed Jesus as her sovereign and omnipotent **Lord**. She had heard of the

Messiah's great power and also sensed His great goodness; and she treated Him with both dignity and expectancy. She approached Him in the same reverent, trusting spirit as the leper who met Jesus after the Sermon on the Mount "and bowed down to Him, saying, 'Lord, if You are willing, You can make me clean'" (Matt. 8:2).

After the irreverent treatment of the Lord by the scribes and Pharisees—who had called Him a drunk, a companion of sinners, and demon-controlled—it must have been refreshing for Jesus to hear this Gentile woman come to Him with such respect and submission. Although she did not yet understand the full meaning of Christ's lordship or messiahship, she came with a sense of awe and wonder.

This woman loved her young **daughter** more than her own life, and she came to the only source of help she knew of. Her faith was great because she turned from faith in false gods, dumb idols, and pagan deities to faith in Jesus Christ. Her trust in Astarte may have seemed satisfactory while things were going well; but when her **daughter** became **cruelly demon-possessed,** the mother discovered she could get no help from a goddess of stone. She therefore left her religious system, left her pagan family and friends, left her false belief that had no answers or power, and came to the only One who could help her. By her appeal to Christ, she publicly affirmed His power over her former gods of wood and stone and metal. Like the Thessalonian believers, she had "turned to God from idols to serve a living and true God" (1 Thess. 1:9).

PERSISTENT

But He did not answer her a word. And His disciples came to Him and kept asking Him, saying, "Send her away, for she is shouting out after us." But He answered and said, "I was sent only to the lost sheep of the house of Israel." (15:23-24)

Great faith does not give up; it is not deterred by obstacles, setbacks, or disappointments. Jesus therefore tested the faith of this woman by setting up a series of barriers. Some people have to struggle against strong doubts before they come to fully trust Christ for salvation. Others have to struggle against the objections and arguments of friends and family. Still others struggle to believe because they have never heard the gospel clearly presented or because they see inconsistencies in the lives of Christians they know. This woman, however, had barriers placed in her way by the Savior Himself.

Sometimes the hardest response to accept is no response at all, and that is what this woman received from Jesus as **He did not answer her a word.** The disciples apparently interpreted Jesus' ignoring the woman as a sign of unconcern and wondered why He did not dismiss her. As she continued to plead with Jesus and He continued to ignore her, **His disciples** became more upset with the woman and more puzzled about the Lord. In frustration they **came to Him and kept asking Him** to do something about this nuisance who not only was getting on their nerves and but was attracting attention at a time when Jesus wanted to get away from the pressures and demands of the crowds. Finally they said, **"Send her away, for she is shouting after us."**

The disciples response was insensitive and prejudiced. They did not want to be bothered by this Gentile woman who was interfering with their plans and peace of mind. In advising the Lord to **send her away,** they may have had in mind His healing the daughter first, sensing that that would be the only thing that would make the woman leave. And on the surface it seems as if Jesus was equally, if not more, insensitive, because He did not even acknowledge her presence. Commenting on the Lord's seeming indifference, the early church Father Chrysostom wrote, "The Word has no word. The fountain is sealed. The Physician holds back his remedy."

But Jesus did nothing unloving and nothing without a divine purpose. He had had enough of superficiality and shallowness, of the pretended faith of those who selfishly got what they wanted from Him and left. But more than that He wanted to test the woman's faith to bring it to full flower. He put up the barriers not to keep her away but to draw her closer. He also used the occasion to show the disciples the value of persistent faith and to help them distinguish between the genuine and the superficial. He erected barriers that only genuine, persistent faith could hurdle. (Cf. Matt. 19:16-22, where Jesus placed barriers before the young man to test the genuineness of his plea for eternal life.)

Speaking directly to the disciples, but within the hearing of the woman, Jesus said, **I was sent only to the lost sheep of the house of Israel.** The hardness of heart suggested by His silence now seemed to be confirmed by His words. We do not know what the disciples thought of Jesus' comment, but they must have wondered why He had so willingly healed the servant of the Roman centurion and offered the water of life to the Samaritan woman at Sychar but now refused to help this woman simply because she was not **of the house of Israel.**

But by those words Jesus assured the disciples that His plan of redemption was still on course. Israel was still the Lord's chosen people and the kingdom was still offered first to the seed of Abraham. Despite their hostility, resentment, and rejection, the Lord would continue to call **the house of Israel** to repentance. His primary ministry was still to the children of the covenant. It was not yet time to move to the Gentile nations, because the full opportunity to Israel had not as yet been presented. It is important to note that even after the crucifixion and resurrection, Peter still referred to Israel as "the sons . . . of the covenant," to whom Jesus was first sent for blessing and cleansing (Acts 3:25-26).

Whatever effect Jesus' response had on the disciples, it must have been a painful blow to the woman. Most people would have indignantly said, "So much for your God of love, your message of compassion, and your narrow, bigoted religion. I want nothing to do with a God or religion like that." But this woman had no resentment or bitterness, only an abiding love for her afflicted little girl and a determination to have her freed from her demonic torture. She also knew that the gods her people worshiped did not care. She knew Jesus was the only hope and that she had nowhere else to turn. She said in effect what Peter had said not long before: "Lord, to whom shall we go?" (John 6:68).

But she came and began to bow down before Him, saying, "Lord, help me!" And He answered and said, "It is not good to take the children's bread and throw it to the dogs." But she said, "Yes, Lord; but even the dogs feed on the crumbs which fall from their master's table." (15:25-27)

To bow down is from *proskuneō,* which literally means to prostrate oneself and is frequently translated "to worship." Whether or not the woman's bowing down was intended to be worship, it was clearly an act of humility. She threw herself at Jesus' feet and pleaded with even greater desperation, **Lord, help me!**

But again Jesus put her off, saying to her the same basic truth He had just pointed out to the disciples (v. 24): **It is not good to take the children's bread and throw it to the dogs.**

Two different Greek words are used in the New Testament for **dogs.** One refers to the mangy and often vicious mongrels that ran in packs and lived largely off garbage and carcasses of dead animals. The **dogs** referred to here, however, were household pets that were sometimes treated almost like family.

Even so, Jesus' remarks were far from a compliment. The woman knew that **children's** referred to Jews and **dogs** referred to Gentiles, because both figures were commonly used by Jews. Jesus' words sounded much like the insults Jews frequently cast at Gentiles and that the woman had probably heard many times before.

But she was undaunted, and in an incredible flash of insight she picked up on Jesus' own illustration, saying, **Yes, Lord; but even the dogs feed on the crumbs which fall from their master's table.** She knew she was sinful and unworthy of anything He had to offer and was willing to concede that she was less deserving than Jews. In doing so she demonstrated a complete absence of the pride, self-reliance, and self-righteousness that characterized most Jews. She was willing to settle for **the crumbs which fall from their master's table,** because that would be enough to meet her needs. A tiny leftover of Jesus' great power could heal her daughter, and that was all she asked.

Although Jesus' priority mission was to the Jews, the crumbs of the gospel did indeed fall from their table and feed humble Gentiles who hungered for the Bread of Life.

THE LORD'S RESPONSE

Then Jesus answered and said to her, "O woman, your faith is great; be it done for you as you wish." And her daughter was healed at once. (15:28)

473

After putting up a barrier of silence and then a double barrier of seeming rejection, Jesus heard what He wanted to hear. Her seeking heart would not give up. Like Abraham, she grew strong in faith through God's testing (Rom. 4:20), and like Jacob wrestling with the Lord (Gen. 32:26), she would not let go until He blessed her. She fulfilled the pledge of Jeremiah 29:13-14, "'And you will seek Me and find Me, when you search for Me with all your heart. And I will be found by you,' declares the Lord."

Highly pleased with the woman's response, **Jesus** declared, **O woman, your faith is great.** Without having heard the Sermon on the Mount, she came with the humble, mourning, meek, and seeking heart that God requires for kingdom entrance (Matt. 5:3-6). She exhibited the attitude expressed in Luke 16:16 of vigorously pressing forward (from *biazomai*) into the kingdom and in Luke 13:24 of striving, struggling, straining every nerve (from *agōnizomai*) to enter it.

Because of her great faith, Jesus granted her **wish** that her little child be delivered from the demon, **and her daughter was healed at once.** As Spurgeon observed, "The Lord of glory surrendered to the faith of the woman." She kept asking until she received, seeking until she found, and knocking until it was opened to her (cf. Matt. 7:7).

BIRDVILLE
BAPTIST CHURCH
LIBRARY

Compassion for the Outsider (15:29-39)

43

And departing from there, Jesus went along by the Sea of Galilee, and having gone up to the mountain, He was sitting there. And great multitudes came to Him, bringing with them those who were lame, crippled, blind, dumb, and many others, and they laid them down at His feet; and He healed them, so that the multitude marveled as they saw the dumb speaking, the crippled restored, and the lame walking, and the blind seeing; and they glorified the God of Israel.

And Jesus called His disciples to Him, and said, "I feel compassion for the multitude, because they have remained with Me now three days and have nothing to eat; and I do not wish to send them away hungry, lest they faint on the way." And the disciples said to Him, "Where would we get so many loaves in a desolate place to satisfy such a great multitude?" And Jesus said to them, "How many loaves do you have?" And they said, "Seven, and a few small fish." And He directed the multitude to sit down on the ground; and He took the seven loaves and the fish; and giving thanks, He broke them and started giving them to the disciples, and the disciples in turn, to the multitudes. And they all ate, and were satisfied, and they picked up what was left over of the broken pieces, seven large baskets full. And those who ate were four thousand men, besides women and children. And sending away the multitudes, He got into the boat, and came to the region of Magadan. (15:29-39)

The God of Scripture is a God of compassion. He suffers with people; He feels their pain and their sorrow and seeks to alleviate it, because He deeply cares for their welfare and happiness. John 3:16 could be translated, "God had such compassion on the world, that He gave His only begotten Son, that whoever believes in Him should not perish, but have eternal life." It is God's compassion for man that, from the time of the Fall, has offered the way back to Him. Jeremiah declared, "The Lord's lovingkindnesses indeed never cease, for His compassions never fail" (Lam. 3:22). The Authorized Version of that verse reads, "It is of the Lord's mercies that we are not consumed, because his compassions fail not." The Lord's compassion restricts his judgment and extends His mercy, giving fallen mankind opportunity to repent and be saved.

Over and over again God showed compassion on His people when they were in need, despite their sin and rebelliousness against Him. During their time of oppression under Aram, "the Lord was gracious to them and had compassion on them and turned to them because of His covenant with Abraham, Isaac, and Jacob, and would not destroy them or cast them from His presence until now" (2 Kings 13:23). During the time that Babylon ruled Judah, Zedekiah, the appointed Jewish king at Jerusalem, not only rebelled against Nebuchadnezzar but also against God, Jeremiah, and the other prophets. The priests and the people were also unfaithful and wicked. Yet "the Lord, the God of their fathers, sent word to them again and again by His messengers, because He had compassion on His people" (2 Chron. 36:13-15).

From the earliest part of His ministry, Jesus felt compassion for the multitudes, "because they were distressed and downcast like sheep without a shepherd" (Matt. 9:36). He had special compassion for the sick and suffering, whom He healed of every sort of affliction (14:14; cf. 4:23; 8:16; 9:35). His compassion was not limited to His own Jewish people; and as He ministered to all men, He found unusual faith among many of the Gentiles, such as the Roman centurion whose servant He healed (Matt. 8:5-13) and the Syrophoenician woman whose daughter He had just delivered from demon possession (15:22-28).

After **departing from there,** the region of Tyre and Sidon where that woman lived (v. 21), **Jesus went along by the Sea of Galilee, and having gone up to the mountain, He was sitting there.** We learn from Mark that Jesus went around the Sea of Galilee, apparently on the east side, stopping in "the region of Decapolis" (Mark 7:31), another Gentile area. Although His primary ministry was still to the Jews, the Lord continually reached out beyond the covenant people, giving a preview of the extension of the kingdom into the whole world (cf. Matt. 28:19; Acts 1:8).

During His three-year ministry, Jesus gave many such previews of the coming kingdom. In the transfiguration He previewed His return in great glory at the second coming to establish the millennial kingdom on earth. His choosing twelve men to be His apostles prefigured the reestablishment of the twelve tribes of Israel, over which those apostles would one day reign (Matt. 19:28). His healing of all who came to Him prefigured His ultimate external "healing of the nations" (Rev. 22:2). His teaching about the kingdom prefigured the fulfilled kingdom when "the earth will be full of the knowledge of the Lord as the waters cover the sea" (Isa. 11:9).

As already mentioned, this ministry of several months in Gentile land prefigured the coming kingdom that would embrace Gentile and Jew alike. On these and other occasions, Peter had therefore been repeatedly and dramatically exposed to the truth that the gospel was for all men—long before his vision of the unclean animals and his encounter with Cornelius, through which He was finally convinced "that God is not one to show partiality" (Acts 10:1-34; cf. vv. 45-47).

The region of Decapolis, where Jesus had just arrived, was on the southeast side of the Sea of Galilee, directly south of the modern Golan Heights. Decapolis means "ten cities" (from the Greek *deka,* "ten," and *polis,* "city") and derives its name from the ten city-states located within its boundaries. This somewhat independent territory was wedged between the region to the north ruled by Philip the tetrarch and the regions to the south and west ruled by Herod Antipas. In and around these ten cities archaeologists have discovered the ruins of elegant amphitheaters, forums, and countless pagan statues and monuments honoring the various gods of the Greek pantheon—including Zeus, Aphrodite, Athene, Artemis, Hercules, Dionysus, and Demeter.

From the time that Jesus fed the five thousand until this feeding, some time had elapsed. In the earlier miracle He had commanded that multitude "to recline on the grass" (14:19), whereas He instructed the multitude in Decapolis "to sit down on the ground" (15:35). In that part of Palestine the grass lasts only from early spring until early summer, when most of it withers from the heat. The multitude of Jews near the northeast shore of Galilee had been able to sit on grass, whereas the crowd of Gentiles in the Decapolis had to sit on bare ground, indicating that as much as several months may have elapsed between the two feedings.

Although Jesus had not gone to the district of Tyre and Sidon for the purpose of ministering, He was immediately recognized there and was eager to help those who came to Him—no doubt including many others besides the Canaanite woman. When He arrived in the region of Decapolis He was also recognized, because from the earliest days of His ministry people from that area had come to hear Him speak and to be healed (Matt. 4:24-25). Therefore, when word spread that Jesus was actually visiting their own territory, **great multitudes came to Him.**

Jesus had gone up to the mountain and was some distance from populated areas. It therefore took several days for word of His presence to spread and for the **multitudes** to get to Him from various parts of the region. Travel was of course especially slow for the ones who were **bringing with them those who were lame, crippled, blind, dumb, and many others.**

Crippled (from *kullos*) refers to any part of the human body that is deformed or unable to be used, and includes mutilation or total loss. Jesus used the term to described a person who has had a hand or foot cut off (Matt. 18:8). The people seeking help therefore included the most seriously deformed.

When the friends and relatives found Jesus, **they laid** their afflicted loved ones **down at His feet; and He healed them. Laid** is from *rhiptō*, which means to cast or throw down in haste but not carelessly. They could not reach Jesus too quickly or get too close. The crowd eventually numbered "four thousand men, besides women and children" (15:38), and therefore could have totaled as many as twenty thousand. We do not know how many of that number had come for healing, but it must have been many hundreds and perhaps several thousand. The people did not all arrive at the same time, and those who were healed moved away to make room for others. But at any given time Jesus would have had hundreds of people crowding around Him.

None of the gospel writers gives details of the healings; we are simply told that **He healed them**. But it is not hard to imagine the cries for help that mingled with shouts of joy, as some came to Jesus diseased and deformed while others were leaving healthy and whole. People who were sick went away cured; people who came with only one functioning arm or leg went away with two; and people who came blind and deaf went away seeing and hearing. People who had never spoken a word were now shouting praises to Jesus. People who had never walked a step were now jumping and running for joy. It is hardly surprising that **the multitude marveled as they saw the dumb speaking, the crippled restored, and the lame walking, and the blind seeing**.

No doubt many of **the multitude** had seen Jesus heal before, but that made the sight no less amazing. **Marveled** is from *thaumazō*, which means to be struck with awe. The people were seeing something that defied human explanation, and they were dumbfounded at the uninterrupted flow of instantaneous and complete healings. Mark says "they were utterly astonished, saying, 'He has done all things well'" (7:37). The wonder of these Gentiles was greater than the wonder of the Jews, whose awe was often tempered by spiritual pride and skepticism. When the crowd at Decapolis saw the perfection of the healings, they knew the power behind them was divine—in great contrast to the Pharisees who charged Jesus with casting out demons by Satan's power (Matt. 12:24).

Knowing that their pagan gods could not perform such marvels, and would not have been inclined to perform them if they could, the people from Decapolis **glorified the God of Israel**. They were not fully aware of who Jesus was, but they knew He was a Jew and that He served **the God of Israel**, and they glorified His **God** in praise and reverent fear. Their excitement and gratitude over being healed or seeing their loved ones and friends healed made them spontaneously praise the Lord.

The multitudes were so large and the needs so great that the healings continued for several days. After that miraculous but exhausting time, **Jesus called His disciples to Him and said, "I feel compassion for the multitude, because they have remained with Me now three days and have nothing to eat.**

I feel compassion is from the verb *splanchnizomai*, which literally means to be moved in one's inward parts, in the bowels or viscera, which the ancients considered the seat of emotions. The English word **compassion** is taken from the Latin, which means to suffer with, but it has come to mean much more than that. According to one definition, it is "a feeling of deep sympathy and sorrow, accompanied by a strong desire to alleviate the pain and remove its cause."

Jesus had **compassion** for people's spiritual needs, which were eternal in their consequences. He had **compassion** for their physical afflictions, which were often lifelong in their effect. But He also had **compassion** in regard to their food, which sustained them from day to day. In His model prayer the Lord tells us to ask our heavenly Father to "give us this day our daily bread" (Matt. 6:11), because He cares about the practical needs of our daily lives.

Despite the great excitement of the people and the fact that for many of them this was the first time in their lives they had been physically well and whole, **three days** without food was a long time. Jesus therefore did **not wish to send them away hungry, lest they faint on the way.** The idea behind **faint** is that of collapsing, as a bowstring goes limp when unstrung. The Lord was determined that the needy multitude would not go home on empty stomachs and become **faint on the way.**

At first glance the disciples' response seems to be essentially the same as it was when He asked them to feed the five thousand near Bethsaida Julias (14:16-17). Because in Decapolis the disciples appeared to act as if this were the first time Jesus had requested such a thing of them, many liberal commentators have maintained that Matthew gives two accounts of the same feeding, with differing and even conflicting details. But as a former tax collector, who was used to keeping accurate records, Matthew was much too astute to have missed the contradictions; and it would make no sense to fabricate them. He was with Jesus throughout His ministry and it is inconceivable that he would be so confused about such a dramatic event that he thought it happened twice instead of only once. Nor would the Holy Spirit, who inspired the gospels, have allowed such misrepresentation. The necessity of food is so basic that it may be assumed there were other such feedings not recorded in the gospels (cf. John 21:5).

Why, then, did the disciples again ask Jesus, **Where would we get so many loaves in a desolate place to satisfy such a great multitude?** Why did they not simply expect Jesus to perform a miracle like the one He had performed only a month or so earlier? They probably did. They could not possibly have forgotten the earlier occasion, especially since they were directly involved in distributing the food to some twenty-five thousand people as Jesus multiplied it. The reason for their question about where to find food seems to be that they were simply acknowledging again their own lack of resources. They were saying, in effect, "Lord we are no more able to feed this crowd by ourselves than we were able to feed the other one. This group is smaller, but four thousand men and their families are just as impossible for us to feed as five thousand."

The region of the Decapolis was probably a more **desolate place** than the area near Bethsaida Julias, and if they could not have found food there, they could certainly not find it here. The disciples did not doubt that Jesus could also miraculously feed this group; nor had they forgotten the previous feeding. The first idea is totally improbable and the second is impossible. Rather, their reply to Jesus emphasized that they knew the Lord could **satisfy such a multitude** but that they could not. He had no less power than before, and they had no more.

Jesus then asked them, **"How many loaves do you have?" And they said, "Seven, and a few small fish"**; and again (cf. 14:18) they brought what little they had to Him. Also as before, Jesus **directed the multitude to sit down on the ground.** Because this crowd was almost as large as the previous one that was fed, it seems likely that Jesus also had this group sit in groups of hundreds and fifties (see Mark 6:40) in order to simplify the distribution.

Then **He took the seven loaves and the fish; and giving thanks, He broke them and started giving them to the disciples, and the disciples in turn, to the multitudes.** The verb translated **started giving** could also be rendered "kept giving." In either case the idea is that of repeated **giving** out of the food as it was multiplied. When his basket of food was emptied, a disciple would bring it back to the Lord for refilling, until all **the multitudes** were fed.

The Lord could have miraculously distributed the food as easily as He had miraculously multiplied it. He had provided manna for the children of Israel in the wilderness fresh every morning, distributed across the entire wilderness area in which they were encamped, so that the people needed go only outside their tents and gather what was needed (Ex. 16:14). But Jesus was teaching the disciples as well as feeding the multitudes. He wanted them to learn the practical as well as the theological reality of His compassion. He wanted them to participate first hand in God's concern for the daily needs of people as well as for their eternal redemption and physical wholeness, because divine compassion embraces every dimension of human need.

No one went away hungry, because **they all ate;** and no one went away half full but completely **satisfied.** After everyone had eaten all he wanted, the disciples **picked up what was left over of the broken pieces, seven large baskets full.**

The **seven large baskets** mentioned here are of a different type than the twelve baskets used in the feeding of the five thousand. The type of basket used at the previous feeding was a small Jewish container called a *kophinos,* used by an individual when traveling to carry food for one or two meals. The **baskets** used in the Decapolis feeding, however, were *spuridas,* which were distinctly Gentile and quite **large.** They could even hold a grown man, and it was in such a basket that Paul was lowered over the wall in Damascus (Acts 9:25). Therefore these **seven large baskets** held considerably more food than the twelve small baskets used in the other feeding (Matt. 14:20). Because this crowd had not eaten for three days, they would have consumed more than the other, which was without food for only one day (14:15).

Alfred Edersheim observed that "the Lord ended each phase of His ministry with a feeding. He ended the ministry in Galilee with the feeding of the five thousand. He ended the ministry in the Gentile area with the feeding of the four thousand. And He ended the Judean ministry before His death on the cross with the feeding of His own in the upper room."

After the **four thousand men, besides women and children,** had been fed, **sending away the multitudes,** Jesus **got into the boat, and came to the region of Magadan.** The identity of **Magadan** is not certain, because there is no other biblical, historical, or archaeological information about it. Mark reports that they went "to the district of Dalmanutha" (8:10), but that location is also uncertain. Because no land travel is mentioned, the **region** apparently bordered the Sea of Galilee.

From Jesus' ministry to the Gentile crowd in the Decapolis a number of important lessons can be learned.

First, we see again Jesus' unrivaled divine power. Because only God can create, only God could have multiplied those seven loaves of bread and a few fish even one-fold, not to mention many thousand-fold. He is the God of Abraham, who believed in Him "who gives life to the dead and calls into being that which does not exist" (Rom. 4:17). Just as He had created healthy tissues to replace diseased ones, whole limbs to replace deformed and missing ones, and seeing eyes to replace blinded ones, He also created a superabundance of food to replace a little.

When the apostles were establishing the early church, many miracles were performed through them. But their miracles were performed in the name and by the power of Jesus Christ, for whom they served merely as instruments. Jesus, however, performed miracles in His own name and power, because He was the source of the power. He did not heal, deliver, raise the dead, and multiply food as God's agent but as God.

Second, the fact that He not only cured diseases and restored hearing and sight but restored those who were *kullos* (maimed and sometimes completely without arms, legs, eyes, or other parts of the body), He set Himself totally apart from self-proclaimed divine healers of past years and modern times. You look in vain among those healers for verified accounts of anyone who was given an arm, leg, or eye to replace one that was missing. Their "cures" are at best psychosomatic and are extremely minor compared to those the Lord performed during the three years of His earthly ministry.

God is still capable of sovereignly healing the most hopeless disease and of creating new limbs where there are none. But the only age of healing in the church was the time of authenticating the Messiah Himself and of His Word through the apostles. Once those ends were accomplished, the gift of miracles ceased. (For a more complete discussion of this subject, see the author's book *The Charismatics*, published by Zondervan.)

Third, we learn that the goal of ministry is worship. Although most, if not all, of the multitudes in Decapolis were pagan Gentiles, when they saw the magnitude and perfection of Jesus' healing power, they not only were astonished beyond measure but also "glorified the God of Israel" (v. 31). Witnessing such a divine display demanded much more than awe; it demanded reverential worship, which those Gentiles offered as best they knew how.

Their worship was Jesus' supreme goal. He had unqualified compassion to heal their broken bodies and to fill their empty stomachs. But He was infinitely more concerned that, through their trust in Him as Lord and Savior, He could also save their souls from eternal damnation and make them citizens of His heavenly kingdom.

Christ's followers are likewise called to minister not only to people's physical and temporal needs but to lead them to glorify God, "that the grace which is spreading to more and more people may cause the giving of thanks to abound to the glory of God" (2 Cor. 4:15). The goal of evangelism and of Christian living is to "worship the Father in spirit and truth; for such people the Father seeks to be His worshipers" (John 4:23). Only when devotion to the Lord is sincere and unqualified, service to others truly selfless, and daily living consistently Christlike, will God be glorified.

That is an especially important lesson for our day, in which self-love and self-satisfaction have become accepted and touted even in much of the church. We are tempted to offer the gospel simply for what it can do for a person, with no suggestion of the need to turn from self to God and from our own priorities to His. We like to make the way of salvation seem wide, although the Lord says it is narrow (Matt. 7:14). We want to make the Christian life appear easy, although Jesus declared that "he who does not take his cross and follow after Me is not worthy of Me" and that only "he who has lost his life for My sake shall find it" (10:38-39).

Fourth, this story teaches the necessity of relying on divine resources. Like the disciples, we are most usable to the Lord when we acknowledge our own lack of resources and turn to Him. Whatever we may have in ourselves is never enough to meet the needs of others or to accomplish anything for God. Jesus did not command the apostles to be His "witnesses both in Jerusalem, and in all Judea and Samaria, and even to the remotest part of the earth" until He had first promised, "You shall receive power when the Holy Spirit has come upon you" (Acts 1:8). "Every good thing bestowed and every perfect gift is from above, coming down from the Father of lights," James says (James 1:17).

I was once asked to visit a elderly lady who was dying and did not know Christ. She was frail and sick, and I did not want to upset her; yet I knew that above everything else she needed Christ. All the way over there I prayed that God would help me know what to say and how to say it; but as I neared her apartment door I became more and more uneasy. When one of her friends let me in and I walked over to her bed, the first thing she said was, "Before you say anything, I just want to tell you that yesterday my sister led me to Christ." After a time of reading some psalms and prayer, I said, "You don't need to fear death any more"; to which she replied, "Fear death? I don't fear death. I don't fear death at all." By the time our visit was over, I felt she had ministered to me more than I had to her. I had been totally inadequate to meet her needs; but as I went in dependence on our gracious Lord, I found He had already preceded me and made full provision.

Fifth, we learn from this story that God's resources are never diminished, much less exhausted, because He has an infinite capacity to create. He did not need the seven loaves and few fish in order to feed the multitude. He could just as easily have made the food from nothing, just as He created the world from nothing. He used the loaves and fish in order to involve the disciples and to help teach them to give what they had into His care. "Give, and it will be given to you; good measure, pressed down, shaken together, running over, they will pour into your lap. For by your standard of measure it will be measured to you in return" (Luke 6:38). God's people would never lack resources to do what He calls them to do if they trusted that promise.

Sixth, we learn about the servant's usefulness. Although the Lord is able do His work without us, He chooses to do it through us. He did not need the disciples' help to distribute the food any more than he needed the seven loaves and the fish to make the food. He could have done in an instant what took them several hours to do. But in His infinite wisdom and mercy God chooses to use human instruments to do His divine work of carrying the gospel to the world and of ministering to its needs. In submissively serving others in our Lord's name and power, we learn to serve Him—in preparation for serving Him for all eternity in dimensions we cannot now conceive.

Seventh, we learn that God gives liberally, in "good measure, pressed down, shaken together, running over" (Luke 6:38), as we have already seen. Everyone on the mountainside ate until he was completely satisfied. There was even more than enough, so that seven large baskets of food were left over.

Eighth is the lesson of spiritual investment. When the disciples gave all they had to Jesus and then helped Him give it away to others, they had seven full baskets remaining for themselves. "He who sows sparingly shall also reap sparingly; and he who sows bountifully shall also reap bountifully" (2 Cor. 9:6).

The ninth and overarching lesson is the limitless compassion of Jesus Christ. He has compassion for all our needs—eternal, lifetime, and daily. He has compassion on Jews and on Gentiles, on the severely afflicted and the merely hungry. Following the example of our Lord, we are to "do good to all men, and especially to those who are of the household of the faith" (Gal. 6:10). Our compassion is not measured by our feelings but by our giving.

John Wanamaker, founder of the famous Philadelphia department store that bears his name, was a devoted Christian. On a trip to China to observe Christian mission work there, he came across a small village where a group of Christians had begun building a church but lacked money to complete it. In a nearby field he noticed the strange sight of a boy yoked together with an ox as they together pulled a plow held by his father. Mr. Wanamaker's guide explained that the boy had promised his father, "If you will sell one of the oxen and give the money for the building of the church, I will take the oxen's place pulling the plow." Mr. Wanamaker is said to have fallen to his knees and said, "Lord, let me be hitched to a plow that I may know the joy of sacrificial giving."

Bibliography

Barclay, William. *The Beatitudes and the Lord's Prayer for Everyman*. New York: Harper & Row, 1964.

_____. *The Gospel of Matthew*, vol. 1. Philadelphia: Westminster, 1958.

Boice, James Montgomery. *The Sermon on the Mount*. Grand Rapids: Zondervan, 1972.

Broadus, John A. *Commentary on the Gospel of Matthew*. Valley Forge: Judson, 1886.

Eerdman, Charles R. *The Gospel of Matthew*. Philadelphia: Westminster, 1966.

Gaebelein, Arno C. *The Gospel of Matthew*. Neptune, N.J.: Loizeaux, 1961.

Hendriksen, William. *New Testament Commentary: Exposition of the Gospel According to Matthew*. Grand Rapids: Baker, 1973.

Lange, John Peter. *Commentary on the Holy Scriptures: Matthew*. Grand Rapids: Zondervan, n.d.

Lenski, R. D. H. *The Interpretation of St. Matthew's Gospel*. Minneapolis: Augsburg, 1964.

Lloyd-Jones, D. Martyn. *Studies in the Sermon on the Mount*. Grand Rapids: Eerdmans, 1977.

Morgan, G. Campbell. *The Gospel According to Matthew*. Old Tappan, N.J.: Revell, 1939.

Pentecost, J. Dwight. *The Sermon on the Mount*. Portland: Multnomah, 1980.

Pink, Arthur W. *An Exposition of the Sermon on the Mount.* Grand Rapids: Baker, 1953.

Plummer, Alfred. *An Exegetical Commentary on the Gospel According to St. Matthew.* Grand Rapids: Eerdmans, 1963.

Sanders, J. Oswald. *Bible Studies in Matthew's Gospel.* Grand Rapids: Zondervan, 1973.

Tasker, R. V. G. *The Gospel According to St. Matthew.* Grand Rapids: Eerdmans, 1977.

Watson, Thomas. *The Beatitudes.* Carlisle, Pa.: The Banner of Truth Trust, 1975.

Indexes

Index of Greek Words

Index of Hebrew/Aramaic Words

Index of Scripture

Index of Subjects

Moody Press, a ministry of the Moody Bible Institute, is designed for education, evangelization, and edification. If we may assist you in knowing more about Christ and the Christian life, please write us without obligation: Moody Press, c/o MLM, Chicago, Illinois 60610

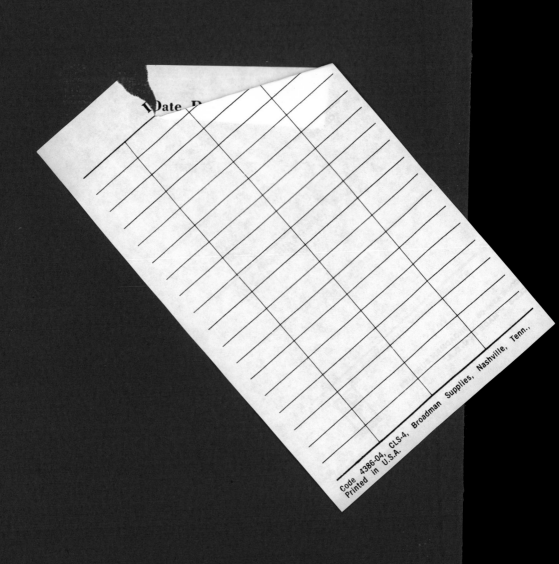

Date

Code 4386-04, CLS-4, Broadman Supplies, Nashville, Tenn.,
Printed in U.S.A.